ACCOUNTING FOR MANAGERS

ACCOUNTING FOR MANAGERS

Second Edition

JOHN J. GLYNN • JOHN PERRIN • MICHAEL P. MURPHY

THOMSON

LEARNING

Australia • Canada • Mexico • Singapore • Spain • United Kingdom • United States

THOMSON

LEARNING

British Library Cataloguing-in Publication Data
A catalogue record for this book is available from the British Library

First published 1994 by Chapman & Hall
Reprinted 1995 by Chapman & Hall
Reprinted 1996 by International Thomson Business Press
This edition published 1998 by International Thomson Business Press
Reprinted by Thomson Learning 2000 , 2001
Typeset by The Florence Group, Stoodleigh, Devon
Printed in Singapore by Markono Print Media Pte. Ltd.

ISBN 1-86152-261-4

Thomson Learning
Berkshire House
168–173 High Holborn
London WC1V 7AA
UK

http://www.thomsonlearning.co.uk

Contents

Preface

The four years since the first edition of this book was published have witnessed a number of important changes in accounting. Some of these changes relate to financial reporting and the activities of the ASB; some relate to continuing efforts of the IASC and others to harmonise financial reporting practice on an international basis; others relate to the increasing influence of newer approaches to costing, such as activity-based costing; while others relate to the changing role of the accountant in the context of the strategic management of companies and the introduction of new management accounting practices. In this second edition we have attempted to reflect these and other changes by introducing new material as well as revising and updating the topics covered in the first edition. In doing this we have been conscious of the need to avoid information 'overload' as the book is intended principally for management students and for practising managers.

The challenge faced by management, both in the private and public sectors, is that of planning and controlling the use of resources to achieve organisational objectives. At the same time, they have a duty of accountability to the providers of those resources to demonstrate that the resources have been properly applied and how effective their management has been. Accountants have an important role to play in both areas: they maintain the financial records of an organisation's economic trans-actions, they prepare regular financial reports based on these records for management, they help management to plan (in large part via the budgetary process), and they prepare the external financial statements of the organisation. The work of accountants permeates all aspects of management, and the key purpose of accounting is that of providing useful information both for managers and for external parties. The more accounting is able to achieve this successfully, the more efficient and effective will be the management of organisations, and the efficiency with which individuals and society at large allocate resources will be much improved. It is important that accountants and managers understand each other's needs and work together.

This book is designed principally for post-experience management students, such as those pursuing DMS and MBA qualifications, and for practising managers who need to obtain a better understanding of the work of accountants. However, it will also be of use to undergraduate accounting and management students, given its integrated coverage of financial and management accounting. No previous knowledge or experience of accounting is assumed. The book explains the conceptual bases of accounting and examines a number of the techniques that have been developed to help accountants provide the useful information which is their core objective. Throughout the book we provide illustrations of these techniques, and at the end of each chapter there are exercises and discussion topics as appropriate, as well as suggestions for further reading for those who would like to go into more detail about particular topics. At the end of the book we also provide a bibliography of reading references and a glossary of accounting terminology to help demystify the sometimes hieratic language of accountants.

The book commences with a review of the history, nature and purposes of accounting. This first chapter also introduces the distinctive roles of financial accountants and management accountants. The next seven chapters concentrate primarily on the work of financial accountants. They commence with a discussion of the core principles of maintaining financial accounting records, and this is followed by a review of the primary financial statements and an examination of the legal framework of financial reporting. There is then a discussion of taxation and its impact on enterprises, followed by a chapter on the work of auditors in relation to accountability systems. The next chapter discusses the interpretation of the data contained in financial statements and the use of accounting ratios. This section concludes with a new chapter which looks at international dimensions of financial reporting and the moves towards 'harmonisation'.

Chapter 9 provides a bridge between the work of financial accountants and that of management accountants by reviewing the considerations that need to be taken into account in the design and implementation of effective management accounting systems. The ensuing eight chapters build on this review, initially by discussing concepts of costs and identifying relevant costs for short-term decision-making. Included here is a new chapter dealing with accounting for overhead expenditure and activity-based issues. This is followed by a chapter which discusses longer-term decisions, reflecting the time value of money. Chapter 14 introduces budgeting and the many roles that budgets can be used for, and is followed a chapter on the role that accounting can play in the achievement of effective control in organisations. This theme is pursued further in Chapter 16 in the context of accounting and internal markets. This section of the book concludes with a discussion of working capital management and techniques for improving it.

The final chapters are new to the book and concentrate on some of the new directions in accounting. The first of these chapters focuses on social responsibility and environmental accounting, while the second looks at the role that accounting is increasingly playing in the strategic management of organisations.

Many people have helped us in the preparation of this book. In particular, our thanks are due to Sarah Henderson and Dominic Recaldin at International Thomson for their support and encouragement, and to colleagues at Canterbury Business School, most notably Robert Jupe, Rennie Tjerkstra and Bruce Pollard for their helpful comments on the manuscript. An enormous debt of gratitude is owed to Ann Hadaway and Elaine Holland for their efforts in deciphering our handwriting and preparing the final manuscript.

In conclusion we would like to thank our wives and families – Lourdes (Glynn), Sue and Abigail (Murphy) and Jennifer (Perrin) – for their patience and understanding, without which we would have been unable to complete our work.

John Glynn
University of Wollongong

Michael Murphy
Canterbury Business School

John Perrin
University of Warwick (Emeritus)

Abbreviations

AAA	American Accounting Association
ABC	activity-based costing
ABM	activity-based management
ACCA	Chartered Association of Certified Accountants
ACT	advanced corporation tax
APB	Auditing Practices Board
APC	Auditing Practices Committee
ARR	accounting rate of return
ASB	Accounting Standards Board
ASC	Accounting Standards Committee
ASSC	Accounting Standards Steering Committee
CAPM	capital asset pricing model
CBA	cost–benefit analysis
CBI	Confederation of British Industry
CCAB	Consultative Committee of Accountancy Bodies
CEA	cost-effectiveness analysis
CIMA	Chartered Institute of Management Accountants
CIPFA	Chartered Institute of Public Finance and Accountancy
DCF	discounted cash flow
ED	Exposure Draft
EMH	efficient markets hypothesis
EOQ	economic order quantity
EU	European Union
FASB	Financial Accounting Standards Board
FEE	Fédération des Experts Comptables Européens
FIFO	first in, first out
FRC	Financial Reporting Council
FRED	Financial Reporting Exposure Draft
FRRP	Financial Reporting Review Panel
FRS	Financial Reporting Standard
GAAP	Generally Accepted Accounting Principles
GP	general practitioner

IAPC	International Auditing Practices Committee
IAS	International Accounting Standard
IASC	International Accounting Standards Committee
ICAEW	Institute of Chartered Accountants in England and Wales
ICAI	Institute of Chartered Accountants in Ireland
ICAS	Institute of Chartered Accountants of Scotland
IFAC	International Federation of Accountants
IIA	Institute of Internal Auditors
IOSCO	International Organization of Securities Commissions
IRR	internal rate of return
IT	information technology
JIT	just in time
LIFO	last in, first out
MBO	management by objectives
MIS	management information system
NAO	National Audit Office
NHS	National Health Service
NI	national insurance
NNDR	national non-domestic rate
NPV	net present value
OED	*Oxford English Dictionary*
OFR	operating and financial review
PAYE	pay as you earn
PB	programme budgeting
PPBS	planning, programming and budgeting systems
R&D	research and development
RI	residual income
ROCE	return on capital employed
ROI	return on investment
SAS	Statement of Auditing Standards
SMEs	small and medium-sized enterprises
SORP	Statement of Recommended Practice
SSAP	Statement of Standard Accounting Practice
UBR	uniform business rate
UITF	Urgent Issues Task Force
VAT	value-added tax
VFM	value for money
ZBB	zero-base budgeting

1 The nature and purposes of accounting and its management interface

Objectives

Accounting (or accountancy), like taxation, has been a function of organised society throughout history. Accounting is the recording, reporting and, sometimes, interpretation of all the financial (money-value) transactions and resources of individuals, enterprises and other formal organisations (accounting entities). The main branches of accounting are **financial accounting** and **management accounting**. Financial accounting has as its principal roles the keeping of accurate records of economic events and transactions affecting entities, and their use for the preparation of relevant and useful reports, primarily intended for the benefit of external stakeholders.

Management accounting, often using the same base data/records as financial accounting, but also taking data from other sources, and applying analytic techniques especially relevant to planning, decision-taking and control, has the particular role of providing information and advice to managers to aid them in their work. Management accounting has evolved from earlier **cost accounting** methods, and the measurement and control of production and other costs remains a major task. Other such tasks include the preparation and monitoring of budgets, capital-expenditure evaluation, and participation in **management information systems** (MIS) design and implementation.

The nature of accounting

Accounting has existed throughout history. In all societies, and at all stages of history, accounting systems have been used as a basis for planning, deciding and controlling economic activity. Accounting records have been used to provide information for the management of the granaries belonging to the Pharaohs of Ancient Egypt; to control the tax revenues of the emperors of Ancient China; to ensure the accountability of the stewards of medieval nobility; and to provide information about the activities of modern multinational enterprises in market economies. Throughout history and across all forms of economic structures, accounting has been important, and the genesis of modern capitalist economies was perhaps the development of double-entry bookkeeping in the Middle Ages.

Although accounting has been present throughout history, it has existed, and continues to exist, in many different forms. The key to a successful accounting system is ensuring that it mirrors the needs of the society and organisations in which it exists. An accounting system which was appropriate for the monarchs of medieval Europe is unlikely to be appropriate in the twentieth century. Similarly, an accounting system appropriate for a centrally planned economy is unlikely to be appropriate for a society operating within the disciplines of a market economy. Even within market economies there are differences in the demands made of accounting, and hence in accounting systems, although there is an increasing emphasis on harmonisation – in part caused by the internationalisation of business throughout the modern world economic environment. Prime examples of this are the Company Law Harmonisation Programme of the European Union and the work of the IASC and related bodies. However, even within this drive towards harmonisation and standardisation of accounting practice there is a recognition that different societies are at different stages of development; have different political systems; have different economic infrastructures; and have different histories. The emphasis of harmonisation is on identifying common ground and using this as a basis on which to build, rather than on stating that there is just one correct way to do things. The more that societies move towards common structures and goals, the more this common ground expands and the more a common philosophy of accounting becomes appropriate.

The focus of this book is on the contribution that accounting and accountability systems can make towards the more efficient and effective management of business enterprises operating in a market economy. It is intended to be of practical use and, as such, contains examples of the ways in which accounting can be used to provide useful information to those concerned with the activities of business enterprises. However, one book cannot cover all aspects of accounting systems, processes, concepts, techniques and the contribution that accounting can make towards the success of enterprises. It has been necessary to concentrate on aspects of accounting of particular relevance to management. These are normally termed **financial accounting**, where the focus is on the recording of transactions and the annual financial reporting of enterprises, together with **management accounting** and **cost accounting**, where the focus is on internal decision taking within enterprises. However, the distinction between these different 'accountings' is not clear cut. Frequently, although they have different emphases, they use the same data as their starting point. These data are those contained in the basic accounting records of the enterprise, and the most common approach to recording these data is that of double entry bookkeeping. This holds true whether the data are recorded manually in 'books of account' or maintained using modern computer-based systems.

It is a feature of all societies that organisations and individuals within them have particular roles and contributions to make towards that society, and that they are provided with resources, of whatever type, to enable them to perform these roles and make these contributions. The possible roles, contributions and resources involved are many and various. However, a crucial element of the overall process is that the organisations and individuals in question must be **accountable**. This accountability may take a variety of forms: it may relate simply to the safe custody of the resources, or it may relate to the outcomes and outputs of the activities for which managers are responsible while using the resources entrusted to them. The particular contribution of accounting to this process is its focus on the financial consequences of the activities of organisations and individuals.

The need for external financial accounting reports

A feature of modern economic organisation, in whatever form, is that the owners of the resources employed in economic activity frequently do not have direct control over the day-to-day management of these resources. There is a separation between the ownership and the management of resources, and this separation is increasingly common as enterprises become larger. In the case of a small business enterprise, such as a garage, there may be only one owner of the enterprise who also has control over the management of its resources. In such cases there is no separation of ownership and control. Enterprises of this sort are commonly referred to as 'proprietary businesses' as the owner (proprietor) is also responsible for the management. In the case of a business owned by the members of a family the situation may be different. Perhaps not all the members of the family participate in the management of the business. If this is the case those who do so will need to account for their management of the business to the rest of the family. To do this they will need to maintain accounting records of the transactions into which they enter on behalf of the business, and of the consequences of their business decisions. These records will then form the basis of 'statements of account', showing the results of their management of the business, which they will then render to the other members of the family. At the same time, the accounting records will help them in their day-to-day management of the business as these will provide information about such items as the costs and revenues associated with different aspects of the business. Thus, the accounting records provide the basis of 'statements of account' (financial reporting) from managers to owners and, at the same time, provide information that managers can use in their management of the business (management accounting).

The separation of ownership and control is at its most noticeable in the case of a large business enterprise where the owners of (shareholders in) the enterprise appoint professional managers to conduct the activities of the enterprise. There may be many such shareholders. In the case of some previously state-owned enterprises which have been privatised in the United Kingdom (e.g. telecommunications, water and electricity companies) there may be millions of shareholders. These shareholders appoint, via a General Meeting, the senior managers (directors) of the company, who are charged with managing the resources of the company to achieve its objectives. However, it is worth noting that it is normally the existing board of directors which nominates replacement or additional directors to such a General Meeting, and these nominations are normally accepted by the shareholders. In the case of a company, the objectives will typically relate to generation of profits, which can then be distributed to the owners of the enterprise, although there may also be other objectives. For example, a listed company may seek to achieve increases in its share price – this would afford shareholders the opportunity of making capital gains; it might also make the company less vulnerable to a takeover and make it easier for it to acquire other companies. The separation of ownership and control means that there is a need for a formal structure of accountability between the managers of the resources and the owners of these resources, of which annual financial statements are an important, but not the only, element. The larger the enterprise and the greater the number of shareholders, the more important it is that there is a formal and regulated structure. Virtually every country which operates, or is seeking to operate, a market economy has passed legislation to provide such a formal and regulated structure of accountability, although the detail of the legislation varies from country to country. In the United Kingdom the core of this legislation is the Companies Acts.

The simple agency relationship between owners and managers summarised above ignores the many other parties who have an interest in the activities of a business enterprise. Employees, customers, suppliers, finance providers and society at large all have interests in the way in which the managers of a business enterprise use the resources entrusted to them and conduct the business of the enterprise. An alternative view is that of 'stakeholders' in an enterprise, whereby the stakeholders are all those groups which society regards as having reasonable rights in, and claims against, the enterprise and which have corresponding rights to information about the activities of the enterprise. This information is necessary to help them make decisions about their relationships with the enterprise.

The range of stakeholders, their interests in enterprises and their information needs have frequently been debated in western market economies. Table 1.1 shows extracts from three influential statements on this subject by major professional accountancy bodies. It should be noted that none of these statements includes the management of an enterprise as a user group. This is because the focus of all three statements is upon the external financial reporting of (accountability of) enterprises and its regulation. This is not to deny the importance of financial information to managers or their rights to such information. Rather, the focus is on management reporting on the activities and resources of the enterprise under their control to outside stakeholders in the enterprise. At the same time, they will be using the services of accountants to provide them with information useful in the operational and strategic management of the enterprise. The requirements of these different groups for financial information about the activities of an enterprise can be summarised by considering the types of decision that they have to make about their links with the enterprise. Table 1.2 provides some examples.

Table 1.1   Stakeholder groups

Source A	Source B	Source C
The equity–investor group	Investors	Investors
The loan–creditor group	Lenders	Lenders
The employee group	Employees	Employees
The analyst–advisor group		
The business contact group	Suppliers and other trade creditors	Suppliers and other creditors
	Customers	Customers
The government	Government	Government and their agencies
The public	Public	Public

Sources: **A**: ASSC (1975a).
       B: IASC (1989).
       C: ASB (1995a).

Table 1.2 Examples of the differing information requirements of user groups

User group	Example of decision
The equity–investor group	Buy/hold/sell shares
The loan–creditor group	Increase/hold constant/reduce levels of credit and loans and on what terms
The employee group	Submit claims for wage increases; ability to take industrial action
The analyst–advisor group	Which investments to recommend to clients
The business contact group	What trade to do and on what terms (e.g. credit)
The government	Central and local taxation and industrial policy; environmental and employment issues etc.
The public	Assess economic and social impact of firm; policy and implementation issues

Definitions of financial accounting/reporting

We have already seen that many groups have a need for financial information about the activities of business enterprises and the outcomes of these activities. In market economies the principal, but not the only, means of providing this information is the annual financial accounts prepared by management. These accounts, which are almost universally required by legislation, are based on the accounting records maintained by an enterprise and are intended to provide their readers – the stakeholder groups – with the information that they require. They are a vital communication and accountability mechanism in market economies. Unsurprisingly, the structure and objectives of these financial statements have been the subject of much comment. The following quotations are from pronouncements issued by influential accounting bodies about financial statements and the annual corporate reports which contain them:

> The objective of financial statements is to provide information about the financial position, performance, and financial adaptability of an enterprise that is useful to a wide range of users for assessing the stewardship of management and for making economic decisions.
>
> (ASB 1995a: para. 1.1)

> [serving] . . . the informational needs of external users who lack the authority to prescribe the financial information they want from an enterprise, and therefore must use the information that management communicates to them.
>
> (FASB 1978: para. 28)

> The fundamental objective of corporate reports is to communicate economic measurements of, and information about, the resources and performance of the reporting entity useful to those having reasonable rights to such information.
>
> (ASSC 1975a: 28)

As can be seen from these pronouncements, there is a strong measure of agreement about the purposes of the annual financial statements of enterprises. They exist to supply the information requirements of the stakeholders in the enterprise. In most cases these statements are public documents available for inspection by anyone (although some countries offer exemptions in this respect for smaller companies), and their contents are prescribed by legislation and professional accounting statements.

Desirable characteristics of accounting information

If annual financial statements are to satisfy the information needs of their users the information that they contain must have characteristics related to the needs of these users. This has been an area of great – and still, to some extent, unresolved – debate. The debate is not so much about what these desirable characteristics are as about the extent to which it is possible to provide accounting information which has all these characteristics. These characteristics will be examined in some detail later in this book. For the present we want simply to identify them and comment briefly upon them (see Table 1.3). Many desirable characteristics for accounting information have been identified, and to some extent a number of these overlap. Below we summarise current views on the most important of these characteristics and the way in which they are interpreted for the preparation and analysis of accounts.

- **Understandable**: if the information contained in the financial statements cannot be understood by the readers of those statements the whole purpose of preparing the statements is rendered futile. Traditionally, financial statements have concentrated on the presentation of information in the form of numerical tables accompanied by some limited explanatory text. Increasingly, it is believed that this needs supplementation by other forms of presentation, including graphs, pie charts, etc., and commentaries on the financial information such that the information is

Table 1.3   Desirable characteristics of financial accounting reports

Characteristic	A	B	C	D
Understandable	y	y	y	y
Objective	y	y	y	
Comparable	y	y	y	y
Realistic	y	y	y	
Relevant	y		y	y
Reliable	y		y	y
Consistent	y	y		y
Timely	y		y	y
Prudent		y		y
Economy of presentation		y	y	y
Materiality			y	y
Usefulness			y	y
Faithful representation				y
Substance				y
Neutrality				y
Completeness				y
Cost/benefit				y

Sources: **A**: ASSC (1975a).
　　　　　B: Inflation Accounting Committee (1975).
　　　　　C: FASB (1980).
　　　　　D: ASB (1995a).

rendered more accessible to readers who have not had formal accountancy training. In addition to the way in which they present information, a major obstacle to the understandability of financial statements is accounting 'jargon'. Accountants, like other professional groups, use language in a very precise way. In particular, they attach very precise meanings to ordinary words. Unfortunately, these meanings are not always those which 'non-accountants' attach to these words. Effectively, accountants use these words as a 'code' which enables them to convey a great deal of information to those who understand the code, but this means that readers who do not know the code can all too easily misinterpret the information that the financial statements are intended to convey. One of the purposes of this book is to provide a decoding manual for non-accountants. It does this in two ways. First, the Glossary at the end of the book provides definitions and explanations of the more common accounting terminology, and, second, throughout the book examples and illustrations are given of the practical implementation of accounting terminology.

■ **Objective**: the information presented in financial statements needs to be objective and unbiased if it is to meet the needs of users. It needs to be neutral, in that it should not be biased towards the interests of any one stakeholder group. The principles employed in the preparation of the financial statements, and the accountants themselves, must not favour any particular interest group. Historically, there has been a strong tradition in accounting whereby 'objective' has been interpreted as meaning 'verifiable'. According to this tradition, information could not be objective unless it could be independently verified, for example by an auditor. This meant that all sorts of potentially useful information which could not be verified in this way was excluded from financial statements. More recently, the emphasis has switched to the view that 'neutrality' is at least as important as 'verifiability'. Financial statements increasingly contain information which, although neutral, is not verifiable in the traditional sense. An example of such information is the inclusion of the values of intangible assets such as 'brand names'. However, the concept of verifiability retains an important influence on the information that is contained in financial statements, particularly where an independent audit is required. The modern view has been expressed thus:

> The information contained in financial statements must be neutral, i.e. free from bias. Financial statements are not neutral if they include information that has been selected or presented in such a way as to influence the making of a decision or judgement in order to achieve a predetermined result or outcome.
>
> (ASB 1995a: para. 2.19)

■ **Comparable**: unless the information contained in a set of financial statements can be compared and contrasted with information from elsewhere its usefulness is greatly diminished. Readers of the information need to be able to compare it with their expectations, with information about the previous performance of the enterprise, with information about the performance of other enterprises and with information derived from other sources. There is a need for consistency in the preparation and presentation of financial information. This consistency must apply to the financial statements of an individual enterprise over time (enabling comparison of current performance with previous and with anticipated performance).

Equally, it must apply across different enterprises (enabling the performance of one enterprise to be compared with another). This need for consistency has been a major influence in the drive towards the 'harmonisation' and 'standardisation' of accounting practice within and across individual countries. The 'harmonisation' and 'standardisation' movement is discussed further in Chapters 4 and 8.

■ **Realistic**: if financial statements are to be of any use to their readers they must be realistic: they must reflect the world and the enterprise as they are. The problem here is what is meant by 'reality', because there may be more than one view of reality. For example, there may be an 'economic reality' and a 'legal reality'. This is a problem where the parties to a contract adopt a particular legal form for the contract because it is convenient but acknowledge that the economic reality is different. The issue then is whether financial statements should reflect the legal position or the acknowledged economic position. This is currently the focus of major debates. In general, the accounting profession favours reporting the economic 'reality' in financial statements, while the legal profession favours reporting the legal 'reality'. This debate is often referred to as the economic (substance) v. legal (form) debate. The professional accounting view is that:

> If information is to represent faithfully the transactions and other events that it purports to represent, it is necessary that they are accounted for and presented in accordance with their substance and commercial effect and not merely their legal form. . . . The substance of transactions and events is not always consistent with that which is suggested by their legal form: although the effects of the legal characteristics of a transaction are themselves part of its substance and commercial effect, they have to be construed in the context of the transaction as a whole (including any related transactions).
>
> (ASB 1995a: para 2.18)

This view is expounded at some length in a statement, issued by the ASB (1994a), dealing with reporting the substance of transactions, an issue which is discussed further in Chapter 4.

■ **Relevant**: as we have already seen, the purpose of financial statements is to provide information to stakeholders in the enterprise such that they will be able to make 'informed judgements and decisions' (AAA 1966: 1). The information they contain needs to be relevant to those decisions. The problem is that different decisions may require different information and that all decisions ideally require information about the (likely) future consequences of those decisions. Definite information about the future is, of course, not available; we have to predict the future using information about the past (predictive value being another desirable characteristic of financial statements) in conjunction with specific assessments as to how the future may differ from the past. This obviously raises the question as to what information has predictive value, and the balance between predictive and confirmatory value of information. The current position in most market economies is that financial statements must provide information about an enterprise's assets and liabilities, its revenues and expenditures, and its cash flows. Thereafter, it is up to the readers of the financial statements to make their own assessments in the context of the decisions they need to make. In general 'Information has the quality of relevance when it has the ability to influence the decisions of users by helping them to evaluate past, present or future events or confirming, or correcting, their past evaluations' (ASB 1995a: para 2.8).

■ **Reliable**: if readers of financial statements are to rely on the information such statements contain in making their decisions, then they must have confidence in that information. In most market economies this confidence is reinforced by a requirement to have the financial statements audited by an independent auditor. The regulations in this respect vary from country to country, but the requirement for such an audit is almost universal. The concept of reliability has been summarised thus: 'Information has the quality of reliability when it is free from material error and bias and can be depended upon by users to represent faithfully what it either purports to represent or could reasonably be expected to represent' (ASB 1995a: para. 2.13).

■ **Consistent**: we have already referred to the need for readers of financial statements to be able to compare the information contained in financial statements with information from other sources. If this is to be worth doing the information from these various sources must be consistent in its scope and methods of preparation and presentation. Thus consistency is crucial to comparability. The problem is that as the circumstances of an economy or enterprise change, the requirement for 'realism' may dictate a change in the way that the financial statements are prepared, thereby removing consistency of treatment. Where this is necessary, it is important that the financial statements disclose the impact of these changes. In general, realism is regarded as being a more important characteristic than consistency – provided that the impact of any changes is adequately disclosed. This is because, ultimately, sound decisions can be based only on relevant and realistic information.

■ **Timely**: if the information in financial statements is to have value to its readers it must be timely. Stale news is no news. If the information is out of date it will not help its readers make sound decisions. Financial statements need to be published as quickly as is consistent with the need for them to be relevant and reliable. If there is undue delay the information they contain may lose its relevance. In a number of countries timeliness is ensured by legislation; for example, in the United Kingdom a company must publish its financial statements within a specific time of the period to which they relate.

■ **Prudent**: the nature of financial statements is that they contain information on both complete and incomplete transactions. An incomplete transaction is one in which all of the cash consequences have not yet been realised (for example a credit sale where the customer has not yet paid for the goods/services as at the date of the financial statements). Because the cash consequences have not been fully realised there is inevitably an element of doubt as to what these will ultimately be (for example, the customer may be unable/unwilling to pay for the goods or services received). If too optimistic a view is taken as to the ultimate cash consequences there is a danger that the enterprise or the stakeholders associated with it will enter into commitments which they will then not be able to meet. The general principle underlying the preparation of financial statements is that they should present a 'prudent' picture of the enterprise's profit, its assets and liabilities. However: 'Prudence is the inclusion of a degree of caution in the exercise of the judgements needed in making the estimates required under conditions of uncertainty, such that income or assets are not overstated and expenses or liabilities are not understated' (ASB 1995: para 2.20).

■ **Economy of presentation**: the maintenance of the detailed accounting records of an enterprise, the preparation of financial statements and the audit thereof constitute a costly process. In fact, it is a process the cost of which may often be underestimated. It is necessary to ensure that the benefits derived from this process exceed its costs, as otherwise society will suffer a net loss. The problem is that the benefits and costs of this process are not easily assessed. Thus, there is often a 'political' dimension to decisions about the maintenance of accounting records and the dissemination of financial statements.

> The evaluation of benefits and costs is, however, substantially a judgmental process. Furthermore the costs do not necessarily fall on those users who enjoy the benefits . . . it is often difficult to apply a cost–benefit test in a particular case.
>
> (ASB 1995a: para 2.38)

■ **Materiality**: while all the transactions of an enterprise must be properly and fully recorded, however small they might be, when it comes to the preparation and publication of financial statements it is necessary to aggregate these transactions into larger wholes. This inevitably requires that decisions are made about the amount and extent of such aggregation. The problem is twofold: the higher the level of aggregation, the greater the risk of useful information not being disclosed in the financial statements; while, on the other hand, the lower the level of aggregation, the greater the volume of information that has to be disclosed, with all the associated problems of information overload and cost. Materiality is an accounting concept which recognises the fact that it is impractical to record, or at least report, every detail of an enterprise's activities and that to do so would be of little benefit to the users, while acknowledging at the same time that information which is too highly aggregated would be of equally little benefit. A balance has to be struck:

> Information is material if it could influence users' decisions taken on the basis of the financial statements. If that information is misstated or if certain information is omitted the materiality of the misstatement or omission depends on the size and nature of the item in question judged in the particular circumstances of the case.
>
> (ASB 1995a: para. 2.6)

■ **Usefulness**: in many ways, this is the ultimate yardstick for the information contained in financial statements. If it is not useful it is not worth preparing. The concept of usefulness goes right back to the definitions of financial statements and accounting which were mentioned earlier in this chapter. It is effectively a conflation of all the other characteristics, and the ultimate question is whether better decisions are made because of the existence and use of the financial statements. The real-world usefulness of financial statements is inevitably a result of 'trade-offs' between all the characteristics, and perhaps the most important such 'trade-off' is that between **relevance** and **reliability**.

The edifice of financial reporting and its desirable characteristics, as outlined above, will be built on sand unless it is based on a reliable structure of financial records which record the economic events and transactions affecting the enterprise. Thus, financial accountants have two key roles:

1 They must ensure that the enterprise has in place a system of financial recording that properly records all its trading and other economic transactions. This must be their primary responsibility. In the absence of such records (i.e. a lack of 'proper books of account') there can be no reliable financial reporting, nor could there be any effective management accounting. Chapter 2 discusses core issues involved in the design and implementation of financial recording systems.
2 They must extract from the financial records the periodic financial statements of the enterprise. Chapter 2 also discusses the essentials of such extraction and provides a basis from which Chapter 3 goes on to discuss the 'primary financial statements' of enterprises. Thus, financial accountants are traditionally viewed as being responsible both for the maintenance of the core accounting records of an enterprise and for the preparation of external financial reports based upon these records.

Cost accounting and management accounting

So far we have not presented any precise definition of management accounting or any clear specification of its specific tasks and the boundaries of its role. Some might argue that this is not necessary on the grounds that management accounting is 'what management accountants do'. Management accounting is not defined in law; management accountants do not have to be members of professional accounting bodies (although many of them are) – auditors are the only accountants who have to have appropriate professional qualifications. The tasks, roles and boundaries of management accounting vary from entity to entity. However, a useful definition of the role of management accounting is provided by the IFAC: 'the process of identification, measurement, accumulation, analysis, preparation, interpretation and communication of information (both financial and operating) used by management to plan, evaluate and control within an organisation and to assure use of an accountability for its resources' (IFAC 1987: para. A). Perhaps the main areas of uncertainty or controversy over the role and boundaries of management accounting relate to how far it should take responsibility for and control of the enterprise's total, or integrated MIS, and the extent to which the management accountant should have the authority to be proactive – going beyond a purely advisory role towards more interventionist participation in management decision-making.

Historically, management accounting has evolved from cost accounting, but with cost accounting remaining a major subordinate component of the management accounting process. Costs have been recorded, reported and controlled since the time of the Pharaohs, and before. However, until modern times 'costs' usually meant simply 'cash expenditures', and, indeed, to this day this remains the case in some parts of the public sector (and in many very small businesses). We shall see in later chapters how many different ways there are of defining and measuring costs.

Modern systems of cost accounting began to develop after the start of the Industrial Revolution, when production processes became more complex, enterprises grew larger, and top management could no longer maintain awareness and control of efficiency by personal observation and oversight. The First World War encouraged the wider use of cost accounting through the introduction of 'cost-plus contracts', where cost data had to kept and made available for checking and audit against bills rendered. By the end of the Second World War cost accounting had become more sophisticated and influential, and the terms 'managerial accounting' and 'management accounting' began to be used, especially in the USA and in academic writing.

Traditional cost accounting first came under criticism from economists, and then from academic accountants who had a background in economic education (Dean 1951; Solomons 1952) and from management scientists (Goetz 1949). Traditional cost accounting had as its main functions the control of costs in factories, mines, railways, etc. and the provision of cost data for the valuation of stocks. It was the work of critics such as those mentioned above which helped cost accounting evolve into management accounting, with the more intellectual role of helping managers to plan, to evaluate alternative courses of action and investment, and to reach (hopefully) optimal decisions. (For a modern viewpoint on the origins of management accounting, see Johnson and Kaplan 1987; Hopwood 1988.) The contemporary scene in management accounting shows four major developments:

- There is a growing awareness that simply providing managers with information is not sufficient. Managers have difficulties interpreting accounting information, and may also have personal priorities and agendas which differ from the 'rational' pursuit of optimisation of corporate goals. Thus there is a behavioural dimension to the use of accounting (and other) management information, and approaches are being sought to improve the communication and interpretation of accounting information, and its use in assisting good planning, decision-making and control.
- Some academics believe that much accounting information, far from being objective or neutral, is instead consciously biased or distorted to support narrow managerial objectives which may be against the interests of workers or society (for example information made available during successive rounds of pit closures in (the then) British Coal). They are working to develop forms and conventions of accounting which might overcome such problems.
- Traditional cost accounting, and even much modern management accounting, has been fixated mainly on manufacturing and other industrial activity. But modern market economies are characterised by a contraction in industrial employment and the relative expansion of the service sector. (Even ignoring the current recession in manufacturing industry, the rapid spread of automation and robot technology inevitably means a continuing fall in the proportion of the population employed in blue-collar jobs in industry.) So management accountants are working to develop accounting systems which are more tailored to service businesses (including retail operations), professional offices, and public-sector enterprises such as the NHS, schools and universities, and local and central government.
- Given the increasing automation of industry, and the adoption of new forms of management organisation and of the organisation and control of work (many of these coming from Japan, and some from the USA (Lee 1987)), it is argued that conventional management accounting is today inadequate even for manufacturing industry. This is leading to the development of new accounting technologies and approaches sometimes termed **strategic management accounting**.

The basic problem is that accounting is not an exact science. As we will see in later chapters, many of the precise-looking numbers used in accounting reports are in fact only estimates, or values chosen from a range of alternative measurement methods, each with some validity in a particular context (for example factual but misleading accounting numbers from past records as opposed to realistic estimates of present or future costs after allowing for inflation, currency devaluation, market forces, etc.). Good accountants are always in search of the truth, although, if they find it, top management sometimes prevents its disclosure. More often, the problem is that the 'truth' is uncertain and arguable, rather like many cases in a court of law or issues before Parliament. Accounting is a human artefact – different truths lie in the eyes of different beholders.

Tasks of management accounting

The tasks (and roles) of management accounting vary from enterprise to enterprise, according to the organisational structures and requirements set by top management, but the following comprise the principal ones and closely parallel the tasks of management – this is hardly surprising, as management accounting is intended to help management in the discharge of its responsibilities:

1 Planning:
   - Liaise with other management functions on medium- and long-term (corporate) plans, including capital-expenditure proposals.
   - Prepare three- to five-year outline medium-term budgets.
   - Administer the annual budget cycle, linked to the enterprise's managerial responsibility structure.
   - Develop cost and other financial information systems to monitor achievement in realising plans.
2 Control:
   - Measure the outturn (results) of costs, sales, etc. against annual budgets and agree cost and performance 'standards'.
   - Prepare cost, sales and budget reports, and circulate them to responsible managers (reports are normally at least monthly, but the goal is real-time systems where up-to-date information is available constantly on managers' terminals).
   - Follow up reports with advice, supplementary studies, if helpful, and sometimes pressure to conform to agreed plans, budgets and standards.
3 Decision-making:
   - Provide information for decisions (very often the cost and other financial information routinely available for planning and control is not fully relevant for particular strategic or operational decisions – this issue is discussed in later chapters).
   - Provide advice and participate in the decision process where multi-function management is an accepted part of the enterprise culture.
4 Capital projects:
   - Participate in planning capital programmes, including liaison with financial management regarding the raising and timing of capital funds.
   - Reconcile the capital programme with corporate plans, and prepare medium- and long-term capital budgets.
   - Prepare detailed cash-flow budgets for capital funding and expenditure for the year ahead.
   - Monitor the progress of capital spend against budget.

5 Performance evaluation:
- Agree procedures with personnel and top management regarding ways to include budgets and other financial measures within the performance evaluation of individual managers, departments, divisions, etc.
- Circulate, explain and follow up performance reports.

6 Costs for financial accountants:
- Supply the cost information needed by financial accountants for preparing annual accounts and other external reports (these costs, mainly relating to production operations and stocks in hand, may be measured or classified on a different basis from the relevant costs used for managerial planning, decision-making and control).

7 Wider roles:
- As with other management jobs, management accountants may sometimes expand their roles (or empires!) to take on additional tasks. This may occur especially in small to medium-sized enterprises (SMEs), perhaps because the finance or marketing functions are weak, or if there is no corporate planning function. The management accountant may become involved in tasks such as economic and strategic reviews or management-by-objective programmes.

Accounting and management information systems

Historically, most of the accounting data for production and other operations were collected and entered into records by the cost accounting department. At intervals, these data were transferred to a financial accounting department in full, or in a condensed, aggregated form if that was required. With the spread of large mainframe computers in the 1960s, there was a logic in centralising all accounting data, recording in one computer centre managed by the financial accounting department or by a computer specialist reporting direct to the chief accountant or finance director. Such organisational arrangements have tended to persist even after the introduction of PCs and diffused-terminal networks.

Accounting measurements – or, more precisely, 'money-value measurements' – provide the only common measurement system or common language for business. Costs, revenues and asset values can all be aggregated or compared – in the common denominator of money. In contrast, physical units of output or sales comprising, for example, bolts, nuts, screws, nails and steel girders provide meaningless disinformation if aggregated together. Nevertheless, this information is essential in its unaggregated form for the accurate measurement of costs. The need is to measure costs per unit or batch of output for separate kinds of product, or the cost or value of each separate kind of asset:

Unit price of inputs × Volume of inputs = Cost
Unit selling price × Volume of sales   = Sales revenue

The accountant has direct access to invoices and price lists for these cost and revenue calculations, but normally must rely on other managers for the accurate collection of data on the volume of sales, inputs, and each separate important 'activity' involved in the production or sales processes whose cost needs separate identification and measurement in order to facilitate understanding and control of the efficiency of resource utilisation. Managers themselves also need physical measures of inputs and activities for their own personal use in good management – indeed, many managers prefer to manage mainly on the guidance of the physical measures they collect rather than the accounting measures of these inputs and activities, which may only become available to them after some delay.

As indicated above, there are a number of different types of information which management needs in addition to that relating to costs and revenues – what is sometimes referred to as the 'broad scorecard'. Examples include personnel information regarding skills, training, absenteeism and labour turnover; and quality-control and performance information regarding the meeting of completion/delivery dates. If all this information can be combined together in one, normally computer-based, system there exists an MIS, which to be fully integrated must also contain accounting information. A fully integrated MIS is easier to describe than to implement.

The public sector

This book is about accounting for managers. It is expected that the majority of these managers will be in the private sector. However, it is acknowledged that managers in the public sector face similar problems. The phenomenon of the **new public management**, arising from the introduction of commercial principles (business-style management, contracting, control and accounting methods), wherever possible, into the public sector, emphasises this similarity. For example, NHS Trusts have been expected to account commercially and to aim to at least 'break even' (after allowing for financing costs), while 'trading' within the so-called 'internal market' of healthcare, which itself is globally limited by annual government budget allocation. Universities now operate broadly on commercial accounting principles and seek to earn a surplus, or 'profit' (for reinvestment within the university). But there remain large areas of central and local government which are expected to spend all their budget allocation and thus end the year with no surplus or profit. Here full commercial accounting standards of financial reporting, costing and budgeting are increasingly being demanded and developed.

Financial management

A manager without accurate, up-to-date and relevant management information is like the captain of a submarine all of whose navigational and control instrumentation has failed. Such managers are floundering, unlikely to reach their objectives safely, or at least efficiently. Much of the navigational (i.e. planning) and control information needed by managers to aid their decision-making and action is provided by accounting. Whereas financial accounting focuses mainly on the information which must be reported externally to satisfy the law, tax collectors, shareholders and major creditors, and maintaining the underpinning accounting records, management accounting exists mainly to provide internal information to assist managers in their planning, decision-making, and control of activities, resources and capital projects. There is another element that must be considered: **financial management**, where the core role is that of securing the necessary finance (both long-term and short-term capital, the latter commonly termed 'working capital'). This role involves ensuring that capital is available when needed and balancing the desire to minimise the 'cost of capital', while at the same time minimising the risk of insolvency or loss of credit status. Financial management must establish rapport and trust with major sources of finance, and has to cooperate with financial accounting in deciding the detail and form of external financial reporting and information disclosure.

Financial management is often seen as a key 'survival' function of the enterprise, whereas accounting may be viewed as a 'facilitating' function of lower status. Often a finance director will be responsible at board level, not just for finance, but for accounting as well; and the two main branches of accounting may be brought together in larger firms under a chief accountant (often termed 'controller' in American firms and business literature). In smaller firms there may not be enough work to justify the cost of an expert finance specialist and, since most accountants have some expertise in finance, the de facto chief accountant will often take on the finance role as well and operate at board level as financial director or controller. In firms large enough to justify a specialist finance department and head of finance (treasurer), the finance director will often be an accountant who has moved across to specialise in finance, although there is an increasing tendency (already pronounced in the USA) to view the finance function as quite separate from accounting, with senior finance staff being recruited from masters in business administration (MBAs), postgraduate specialists in finance, or persons trained in merchant banks or other relevant financial institutions.

At board and top-management level managers will need interface and contact with, as well as information and advice from, all three functions: financial management, financial accounting and management accounting. In contrast, at middle- and junior-management levels the main contact of the managers will be with management accounting. However, at all levels the accountants – as 'ring-holders' of useful information (which managers may not even realise the accountants hold, or can assemble and provide) – should be proactive in offering information and advice, and in making it clear what aid they can provide to managers.

Interactions in accounting and finance

Figure 1.1 illustrates the interactions, or interdependent interests, in accounting and finance: The major interactions or interdependent interests, represented in Figure 1.1 by the notation A–D, are summarised below:

A: The main link between management accounting and financial management is a shared concern for the efficient and effective use of capital. This is sometimes termed 'resource management'. There is a particular concern for new capital outlays which commit the firm to particular markets, products or technologies for years ahead, and how they are to be financed. The management accountant has to verify all the costs, both of the outlay itself and of the future activities for which the capital outlays will be used. A 'capital appraisal' (termed 'option appraisal' in some public services) must be undertaken to assess whether profitability will be acceptable. In addition, the financial manager will be concerned with the risk or uncertainty involved, and with the timing of cash flows relative to the future needs to meet payment obligations to creditors and shareholders.

B: The main link between financial accounting and financial management is a shared concern for the measurement of profits and asset values; for the form and detail of financial reports; and for the impact these will have on interested parties external to the enterprise. One frequent problem here is that financial managers (and the board of directors) may want a more 'rosy' picture of the firm's profits and financial position to be projected externally than a cautious and objective accountant would want to endorse. This puts pressure on accountants, when there are doubts over facts or contingencies – or where there is a choice of accounting methods allowed by professional bodies, government or the Stock Exchange – to report only the most optimistic accounting measurements. This results in what is often termed 'creative accounting'.

C: The main link between financial accounting and management accounting is the collection of data, maintenance of accounting records and exchange of information relevant to the needs of the two branches of accounting. In particular, the management accountant is typically in charge of the method and detail of collecting data and compiling information on the costs of production, selling and other activities. This information is important for the costing and valuation of unsold stocks of goods for sale (including work still in progress and incomplete), and for the calculation of enterprise profit or loss required from the financial accountant.

D: This is the cross-over area of interests shared by all three of the accounting and finance specialisms. Prominent here is taxation, which affects choices in financing, profit calculation and reporting, and assessment of the effects of both current operations and future choices of operations, other activities and alternative uses of new capital investment. Also important is the measurement and control of cash flow, perhaps with particular concern for the balance between debtor receipts and creditor payments, and the locking-up of cash in raw materials, work-in-progress and unsold finished goods relative to the current and foreseeable rate of sales and cash realisation from sales. Again, there is shared concern for the rate of return achieved from existing capital investment and for realistic forecasting of the expected rate of return from new capital investment and the risk associated therewith.

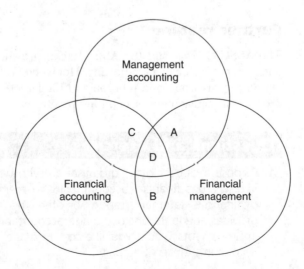

Figure 1.1
Interactions in accounting and finance.

Conclusions

The theme of this chapter has been to introduce readers to the purposes and roles of accounting, to the main branches of accounting and the differences of function between them, and to some of the key tasks they carry out. In essence, the accountant exists to provide information and advice. This book emphasises those aspects of accounting which impinge on the work and understanding of managers. These do not just include management accounting, but also require sufficient understanding of financial accounting and financial management to allow the manager to see how these activities affect the enterprise and the overall management process.

Accounting has a long history, involving recording and reporting on cash and other property, and amounts owing to and by organisations. From this has grown modern financial accounting, with its particular concern for accountability to various stakeholders, especially the shareholders of public companies, and for financial reporting to stakeholders in accordance with the law and standards set by professional institutes. *Inter alia*, financial statements should be understandable, objective, comparable, realistic, relevant, reliable, consistent, timely, prudent, economical in presentation and material in content.

Earlier systems of cost accounting have come to be incorporated within the much wider approach of modern management accounting, where the objective is to provide information on costs, revenues, the use of capital, etc. in such detail and form as will assist managers in planning, decision-making, and control of their activities and organisational units. Annual budget planning and monitoring have become very important in all enterprises, but perhaps especially in public-sector enterprises with fixed allocations and no profit to measure or relate to incentives. Management accountants supply advice as well as routine reports, and increasingly their role is proactive, to link up with management information systems and wider management strategy.

Further reading

The ASSC (1975a) and the ASB (1995a) provide professional views on the nature and purposes of financial reporting. Hopwood (1988) discusses the role of accounting within organisations, and Johnson and Kaplan (1987) provide a critique of the development of management accounting practices.

Questions and exercises

1 Choose a club or other organisation with which you are familiar. Explain how it discharges financial accountability to members and others through the use of financial statements/reports or other mechanisms. Do you consider that this provides adequate disclosure and accountability – and why, or why not? What improvements would you like to see made in the organisation as regards its accounting or accountability?

2 Explain (a) the common features of and (b) the distinctive differences between financial accounting and management accounting, as regards their purpose, scope and tasks.

3 Referring to the table of 'desirable characteristics of accounting reports' in this chapter, why do you think the terms 'accurate' and 'truthful' do not appear in the list?

4 Why do you think it might be that among all the desirable characteristics of accounting reports and financial statements mentioned in this chapter it has been suggested that the most important 'trade-off' (that is, compromise where separate characteristics may appear to conflict with each other in respect of the accounting measurements or disclosure which would result) is that between 'relevance' and 'reliability'?

5 Some kinds of management decision can use routine accounting information supplied for control purposes, while other kinds of decision may need specially prepared accounting (and other) information. Speculate on why this may be true and on what the kinds of decisions are which might benefit from non-routine accounting information.

6 Why is it that management accountants cannot do their job properly without the assistance and cooperation of managers? What kinds of assistance or co-operation do you think accountants may need from managers?

7 What, if any, difficulties or disadvantages might arise if the accounting function takes over and develops the enterprise's MIS? Is there any other organisational framework which would be likely to work better for the corporate benefit – and why, or why not?

8 How do you think financial management imperatives might differ between enterprises in the private and public sectors? To what extent are such differences a function of the differing nature of the accountabilities in these sectors as opposed to anything inherent in the discipline of accounting?

9 Assume you (or your family) comprise an 'enterprise', albeit a domestic one. You want to borrow from the bank for capital purposes, to invest in a car. The bank manager has asked you to submit a financial statement for your domestic enterprise. Prepare an accounting statement to show your revenues, costs/ expenses and residual profit/loss (surplus/deficit). You may use disguised or simulated numbers. Think carefully about the amount of detail, the best layout, and the clearest (yet concise) captions to use in order to achieve clarity, to discharge your accountability honestly, and to enable the bank manager quickly to obtain a relevant and reliable understanding of your financial position.

10 'It is not possible to be an effective manager without at least a grounding in accounting because it is the language of business.' Do you agree with this statement?

2 The background to traditional accounting statements

Objectives

This chapter reviews the background to traditional financial statements by examining the fundamental accounting identity and its extensions which provide the conceptual basis for such statements, and the justification for double entry bookkeeping. In this context it examines the meaning of the terms 'asset', 'liability' and 'equity', as well as income and expenses. Attention is paid to the core requirements of an effective system of accounting records from which external financial reports and management information can be extracted. The distinction between the cash and accruals basis of accounting is discussed, as are the fundamental accounting concepts upon which all external financial reports are based.

The origins of accounting

As indicated in the previous chapter, accounting has a long history, the origins of which lie in the need of owners and managers of resources to plan, control and account for the use of these resources. The origins of accounting and auditing lie in government accounting dating back to Ancient Egypt and Imperial China. Prior to the emergence of joint-stock companies there was little external financial reporting; most accounting information was internally focused, although it did incorporate accountability reports from stewards to their masters regarding the discharge of their duties. To enable such reports to be prepared and verified, and to enable control to be maintained over the use of resources, it was necessary to develop systems for recording resources and their movement. In the early days of accounting such recording systems tended to focus on physical resources (including cash). As commerce and trade developed it increasingly became necessary to develop more sophisticated systems for recording commercial transactions and their outcomes. A major breakthrough in this regard was the invention of double-entry bookkeeping in Italy in the fifteenth century. Later in this chapter we will examine the relationship between modern financial reporting systems and double-entry bookkeeping. Before doing so, it is important to emphasise that such reporting could not exist without a system for recording, in a structured way, the individual transactions that an enterprise engages in and the changes that these transactions lead to in its assets and liabilities.

If accounting is to be worth anything it must be based on the proper and accurate recording of transactions. In this chapter we review what is necessary to enable such recording to take place. Once this base is established it can be built on to provide information for both internal and external users. The most visible part of this whole process is the publication of the annual financial statements of enterprises. Such statements are an end product of the accounting system. Underpinning them and (the less visible) internal management accounting reports and statements is the core process of capturing in the base accounting records all the economic activities of the organisation. In the main, this is still based on the basic principles of double-entry bookkeeping, although increasingly it utilises the flexibility afforded by modern computer database systems.

In the remainder of the chapter we discuss the bases on which this 'core' recording of the economic activities of an enterprise takes place. The perspective adopted in this discussion is that of the accounting records necessary to enable enterprises to prepare their annual financial statements – their external financial reports. However, it must be borne in mind that these accounting records will also form the basis of the internal accounting reports used by management to plan and control the activities of the enterprise, and we will refer to this as well.

The fundamental accounting identity

Derived from the double-entry bookkeeping approach to recording the economic activities of commercial enterprises and underpinning traditional external financial reporting is a key assumption. This assumption is that the assets of an enterprise are exactly equal in value to the claims against those assets. It is this assumption which ensures that balance sheets do in fact balance and which ultimately provides the linkage between balance sheets and profit and loss accounts. It is commonly expressed in the form of an equation, which is often referred to as the **fundamental accounting identity**. This equation is:

$$\text{Assets} = \text{Claims (against the assets)} \tag{2.1}$$

Associated with this key assumption is another, no less important. This second assumption is that the enterprise is an entity distinct from its owners. We will see the importance of this later, when we discuss the legal aspects of external financial reporting. The range of potential accounting entities is very large; some of these are business entities and some are legal entities. Table 2.1 lists some examples. The financial reporting requirements for these different entities will vary depending on their legal status. This is addressed in Chapter 4.

Before proceeding further, it is important to clarify what is meant by the word 'asset'. The ASB defines assets in the following terms:

> Assets are rights or other access to future economic benefits controlled by an entity as a result of past transactions or events.
>
> (ASB 1995a: para. 3.5)

Thus, an asset is something an enterprise controls (owns) and which has a value. This value derives from the future economic benefits, such as cash inflows, which the enterprise will enjoy because of its ownership of the asset. The range of assets

Table 2.1   Accounting entities

Business entities:
Sole trader (F.A. Smith, Newsagent)
Partnership (Price Waterhouse & Co., Chartered Accountants)
Unlimited-liability company (Jones & Co.)
Limited-liability company (J.A. Smith Ltd.)
Public limited-liability company (Marks and Spencer plc)
Group of companies (the Smith Kline Beecham plc Group of Companies)
Division or other responsibility centre of a company or group of companies (GEC Turbine
   Generator Division)

Non-business entities:
Charity (Oxfam)
Clubs and other associations (Polo Farm Sports Club)
Local authorities (Kent County Council)
Health authorities (South Thames Regional Health Authority)
Statutory agencies (Driver and Vehicle Licensing Centre)
Educational institutions (University of Kent at Canterbury)

---

owned by enterprises is wide, but typically will include such items as cash in hand and at bank, debtors, stocks and work-in-progress, plant and machinery, land and buildings, investments, etc. What should be recognised as assets for the purposes of financial reporting and how such assets should be valued are, and have been for some time, major areas of debate in financial accounting. For the present it is sufficient to regard assets as things controlled by an organisation which confer economic benefits on it and to which accounting assigns a monetary amount (value).

However, an enterprise could not have acquired such assets unless it was first provided with the funds to do so. The providers of such funds then have claims against the enterprise, and specifically against the assets of the enterprise, for their repayment. The repayment terms will form part of the contract between the enterprise and the fund providers. Thus, given the structure of commercial enterprises and their separate legal personality (except in the case of sole traders), the assets owned by the enterprise must, by definition, be exactly matched by the claims of the different fund providers against those assets. This is the basis of the fundamental accounting identity stated in equation (2.1).

However, there are two different categories of claims:

- **liability claims**: the claims of **creditors** for goods, services or money supplied, or lent, to the enterprise;
- **ownership claims**: the claims of the **owners** of the enterprise to the balance of the assets after all liability claims have been provided for, often referred to as equity claims.

Thus equation (2.1) can be rewritten as:

$$\text{Assets} = \text{Liability claims} + \text{Equity claims} \qquad (2.2)$$

or, more usually as:

$$\text{Assets} = \text{Liabilities} + \text{Equity} \qquad (2.3)$$

However, to emphasise the fact that equity is a residual item left over after all liabilities have been provided for, equation (2.3) is more usually written as:

$$\text{Assets} - \text{Liabilities} = \text{Equity} \tag{2.4}$$

A more formal definition of liabilities is provided by the ASB:

> Liabilities are obligations of an entity to transfer economic benefits as a result of past transactions or events.
>
> (ASB 1995a: para. 3.21)

Individuals or corporate organisations who have liability claims against an enterprise are normally referred to as creditors. As is the case with assets, enterprises can have a wide range of liabilities, but common examples include trade creditors, bank loans and overdrafts, other loans and taxation payable. The general accounting principle regarding the inclusion of liabilities in financial statements is that they should be stated at the amount that will have to be paid to settle them in full, regardless of when payment is actually due. Having said this, we should point out that there is one unusual category of liability which is not normally included in financial statements. This is the category of 'contingent liabilities'. A contingent liability is a liability which will only crystallise if some future event happens. Thus a contingent liability might be the damages that the enterprise would have to pay if it lost a legal action, or the additional amount it might have to pay to a vendor where a sale agreement specified that the consideration payable was dependent on profit. Contingent liabilities have not always been well, or adequately, disclosed in financial statements, and sometimes when they have crystallised they have led to the insolvency of enterprises. Smith (1996) provides some good examples of the potential importance of contingent liabilities.

A formal definition of equity (ownership interest) is:

> Ownership interest is the residual amount found by deducting all of the entity's liabilities from all of the entity's assets.
>
> (ASB 1995a: para. 3.39).

In financial statements, equity is normally regarded as having three components. These are:

1 The amount of any funds supplied by the owner(s) to the enterprise to fund its activities. The accounting presentation of these funds will vary according to the nature of the enterprise in question. In the case of limited-liability companies incorporated under the Companies Acts these funds will be the amount of the nominal value of the share capital subscribed by the shareholders in the company plus any share premium resulting from the issue of shares for consideration in excess of their nominal value.
2 The amount of the accumulated surpluses/deficits (profits/losses) resulting from the enterprise's trading and other activities. Such surpluses/deficits are, of course, stated after taking into account monies distributed as dividends to the owners (shareholders) from surpluses (profits).
3 The amount of any other reserves that have arisen since the foundation of the enterprise. Such reserves might include surpluses arising on the revaluation of assets to reflect current market values.

The main reason for showing these three components separately is derived from the legal regulation of the affairs of limited-liability companies. The Companies Acts lay down a number of detailed and stringent requirements relating to equity, which are discussed further in Chapter 4. An underlying principle of these requirements is that of creditor protection, based on a view that the share capital comprises a type of 'reserve fund' or 'safety net' from which creditors will be able to recover the monies due to them if the enterprise runs into financial difficulties. This is, of course, an oversimplification, but the underlying principle is that the share capital is the risk capital of the enterprise, and that the shareholders should receive monies from the enterprise only if it has been successful and generated surpluses/profits. Thus, under the Companies Acts, dividends can be paid to shareholders only out of 'realised profits' – a technical concept which we will examine in Chapter 4. Enterprises such as sole traders and partnerships, which are not incorporated under the Companies Acts, do not face the same legal strictures. However, their accounts tend to be prepared on the same principles as regards 'equity', although the terminology differs because they do not have share capital as such.

Equation (2.4) is the basis of one of the primary financial statements of enterprises, the **balance sheet**. An enterprise's balance sheet summarises its assets, liabilities and equity at a given point in time. The structure and content of balance sheets is examined in detail in Chapter 3. For the present it is sufficient to note that a balance sheet is an amplification of the fundamental accounting identity for a given enterprise at a given point in time. It provides those who read it (and hopefully understand it) with useful information to help them assess their links with the enterprise.

Equation (2.4) represents a static position: assets, liabilities and equity at a point in time. It can be developed to cover a period of time by focusing on the changes in its components over such a period. Thus, over a particular period in time, a financial year for example:

$$\Delta(\text{Equity}) = \Delta(\text{Assets}) - \Delta(\text{Liabilities})^1 \qquad (2.5)$$

Given the fact that equity is the residual ownership interest it can be seen that there are three types of events/transactions an enterprise can engage in which might lead to a change in equity during a financial reporting period.

- **Financing transactions**: these are transactions by means of which owners either invest new equity capital/funds into the enterprise or withdraw/have returned to them part of their existing equity, for example by dividend payments out of surpluses (profits).
- **Trading transactions**: these are transactions in which the enterprise buys and sells goods or services, and which result in it making either surpluses (profits) or deficits (losses).
- **Revaluations**: from time to time the market value of the fixed assets of an enterprise will vary significantly from the value at which they are currently shown in the enterprise's accounts (e.g. from the original cost). In these circumstances the enterprise may, subject to some restrictions, restate the assets at their current market value. This will lead to a corresponding increase/(decrease) in the residual equity.

If we assume that an enterprise has no financing transactions or revaluations during a given period then any change in equity during that period must come from a profit or loss resulting from its trading transactions. Thus, we can rewrite equation (2.5) as:

$$\Delta(\text{Equity}) = \text{Profit}/(\text{Loss}) = \Delta(\text{Assets}) - \Delta(\text{Liabilities}) \qquad (2.6)$$

This gives us a link between a position statement, the balance sheet and a flow statement which summarises the changes in equity during a financial period. This flow statement is the **profit and loss account**. Conventional wisdom tells us that:

$$\text{Profit}/(\text{Loss}) = \text{Income} - \text{Expenses} \qquad (2.7)$$

The income of an enterprise is the revenues it is entitled to receive from third parties. Examples of income include the revenues derived from the sale of goods or services, rents, royalties and other entitlements. The key point is that as a result of the generation of income the enterprise – and therefore ultimately its owners/shareholders – is better off. On the other hand, expenses (costs) represent a diminution in the wealth of the enterprise (and therefore, ultimately of its owners/shareholders). Normally this diminution will have been accepted in order to obtain resources (goods, labour, knowledge, etc.) which enable the enterprise to generate future income greater than the amount of the expenses incurred to obtain the resources in question.

The relationship between an enterprise's income and its expenses – its profit/(loss) – is the essence of the profit and loss account, which summarises and analyses the trading transactions of an enterprise, grouping like items together, to provide users with information about the outcome of the trading transactions during a particular financial period.

However, as indicated above, a change in equity may also be the result of the revaluation of assets or liabilities, rather than of trading transactions. This can be allowed for by introducing the concepts of **gains** (which subsume income) and **losses** (which subsume costs). These concepts have been defined by the ASB in the following terms:

> Gains are increases in ownership interest, other than those relating to contributions from owners. . . .
> Losses are decreases in ownership interest, other than those relating to distributions to owners.

> (ASB 1995a: para. 3.47)

We can integrate these different approaches by combining equation (2.7) with equation (2.6) and using the concepts of gains and losses, to obtain the following equation:

$$\text{Gains} - \text{Losses} = \Delta(\text{Assets}) - \Delta(\text{Liabilities}) \qquad (2.8)$$

However, given our earlier assumption, this ignores the possibility of changes in equity, and hence in assets or liabilities, having arisen because of financing as opposed to trading transactions. Such changes are either the result of fresh equity capital being introduced into the enterprise – referred to by the ASB (1995a) as a **contribution** – or part of the existing equity capital being returned to the owners – referred to by the ASB (1995a) as a **distribution**. Thus equation (2.8) needs to be extended to allow for this as follows:

$$\text{Gains} - \text{Losses} + \text{Contributions} - \text{Distributions} = \Delta(\text{Assets}) - \Delta(\text{Liabilities}) \; (2.9)$$

We also need to recognise that changes in assets and liabilities can be either increases or decreases, so the full statement of equation (2.9) is:

Gains – Losses + Contributions – Distributions
= Increases in assets – Decreases in assets – Increases in liabilities
+ Decreases in liabilities　　　　　　　　　　　　　　　　(2.10)

Equation (2.10) can be reorganised in terms of the arithmetic signs of its components, as follows:

Losses + Distributions + Increases in assets + Decreases in liabilities =
Gains + Contributions + Decreases in assets + Increases in liabilities　(2.11)

This extended version of the accounting identity is called the **bookkeeping equation**; it is the basis of that system of recording the transactions of enterprises which is normally referred to as **double entry bookkeeping**, on which most modern financial accounting and reporting is ultimately based. Conventionally, items on the left-hand side of the equation are called **debits** and items on the right-hand side are **credits**.

Historically, the different items in the equation were recorded by accountants (bookkeepers) in ledger accounts contained, literally, in the books of account. However, in more recent times these ledgers have been replaced, first by machine accounting systems and more recently by computer-based accounting systems. Throughout this period of transition the basic principle has remained the same: the bookkeeping equation must remain in balance. Thus every transaction (economic event) affecting an enterprise must have two sides: an increase in one element of the equation and a decrease in another.

Accounting records and bookkeeping

It is not the purpose of this book to go into great detail about traditional bookkeeping, or more modern database systems of accounting. However, some key elements of any effective accounting system must be recognised. These are outlined below.

Chart of accounts

An effective accounting system needs to record the transactions (economic events) affecting an enterprise. To do this it needs a structure or framework according to which these transactions can be classified, and such a structure is normally called the **chart of accounts**. The objective of a chart of accounts is to map out the way in which the enterprise's transactions will be recorded and like items grouped together. In the UK, unlike a number of other European countries, there are no externally imposed detailed requirements for an enterprise's chart of accounts. Instead, it is the responsibility of the individual enterprise to design its own chart of accounts. In doing this it will be influenced both by its legal obligation (if it is a company) to keep accounting records sufficient to record and explain the company's transactions, and to enable balance sheets and profit and loss accounts to be prepared (Companies Act 1989: s. 221), and by its own management information requirements. Thus, subject to Companies Act requirements, an enterprise can itself determine the degree of analytical detail in its basic accounting records. Important considerations in this respect will be:

- maintaining control over its transactions: the level of detail must be sufficient to enable management to discharge its fiduciary obligations with respect to the enterprise's assets and liabilities;

- reporting requirements: the accounting records must be such as to enable management to prepare proper annual financial statements from them, as well as any periodic internal management accounting reports it requires;
- decision making needs: the accounting records need to provide information which facilitates managerial decision making, as well as facilitating control over costs and budgetary performance;
- cost: maintaining accounting records is a costly process and the more detailed the analysis provided by these records, the more costly maintaining them is likely to be; the cost of accounting should not exceed the value to management of the information provided.

The end product is a chart (schedule) of accounts with their associated titles and codes. An example is shown in Table 2.2.

This illustration is of a very simplified chart of accounts. In reality, even a small business will require a much more extensive chart of accounts. Larger businesses have charts of accounts involving several hundred, or even more, different accounts because management has decided that it needs to have such extensive analysis to be able to obtain the information it requires to manage the business effectively. A large company organised on a divisional basis might have a chart of accounts structured along the following lines:

Division	*Budget centre*	*Main code*	*Sub-code*
01–99	001–999	001–999	001–999

This would result in individual account codes having eleven digits and provide a basis for a detailed analysis of the enterprise's operations. In practice, the authors have encountered account codes of seventeen digits in multinational enterprises. While such an extensive chart of accounts provides the facility for very detailed analysis of operations, it also carries dangers. The principal dangers are an increased opportunity for error (the more digits in an account code, the greater the probability of miscoding) and information overload (there is a natural human tendency to ask for all the information available and where extensive analysis is available it tends to be produced, leading to a danger of management being overloaded by detail and unable to see the 'wood for the trees'). Care needs to be exercised to ensure that management, at different levels, is provided with the analysis and information that it does in fact require and is neither overburdened with detail nor provided with insufficient detail. There needs to be effective consultation between management and the enterprise's accountants to ensure that this happens and that the chart of accounts, and the reports

Table 2.2 Example of a chart of accounts

Main code	Sub-code	Account title
001		**Fixed assets**
	001	Freehold land and buildings – cost
	002	Leasehold land and buildings – cost
	003	Motor vehicles – cost
	004	Plant and machinery – cost
	005	Furniture and fittings – cost

Main code	Sub-code	Account title
	101	Freehold land and building – accumulated depreciation
	102	Leasehold land and buildings – accumulated depreciation
	103	Motor vehicles – accumulated depreciation
	104	Plant and machinery – accumulated depreciation
	105	Fixtures and fittings – accumulated depreciation
	201	Freehold land and buildings – depreciation charge
	202	Leasehold land and buildings – depreciation charge
	203	Motor vehicles – depreciation charge
	204	Plant and machinery – depreciation charge
	205	Fixtures and fittings – depreciation charge
002		**Current assets**
	001	Raw material stock
	002	Work-in-progress
	003	Finished goods stock
	101	Trade debtors
	102	Other debtors
	103	Prepayments
	201	Cash in hand
	202	Cash at bank
003		**Current liabilities**
	001	Materials suppliers
	002	Other suppliers
	003	Payroll creditors
	004	Taxation payable
	005	Dividends payable
	006	Interest payable
	007	Accruals
004		**Income**
	001	Product sales
	002	Service sales
	003	Interest receivable
	004	Other income
005		**Costs**
	001	Cost of goods sold
	002	Payroll costs
	003	Premises costs
	004	Marketing costs
	005	Administration costs
	006	Finance costs
	007	Bad and doubtful debts
006		**Equity**
	001	Share capital
	002	Retained profits
	003	Other reserves
007		**Loans**
	001	Long-term loans
	002	Medium-term loans

derived from it, are appropriate to the needs of management. Unfortunately, all too often charts of accounts and accounting reports are designed solely by accountants.

Internal control

Whatever the structure of the chart of accounts decided on by management, it will be important to ensure that it is implemented in practice by the enterprise and its staff. To achieve this, management needs to design and implement detailed financial and operating procedures. The generic term for such procedures is an **internal control system**, which has been defined as:

> all the policies and procedures (internal controls) adopted by the directors and management of an entity to assist in achieving their objective of ensuring, as far as practicable, the orderly and efficient conduct of its business, including adherence to internal policies, the safeguarding of assets, the prevention and detection of fraud and error, the accuracy and completeness of the accounting records, and the timely preparation of reliable financial information.
>
> (APB 1995a: para. 8)

Prime documents

Prime documents are the basic inputs into the accounting system of an enterprise. They are documents that are raised, or received, by the staff of the enterprise as it engages in economic and other transactions. They are the source material for the whole of the accounting process and the underpinning of all the accounting records. As such, they are crucial to the whole process, and as part of its internal control system management needs to ensure that they are designed to capture all the necessary information required for accounting purposes, that they are properly prepared in a timely and controlled manner, and that they are transmitted to the accounting function. Examples of prime documents include goods-received notes, stock requisitions, delivery notes, purchase invoices, sales invoices, cheque requisitions, contracts. For example, a sales invoice would typically need to record the following information:

- customer name, address and account number;
- quantities, types and prices of merchandise/services;
- quantity discounts;
- total sales value;
- value-added tax;
- settlement terms;
- delivery details;
- date.

Prime records

Prime records are what were historically called the 'books of prime entry'. They are the first level of accounting records. In practice they may take many forms, but their function is to record the information contained in the prime documents referred to above. Examples of prime records include sales day books, purchase day books, cash payment and cash received records. As well as recording the prime documents, the prime records have another function – they are the first stage in the analysis of economic transactions. They analyse these transactions into the various categories and classifications specified by the chart of accounts. The information content of a prime record can be illustrated with an extract from a cash payment prime record, as shown in Table 2.3.

In real life the analysis of the cash payments would be much more extensive than that shown in Table 2.3, reflecting the (probably) extensive nature of the chart of accounts. Similarly, there will need to be a separate cash payments (and receipts) prime record for every cash fund. Extending the definition of cash to include bank accounts, there will need to be a separate record for every bank account. An enterprise will need a number of prime cash payment (receipt) records, relating to each of its bank accounts and cash (petty cash) funds. These records are normally referred to as cash books (and will normally deal with cash receipts as well as cash payments). The bases for their maintenance are the prime documents referred to earlier and the internal control system, which needs to be such as to ensure that all prime documents (cheque requisitions, cheques, petty cash vouchers, receipts, etc.) are properly recorded in the relevant cash records (or other prime records for other types of transactions/prime documents).

Ledgers

Ledgers are the practical implementation of the chart of accounts. Each of the individual account headings specified by the chart of accounts will have its own ledger account. The purpose of this ledger account is to collect together all the transactions for the account heading in question. Periodically, typically every week or every month, the information from the prime records will be transferred to the ledgers (a process often referred to as 'posting'). In a traditional manual system this 'posting' will be done by the physical process of writing the relevant totals from the prime records into the ledgers. Nowadays, with modern computerised systems, the process is likely to be automated. Thus each ledger account records increases or decreases in the monetary value of the item to which the account heading relates. The ledger

Table 2.3 Example of a cash payments prime record

				Analysis		
Date	Ref.	Payee	Amount £	003–001 £	003–002 £	005–005 £
1/1/9X	00245	Bloggs	156.89		156.89	
2/1/9X	00246	Smith	45.21	45.21		
3/1/9X	00247	Hill	269.00			269.00
4/1/9X	00248	Johns	14.23		14.23	
5/1/9X	00249	Hughes	85.11			85.11
6/1/9X	00250	Jones	139.84		139.84	
7/1/9X	00251	Smith	84.00			84.00
			794.28	45.21	310.96	438.11

as a whole is simply the aggregation of all the individual ledger accounts. The precise layout of the ledger accounts will vary from enterprise to enterprise, according largely to the technology it employs to maintain the accounting records. However, the typical format of a ledger account under the classical manual system of maintaining accounting records is shown in Table 2.4.

The double-entry system of bookkeeping (derived from the fundamental accounting identity) requires that for each and every entry there is a balancing entry in the accounting records. The balancing entries in relation to the example in Table 2.4 would be:

■ account no. 004–001 (Product sales) a credit entry of £43 241.00;
■ account no. 004–002 (Service sales) a credit entry of £9 326.76;
■ account no. 002–202 (Bank account, assuming all customer receipts were paid into the bank account) a debit entry of £39 671.07.

Within the ledger(s) as a whole there would be many such ledger accounts similar to the trade debtors account illustrated in Table 2.4. While the number of ledger accounts is influenced by the criteria referred to above, the bottom line is that there needs to be an individual ledger account for each separable and significant asset or liability, and for each separable and significant category of income or expense. This is perhaps not too great a problem as regards the income and expense categories, depending on the analysis required by management. However, it can be a major problem as regards the individual assets and liabilities.

Debtors can again be used as an example. An enterprise will need a separate ledger account for each individual customer to whom it offers credit terms. If it does not keep such a separate account it will not know how much it is owed by that customer at any point in time, and therefore management will have failed in the discharge of its fiduciary duties. Large enterprises may have many thousands, even hundreds of thousands, of individual customers; consider, for example, electricity companies, large retail chains and the clearing banks. Correspondingly, large enterprises may have many different individual suppliers, and may need to maintain complex analyses of their income and expenses from different sources. Such organisations could have in excess of a million different individual ledger accounts.

Table 2.4 Example of a ledger account

		Account no. 002–101 Account title: Trade debtors	
Date	Description	Debit £	Credit £
1/1/9X	Opening balance	19 678.95	
7/1/9X	Product sales	43 241.00	
7/1/9X	Service sales	9 326.76	
7/1/9X	Customer receipts		39 671.07
	Closing balance		32 575.64
		72 246.71	72 246.71
8/1/9X	Opening balance	32 575.64	

Thus, while the fundamental accounting identity and its derivative, the bookkeeping equation, look very simple in their pure forms, their practical implementation is a major problem for enterprises. The volume of individual ledger accounts and the even larger volume of individual transactions that have to be recorded in these ledger accounts impose great demands on the accounting system. Unless this system is properly specified and properly resourced it will fail. The consequences of such failure can be disastrous. It will not simply be a question of the accounts being wrong. The management of the enterprise will not know who owes money or for how long they have owed it, and this will make it very difficult for management to ensure that it collects all the monies due to the enterprise. Management will not know to whom the enterprise owes money and when it is due for payment, and this will make it very difficult for management to ensure that the enterprise only pays money to those entitled to such payments. Management will not know what the enterprise is spending money on, what income it is generating and what expenses it is incurring. Effective management will be impossible and the enterprise will almost certainly be a rapid candidate for insolvency, and its directors may be liable to a charge of failing adequately to discharge their fiduciary responsibilities. To prevent this, management must be prepared to invest sufficient resources in the accounting function. It is not good enough to regard the accounting function as an overhead expenditure to be minimised. It is an essential activity of an enterprise which must be optimised, that is, it must be resourced adequately to enable it to perform its functions, but – and it is an important 'but' – management must ensure that it is getting value for money from this resourcing. It must ensure that it is obtaining an appropriate amount of relevant and reliable information from the accounting function. This is an issue to which we will return later.

Journals

While the prime records will record the vast majority of the economic transactions of an enterprise, there will inevitably be exceptional events with which they cannot cope. The range of these events is wide, but their frequency limited. Journals are effectively a supplementary system of prime records intended to cope with these exceptional transactions. In addition to this, they are also designed to cope with economic events which do not of themselves involve a transaction. Examples of such events include charging the annual depreciation on fixed assets, providing for bad and doubtful debts, and providing for excess and obsolete stocks. In practical terms, journals serve the same function as prime records and lead to appropriate ledger entries. It is their source that distinguishes them from the mainstream system of prime documents being entered in the prime records and thereafter being posted to the relevant ledger accounts. Because the economic events recorded by journals are outside the mainstream events affecting the enterprise, they need to be carefully monitored and controlled. This is not to say that they are necessarily unusual; it is simply that they are not captured by the prime documents. Typically, accounting entries processed via journals require significant amounts of verification and authorisation. Table 2.5 illustrates the usual double entry form of journals.

This example deals with the annual depreciation charge for the financial year. The entries it contains will be the result of detailed calculations based on the types, values and economic lives of the various fixed assets owned by the enterprise. Chapter 3

Table 2.5   Illustration of a journal entry dealing with depreciation

Date	Description	Code	Debit £	Credit £
31/12/9X	Depreciation charge for year on freehold land and buildings	001–201	3 000.00	
	Accumulated depreciation on freehold land and buildings	001–101		3 000.00
	Depreciation charge for year on leasehold land and buildings	001–202	9 000.00	
	Accumulated depreciation on leasehold land and buildings	001–102		9 000.00
	Depreciation charge for year on motor vehicles	001–203	6 500.00	
	Accumulated depreciation on motor vehicles	001–103		6 500.00
	Depreciation charge for year on plant and machinery	001–204	3 700.00	
	Accumulated depreciation on plant and machinery	001–104		3 700.00
	Depreciation charge on fixtures and fittings	001–205	8 600.00	
	Accumulated depreciation on fixtures and fittings	001–205		8 600.00
			30 800.00	30 800.00

discusses the meaning and methods of calculation of depreciation charges. For the present, it is sufficient to recognise that, while depreciation is a real cost that needs to be reflected in the accounting records and accounts of an enterprise, it is not a cost which emerges from the normal system of prime documents and prime records. Accordingly, it requires the preparation of a journal entry. Another item in the same category is the provision for bad and doubtful debts. All businesses incur bad debts (i.e. customers who, for whatever reason, fail to pay the monies that they owe) and it is normal practice to provide for this. The normal system of prime documents and prime records will ensure that the debt is properly recorded, but it will not record the possibility of non-payment. This is a matter of managerial judgement, which, once made, needs to recorded. Table 2.6 illustrates a journal entry dealing with bad-debt provisions.

Every business enterprise will encounter events/transactions which need to be recorded in the accounting records via journals. The internal control system needs to ensure that all such events/transactions are in fact recognised and recorded; that the journal entries are properly prepared and authorised by responsible personnel; and that unauthorised personnel are not able to initiate and process journal-entry transactions.

Trial balance

The volume of ledger accounts and the even larger volume of individual transactions means that there is great scope for unintentional error in accounting records. However, the double entry system also provides quite considerable scope for

Table 2.6   Illustration of a journal entry dealing with bad and doubtful debt provisions

Date	Description	Code	Debit £	Credit £
31/12/9X	Bad and doubtful debts charge	005–007	4 500.00	
	Trade debtors	002–101		4 500.00
			4 500.00	4 500.00

detecting such errors. This is because of its requirement that the bookkeeping equation always be in balance. If it is not in balance an error must have occurred. A trial balance is nothing more or less than a listing of the balances on all the individual ledger accounts. By definition, each of these balances will be a debit balance (where the value of the debit entries on an individual ledger account exceeds the value of the credit entries) or a credit balance (where the value of the credit entries exceeds the value of the debit entries). The trial balance totals the value of the debit balances and the value of the credit balances. These should be equal. If they are not, there must be an error somewhere in the ledger accounts. Examples of such errors include incorrect arithmetic (where an arithmetical error has been made in computing the balance on a ledger account(s)), single-sided entries (where one part of an event/transaction has been recorded in the ledger accounts but not the other part) and unbalanced entries (where the amount at which the event/transaction has been recorded differs between the ledger accounts in which it has been recorded). Table 2.7 illustrates the structure of a trial balance.

Table 2.7   Illustration of a trial balance

Main code	Sub-code	Account title	Debit £	Credit £
001		Fixed assets		
	001	Freehold land and buildings – cost	67 000.00	
	002	Leasehold land and buildings – cost	85 000.00	
	003	Motor vehicles – cost	32 000.00	
	004	Plant and machinery – cost	49 500.00	
	005	Furniture and fittings – cost	18 700.00	
	101	Freehold land and buildings – accumulated depreciation		77 00.00
	102	Leasehold land and buildings – accumulated depreciation		77 00.00 98 00.00
	103	Motor vehicles – accumulated depreciation		10 250.00
	104	Plant and machinery – accumulated depreciation		11 200.00
	105	Furniture and fittings – accumulated depreciation		67 00.00
etc.	etc.	etc.		
		Totals	£	£

However, even if the trial balance balances this does not provide a guarantee that the recording in the ledger accounts of the transactions is correct. This is because there are some types of error which do not have an impact on the balancing of the bookkeeping equation. Examples of such errors include a debit or credit entry being correctly recorded except that it is recorded in the wrong ledger account; a transaction not being recorded at all (i.e. neither a debit nor a credit entry relating to it has been made); and the recording of a transaction being duplicated (i.e. the relevant debit and credit entries have been repeated). Thus, while the trial balance provides a valuable check on the integrity of the accounting records, it does not provide a foolproof one. This reinforces the need for an adequate system of internal control to ensure that all transactions are recorded, that they are recorded in the correct ledger accounts and that they are not duplicated.

Recognition of elements of accounts

So far we have reviewed the structure of accounting records in the light of the fundamental accounting identity and bookkeeping equations. In doing this, we have referred to the recording of economic events (transactions) affecting an enterprise. What we have not looked at are the circumstances in which such an event (transaction) should be recognised/recorded for accounting purposes. In this respect there are two main issues to be considered:

1 Recording of an event (transaction) in the core accounting records: this will take place at the time the event itself takes place. Such an event may be a purchase transaction, a sales transaction, a payment transaction, a receipt transaction or any of a wide range of other possible transactions that the enterprise might enter into. The recording will take place at the monetary value of the transaction, for example purchase price, sales price, payment amount. The actual recording will be stimulated by the event/transaction itself and, more particularly, by the prime document which is associated with the event. Thus, a cheque payment will involve the preparation of a cheque requisition and its authorisation, the physical preparation of the cheque, its recording in a cheque payments record, and (along with other such payments) its analysis and processing to the ledger accounts. The internal control system of the enterprise should be such as to ensure that all events/transactions take place within a structured and controlled environment so that no events/ transactions can be overlooked, and all lead to the appropriate documentation being raised and the appropriate accounting entries being made.

2 Preparation of the financial statements from the core accounting records: of prime concern here is the basis on which the financial statements are to be prepared. Closely associated with this is another consideration, whether or not the monetary value at which the event is shown in the core accounting records is an appropriate one for inclusion in the financial statements.

Let us look first at the basis on which the financial statements are to be prepared. There are two main such bases:

■ **Cash basis**: using this basis, only cash and cash-at-bank transactions are recognised in the financial statements. The only income recognised is cash receipts. The only expenditure recognised is cash payments. The only asset (or liability) recognised is cash in hand and at bank (or bank overdraft). No transactions other than those involving an exchange of cash are recognised in the financial statements. If the enterprise has more cash and cash at bank at the end of the financial period than it had at the start it has made a surplus/profit. If it has less it has incurred a deficit/loss. Given the range of assets and liabilities that modern commercial enterprises have and the volume of credit transactions in which they engage, financial statements prepared on a cash basis could only give a very incomplete picture of the activities of an enterprise. In addition, such financial statements would be very susceptible to manipulation, for example by delaying payments to creditors. The picture that they give of the enterprise could be changed dramatically by altering the timing of the receipts and payments. Nowadays, the use of cash accounting is mainly restricted to some professional practices and to various aspects of government accounting, and in government accounting there are strong moves away from cash accounting to the other basis of accounting, the accruals basis.

■ **Accruals basis**: virtually all financial statements are prepared on this basis nowadays. It recognises the existence of assets and liabilities other than cash, and it recognises the existence of transactions other than those involving the exchange of cash. In fact, it goes beyond simply recognising the existence of these things; it maintains that without doing so it would be impossible to provide an adequate portrayal of the activities of an enterprise and of the outcomes of these activities. Thus, financial statements prepared on this basis 'provide the type of information about past transactions and other events that is most useful to users in making economic decisions' (IASC 1989: para. 22). However, the range of potential assets and liabilities, income and expenses that can be recognised in financial statements prepared on the accruals basis is complex and contentious. There is great scope for differing accounting representations of the same set of economic events and, as we shall see in Chapter 3, there is evidence of use being made of this scope by management to prepare financial statements giving rather rosy pictures of corporate performance.

The second consideration is that of assessing whether or not the monetary value at which an item is recorded in the core accounting records and a trial balance is in fact appropriate for inclusion in a set of financial statements. There are a number of circumstances in which this value may not be appropriate. In identifying some of these circumstances it should be noted that we are concentrating on the accruals basis of accounting.

For example, while a credit sale may have been made to a customer during the financial period and been correctly recorded in the ledger at the value of the sale, the customer may have become insolvent and unable to pay the debt. Thus the debt is not worth the amount shown in the ledger and an adjustment is required. Equally, there may be transactions recorded correctly in the ledger which affect more than one financial period. For example, an enterprise with a 31 December financial year end may, on 1 July, have paid insurance premiums relating to the coming twelve-month period. In such a case the payment recorded in the ledger needs to be apportioned between two financial years in preparing financial statements. Similarly, an enterprise may have paid rent in advance at the end of the financial period. In such circumstances an adjustment, normally called a prepayment, to the core accounting information (trial balance) will be required when financial statements are being prepared.

There may also be economic events affecting the financial period which have not yet been recorded in the ledger. For example, an enterprise might not, at the year-end, have received an invoice for the electricity it has consumed during the last couple of months of the financial year. Accordingly, no expense for this electricity will have been recorded in the ledger. In these and similar instances an adjustment, called an 'accrual' (the noun from the verb 'to accrue'), to the information contained in the core accounting records will be required before the financial statements can be prepared.

Typically, adjustments for prepayments and accruals are made by journal entries raised at the end of the financial period. Such journal entries are similar to those illustrated earlier regarding depreciation charges and bad/doubtful provisions. In the case of a company having paid insurance premiums of £5000 relating to the period 1 July 19X0 to 19X1 and having a financial year ending on 31 December, Table 2.8 illustrates the relevant journal entry.

As at 31 December 19X0 the company has paid in advance for six months' insurance and therefore the amount of the prepayment was 50% of the premium, i.e. £2500. Within the structure of the company's chart of accounts, insurance premiums are charged to administration costs. It is relatively easy for most enterprises to identify their prepayments because their accounting system will have recorded the payment and documentation will be available on which to base the computation of the prepayment. In the case of accruals the position may be more difficult. While the enterprise may recognise the need to make an accrual, for example as regards electricity, it may well have to estimate the amount of a necessary accrual in the absence of a supplier's invoice at the time when the accounts are being prepared. In such circumstances it will need to base its estimates on previous invoices, price levels and estimates of

Table 2.8 Example of a journal entry recording prepayments

Date	Description	Code	Debit	Credit
31/12/9X	Prepayments	002–103	2 500.00	
	Administrative costs	005 005		2 500.00
			2 500.00	2 500.00

Being prepaid insurance premiums as at 31/12/9X

Table 2.9 Example of a journal entry recording accruals

Date	Description	Code	Debit	Credit
31/12/9X	Premises costs	005–003	350.00	
	Accruals	003–007		350.00
			350.00	350.00

Being accrued electricity costs as at 31/12/9X

consumption. If a company estimates that it needs to accrue £350 for electricity charges then it will need to process a journal entry such as that shown in Table 2.9.

The core principles for the initial recognition of economic events and transactions affecting an element in the accounting records and in financial statements are that:

(**a**) there is sufficient evidence that the change in assets or liabilities inherent in the element has occurred (including, where appropriate, evidence that a future inflow or outflow of benefit will occur); and

(**b**) it can be measured as a monetary amount with sufficient reliability.

(ASB 1995a: para. 4.6)

Similar principles apply to the subsequent remeasurement of an element or, ultimately, the derecognition of an element. In this context an element is an asset, a liability, equity, a gain or a loss (definitions of which have already been provided). Most of the time the prime documents and the resultant prime records and ledger accounts will ensure that events/transactions that need to be recorded in the accounts will in fact be so recorded. However, as we have indicated, enterprises need to ensure that they have set up internal control systems which will ensure that *all* events/transactions meeting the recognition criteria are in fact recorded, and this will involve the use of journal entries to supplement the system of prime records. This may well require an extension to the trial balance for the preparation of financial statements. Table 2.10 illustrates such an extension.

Ignoring the column of codes, the first two columns in Table 2.10 are the trial balance as derived from the core ledger accounts maintained by the enterprise. The next two columns represent the 'post-trial balance' journal entries needed to comply with the recognition criteria outlined above, and the final two columns represent the final trial balance on which the enterprise's final statements will be based. Of course, these final adjustments will need, at some point in time, to be incorporated into the ledger accounts of the enterprise. This is particularly important as the final balances on the ledger accounts will be the basis of the accounting records for the next financial year.

Table 2.10   Illustration of a final trial balance

Account code	Ledger account balances		Final accounts adjustments		Final accounts balances	
	Debit £	Credit £	Debit £	Credit £	Debit £	Credit £
001–001	XXX				XXX	
001–002	XXX				XXX	
001–003	XXX				XXX	
001–004	XXX				XXX	
001–005	XXX				XXX	
001–101		XXX		XXX		XXX
001–102		XXX		XXX		XXX
etc.						
	XXX	XXX	XXX	XXX	XXX	XXX

Monetary value

As has already been stated, the first stage of accounting is principally concerned with recording the economic events/transactions affecting an enterprise, and in particular recording the monetary values attaching to these events/transactions. Subsequently, and largely based on this initial recording, management information and external financial statements are prepared. This immediately raises the question of what monetary values should be used for this purpose (as opposed to the initial recording). This is a very difficult question to answer, given the various groups interested in accounting information and their differing information requirements. The identification and reporting of the appropriate monetary value of assets/liabilities/gains/losses is a major concern of this book and a theme which recurs at many points. For the present it is sufficient to recognise that there are different bases for attaching monetary values to economic events/transactions, and to individual assets and liabilities resulting from such events/transactions. The measurement bases that could be used, each having its own advantages and disadvantages in relation to the purposes for which the accounting information is required, include:

- **Historical cost**: this is the cash-equivalent value attaching to an event/transaction at the time that it took place. Thus the historical cost of an item of stock or a fixed asset such as a motor vehicle owned by an enterprise is the amount that it paid to acquire it.
- **Replacement cost**: this is the current cash amount that an enterprise would have to pay to replace an asset that it currently owns. Thus if it owns an item of stock which it acquired at an historical cost of £100 and it would now cost £150 to purchase a similar item, the replacement cost of the item of stock it owns is £150.
- **Net realisable value**: this is the amount for which an asset could be sold, net of any expenses incurred in the sale.
- **Net present value**: this is a slightly more difficult concept, but one which is closely related to the definition of an asset given earlier. The net present value of an asset is the current-value equivalent of all the cash flows that an enterprise will receive deriving from its ownership of the asset, allowing for the fact that money has a time value, i.e. that money now is worth more than money in the future. The time of value of money is covered in detail in Chapter 13.

Fundamental accounting concepts

As we pointed out earlier, the accruals basis of accounting is both more complex and more contentious than the cash basis, and can lead to many different accounting representations of similar economic events. To help guard against unnecessary diversity in accounting presentation certain **fundamental accounting concepts** have been enunciated. These were formally presented by the ASSC in SSAP 2 in 1971. (The role and objectives of the ASSC are discussed in Chapter 4; for the present it is sufficient to note that its prime concerns were to make financial statements more understandable and comparable across enterprises.) Subsequently, these fundamental accounting concepts were given the force of law and incorporated into the Companies Acts. Associated with these fundamental accounting concepts, but not formally part of them, is the view that accounting records should be maintained and financial statements prepared on the historical-cost basis of accounting; that is, all assets, liabilities, income and expenses should be stated in the records and financial statements at the monetary amount at which transactions took place. We will see later in this chapter, and in Chapter 3, that there are occasions when this assumption is breached. However, all events/transactions should initially be recorded at their historical cost. Any later deviations from this are a matter for specific decision and full disclosure in any external financial statements.

There are four fundamental accounting concepts:

1 **The matching concept**: this requires that once any part of a transaction is recognised all the other elements of that transaction must also be recognised. Thus if an item of income is recognised in financial records and statements all the costs of generating that income must be recognised, as must any associated changes in assets and liabilities. For example, a credit sales transaction involving merchandise which the enterprise previously held in stock will involve the following elements, each of which must be recognised (recorded):

- income (the revenue from the sale);
- an increase in debtors (resulting from the sale);
- a reduction in stock (resulting from the transfer of the stock to the customer);
- an increase in costs (the cost to the enterprise of giving up the asset, stock, which it previously owned).

All of these different elements need to be recorded if the matching concept is to be adhered to. If they were not recorded the accounting records and any resultant financial statements would tell only part of the story.

2 **The going-concern concept**: this requires that, in the absence of evidence to the contrary, accounting records should be maintained and financial statements prepared on the assumption that the enterprise in question will continue to exist in the future and that it will continue to trade. The implication of this assumption is that the assets of the business will not be the subject of a forced sale and that any contingent liabilities of the enterprise which would arise if it ceased to trade remain contingent. This is a significant assumption, because the forced-sale value of the assets of an enterprise may well be significantly lower than their historical cost or other reported value. For example, it is widely recognised that debts will be difficult to collect and work-in-progress difficult to sell in the event of an insolvency.

3 **The prudence concept**: as we saw earlier, the accruals basis of accounting recognises the existence of items other than cash. The ultimate case value of items recognised in this way must, by definition, be more or less uncertain. How much can the stock be sold for? Will the enterprise receive all the money it is owed by debtors? There may be similar uncertainties regarding the amount that will ultimately be paid by creditors. This uncertainty is the focus of the prudence concept, which was referred to in Chapter 1.

> Prudence is the inclusion of a degree of caution in the exercise of the judgements needed in making the estimates required under conditions of uncertainty, such that incomes or assets are not overstated and expenses or liabilities are not understated.
>
> (ASB 1995a: para. 2.20)

4 The consistency concept: this concept recognises that differing accounting bases and policies are available to an enterprise preparing financial statements. The concept requires that an enterprise be consistent in the bases and policies it adopts. If this were not to be so it would be impossible for the users of the financial information provided by the enterprise to use it with confidence or to compare information relating to one financial period with that relating to another.

These four fundamental concepts, together with the core accounting records based on the fundamental accounting identity and bookkeeping equation, are the underpinning of the traditional financial statements, which we examine in Chapter 3.

Conclusions

The theme of this chapter has been that reports produced by accountants can be of value to their readers, whether internal or external, only if they are prepared from core accounting records based on the timely and accurate recording of economic activities. It has also sought to define the various elements of the accounting framework and raise some of the issues involved in the extraction of financial statements from the underpinning accounting records. Management has an important role to play in identifying the nature and extent of the analysis of transactions that it needs to help it discharge its managerial responsibilities, and in setting up internal control

The origins of accounting lie in the need for the owners and managers of resources to have information to enable them to plan and control the use of these resources. The nature of the accounting records needed to provide this information has developed over time, although a landmark in this was the development of double-entry bookkeeping in the fifteenth century. Modern accounting systems have their roots in this development, although the introduction of computer database systems has led to major changes in the implementation of accounting systems. The principles of double-entry bookkeeping have also been influential in the structure of the financial statements of companies.

Any system of accounting, if it is to achieve its core objective of providing useful information, needs to be based on the maintenance of accounting records which reflect the economic activities of the enterprise in question on a timely and accurate basis. To achieve this, management needs to institute a system of internal control. Such a system of internal control will need to:

■ provide assurance that management's operating policies are being properly implemented;

■ provide an adequate system of prime documents and prime records to ensure that the impact on the enterprise of all its economic activities is captured in the accounting records;

■ provide adequate procedures for the preparation of accounting reports, whether internal or external, from the accounting records;

■ have regard to legal and quasi-legal requirements, as well as those of management, in the design of the enterprise's structure of accounting records.

systems which will ensure that the policies it determines, whether relating to operating or financial matters, are properly implemented.

Further reading

The ASB (1995a) provides a professional view on the concepts and principles which should underpin financial reporting. Nobes (1997) gives an explication of the basics of financial accounting, as do, at a more advanced level, Alexander and Britton (1996). Smith (1996) offers insights into the ways in which companies can use the flexibility inherent in financial reporting to their advantage.

Questions and exercises

1 Using the chart of accounts shown in Table 2.2, design a cashbook layout to record the following transactions and record the transactions shown below in this layout:
   (a) the payment of £10 000 for a new delivery van;
   (b) the payment of £250 for an advertisement in a local newspaper;
   (c) the payment to a supplier of £2500 for goods originally supplied on credit terms;
   (d) the repayment of £10 000 of a long-term loan;
   (e) the receipt of £2000 from a customer who had been supplied with goods on credit terms;
   (f) the receipt of £20 000 from the issue of new share capital;
   (g) the payment of wages amounting to £6000.
2 The prime records of Suppliers Ltd contain the following summaries of its transactions for the week ending 7 January 19XX. These need to be transferred to its ledger accounts. Prepare journal entries which will do this, using the chart of accounts contained in Table 2.2.
   (a) credit sales to customers amounting to £60 000 of merchandise which originally cost £30 000;
   (b) cash sales to customers amounting to £7000 of merchandise which originally cost £3700;
   (c) purchases of materials from suppliers on credit terms amounting to £35 000;
   (d) payments to suppliers, for materials supplied on credit terms amounting to £18 000;
   (e) payments to staff of salaries and wages amounting to £6000.
3 Magic Ltd is in the process of preparing its annual financial statements for the financial year ended 31 December 19X0. Its accounting records are up to date and it has prepared a trial balance from these records which balances. However, there are some economic events needing to be incorporated in the financial statements which have not as yet been recorded in the accounting records. Accordingly, journal entries need to prepared to record these events, which are:
   (a) Smith Ltd, which owes Magic £2000, has been put into liquidation and the liquidators have informed creditors that they do anticipate being able to make any distributions to creditors.
   (b) On 1 November 19X0 Magic paid an advance rental for its sales office in

Guildford. This rental payment was in the amount of £10 000 and related to the period 1 November 19X0 to 31 January 19X1.

(c) The last telephone bill that Magic received was for £397.81 and related to the quarter ended 31 October. The bill comprised £100.00 for the rental of facilities for the coming quarter and £297.81 for call charges for the previous quarter. Historically, Magic's telephone bill has been fairly constant each quarter.

(d) On 30 December 19X0 Magic received a special delivery of goods from Jones Ltd with a purchase price of £8000. The invoice from Jones was not received until January 19X1, after the trial balance had been prepared.

(e) As at 31 December 19X0 Magic owned plant and machinery which had cost it £100 000 to acquire. It had analysed this plant and machinery and had calculated that it needed to incorporate a depreciation charge of £15 000 in its financial statements for the period ending 31 December 19X0.

Using the chart of accounts contained in Table 2.2, prepare journal entries to incorporate the above information in the final trial balance, and hence accounts, of Magic.

4 John Smith is about to set up in business as a newsagent in rented premises. He has asked you to help in designing a chart of accounts for this business which will provide him with the information he needs to manage the business in a cost-effective way. Prepare a chart of accounts which would be suitable for a small newsagent business.

5 Makeit Ltd is a small company which specialises in the manufacture of wrought-iron gates to customer specifications. It employs three specialist blacksmiths, a salesman/negotiator and an office administrator, and offers its customers thirty-day credit terms. Prepare a schedule listing the prime documents that it needs to have as a basis for the maintenance of its accounting records.

6 Unification plc is a large, diversified company in the electronics industry. It has a well-established accounting and internal control system. However, in preparing its financial statements each year it finds it necessary to make a number of adjustments to the information recorded in its accounting system. List the areas in which you believe that it finds it necessary to make such adjustments.

7 If a trial balance does not balance it indicates that there have been errors in the recording of transactions. What are the types of errors that an 'unbalanced' trial balance might indicate? Are there any types of recording errors which would not lead a trial balance 'not to balance'? If so, what are they?

8 Discuss the things that management should take into account in determining the design of an accounting system which will satisfy both its own information requirements and its obligation to provide external reports on the entity which it manages.

9 There are several possible approaches which accountants can employ in the measurement of the economic activities in which enterprises engage. Assess which measurement bases are most likely to provide the different stakeholders associated with an enterprise with the information that they require.

10 Accountants have developed criteria which they employ for the recognition of the economic activities of enterprises. How appropriate are these criteria for stakeholders who may wish to make decisions about their relationships with an enterprise?

3 The principal accounting statements

Objectives

In this chapter we examine the structure and content of the primary financial statements. Originally these were the balance sheet and profit and loss account. However, in more recent years cash-flow/funds-flow statements have also come to be regarded as primary financial statements, and in 1992, a further primary financial statement, a statement of total recognised gains and losses, was introduced. We will see that the purpose of these statements is to provide useful information to the users of the financial statements about the financial position, performance and adaptability of the enterprises to which they relate.

Attention will be paid to the ways in which accountants classify and present information in financial statements – including the distinction between fixed and current assets in balance sheets, and the debate regarding the nature and disclosure of ordinary and extraordinary items in the profit and loss account. Reference will also be made to the influence of legislation and the statements of professional accountancy bodies on the structure and content of the financial statements of enterprises, although this influence is dealt with in more detail in Chapter 4. Emphasis is placed on the need for financial statements to provide an effective communication channel accessible to interested parties.

The primary financial statements

The primary financial statements are the principal means via which the managers of an enterprise communicate information to the differing stakeholders associated with it. These statements are based on the accounting records of enterprises (the bases of which were described in Chapter 2) and have to comply with requirements of both law (principally the Companies Acts) and quasi-law (pronouncements of professional accounting bodies and other organisations such as the Stock Exchange). They deal with three main aspects of the financial affairs of enterprises:

- resources and the funding of resources – this is the focus of the balance sheet;
- performance in terms of the increases (gains) or the decreases (losses) in ownership

interest over a financial period – this is the focus of the profit and loss account and the statement of total recognised gains and losses;

■ the sources of the enterprise's cash inflows and the ways in which these have been applied – this is the focus of the cash-flow statement.

Taken together, these statements can provide a rich source of information for assessing the financial affairs of enterprises, particularly when interpreted in conjunction with other sources of information.

Balance sheets

The purpose of a balance sheet has been stated by the ASB as:

> The balance sheet (together with related notes) provides information about an entity's assets and liabilities and its ownership interest and shows their relationships to each other at a point in time. The balance sheet delineates the entity's resource structure (major classes and amounts of assets) and its financial structure (major classes and amounts of liabilities and ownership interest).

> (ASB 1995a: para. 6.34)

With this definition in mind, we look at the basic framework of a balance sheet and then proceed to examine its various components in more detail. Broadly speaking, the balance sheets produced by many public-sector organisations are similar to those produced by private-sector companies, although the detailed requirements of various parts of statute law and the requirements of sponsoring ministries mean that there may be differences in their detailed contents. For the present the reader can assume that the following description of balance sheets is equally applicable to private- and public-sector organisations.

A useful first step is to look at the principal balance sheet headings and the overall framework of balance sheets. This approach is particularly relevant given the increasing tendency of some large public companies to keep their balance sheets free from what they regard as unnecessary detail. Such companies seek to emphasise the key elements and relationships in the balance sheet and provide more detailed information in supplementary notes. This style of financial reporting is potentially very useful because it provides informed readers with key figures on which to concentrate. However, it can also be argued that it might lead to important issues being relegated to supplementary notes which may not be read by many users of the financial statements. The issue of the balance between the information content of the primary financial statements themselves and the information content of amplifying/supplementary information is considered in more detail in Chapter 4. However, the key point is that such supplementary disclosures should serve to provide only additional information which expands on and is consistent with the core information disclosed in the primary financial statements. It should not contradict or otherwise be at variance with the information in the primary financial statements. Unfortunately, as we shall see, this has not always been the case.

The essential structure of a balance sheet, based on the fundamental accounting identity discussed in Chapter 2, is shown in Table 3.1. The first point to note about

Table 3.1 Framework of a balance sheet

Summary balance sheet of XYZ plc as at 31 December 1997				
	1997		1996	
	£000s	£000s	£000s	£000s
Fixed assets		X		X
Current assets	X		X	
Current liabilities	X		X	
Net current assets		X		X
Long-term liabilities		X		X
Total net assets		X	X	
Share capital		X		X
Reserves		X		X
		X	X	

this balance sheet structure is its identification. The title clearly states the name of the entity and the point in time to which the balance sheet relates. Without this information the statement would be useless. It also reinforces the fact that the balance sheet is a position statement showing the assets, liabilities and equity of a specific entity at a specific point in time. The second point to note is the provision of comparative figures relating to the previous year. Stakeholders in the entity will want to know how the structure of its assets, liabilities and equity has changed during the period to which the financial statements relate. The provision of comparative figures enables them to do this. In practice, particularly for large companies which have their shares listed on the Stock Exchange, a separate part of the annual report will be a financial review which shows comparative data for five, ten or twenty years, enabling trends in the financial structure and performance of the company to be identified.

As can be seen from the framework shown in Table 3.1, for financial reporting purposes, accounting conventionally classifies assets (which were defined in Chapter 2) into two main categories, fixed assets and current assets. The core of this distinction is the purpose for which an enterprise holds the assets and the duration of time for which it intends to hold them. It is not concerned with the physical nature of the assets.

Fixed assets

These are assets which the enterprise intends to hold for the long term (normally deemed to be more than twelve months) and which it owns, or has exclusive use of, for the generation of profit on an ongoing basis. Examples of fixed assets include land

and buildings, plant and machinery, furniture and equipment, motor vehicles, etc. It may be the case that an enterprise owns two physically identical assets, one of which will be classified as a fixed asset and one of which will not. Consider a motor dealer owning two identical vans. One van may have been acquired with a view to using it in the business over a long period of time for carrying spares, making deliveries, etc. This would be classified as a fixed asset. The other may have been acquired with a view to making a profit from reselling it. Such a van, which will typically spend a short period of time with the enterprise, perhaps in a showroom until it is sold, would not be classified as a fixed asset. It would be classified as a current asset.

Fixed assets are generally stated in financial statements at their original cost (or sometimes at a subsequent revaluation) less accumulated depreciation. The monetary value at which fixed assets are included in financial statements is a frequent source of confusion to non-accountants and it is worth spending some time on examining the bases on which it is normally computed. The starting point in the process, like that for other accounting events and transactions, is the price that was originally paid for the asset – its original cost. This will be recorded in the core accounting records just as would any other asset or liability, and it will also be recorded in some form of subsidiary register, where the physical details and location of the asset will be shown. However, the use of the asset by the enterprise in the generation of income will involve a cost which needs to be recognised.

To illustrate this, let us assume that an enterprise purchased a fifty-year lease on a factory for £100 000 on 1 January 1980, and that the enterprise's financial year-end is 31 December each year. At 31 December 1980 the accounting records and trial balance will show an asset of £100 000. However, the enterprise will have used the factory during 1980 in its activities, and a charge needs to be made in its profit and loss account for that year to reflect the cost of this use (so as to conform with the matching principle). This is because the lease on the factory is a wasting asset – at some point in the future (at the end of the lease period) the asset (the lease) will disappear and have no value at all. Thus we are faced with a problem: the enterprise paid £100 000 for something in 1980 which it is going to use for a long period of time (fifty years), at the end of which it will be worthless. How are we to account for this? The accountant's answer is depreciation (or a word which means the same in the case of leasehold property, amortisation).

The accounting problem which depreciation addresses is that of an enterprise incurring a cost (spending money) on something with a long but limited life, and how this cost should be allocated over the life of the resource (asset) that was acquired. Depreciation is simply the accounting device via which this is achieved; it spreads (allocates) the cost of the asset to the individual accounting periods comprising the life of the asset. Thus in the case of the factory lease the £100 000 cost of the lease has to be spread over its fifty-year life. The easiest way of doing this is simply to allocate the same amount, i.e. £100 000/50 = £2000, to each of the years involved. This is the easiest and most common way of calculating depreciation and is called the 'straight-line' method of depreciation. The reason it is called the straight-line method is that the accounting value of the asset reduces each year in a linear fashion, the amount of the reduction being the constant annual depreciation charge (see Figure 3.1).

There are, of course, instances where companies will intend to replace assets before the end of their useful lives. For example, an enterprise might have a policy

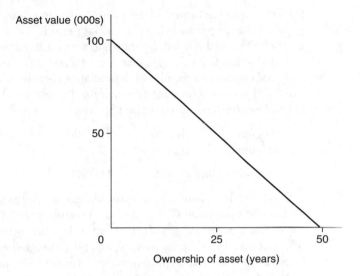

Figure 3.1
Straight-line
depreciation.

of disposing of its motor vehicles after four years of ownership to ensure that its vehicle fleet maintains an appropriate level of reliability. In such a case it would not be right to charge the whole of the original cost of a vehicle to the four years for which the enterprise owns it. Only the difference between the original cost and the amount for which the vehicle is disposed of at the end of the four years, i.e. the difference between original cost and any salvage value, should be charged. Continuing to use the straight-line idea of depreciation, we can identify a formula for computing the amount of depreciation to be allocated to each of the years for which a fixed asset is owned and used by an enterprise. This formula is:

$$D = \frac{C - S}{N} \qquad (3.1)$$

where: D = the amount of the depreciation to be allocated to each year of the asset's
life;
C = the original cost of the asset;
S = the estimated salvage value of the asset;
N = the estimated life of the asset in years.

Each year the amount of the depreciation charge (allocation) will be included as a cost in the profit and loss account of the enterprise. However, the bookkeeping equation requires that whenever one of its components is changed so must another be, to ensure that the equation remains in balance. In this instance we have changed one element (costs) by the amount of the depreciation charge, and so we must change another element by the same amount. This other element is assets, in particular the accounting value of the fixed asset to which the depreciation relates. This is achieved via the concept of accumulated depreciation. Accumulated depreciation is simply the total amount of depreciation that has been charged (allocated) in relation to an individual fixed asset since it was acquired by the enterprise. It is deducted from the cost of the asset in the balance sheet. Returning to our example of the factory lease, after the enterprise has occupied the premises for ten years it will have charged (allocated) depreciation to ten individual financial periods, i.e. a total amount of £2000 × 10 = £20 000. This £20 000 will be shown as accumulated depreciation in the balance sheet as a deduction from the original cost of £100 000. The resultant net monetary value (original cost less accumulated depreciation) is referred to as the net book value of the asset and is the net amount at which fixed assets are shown in a balance sheet. In our example of the lease it would be £80 000, made up of:

Original cost of the lease	£100 000
Accumulated depreciation	20 000
Net book value	£80 000

So far we have assumed that the difference between the original cost of an asset and any salvage value is allocated on a simple straight-line basis to each of the years for which it is owned (used), that is the key factor in the computation of depreciation is time. In addition to straight-line depreciation, there are other methods of calculating depreciation in which time remains the key factor in computing depreciation. Consider, for example, an enterprise purchasing a new car which it will keep for four years and the change in the value of that car over the four-year period – it is most unlikely that the value of the car will decline in a linear way. It is much more likely to decline in the way indicated in Figure 3.2.

As we have seen, the objective of depreciation is to allocate the difference between the original cost of the asset and any ultimate salvage value over the life of the asset. The straight-line method assumes that each of the years comprising this life should bear an equal amount of this difference. However, as the example of the car shows, this may not reflect the way in which the asset in fact loses value over time. To deal with this, other methods of time-based depreciation have been devised which do attempt to reflect the pattern of loss in value illustrated in Figure 3.2. The most notable of these is the reducing-balance method of depreciation. In this method each

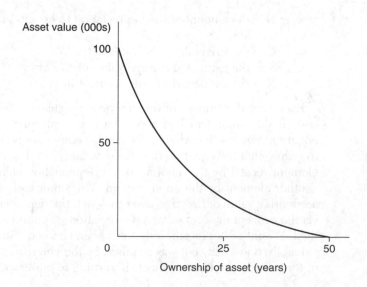

Figure 3.2
Reducing-balance
depreciation.

year's depreciation allocation is based, not on the original cost of the asset, but on its net book value at the start of the financial year in question. The formula for computing the annual depreciation charge under the reducing-balance method is:

$$D = 1 - \sqrt[n]{\frac{S}{C}} \qquad (3.2)$$

where: D = depreciation percentage (of opening net book value) per annum
n = estimated life in years
S = forecast salvage value
C = original cost

As noted in Chapter 5, the Inland Revenue in the UK use a form of reducing-balance depreciation to calculate capital allowances (taxation depreciation), which are used as a basis for assessing taxable income.

Apart from the time-based methods of computing depreciation, there are a number of other methods, mostly based on the amount of usage of the asset during a given financial period. The underlying principle of these methods is that of specifying a 'usage capacity' for an asset when it is first acquired. This 'usage capacity' might be specified as 100 000 miles in the case of a lorry, 40 000 operations in the case of a machine, or 35 000 flying hours in the case of an aeroplane. Using the original cost, an estimate of salvage value and the estimated 'usage capacity', a depreciation charge is calculated for each mile driven, operation performed or hour flown. Thereafter, depreciation is charged in each financial period based on the number of miles driven, operations performed or hours flown in that period, multiplied by this charge.

In the UK there are no legally specified methods for computing depreciation (the directors of an enterprise have to select the one they believe is most appropriate to their circumstances), although SSAP 12 (ASC 1992) deals with accounting for depreciation. Given the range of different methods available for computing depreciation and the critical importance of forecasts (salvage value and asset life) in this computation, a reader of an enterprise's annual financial statements would not be able properly to understand its financial state of affairs without knowing on what basis depreciation had been calculated and what were the key estimates that had been used in its computation. As we shall see in Chapter 4, the policies an enterprise employs in computing depreciation are regarded as a significant item of information for the readers of financial statements and must be disclosed as part of those statements, normally via the supplementary notes.

So far we have focused on valuing fixed assets in financial statements at original cost less accumulated depreciation. However, we have already acknowledged that they could be stated at a valuation less any subsequent accumulated depreciation. Why is this? The problem is that because fixed assets are, by definition, assets that an enterprise holds for the long term, the *market value* of such assets may diverge significantly from their net book value based on original cost and, while the basic accounting concept is that they are not held for resale, such resale is always an option. If values have risen significantly since the asset was acquired shareholders, in particular, will be interested in whether or not it would be financially better from their point of view if fixed assets were to be sold rather than continuing to be employed in the activities of the enterprise. On the other hand, if values have fallen significantly lenders might want to review their relationship with an enterprise, particularly if their lending is secured on the value of the assets in question.

One way around this difficulty is for enterprises periodically to revalue the fixed assets in their financial statements so as to reflect their current market values. This has been a common practice by enterprises throughout recent years. The consequence of such revaluations is that balance sheet carrying values give a better indication of the economic value of properties and that depreciation charges in the profit and loss account better reflect the economic value of the resources being consumed by the enterprise in carrying out its activities. Thus users of accounts have much more relevant information on which to assess their economic relationship with the companies.

However, there is a conceptual conflict underpinning the whole issue of revaluing fixed assets in financial statements. What is the purpose of balance sheets? Is it to show the 'true' net market value of the assets and liabilities owned/controlled by an enterprise? If so, then surely everything should be stated at current market value (assuming this can be estimated) and historical cost has no place. If this is not the case, are balance sheets meant simply to show the way in which management has used the resources entrusted to it by shareholders and other providers of funds (the stewardship view)? In some ways, the debate about the purpose of financial statements is at its most pointed when it comes to the ways in which fixed assets are valued in balance sheets and depreciated in profit and loss accounts.

Associated with this is the fact that, as is evident from the foregoing, the valuation of fixed assets in the balance sheets of enterprises involves judgement (of estimated life, of estimated salvage value, of current market value). Unfortunately, all the evidence points to the fact that many intended users of financial statements do not appreciate the amount of judgement contained in financial statements, and not just as regards fixed assets. As we shall see later, there are many other areas where managerial judgement is of importance in the preparation of financial statements. The only item in a set of financial statements that does not involve the making of forecasts and judgements is cash in hand, i.e. actual money. Even cash at bank involves a judgement – that the bank will remain solvent and be able to meet its obligations to its depositors. The example of the Bank of Credit and Commerce International illustrates that this will not always be the case. Unfortunately, most readers of financial statements assume them to be stating matters of fact rather than to be based on forecasts, assessments and judgements. In the words of Ian Tegner (then chairman of the 100 Group and senior vice-president of the Institute of Chartered Accountants in Scotland):

> What fails to be appreciated is the degree of judgement in accounts. . . . The only important items in accounts really are those that reflect judgements about the future, which then determine management's assessments of the carrying value of various assets.
>
> (Ian Tegner; quoted in Singleton-Green 1990: 82)

Current assets

These are the short-term assets of an enterprise, which are either held for the purposes of trading transactions intended to generate a profit or result from such transactions. The old name for assets of this type was 'circulating assets', a descriptive term which emphasised the way in which they circulate through the business: cash is used to purchase stock (or to pay creditors if the stock is purchased on credit terms); this stock is then sold, resulting in debtors; these debtors then pay what they owe, resulting in the circle coming back to cash.

As with fixed assets, current assets will initially be stated in the accounting records of an enterprise at historical cost. Thus stock will be stated 'at the cost of bringing the product ... to its present condition and location' (ASC 1988: para. 17). Similarly, debtors will initially be stated at the monetary amount they owe the enterprise as a result of their contractual relationships with it. However, the reasons that an enterprise owns such assets are probably to facilitate its trading activities and help in the generation of sales which will eventually lead to increases in cash. Its ultimate objective is that, in the short term, all its current assets will be recycled into cash. Thus, unlike fixed assets, the current market (cash-equivalent) value of current assets is an important piece of information for understanding the financial affairs of an enterprise – it indicates how much cash the enterprise is likely to realise (as a minimum) from these assets. We say 'as a minimum' because of the fundamental accounting concept of prudence. As we saw in Chapter 2, this requires that financial statements are prepared on a prudent basis, i.e. one which does not anticipate profits until their ultimate cash realisation is reasonably certain. This is particularly relevant in the case of stocks. Stocks may have a cash-equivalent value in excess of their original cost *if they can be sold*. However, the fact that they are stocks indicates that they have not yet been sold, and therefore it is not certain that they will ultimately realise current market prices. Accordingly, their carrying value is not revalued upwards to such market prices and profits are not anticipated.

The concept of prudence goes further. It requires not only that profits are not anticipated, but also that losses *are* anticipated. The practical implementation of this with regard to current assets is that if the market (net realisable) value of a current asset becomes less than its original cost, then for financial statement purposes the monetary value of such an asset must be reduced from original cost to market value. This is usually referred to as the 'lower of cost and market value principle'. If it seems that a debtor will be unable to pay the whole of his/her debt, then for financial statement purposes the monetary value of the debt should be reduced to the estimated amount that will ultimately be received from the debtor. Similarly, if the market value of an item of stock falls below what it was originally purchased for, then its monetary value for the financial statements should be reduced. The core concept underlying the monetary valuation of current assets in a balance sheet is that of trying to provide readers with a prudent statement of the amount of cash which the enterprise is likely to have available to it, in the short term, resulting from its ownership of these assets.

However, as was pointed out above, this involves the preparers of the accounts (managers) in making judgements in relation to these current assets. For example, with respect to debtors, they have to judge whether the whole face value of the debt will be recovered. They have to make even more complex judgements with regard to stock. They first of all have to decide on the accounting policies they will use in measuring its cost, and there are a number of different ways in which this can be done. The most notable are the first in, first out (FIFO) method (which effectively assumes that the oldest items of stock are disposed of first) and the last in, first out ((LIFO) method (which assumes that the newest items of stock are disposed of first), popular for taxation reasons in the USA. In the UK the normal method is the FIFO method. However, even within this method there are other judgements to be made. SSAP 9 (ASC 1988: para. 19) states that cost should include production overheads but goes on to say that 'problems arise on the allocation of overheads which must usually involve the exercise of personal judgement in the selection of an appropriate convention' (ASC 1988: app. 1, para. 3). It is beyond the scope of this chapter to discuss methods of overhead allocation (these are dealt with in Chapter 12), but, as the standard recognises, they inevitably involve a great deal of judgement. In fact, many practising accountants maintain that the extent of the judgement involved in the valuation of stocks is one of the biggest practical problems in accounting – and one that has significant real-world consequences.

Most of the assets owned by enterprises fall fairly readily into the fixed and current assets categories. However, there will always be assets whose classification is more problematic. Such assets may include investments and intangible assets. In such instances the Companies Acts specify how they should be shown in the balance sheet.

An important issue for the purposes of this book is the principles on which the recognition of assets in financial statements is based in the first place. In Chapter 2 we saw that assets are things of value owned/controlled by an entity as a result of economic transactions; that the financial statements should recognise assets when it is reasonably certain that future economic benefits will flow to the entity as a result of its ownership/control; and that these benefits can be quantified with reasonable certainty. With some assets this can be a problem. In recent years both Smith (1996) and Griffiths (1995) have provided very readable demonstrations of the ways in which a number of enterprises have been very imaginative, first, in identifying items of value they own and control and, second, in measuring their value. It is unquestionably the case that during the latter part of the 1980s and, to some extent, in the early 1990s enterprises increasingly sought to include as assets in their financial statements items that they would not previously have done. This was undoubtedly the result of the commercial pressure to report good performance under which they found themselves, and of the desire to reflect in the financial statements better measures of 'shareholder value'. However, this increasingly placed the somewhat pragmatic nature of financial reporting and auditing under sometimes intolerable pressures. How can an auditor verify the value of a brand name or of a milk quota? This trend was, at least in part, responsible for the Dearing Committee Review of financial reporting and the formation of the FRC (both of which are discussed in Chapter 4), as well as the APB's review of the role and scope of auditing (which is discussed in Chapter 6).

Current liabilities

Current liabilities are grouped with current assets on the balance sheet. This is because they too have a short-term focus. Current assets are assets which the enterprise expects to turn into cash within the next twelve months; current liabilities are liabilities which the enterprise expects to have to settle for cash within the next twelve months. As we have already seen, a liability is an amount of money owed to a person or organisation who has either lent the enterprise money or supplied it with goods or services on a credit basis and who has not yet been paid. These are the principal types of creditors. However, there are others as well. The most notable of these are the government (for taxation arising in relation to the enterprise's activities) and shareholders (for amounts due to them for unpaid dividend payments). In some ways these are the complete opposite of each other. The enterprise has no choice about the taxation; if it has engaged in certain types of transactions with particular outcomes it will incur a taxation liability and the government will pursue it to recover the amount it is owed. In fact, various government agencies, notably the Inland Revenue and HM Customs & Excise, are among the most frequent instigators of insolvency proceedings against business enterprises. With regard to shareholders, the most common liability here is for dividends, and it is within directors' own power whether or not to propose that a dividend be paid to shareholders. However, the financial market pressures in this respect should not be ignored.

Accounting for current liabilities is, in principle, reasonably straightforward. They should be stated at the amount of money that the enterprise expects to have to pay to its creditors during the course of the twelve months following the date of the balance sheet. There should be none of the valuation problems involved with the balance sheet valuation of fixed and current assets.

Net current assets

By showing the net of current assets less current liabilities the balance sheet is directing the reader's attention to a key indicator of the enterprise's financial well-being: whether or not it will be able to meet its short-term liabilities from its short-term assets. If it cannot, it may have to resort to further borrowing to do so or it may have to contemplate fixed-asset disposals, thereby reducing its operating capacity. This is an issue which we take up in further detail in Chapter 7, when we will see that different types of enterprise have different amounts of net current assets, depending on their trading and financing structures and relationships. For the present, we need to note that it is a key measure, highlighted by the balance sheet, but, as with all financial measures, it needs to be interpreted in the light of other information.

Another name used to describe net current assets is 'working capital'. This other name reflects the fact that, while the fixed assets of an enterprise provide it with its long-term operating capacity, it is the short-term assets and liabilities that are often the day-to-day working focus of management. In exactly the same way that investments in operating capacity (fixed assets) should be justified and evaluated in terms of their contribution to the overall profitability of an enterprise, so should its investments in short-term assets. (Chapter 17 examines this issue in more depth.)

Long-term liabilities

These form part of the longer-term financing of the enterprise and comprise liabilities that are not due for settlement by the enterprise within the twelve months following the balance sheet date. Typically, they will be medium- or long-term loans provided by financial institutions. The range of terms on which such medium- to long-term finance is available is very wide. It is important that users of financial statements have a full understanding of the financing of the enterprise to which they relate. Accordingly, such financial statements, or their supporting notes, need to provide full details of the terms of all long-term loan finance. These details should provide information on when the loan finance is repayable, the interest rates which are being charged and what security, if any, has been pledged to secure the loans. The due dates for the repayment of loan finance need to be continually reassessed to ensure that any amounts which are in fact repayable within twelve months of the date of the financial statements are included in current rather than long-term liabilities.

Equity

In the previous chapter we saw that the balance sheet equation was:

$$\text{Equity} = \text{Assets} - \text{Liabilities} \tag{3.3}$$

So far in this chapter we have seen how the overall balance sheet framework deals with the items on the right-hand side of this equation by providing details of the assets owned by an enterprise (fixed and current) and of its liabilities (current and long term). The remaining part of the balance sheet deals with the left-hand side of the equation, equity in the enterprise. As we have already seen, the equity of an enterprise comprises three main elements: the amount of the risk capital invested by the owners; any accumulated surpluses (profits)/deficits (losses); and other reserves, generated by, for example, revaluations. In the case of companies incorporated under the Companies Acts, the risk capital invested by the owners is the share capital and any associated share premium. Depending on the precise constitution of a company, there can be a number of different types of share capital, each of which has different rights attaching to it. In the 1950s there was a tendency for companies to have quite complex share-capital structures involving ordinary shares, non-voting shares and various different types of preference shares. Nowadays the tendency is for companies to have rather simpler structures of share capital, although more complex financing instruments do still exist.

On the company's initial formation its constitution, as reflected in its Articles and Memorandum of Association, will provide for it to have an authorised amount of share capital, divided into a given number of shares of various types. In the simplest case all of these shares will be ordinary shares. For example, a company might have an authorised share capital of £1 million divided into 1 000 000 ordinary shares of £1 each. This £1 value is called the nominal, or par, value of the shares. The Companies Acts require that the number of authorised shares and their par value be disclosed in the financial statements. However, not all the authorised shares may have been issued by the company; and the full amount of the par value need not have been subscribed by the shareholders. Thus the financial statements need to show the number of shares that have actually been issued by the company and the amount that the shareholders have subscribed in relation to these shares. Taken together, the information about the authorised and issued shares provides readers with the information they need about the share capital of the company. For example:

Share capital:
Authorised: £1 million divided into ordinary shares of £1 each
Issued: 500 000 ordinary shares of £1 each with 50p paid   £250 000

The £250 000 is the subscribed amount of the share capital which represents the amount of risk capital that the shareholders have invested in the company. It should be noted that the unpaid balance of the issued shares effectively represents a reserve fund and the shareholders may (almost certainly will) be called upon to pay this amount at a later date. The share capital, as represented by its par value, cannot be returned to shareholders unless the company is liquidated or a court authorises a capital reconstruction. Similarly, there are various forms of reserve which cannot be returned to shareholders or paid out to them as dividends. These non-distributable reserves arise in two main ways.

The first relates to the price at which the shares are issued to the shareholders. While this cannot normally be less than the par value, it may be more. The actual price will, of course, depend on the capital market's assessment of the value of the shares. But, for example, £1 ordinary shares might be issued at a price of £1.50. In such a case the difference between the par value and the issue price (here 50p) is called the share premium. The amount of such share premiums is a non-distributable reserve and is shown as such in the accounts.

The second main way in which non-distributable reserves come into being is when an enterprise revalues its fixed assets. In such cases the difference between the previous net book value and the revaluation amount is transferred into a revaluation reserve. Such reserves are not distributable until the asset is disposed of and the revaluation surplus (more or less) realised. Again, revaluation reserves are shown in the equity section of the balance sheet as non-distributable reserves.

The other main component of the equity part of the balance sheet is retained profits/(losses). This simply represents the amount of the accumulated profit, generated by the enterprise since it was founded, which has not yet been distributed to shareholders. It increases or decreases each year in accordance with the amount of the retained profit or loss for that year.

Readers should note that the market price of the shares in a listed company may vary significantly from the nominal/par value of the shares, even allowing for retained profits and other reserves. Market price reflects the capital market's assessment of a business and financial prospects of a company.

The balance sheet in summary

The structure of a balance sheet mirrors the fundamental accounting identity, providing information on the assets, liabilities and equity of an enterprise. In the framework we used earlier in this chapter only a limited amount of information is given. A fuller version of a balance sheet is shown in Table 3.2, giving more information and conforming to current practice and requirements. In practice, even a balance sheet like this would have a large number of supplementary notes giving more detail about the items in the balance sheet.

There are many detailed legal and quasi-legal requirements regarding the preparation of balance sheets and the supplementary information that has to be given, details of which are contained in Chapter 4. To summarise, the key features of balance sheets are:

- Their objective is to provide users with information about the financial position of an enterprise at a point in time, thereby helping the user appreciate its resource and funding structure.
- They have three main components: assets, liabilities and equity, and are an elaboration of the fundamental accounting identity.

Table 3.2   Balance sheet

Balance sheet of XYZ plc as at 31 December 1997			
	1997		1996	
	£000s	£000s	£000s	£000s
Fixed assets:				
Property				
– at cost	X		X	
– accumulated depreciation	X	X	X	X
Equipment				
– at cost	X		X	
– accumulated depreciation	X	X	X	X
		X		X
Current assets:				
Stock	X		X	
Debtors	X		X	
Cash	X		X	
	X		X	
Current liabilities:				
Creditors	X		X	
Taxation	X		X	
Dividends	X		X	
	X		X	
Net current assets		X		X
Long-term liabilities		(X)		(X)
		X		X
Share capital: shares of £1 each				
authorised, issued and fully paid		X		X
Share-premium account		X		X
		X		X
Retained profit		X		X
		X		X

- Because of the way they state fixed and current assets, balance sheets are not statements of the value or worth of either individual assets or the business as a whole.
- The preparation of balance sheets involves significant amounts of judgement.

Statements of financial performance

The second main type of financial statement is statements of financial performance. There are two such statements: the profit and loss account and the statement of total recognised gains and losses. The purposes of these statements have been described by the ASB in the following way:

> Statements of financial performance contribute to the purposes of financial reporting by:
>
> (**a**) giving an account of the results of the stewardship of management to enable users to assess the past performance of management and to form a basis for developing future expectations about financial performance; and
>
> (**b**) providing feedback to users so that they can review their previous assessments of the financial performance for past periods and, if necessary, modify their assessments for future periods.
>
> (ASB 1995a: para. 6.19)

These statements are concerned with reporting on the outcomes of an enterprise's activities over a period of time, typically a financial year. Whereas balance sheets are position statements, statements of financial performance are flow statements. The same fundamental accounting principles as apply to balance sheets (going concern, matching, prudence and consistency) also apply to these statements, and particularly to profit and loss accounts, which are commonly regarded by the capital markets as providing key indicators of financial performance because they show the success of an enterprise in achieving its core objective of making profits.

We begin by looking at the traditional format of a profit and loss account as produced in recent years (Table 3.3). Later, we will look at the changes introduced by the ASB (1993a) via FRS 3. As can be seen, a traditional profit and loss account summarises all the principal components of the trading activities for a financial year and of the costs of finance for the year in question. As does the balance sheet, the profit and loss account commences with identification of the enterprise and the financial period to which it relates. Similarly, it shows figures both for the current and for a comparative period. The rationale here is the same as that for the balance sheet – to enable comparisons to be made and trend analysis started. The concept of consistency is obviously of great importance here. If the financial statements have not been prepared on a consistent basis a true comparison will be difficult, if not impossible.

A profit and loss account commences with the sales turnover of the enterprise for the relevant financial period, stated net of any value-added taxation, and then deducts from this the cost of sales, again net of any value-added taxation, to calculate the gross profit of the enterprise. This first part of the profit and loss account reflects how successful the enterprise is in the marketplaces in which it operates. This is because it relates the revenues obtained from selling goods and services in the market the enterprise is operating in to the costs of obtaining or producing these goods and services. Frequently, the relationship between gross profit and sales revenue is expressed as a percentage, called the 'gross profit percentage'. Changes in this percentage over time will indicate changes in the success of the enterprise and its management policies in the markets, both buying and selling, in which it operates.

The next section of a profit and loss account summarises the expenses that the enterprise has incurred in supporting its trading activities. In Table 3.3 it shows administrative and distribution costs and the interest that has been paid on borrowed

Table 3.3   Profit and loss account

Profit and loss account of XYZ plc for the year ended 31 December 1997			
	1997		1996
	£000s	£000s	£000s	£000s
Sales turnover		X		X
Cost of sales		X		X
Gross profit		X		X
Distribution costs	X		X	
Administrative expenses	X		X	
Interest payable	X	X	X	X
Profit on ordinary activities before taxation		X		X
Taxation on ordinary activities		X		X
Profit on ordinary activities after taxation		X		X
Extraordinary income	X		X	
Extraordinary charges	X		X	
Extraordinary profit/loss	X		X	
Taxation on extraordinary profit/loss	X	X	X	X
Profit/loss for the financial year		X		X
Dividends		X		X
Retained profit for the financial year		X		X

funds. The amount of detail shown in this section is to some extent a matter of management's judgement. For the annual external financial statements of companies the Companies Acts lay down the minimum amount of disclosure. In practice, much of the necessary disclosure, for example regarding depreciation charges and directors' remuneration, is provided in the supplementary notes to the accounts rather than on the face of the balance sheet or profit and loss account. For internal management accounts the level of detail may be extensive, depending on the amount of analysis management feel it needs for decision taking and control purposes.

The result of deducting these support expenditures from the gross profit is the profit for the year on ordinary activities, from which allowance is made for the appropriate taxation charges. The next section of the profit and loss account deals with extraordinary items. Adjusting the profit on ordinary activities by these items, the profit and loss account then shows the final profit for the financial period.

The phrase 'ordinary activities' and the concept of 'extraordinary items' require some explanation. The purpose of a profit and loss account is to provide users with information on how an enterprise has performed in a financial period. In part, this is to provide them with feedback information so that they can assess this performance against their earlier expectations. In part, it is to help them in making assessments of the likely future performance of the enterprise. To enable them to make these assessments of future performance, users need to know, not just the amount of the various components of profit (sales, cost of sales, expenses, etc.), but also whether or not these components include any unusual items – that is, items which, for whatever reason, are unlikely to recur in the future. Such knowledge may significantly improve their ability to make reliable forecasts. This issue was addressed by the ASSC in 1974 in SSAP 6 and later revisited (ASC 1986). SSAP 6 introduced the concepts of ordinary activities, exceptional items and extraordinary items. It defined these in the following terms:

> Ordinary activities are any activities which are usually, frequently or regularly undertaken by the company and any related activities in which the company engages in furtherance of, incidental to, or arising from those activities. They include, but are not confined to, the trading activities of the company.
>
> (ASC 1986: para. 28)

> Exceptional items are material items which derive from events or transactions that fall within the ordinary activities of the company, and which need to be disclosed separately by virtue of their size or incidence if the financial statements are to give a true and fair view.
>
> (ASC 1986: para. 29)

> Extraordinary items are material items which derive from events or transactions that fall outside the ordinary activities of the company and which are therefore expected not to recur frequently or regularly. They do not include exceptional items. . . .
>
> (ASC 1986: para. 30)

The view of the ASC was that achievement of the core objective of providing users with the information needed for a proper understanding of the profit and profitability of the enterprise would be facilitated by showing these three separate categories of income and expenditure separately on the face of the profit and loss account. Perhaps the best way to illustrate this view is to give examples of the unusual (exceptional and extraordinary items).

First, exceptional items were to be shown in that section of the profit and loss account dealing with ordinary activities, but emphasised by being shown as individual line items or perhaps highlighted in the notes to the accounts. Amongst the examples of exceptional items given by SSAP 6 were redundancy costs relating to continuing business segments; profits or losses on the disposal of fixed assets; and abnormal charges for bad debts and write-offs of stock and work-in-progress. These are the sort of income and expenses which form part of the ordinary and continuing activities of the enterprise but which may be unusual in the year in question because of their size. For example, an exceptional bad-debt expense might be one which arises because of the inability of a major debtor to pay. The key point is that exceptional items are included in computing the profit on ordinary activities, albeit disclosed separately because of their materiality, because they arise from the ordinary activities of the enterprise. However, a cynical view might be that management could be more strongly tempted to classify costs than revenues as exceptional, i.e. unusual, and there is some evidence that this is the case. Both Griffiths (1995) and Smith (1996) provide examples of this.

SSAP 6 gave six examples of extraordinary items, including the discontinuance of a business segment and the expropriation of assets. However, it pointed out that these examples were not intended to be exhaustive (ASC 1986: para. 4). The standard effectively gave a licence to management to look for extraordinary items, although via its definition it imposed some limits to creativity. Again, Griffiths (1995) and Smith (1996) provide examples of this.

There is little doubt that the classification of profit and loss account items offered by SSAP 6 lent itself to abuse, and this was an immediate cause of concern to the ASB on its formation in 1990. Following a discussion draft and exposure draft, in October 1992 it issued FRS 3, subsequently amended in 1993 (ASB 1993a). This standard introduced a number of significant changes to the information provided by profit and loss accounts, including the withdrawal of the licence to creativity afforded by SSAP 6. FRS 3 is a very technical document. In many ways this is inevitable given that it is attempting to redress existing abuses. Technical as it may be, there is no doubt that FRS 3 represented a major shift in the presentation of information about the financial performance of enterprises.

The principal reforms introduced by FRS 3 relate both to the way in which information about financial performance is presented in financial statements and to the bases on which this information is prepared. The changes relating to presentation require the following:

- A new layered structure for the profit and loss account (illustrated in Table 3.4). This new structure attempts to give readers of financial statements more useful information for assessing the performance of the enterprise. It separates out the results of continuing operations, the results of operations acquired during the financial year and those of parts of the enterprise disposed of, discontinued, during the year. It also requires disclosure of 'exceptional items' such as profits (losses) on the disposal of properties. It is hoped that this revised format will provide users with a fuller understanding of the results of the enterprise in a financial period. It should also assist them in forming a better assessment of its likely future performance by providing them with information about the results of the continuing activities of the enterprise and about 'exceptional items' forming part of its ordinary activities. It does allow for 'extraordinary' items, but the whole tenor of FRS 3 is that the meaning of the word 'extraordinary' is much closer to that of common parlance, i.e. extraordinary items are meant to be extremely rare.
- A statement of total recognised gains and losses. This is viewed by the ASB as being of sufficient importance to be regarded as a primary financial statement in its own right, and as such is given equal prominence to the other primary financial statements (balance sheet, profit and loss account, cash-flow statement). The reason for FRS 3 introducing this new primary financial statement was a concern that not all the elements of the financial performance of an enterprise would normally be reported in its profit and loss account. This applies particularly to asset revaluations, which historically would have been recorded as movements in reserves rather than as part of the overall 'gains' of an enterprise. The new statement seeks to show all the gains and losses recognised in a financial period, whether or not they are incorporated in the profit and loss account. Table 3.5 provides an illustration of such a statement.

Table 3.4 Specimen profit and loss account based on FRS3

Profit and loss account of XYZ plc for the year ended 31 December 1997			
	1997		*1996 as restated*
	£000s	*£000s*	*£000s*
Turnover:			
Continuing operations	X		X
Acquisitions	X		
	X		
Discounted operations	X		X
		X	X
Cost of sales		X	X
Gross profit		X	X
Net operating expenses		X	X
Operating profit:			
Continuing operations	X		X
Acquisitions	X		
	X		
Discounted operations	X		X
		X	
Profit on sale of properties in continuing operations		X	X
Profit on ordinary activities before interest		X	X
Interest payable		X	X
Profit on ordinary activities before taxation		X	X
Taxation on profit on ordinary activities		X	X
Profit on ordinary activities after taxation		X	X
Minority interests		X	X
Profit before extraordinary items		X	X
Extraordinary items (included only to show positioning)		X	X
Profit for the financial year		X	X
Dividends		X	X
Retained profit for the financial year		X	X

In addition, FRS 3 introduced other requirements, including a reconciliation of the movement in shareholders' funds and a note of historical cost profits and losses. Taken as a whole, this new presentation of financial-performance information undoubtedly provides a much richer information base for the users of financial statements. However, this information base is much more complex than that which was previously available, and there is a danger that the unsophisticated reader of financial statements will find it overpowering, even to the extent of ignoring most of it

Table 3.5   Specimen statement of total recognised gains and losses

Statement of total recognised gains and losses for XYZ plc for the year ended 31 December 1997

	1997	1996 as restated
	£000s	£000s
Profit for the financial year	X	X
Unrealised surplus on revaluation of properties	X	X
Unrealised (loss)/gain on trade investment	X	X
	X	X
Currency translation differences on foreign currency net investments	X	X
Total recognised gains and losses relating to the year	X	X

and simply concentrating on the 'bottom line' of profit after taxation. The overall thrust of FRS 3 is summarised in its first paragraph:

> To require reporting entities . . . to highlight a range of important components of financial performance to aid users in understanding the performance achieved by a reporting entity in a period and to assist them in forming a basis for their assessment of future results and cash flows.
>
> (ASB 1993a: para. 1)

In summary, the objective of statements of financial performance is to provide users with information about the gains an enterprise has generated from its activities and the principal components of such gains. They summarise the outcomes of the activities of the enterprise using the accruals basis of accounting and highlight key aspects of these outcomes. FRS 3 goes some way to reducing the earlier 'creativity' that was available to corporate management, by requiring more detailed disclosure of the various 'gain' components so as to promote a fuller appreciation of their amount and significance, and revising the ASC's earlier definitions of ordinary activities, exceptional items and extraordinary items. It also seeks to promote a greater emphasis on the articulation between the statements of financial performance (profit and loss account and statement of total recognised gains and losses) and the balance sheet, so as to prevent the possibility of users being misled by apparently strong profit performance at the expense of a weakening of the balance sheet. Paragraph 13 of FRS 3 emphasises that:

> Gains and losses may be excluded from the profit and loss account only if they are specifically permitted or required to be taken directly to reserves by this or other accounting standards or, in the absence of a relevant accounting standard, by law.
>
> (ASB 1993a: para. 13)

Cash-flow statements

As we have already pointed out, a positive cash flow is crucial to the continuing success and existence of enterprises – companies become insolvent when they run out of cash to pay their bills. However, the accounting profession was slow in requiring the provision of cash-flow information in financial statements, perhaps because of a reluctance to abandon profit as the ultimate indicator of corporate performance (although profit is nothing more than an intertemporal allocation of cash flows). Initially, the accounting standard setters favoured funds-flow statements (ASSC 1975c) rather than cash-flow statements, but shortly after its formation in 1989 the ASB came down in favour of cash-flow statements by issuing FRS 1 (ASB 1991). In 1995, following a consultation exercise about the impact of FRS 1, the ASB proposed a number of primarily technical and presentational changes via FRED 10 (ASB 1995b), which resulted in FRS 1 being revised in 1996 (ASB 1996).

The principal reasons why cash-flow statements have ultimately prevailed are as follows:

■ Cash flow is the best indicator of viability and liquidity. Enterprises fail because they run out of cash, not because they run out of working capital. Working capital includes stocks and debtors, neither of which are of much use in paying creditors if a business is short of money.
■ Some users will incorporate net present value models in their evaluation of enterprises. These models require an assessment of future cash flows, and cash-flow reporting is likely to be more useful for this purpose than funds-flow reporting.
■ Funds-flow statements are basically a reorganisation of the information already contained in balance sheets and profit and loss accounts. As such, they do not provide additional information to users, whereas cash-flow statements do provide new information.
■ Cash flow is a normal business concept and, as such, is easier to understand and use than funds flow. It is also a measure of corporate performance to which management pays a great deal of attention and thus provides a useful indicator of managerial performance.

In the words of the ASB:

> The objectives of financial reporting indicate that users need information about cash inflows and outflows to help with assessments of liquidity, solvency and future cash flows and to provide feedback about previous assessments. A statement of cash flows . . . provides useful information about an enterprise's activities in generating cash through operations to repay debt, distribute dividends, or reinvest to maintain or expand operating capacity; and about its investing and financing activities, both debt and equity, in so far as they relate to receipts and payments of cash. Important uses of information about an enterprise's current cash receipts and payments include helping to assess factors such as an enterprise's liquidity, solvency and financial adaptability, the way in which profits are converted into cash and risk.'
>
> (ASB 1991: para. 26)

Table 3.6 gives an illustration of the layout and information content of a cash-flow statement based on the revised requirements of FRS 1. The standard identifies eight main components of an enterprises' cash flows. These are:

■ **Net cash flow from operating activities**. This is the cash flow that the enterprise has generated (incurred) during the financial period from its trading

Table 3.6 Example of cash-flow

Cash-flow statement for XYZ plc for the year ended 31 December 1997	
	£000s
Operating profit	X
Depreciation charges	X
Loss/(profit) on sale of tangible fixed assets	X
Decrease/(increase) in stocks	X
Decrease/(increase) in debtors	X
Increase/(decrease) in creditors	X
Net cash flow from operating activities	X
Returns on investments and serving of finance	X
Corporation tax paid (including advance corporation tax)	(X)
Capital expenditure	(X)
	X
Equity dividends paid	(X)
Management of liquid resources	X
Financing	X
Increase/(decrease) in cash	X

transactions, independently of how long-term finance has been provided for these activities. As such, it is a prime indicator of how successful the management of the enterprise has been in managing its trading activities and the cash-flow consequences of these trading transactions. However, FRS 1, seeking to emphasise the articulation between the differing primary financial statements, requires that the cash-flow statement start with a reconciliation of the operating profit (shown in the profit and loss account) with the net cash flow generated by operating activities. The import of this is that, while, from time to time in its life, an enterprise might have a net cash outflow from operating activities (for example, a relatively new enterprise undergoing a period of expansion may require significant increases in its investments in inventories and debtors), it would normally be expected that this cash flow would be positive. However, it should also be recognised that an unduly high cash inflow might be indicative of a declining enterprise, as it reduces its investment in inventories and debtors. The amount of the cash flow from operating activities, while it is a prime performance indicator, should not be looked at in isolation. As with many other items of information contained in financial statements, it should be interpreted in conjunction with other information, both from the financial statements and from elsewhere.

■ **Returns on investments and servicing of finance**. This is the net cash flow resulting from the costs of the finance (other than equity finance) that the enterprise has employed during the year, together with any interest that it has been able to generate from the management of its cash resources. Its focus is essentially the cash-flow cost of the enterprise's finance. As such, it is information which enables users of financial statements to assess the consequences of financing and financial-management decisions.

■ **Taxation**. So far the information in the cash-flow statement has concentrated on the cash-flow consequences of decisions that are primarily under management control. Here, the statement recognises that these decisions have another consequence (taxation) which is largely related to the profit that the enterprise generates. Chapter 5 discusses the various forms of taxation affecting enterprises in the UK. Here, it is sufficient to recognise that the generation of profit will lead to taxation liabilities being incurred and that the timing of the settlement of these taxation liabilities may be very different to their recognition for accounting purposes. Thus users of financial statements need to know, not just the overall amount of the taxation liability, but how much has actually been paid.

■ **Capital expenditure**. The focus here is the amount of cash that the enterprise has spent on fixed assets during the financial period and the amount that it has recouped from the sale of such assets. In general, successful, thriving enterprises will invest cash in acquiring operating capacity via a continuing programme of investment in fixed assets, while declining enterprises may seek to stabilise themselves via the sale of fixed assets. However, it should be noted that fixed assets – or more generally, operating capacity – can be acquired by other means than cash purchase, for example by purchase on deferred payment terms or by leasing. This, again, emphasises the point that items of information contained in financial statements – in this case information about net cash outflow on investing activities – need to be interpreted in the light of other relevant information.

■ **Acquisitions and disposals**. This part of the statement, which only fully applies to groups of companies, shows the cash-flow consequences of the purchase or sale of subsidiary companies and, as such, is a counterpart of the previous item.

■ **Equity dividends paid**. This item shows the cash-flow consequences of the dividends paid to the equity shareholders in the company during the financial period.

The statement then contains an important subtotal, the net cash flow before the use of liquid resources and financing. This subtotal represents the overall net cash-flow position of the enterprise from all its activities other than the management of liquid resources and the raising or repayment of long-term finance, both equity and debt. This is a key indicator of the overall financial viability of the enterprise. Is it generating net cash inflows which it will be able to employ in future expansion and the generation of further benefits for the shareholders and other stakeholders? Or is it a net spender of cash which might, if this continues, start to encounter liquidity and solvency problems? Again, the information content of this net cash flow needs to be viewed in the light of other broader information about the enterprise's circumstances.

The next item in the statement is net cash flow arising from the management of liquid resources. Here the focus is on the cash flows associated with the enterprise's investments in liquid resources. These are current-asset investments which are readily disposable at defined cash values without affecting the enterprise's operating capacity. Typically, they will include items such as investment in term deposits and government securities. As such, they are likely to be an important element in the enterprise's treasury management.

The final part of the cash-flow statement deals with the enterprise's financing transactions. It shows the extent of any additional finance raised during the year (from the issue of new share capital or the raising of loans) and the amount of any financing repaid during the year, as well as any transaction costs associated with this raising/ repayment of finance. Again, this is undoubtedly useful information as it highlights the cash-flow consequences of any changes that have taken place in the financial structure of the enterprise. However, as with many other areas of financial information, its focus is historical – it shows what has happened. Equally useful, but unfortunately not revealed here, is the extent of the enterprise's future access to finance. It would be very helpful, for example, to have information about an enterprise's credit lines, as this would enable users to form an assessment of their adequacy.

Overall, the cash-flow statement required by FRS 1 is undoubtedly a significant addition to the information about the activities of enterprises contained in their financial statements. This is because:

- it supplements the information contained in the balance sheet and profit and loss account;
- it focuses on the flow of cash through the enterprise and addresses key issues such as:
  - how successful is the enterprise in generating cash flow from operating activities?
  - what investment activities has it undertaken?
  - what are the cash costs of its financial structure?
  - what are the taxation cash flows associated with its activities?

In summary, the cash-flow statement directly addresses the cash-flow/financial-management decisions of the enterprise and their consequences for its financial health.

The concept of financial adaptability

Modern commercial enterprises exist in a fast-changing competitive environment. One has only to consider the rapid advances in technology in recent years, and the political reform and political changes that have taken place in Central and Eastern Europe to recognise the pace and scale of the changes in the commercial environment. These changes present new opportunities for enterprises and new threats. New product and market opportunities are continually emerging, and old products and markets are disappearing. To remain successful, enterprises need to be able to respond to these changes – they need to be adaptable. In part, this adaptability will be a function of corporate visions and cultures, of management's styles and abilities. However, it will also be, in part, a function of enterprises' finances. Are their financial structures, the patterns of their resources and liabilities, and the patterns of their cash flows such as to enable them to respond to challenges and opportunities? If so, then, ceteris paribus, they will be more successful. Users of financial information will seek to assess the financial adaptability of enterprises, and each of the primary financial statements has a role to play in this. The balance sheet provides information on the pattern and amounts of assets and liabilities; the profit and loss account shows how successful the enterprise has been in the past at generating profits from its activities; the statement of total recognised gains enables users to assess overall economic changes as regards the resources of the enterprise; and the cash-flow statement provides information about the flow of the ultimate resource, cash, through the enterprise. In the words of the ASB:

Financial adaptability consists of the ability of an enterprise to take effective action to alter the amount and timing of cash flows so that it can respond to unexpected needs, events and opportunities. All the primary financial statements provide information that is useful in evaluating the financial adaptability of an enterprise.

(ASB 1995a: para. 1.13)

Conclusions

In this chapter we have identified that the major purpose of external financial statements is to provide useful information to stakeholders about the financial affairs of enterprises. The principal way in which they achieve this is via the primary financial statements themselves, together with any supplementary notes. The extent to which these statements in fact achieve their objective of providing useful information is a matter of continuing debate.

Financial statements are intended to provide their readers with useful information about enterprises so as to help them assess their economic and other relationships with such enterprises. The principal financial statements are:

- **The balance sheet**: this is a position statement intended to show, at a specific point in time, the resources owned by an enterprise (its assets) and how these resources have been financed by liabilities and equity. The historical-cost basis of accounting, which is the normal basis on which financial statements are prepared, although it may be adjusted by the use of revaluations, means that balance sheets are not statements which show the current value either of the enterprise in total or of its individual assets.

- **The profit and loss account**, in conjunction with the statement of total recognised gains and losses: these are flow statements reflecting the financial performance of an enterprise over a period of time, normally a financial year. They summarise an enterprise's trading activities, providing information about its sales revenues and the costs that have been incurred to generate these revenues, and other significant changes in ownership interest.

- **The cash-flow statement**: this is a flow statement summarising the receipts and payments of cash by an enterprise during a given time period, normally a financial year. It analyses these receipts and payments according to their economic purpose and origins, providing information such as the net cash flow generated from operations and from the raising of additional long-term finance.

Taken together with other information available to users, such as that contained in the directors' report and the financial and operating review, the primary financial statements help users to assess the financial adaptability of an enterprise – its financial ability to respond to new opportunities and to meet challenges.

Further reading

The ASB (1995a) provides a statement on the concepts and principles which it believes should underpin financial reporting, and applies these to the reporting of financial performance (ASB 1993a) and the reporting of cash flows (ASB 1996). Alexander and Britton (1996) provide a discussion of financial reporting principles, while Griffiths (1995) and Smith (1996) examine financial reporting practice.

Questions and exercises

1 The accounting records of Hendy Ltd contained the following balances as at 31 December 19XX. Using these balances, draft a balance sheet and a profit and loss account for Hendy as at that date.

	Debit £	Credit £
Cash and bank balances	1 000	
Debtors	17 158	
Creditors		9 538
Stocks	19 431	
Fixed assets (at cost)	65 098	
Fixed assets (accumulated depreciation)		16 751
Depreciation for year	6 984	
Bank overdraft		7 423
Credit sales		89 649
Cash sales		57 053
Cost of goods sold	76 030	
Operating costs	41 582	
Loan repayable 31 December 19X2		10 000
Share capital		30 000
Retained profit as at 1 January 19XX		6 869

2 On 1 January 1989 Jehosophat Ltd purchased a new machine for £244 000. The machine was expected to have a useful life of five years and be able during this period to perform a total of 40 000 individual operations. At the end of this time the machine was expected to have a residual value of £24 000. The planned use of this machine during the five-year period is:

Year ended 31 December	No. of operations
1989	8 000
1990	12 000
1991	10 000
1992	5 000
1993	5 000

Calculate the annual depreciation charges for each of the five years during which the machine will be owned:

(a) on the straight-line basis;

(b) on the reducing-balance basis;

(c) on the usage basis.

Plot a graph showing the net book value of the machine at the end of each financial year.

3 The trial balance of Granite Ltd as at 31 December 1997 was as shown below:

	Debit £000s	Credit £000s
Sales		508
Income from trade investments		10
Loss on sale of trade investments	24	
Freehold property – cost	500	
– accumulated depreciation		300
Cost of sales	255	
Depreciation	51	
Bad debts	20	
Selling and distribution expenses	33	
Administration expenses	28	
Taxation expenses	25	
Taxation payable		25
Trade creditors		37
Share capital		300
Retained profit as at 1/1/97		226
Dividends paid	30	
Trade investments	75	
Equipment – cost	280	
– accumulated depreciation		104
Stock	102	
Debtors	56	
Cash	31	
	1510	1510

The following additional information is available:

(a) The freehold property was acquired in 1966 and since then has been depreciated on a straight-line basis on the assumption of a fifty-year life. However, no depreciation has been provided for 1997 because of plans to revalue the property. This revaluation has now been carried out but is not reflected in the trial balance. The value as at 31 December 1997 has been estimated at £600 000 and the remaining useful life at that date as thirty years. The property in question is used by the selling department of the company.

(b) The depreciation expense comprises:

	£000s
Current year charge in respect of selling-department equipment	22

Current year charge in respect of administration-department
equipment   13
Additional depreciation in respect of some selling-
department equipment arising from revised estimates
leading to a shorter anticipated working life   16
                                                                                                        —
                                                                                                        51
                                                                                                        —

(c) Bad debts are very rare in the company's trade. The charge for 1990 arises
from a single customer who defaulted on payment.
(d) The taxation expense comprises:

	£000s
Tax on normal activities	32
Relief for loss on sale of investments	7
	25

Prepare the balance sheet, profit and loss account and statement of total
realised gains and losses of Granite as at 31 December 1997, complying, so
far as possible on the information provided, with the requirements of the
Companies Acts and accounting standards. Comment briefly on how you have
dealt with the various non-routine items in the accounts.

4 Write a short explanation of the following concepts, which have been discussed
in this chapter:
(a) fixed assets;
(b) current assets;
(c) depreciation;
(d) current liabilities;
(e) cash flow.

5 Moors Ltd is a motor-vehicle distributor operating from premises in Canterbury
which has the following assets and liabilities. Identify which of them are current
assets, which are fixed assets, which are current liabilities and which are long-
term liabilities.
(a) a van used for the transport of spare parts and making deliveries to customers;
(b) electronic engine-testing equipment;
(c) spare parts held in its service-department stores;
(d) petrol and diesel oil;
(e) amounts due from credit customers;
(f) amounts due to suppliers;
(g) a mortgage on its premises;
(h) spanners, screwdrivers and socket sets.

6 It is sometimes said that depreciation is a method of providing for the replacement of fixed assets when they come to the end of their useful lives. Do you
agree with this view or not? Justify your answer.

7 Clearly explain the principal changes which FRS 3 has introduced in the
reporting of the financial performance of companies and why the ASB felt it
appropriate to introduce these changes.

8 It is often said that unsophisticated readers of financial statements do not appreciate the amount of judgement involved in the preparation of such statements. Identify the principal areas of such judgement in relation to the following:

(a) fixed assets;

(b) stocks;

(c) debtors;

(d) trade marks.

9 How can financial statements provide useful information to their readers if they do not show the current values of an enterprise's assets and liabilities?

10 FRS 1 introduced a requirement for companies to publish cash-flow statements as part of their annual accounts. Why did the ASB believe that it was important for companies to publish such statements?

4 The legal and quasi-legal background to financial reporting

Objectives

In the previous chapter the focus was on the structure of the primary financial statements. In this chapter it is on the other elements of the annual reports of companies, and on the legal and quasi-legal framework within which such reports are produced. Attention is paid to items such as the **directors' report**, **notes to the financial statements** and **operating and financial reviews**. Some of these items are required by statute law and some by quasi-law. In this context quasi-law means financial reporting requirements which are not directly imposed by statute law, but which are required by influential professional accountancy bodies and by other organisations such as the Stock Exchange. The increasing tendency to incorporate such quasi-legal requirements into statute law will also be discussed, as will the 'standardisation' debate relating to the efforts that have been made in the UK (and elsewhere) since the late 1960s to reduce the amount of flexibility available to companies in their choice of accounting policies and bases when presenting information in their annual reports. The principal purpose of the other elements of annual reports is to amplify and explicate the information contained in the primary financial statements, thereby enabling stakeholders better to assess their relationships with the company. This is also increasingly the case with financial reporting in many areas in the public sector.

Company annual reports and their contents

Before looking at the detailed legal and quasi-legal regulation of the annual financial and associated statements of companies, it will be useful to identify the normal components of the annual reports of companies of which such statements are part. For completeness, this will be done with regards to what is required of a company listed on the London Stock Exchange and having subsidiary companies. It must, therefore, be recognised that smaller non-listed companies may not be required to produce all the information and statements listed below (in fact the Companies Acts specifically exempt smaller and medium-sized companies from a number of financial reporting requirements). For convenience, except where we need to talk specifically about groups of companies, we will use the terms 'company' and 'groups of companies' interchangeably (Appendix 4.A discusses the definition of groups of companies and reporting requirements directed specifically at such groups). Typically, the contents of an annual report will include the following elements:

- **Chairman's statement**: this will normally be a relatively brief (one- or two-page) statement giving an overview of the state of affairs of the company and the principal commercial factors affecting it during the financial year just ended, and those likely to affect it in the future. This statement is not subject to a formal audit, although auditors would normally be expected to ensure that it does not contain statements significantly at variance with the audited accounts.
- **Chief executive's report** (operating and financial review): this will normally be a more detailed review of the company's operations providing information about the performance of the principal operating units/segments and may run to several pages. Again, this statement does not legally have to be audited, although prudent auditors (APB 1995c) will review it for consistency with the audited statements. Such reviews are discussed later in this chapter in the light of the ASB (1993c) statement regarding them.
- **Directors' report**: this is a statutory requirement and, while it does not form part of the audited accounts, the auditors have an obligation to ensure that its contents are in conformity with those accounts.
- **Statement of directors' responsibilities**: the current debates on corporate governance have led to the requirement for a clear statement of such responsibilities, particularly with respect to the nature and discharge of their fiduciary duties.
- **Statement of auditor's responsibilities**: auditors (and others) have in recent years become increasingly concerned about the public's misunderstanding of their role and responsibilities. This statement attempts to ensure that there is clarity about these, and it is a counterpart to the statement of directors' responsibilities.
- **Consolidated balance sheet**: this is a legal requirement, and a statement which aggregates the external assets and liabilities of all the individual companies in the 'group' of companies.
- **Parent-company balance sheet**: again, this is a legal requirement, and a statement which summarises the assets, liabilities and equity of the parent company in its own right.
- **Consolidated profit and loss account**: again, this is a legal requirement, and a statement which incorporates all the trading transactions of companies within the group.
- **Consolidated cash-flow statement**: this is a statement required by FRS 1 covering the activities of all the individual companies within the group.
- **Notes to the accounts**: these provide further details about the items contained in the primary financial statements, as well as other information required by law or quasi-law. They form part of the overall financial statements and are subject to audit.
- **Auditor's report**: a statement required by statute law from the company's auditors as to whether or not the financial statements, taken as a whole (primary financial statements and notes to the accounts), provide a 'true and fair view' of the company's (group's) financial position and performance.

In addition to these, the annual report may (will) contain other information such as notification of the company's Annual General Meeting, five- or ten-year financial summaries, and miscellaneous statements on such diverse topics as environmental performance and corporate citizenship.

Overall, the annual report may be very extensive. In some cases they reach nearly 100 pages of information. Some of this information is required by law and quasi-law, and as such is regulated to a greater or lesser extent. Some of it is subject to formal audit and some of it is not. Some of it is the result of the company and its management attempting to convey what they regard as being key messages to stakeholders and potential stakeholders, for example regarding concern for the environment. It may be more or less glossy and include promotional material (it is widely accepted that financial public relations has been a growth sector in recent years). Overall, the annual report is a compendium of information, and one problem faced by users is knowing which bits are which, which bits are audited (and hopefully more reliable as a result) and which bits are not. In the remainder of this chapter we concentrate on those elements of annual reports which are the subject of regulation in one form or another.

Types of commercial enterprise

Within the UK there are three principal forms of commercial organisation. These are:

- **Sole traders**: historically, this is the oldest form of business structure and is simply an individual engaging in commercial activities in his/her own right. There is very little specific legal regulation regarding the activities of sole traders, although they are subject to the requirements of the law in general. In particular, they are not required to prepare (other than for taxation purposes) or publish annual financial statements.
- **Partnerships**: a partnership exists when two or more individuals collaborate in a business operation with a view to generating a profit. The rights and obligations of the individual partners will normally be enshrined in a partnership agreement, which is essentially a contract between the partners, although the Partnership Acts do lay down a framework for the legal regulation of partnerships. There are relatively few statutory legal requirements relating to partnerships and, as is the case with sole traders, they are not required to publish annual financial statements.
- **Companies**: there are a number of different forms of company within the UK, including limited-liability companies, unlimited-liability companies and public companies. However, in all cases companies are subject to legal requirements imposed by the Companies Acts. Amongst these requirements are those of preparing annual financial statements, having them audited and publishing them. As the most common form of company is a limited liability company it is upon this that we shall concentrate. There are, of course, many areas other than accounting in which the Companies Acts regulate the affairs of companies, but these are beyond the scope of this book. Readers who require further information about these legal requirements should consult a company law text such as Sealy (1996).

The Companies Acts and financial reporting

The Companies Acts date back to the middle of the nineteenth century, when, for the first time in the UK, it became possible to form a company by a simple process of registration. Prior to this, company promoters had to ask Parliament to pass a special Act to enable a company to be formed. From the very earliest days the Companies Acts recognised the need for companies to produce financial information about their activities and to have such information audited. In the first instance, this information was primarily intended for the benefit of the providers of the risk capital, the shareholders. However, the nineteenth century was also an era of the fraudulent promotion and management of companies. The financial information produced by companies rapidly came to be regarded as a means of creditor protection as well, and in the latter part of the century there were a series of legal actions dealing with accounting and financial reporting matters, particularly the distribution of dividends. A good review of the principal issues in this regard can be found in French (1977). This was the era in which the rather pragmatic fundamental accounting concepts of matching and prudence were first formally enunciated.

Initially, legal requirements regarding the provision of financial information focused on the balance sheet, as this was regarded as the statement which provided information about the asset backing of the business and its financial soundness and probity. Towards the end of the nineteenth century and in the early twentieth century increasing emphasis started to be placed on the profit and loss account. Table 4.1 summarises the principal changes in financial reporting requirements introduced by the various Companies Acts. The mid- to late nineteenth century was also the era when professional accounting bodies, which were the precursors of the current professional institutes of accountants, were founded. The formation of these bodies was an important element in the development of financial statements, because the financial reporting

Table 4.1   Principal financial reporting changes introduced by the Companies Acts

1844	Formation of companies by registration with the Board of Trade and the production of a 'full and fair' balance sheet
1855	Granting of limited liability to all registered companies
1856	Introduction of 'model regulations' for companies, including a model balance sheet
1862	Dividends only to be paid out of profits
1900	Introduction of a compulsory annual audit
1907	Audited balance sheets to be filed with Registrar of Companies and requirement for a number of specific disclosures
1928/29	An income statement to be produced and distributed to shareholders (although it did not have to be audited or filed with the Registrar of Companies) and further specific disclosure requirements
1947/48	Requirement for the auditor to be professionally qualified; requirements for the presentation of annual balance sheets and profit and loss accounts; and the preparation of consolidated accounts as well as further specific disclosures
1967	Increase in the number of specific disclosures and a requirement for a directors' report
1972	Implementing the 1st EC Directive regarding *ultra vires*
1980	Implementing the 2nd EC Directive regarding public companies
1981	Implementing the 4th EC Directive regarding rules of accounting and accounts formats
1985	Consolidating Act
1989	Implementing the 7th EC Directive regarding group accounts and 8th EC Directive regarding regulation of auditors

Table 4.2 The accounting profession in the UK

Professional body	Founded	Members
The Institute of Chartered Accountants in England and Wales (ICAEW)	1870	109 200
The Institute of Chartered Accountants of Scotland (ICAS)	1854	14 000
The Institute of Chartered Accountants in Ireland (ICAI)	1888	9 500
The Chartered Association of Certified Accountants (ACCA)	1891	50 000
The Chartered Institute of Management Accountants (CIMA)	1919	42 000
The Chartered Institute of Public Finance and Accountancy (CIPFA)	1885	12 000

Source: AGCAS (1997).

requirements of the early Companies Acts in many ways reflected a traditional UK respect for the expertise of professional groups. Until relatively recently, the Companies Acts concentrated on specifying what types of financial statements companies had to produce and which items of information had to be disclosed. The detailed and practical implementation of these rather broad requirements was largely left to the accounting profession, operating within a fairly loose legal framework, an implementation not helped by the diversity of this profession. (Table 4.2 provides an overview of the current major professional accounting bodies in the UK.)

The detail of determining accepted accounting bases was not, as was the case in many other European countries, specified by the legislature. There was, and still is, no UK equivalent to the *plan comptable* of France or the Spanish National Chart of Accounts, laying down in detail the ways in which enterprises should account for their activities. One consequence of this was, as is discussed in Chapter 5, a divergence between the principles and practices involved in financial reporting and those associated with the calculation of taxation liabilities. A related consequence of 'leaving it to the profession' in this way was the emergence of a wide range of different accounting practices, each of which could be justified in terms of the fundamental accounting principles. The choices that an enterprise made between these different accounting practices could have a significant impact on the balance-sheet valuation of its assets and liabilities and upon its reported profit. This flexibility in the selection of accounting practices has for the last thirty years or so (and before that by a number of informed commentators) been widely viewed as being one of the two major problems of financial reporting and has led to strenuous efforts by the accounting profession and other interested parties to reduce the range of choice open to enterprises in their preparation and presentation of financial statements. Later in this chapter we shall examine the accounting standards movement, and its attempts to make accounting practices and financial statements more comparable and standardised.

The other main issues which have provoked ongoing debate are the rationale for requiring companies to produce annual financial statements in the first place and the types of information that should be contained in such statements. Prior to the emergence of modern capital markets and of the view that there are a number of different groups of stakeholders, each of which has 'rights' to information about the activities of the commercial enterprises with which they are associated, the purpose of the annual financial statements of companies was mainly perceived as that of being stewardship reports from the company directors to the shareholders. According to this – still influential – view, financial statements should focus on the ways in which the directors have applied the monies with which they have been entrusted so that the regularity and probity of these applications can be assessed (ASB 1995a; Page 1992a, 1992b).

The widely held view nowadays is that financial statements are a means of providing information to a broad group of interested parties. Implicitly, this view is endorsed by the Companies Act requirement that companies must file their accounts with the Registrar of Companies, thereby making them available to all interested parties, as well as sending copies to their shareholders. This view has led to an increasing debate as to whether or not, in their traditional form, financial statements provide the type and quality of information needed by their users. (Examples of the arguments in this debate can be found in Arnold *et al.* 1990; ICAS 1988; ICAS/ICAEW 1991; CIMA 1990.) The core of the debate is the extent to which historical-cost-based financial statements as currently prepared do, or do not, provide the future-oriented information needed by stakeholders/decision takers, and the extent to which new forms of financial statements could be devised better to provide this information. The debate is a difficult one. Unquestionably, it would be very useful to provide stakeholders and potential stakeholders with future-oriented information relevant to the decisions that they need to make. However, how practicable are such statements? By definition, if they have a future orientation they will increase the amount of judgement and estimation involved in the preparation of such statements, and, almost inevitably, increase the difficulties faced by management and auditors in preparing and attesting to such statements. Perhaps at the end of the day it boils down to a question of relevant versus reliable information. It would be very useful to have information which was both relevant (future-oriented) and reliable (or at least verifiable). However, as the ASB itself points out (ASB 1995a), there is an inevitable trade-off between these characteristics. The depressing part of the whole debate is the extent to which it is being conducted by the providers of the information (companies, their representatives and accountants) and how little the users are involved. *Plus ça change, plus c'est la même chose.*

The debate, although extensive, has not as yet led to any changes in the statutory requirements regarding financial statements, although the relevance and importance of the debate is recognised by the ASB and may well influence the future of accounting standards and financial reporting in the UK. There is also an underlying tension in the debate. This, at least in part, stems from the different perceptions of the role of financial statements. The continental tradition, which will naturally be influential in the determination of EU Directives, is largely a legalistic, historic-cost-based tradition. The ideas being canvassed within the UK about 'future-decision-oriented financial statements' are significantly at variance with this tradition, and major conflict between the professional bodies – which are implicitly endorsing the ideas being canvassed within the UK – and the need to facilitate European harmonisation could be on the horizon. Correspondingly, if the European harmonisation view wins out there could be tensions between the UK (EU) and other accounting philosophies (e.g. those espoused by the USA and the IASC).

The debate about the objectives and practices of corporate financial reporting is a complex and continuing one. In some ways it is a debate between pragmatists (what can we sensibly do in a verifiable way) and theoreticians (what do users want and how can we provide it). It is a debate which has been around for many years and is likely to continue into the future. There is no absolute right or wrong in financial reporting – it all depends where you are starting from. In many ways this means that, while we must understand the reasons for the debate, we must keep our feet on the ground and understand what the current legal and quasi-legal requirements are, and *why* they are what they are.

Associated with the debate about the structure and content of financial statements is another debate – on the extent to which potential users of financial statements read and understand their contents. Research findings (e.g. Lee and Tweedie 1975a, 1975b, 1977; Bartlett and Chandler 1997) have long shown that many potential users of accounts, most notably private shareholders, read little of the content of annual corporate reports and have problems understanding what they do read. Other research findings (Macdonald Commission 1988; Steen 1989; Humphrey *et al.* 1991, 1992; Sikka *et al.* 1992) have also shown that there is widespread misunderstanding about the role of auditors in respect of company financial statements. This is an issue addressed at more length in Chapter 6 but is generally referred to as the 'expectations gap' – a divergence between the views of the professionals (accountants) associated with the audit of financial statements and the lay users of such statements. In summary, the current state of financial reporting is the subject of much discussion on its usefulness and how it could be improved.

Companies Act requirements

Until relatively recently, statute law regarding the financial statements of companies concentrated on two areas:

- **Requiring specific disclosures**. As Table 4.1 shows, the trend has been one of requiring increasing amounts of disclosure, regarding both the financial statements to be published and the detailed information to be included in these statements. Until the 1981 Companies Act, legislation was largely silent about the bases on which the published information was to be prepared. This was left to the accountants.
- **Attempting to ensure the reliability of the information contained in financial statements**. Since their earliest days the Companies Acts have required that the financial statements of enterprises be audited, and they have continued to lay down an overall quality yardstick regarding the information contained in accounts. Over the years these detailed audit and quality-yardstick requirements have varied. The current position, as first specified in the 1947 Companies Act, is that financial statements should present 'a true and fair view' of the company's financial position and performance. It is the *directors'* duty to prepare financial statements which give 'a true and fair view' of a company's financial position and performance. The *auditor's* responsibility is to give a professional opinion as to whether or not the financial statements do in fact give such a view.

The 1981 Companies Act implemented the EU 4th Directive on Company Law and involved a significant shift in direction from what had gone before, although still retaining the 'true and fair' requirement. The principal changes introduced by the 1981 Act were:

- It specified legally for the first time that financial statements should use the historic-cost basis of accounting. However, some flexibility was allowed and companies were still permitted to use alternative bases of accounting, subject to adequate disclosure.

■ It specified legally for the first time the fundamental accounting principles (going concern, prudence, matching and consistency). Previously these had been specified in SSAP 2 (ASSC 1971).

■ It specified legally for the first time the formats of balance sheets and profit and loss accounts, although more than one format was permitted and companies were allowed to choose between them. These formats are contained in the 4th Schedule to the Act.

■ It introduced for the first time, reporting exemptions for small and medium-sized companies. Prior to this all companies, whatever their size, had to produce full accounts, although there were filing exemptions for some 'private' companies. This change brought the UK into line with most continental countries, where smaller companies are given reporting exemptions to reflect their relatively small economic importance and to spare them the sometimes substantial cost of preparing and publishing full sets of financial statements.

The changes introduced by the 1981 Act have continued throughout subsequent Companies Acts, the most notable being the 1989 Act. This implemented the EU 7th Directive (relating to the definition of, and financial statements of, groups) and the EU 8th Directive (relating to the regulation of auditors). It further increased the amount of detailed disclosure required in financial statements but, more importantly, it also gave the secretary of state new powers regarding the content of corporate financial statements and changed the position regarding 'professional' statements on accounting practices by giving them statutory backing.

To summarise, the general legal rules regarding the annual financial statements of enterprises are:

1 They shall comply with the requirements of the Companies Acts, in particular with the requirements of the 4th Schedule to the Act, which lays down the detailed statutory requirements, and, in particular:
   ■ they shall give a 'true and fair view' of the state of the company's affairs and its financial performance;
   ■ they shall comply with the formats specified in the Acts;
   ■ they shall disclose all significant accounting policies and practices employed in their preparation (e.g. as regards depreciation, stock valuation, foreign-currency translation, research and development expenditure, leases and goodwill);
   ■ they shall comply with the fundamental accounting concepts of going concern, prudence, consistency and matching;
   ■ they shall include comparative figures;
   ■ they shall be dated and signed.
2 The overriding legal requirement is that the accounts shall present a 'true and fair view'. This introduces some difficulties because there is no formal legal definition of 'a true and fair view', an issue we explore later. At this point, we should note that:
   ■ if compliance with the Act gives insufficient information to provide such 'a true and fair view' additional information must be provided;
   ■ if compliance with the Act would prevent 'a true and fair view' (even with the incorporation of additional information) the requirements of the Act must be departed from and details of such departure provided.

The meaning of 'a true and fair view' and its application in practice are crucial to the legal requirements for corporate financial reporting in the UK. However, before we can look in detail at these we first need to examine the role of the profession in relation to accounting policies and practices.

Professional statements and financial reporting

A consequence of the position before the 1981 Act and the lack of detailed statutory specification of accounting and financial reporting practices and bases was that the accountancy profession was largely free to develop a range of accounting practices and bases which it felt were appropriate to particular economic circumstances and events, while still adhering to the requirements of the fundamental accounting concepts. Different accounting bases emerged in such important areas as depreciation, foreign-currency translation and inventory valuation. The extent of this diversity was increased by the fact that, in the main, the emergence of these differing practices and their acceptability in the case of the economic circumstances of particular companies were matters for the exercise of the 'professional judgement' of individual accountants. Such judgement was, of course, informed by the codification of what was regarded by the profession as being acceptable. This codification was supported by the training given to budding accountants and the syllabuses of the examinations administered by the professional bodies. It was also supported by the emergence of accounting textbooks towards the end of the nineteenth century.

It was not until after the Second World War that the professional bodies in the UK really started to make formal pronouncements on accounting practices. Even when they did, in the first instance they tended to be little more than statements about what were considered to be 'generally accepted accounting principles' (GAAP) in particular areas of accounting, that is, the practices that were regularly employed by members of the profession and conformed with the fundamental principles. At this time little comment was made by the professional bodies on what they regarded as being 'best practice' and little attempt was made to ensure that such 'best practice' was employed. Thus, for example, the ICAEW introduced in 1942 a series of what were called Recommendations on Accounting Practice (the N series).

By the 1960s a vast array of accounting bases had come to be regarded as GAAP and, as such, suitable for use in the preparation of financial statements. Because of this, it was possible for a company to prepare a vast number of different sets of financial statements to represent the same set of economic events while remaining within the bounds of GAAP. The extent of the variation possible in reported results can be illustrated with an example. Table 4.3 provides such an example.

Using accounting bases which remain within the bounds of GAAP, very different financial statements could be produced to represent the economic events outlined in Table 4.3. Thus:

1 **Cost of sales**: GAAP would normally require that year-end inventories should be valued at cost and that cost should include an appropriate share of the overhead costs. Within this framework there are two areas of significant variability:
   - **What to include as an appropriate share of overhead costs**. In the case of Imagination, this could, at one extreme, be all the manufacturing overheads

Table 4.3   Illustration of the flexibility of GAAP

Imagination Ltd is a company which commenced operations on 1 January 19XX. During its first year of operations it engaged in the following transactions:

(a) Incurred the following expenses:

	£000s
Direct materials	200
Manufacturing labour	100
Manufacturing overheads	200
Factory administration	100
Head office administration	50
Selling and distribution costs	50
	700

   (i)   the cost of direct materials increased by 50% half way through the year;
   (ii) 20% of the year's production of 8000 units remained unsold at the year end;
   (iii) at the end of the year there were no unused materials or work in progress.

(b) Bought the following assets:
   (i)   freehold land for a cost of £100 000, one quarter of which was resold immediately for £60 000 as it was surplus to the company's requirements;
   (ii) a leasehold building on a twenty-year lease for a cost of £400 000 – the market value of this building at the end of the year was £500 000;
   (iii) plant and equipment with a cost of £300 000, an estimated useful life of five years and a forecast residual value of zero.

(c) Spent £2000 000 on research and development.

(d) Sold goods with a sales value of £1 050 000.

---

plus the factory administration costs, i.e. £300 000 (or £37.50) per manufactured unit (i.e. £300 000/8000 units). At the other extreme it could be zero, on the basis that none of the overhead costs should be included (regarded as 'appropriate'). In practice, of course, there is a wide range of middle ground. However, here we are looking at extreme choices falling within the bounds of GAAP. Effectively, the choice is about what to regard as 'period costs', i.e. costs relating to the provision of general facilities for the time period to which the financial statements relate, and what to regard as 'product costs', i.e. costs attaching to the products produced during that time period.

■ **Assumptions about the flow of stock through the business** and, associated with this, the flow of costs. The two extremes here are the FIFO assumption, via which it is assumed that the earliest purchased (manufactured) items are the first to be disposed of, and the LIFO assumption, via which it is assumed that the most recently purchased (manufactured) items are the first to be disposed of.

   In the case of Imagination, the purchase price of direct materials rose by 50% half-way through the year. Thus the purchase price during the first half of the year would have been £20 per unit (£80 000/4000). During the second half of the year it would have been £30 per unit (£120 000/4000). On the FIFO basis the £20 per unit would be included in cost of sales; on the LIFO basis £30.
The direct labour cost was £100 000. Thus the per-unit direct labour cost would have been £12.50 per unit (£100 000/8000).

Table 4.4 Cost of sales for Imagination

	Low cost of sales £	High cost of sales £
Direct materials	200 000	200 000
Manufacturing labour	100 000	100 000
Manufacturing overheads	200 000	200 000
Plant depreciation (see 4 below)	60 000	164 000
Factory administration	100 000	100 000
Total costs	660 000	764 000
Less: Value of closing stock		
No overheads plus LIFO (£12.50 + £20)		52 000
Overheads plus FIFO (£12.50 + £30 + £37.50)		
+ £12 000	140 000	
Cost of sales	520 000	712 000

Based on the foregoing, the extreme values of the cost of sales, remaining within GAAP, are as shown in Table 4.4.

2 **Freehold land**: GAAP does not normally require the depreciation of freehold land. In the case of Imagination we have an immediate gain. The quantum of this gain would normally be assessed as being £35 000, i.e. £60 000 − (0.25 × £100 000). However, GAAP would allow alternatives as to how this gain should be presented in the financial statements. These include:

- showing the gain as part of the ordinary operating profit for the year;
- showing the gain as part of the operating profit for the year but highlighting it as an exceptional item;
- showing the gain as an extraordinary item;
- not showing the gain as part of the profit for the year but taking it direct to reserves.

3 **Leasehold property**. GAAP would require this to be amortised over the period of the lease. However, the lease could be revalued from cost (£400 000) to market value (£500 000). Thus, the amount of the amortisation could be based on either the original cost (i.e. 5% of £400 000 = £20 000) or the market value (5% of £500 000 = £25 000).

4 **Plant**: GAAP would normally require this to be depreciated over its anticipated useful life. However, as we saw in Chapter 3 there are differing methods for computing depreciation. If we concentrate on the time-based methods the two extremes are the straight-line method, which gives a depreciation charge of £60 000 for the year, and the reducing-balance method, which gives a depreciation charge of £164 000 for the year. Presumably, as this depreciation relates to plant, it could be regarded as a 'product' cost, meaning that some of it (0.20 × £60 000 = £12 000) should be carried forward in the value of closing stock in the case of the low cost of sales scenario. Thus, the low cost of sales scenario is £520 000 and the high cost of sales scenario is £712 000.

5 Research and development: GAAP would normally require this to be expensed in the year, unless the expenditure had resulted in a viable, marketable product. If this were the case the expenditure could be capitalised and then amortised over the life of the product. Thus the two extremes, based on managerial judgement about the outcome of the expenditure, are immediate write-off or capitalisation.

Putting these various items together we can prepare alternative extreme profit and loss accounts for Imagination as shown in Table 4.5. As Table 4.5 demonstrates, within the bounds of GAAP (admittedly being somewhat creative) it would be possible to prepare financial statements for Imagination showing either £445 000 profit or £13 000 profit, i.e a variance of nearly 3500%. Imagination is obviously an artificial example. However, during the 1960s there were a number of real-life examples of the use of the flexibility available within accounting policies and practices. Some of these cases were very 'high profile', leading to a great amount of criticism of accounting and the accountancy profession in the financial press and in Parliament. In essence, the critics were saying that accountants were failing in their job and that unless something was done Parliament would have to intervene and legislate on accounting bases, that is, take away the determination of acceptable accounting practices from the profession. This criticism was both strident and prolonged.

The response of the profession was the formation, in January 1970, of the ASSC by the ICAEW. Later the other major professional bodies joined and by 1976 all the major UK professional accountancy bodies were members of the ASSC. Subsequently its name was changed to the ASC and it is by that name we shall refer to it henceforward.

The objectives of the ASC when first formed included:

- the definition of accounting concepts;
- the narrowing of differences in financial reporting between companies;
- the codification of 'best practice' in financial reporting.

Table 4.5 Alternative profit and loss accounts for Imagination

	High profit £000s	Low profit £000s
Sales revenue	1 050	1 050
Cost of sales	520	712
Amortisation of lease	20	25
Research and development	–	200
Head-office administration	50	50
Selling and distribution	50	50
	640	1 037
Gain on sale of freehold property	35	–
Profit for the year	445	13

The way in which the ASC went about achieving these objectives was by the development and promulgation of SSAPs. The intention was that these SSAPs would lay down standardised bases for accounting and financial reporting which would be used in the preparation of annual financial statements. In particular, the requirements of the SSAPs would have to be followed in all financial statements intended to present a 'true and fair view', and the enforcement mechanism would be via the auditors. The auditors would have to comment in their audit report on any deviation from the requirements of SSAPs and to state whether or not such a deviation was appropriate given the circumstances of the enterprise. The hope of the ASC was that a new era of financial reporting would be born and that this new era would be characterised by financial statements which:

- were based on 'best practice' as codified in the SSAPs;
- were understandable because the bases on which they were prepared were known and laid down in the SSAPs;
- were comparable because all enterprises would be preparing their financial statements on the same bases;
- provided reliable and useful information to readers because the bases on which they were prepared would have been determined by experts (the ASC) in consultation with other interested parties and the implementation of these bases would have been verified by the auditors.

The work of the ASC represented the first major attempt in the UK to put order and consistency into corporate financial reporting at a detailed practical level. Other countries were also making similar efforts. In some, such as the USA, these efforts had started earlier, and in others, such as Australia, they started later. There was also the IASC, which was attempting to achieve similar objectives on a transnational scale. Thus, the 1970s were the period in which the need to standardise accounting practice really started to be addressed in a major way in the UK.

The process by which the ASC attempted to standardise accounting practice in the UK involved two stages. First, having identified an area in which standardisation was felt to be needed, it developed a proposed standard which it then issued for comment as an Exposure Draft (ED). Following a period of consultation, an SSAP based on the ED would be issued or, perhaps, a revised ED would be issued to take into account points made during the consultation process. Prior to its demise in 1990 the ASC had issued some fifty-four EDs and some twenty-four SSAPs.

The ASC faced a major problem in that, while it was trying to standardise accounting practice, there was no agreed underpinning conceptual framework for financial reporting on which its accounting standards could be based. Instead, there was a long history of pragmatic solutions to specific accounting problems. This meant that the ASC sometimes found it difficult to justify its proposed standards as being the best/most appropriate technical solutions to accounting problems. It also meant that they could not argue that their standards had overall applicability, justified on the basis of an agreed set of core concepts. Great efforts were made during the 1970s and early 1980s to generate an agreed conceptual framework, particularly in the USA. However, these efforts proved unsuccessful. The result of this was that the work of the ASC was in many ways a continuation of what had gone before, albeit producing authoritative professional statements which, undoubtedly, in their early days had great

influence on financial reporting in the UK. The standard-setting process was characterised by a 'fire-fighting' approach. Rather than proceeding from an agreed set of
first principles and developing a logical and coherent set of standards, it was forced
to react to what were perceived as being particular problem areas. In many ways this
made its task even more difficult because, by their very nature as problems, such areas
included some of the more intractable issues of financial reporting.

The difficulties faced by the ASC were compounded by the real-world economic
consequences of financial statements and the accounting bases on which they are prepared. Such statements influence economic relationships; they are a major information
source in the decisions that stakeholders and potential stakeholders make about their
relationships with an enterprise; and they may also be a factor in contractual relationships. They constrain the amount that can be paid as dividends to shareholders, as such
dividends can only be paid out of realised profits; they influence the amount of performance-related bonuses and pay, as these will normally be based on reported profits or
earnings per share; they may even influence contract prices if these are based on a
return on capital employed formula. Financial statements may be determinants of the
economic benefits to be received by stakeholders rather than simply being neutral
reports of economic events. Any change in the accounting bases used for their preparation will therefore lead to a change in the distribution of economic benefits. In these
circumstances it is hardly surprising that interested parties would seek to ensure that
the bases endorsed by the ASC, via its EDs and SSAPs, were ones which, at the very
worst, would not disadvantage them and preferably would advantage them. The standard-setting process proved, inevitably, to be highly politically charged.

If the objectives of the ASC were to be achieved it was essential that their pronouncements were followed in practice by enterprises in the preparation of their annual
financial statements. However, the ASC was not a statutory body and it had no legal
powers with which to enforce its standards. The enforcement mechanism it sought to
use was the audit process, that is by the involvement of other professional accountants.
If companies departed from the requirements of SSAPs auditors were expected to comment on this in their audit reports. In the early days of the ASC this did happen, and
adverse comments by auditors were taken seriously by the capital markets. However, as
time passed the number of what were increasingly perceived as 'technical' qualifications
by auditors grew and they ceased to be as influential, particularly as auditors showed an
increasing tendency to concur with departures from SSAPs. In addition, the SSAPs
themselves became increasingly less specific in their requirements. As the problems
they addressed became increasingly intractable, the SSAPs permitted more and more
flexibility. They became more statements of good intent than clearly specified standards. More and more different accounting bases could be justified as falling within the
terms of the standards, and the narrowing of the areas of difference and variety of
accounting practice which the ASC was originally set up for was not being achieved. The
accountancy profession recognised this and the CCAB set up a committee to investigate
what could be done. This committee reported in 1988 (Dearing 1988) and recommended significant changes. In particular, it recommended that accounting standards
should be given statutory backing. Many of the recommendations of the Dearing Committee Report were implemented in the 1989 Companies Act and in 1990 the government created a new body, the FRC, with powers delegated to it by the secretary of state
for the oversight of financial reporting by companies in the UK.

In November 1991 the FRC published a review of the state of financial reporting in the UK (FRC 1991), part of which related to its own remit. This remit was defined (FRC 1991, appendix b, paragraph 1) as being:

To promote good financial reporting . . .

To provide guidance to the Accounting Standards Board (a committee of the FRC) on its work programmes and on broad policy issues.

To verify that the new arrangements are conducted with efficiency and economy and that they are adequately funded.

(FRC 1991: app. b, para. 1)

The membership of the FRC is drawn from preparers, users and auditors of financial statements, and it has observers from the relevant government departments. Under the auspices of the 1989 Act and the FRC, two other new bodies were created. These were the ASB and the FRRP. The role of the ASB is to take over the work of the ASC in the formulation and promulgation of accounting standards. The role of the FRRP is to identify defects in the financial statements of companies, in particular failures to comply with the requirements of the Companies Acts and material departures from accounting standards. Where it identifies such defects it seeks to obtain corrective action from the company in question by voluntary means, but if this fails it has the authority to ask a court to compel companies to take any necessary corrective action, including in extreme cases the preparation and publication of revised accounts.

The work of the FRC, the ASB and the FRRP is the practical implementation of the 1989 Companies Act and the recommendations of the Dearing Committee. Of particular importance are those sections of the Act which:

■ require companies to state whether or not accounts have been prepared in accordance with applicable 'accounting standards' and to provide details of, and the reasons for, any departures from such standards;
■ give statutory recognition to accounting standards and empower the ASB to issue such standards;
■ authorise the FRRP, via powers delegated from the secretary of state, to apply to the courts for a revision of accounts to remedy defects – if such an order is granted, the costs of complying with it will be borne by the directors who were responsible for the authorisation of the defective accounts.

The 1989 Act, and the bodies that were created pursuant to it, introduced major changes in financial reporting in the UK, particularly for larger companies, which are the focus of the FRRP's attention. For the first time, accounting standards have been given legal force and a proper enforcement mechanism has been set up. At the same time, the resourcing of the standard-setting process (now under the control of the ASB) has been improved. It could be argued that the reform came not a day too soon (and possibly too late) given some of the financial *causes célèbres* that emerged at the end of the 1980s and in the early 1990s. Cases such as those of Colloroll, BCCI, Maxwell, Polly Peck, British & Commonwealth and others all indicate that reform of the financial reporting process was necessary. While the work of the FRC and its associated bodies focuses largely on accounting issues, there was a similar move for reform in auditing, as we shall see in Chapter 6. As the ASB gets increasingly into its stride the scope for 'creativity' in financial reporting will be greatly diminished and that, at last, the original objectives of the ASC, dating back to 1970, will finally come to be realised.

The principal mechanism via which the ASB issues accounting standards is a new form of document, known as FRSs. These will gradually replace the SSAPs extant when the ASB was formed. Pending this, these SSAPs remain in force. FRSs are preceded by the issue of FREDs, which lay out the ASB's intent, and FREDs will normally be preceded by the issue of Discussion Papers, which will examine the issue under consideration. As at the end of 1997 the ASB had issued the following FRSs (as well as a number of FREDs and Discussion Papers):

- FRS 1: cash-flow statements;
- FRS 2: accounting for subsidiary undertakings;
- FRS 3: reporting financial performance;
- FRS 4: capital instruments;
- FRS 5: reporting the substance of transactions;
- FRS 6: acquisitions and mergers;
- FRS 7: fair values in acquisition accounting;
- FRS 8: related party disclosures;
- FRS 9: associates and joint ventures;
- FRS 10: goodwill and intangible assets.

The ASB has also set up a UITF. The role of this body is to examine areas of emerging difficulties in financial reporting as a matter of urgency and to attempt, wherever possible, to arrive at consensus judgements. Much of its work is likely to relate to the interpretation of accounting standards or the provisions of the Companies Acts, and its pronouncements will be viewed as authoritative.

The hope is that the work of the FRC, the ASB, the FRRP and the UITF signals a new dawn for financial reporting in the UK by the introduction of a new, more standardised and more regulated system. In many ways this new system bears similarities to that in the USA, as the work of the new bodies parallels much of the work undertaken by the Securities and Exchange Commission and the FASB in that country. It also, in different ways, brings the UK closer to some of the legally driven systems of accounting which exist in continental Europe, while still maintaining the divorce between the regulation of financial reporting and taxation legislation. The ASC was born as a response to a number of abuses of financial reporting in the 1960s, and while it created a major impact in its early days its work became increasingly less influential as time progressed. It is to be hoped that the work of the new system and structures will not go the same way.

True and fair view

In this chapter, and earlier in this book, reference has been made to the requirement that financial statements should present 'a true and fair view' of a company's financial position and performance. This is regarded as being the ultimate yardstick for the quality of the information that financial statements contain. The directors of a company have a clear legal obligation to prepare financial statements which comply with this requirement (s. 226(2) of the Companies Act). Unfortunately, although they require this 'true and fair view', the Companies Acts themselves do not define the meaning of the phrase. Given the importance of the phrase as an overriding quality-assurance standard, this might be viewed as unfortunate. Alternatively, the absence of such a definition and the wording of the phrase itself might be viewed as being a clear indication of the role that judgement must inevitably play in the preparation of financial statements. If this is the case it is a message that many users of financial statements have failed to understand, instead interpreting an audit report which states that the financial statements do in fact give 'a true and fair view' as being confirmation that they are 'right'. This misapprehension is part of what is commonly referred to as the 'expectations gap', an issue which is discussed further in Chapter 6.

In part, the problem has been the absence of unambiguous and definitive guidance, both by the Companies Acts and by the accounting profession, as to what constitutes 'best accounting practice' in all the circumstances which commercial enterprises might encounter. There is no accounting and financial reporting 'rule book'. Many would argue that the very diversity of economic circumstances would prevent a meaningful rule book ever being prepared. Others would argue that it is the very absence of such a rule book which has, together with an insufficiently independent-minded stance by auditors, fostered the sort of 'creativity' in financial reporting commented on by writers such as Griffiths (1995) and Smith (1996). Even if such a rule book defining the meaning of 'a true and fair view' did exist and financial statements were prepared in accordance with it, another problem would remain. This is what is usually referred to as the issue of 'substance over form'. It is likely that a rule book would say that transactions of particular types (legally defined) should be accounted for in particular ways to present the requisite 'true and fair view'. This is fine so far as it goes, but the issue then arises as to whether or not the financial statements should seek to represent the legal form of economic events and transactions, or their underlying economic substance (reality). It is all too possible that there might be a conflict between truth (legal form) and fairness (economic substance). The consensus within the accounting profession is that financial statements should try to present the economic substance in a truthful way. This is an issue which has recently been addressed by the ASB, in FRS 5.

The core of the problem which FRS 5 addresses is that enterprises can engage in transactions having a legal form which suggests that they should be reported on in a particular way (in accordance with their legal form) but whose economic substance would suggest a different form of reporting. Perhaps the simplest example of this is a hire-purchase contract. Legally, this is a bailment to hire (rental agreement) with an option to purchase. In reality, of course, it is nearly always a purchase agreement, with the purchase consideration being payable on extended credit terms. If the legal form were followed, the presentation in the accounts (pending the payment of the amount associated with the option to purchase) would be that there would be no entries on the balance sheet (because there would be no assets or liabilities under the agreement) and that rental payments would be shown in the profit and loss account as they were incurred. The underlying economic reality of the transaction would not be shown; this is why accountants are in favour of the 'substance over form' doctrine. Far more complex examples of this problem exist, many devised by the corporate-finance departments of merchant banks and other financial advisors. The key issue is, given that enterprises can acquire the control and use of assets while not legally owning them, how should such events be recorded in financial statements. The generic term for this sort of activity is 'off balance sheet finance'. It enables enterprises to control and use assets in generating profits without these assets (and any corresponding liabilities) appearing in their balance sheets (if balance sheets are based simply on the legal form of the economic events). This has a number of potential advantages for an enterprise. First, it enables them to increase their effective borrowings without the associated liabilities being recorded in the financial statements. This can be of great benefit to companies whose borrowing powers are restricted by their constitution to a fixed proportion of their net assets. Second, it reduces the asset and capital base on which return on capital employed calculations are based, thereby improving their apparent profitability. Third, it can mask the 'true' risk profile of the enterprise. 'Off balance sheet financing' effectively enables enterprises to disguise the true state of their financial position, performance and commitments when assessed in economic rather than strictly legal and contractual terms; hence the importance of reporting substance over form (at least in the view of the accounting profession). In the words of the ASB:

> The objective of this FRS is to ensure that the substance of an entity's transactions is reported in its financial statements. The commercial effect of the entity's transactions, and any resulting assets, liabilities, gains or losses, should be faithfully represented in the financial statements.
>
> (ASB 1994a: para. 1)

FRS 5 is a very technical document discussing issues such as 'quasi-subsidiaries', 'linked transactions' and control of entities. In many ways it is a prime example of the problems faced by regulators of financial reporting. Corporate management and its financial advisors are all too aware of the importance of the contents of the annual financial statements for themselves and the future of the entities which they manage. They have major incentives to ensure that such statements present acceptable portrayals of this performance, and they have access to highly expert advice in achieving this. The range of options open to them is enormous, and to prevent abuse the ASB and related organisations are increasingly having to become very technical and legalistic in their pronouncements, engaging in a considerable amount of 'second-guessing' about what sorts of arrangement companies might devise in the future. This emphasises the importance of the UITF as a mechanism for dealing rapidly with emerging issues and perceived abuses of the system.

As can readily be seen, the role of judgement is crucial in the determination of what does and does not constitute 'a true and fair view' in any particular set of circumstances, particularly when the question of 'substance v. form' is taken into account. This means that it is crucial that such judgement is properly and honestly made, and that safeguards are set up to ensure that this is the case. The institution of procedures to assure this was one of the issues addressed by the Cadbury Committee (1992) and by an ICAS Discussion Document (ICAS 1993). Both placed great emphasis on the need for non-executive directors to play major roles in such procedures. However, it is still necessary to have a framework with reference to which such judgement can be exercised, and counsel's opinion has been sought by professional accounting bodies in relation to such a framework. Based on such opinions and on received wisdom within the accounting profession, the position appears to be that in order to present a 'true and fair view' financial statements should:

- be free of intentional bias;
- not be misleading or misrepresent the economic circumstances of the company;

- disclose all material facts;
- reflect an appropriate selection of accounting policies and practices based on the underlying economic realities of an enterprise, with these policies having been properly applied;
- comply with accounting standards – while such compliance was relevant before the 1989 Companies Act insofar as such standards would shape the expectations of the readers of financial statements, it is even more relevant now given the new status accorded to accounting standards by that Act.

The importance of accounting standards (i.e. the SSAPs previously issued by the ASC and the FRSs now being issued by the ASB) has been emphasised by the Counsel's Opinion issued by the ASB as an appendix to its *Foreword to Accounting Standards* (ASB 1993c). This appendix emphasises the following:

- Courts asked to interpret the truth and fairness of financial statements cannot do so without evidence as to the practices and views of accountants.
- [A]ccounting standards are authoritative statements of how particular types of transactions and other events should be reflected in financial statements and accordingly compliance with accounting standards will normally be necessary for financial statements to give a true and fair view' (ASB 1993c: app., para. 3).
- [I]t is now the norm for accounts to comply with accounting standards. ... Just as a custom which is upheld by the courts may properly be regarded as a source of law, so too ... does an accounting standard which the court holds must be complied with ... become ... a source of law in the widest sense of that term. (ASB 1993c: app., para. 15).

Hopefully, in the future the work of the FRRP and the UITF, in conjunction with that of the ASB itself, will provide increasingly specific guidance as to what can be regarded as constituting 'a true and fair view'.

Other legally required information and reports

Apart from the primary financial statements there are a number of other legal requirements regarding the provision of information about the financial affairs of companies. The principal of these is the requirement for the annual reports of companies to include a directors' report and notes to the accounts:

- **Directors' report**: the requirement for a directors' report was introduced by the 1967 Companies Act. The precise requirements for the contents of such a report are set out in section 234 of the 1985 Act and in the 7th Schedule to the Act. In addition, the Stock Exchange imposes additional requirements for listed companies. The principal objective of the director's report is that it should provide an overview of the company's financial condition and performance, as well as highlighting particular items of information. Amongst other things, it should contain a fair review of the business of the company, a summary of its principal activities, particulars of any important events affecting the company or its subsidiaries, details of the appropriation of profits, details of significant changes in fixed assets, names of the directors and their interests in the shares of the company, information about the company's employees and details of any political or charitable donations made by the company.

In addition to the director's report, the annual reports of many companies, particularly listed companies, also contain a statement from the chairman commenting on the company's performance and prospects, as well as a more detailed analysis of the company's operations. Such analyses can be both extensive and informative. However, it should be noted that they do not form part of the legally required, and thus audited, statements, whereas the directors' report is legally required and the auditors have a responsibility to ensure that its contents are in conformity with the audited statements. The ASB (1993b) has issued a statement regarding operating and financial reviews of this sort.

■ **Notes to the accounts**: the 4th Schedule to the 1985 Act specifies a wide range of items which must be disclosed either on the face of the accounts or in notes to the accounts. These notes form part of the accounts and are subject to audit in the same way as the main body of the accounts. Increasingly, companies include much of the statutorily required disclosure in supplementary notes rather than on the face of the financial statements themselves. This has led to the notes, particularly for large companies, becoming both extensive (sometimes running to over twenty pages) and technical because of the nature of the disclosures. In addition to the statutory disclosures, further disclosures are required by accounting standards and Stock Exchange regulations. Notes to the accounts are a potentially very rich source of information to users. However, their length and complexity mean that a large proportion of readers of accounts do not in fact read them, so that they will at best, acquire only partial information and may perhaps misunderstand information contained on the face of the accounts. As a point of principle, the information contained in the notes to the accounts should serve to amplify the information contained in the body of the accounts; it should not restate, reinterpret or contradict such information. This is particularly important given the relatively limited readership of the notes.

The range of disclosure required by the Companies Acts, accounting standards and the Stock Exchange is wide. The legal requirements regarding information which must be contained either on the face of the accounts or in the notes to the accounts are contained in the 4th Schedule to the 1985 Act. The accounting standards requirements are set out in SSAPs and FRSs, and the Stock Exchange requirements are set out in the 'Yellow' and 'Green' Books published by the Stock Exchange. (It is beyond the scope of this book to list all the disclosures that are required, but a useful overview can be found in Aldis and Renshall 1990).

A very important requirement is the disclosure of the accounting policies adopted in the financial statements. Unless readers are informed about the company's choice of accounting policies it will not be possible for them to obtain an adequate appreciation of the company's financial condition from the financial statements. The Companies Acts require disclosure of significant accounting policies, as do a number of accounting standards, most notably SSAP 2. Examples of these further disclosure requirements include:

■ a statement of compliance with, or departures from, accounting standards;
■ information about authorised, issued and paid-up share capital;
■ information about debentures;
■ information about cost, depreciation and revaluation of fixed assets;
■ details of reserves and provisions;

- a considerable amount of detail about the company's indebtedness;
- information about guarantees and other financial commitments;
- information about components of the profit and loss account;
- information about the number and remuneration of employees;
- information about subsidiary and associated companies;
- extensive information about the emoluments of directors.

The foregoing is just a sample of the principal areas in which disclosure of the financial affairs of enterprises is required. The complete range of required disclosures, particularly for large listed companies having subsidiary undertakings, is very extensive. As was pointed out earlier, the notes to the accounts are a potential mine of information for users. However, the very extent of this information, together with its technical complexity, makes it very daunting to the lay reader, although of potentially great value to a professional reader such as an investment analyst. In part, this complexity is one of the factors which led to the introduction of the possibility of companies producing summary accounts, which was introduced by the 1989 Act.

Operating and financial review

As will have been evident from the foregoing, the annual reports of a modern large corporation are complex and technical documents which many readers will have great difficulty in understanding. In addition, there may be significant pieces of information which by their very nature may not be adequately highlighted in the accounts as such, for example ones relating to competitive and market prospects and other commercial information. As pointed out above, many companies (principally listed ones) have long supplied reviews of their operations as part of their annual reports. In 1993 the ASB issued what it called 'a statement of best practice' to give guidance as to what it believes should be contained in such reviews (ASB 1993b). This is not a standard per se, and it is intended to be persuasive rather than mandatory. However, it has the support of the FRC, the Hundred Group of Financial Directors and the London Stock Exchange. It defines an OFR as 'a framework for the directors to discuss and analyse the business's performance and the factors underlying its results and financial position, in order to assist users to assess for themselves the future potential of the business' (ASB 1993b: para. 1).

The ASB document is far from prescriptive as to what the structure and content of an OFR should be. Instead, 'directors should consider what matters are of significance in the circumstances of their business' (ASB 1993b: para. 6). It does, however, outline a framework for such reviews which suggests that they should incorporate:

1 *An operating review*, to include:
- a discussion of the operating results for the period, focusing on both the business overall and such segments of the business as are relevant to a proper understanding of the overall business;
- a discussion of the dynamics of the business, i.e. those factors that may be influential in the future prosperity of the business, including the main risks and uncertainties it faces and how management intends to deal with them;
- a discussion of the business's investing activities, both current and prospective, and the hoped-for returns from such investment;

- a discussion of other activities which the business is undertaking to enhance its future prospects, e.g. marketing campaigns, training programmes, research;
- a discussion of the results for the year from the perspective of the shareholders and the returns available to them;
- an indication of any areas where the reported performance of the company is particularly sensitive to the application of accounting judgement.

2 A *financial review*, to include:
- a discussion of the company's capital structure and treasury policy;
- a discussion of the make-up of taxation charges and liabilities, with a commentary on why they differ, if they do, from 'standard' charges;
- a discussion of the business's cash-flow sources and obligations, and a commentary on its current liquidity;
- a confirmation that, in the directors' opinion, the company is a going concern;
- a commentary on the company's resource structure, with particular reference to where the strengths of this structure may not be adequately reflected in the balance sheet, for example as regards intangible assets.

The statement then goes on (ASB 1993b: para. 38) to suggest that directors should comment on the extent to which they have complied with the principles it sets out. The statement is to be welcomed, because (as was commented on earlier) annual reports are increasingly complex and difficult for the lay reader to understand. Such a reader would certainly find an informed yet objective commentary on the financial performance of an enterprise of great value, and it is to be hoped that the statement engenders this. As the statement itself states, many companies already provide such commentaries; the hope is that the statement will encourage *all* companies to do so.

Summary accounts

As has already been pointed out, the annual reports of major listed companies can be daunting documents. Accordingly, it is hardly surprising that many of their intended recipients, the archetypal private shareholders, read at best only part of them and tend to concentrate on the more accessible parts, such as the chairman's statement and the operating review. This, of course, means that they may neglect the key financial information. In an attempt to remedy this problem the 1989 Companies Act introduced the possibility of companies preparing much shorter 'summary accounts' to help lay readers access the key information regarding companies' finances. Taken in conjunction with the operating and financial reviews proposed by the ASB (1993b), such accounts could provide a useful framework for such readers to get a core understanding of the company and its financial position and performance. At the very least, they could provide a basis for a discussion between a private shareholder and his/her financial advisor. The provisions introduced by the Act relate to listed companies and such of their members as wish to receive summary financial statements as opposed to the full set of accounts. Companies still have to prepare full accounts and file them with the Registrar of Companies, and prior to the issuing of summary as opposed to full accounts they have to obtain the wishes of their shareholders. The Act lays down procedures for doing this.

The Act lays down the required contents of such summary financial statements. The key requirements are that they must be consistent with the information in the full financial statements and that they must be accompanied by an auditor's report confirming this. There is, of course, an issue here relating to whether or not such summary financial statements can, in practice, give readers a full appreciation of the financial condition of the enterprise. If they can, why is it necessary to produce the full set of accounts? Do these contain redundant and gratuitous information?

Conclusions

The principal sources of regulation regarding the financial statements of companies in the UK are the Companies Acts, supplemented by the work of the FRC (and most notably the ASB) and the Stock Exchange. Historically, the accountancy profession was given a great deal of freedom in the development and implementation of the bases and policies involved in the preparation of such annual financial statements. While this is still true to a great extent, there is an increasing tendency towards the standardisation of these bases and policies, and for them to be incorporated in statute law, either directly, or indirectly via the work of organisations such as the ASB. This tendency is likely, in the coming years, to impose significant restrictions on the freedom of enterprises to select those accounting bases and policies they feel best suit their particular circumstances, but, at the same time, it is likely to improve the extent to which the financial statements of different enterprises can be compared.

The principal source of regulation for the financial statements of companies is the Companies Acts. They specify the format and detailed content of balance sheets and profit and loss accounts, and lay down that such financial statements should be audited and present a 'true and fair view'. Within the Acts, the majority of these requirements relating to the structure and content of the financial statements are contained in the 4th Schedule to the 1985 Act. The second principal source of regulation is accounting standards. These are now issued by the ASB, and, since the 1989 Companies Act, companies have to confirm that they have followed the requirements of such standards, or explain and justify any deviation from them. The 1989 Act provided a statutory framework for the enforcement of accounting standards, and in 1990 the government set up a new oversight body, the FRC. Increasingly, the trend is for more and more detailed regulation of corporate financial statements, and there is an increasing convergence of financial reporting in the private and public sectors.

Further reading

The ASB (1993c) summarises the purposes of the accounting standardisation movement in the UK, while Aldis and Renshall (1990) provide a summary of the financial reporting requirements of the Companies Acts. Alexander and Britton (1996) provide a discussion of financial accounting concepts and practices in the light of the standardisation movement.

Questions and exercises

1 Current trends in the regulation of the financial statements of companies are likely to lead to an increasingly legally driven system. Do you think that such a system will lead to a greater degree of comparability between the accounts of different companies? If so, why will this be the case?

2 Ask five people what they understand the meaning of 'a true and fair view' to be. Analyse how closely their opinions conform with those of counsel as obtained by the ASC and the ASB.

3 Do you believe that the directors of a company should be free to select the accounting bases and policies that they believe are most appropriate to the circumstances of their company so as to present 'a true and fair view', or should they be required to comply with an externally and legally imposed set of such bases and policies?

4 Given that the financial statements of commercial enterprises are supposed to communicate useful information to their readers, how could legislation help to improve the accessibility of the information contained in such statements to their intended readership?

5 At present, legislation requires that the financial statements of companies are distributed to shareholders as of right and are made available to other stakeholders via their lodgement with the Registrar of Companies. Given the balance of interest of stakeholders, do you believe that this pattern of distribution is appropriate?

6 Do you believe it to be right that the annual reports of companies include a mixture of audited and non-audited information? If not, what would you propose?

7 Obtain the annual reports of a listed company from each of the following sectors:
(a) retailing;
(b) manufacturing;
(c) construction.
Compare the structures and types of information contained in the financial statements of these reports.

8 Contrast the information collected to answer question 7 with the information in the chairman's statements and operating and financial reviews.

9 Do you think the work of the FRC should be restricted to listed companies?

10 To what extent do you believe that the new structures of the regulation of financial reporting are appropriate for smaller, unlisted, companies?

Appendix 4.A: Groups of companies

There are some quite complex definitional issues about what constitutes a 'group' of companies and exactly how such a 'group' should prepare its financial statements. The detailed requirements in this respect are contained in the 1989 Companies Act and in accounting standards produced by the ASB, and they are beyond the scope of this book. The underlying issue, however, is a fairly straightforward one. This is that many companies, both large and small, have acquired ownership and control of other companies, and thereby of their resources and activities. Most of the major companies listed on the London Stock Exchange have a number of such subsidiary companies, sometimes running into hundreds, which they have either acquired or formed over a number of years. In the case of acquisitions, subsidiaries may have been acquired on an amicable basis or as a result of keenly contested 'takeovers'. From a financial reporting standpoint, whether it was a friendly or a hostile takeover does not matter. What is important is that in the financial statements of the parent company (the one which has carried out the acquisition) the investment in the subsidiary companies will simply be recorded at the cost of the acquisition, and the financial performance of the subsidiary companies will be reflected in the accounts of the parent company only as and when it receives dividends from them. The situation is rather more complex in the case of the relatively small number of companies which can truly be said to have merged rather than one being taken over by the other. (Readers who want to pursue this complexity further should look at FRS 2, FRS 6 and FRS 7, issued by the ASB.) The key issue is that the financial statements of the parent company alone will give a very incomplete picture of the financial performance and position of the totality of the resources and activities it controls (particularly when the subsidiary companies were acquired some years ago, or there is significant trading between the parent company and its subsidiaries). The more and the larger the subsidiary companies, the greater this problem will be.

The way out of this problem is to require the parent company to prepare 'consolidated' or 'group' accounts. These are intended to aggregate the financial performance and position of all the companies in the group (parent company and its subsidiaries). They aggregate all the resources and liabilities of the parent company and its subsidiaries (eliminating any commonality between these assets and liabilities, e.g. monies owed by one group company to another), and all the trading transactions between group companies. Their aim is to be a set of financial statements of the 'group' as a single commercial entity, rather than as a number of separate legal entities. Such 'group' accounts concentrate on the interface between the companies in the group and the rest of the commercial world to present a financial picture of the group as opposed to its individual members.

The situation is complicated further by the fact that a 'parent' company may acquire significant or effective control/influence over the activities and resources of another company without owning the majority of the voting shares in such a company. In such a case the non-parent company is regarded as being as 'associated' company of the parent company and the 'parent company' needs to incorporate its share of the 'associated' company in its group accounts.

The essence of the legal and professional requirements of reporting for groups of companies is that they should include:

■ a consolidated (group) balance sheet which reflects all the assets controlled by the group and all its external liabilities;
■ a consolidated (group) profit and loss account which reflects all the trading activities of the group with external parties;
■ a consolidated (group) cash flow statement which reflects all the cash flows of the group with external parties.

5 Business taxation

Objectives

In this chapter we focus on the impact of taxation on incorporated businesses. Whilst the profits of unincorporated businesses, for example sole traders and partnerships, are liable to income tax, most limited companies and many other corporate bodies are subject to corporation tax on their taxable profits. Income tax was first introduced into Britain during the Napoleonic Wars but only became a permanent feature of the British tax system in 1842. The history of corporation tax in the UK is much shorter, it having been introduced only in 1947.

The objectives of this chapter, from the viewpoint of both financial reporting and the impact of taxation on business decisions, are:

- to provide an overview of the system of corporation tax as it operates at present;
- to examine the impact of three other taxes on companies – capital gains tax, national insurance contributions and value-added tax;
- to summarise the financial reporting requirements as regards corporation tax;
- to consider the influence that taxation has on financial decision-making.

Background to UK taxation

Within the UK the types and rates of taxation are determined annually by Parliament via the Finance Bill, which enacts the proposals outlined by the Chancellor of the Exchequer in his budget statements to the House of Commons. The principal forms of taxation in the UK are as set out in Table 5.1. The focus of this chapter is on those taxes which affect business enterprises. In this respect we will pay particular attention to the taxation of companies rather than the taxation of sole traders and partnerships. Such taxation is normally referred to as corporation tax. However, there are many similarities in the determination of the taxable income of companies and that of other trading entities such as partnerships, and it is therefore appropriate to start with an overview of the types of income which are assessable for taxation purposes whatever the legal status of the enterprise generating the income.

Table 5.1 Principal forms of UK taxation

Income tax	levied on the earnings and investment income of individuals, whether from wages or salaries, or from the profits of a trade, profession or vocation
Corporation tax	levied on the profits of companies
Advanced corporation tax	imputed on the dividend distributions of companies and recoverable against mainstream corporation tax (the terms imputed and mainstream corporation tax are explained in more detail later in this chapter)
Value-added tax	levied on the provision of goods and services at varying rates based on the 'output' value of such goods and services
Excise duties	levied on particular goods such as petrol, tobacco and alcohol
National insurance	effectively a payroll tax levied on both employers and employees
Council tax	a form of quasi-personal tax which has replaced the Community Charge, which itself replaced the domestic rate system of taxation and is a local rather than a national tax
Local business rate	a local tax on businesses which replaced the previous rate system, but based on property values

The general rules for the computation of corporate taxation are largely based on income-tax principles, at least with respect to what income is assessable to tax, or not, and what charges are allowable, or not, against that income. There is no overall statutory definition of income, other than a bland statement that 'income is taxable if it falls within one or other of the Schedules of the Taxes Act 1988' (ICTA 1988: s. 5(i)). There are four schedules to this Act, which are shown in Table 5.2.

Table 5.2

Schedule	Category of income
A	Annual profits or gains arising from rent, or similar payments, from land in the United Kingdom
D	Annual profits or gains which fall within one of the following six cases:
	I Profits or gains arising from any trade
	II Profits or gains from a profession or vocation
	III Interest, annuities, other annual payments, discounts and public-revenue dividends
	IV Profits or gains arising from securities outside the UK
	V Profits or gains from possessions held outside of the UK
	VI Annual profits or gains not falling under any other case or schedule
E	Emoluments from an office or employment
F	Distributions by companies resident in the UK

In essence, the application of those principles to corporate commercial enterprises means that any income that they receive is liable to taxation. However, the emphasis on profits appears to indicate that such enterprises can deduct the costs that they incur in generating the taxable income for the purposes of computing their taxable profits. In practice, this is largely true – except that in a number of areas the government has laid down detailed regulations regarding what costs will and will not be deductible from income in the computation of taxable profit.

Apart from direct manufacturing or service delivery costs, allowable business expenses include repairs and maintenance, rent and rates, salaries and wages, finance charges, training and professional fees. Disallowable expenses include expenses not directly associated with manufacture or service delivery (for example the payment of the private school fees of directors' children), distribution of profit, capital expenditure and depreciation, some accounting provisions (such as for general bad-debt provision), donations, entertainment expenses and gifts. Income from overseas trading is assessed, whether actually received or not, but overseas taxation is normally an allowable deduction.

In the UK there is a difference between accounting profit and taxable profit. Subject to the restrictions imposed by accounting standards and the provision of the Companies Acts, companies are largely free to choose the specific accounting policies that they feel are appropriate to their circumstances for the determination of the profit that they report to their shareholders. This is not the case when it comes to the determination of their *taxable* profits. Here, they are required to comply with the requirements of taxation legislation. Thus, in the UK, in contrast to many other European Community countries, there can be significant variations between the profit reported in the accounts and the profits which are assessed to tax.

As is indicated above, the major areas of difference are:

- **Depreciation**: if the government were to accept for taxation purposes a company's own assessment of the amount it needed to charge in a financial year for depreciation (in an attempt to match the costs of using fixed assets with the revenues generated from use in that financial year) it would, given the highly judgemental nature of accounting depreciation, be exposing itself to abuse. To prevent this, and also to allow itself to influence the investment decisions of companies as part of its economic policies, the government has determined that depreciation will not be an allowable deduction from income in determining taxable profits. Instead, it has set up its own system of **tax depreciation**, called capital allowances. The effect of this is to standardise taxation allowances for the use of fixed assets across companies and to allow the government to use changes in the rates of such allowances as instruments of economic policy. If it wants to encourage investment it can increase them, and vice versa. The point as regards corporate accounts is that there is no necessary relationship between the rates of depreciation that a company believes appropriate (given the present economic lives and forecast salvage values of its fixed assets) and the corresponding rates of capital allowances. In fact, there will almost certainly be differences between the two, leading to a difference between accounting profit and taxable profit. Thus, for example, the 1996 reduction in capital allowances for plant and machinery from 25% to 6% for equipment with a working life of more than twenty-five years.
- **General accounting provisions**: this principally relates to bad and doubtful debts. While specific bad-debt provisions against defaulting debtors are allowable for taxation purposes, general bad-debt provisions are not. For companies with relatively few credit customers this does not cause a problem, but it can do for those dealing with large numbers of customers, for example retailers and the clearing banks. Such businesses frequently make a general bad-debt provision in their accounts based on previous experience, say 2% of debtor balances, because

the vast number of debtor balances means that it would not be cost-effective to do so on an account-by-account basis. However, the consequence of this is that they cannot obtain tax relief until they are able to identify the bad debts individually, for example when they finally write them off.

■ **Disallowable expenditure**: as indicated earlier, some categories of expenditure are simply not deductible for taxation purposes, although they may in the view of the company be perfectly legitimate expenditure, for example business entertainment expenses.

Table 5.3 illustrates, in broad terms, how this works.

The consequence of the foregoing is that there will almost certainly be differences between a company's accounting profit and its taxable profit, and this difference may be significant. This difference is the result of what accountants refer to as 'timing differences'. These differences may be permanent (i.e. they will never be reversed – this is the case with items of expenditure which the government has decided are not allowable for taxation purposes) or they may be temporary (i.e. they will be reversed in the fullness of time). The main temporary timing differences would arise from depreciation/capital allowances. Although these may be at different rates while the company owns the asset, when it comes to sell it the resulting balancing charge/allowance and the accounting profit or loss on disposal will remove the difference, as both will reflect the cash the company originally paid for the asset when it acquired it and the cash it received when it disposed of it.

Accountants have devised the concept of **deferred taxation** to reflect these timing differences. Deferred taxation seeks to provide in the financial statements of companies for the taxation consequences of the types of timing differences we have described. These timing differences are differences between profits or losses as computed for tax purposes and those shown in financial statements, and they arise from the inclusion of items of income and expenditure in tax computations in periods different from those in which they are included in financial statements. Timing differences originate in one period and are capable of reversal in one or more subsequent periods, except for disallowable items of expenditure. An obvious timing difference, referred to earlier, arises from the differences between depreciation as measured by accountants and capital allowances determined by the Inland Revenue. Table 5.4 illustrates this basic concept of **timing**. Other examples that can arise include when a loss for tax purposes is available for relief in future years or when assets are revalued. Deferred tax relating to the non-trading activities of a company should be shown separately as a part of the tax on profit or loss on ordinary activities, either

Table 5.3   Taxation computation

Profit per the financial accounts	£X
Add back disallowable items (e.g. depreciation and general bad-debt provisions)	X
	X
Deduct capital allowances	X
Taxable profit	X

Table 5.4 Timing differences – accountant's depreciation/Inland Revenue's system

Year	1 Straight-line depreciation (10%) £	2 Writing down allowance (25%) £	3 Timing difference £
1	100 000	250 000	–150 000
2	100 000	187 500	– 87 500
3	100 000	140 625	–40 625
4	100 000	105 468	–5 468
5	100 000	79 102	+20 898
6	100 000	59 326	+40 674
7	100 000	44 495	+55 505
8	100 000	33 371	+66 629
9	100 000	25 028	+74 972
10	100 000	75 085	+24 915
	£1 000 000	£1 000 000	£ 0

Note: These calculations relate to two methods of recognising the depreciation of assets purchased for £1 million. In column 1 the accountant's straight-line method is illustrated, the assumption being that the assets will last for ten years. In column 2 we have the capital allowance (depreciation) as determined by the Inland Revenue based on a reducing balance of 25% per year. Note that at the end of year 9 these assets have a written-down value of £75 085. If we assume that these assets have a zero disposable value, then this balance can be written off in year 10. In the third column we have the timing differences between these two methods. It can clearly be seen that in year 1 the accountant's profit is further reduced by an additional £150 000 of allowable expenditure, which, at 35%, reduces the corporation tax liability by £52 500. On the same principle, liability to corporation tax is reduced in the subsequent three years. Thereafter, this trend starts to be reversed as the revenue's recognition of depreciation becomes lower than that recognised by the accountant. These timing differences are credited and debited to a deferred taxation account but over the ten-year period net out to zero.

on the face of the profit and loss account or in a note. Deferred tax arising as a result of an extraordinary item should similarly be shown separately. Over time, the rate of corporation tax and tax allowances are liable to change. If these changes are significant the deferral impact should also be regarded as an extraordinary item. The deferred tax balance should be disclosed in the balance sheet or supplementary notes. Transfers to and from the account should also be shown in these notes.

Corporation tax

Corporation tax is the general name for the taxation of the activities of companies. Before 1947 the taxation of corporate profits was integrated with the system for personal income tax, using the categories of income indicated in Table 5.1. Then, 'In 1947 the system was rationalised by raising the rate of profits tax and exempting individuals and partnerships from the tax altogether. In effect, in addition to income tax there was a separate tax on corporate profits' (Kay and King 1978: 176). During the last forty or so years there have been a number of important changes to the system of corporation tax. In 1965, for example, the **Classical System** was introduced. Under the Classical System, corporation tax was based on the profits of the company. If the company chose to distribute any of these profits to its shareholders the distribution was income in the hands of the recipient and so was charged to income tax in addition to the company's corporation-tax charge. In effect profits distributed to shareholders, having already been taxed once, were taxed again. This system still exists in some other countries, such as the USA. In 1973 this system was repealed in the UK and the current **Imputation System** was introduced. This latter system has also been adopted by other EC countries.

The Imputation System followed from the Report of the Select Committee on Corporation Tax (HCP 622), which considered various ways of reforming the structure of corporation tax so as to remove the (then) discrimination against distributed profits. This was felt to be important so that 'neutrality' in the fiscal system could be achieved. The degree of discrimination depended critically on the tax position of the individual shareholder because of marginal tax rates, and much of the discussion in considering the change was taken up with whether a **two-rate system** (one rate for retentions and one rate for distributed profits) or the present Imputation System should be introduced. Not everyone supported the change to the Imputation System. Professor Kaldor (HCP 622: app. 15, p. 253), who saw tax as an instrument of economic policy, argued for the retention of the Classical System as being more conducive to both investment and the efficient allocation of resources. According to him, new shares would always be taken up by the capital markets provided that the terms of issue made them attractive relative to existing financial investments. It was claimed that no evidence existed to suggest that previous changes in France and Germany had noticeably stimulated investment.

With the Imputation System shareholders receive credit for tax paid by the company, and this credit may be used to offset their income-tax liability on dividends. In essence, part of the company's tax liability is **imputed** to the shareholders and regarded as a prepayment of their income tax on dividends. Companies pay tax on their profits at the rate of corporation tax, and any profits which are subsequently distributed are regarded as having already been charged income tax at a specified rate – the **rate of imputation**. In the UK the rate of imputation has traditionally been set at a rate equal to one of the rates of income tax, currently the lower rate. Income tax is imputed to dividends at the lower rate of 20%, although higher-rate taxpayers are taxed at a rate of 40% on their gross dividends. Shareholders, therefore, pay additional income tax on their dividends, if they are liable to higher-rate income tax; pay nothing, since tax on savings income is limited to the lower rate of 20% for non-higher rate taxpayers; or if they are not liable to income tax and are not bodies corporate, can claim a refund of tax from the Inland Revenue. From April 1999 no individual or pension funds will be able to claim a refund.

The Imputation System is, in essence, only another form of the two-rate system. This can be simply illustrated. Consider a company with a before-tax profit of £100, which can be either fully distributed by way of a dividend or fully retained by the company. Suppose that corporation tax is at 31% and the imputation credit is ¼th (given a lower rate of income tax of 20%) based on $I/(100–I)$, where I = the lower rate of income tax. The situation would be as shown in Table 5.5. If this is fully distributed, shareholders receive £86 and the effective tax rate is 17%. What we have, in effect, is a two-rate system: corporation tax on retained profits of 31% and corporation tax on distributed profits of 17%. This example neatly demonstrates why some governments prefer this system as they believe it promotes an efficient market.

Table 5.5 Example of the imputation system

Profit fully distributed	(a) Profit retained £	(b) £
Profit	100	100
Corporation tax (31%)	31	31
	69	69
Imputed credit (¼)	–	17
Shareholders' gross income		86

The dividend actually paid by a limited company to its shareholders is a net figure after the deduction of basic-rate income tax. The income tax thus imputed to the dividend is payable to the Inland Revenue on the quarter date following payment of the dividend. This payment, termed **advance corporation tax** (ACT), is credited against the (**mainstream**) corporation tax due from the company.

Rates of tax

Since 1988/9 a lower rate of corporation tax has been applied to what are termed small companies, currently set at 21%. However, given that it is based on the level of profits it could perhaps be better described as a small-profits tax rather than a small-companies tax. Larger companies pay at the standard rate of 31%. Small companies are classified as those with profits, including dividends received plus tax credit, of up to £300 000 (ICTA 1988: s. 13). Where profits are above this limit but less than £1 500 000 (ICTA 1988: s. 13(2)) marginal relief applies. The basic formula is that marginal relief consists of the standard company rate on the profits less 1/40th of the amount by which the profits fall short of the upper limit of £1 500 000.

For example, if profits were £750 000 the corporation tax would be:

31% on £750 000	232 500
less $\dfrac{£1\,500\,000 - £750\,000}{40}$	18 750
	213 750 i.e. an average rate of 28.5%

However, it should be noted that the effect of the marginal relief is to give a **marginal tax rate** of 33.5% on profits between £300 000 and £1 500 000.

Basis of assessment and computation of profit

Limited companies are assessed to corporation tax on their taxable profits, as discussed earlier, less 'capital allowances', for each accounting period. Taxable profits include profits from all sources, including capital gains but excluding dividends received from other UK companies. Income tax suffered by imputation from dividends received by the company can be offset against any ACT due. Corporation tax rates are fixed for the government (or public-sector) fiscal year, beginning 1 April each year. Where, as is often the case, the company's accounting year-end is different from the government fiscal year, typically following a calendar basis, the profits will need to be apportioned to the relevant fiscal year to establish the appropriate tax rates needed to compute the liability. Payment is due to the Inland Revenue nine months after the end of the company's accounting period.

Capital gains made by companies are chargeable to tax at the normal rates of corporation tax, in accordance with capital-gains-tax principles. Individuals, on the other hand, are liable to capital gains tax at their marginal rate of income tax. A capital gain, or loss, can be defined as the difference, net of transaction costs, between the original cost of an asset and its subsequent sale proceeds, subject to 'rebasing'. Rebasing applies to assets held at 31 March 1982. Assets acquired before that date are reassessed (rebated) for disposals after 5 April 1988. Gains after 31 March 1982 are reduced, although gains cannot thereby be reduced below nil, by applying to the cost the rise in the retail price index since acquisition. From 4 July 1987 indexation cannot be applied to shares in building societies or industrial and provident societies.

Illustration:

Minethorpe plc bought some shares in March 1983, when it had quite a lot of surplus funds, and sold them January 1997:

		£	£
1/1/97	Proceeds received on sale	108 000	
less	Incidental expenses of sale	8 000	
	Net proceeds of sale		100 000
31/3/83	Price paid on acquisition	14 500	
add	Incidental expenses of purchase	500	
	Total cost of acquisition		15 000
	Gain before indexation		85 000
less	Indexation allowance (0.852 × 15 000)		12 780
	Net gain		72 220

The indexation allowance factor, in this case 0.852, is provided in tables available from the Inland Revenue.

Of course, most assets sold by a business are replaced, and in such cases **rollover relief** applies. This relief applies to land and buildings, fixed plant, ships and aircraft, and property let commercially. Moveable plant or machinery and motor vehicles are not covered. In the case of land and buildings, regarded as non-depreciating assets, the capital gain is offset against the new asset, and is thus not payable until the new asset is sold.

With depreciating assets, the capital gain is not deducted from the cost of the replacement but is postponed for ten years, unless in the meantime the new asset is sold or replaced by a non-depreciating asset. Depreciating assets are considered to be those with a predictable life of under fifty years and leases with an unexpired term of sixty years. It is usual that the new asset must be acquired not earlier than one year before and not later than three years after the sale of the old asset. In cases where the new asset cost is less than the gross proceeds from the sale of the old asset, the difference (if less than the gain) represents the capital gain on which tax must be paid and only the balance of the gain can be rolled over.

Financial reporting requirements for corporation tax

Two accounting standards apply to the reporting requirements of corporation tax: SSAP 8, The Treatment of Taxation Under the Imputation System in the Accounts of Companies, and SSAP 15, Accounting for Deferred Tax. These standards were originally issued by the ASC and, while this has now been superseded by the ASB, they remain in force pending their replacement by new FRSs. The main purpose of SSAP 8 was to establish a standard treatment of taxation in company accounts, with particular reference to ACT and 'mainstream' corporation tax. The seven main accounting problems arising from the imputation system are:

■ the treatment in the profit and loss account of outgoing dividends and the associated ACT;
■ determination of the recoverability of ACT against mainstream corporation tax;
■ the treatment of irrecoverable ACT arising from the payment or proposed payment of dividends;
■ the treatment of any unrelieved overseas tax;
■ the treatment of franked investment income;
■ the balance-sheet treatment of taxation liabilities, recoverable ACT and dividends;
■ the treatment of preference shares.

Each of these problems is briefly dealt with below. The first problem centres on whether ACT should be treated as part of the cost of the dividend or as part of the company's profits. The fact that the dividend will carry a tax credit is a matter affecting the recipient rather than the company's method of accounting for the dividend. Accordingly, it is considered appropriate that dividends shown in the profit and loss account should be shown at the amount paid, or payable, to the shareholders, and that neither the related ACT nor the imputed tax credit should be treated as part of the dividend. It follows that the charge for taxation in the profit and loss account should include the full amount of corporation tax and not merely the reduced liability after ACT is offset.

As was explained earlier, ACT is primarily recovered by being offset against the mainstream corporation tax on the income of the year in which the distribution is made. For accounting purposes it is necessary to decide whether recovery of the ACT is reasonably certain or foreseeable, or whether it should be written off in the profit and loss account. If the mainstream corporation tax on the income of the year under review and the amounts available from the preceding year are insufficient to cover the ACT, then recoverability of ACT will depend on the extent to which corporation tax payable in future periods is in excess of ACT on dividends paid and proposed, or on the existence of a deferred taxation provision of adequate size.

When the recoverability of ACT is not reasonably certain it is deemed prudent to write it off in the profit and loss account in which the related dividend is shown, or in the first subsequent period in which ACT previously regarded as recoverable is now deemed irrecoverable. The standard also considers that unrelieved overseas tax cannot be carried forward and that the accounting treatment is similar to that of irrecoverable ACT.

Franked investment income comprises the amount of a qualifying distribution received from another UK resident company, with the addition of the related tax credit. The net amount received can be redistributed to shareholders of the recipient company without payment of ACT and the related tax credit remains attached from the viewpoint of the shareholder. In order to recognise this income appropriately, both at the pre-tax and after-tax stage, it is expected that incoming dividends from UK resident companies be included at the amount of cash received or receivable plus the tax credit.

In most cases the balance sheet will contain one liability for corporation tax, being that on the profit of the year, which is generally payable within six months of the end of the accounting period and thus is shown as a current liability. If ACT is to be offset against corporation tax on the income of the year under review no separate liability for ACT should be shown. If this is not possible ACT should be shown as a separate liability. The related ACT on dividends proposed but not to be paid until after the company year-end is not due for payment until 18 months later and is to be regarded as a separate non-current liability. ACT regarded as recoverable only in future years should be shown as a non-current asset.

Where the title of a class of preference shares issued before 6 April 1976 includes a fixed rate of dividend, the fact that the rate in the title now includes a tax credit should be indicated.

For further detail on the reporting requirements of corporation tax, readers are advised to refer to SSAPs 8 and 15 directly. However, it should be noted that the Finance (No. 2) Act 1997, has made some changes to the imputation system, in particular that companies receiving dividends from UK companies will not be able to receive any refunds in respect of tax credits. Further changes to the system are expected in 1999. As a result, the ASB has issued (October 1997) an exposure draft proposing amendments to SSAP 8.

Readers interested in the accounting practice relating to value-added tax (VAT) can consult SSAP 5 Accounting for value added tax. The major item of concern here is that turnover in the profit and loss account should exclude VAT on taxable outputs, and that irrecoverable VAT allocatable to fixed assets and other items should be included in their cost.

The impact of taxation on financial decision-making

Taxation, in addition to being a key element in government fiscal policy and leading to a number of presentational issues in financial statements, also has important implications for the financial management and the overall performance of a company. Clearly, taxes levied on a company's products, such as VAT, have a direct effect on consumer demand. Also, taxes on the income of the organisation will impact upon financial decisions and possibly cause management to adopt tax-avoidance strategies. When it comes to financial-management decisions, taxation has an influence in three key areas: the possibility of profits (or more precisely cash flows from operations) being used for reinvestment or distributions to shareholders, the preferential tax treatment of debt capital, and tax planning.

First, the amount of corporation tax payable by a company has a direct impact on the funds available from retained earnings for investment or distribution. Second, the tax system provides an incentive for companies to raise finance from debt rather than equity. This arises because loan interest is deductible in arriving at profits subject to corporation tax, whereas dividends are not. Tax planning offers opportunities, through the coordination of tax affairs, especially within groups, to reduce the tax payable. Two examples can be cited to illustrate this last point. An ACT avoidance measure is the use of scrip dividends, whereby the shareholder is given the option of either a cash dividend or a scrip dividend of shares to the same value. No ACT is due from the paying company for scrip dividends, giving a cash-flow saving to the extent that the scrip option is adopted. For a group with overseas operations, further planning opportunities exist. As Collier *et al.* state:

> These relate to the organisational set-up and the extent to which overseas taxes can be offset against UK liability. The main choices for organisation of overseas operations are overseas resident subsidiary and branch. The taxation treatment is very different. In the former case, defined when control and management are abroad, no UK tax becomes payable until profits are remitted (but note there is no relief for losses against UK income either), while in the case of branches profits and losses these form part of the results of the UK company and are fully liable to UK taxation. However, both branches and overseas subsidiaries will be liable to tax in the location abroad. In effect they are double taxed. Normally relief to instigate this can be obtained through double-taxation agreements, whereby tax paid abroad can be offset against UK liability on the same income up to the limit of the UK tax due.
>
> (Collier *et al.* 1988: 40)

The UK has a fairly extensive network of reciprocal taxation agreements, covering more than eighty countries. If no such reciprocal agreement exists the UK usually grants unilateral relief to UK registered companies.

In any investment decision the impact of corporation tax has to be considered, both in terms of the corporation-tax liabilities arising as a result of the additional profits generated and in terms of the impact of corporation tax on the capital funding requirements of the project. 'Investment decisions' do not imply just strategic opportunities to expand activity; quite the most common investment decision concerns the replacement of existing assets because they have become worn out and/or technically obsolete. Chapter 13 deals with investment appraisal in some detail, but here we consider some of the taxation issues in advance of this more detailed discussion.

The distinction between accounting profit (based on the accruals accounting convention) and economists' views of profit (based on net cash inflows) has already been drawn. Clearly, all investment opportunities should be undertaken if as a result of cost reduction or increased net cash inflows the value of shareholders' investment is increased. The value of a company's shares is based on its projected future dividends; that is, cash distributions. Whilst accounting profit is an important concept, businesses go bankrupt because they become insolvent (i.e. run out of cash), not because they fail to make adequate accounting profits. It follows, therefore, that investment decisions ought to be considered in the light of their cash-flow impact on the business. This being the case, a number of taxation-related issues potentially arise. Taxation, since it is a cash-based cost to the business, should, in theory, be included in the relevant project cash flows. This should imply that these 'net-of-tax' cash flows should be discounted by a 'net-of-tax' discount rate. (The process of discounting cash flows is explained in much more detail in Chapter 13.). In order to arrive at net-of-tax cash flows the calculation of the corporation-tax charge in each year requires reference to the accounting profit, which is then adjusted by adding back what the Inland Revenue regards as non-allowable deductions and subtracting capital allowances. The discount rate needs to reflect the fact that debt interest is an allowable business expense. If this were not so the tax charge would be proportionally higher. If a company's debt (D) was at, say, 10%, then its net-of-tax cost $(1 - C$, where C, the tax rate, $= 31\%)$ would be 6.9%. This value would need to be recorded in the calculation of the company's overall weighted-average cost of capital, along with the other major capital component of equity (see Appendix 13.A).

The principle, to be further discussed later (in Chapter 13), is that all investment opportunities are acceptable provided that the overall opportunity cost of the capital that it is proposed to allocate is covered. One should never simply look to satisfying the cost of, say, borrowed capital. To do so would only increase the financial risk associated with the return expected by the company's equity investors.

National insurance

As originally conceived, the national insurance (NI) system set up in 1946 was intended to be different from a system of taxation. As stated in a Parliamentary command paper:

> The distinction between taxation and insurance contributions is or should be related to assumed capacity to pay rather than to the value of what the payee may expect to receive, while insurance contributions are or should be related to the value of the benefits and not to the capacity to pay.
>
> (Cmnd. 6404: para. 272)

The National Insurance Fund is a separate fund used solely to pay the state retirement pension, widow's benefit, invalidity benefit, sickness benefit, maternity allowance, guardian allowance, child's special allowance, Christmas bonus to pensioners and redundancy payments – estimated in 1996/7 at over £40 billion.

Although the contributory principle is still alive, NI has many of the hallmarks of taxation – being, for many workers, a proportional tax. The concept of insurance is in fact a myth since, particularly with respect to the state pension, those that contribute today basically pay the pensions of the generation now retired. *Butterworth's UK Tax Guide 1992–93* notes that:

> in the General Election of 1992 the national insurance system for the first time in many years became a major issue in British politics, although it cannot be said that the contributory principle as such was widely debated. In fact the programmes of the opposition parties entailed abolition of the contributory principle completely: Labour by its proposed removal of the upper earnings limit for employee contributions and the Liberal Democrats by their proposed assimilation of national insurance contributions to the income tax system.
>
> (Butterworth's 1992: 1204)

Table 5.6 National insurance contributions for 1997–8

Class 1			
	Employee		Employer
Pay per week £	first £62/week %	excess up to £465/week %	on all earnings %
below 62.00	0	0	0.0
62.00–109.00	2	10	3.0
110.00–154.99	2	10	5.0
155.00–209.00	2	10	7.0
210.00–465.00	2	10	10.0
over 465.00	2	10	10.0

From its inception, the employer contributions have been nothing other than a direct tax on employment – a payroll tax. The employer gains little from the payments of these monies. In companies, employees and employers pay what are termed **Class 1 contributions**. No contribution arises unless the employee's weekly wage exceeds a threshold termed the lower earnings limit. If earnings do exceed this threshold contributions are payable on the earnings up to as well as above this limit. Table 5.6 provides the standard rates for Class 1 contributions in 1997/8. There are two other sets of rates: contracted-out rates and the reduced rate. The former rate(s) relates to when an employee is on an approved contracted-out occupational pension scheme. The latter rate applies in the case of certain married women and widows who prior to 12 May 1977 had elected to pay reduced contributions into the scheme and have not subsequently revoked the election or lost the right to pay reduced contributions.

Class 1 contributions are normally payable under the PAYE system, the employer being liable for the deduction of employee contributions and for payment, together with the employer's secondary contributions, to the Collector of Taxes within fourteen days of each month-end. The Revenue subsequently surrenders these monies to the Department of Social Security for payment into the NI Fund.

Value added tax

Value added tax (VAT) was introduced in 1973. Since 1 April 1991 the rate on all taxable goods and services not zero-rated is 17.5%. VAT is, as its name implies, an indirect tax on value added. VAT is largely removed from business costs, being confined to consumer expenditure. The tax suffered by a business on its purchases is called **input tax** and that which it charges its customers is called the **output tax**. The system operates right through the chain of importation or production of goods, through distribution via wholesalers, until the final sale from the retailer to the consumer. It is thus the ultimate consumer who bears the tax on the sale price of purchases – a tax on the value added to basic raw materials. Table 5.7 illustrates this chain effect. VAT is a tax administered by HM Customs & Excise.

Various categories of goods and services are zero-rated (although they are in theory taxable, the tax rate is nil). This means that the trader cannot charge customers with

Table 5.7 VAT – the chain effect, who pays?

Stages	£	£
1 A manufacturer buys, for example, raw materials at a basic price of	5 000	
on which his supplier charges VAT (17.5%)	875	
Total cost to manufacturer	5 875	
2 Supplier pays to Customs & Excise	VAT (875)	875
3 Manufacturer turns the raw material into finished goods, which are despatched to a wholesaler at a basic price of	15 000	
to which VAT (17.5%) was added	2 625	
Wholesaler pays	17 625	
4 Manufacturer pays to Customs & Excise: VAT (£2 625–875)		1 750
5 The wholesaler sells the goods on to a retailer	18 000	
to which VAT (17.5%) was added	3 150	
Retailer pays	21 150	
6 Wholesaler pays to Customs & Excise: VAT (£3 150–£2 625)		525
7 The retailer sells the goods to customers (in total) at	24 000	
to which VAT (17.5%) was added	4 200	
Customers pay (in total)	28 200	
8 The retailer pays to Customs & Excise: VAT (£4 200–£3 150)		1 050
Total tax received by Customs & Excise:		4 200

the tax but can claim back the relevant input tax. A list of zero-rated supplies is provided in Table 5.8. Also, a large number of goods and services are exempt from VAT (see Table 5.9), but the trader cannot recover any associated input tax, so that this becomes a cost to him to be recovered in the price charged to customers. All traders whose turnover exceeds £48 000 are obliged to register for VAT with the Customs & Excise. They are expected to keep suitable records and a 'tax account' in which their total liabilities or claims in respect of VAT are recorded. These records are subject to audit. Where a supplier has suffered a bad debt by reason of a customer becoming insolvent, it is normally possible to reclaim the VAT paid on the supplies concerned.

Table 5.8 VAT – zero-rated supplies

These groups are as set out in Schedule 8, VAT Act 1983: The Schedule contains a number of groups, which are listed here with some important examples of zero-rated goods and services.

Group 1	Food
	Including:
	▪ food of a kind used for human consumption
	▪ animal feeding stuffs
	Exceptions include:
	▪ supply in the course of catering, including all food which is consumed on the premises and all hot food
	▪ ice cream, confectionery and chocolate biscuits
	▪ spirits, beer and wine
	▪ pet food
Group 2	Sewerage services and water
Group 3	Books
	Including:
	▪ books, booklets, brochures, pamphlets and leaflets newspapers, journals and periodicals
	▪ Individual knitting patterns are taxable supplies but booklets containing more than one pattern are zero-rated.
Group 4	Talking books for the blind and handicapped, and wireless sets for the blind
Group 5	Construction of buildings etc.
Group 6	Protected buildings
Group 7	International services
Group 8	Transport
Group 9	Caravans and houseboats
Group 10	Gold
Group 11	Bank notes
Group 12	Drugs, medicines, aids for the handicapped
Group 13	Imports, exports, etc.
Group 14	Tax-free shops
Group 15	Charities etc.
Group 16	Clothing and footwear

Business rates

Finally, in this section it should be noted that businesses used to pay rates based on the value of their properties. This system was revised in April 1990 to a 'uniform business rate' (UBR). This rate is set centrally by central government, collected locally and reapplied nationally to local councils pro rata to population. During the passage of the legislation through Parliament the UBR became the national non-domestic rate (NNDR).

Conclusions

Each year the taxation and allowances outlined in Chancellor's Budget have an impact on companies' overall profitability. Managers therefore need to keep up to date with these developments, understand what impact they have on their company's reported profit and how these pronouncements effect their strategic investment decisions.

Table 5.9 VAT – exempt goods and services

Group 1	The grant of any interest in or right over land, but not the letting of accommodation, parking or camping facilities, or fishing or taking game Bedroom accommodation in hotels is taxable but not other accommodation in hotels or elsewhere From 1 August 1989 an election (subject to many qualifications) can be made to waive this exemption and thus recover input tax
Group 2	Insurance, covering also services provided by brokers and agents; but most marine, aviation and transport insurance is zero-rated
Group 3	Postal services, but not cable services
Group 4	Betting, gaming and lotteries, but admission charges, club subscriptions and taking from gaming machines are taxable
Group 5	Finance, i.e. dealing in money or credit, banking and the sale of securities; but stockbrokers' commissions and unit trust management fees are taxable The charge made by credit-card companies on retailers is exempt in 1985/6 and onwards
Group 6	Education, including the supply of incidental services, and covering the facilities provided by youth clubs and similar organisations
Group 7	Health, covering goods and services provided by medical practitioners, dentists (although no longer wholly exempt from 1 September 1988), opticians, nurses, pharmaceutical chemists, hearing-aid dispensers, hospitals, etc Protective boots and helmets purchased by businesses are chargeable from 1 April 1989
Group 8	Burial and cremation services
Group 9	Trade unions and professional bodies
Group 10	Sports, sports competitions and physical education
Group 11	Works of art etc
Group 12	Fundraising events by charities and other qualifying bodies

Most of the larger accounting firms regularly produce information on taxation, which is provided free to their clients. The Inland Revenue and Customs & Excise also produce a range of free publications that can provide much useful information to the general manager.

Although companies pay taxes they do not suffer the burden of them; in the end, only individuals suffer the burden, whether as consumers, employees or shareholders. Nevertheless, financial managers need to be aware of the tax consequences of their proposed decisions since tax may affect their prices, their wage bills or the returns they achieve for their shareholders. In essence, regard has to be had to three aspects:

■ the amount of the tax payments;
■ the timing of the tax payments;
■ compliance with tax regulations.

It may be possible to reduce the amount of the payments by tax planning; this applies most obviously to corporation tax. It may also be relevant to employee national insurance contributions and to VAT, where it may be possible to bring a product within zero-rate provisions and so be able to lower the price to the final consumer. The timing of tax payments is significant because, as with any payment, delay reduces the cost: tax postponed is tax saved. This applies to any tax payment. Compliance with the tax regulations inevitably imposes costs, but failure to comply may incur penalties, which are, or should be, an avoidable cost.

Further reading

For managers, two very readable texts are James and Nobes (1997) and Hancock (1997). Both texts are revised annually following the presentation of the Chancellor's Annual Budget. The first of these sets out to provide an introduction to the economic theory of taxation, together with a detailed account and discussion of the tax system operating in the United Kingdom, with some overseas comparisons. The book assumes that the reader has some general background knowledge of basic economic principles. The most recent edition, at the time of writing, contains a separate chapter on international aspects of corporation tax, including issues related to European Union harmonisation. Hancock provides a more practical appreciation of tax, primarily for students preparing for professional exams. As such, his is a text that can assist the reader with independent study and is therefore a very readable text for managers. Each chapter has self-test questions, and answers are provided at the end of the text.

Questions and exercises

Unlike most of the other chapters in this book, there are no self-test questions associated with this chapter. Instead, a series of investigative questions is provided, the answers to which all managers should be broadly familiar with.

1 For an organisation with which you are familiar, attempt to estimate, in general terms, the compliance costs to the organisation of being a tax collector on behalf of the government. (Consider the compliance costs for the calculation and collection of corporation tax, PAYE/NI and VAT.)
2 Why is taxable profit different from financial accounting profit? Illustrate your answer with examples.
3 Why does the Inland Revenue not allow depreciation as a taxable allowance in the calculation of taxable profit but, instead, prefers to promote capital allowances?
4 What impact do capital allowances have on long-term investment decisions?
5 Why have accountants devised the concept of deferred taxation?
6 What is the 'Imputation System' of corporation tax? Why was this system adopted in the UK in 1973?
7 What impact does the imposition of VAT have on consumer demand?

8 'Taxation is nothing more than another business expense.' Discuss.
9 Should the management of taxation be a centralised or decentralised management responsibility?
10 Is taxation a critical factor when undertaking investment decisions or should its impact be seen as a residual issue?

6 Auditing and management

Objectives

Like accounting, auditing has been around for a very long time. Historically, its principal focus has been to ensure that the accountability reports (financial statements) prepared by managers (stewards) have been reliable, and that owners (shareholders) could use these reports with confidence. Thus, the original focus of auditing was the 'correctness' of accountability reports. Closely following this was the idea of regularity – auditors were expected to confirm that resources had only been applied for authorised purposes. Later, and particularly in the late twentieth century, have come ideas of auditors ensuring that 'value for money' is being achieved by the expenditure of resources, particularly in the public sector.

In this chapter we concentrate, first, on the overall principles of accountability. From this base we proceed to examine the history of the auditing of the financial statements of private-sector companies and to examine the fundamental concepts underpinning this process. Thereafter we review the role of the internal audit process and look at trends in auditing in the public sector.

The varieties of auditing

Auditing has existed in various guises throughout history. Wherever stewards (managers) have been entrusted with the management of resources by the owners of those resources the owners have required statements of account from the managers on the use of such resources. Thus there is an accountability relationship between the managers and the owners. The terms of this accountability relationship will vary depending on the reasons the owners entrusted their resources to the managers in the first place. This might simply have been for safekeeping (in which case the statement of account might simply state how the resources have been kept safe and confirm that they are still safe); it might have been to expend the resources in some approved way (in which case the statement of account would demonstrate how they have actually been expended); it might have been to generate a surplus by using the resources in some form of commercial venture (in which case the statement of account would focus on the trading transactions entered into and their outcomes); it might have been to use the resources as efficiently and as effectively as possible to achieve some given objective (in which case the statement of account should demonstrate the efficiency and effectiveness achieved).

However, in all cases the managers will have a vested interest in demonstrating that they have fulfilled their obligations under the accountability relationship, and this might lead to them preparing biased statements of account. Accordingly, owners will normally require reassurance that the statements of account are in fact reliable, and this is where the auditor comes in. The role of the auditor, in general terms, is to confirm the reliability of the statements of account and, in some circumstances, to go behind them to ensure that the detailed conditions of the accountability relationship have been complied with. As accountability relationships vary and as the terms of the auditing contract (between the owner and the auditor) vary, so the nature of the audit will vary.

The principal forms of audit within the UK are:

- **External audit**: this phrase is normally used to refer to the audit of the annual financial statements of companies (or other entities) by professionally qualified and legally registered accountants. Such audits are required by the Companies Acts, although there are exemptions from these requirements for small companies, which also lay down the objectives of the audit. External audits are not, however, restricted to the private sector. They also exist within the public sector. Here the Audit Commission and the National Audit Office have legal responsibilities to carry out external audits of public-sector organisations or arrange for them to be carried out. However, as we will discuss later, because the accountability relationships in the public sector differ from those in the private sector, so do the nature and objectives of the audits that are carried out.
- **Internal audit**: this phrase relates to those audits that management decides to have carried out within its enterprises. The objectives and scope of such audits are determined by management. They are normally carried out to provide management with reassurance that the enterprise's internal control systems are being complied with, although increasingly in recent years they have also been used to examine broader resource-utilisation issues such as efficiency and effectiveness.

External audit in the private sector

External audits of the financial statements of companies have been envisaged by the Companies Acts since the middle of the nineteenth century, although the precise legal requirements have varied over time. Of particular interest is the way in which the objectives of such audits have varied. T. A. Lee (1986) provides a useful summary of these changes, emphasising the move from 'fraud and error detection' as the primary audit objective to 'attesting the credibility of financial statements'. In many ways these changes in audit objectives are the origins of much of the current debate about the role of auditing and how well this role is being discharged. There is widespread misunderstanding about the role of auditors and auditing. In essence, this misunderstanding relates to the different perceptions that the accountancy (auditing) profession and the public at large have about the purpose of auditing, and it is normally referred to as the 'expectations gap'. Before looking at the expectations gap in detail and examining the response of the profession to it we shall first review the purpose and role of auditing as commonly understood by accountants and as currently incorporated in legislation.

The Companies Act 1985, as amended by the 1989 Companies Act, contains a number of sections relating to audit requirements, the principal of which are:

- **Section 236**: this requires that the auditor's report state whether or not accounts have properly been prepared in accordance with the requirements of the Act, and whether or not they give a 'true and fair view' of the company's financial position and performance.
- **Section 237**: this requires that the auditor comment, on an exception basis, on other matters, for example the maintenance of proper accounting records, agreement between the accounts and the underlying accounting records, receipt of the information and explanations deemed necessary for the audit, and that the information contained in the director's report is consistent with that in the accounts.

Thus, while the core objective of the audit as required by the Companies Acts is the expression of an expert professional opinion as to whether or not the accounts present a 'true and fair view', there are other objectives related to the reliability of information and the regularity of the company's actions. The Companies Acts also lay down a number of requirements regarding the regulation of the auditing process. These include the appointment of auditors (by the shareholders in general meeting; section 384); giving the auditors the right to inspect the company's accounting records and obtain information and explanations from company officials (section 237); and giving auditors the right to communicate with shareholders (section 392). Fuller details of these requirements can be found in Aldis and Renshall (1990). They can be broadly summarised as providing the auditor with the legal back-up needed to ensure that a full and proper audit can be carried out.

The accountancy profession has defined the role of auditors as being 'to provide objective assurance on an entity's published financial reports, principally for the benefit of primary stakeholders to whom the auditors owe a duty of care, but also for the information of other stakeholders' (APB 1994: para. 4.7). Received professional wisdom in recent years has been that the core objective of the external audit of the annual financial statements of companies is to provide users with an independent, expert opinion on the statements. This is generally referred to as the 'attest' function of the auditor. Effectively, via this opinion, the auditor is attesting to the credibility of the information contained in the statements. This attest function is generally regarded as being necessary because 'The accounting information in the main annual financial statements of the generality of companies lacks sufficient credibility, without a formal audit, to be used with complete confidence by shareholders and other report users' (T. A. Lee 1986: 74). Underpinning this traditional 'attest' function of the auditor are four core concepts of auditing: independence, truth and fairness, responsibility and evidence. These are explained in detail below.

Independence

The prime reason for having an audit in the first place is the potential lack of objectivity in accountability reports produced by managers leading to a 'credibility gap'. The role of the auditor is to reintroduce objectivity into the accountability reporting process by requiring an *independent* expert opinion. Thus the independence (objectivity) of the auditor is critical to the value of auditing. Ceteris paribus, the less independent the auditor, the lower the level of objectivity and the less the credibility of the statements which are the subject of the audit will be enhanced. Ultimately this independence is a function of the state of mind of the auditor in relation to any particular audit assignment. However, such a state of mind cannot be observed or assessed by shareholders and others. Accordingly, to reassure users of financial statements there are regulations which define situations and relationships which might be perceived as threatening the independence of auditors, and auditors are required to avoid such situations. Some of these regulations are contained in the Companies Acts (e.g. those relating to the appointment and removal of auditors), while others are the subject of statements by professional accountancy bodies whose members are authorised to carry out audits. The main threats to independence are normally regarded as those given below:

1 **Fee income**: there are two issues here that are commonly regarded as being threats to the auditor's independence, both relating to the financial relationships between the auditor and the client company:

■ **audit fees**: these are the fees the auditor receives for carrying out the audit and they are paid by the company whose financial statements are the subject of the audit. For large groups of companies such audit fees may be very substantial. In theory, the amount of the audit fee, as with the appointment of the auditors, is determined by the shareholders in general meeting. In practice it is the directors who nominate the auditors (it is very unusual for the shareholders to dissent from such a nomination) and fix the level of the audit fees (the shareholders authorising them to do so). Thus directors of companies have a significant degree of influence over who the auditors are and how much they will be paid. This influence is commonly regarded as posing a threat to the independence of the auditor. To counter this threat professional and/or statutory regulations impose limits on the proportion of fees that an audit practice derives from any single client. The idea is that imposing these limits makes it less likely that the directors of any particular client will be able to exert undue influence on the auditors. In the UK the current position is that the fees from any client, or group of clients, should not exceed 10% of the auditors' gross fee income.

■ **fees for other work**: apart from providing audit services modern accountancy practices frequently provide a range of other professional services to their client companies. These other services include taxation advice, management consultancy advice and specialist financial investigation services. The income that practices derive from these services may be very large and, unlike the audit fee income, it is purely discretionary, i.e. the work involved (and therefore the fees) does not have to be awarded to the company's auditors, although it frequently is. There is therefore a fear that auditors might be tempted to compromise their audit independence to ensure that they are awarded this other work. The 1989 Companies Act (section 390) introduced a new requirement to ensure that the full extent of the financial relationships between the auditor and the auditee company are disclosed. In some countries, notably the USA, there are strict limits on the extent of the other services that auditors can provide to their audit clients. However, it has been argued (e.g. Goldman and Barlev 1974) that specialist expertise in these other services may actually reinforce an auditor's independence as corporate management could be unwilling to lose access to such expertise.

In recent years a new strand to the debate about auditors' financial links with companies has emerged. This is a phenomenon usually referred to as 'lowballing', which reflects the increasingly competitive market in which the major accountancy practices find themselves. In its purest form 'lowballing' is the practice of quoting very low (perhaps below economic) audit fees to potential clients in order to secure the assignments. The incentives for doing this are various, but could include obtaining access to other work for the client (and the associated fees), obtaining prestige/profile in the financial services market by securing the audit of a 'blue-chip' company, or simply reinforcing the overall financial base of the accountancy practice. It is analogous to the use of 'loss leaders' in the retail trade. The danger of 'lowballing' is that the fees generated might not be enough to cover the costs of carrying out an proper audit to the required standards and that budgetary pressure might therefore lead to the quality of the audit being compromised.

2 **Personal relationships**: if the auditor is closely associated on a personal basis with senior personnel of the company whose accounts are being audited, then users of the accounts who are aware of such relationships may perceive the auditor's independence as being compromised. It is at least possible that an auditor will be unwilling to express opinions on matters which may adversely affect people having a close personal relationship. This obviously includes family members (spouses, children, etc.), but could also include close friendships or even people with whom the auditor might be expected to feel an instinctive empathy. This latter is obviously something of a problem given the undoubted existence of a group of people in the City who share common backgrounds, values and beliefs. Personal relationships of this sort are not specifically covered by the Companies Acts, and the professional guidelines, perhaps inevitably, are not very specific in this area other than stating that such potentially compromising links should be avoided.

3 **Financial involvement**: the professional guidance is much more specific here, going into some detail as to what an audit practice should do to avoid its perceived independence being compromised by financial links between partners or audit staff and the company being audited. In essence, what the guidance states is that no one having a financial involvement in the company whose accounts are being audited should be involved in the audit of that company (unless such an involvement is on a normal disinterested commercial basis, such as normal banking transactions with a bank); least of all should they have any beneficial ownership interest. The professional guidance is somewhat detailed, but its essence is the need to avoid the potential for any perceived loss of independence.

4 **Conflicting interests**: there is a wide range of situations which could put the auditor into a position where conflicting interests might lead to a perception of a loss of independence by users of the audit report. The most notable of these is the potential conflict between the management consultancy advice an audit practice might give to clients and the audit of financial statements based, at least in part, on such advice. Thus a situation might arise where an accountancy practice, acting as a management consultancy, offered advice on the suitability of a particular accounting system or software package from a management consultancy perspective, and then the audit arm of the practice, when it came to carry out the audit,

found that it was deficient in some way from an audit perspective. A similar situation might arise if the practice was to supply accountancy services (maintaining the core accounting records) and then audit such records. The basic position of the professional recommendations is that accountancy practices should avoid such conflicts of interest to protect their independence. However, the specific recommendations of the professional statements are far from all-encompassing (which is hardly surprising given the range of potential conflicts of interest).

The range of threats to the perceived and actual independence of auditors is wide and we need to recognise that accountancy practices do exist in a real commercial world. While it might be ideal to have auditing hermits emerging from their caves to carry out wholly independent and disinterested audits, this is not a realistic proposition. We might also query whether such hermits would have the commercial knowledge to carry out effective audits. What is encouraging is the degree to which the major accountancy practices recognise the need for independence and try to ensure that they comply, not just with the letter of the law and the professional statements, but with their spirit. Virtually all major practices have clearly defined and policed procedures to avoid situations which might be perceived as compromising independence. Inevitably, given the numbers of people involved in such practices, the breadth of their family and personal circumstances and the complexity of the financial structures of modern multinational corporations, mistakes are going to happen from time to time. However, the reputations of such practices are among their most important assets and they seek assiduously to preserve these reputations.

Having said this, the one thing they can do little about is the fact that the audit fee is paid by the company being audited, and that the directors have effective control over the appointment of auditors and the determination of the audit fee. This has been a major area of suggested reform. Suggested reforms have included the periodic rotation of auditors (i.e. the audit appointment should be for, say, three, five or seven years, after which new auditors will be appointed); that the appointment of auditors and the determination of their remuneration should be a matter for an 'audit committee' of non-executive directors; and that audits should be carried out by public servants, with the fees payable being based on measures such as turnover or net assets. These suggested reforms are part of a wider debate on the role, purpose and structure of the audit process, and demand for them tends to become more vocal whenever apparent audit failures are revealed.

Responsibility

The auditor is a professional person giving an independent, expert opinion on the financial statements of a company in return for a – sometimes very substantial – fee. Thus there need to be mechanisms via which an auditor can be held accountable for the quality of the audit and the resultant audit opinion. There are two main elements to this: for what the auditor can be held responsible and to whom the auditor owes a duty of responsibility.

1 **For what can the auditor be held responsible?** This ties in very closely with the objectives of the audit process and is the subject of much debate insofar as the public at large have rather different perceptions of the objectives of the audit than those the auditing profession has. However, the legal position at present appears to be that

dictated by the Companies Acts, that is that the auditor's duty is to give an opinion on the truth and fairness of the financial statements, and report (principally by exception) on a number of other items. We will discuss later how this differs from broader perceptions of the role of the auditor. To have a reliable basis for such an opinion the auditor will have to ensure that the audit has been properly carried out. The requirements for this are the subject of statute law (the Companies Acts), case law (there are a large number of cases dating back to the nineteenth century regarding what constitutes adequate conduct of an audit) and professional guidance (Auditing Standards and Guidelines). T. A. Lee (1986: 104–5) provides a good summary of these requirements, the key points being:

- familiarity with statutory duties, rights and powers;
- familiarity with relevant professional standards, i.e. SSAPs (and now FRSs) and Auditing Standards and Guidelines;
- maintaining independence;
- adequately planning the audit to obtain the necessary evidence (see below);
- obtaining sufficient evidence to support the audit opinion;
- using best (current) practice in carrying out the audit;
- reporting the opinion in the way prescribed by law and professional standards;
- ensuring adequate supervision of all staff employed on the audit.

More recently the APB (1996) has commented on what it regards as the 'enduring principles of auditing' with which all auditors are expected (have a responsibility) to conform. These are:

- integrity;
- objectivity and independence;
- competence;
- rigour;
- accountability;
- judgement;
- clear communication;
- providing value;
- association.

If an auditor should fail in the discharging of any of these requirements there is the possibility of a suit for negligence being raised by parties who have suffered loss as the result of a deficient (negligent) audit having being carried out. There is also the possibility of a report being made to the relevant professional organisation and the auditor being subject to disciplinary action. In an extreme case this might result in the auditor's right to practise being withdrawn. Historically, the major focus has been on claims for damage arising out of auditor negligence in the conduct of the audit, although this is changing with the increased regulation of the auditing profession following the implementation of the EC 8th Directive in the 1989 Companies Act.

2 **To whom does the auditor owe a duty of responsibility?** There is a substantial history of legal action against auditors whose work has been regarded as deficient (negligent) by interested parties who claim to have suffered loss as a result. Many of these cases have concentrated on matters of fact (i.e. was the auditor in fact negligent) and there is now a well-established body of case law in this regard (for a

summary, see T. A. Lee 1986: ch. 5). However, equally important is the question of who has a right of action against an auditor if they have suffered loss as a result of a deficient audit. The key principle here is that the audit contract is between the company and the auditor. Thus the company has an obvious right of action against a negligent auditor if it has suffered a loss. The difficulty with this is that all too often deficiencies in the audit emerge only when the company becomes insolvent and is being wound up, and many actions against auditors are in fact launched by receivers/liquidators of companies in the company's name. However, case law has established that the audit is for the benefit of the shareholders, although they are not direct parties to the audit contract. Accordingly, it is generally accepted that they have a right of action. The position regarding other parties (e.g. potential share-holders, employees and trading partners) is somewhat more difficult. Historically, the law has generally been disinclined to give a right of action to parties who suffer economic as opposed to physical damage from the negligent performance of a contract (in this case the auditing contract between the company and the auditor). This is largely because of perceived difficulties in relating the economic loss directly to the negligence (the 'proximity' question). In the famous words of an American judge, Cardozo C. J. (*Ultramares Corporation v. Touche*, 1931, 255 N.Y. 170, 174 N.E., 441, 74 A.L.R. 1139), the danger is regarded as one of creating 'liability in an indeterminate amount for an indeterminate time to an indeterminate class'.

More recently there was something of a tendency for courts in the UK to relax this attitude and to contemplate third parties having rights of action against auditors and accountants where they relied on statements made by auditors and accountants as part of their decision-making process. Such cases include *Candler v. Crane, Christmas & Co.* (1951, 2 K.B. 164, 1 All E.R. 426, 1 T.L.R. 371), *Hedley Byrne & Co. Ltd v. Heller & Partners Ltd* (1964, A.C. 465; 1963, 2 All E.R. 575, 3 W.L.R: 101) and *JEB Fasteners Ltd v. Marks Bloom & Co.* (1981, 3 All E.R. 289). In various ways these cases seemed to extend the rights of third parties against auditors, but perhaps not so significantly as some commentators have indi-cated. In the Caparo case (*Caparo Industries PLC v. Dickman and Others*, (1990, 1 All E.R. 568, 2 A.C. 605, 2 W.L.R. 358 H.L.) and others (*Al-Saudi Banque v. Clark Pixley*, 1990, Ch. 313; *James McNaughton Papers Group Ltd v. Hicks Anderson & Co.*, 1991, 1 All E.R. 134, A.C.L.C. 3091; 1990, B.C.C. 891; and *Berg & Sons Ltd v. Mervyn Hampton Adams*, 1993, B.C.L.C. 1045) this apparent relax-ation was halted, and the current position appears to be that very few third parties will have a right of action against auditors, and then only in restricted circum-stances. This is a difficult area of the law as it is part of the more general law of tort rather than law specifically oriented to accounting and auditing. Accordingly, it is the subject of broader legal developments.

Many people strongly hold the view that auditors should have a duty of respon-sibility to people who rely on the 'enhanced credibility' which the audit is supposed to afford to a company's financial statements. Some argue that if this broader set of users were not supposed to be the beneficiaries of this 'enhanced credibility' there would be no reason for a statutory audit to be required and for the audited accounts to be publicly available (via the Registrar of Companies)? They argue that this very process fosters a sense of reliance on the audit opinion and that therefore the auditor owes all users a duty of responsibility.

In part this debate also relates to the financial resources which accountancy practices have available to them to meet any damages awarded by the courts if they are found to have acted negligently. If they are constituted as unlimited partnerships the partners are jointly and severally liable for any award of damages, and such damages are potentially huge, running into tens or hundreds of millions of pounds. The question then arises whether or not such potential liabilities are a fair burden to place on auditors. Prudent auditors will take out professional indemnity insurance wherever possible, but is questionable whether they will always be able to obtain sufficient insurance given the scale of potential claims. An alternative approach, and one envisaged by the 1989 Companies Act, is to permit at least a degree of limited liability to auditors. However, as yet few accountancy practices have been able to do this, although it remains a very live issue.

Truth and fairness

As we saw in Chapter 4 the concept of a 'true and fair' view is fundamental to the system of corporate financial reporting in the UK, and yet it is a concept which lacks a precise legal definition. We do not want to repeat the earlier discussion here. Instead, we will concentrate on the means via which the auditor's opinion on the truth and fairness of the financial statements is communicated to interested parties via the audit report. Audit reports have been the subject of auditing standards since the early 1980s, the most recent standard being issued by the APB (1993). The format is:

Auditors' report to the shareholders of XYZ Ltd

We have audited the financial statements on pages . . . to . . . , which have been prepared under the historic-cost convention (as modified by the revaluation of certain fixed assets) and the accounting policies set out on page . . .

Respective responsibilities of directors and auditors
As described on page . . . , the company's directors are responsible for the preparation of the financial statements. It is our responsibility to form an independent opinion, based on our audit, on those statements and report our opinion to you.

Basis of opinion
We conducted our audit in accordance with Auditing Standards issued by the APB. An audit includes examination, on a test basis, of evidence relevant to the amounts and disclosures in the financial statements. It also included an assessment of the significant estimates and judgements made by the directors in the preparation of the financial statements, and of whether the accounting policies are appropriate to the company's circumstances, consistently applied and adequately disclosed.

We planned and performed our audit so as to obtain all the information and explanations which we considered necessary in order to provide us with sufficient evidence to give reasonable assurance that the financial statements are free from material misstatement, whether caused by fraud or other irregularity or error. In forming our opinion we also evaluated the overall adequacy of the presentation of information in the financial statements.

Opinion

In our opinion the financial statements give a true and fair view of the state of the company's affairs as at 31 December 19X0 and of its profit (loss) for the year then ended, and have been properly prepared in accordance with the Companies Act 1985.

ABC
Registered Auditors
London
31 January 19X0

Auditors were expected to comply with this new form of report for the audit of financial statements for financial periods ending on or after 30 September 1993. A number of features of this reporting framework are worth highlighting:

- **Addressees**: the report is addressed to the shareholders of the company, thereby highlighting the fact that they are envisaged by law as being the principal beneficiaries of the external audit process.
- **Scope**: the report identifies precisely which pages of the annual report containing the financial statements have been the subject of audit.
- **Accounting policies**: the importance of an appreciation of the accounting policies selected by the directors is emphasised by referring to them specifically in the audit report.
- **Respective responsibilities of directors and auditors**: when the APB issued a consultative document regarding a new format for audit reports (APB 1991) the proposed audit-report structure included a section which dealt specifically with the directors' responsibilities for the financial statements, referring directly to the need for them to comply with the fundamental accounting concepts (consistency, prudence, going concern, and matching) in the preparation of the financial statements and to their responsibilities with regard to the prevention and detection of fraud and error. In the final Auditing Standard this requirement has been changed. The new requirement is that there should be, elsewhere within the financial statements, a separate statement of the directors' responsibilities and that the audit report should simply refer to this section. However, if such a statement is either missing or inadequate the audit report should compensate for this by including a statement of what the directors' responsibilities are.
- **Audit process**: the report stresses that the audit processes carried out meets the professionally specified standards of audit performance ('in accordance with *auditing* standards'). This might seem a powerful statement about the quality of the audit that has been carried out, and certainly many readers of the report will perceive it in this way. Unfortunately, as we shall see later, this might be something of an excessive reliance on the nature of auditing standards. This paragraph also emphasises that the audit is conducted on a 'test basis' (it is not – and could not – be a check on everything).
- **Emphasis on the extent of judgement required in the preparation of financial statements** and the fact that all the auditor can do is assess the reasonableness of such judgements rather than verify their 'correctness'.
- **Nature of an audit**: here the report is attempting to emphasise that an auditor's opinion on the financial accounts is precisely that – an opinion, hopefully an inde-

pendent, expert opinion based on the acquisition and evaluation of evidence to support it. It is not a guarantee of the 'correctness' of the accounts. Unfortunately, there is evidence that a number of users of financial statements perceive it as such.

- **Nature of the opinion**: this will normally be a confirmation that, in the auditor's opinion, the accounts do indeed give a 'true and fair view'. In these circumstances the audit report is normally referred to as an 'unqualified' report, that is the auditor is saying that s/he has no significant reservations about the financial statements which need to be communicated to readers. However, there will be circumstances where the auditor does have such reservations and therefore expresses them in the audit report. Such audit reports are normally referred to as 'qualified'. Where the auditor wants to express such reservations it is vital that they be fully and clearly stated. Unfortunately, all too often these 'qualifications' are expressed in rather technical and recondite language which makes their exact meaning difficult to understand, particularly by readers not educated in accounting jargon.
- **The remainder of the report deals with legalistic issues** such as compliance with the Companies Acts, date and place of issue.

The hope is that the new audit report structure will help better to inform users of financial statements about what, at least from the profession's standpoint, an audit is, and therefore about what the auditor can be held responsible for.

Evidence

Much of the presumed value of the audit derives from the fact that it results in the publication of an independent, expert opinion on the truth and fairness of the financial statements of an enterprise. If this presumption is to be justifiable the opinion itself must be firmly grounded on evidence which justifies it. Thus auditors have a duty to obtain sufficient relevant and reliable evidence to support their final opinions. The planning, collection and evaluation of such evidence are the core of the audit process. They are also the areas which most frequently result in actions for negligence against auditors and, unsurprisingly, the areas in which the APB provides most guidance to auditors by issuing professional-practice statements. Such statements were first issued by the APC and took the form of Auditing Standards (which were mandatory) and Auditing Guidelines (which were supposed to be influential but not mandatory). Since the APC was replaced by the APB the structure and scope of these statements have changed. The current position is that the documents issued by the APB have the following applicability:

- **Statements of Auditing Standards (SASs)**: these state the basic principles and essential procedures which auditors are expected to adhere to. As is usual with such statements, they are issued after the publication of an Exposure Draft and a period for comment by interested parties. The framework which the APB intends to follow was issued in June 1993 (APB 1993a).
- **Practice Notes and Bulletins**: these are intended to assist auditors in applying audit standards and to provide them with guidance on emerging issues. They are intended to be indicative of good practice, but are not mandatory.

There is no doubt that the APB has engaged in a major exercise in this restructuring of professional statements on auditing. What it is seeking is much more structured and extensive than the work which was carried out by the APC, and it will be correspondingly controversial and demanding on resources. However, it fits in with the general trend which we discussed in Chapter 4 of the increasing regulation of issues relating to the financial statements of enterprises.

In its auditing standards the APB will be placing great emphasis on the planning, collection and evaluation of audit evidence (Series 200/299, 300/399, 400/499, 500/599 of the standards deal with issues relating to evidence). The core issues that an auditor has to address in planning the collection of evidence necessary to support an audit opinion are given below:

- *Cost*: evidence, of whatever sort, is expensive to obtain and evaluate. Its acquisition has to be planned and resourced. Its evaluation requires the time of skilled professionals. At the same time, auditing practices are not charities – they are commercial enterprises seeking to make profits by engaging in audit practice. Thus they face a dilemma. They must comply with required standards of professional practice contained in statements such as SASs and yet do so within the cost constraints imposed by the audit fees they are able to negotiate (bearing in mind that, effectively, these fees are negotiated with the auditees – the directors). This is why the profession is so concerned about the issue of 'lowballing' – situations where an auditor pitches the audit fee at too low a level to support the costs of carrying out a competent audit.

- *Availability*: the very notion of an audit of financial statements implies that the information they contain is in fact verifiable, i.e. that evidence to support it can be obtained. In many cases this will be true – an auditor can count cash, inspect physical assets, and verify debtors and creditors by direct communication with them. However, there are areas where it is very difficult to obtain direct evidence to support such information – depreciation rates and policies are a matter of judgement, as is the valuation of intangible assets. In these circumstances the auditor is driven to form assessments about the reasonableness and reliability of judgements formed by others such as directors or external experts. This is a difficult and demanding role, and one which is always at risk of the glare of hindsight proving the assessment wrong.

- *Usefulness*: ideally the auditor will want evidence which enables the formation of a direct assessment of the truth and fairness of the information in the financial statements. An auditor will not want to waste time and money collecting and assessing evidence which does not contribute to this assessment. There are many factors which the auditor will need to take into account in assessing usefulness. These include issues such as relevance, reliability, objectivity, technicality, availability of documentation and source. T. A. Lee (1986) and Mautz and Sharaf (1961) provide extensive discussions of these issues, as, increasingly, do the statements issued by the APB.

A major difficulty faced by auditors is that it is highly unlikely that they will be able to acquire and evaluate any evidence which will directly confirm whether or not the financial statements as a whole present a 'true and fair view'. To counter this they need to break down the overall assertion of 'truth and fairness' into a series of sub-propositions about which they *can* obtain evidence. We can illustrate this process using the amount shown in a balance sheet for debtors as an example. Table 6.1

Table 6.1 Testable audit propositions regarding debtors

Showing debtors as an asset in a balance sheet effectively implies that an enterprise will receive future economic benefits (cash) at least equal to the amount so shown. This overall proposition has a number of testable sub-propositions, of which the following are a selection.

Proposition	Audit test approaches
The enterprise offers credit terms to its customers	Examination of documentation relating to the enterprise's terms of trade (e.g. promotional literature, credit-control authorisations, etc.)
The enterprise's internal control system and prime documents ensure that all aspects of its transactions with customers are properly recorded	Checking the adequacy of the internal control system by assessing its strengths and weaknesses (e.g. as regards procedures for the authorisation of documentation and the transfer of information)
The enterprise's sales ledger correctly records the amounts owed by customers	Testing the accuracy of the sales ledger by tracing its recording of transactions recorded via prime documents (e.g. sales invoices, credit notes, receipts from customers, etc.)
The debts recorded in the enterprise's sales ledger are acknowledged by customers as being payable by them	Contacting customers directly to ask them to confirm that they owe the amounts recorded in the sales ledger
The debts recorded in the enterprise's sales ledger as owed by customers are, in fact, collectible	Looking at customer payment patterns to assess whether or not they are in accordance with their authorised terms of credit in an attempt to identify any problem accounts, and examining the post-year-end receipt of monies from customers

illustrates the sub-propositions regarding debtors. The examples shown in Table 6.1 of auditing propositions and approaches to obtaining evidence to substantiate them are, of course, highly simplified. However, they do illustrate an important point. In collecting evidence to support their ultimate audit opinions auditors use two basic approaches, which are often referred to as compliance and substantive testing. The word 'testing' is important – its very use emphasises the fact that auditors cannot check everything, even if they wanted to, within the time and cost constraints under which they operate. Because of this, they typically adopt a three-part approach to the collection and evaluation of audit evidence:

1 **A review of the enterprise's internal control and operating procedures**. The purpose of this review is to assess the adequacy of these procedures as regards ensuring the compliance of activities with management policies, and the timely and accurate recording of these activities. Such a review seeks to identify areas, either of operations or financial recording, where there is a risk of unauthorised or incorrectly recorded activity. Typically, such systems reviews are very structured, involving the use of internal control questionnaires. A specimen extract of such a questionnaire is shown in Figure 6.1. Systems reviews, whether or not based on the use of questionnaires, inform the basis of the second part of the approach to gathering audit evidence.

Client name:		Bloggs and Company Ltd
Financial reporting period:		31st December 19X0
Control area:		Cash receipts
Completed by:	John Smith	*Date:* 16 January 19X1
Reviewed by:	James Jones	*Date:* 19 January 19X1

Question	*Answer*
1 Is incoming post opened by more than one person?	Yes
2 Are all cheques and postal orders immediately stamped 'account payee only'?	Yes
3 Is a list made of all cheques and postal orders contained in the post by the persons opening it?	No
4 Is this list signed and dated by the persons preparing it?	n/a
5 Is this list subsequently verified with the cash received part of the cash book?	n/a
6 etc.	

Figure 6.1
Illustrative internal control questionnaire.

2 **This involves the sample testing of transactions**. The basis of selecting the type and extent of transactions to be tested will be a combination of the internal control review and a broader assessment of the enterprise's activities and their associated risk of misstatement or error. The objective of this testing is to assure the auditor that the enterprise's accounting and operating procedures can be relied upon to ensure that its accounting records properly and fairly record all economic events affecting the enterprise. In planning this compliance testing the auditor will take into account any weaknesses identified in the systems review referred to above. Where weaknesses have been identified the scope of the audit testing will be extended to ensure that these weaknesses have not in fact led to error or malpractice. Where the internal control systems have been identified as strong there is likely to be less audit testing and the focus of such testing will be on ensuring that the systems are operating as specified. The purpose of the systems review and the compliance testing is to inform the auditor about the likely reliability of the balances in the enterprise's accounting records. In the light of this information, the auditor can then plan the final form of audit testing.

3 **Substantive testing**. The focus here is the verification of the amounts of individual account balances or the underlying information on which they are based. Examples of such testing include the verification of physical inventories, the counting of cash and the direct confirmation of amounts due from customers. The extent of such testing will be heavily influenced by the results of the systems review and the compliance testing. The more reliable the systems appear to be and the better they are complied with, the less will be the extent of the substantive testing that the auditor needs to carry out.

The audit evidence collection and evaluation process is essentially an iterative one. The auditor will initially plan the collection of evidence s/he believes is necessary to support an audit opinion based on the initial appraisals of the enterprise and its control systems. This plan will then be adapted in the light of the evidence obtained from the detailed reviews of the enterprise's systems and whether or not they are operating as specified (as revealed by the compliance tests). It will then be further adapted in the light of the results of the substantive tests. The auditor must never lose sight of the fact that the end product of the audit process is an opinion on the overall 'truth and fairness' of the financial statements, and his/her work should be focused on being able to attest this. Accordingly, s/he must constantly be reassessing this 'truth and fairness' in the light of the evidence being obtained. This may well mean that the original plans for the collection of audit evidence have to be reformed in the light of audit evidence already collected. There is also an extensive body of case law regarding what the courts regard as constituting the adequate planning, collection and evaluation of audit evidence. T. A. Lee (1986: Ch. 7) provides a useful review of these cases, as does Hatherly (1980).

Audit regulation

Auditors and auditing are increasingly becoming subject to more detailed regulation, and this parallels similar developments in financial reporting in general. This regulation is based in part on the work of the APB and in part on EU harmonisation. The EU 8th Directive, as implemented in the 1989 Companies Act, changed the regulation of auditing in the UK. Prior to 1989, members of the ICAEW, ICAS, ICAI and ACCA who held practising certificates issued by these bodies were authorised to carry out the audit of the financial statements of companies. The 1989 Act introduced the new position of 'Registered Auditor' and gave the secretary of state new regulatory powers. Effectively the secretary of state has delegated most of these powers to the professional bodies (who first had to make formal submissions justifying such delegation, particularly with respect to a much closer monitoring of training and the conduct of professional practice). Thus, the power of the professional bodies remains, but it is subject to much closer scrutiny.

The audit debate

In recent years there has been a considerable debate about the role of company auditing and the work of auditors. The APB (1996) provides a good review of this debate and its proposals for a way forward. In part, this debate has been the result of wider debates about corporate governance in general and the role of the audit in this process. Thus the Cadbury Committee's (1992) investigation and report led, amongst other things, to the development of a 'code of best practice' for the governance of listed companies in the UK, including recommendations about the relations among a company, its directors and its auditors. This code recommends a major role for non-executive directors, who should be independent of the management of the company, in ensuring that the company is managed to high ethical standards. Among other things, it recommends that the roles of chairman and chief executive should be separated; that there should be a remuneration committee to deal with executive directors' pay made up wholly or mainly of non-executive directors; and that there should be an audit committee, again made up of non-executive directors, to manage the company's relations with its external auditors. In essence, the role of the audit committee would be to reinforce the independence of the auditor by taking issues relating to the appointment and remuneration of auditors away from the executive directors and providing a forum to receive reports from auditors on their work, and also to monitor the standards to which the audit is performed.

The other main element in the debate has focused on the 'expectations gap' and how to resolve it. There is a considerable and long-established body of research evidence which indicates that many users of financial statements have perceptions about the role and scope of the audit, and about the responsibilities of the auditor, which differ significantly from those of the auditing profession, as supported by statute and case law. These differences include:

- **The nature of the audit opinion**. There is a widespread belief that an unqualified audit opinion means that the financial statements are 'right'. As we have seen in Chapter 3, there is an extensive amount of judgement involved in the preparation of financial statements, and therefore they can never be 'right' in the generally accepted meaning of the word. They can never be more than best estimates of the financial position and performance of an enterprise based on existing knowledge and forecasts applied in a proper way. Thus the audit report cannot be a 'certificate of correctness'. It is, as we have seen, no more than an independent and expert opinion on the interpretation and accuracy of the existing knowledge base and on the suitability of the forecasts on which the financial statements are ultimately based. The revised form of audit report outlined above goes some way to conveying the importance of judgements and estimates in the preparation and audit of financial statements. It could, perhaps, have gone further.

  The new form of audit report also refers to an examination, on a test basis, of evidence. Presumably the purpose of this is to inform users of the audit report that not everything has been checked. However, as it stands this is a rather bland statement. It tells the user nothing about the extent of the testing basis or on what principles the testing was carried out (statistical, judgemental, etc.). It would be unrealistic to expect an audit report to specify these principles in detail, and such a report would make both dry and difficult reading. However, the authors wonder whether or not the wording of the new statement adequately conveys the extent of auditing judgement involved in the 'test basis' and the extent to which this judgement might vary from auditor to auditor.

- **Misunderstandings of the scope of the audit report**. While the new format of the audit report identifies those pages of the company's annual report whose contents have been subject to audit, there is evidence that this limitation is not always appreciated by users of such reports. This may be because such users do not in fact read the audit report, but instead rely on a simplistic view that financial statements have been audited, that the annual report contains the financial statements and that therefore the annual report is reliable. There appear to be two possibilities here. The first is educational – ensuring users of financial statements and annual reports are aware of the need to read the audit report so as to identify exactly what has been audited. This is probably impractical. The second, which has already been addressed by the auditing profession, is to try and ensure that all the other information in the annual reports is at least compatible with and does not contradict the audited financial statements. This is the line which has been suggested by the APB, and is dealt with in SAS 160 (APB 1995c) which requires that auditors should seek to resolve any inconsistencies in such information.

■ **The economic well-being of the company**. There is evidence (e.g. Steen 1989) that a significant number of people believe that the external audit provides a guarantee of the financial soundness of the company being audited. This is a key misunderstanding, as the focus of the external audit is *information risk* (focusing on the reliability and credibility of the information in the financial statements) and not *commercial risk* (the economic circumstances in which the company finds itself), except that it needs to ensure that the information disclosed in the financial statements adequately reflects these commercial risks. A key question here is whether or not the company is in fact a 'going concern', which is one of the fundamental accounting principles discussed in Chapter 3. An audit must incorporate an assessment of the future risks facing a company which might threaten its ability to survive in the future, and the auditors much form an opinion as to whether or not any statements given by the directors on the subject of an entity's going-concern status are justified.

However, there is a danger here. If the auditors cast doubt on a company's future there is a possibility of their assessment (if it is adverse) becoming a reality – creditors concerned about receiving their money might press for settlement, thereby ensuring the demise of the company. Thus the assessment of a company's going-concern status is an onerous responsibility. The APB suggests that the auditors should require a statement from the directors regarding the company's going-concern status, together with supporting evidence, and that the auditors should perform procedures to confirm the directors' view. However, at the end of the day the problem remains that going-concern status relates to the future – and no one (directors, auditors or anyone else) can (or should be expected to) guarantee the future.

■ **The respective responsibilities of the directors and the auditors** regarding the financial statements. The proposed new format for audit reports addresses this issue.

■ **In relation to fraud**. Until the 1940s the detection of fraud was regarded as a primary objective of auditing. Since then the auditing profession has increasingly regarded enhancing the credibility of the financial statements as the primary objective of auditing, with the detection of fraud becoming very much a secondary objective. The prevention and detection of fraud is regarded as being primarily the responsibility of the directors, and while an audit might reveal fraud it is not designed to do so, unless the fraud is on such a scale that it would prevent the financial statements giving a 'true and fair view'. However, if the auditors find any evidence of a fraud during their conduct of the audit they must investigate further. The perception of the general public, however, is somewhat different. There is a widely held view that the detection of fraud, of all kinds, is a primary purpose of an audit. While this view may be understandable, it is fundamentally unrealistic. The time and cost of checking all the transactions of an enterprise to detect any possible fraud would be prohibitive. Accordingly, the emphasis must be on the prevention of fraud in the first place, and the best way of achieving this is by companies having adequate internal control systems and assuring the users of financial statements that this is the case. This is the approach suggested by the APB in line with the recommendations of the Cadbury Committee, which suggests that the auditor should report on the adequacy of a company's internal control procedures (as well as other risk-management controls). Whether or not this will be sufficient to change or satisfy the public's expectations regarding the responsibility of auditors for the detection of fraud remains an open question.

■ **Compliance by the company with legal regulatory requirements**. The position here is rather similar to that regarding fraud, that is that the primary responsibility rests with management rather than the auditors and that an adequate system of internal controls should prevent illegal acts. Again, as with fraud, if an auditor detects illegalities as a result of his/her normal audit procedures these must be pursued because they might impact on the truth and fairness of the financial statements. However, there is an additional dimension here – whether or not such illegalities/irregularities should be reported.

■ **Competence of corporate management**. This has never been regarded as an objective of auditing by the auditing profession. However, a number of studies (e.g. Steen 1989; Humphrey *et al.* 1992) indicate that a large proportion of the public believes that as part of the audit auditors assess how well a company has been managed. As we discuss below, such assessments, looking at issues such as economy, efficiency and effectiveness, are part of the remit of public-sector external auditors, but external auditors of private-sector enterprises have never viewed them as part of their responsibilities. To do so would be to tread a very thorny path as it would inevitably involve an assessment of the economic soundness of management's decisions and it must be questioned whether or not auditors would have the knowledge or competence to do this. In addition, they would be able to look only at the consequences of the choices that management actually made; they would not be able to look at the consequences of options that management rejected. The ultimate arbiter of management competence in the private sector must remain the capital market and the exercise of shareholder power. All that the auditor can do is help to ensure that the market and shareholders have credible information on which to make their assessments of managerial competence.

As the foregoing indicates, there is extensive and ongoing debate about the role and scope of auditing and the extent to which it is meeting the needs and expectations of users of financial statements and the public at large. This debate has been going on for a number of years and is regularly refuelled by corporate scandals such as those involving Polly Peck, Bank of Credit and Commerce International (BCCI) and Maxwell. The contributors to this debate include the financial press, the auditing profession, investors, creditors, employees, pensioners and politicians. It is a debate which is fundamental to the nature of corporate governance in the UK and one which will not be easily resolved. There is a tension between what it is reasonable to expect of the auditing profession (and therefore hold them responsible for delivering) and the demands that users of financial statements would ideally like to make of auditors. The resolution of this debate must ultimately be pragmatic and involve the acquiescence of the auditing profession, because ultimately society cannot compel an individual to be an auditor, and if the responsibilities and risks demanded of an auditor start to become unduly onerous in relation to the financial benefits that auditors enjoy it will be difficult to recruit auditors. One danger is that auditors could be used as scapegoats in corporate failures, in part because of the 'expectation gap'. Another danger is that the auditing profession could become excessively defensive.

It is encouraging that the auditing profession has recognised that change is necessary and that it needs to be responsive to the changing financial environment within which it operates (APB 1996). Hopefully its efforts, and those of others, will lead to a consensus emerging about the roles and responsibilities of auditors.

Internal auditing

There is a close analogy between management accounting/financial reporting and internal/external auditing. In both cases one is the result of management decision and the other is the fulfilment of legal and/or quasi-legal requirements. Thus the role and the work of an internal auditor are not delimited by statutory obligations. They are determined by management, and therefore are able to focus on those aspects of an enterprise's financial and operating systems which management believes to be the most important, and to which management believes the internal audit function can make the greatest contribution.

Historically, the role of internal auditing was mainly confined to ensuring that the internal control systems specified by management were in fact being implemented. The emphasis was on regularity (conformity with the specified systems), particularly as regards financial matters. As such, it was essentially an extension of companies' internal control systems. More recently, the internal audit role has become increasingly proactive, looking not simply at regularity but at the operations of enterprises, and questioning the efficiency and effectiveness of such operations. The APB has defined internal auditing as: 'an appraisal or monitoring activity established by management and the directors for the review of the accounting and internal control systems as a service to the entity. It functions by, amongst other things, examining, evaluating and reporting to management and the directors on the adequacy and effectiveness of components of the accounting and internal control systems' (APB 1995b: para. 3). The traditional role of internal auditing was essentially a relatively low-level operation within the managerial hierarchy and usually involved reporting to the chief accountant (or equivalent). This is still the case in a number of companies. The expanded, more proactive role, implicit in the above definition of internal auditing as an 'appraisal function' (which parallels public-sector audit developments) requires a much more high-profile position and reporting responsibility, sometimes referred to as management auditing (Murphy 1996). It also requires that the internal auditors possess not just traditional accountancy skills but also a broader set of business, management and commercial skills.

Internal auditors are required to evaluate and report to management on corporate operations (as regards their regularity, their efficiency and effectiveness), yet the internal audit function is part of the organisation and as such subject to the same controls as the aspects of the organisation that it is auditing. The scope of the audit remit is ultimately determined by management and internal auditors lack the independence of external auditors. However, because they are part of the organisation they may well have a much better understanding than an external auditor of the way the organisation operates and what are the areas of risk; this knowledge could be of great value to the external auditors, and appropriate reliance on the work of internal auditors can lead to more effective and cheaper external audits. The amount of reliance that an external auditor will feel able to place on the work of internal auditors will depend on a number of factors, including its technical competence and its scope. A very important factor will be the degree of independence that the internal audit function has. It is generally felt that this independence will be higher if the internal audit function reports to an audit committee composed principally of non-executive directors. McInnes (1993) goes so far as to suggest that if the internal audit team is sufficiently strong much of the detailed audit work could be left to its members, and that the work of the external auditor could be largely confined to assessing the work of the internal auditors.

Auditing in the public sector

External audit in the public sector is designed to cover the dual roles of fiscal regularity and value-for-money (VFM) auditing. The former role is the more traditional responsibility and is similar to the role of external audit in the private sector, as discussed earlier. In this section we therefore restrict discussion to the statutory basis of auditing in the public sector and concentrate more on the role of VFM auditing.

Audit responsibility for central government lies with the Comptroller and Auditor General (C&AG), who is head of the National Audit Office (NAO). The NAO performs both financial and VFM audits. The Exchequer and Audit Departments Act of 1866 created the office of the C&AG. More recently, the National Audit Act 1983 updated the powers of the C&AG, including the fact that s/he was to be an officer of the House of Commons and, in Part II of the Act, introducing the responsibility for VFM auditing. Local-government audit has a long history, with references as far back as 1430 (Jones 1985). The most recent legislation for England and Wales is provided by the Local Government Finance Act 1982, which established the Audit Commission for Local Authorities. The Commission came into being on 1 April 1983 with two main responsibilities:

- to secure the continued integrity of local government, so that confidence in the institutions of government is not eroded by concerns over fraud and corruption;
- to help authorities improve the returns on the £25 billion plus as required by Section 15 of the Act.

Similar arrangements were introduced in Scotland by the Local Government (Scotland) Act 1983, which established an Accounts Commission with essentially the same mandate. Both Commissions allocate some of their work to private-sector audit firms.

Up until October 1990 various National Health Service Acts prescribed that the relevant secretaries of state should employ auditors to audit the accounts of health authorities. With the passing of the National Health Service and Community Care Act 1990, the 1992 Act was amended to allow the Audit Commission to become responsible for the appointment of auditors to health-service bodies. The NHS as a whole remains subject to audit by the NAO. It is currently a topic of debate that, with the advent of Trust status for many health authorities, such Trusts might not employ their own private-sector auditors directly without reference to the Commission.

With respect to nationalised industries and other public-sector bodies, it is the relevant secretary of state who appoints a firm of private-sector auditors to carry out financial/regulatory audits. For example, under the provisions of the Transport Act 1962 the secretary of state for transport appoints the external auditors of the accounts of the British Railways Board. The audit reports of nationalised industries merely mirrored the reports of private-sector companies. Perhaps rather surprisingly, no auditor had a mandate to consider whether such bodies provided value for money for the services they provided. For those nationalised industries that have been privatised over the last decade, the question of whether privatisation has actually increased efficiency must therefore remain in considerable doubt since no independent review ever took place before they were privatised. (For a more detailed review of the statutory basis of auditing in the public sector, see Glynn 1993.)

Value-for-money auditing

VFM auditing in the public sector has developed in recent years as a way of expanding the more traditional role of the auditor away from the more straightforward examination of the fairness of the financial statements of an organisation. Although VFM auditing has now been carried out for a decade, there is still much work to be done to develop relevant audit methodologies and techniques. Accountability in the public sector occurs when politicians and the public at large are assured that public funds are being spent efficiently, economically and on programmes that are effective. Some have suggested that VFM auditing is a meld of conventional auditing skills and management consultancy. The terms 'economy', 'efficiency' and 'effectiveness' can be defined as follows:

- **Economy**: acquiring resources of an appropriate quality for minimal cost. Diseconomies can occur when there is overstaffing or overpriced facilities are used.
- **Efficiency**: seeking to ensure that the maximum output is obtained from the resources devoted to a programme, or, alternatively, ensuring that only the minimum level of resources is devoted to a given level of output.
- **Effectiveness**: ensuring that output from any given activity is achieving the desired results. This aspect of the audit recognises that an activity may be efficiently carried out with little outcome or impact or visa versa. The determination of what might constitute approved or desired goals for a particular programme is often far from easy, and it is therefore often difficult to measure exactly what is meant by whether the outcome of a programme proved effective.

In adapting to this expanded mandate the auditor faces many difficulties. There is a need to train and recruit specialist staff, who will have to work with departmental management to determine whether or not it and its staff have been successful in producing the level and quantity of service required by those who formulate policy. The role of the auditor should be to support management by assisting in pointing out deficiencies and advising on possible courses of action. The auditor must be apolitical and not concerned with policy per se, rather with its effects and whether such effects correspond with the intentions of policy. This is a monitoring function, a comparison of the situation that exists with that which might have been expected.

While the notion of economy is straightforward, more ought to be said about efficiency and effectiveness, particularly effectiveness. Efficiency refers to the productive use of resources and ought not to be thought of, narrowly, as productivity. Efficiency is the relationship of output (or productivity) to a standard or target. In order to produce efficiency measures it is necessary to measure both programme outputs and inputs. A useful list of comparison measures might be:

- comparisons over **time**;
- measurements compared **between** geographical areas;
- comparison of actual performance with **standards**, particularly in relation to standardised procedures;
- comparison of actual performance with performance **targeted** at the beginning of the year;
- comparison with similar **private-sector** activities;
- **inter-authority** comparisons.

It is not always easy to measure efficiency. For example, it is relatively easier to determine the efficiency of a hospital pathology department than it is to measure the efficiency of a community policing initiative. In the former example outputs and processes have fairly uniform characteristics and we could, for instance, measure efficiency in terms of the actual time versus standard time to carry out a particular test. In the latter case the measurement of police efficiency in carrying out a particular initiative is difficult given that, generally, police officers are multi-functional and work in teams. Though tasks may be clearly stated (school visits, crime-prevention enquiries, contact with ethnic minorities, etc.), outputs, not being necessarily tangible, cannot be measured.

Programme evaluation, through effectiveness auditing, is measuring the extent to which goals have been attained. The goals are the aims or outcomes that a programme purports to pursue and for which it can be held accountable (where measurable). The audit being a review of programme results, the aim of the auditor is to link programme processes; for example, the number of children receiving a particular immunisation vaccination should be linked to the outcome, perhaps expressed in terms of a decrease in the occurrence a particular illness or infirmity. In some instances it may be possible to produce quantitative data to support recommendations; in other instances it may be provided by the perceived value of a service based on, for example, a consumer or client survey.

Based on their work with the NAO, Glynn *et al.* (1992) have attempted to identify and characterise approaches to the audit of effectiveness. They view effectiveness audit as comprising five separate, but interrelated, elements. The technical and organisational capabilities associated with a programme are examined by an **evaluative audit**. Managerial effectiveness leads on to an examination of output effectiveness and is examined by **output audit**. Both these systems-based examinations are necessary in order to undertake the broader **administrative audit**, which is concerned with managerial accountability. For the auditor, policy effectiveness (the extent to which outputs produce outcomes and impacts consistent with the underlying policy) leads to two types of consideration: first, outcome effectiveness, which is covered by **outcome audit**; and, second, impact effectiveness, which is covered by **impact audit**. Impact audit evaluates programme outputs in a broader sense, going beyond the direct consequences of a programme as it relates to identified stakeholders and considering the impact of the programme in relation to related government policies and strategies. For example, the policy effectiveness of a government retraining programme can be considered both in terms of identified stakeholders (trainees, established employees and employers) and in broader terms, such as the impact of the programme on economic growth, government earnings policy and other government policies to reduce unemployment.

Both when proposing and when commencing an effectiveness audit, the auditor should have a clear vision of the scope of the proposed investigation. The audit could embrace administrative audit, outcome audit and impact audit. But this need not be so. A number of factors need to be considered. The nature of a particular programme might, for example, be such that neither managers nor auditors are able to determine policy effectiveness. Conversely, the auditor may well decide that scarce time and resources could best be concentrated on an outcome audit. Part of this review might, more tangentially, lead to a limited review of broader impact issues. To continue with the above example, a government training programme may well have an impact on other government policies in both intended and unintended ways. Employers might treat training allowances as wage subsidies (an unintended effect) and other employees might be made redundant, thereby increasing unemployment and having a negative impact on other government strategies.

An impact audit may not always be practicable; much depends on the type of programme under review and the associated audit risk. For example, an auditor might feel reasonably confident in examining aspects of the impact effectiveness of tax harmonisation (for example the impacts of revenue collection, equitable treatment of taxpayers and Inland Revenue staffing) but less confident in reviewing the impacts of the government's privatisation programme (for example the broadening of share ownership and quality of service).

Conclusions

In essence, auditing is one of the processes via which accountability relationships are enforced; however, as accountability relationships change so must auditing, and this is the problem that auditors currently face. The role of auditors in the private sector is regarded, at least by the auditing profession itself, as one of attesting to the reliability of the information contained in the financial statements of enterprises. However, many users of audit reports have rather higher expectations of the auditing; they believe auditors have responsibilities which include detecting (preventing) fraud, commenting on the effectiveness of corporate management and ensuring the commercial viability of enterprise. While the profession has historically rejected such views, it is increasingly having to consider them. At the same time, there have been developments in public-sector auditing, commonly labelled VFM auditing, which have required auditors to examine the economy, efficiency and effectiveness of expenditure and activity. Similarly, internal auditing has increasingly started to focus on input/output/value considerations, as opposed to simple regularity. Auditing, in the private and public sectors (both internal and external), is undergoing something of a crisis of identity – what is it supposed to achieve and can it reasonably be expected to do so?

Auditing is a major element in the enforcement of accountability relationships (typically those between owners and managers/stewards). Such accountability relationships typically require that the managers/stewards prepare statements summarising their performance, and they have a vested interest in what such statements show. Accordingly, independent auditors have long been employed to attest to the credibility of such statements. However, it is commonly accepted that the extent to which reliance can be based on auditors' opinions must reflect their expertise, independence, accountability and the existence of a widely agreed focus for their work. Increasingly, all of these issues are being challenged, and there is widespread acknowledgement that new roles are emerging for auditors, that increasing demands are being made of them and that new agreements are necessary.

Further reading

The APB (1996) provides an analysis of the role of the auditor and what can reasonably be expected of the audit process. Mautz and Sharaf (1961) and T. A. Lee (1986) provide a more academic approach to the analysis of auditing, while Glynn (1993) provides an overview of auditing in the public sector.

Questions and exercises

1 In what major respects does the role of external auditing in the public sector differ from that of external auditing in the private sector?
2 Can the role of an auditor be defined independently of an agreed statement as to the nature of the accountability relationship on which s/he will be reporting?
3 You are the auditor of Miniprojects Ltd, a manufacturer of building materials which it sells to the construction industry on credit terms. As part of your audit process, you are evaluating the company's credit-approval procedures. List five key internal controls that you would expect to see as part of such procedures.
4 Some commentators have stated that value for money (VFM) auditing is little different from management consulting. Do you agree?
5 Auditors regularly claim that their sole responsibility is the attestation as to the 'truth and fairness' of corporate financial statements. Given the acknowledged broader expectations of the majority of readers of audit reports, how realistic is this limitation?
6 How can external auditors attest to the 'truth and fairness' of external financial statements in the absence of a legal definition of this concept?
7 As audited financial statements of companies are public documents, should not auditors owe a duty of care to all potential users of these statements?
8 The independence of an auditor is supposed to be a major feature in the enhanced credibility afforded by the audit process to the information in financial statements. However, some commentators state that 'true' independence depends on the auditor's state of mind when carrying out the audit. If this is the case, how can a reader of financial statements assess whether or not an auditor is independent? If s/he cannot do this, how can the audit process ever engender enhanced credibility?
9 To what extent do you believe that it is really possible to standardise the audit process given that different companies will present different audit problems?
10 Identify the auditable propositions inherent in including an amount for 'cash at bank' in a balance sheet.

7 Obtaining useful information from financial statements

Objectives

This chapter focuses on the interpretation of accounting and related information published by enterprises. It concentrates on the information which is published by private-sector companies as part of their annual corporate reports. The approach adopted is an examination of how to use the information in annual accounts, in conjunction with that available from other sources, to address key questions about past corporate performance and likely future performance.

The first part of the chapter concentrates on identifying the potential users of accounting information about corporate entities and the key questions they would like to be able to answer. The chapter then goes on to review the sources of information available to help answer these questions and the techniques that can be used to help interpret such information in a meaningful way. It stresses the fact that a full understanding requires an integration of information drawn from a variety of sources, including, but not limited to, that contained in annual accounts.

User groups

As was discussed in Chapter 1, a wide range of individuals and organisations have financial and other links with companies. Despite this diversity of interests, there is a surprising degree of overlap in the information they would like to enable them to assess the benefits to be derived from continuing or changing these links. This is not to deny that different groups have their own specific interests or that there may sometimes be a conflict between these interests. However, in one way or another, they are all concerned with the performance of the company, its continued existence and its ability to provide them with a positive return in some form, most usually cash.

All of these groups require information to help them evaluate their economic and other links with the company and to decide on the future of these links. Ideally, what each of these groups would like is information about the past performance of the enterprise, about its current state of affairs and, perhaps most importantly, about its future, with all of this information being directed to the group's specific concerns. In practice, with some exceptions, these groups have to make do with general-purpose information rather than tailored information. In the same vein, information about the future is available only in the form of estimates and forecasts, areas which accounting has traditionally fought shy of, at least as regards published information.

Thus great attention is in practice placed on information about the past, and particularly the recent past. This information may be compared with prior expectations, whether formed by members of the user groups themselves or by other interested parties, to help assess the progress of the company. Alternatively, it may be used to identify trends in the performance of the enterprise, as it is widely believed that the identification of trends can help in the forecasting of future performance. Accountants recognise the fact that many users will attempt to identify trends and use these as a basis for forecasting future performance. This recognition underpins the concept of 'maintainable profit' and the emphasis on 'continuing operations' reflected in FRS 3.

A further concern of users is that the information typically available in accounts does not directly address the questions which they want answers to. For example, investors, present and potential, want to know what they are likely to receive in dividends and what is the potential for capital appreciation of their investments; lenders are concerned with the servicing and due repayment of their loans; employees, with the scope for increased remuneration and the security of their employment; suppliers and customers, with the future of their business partnership with the enterprise; and the community, with the broader economic and societal impact of the enterprise. Traditional historical-cost-based financial statements provide little of this information directly. Users have to interpret the information that financial statements provide little of this information directly. Users have to interpret the information that financial statements do in fact contain in conjunction with that available from other sources to satisfy their information needs. Only rarely can they use the information contained in financial statements directly. However, as we have already suggested, there are a number of areas of interest common to all the different users of financial statements. These areas of common interest can be summarised under the following headings:

- **Economic sector**: no company can be appraised independently of the economic environment within which it operates. This environment both constrains the activities of the company and provides it with opportunities. Thus the general state of the economy must be taken into account, as must issues specific to the sector(s) of the economy in which the company operates. Similarly, in a competitive market economy the activities and success of competitor companies must be considered. It is noteworthy that in its radical proposals for the restructuring of corporate reporting the ICAS (1988) called for companies to publish information about their 'economic environment'.

- **Profitability**: the key issues here are whether or not the company's profit represents an adequate return on the resources employed to generate it and whether or not profit performance can be sustained or improved in the future. There are many factors which need to be considered when making such an assessment, including the company's ability to generate profits on the resources available to it, its profit margins, the level of its sales and value-added per employee, its gross profit margin and its cost structure.

- **Solvency**: the key issue here is whether or not the company is generating sufficient cash to meet its present and likely future obligations. In assessing this, attention has to be paid to the balance between liquid assets and short-term liabilities, and to the effectiveness with which the company manages its working capital. The company's management of its debtors, its stocks and its creditors has to be appraised. In doing this, it must be remembered that many businesses fail because they run out of money, even though they are in fact making profits.

- **Growth**: it is a truism that in the modern business world a company cannot stand still. However, although it is a truism its importance for assessing a company is no less. A company's past growth record needs to be examined and an assessment made of its future growth prospects. Key indicators, such as growth in sales and investment in plant and equipment, need to be examined. However, in doing this the emphasis needs to be on real growth, rather than apparent growth resulting simply from price increases.
- **Financing**: the main issues here are whether or not the company has access to sufficient finance to enable it to meet its commitments and whether or not this finance is structured in an appropriate way. Attention needs to be paid to the maturity dates of debt finance, to the balance between debt and equity finance, and to the burden which interest and the repayment of borrowing place on the company's profit and cash flow.
- **Investment performance**: present and potential shareholders want to know how the company is going to perform as an investment. Will it be able to pay constant or increasing dividends? Will they be able to make capital gains? How do the capital markets rate the company? And how does it compare with competitor companies?

Information sources

Corporate annual reports are only one of a wide range of sources of information about the activities and performance of companies available to decision makers. The main sources available can be classified in the following ways:

- **Information required by law or quasi-law and which is publicly available**. A major source here is a company's annual report and financial statements, together with the related information contained in its annual return, which is available for inspection at the Registrar of Companies. This information includes copies of the audited accounts, Memorandum and Articles of Association, the address of the registered office, details of registered charges and other useful items. It should be noted that, because this information is publicly available, those engaging in dealings with the company are deemed in law to be aware of it. Other sources of information in this category include the half-yearly reports required from listed companies, and the prospectuses and circulars issued by companies when they are seeking to raise funds or are engaged in merger or de-merger activities.
- **Information which the company itself voluntarily discloses**. Information in this category includes that available from corporate magazines and newsletters, sales literature, press statements and the like. It can also include corporate advertising, and press and television interviews with company executives.
- **Information available on a subscription or similar basis**. Summaries of company and sector data are available from sources such as Extel, Datastream and similar organisations. Increasingly this data is available via computer database

systems. It is principally factual and incorporates summaries of the accounts, plus related financial ratios, together with other data such as details of dividends. Press cuttings and abstracting services are another useful source of information. Assessments of companies are regularly prepared by financial institutions and made available to their clients, and sometimes to wider audiences. In addition, a wide range of trade associations generate information, and information is also published by organisations such as the CBI, the Institute of Directors and similar bodies.

■ **Other informed comment**. The financial press (notably *The Financial Times*) is constantly producing comment and news about companies and the economy at large. In addition to this, the government produces a range of statistical publications, and organisations such as the Economist Intelligence Unit (EIU) and specialist trade publications provide more detailed sources of information.

These different sources of information have differing attributes with respect to the information needs of those seeking to make decisions about their links with companies. The information required by law and quasi-law tends to have an historical focus and is often the subject of some form of independent verification such as an audit. It is typically regarded as having more reliability than that from other sources. Information from other sources, as well as commenting on a company's past performance, will typically incorporate views on the future of the company and the economic sector in which it operates. Such information may be highly relevant to the decisions that people have to make, but because it concerns assessments of the future and is not normally subject to independent review it may be less reliable. Decision makers have to balance the relevance and reliability of the various sources of information and use a mix which matches their needs.

Analytic review and risk assessment

People who need to make decisions about their financial involvement with companies are in a paradoxical situation. On one hand, because of the wide range of information sources available to them they suffer from potential information overload; on the other hand, they suffer from a lack of the information they really need. The key to this paradox is that the information with which they may be overloaded is all too often not really relevant to their needs (because of a historical focus), although it may be reliable (again because of its historical focus). In many ways this is similar to the problem faced by auditors. When auditing the financial statements of a company, auditors are faced with a plethora of sources of evidence about its affairs. Essential skills for auditors include the ability to identify the evidence they require to enable them to attest to the credibility of the accounts, and the ability to evaluate sources of evidence available to them in terms of relevance and reliability for their needs. Decision makers and their advisers need the same skills. A great deal of information is available to them, not all of it helpful, and they need to develop strategies to help them identify what is relevant, what is reliable and what is useful.

One approach that auditors have developed to help them identify areas for their further attention and to corroborate evidence already obtained from other sources is that of analytic review. In the words of the IAPC of the IFAC, 'The application of analytical procedures is based on the expectation that relationships among data exist and continue in the absence of known conditions to the contrary' (IAPC 1989: para. 12). The focus of analytic review procedures is the identification of relationships between aspects of financial information which might be expected to persist over time and the use of these relationships to identify unexpected variances. The IAPC describes analytical procedures as including:

Comparison of financial information with . . .

- comparable information for a prior period or periods,
- anticipated results such as budgets or other forecasts,
- similar industry information, such as a comparison of the entity's ratio of sales to accounts receivable with industry averages or with other entities of comparable size in the same industry.

Study of relationships . . .

- among elements of financial information that would be expected to conform to a predictable pattern based on an entity's experience, such as a study of gross margin percentages; and
- between financial and non-financial information, such as a study of payroll costs in relation to number of employees.

(IAPC 1989: para. 3)

As the foregoing illustrates, the analytical review approach involves two distinct types of comparison. The first of these is an intertemporal comparison in which financial information for the same enterprise but for different time periods is compared to see whether or not it conforms to past trends and (or) expectations. The second is where financial information about the enterprise is compared with that for other enterprises, either on the basis of an individual enterprise-by-enterprise comparison or by the use of industry/sector averages. Such a comparison enables an assessment to be made of the enterprise in relation to its competitors.

In some ways, the first of these types of comparison should be easier because of the fundamental accounting concept of 'consistency'. The application of this concept means that the user of accounts should, at least in theory, be able to compare accounts from different periods in the knowledge that events and transactions are always treated in the same way and that the accounting information is therefore truly comparable. Unfortunately this comparability may sometimes be more imagined than real. There are two main reasons for this:

- An enterprise may, with justification, change its accounting policies from time to time, for example with respect to stock-valuation methodology or depreciation bases. The impact of such changes, which must be disclosed in the financial statements, needs to be taken into account in any comparisons.
- Enterprises are not at present required to ensure that all the information they present is expressed in terms of a common dimension as regards price levels. Thus a user of accounting information will need to make his/her own adjustment to allow for the impact of changing prices.

Comparison with the financial performance of other enterprises or with sectoral averages also has its dangers. This is partly because different enterprises may not be sufficiently similar to allow a truly realistic comparison and partly because different enterprises may adopt different accounting bases. Accordingly, care must be taken to ensure that the yardsticks being used for comparison are suitable for that purpose.

As suggested above, an important use of the analytical review approach is to identify areas where financial information does not in fact conform to expectations. This may be the result of error, or it may be the result of differential performance. In the case of the audit, this enables the auditor to investigate these areas further, identify the reasons for the difference and ensure that the financial information does in fact properly portray the position. The same would, of course, apply to management if it is using the analytical approach as part of its management control and performance-evaluation systems. The external user of accounts unfortunately is not in either of these privileged positions, having, in general, no right to demand supplementary information. There are, of course, some exceptions to this: a shareholder could ask questions at an annual general meeting of the company, although experience suggests that this is not normally a very productive process; an investment adviser may enjoy preferential access to corporate management and be able to ask for further information, as may a banker. However, in general, an external user of accounts will have to rely on other publicly available information, and it is in this context that the integration of the information in the financial statements with other sources of information becomes so important.

Another audit concept of relevance to the external user of financial statements is that of audit risk, the risk that a set of accounts will contain a material undetected error. As applied by auditors, audit risk is a function of three different types of risk faced by the auditor: inherent risk (the risk that a material error will occur given the nature and activities of the client), control risk (the risk that the client's internal control systems will fail to detect and correct material errors) and detection risk (the risk that remaining undetected errors will fail to be detected during the audit). The external user is not privy to the range of information that the auditor is and so cannot apply the audit risk concept in the same way that an auditor could. However, the concept does suggest that external users of accounting information should not approach it naively; they should consider the probable reliability of the different items of information contained in financial statements. While there would be little excuse for a misstatement in the amount for cash at bank or overdrafts (although this has been known), it would be foolish to believe that the amounts stated for stock and work-in-progress would be equally reliable. This is partly because of the inherent difficulties in valuing stocks, whatever the precise accounting bases used, and partly because of the range of accounting bases that may in practice be used for valuing stock. Similarly, the user needs to be aware that financial statements relating to companies operating in some industrial and commercial sectors inevitably involve more significant judgements than do others. Examples of this might include companies involved in long-term construction or similar contracts, where judgements have to be made about the cost of completing the contracts so that any necessary provisions against future losses can be made, and insurance companies, which have to make estimates of future claims.

Ratio analysis

With this background, we can now look at accounting techniques employing ratio analysis. The essence of these techniques is the linking of significant items of accounting data to compute a ratio and then comparing this ratio with a yardstick. As the IAPC (1989) suggests, these yardsticks can be derived from a number of sources. They can be based on prior expectations; they can be based on budgets; they can be based on previous performance; they may be company-specific or may relate to industry or wider economic averages. The scope is very wide. However, this scope can itself cause problems: ensuring that the measurement bases of the items being compared are the same; ensuring the reliability of the base data being used; and ensuring that useful comparators are used. The user needs to exercise discretion in applying the approach of ratio analysis and, most importantly, needs to bear in mind that ratio analysis will only identify differences in performance. It cannot identify how or why those differences arose, and it is this which may be of prime importance. In many ways financial ratios need to be regarded as access routes to information, rather than as providing information in their own right.

Earlier we identified the key areas in which users require information as the economic sector in which the company operates, its profitability, its solvency, its growth record, its financing and its investment performance. The first of these is not an area in which ratio analysis of accounting information can help us. However, it does provide a context within which the information in the financial statements can be analysed, and this context itself may suggest questions which decision makers will need to ask, including the types of financial ratios they will want to calculate. The other key areas regarding which users want information are all, to a greater or lesser extent, susceptible to financial ratio analysis. In many ways, the ratios resulting from such analysis can be regarded as providing performance indicators, which summarise in quantitative terms the performance of the enterprise and its management in certain key areas.

To illustrate the use of financial ratio analysis we will use the case of Motors Ltd, a company which operates as a motor-vehicle distributor in the South-east of England. It is a family-owned company founded by Albert Johnston, who has recently died after a long illness, and his son, James Johnston, who has been bearing an increasing responsibility for the company as a result of his father's illness, is now eager to sell the company and has approached you as a possible purchaser. He has provided you with an abstract of the accounts of Motors (see Table 7.1) relating to the last two financial years.

Before looking at the information contained in the financial statements in detail a prospective purchaser should consider the context within which the offer for sale is being made. In the case of Motors, issues such as the following would need to be considered:

- To what extent was the business dependent on the expertise of its late founder Albert Johnston for its success?
- Why is James Johnston eager to sell the business?
- What type of motor vehicles does the company sell and what are its terms of trade with the manufacturer whose vehicles it distributes?
- What is the current, and what the likely future, state of trade in the motor industry in general and as regards the type of vehicles that Motors is selling?

These are just a few of the general commercial and sectoral issues that a prospective purchaser would need to address. They provide a background against which the financial statements of the company itself can be examined to see how typical its

Table 7.1   Accounts of Motors Ltd

Balance sheet as at 30 September				
	19X7		19X6	
	£000	£000	£000	£000
Fixed assets:				
Freehold premises:				
Cost	100		100	
Accumulated depreciation	40	60	38	62
Equipment:				
Cost	195		190	
Accumulated depreciation	110	85	80	110
		145		172
Current assets:				
Stock	290		155	
Debtors	130		75	
Cash	20		90	
	440		320	
Current liabilities:				
Creditors	235		130	
Net current assets		205		190
Long-term loans		(100)		(150)
		250		212
Share capital (£1 shares)		150		150
Retained profits		100		62
		250		212

Profit and loss accounts – year to 30 September		
	19X7	19X6
	£000	£000
Sales revenue	1 700	1 950
Cost of sales	1 382	1 575
Gross profit	318	375
Other costs	201	225
Net profit	117	150
Taxation	43	47
Profit after taxation	74	103
Dividends	36	36
Retained profit	38	67

financial performance is and to identify its particular financial strengths and weakness. With this background the financial statements of Motors can be examined in more detail. However, before undertaking a detailed financial ratio analysis an analyst would normally use the financial statements to form an overall/helicopter view of the company's financial performance. In the case of Motors such an overview would be likely to prompt the following issues:

- **Freehold premises**: these have an historic-cost value of £100 000, which has remained the same for 19X6 and 19X7. However, accumulated depreciation has risen from £38 000 to £40 000, i.e. an increase of £2000. Thus the depreciation charge for the year 19X7 relating to freehold premises was £2000. Assuming a straight-line basis for depreciation, this implies that a total of twenty years' depreciation has been charged against the cost of the freehold premises (£40 000/ £2000 = 20). This implies that the company purchased the premises twenty years ago at a cost of £100 000. From the viewpoint of a potential purchaser, a key issue will be what the current value of these premises is. Even taking into account the uncertain state of the property market in recent years, it is likely that such a current value will be considerably in excess of the original cost.

- **Equipment**: the recorded cost of equipment has increased from £190 000 to £195 000 and the accumulated depreciation has increased from £80 000 to £110 000. Although there is no specific information on disposals or purchases of equipment, these figures tend to suggest that there has not been any major investment in new equipment. Also they suggest that, on average, the equipment owned by the company is well past half its forecast useful life. This tends to indicate that the company has not been investing in new equipment, which might be a cause of concern to a potential purchaser.

- **Current assets**: there have been significant changes in these. Stocks have risen from £155 000 to £290 000, an increase of £135 000, or nearly 90%. This might indicate that the business is encountering difficulties in selling its vehicles. A related issue would be what exactly is the nature of these stocks, given that common practice in the motor trade involves the supply of vehicles from manufacturers to distributors on a consignment basis. Similarly, debtors have increased from £75 000 to £130 000, an increase of £55 000, or over 70%. This could indicate that the company is encountering difficulties in collecting money from its customers. A related issue might be why the business has debtors on this scale at all. Customary practice in the motor-vehicle industry is for cars to be sold either for cash or on credit terms provided via finance companies. In neither of these cases would the seller be involved in providing credit to its customers. Accordingly, the source of the debtors would need investigation, as well as the increase. Cash has fallen from £90 000 to £20 000, a fall of £70 000. This is a major change, suggesting that careful attention should be paid to the business's cash-flow position.

- **Current liabilities**: these have increased from £130 000 to £235 000, an increase of £105 000, or approximately 80%. This is a significant increase, which might indicate that the business is encountering problems in meeting its short-term liabilities. Taken together with the decline in cash and the increases in stock and debtors, this increase in creditors indicates a potentially worrying situation.

- **Long-term loans**: these have fallen from £150 000 to £100 000. This suggests that the company has repaid £50 000 during the year, and might further imply that it will need to repay a further £50 000 in each of the next two years. The terms of these long-term loans will need to be ascertained and, given the decline in cash balances mentioned above, a potential purchaser would need to look carefully at the cash-flow position of the business to ensure that it has the capability to fund such repayments.
- **Sales turnover**: this has declined from £1 950 000 to £1 700 000, perhaps reflecting difficult economic circumstances facing the motor trade as a whole. A prospective purchaser of Motors would want to know how this performance relates to that of competitors.
- **Profit after taxation**: this has declined from £103 000 to £74 000. Again, a prospective purchaser would want to know the extent to which such a decline reflects the general economic circumstances facing the industry and the extent to which it reflects the particular circumstances facing Motors and the management responses to these.
- **Dividends**: these have remained the same, despite the decline in profit after taxation. There could be a number of reasons for this, including family members relying on dividends for their income. The exact reason would need to be ascertained.

To summarise, this overview of the financial statements indicates a company which may have a significantly undervalued property asset and is facing difficult trading circumstances which are impacting on its liquidity, while at the same time having to repay loans yet maintaining its dividend payments. With this background, the financial performance of Motors can be analysed in more detail using financial ratios.

Profitability ratios

Profitability ratios focus on the relationship between the profit that an enterprise generates and the resources that it employs to generate these profits. There are two ratios that are commonly used to measure this relationship. These are:

- *Return on equity capital*: this ratio measures the effectiveness with which shareholders' funds have been employed in generating profits for the shareholders. It is calculated as follows:

$$\frac{\text{Profit after taxation}}{\text{Shareholders' funds}} \times 100 \qquad (7.1)$$

The profit after taxation provides a measure of the amount of profit the enterprise has generated which is attributable to the shareholders, and the shareholders' funds provide a measure of the extent of the resources that shareholders have contributed to the enterprise. Thus, the ratio provides a measure of how effectively management has deployed these resources in pursuit of a primary shareholder objective profit.

There is, however, a technical difficulty in the computation of this ratio. This relates to the fact that we are comparing a flow of profit which arises throughout the financial year with a value of capital at a point in time. If the opening equity capital is used for this purpose, then, for a profitable company, the value of the ratio will be overstated because as the company generates profits throughout the year the equity capital base will have increased but this will not have been reflected in the computation. Correspondingly, if the closing equity capital is used this will tend to understate the value of the ratio because management will not have had that closing value of resources available to them throughout the year. This is a problem which is common to the computation of a number of financial ratios and a common response to it is to use averages instead of point-in-time values. Thus in the case of the return on equity capital the average value of the opening and closing equity capital would be used as the denominator. This, however, requires that information about the opening and closing values is available, which may not always be the case for external users of financial statements, although it will normally be so for management. For simplicity, we will illustrate the use of the average method in relation to return on equity capital of Motors and thereafter we will use year-end values.

In the case of Motors the return on equity capital for the two years for which we have information available, and using the average method for the valuation of the capital, is:

$$19\text{X}7: \quad \frac{74\,000}{0.5(250\,000 + 212\,000)} \times 100 = 32.03\%$$

$$19\text{X}6: \quad \frac{103\,000}{0.5(212\,000 + (212\,000 - 67\,000))} \times 100 = 57.70\%$$

There appears to have been a significant decline in the return on equity capital which Motors is achieving. However, in both years the return appears to be a high one; this may be due in part to an understatement of the value of the freehold premises. This is a reflection of a potentially significant problem – most financial statements are based on the historical-cost method of accounting and record assets at the original cost of acquisition by the enterprise rather than their current value. For short-term (current) assets this may not be too great a problem, except in times of rapid price changes. It is more of a problem when it comes to long-term (fixed) assets. In this case there may be significant divergencies between the original cost of the asset and its current value. This seems to be the case in Motors, where freehold premises are shown in the financial statements at their original cost of twenty years ago. The current market value of this asset is likely to be significantly higher. The consequence of this is that any return on capital calculation using historical-cost information is likely to show too high a return on capital. This is because the denominator in the calculation will be understated (being based on historical cost rather than current value) and the numerator will be overstated (insofar as it incorporates depreciation charges based on historical cost rather than current values). Thus in times of price rises return-on-capital calculations will tend to overstate rather than understate the true economic performance of enterprises by showing a higher return on capital employed than would be the case if true economic values were used. This misstatement will be greater the larger the divergence between historic cost and current economic value.

■ *Return on total capital employed*: this ratio measures the effectiveness with which the totality of resources available to management has been deployed, irrespective of how those resources have been financed. It is calculated as follows:

$$\frac{\text{Operating profit}}{\text{Total long-term capital employed}} \times 100 \qquad (7.2)$$

Operating profit is defined as profit before the deduction of finance charges (interest) and taxation. This is a measure of corporate performance which is independent of the way in which resources are financed (by excluding the finance charges) and of taxation charges (which are outside the control of management). Thus the focus of this ratio is on the economic efficiency and effectiveness achieved by management with the resources available. As such it is a prime indicator of overall corporate performance, and is sometimes referred to as the master ratio.

In the case of Motors, assuming that the long-term loans bear interest at a rate of 10% per annum, the returns on total capital employed for the two years (using closing values for capital employed for simplicity of computation) were:

$$19\text{X7}: \quad \frac{117\,000 + 10\,000}{250\,000 + 100\,000} \times 100 = 36.28\%$$

$$19\text{X6}: \quad \frac{150\,000 + 15\,000}{212\,000 + 150\,000} \times 100 = 45.58\%$$

As with the return on equity capital employed, this ratio indicates a decline in financial performance, although not as great. This is, in part, the result of the repayment of £50 000 of the long-term loans.

Without having comparative figures from similar enterprises and more information on the motor vehicle trade as a whole it is not possible to comment on how good the financial performance of Motors has been. However, as suggested earlier, these return-on-capital ratios are perhaps higher than would normally be expected, and this may be due to the use of historic cost rather than current valuation for its freehold premises.

Profitability ratios are the top of a pyramid of financial ratios, summarising overall corporate financial performance. There are numerous subsidiary ratios that can be calculated, each concentrating on a specific aspect of the enterprise's financial and commercial performance. The first tier of these ratios can be derived directly from the core notion of return on capital, as follows:

$$\text{Return on capital} = \frac{\text{Profit}}{\text{Capital}} = \frac{\text{Sales revenue}}{\text{Capital}} \times \frac{\text{Profit}}{\text{Sales revenue}} \qquad (7.3)$$

Thus return on capital can be analysed into two subsidiary measures. The first of these is the capital turnover rate (sales revenue/capital). This indicates the number of times that an enterprise turns over its capital in a financial period. In general terms enterprises seek to turn over their capital as often as possible, as by doing so they will be using such capital effectively. The second subsidiary measure is the rate of profit or profit margin. This relates the profit that an enterprise generates to the sales revenue from which this profit is derived. Different industrial and commercial sectors can have very different capital turnover rates and profit margins even though they may have similar returns on capital. A capital-intensive industry such as heavy engineering may have a low capital turnover rate but a high profit margin. Correspondingly, a labour-intensive industry operating in the service sector may have a high capital turnover rate but a relatively low profit margin. Therefore in analysing the information contained in corporate financial statements it is not sufficient to look at the headline of return on capital; more detailed analysis is required. The first stage in such analysis frequently concerns an analysis of a company's profit, as shown below.

Profit ratios

The next group of financial ratios concentrates on the relationships between the various components of profit and the balance between them. They enable decision makers to examine these relationships and detect changes in them. The highly aggregated nature of the annual financial statements of companies means that there is little scope for detailed analysis of the elements of profit by users of such statements. There is much more scope for such analysis by management, which has access to detailed information about the various components of the profit and loss account. Management also have access to detailed budgetary information with which they can compare actual performance. Accordingly, profit ratios are of much greater use to management than they are to external users of financial statements, who can, at best, use them to make rather broad interpretations of corporate performance. Examples of the sorts of profit ratio commonly calculated include:

■ **Gross margin percentage**: this focuses on the relationships between sales value and the prime costs of providing goods or services. It is concerned with the sharp end of the enterprise's activities and reflects the competitive pressures faced by the enterprise, its market positioning and the effectiveness with which management is controlling prime costs. It is measured as:

$$\frac{\text{Gross profit}}{\text{Sales turnover}} \times 100 \tag{7.4}$$

Thus, for example, a downward trend in this percentage may indicate that the enterprise is coming under increasing pressure from the competition. The possible reasons for such increased pressure are many, ranging from the entry of new direct competitors to the introduction of new products. Alternatively, it may be the result of a deliberate management decision to increase market share by an aggressive pricing policy. If this is the case a user of the accounts would look for indications of sales growth. However, the ratio is not just a reflection of the market in which the enterprise operates. It also reflects the prime costs of supplying this market. Thus a change in the ratio may also be a function of changes in cost structures, the result perhaps of better management control of costs, or of changes in technology:

In the case of Motors the ratio for the two years was:

$$19X7: \quad \frac{318\,000}{1\,700\,000} \times 100 = 18.71\%$$

$$19X6: \quad \frac{375\,000}{1\,950\,000} \times 100 = 19.23\%$$

There has been a decline in this margin of 0.5%, which perhaps reflects the competitive pressure in the motor industry. However, given this competitive pressure, a fall of only 0.5% may represent very good performance by Motors, which has managed to maintain its gross profit margin despite a fall in sales turnover from £1 950 000 to £1 700 000.

- **Net profit margin percentage**: this concentrates on the proportion of the sales revenue of a business that net profit attributable to shareholders constitutes and is calculated as:

$$\frac{\text{Net profit after taxation}}{\text{Sales turnover}} \times 100 \qquad (7.5)$$

In the case of Motors, the ratios for the two years for which information is available are:

$$\text{19X7:} \quad \frac{74\,000}{1\,700\,000} \times 100 = 4.35\%$$

$$\text{19X6:} \quad \frac{103\,000}{1\,950\,000} \times 100 = 5.28\%$$

Thus there has been a decline in Motor's performance over the two years in this key performance indicator, which reflects the net contribution that the sales of the enterprise have made to generating profit attributable to shareholders and reflects the ultimate effectiveness of the enterprise's activities. The net profit margin percentage is potentially very helpful in the prediction of future profits, when combined with a sales forecast. However, it suffers from the disadvantage that it provides a very broad-brush overview. Profit after taxation is the net effect of many different cost and revenue elements under managerial control and of elements outside managerial control such as taxation rates. Further analysis is needed, including the computation of the gross profit ratio, as above.

- **Overhead cost percentage**: the other area of corporate activity which impacts on net profit is that of support or overhead costs. A full understanding of the net profit margin, and changes in it, requires a review of the relationship between these support costs and the level of the enterprise's activities. There is a wide range of ratios that might be computed for this purpose. However, the information available to external users of financial statements means that only a few of them can in fact be calculated. Management, of course, can calculate many more because of its access to the whole range of financial information about the enterprise and its performance. The normal approach is one of measuring the percentage of sales turnover constituted by overhead costs. Given the disclosure requirements imposed by the Companies Acts, the two ratios most commonly calculated are:

$$\frac{\text{Selling costs}}{\text{Sales turnover}} \times 100 \qquad (7.6)$$

$$\frac{\text{Administrative costs}}{\text{Sales turnover}} \times 100 \qquad (7.7)$$

Ratios such as these measure the relationship between the amount spent on a category of overhead support costs and the level of activities being supported, as measured by sales turnover. The main use of these ratios is to provide an indication of the effectiveness with which management is controlling costs of these types relative to sales. The danger is that such ratios may provide a rather simplistic interpretation of the commercial activities of the enterprise because of an implicit assumption that the overhead costs relate to activity in the same period. This may not be true. For example, management may have spent a great deal on a sales promotion campaign, the benefits of which may not arrive until the next financial period, or on the development of new computer systems, the benefit of which will not be achieved till future periods. The essence of the problem is that accounting requires such costs to be expensed because of the 'prudence' concept, and as a result the benefits and the costs are not matched. A reader of the accounts should not simply rely on the ratios but link them with other available information to get a better understanding of such costs. Sources such as the chairman's report, brokers' circulars and press comment may be particularly helpful in this respect.

In the case of Motors the available information is very limited, and the only ratio that can be calculated is that between the other costs and sales turnover, which indicates the following:

$$19X7: \quad \frac{201\ 000}{1\ 700\ 000} \times 100 = 11.82\%$$

$$19X6: \quad \frac{225\ 000}{1\ 950\ 000} \times 100 = 11.54\%$$

Thus there appears to have been little change in the proportion of Motor's sales turnover constituted by overhead costs. However, a more detailed analysis looking at the composition of these overhead costs might prove instructive.

There is a 'standard set' of ratios which analysts tend to compute for all companies, irrespective of the industrial or commercial sector within which they operate, and the ratios commented on above form part of this set. However, in addition to this standard set there are ratios which are more specific to particular industrial and commercial sectors. Examples of such sector-specific ratios include:

- sales (profit) per square metre of selling space, a much used performance indicator in the retail trade;
- research and development expenditure as a percentage of sales turnover, a much used indicator of the future viability of companies operating in high-technology industries such as computing or pharmaceuticals.

The range of financial ratios that can be calculated is very wide. However, not all of them will provide users with useful additional information. A selection of those ratios which will in fact provide such information should be made, based on those elements of corporate performance which are the most important. The need for selectivity goes even further. There are standard formulae for the computation of financial ratios (which are described in this chapter). However, these standard formulae represent nothing more than the way in which such ratios are commonly calculated. They are not the law of God. If the application of the standard formulae will result in the provision of useful information they are worth using. However, there will be many occasions when more useful information can be obtained from the use of different formulae and different ratios. In such circumstances the standard set of ratios should be departed from and different, more useful, ratios calculated. The standard set of ratios is the table d'hôte menu, and discerning decision makers may well find the à la carte menu more beneficial.

Solvency and liquidity ratios

These financial ratios concentrate on the solvency and liquidity of the company (in essence, its ability to pay its liabilities as and when they fall due and its financial adaptability), and, more generally, on the effectiveness with which its working capital (short-term assets and liabilities) is being managed. They focus directly on areas which are crucial to corporate survival and which are the most susceptible to managerial action in the short term. The management of working capital is discussed in more detail in Chapter 17. The two most commonly calculated measures regarding solvency are:

- **Current ratio**: this is an overall comparison of an enterprise's short-term (liquid) assets with its short-term liabilities. It is also known as the working capital ratio and is calculated as:

$$\frac{\text{Current assets}}{\text{Current liabilities}} \tag{7.8}$$

In the case of Motors this ratio is:

$$19X7: \quad \frac{440\,000}{235\,000} = 1.87$$

$$19X6: \quad \frac{320\,000}{130\,000} = 2.47$$

This indicates that there has been a decline in the liquidity of Motors during the financial period to 19X7. Declines in liquidity are generally regarded as being negative indicators of corporate performance. However, the importance of such declines depends, at least in part, on the base from which they result. In the case of Motors, although there has been a decline this has been from a very strong base, in which current assets covered current liabilities by more than a factor of two, to a position where they are still nearly covered twice.

- **Liquid ratio**: this is more focused ratio, which compares an enterprise's liquid assets with its short-term liabilities. Liquid assets are those assets that are readily convertible to cash, which can be used to settle liabilities. Other names for this ratio are the 'acid-test ratio' and the 'quick ratio'. The normal formula for the calculation of this ratio is:

$$\frac{\text{Current assets} - \text{stocks}}{\text{Current liabilities}} \tag{7.9}$$

The reason for deducting stocks from current assets is that they are generally regarded as being relatively illiquid assets because they are the most distant of the short-term assets from being converted into cash. They may need to be transformed by some manufacturing process and they may then have to be sold on credit terms, resulting in a lengthy period before any cash is received. Thus monies invested in stock may not be available for settling short-term liabilities and should be excluded from any assessment of the short-term solvency of an enterprise.

In the case of Motors the liquid ratios are:

$$19X7: \quad \frac{130\,000 + 20\,000}{235\,000} = 0.64$$

$$19X6: \quad \frac{75\,000 + 90\,000}{130\,000} = 1.27$$

This represents a dramatic shift in the liquidity position of Motors. At the end of 19X6 its liquid assets covered its short-term liabilities by a factor of 1.29, while at the end of 19X7 these assets were apparently insufficient to meet its short-term liabilities. Thus on the face of it Motors was facing a potential solvency crisis. However, this might not in fact be the case because there are a number of other issues to be taken into account when considering the solvency of an enterprise, and the normal way in which the liquid ratio is calculated does not take these into account. They are:

■ **The actual, as opposed to the assumed, liquidity of assets**: all too often financial ratios are calculated on the assumption that current assets other than stocks represent the liquid assets of an enterprise. This may or may not be the case. Debtors, for example, may not in reality be liquid assets (liquidity defined as being readily convertible into cash). Typically, debtors take something of the order of sixty to seventy days to pay, which hardly represents immediate liquidity. In addition, accounting conventionally treats amounts receivable within twelve months as a current asset. Thus debtors could include, for example, amounts due on 360-day bills of exchange, where cash will not be received until nearly a year after the balance-sheet date. If this were to be the case, then using the normal basis of computing financial ratios could lead to the liquidity of the enterprises being overestimated.

   The position is complicated by the fact that enterprises may have assets other than current assets which are in fact readily convertible into cash in the short term. This is particularly true of investments which are quoted on the Stock Exchange, but may also apply to fixed assets such as property which can readily be sold for cash. In reality, the liquidity of an enterprise is much more a function of the realisability of its assets than of the accounting classification of those assets into long-term and short-term assets.

■ **Access to finance**: the core issue in assessing the liquidity/solvency of an enterprise is whether or not it has the resources to pay its liabilities as and when they fall due. One source of such resources is the assets of the enterprise, particularly its short-term resources and, most importantly, cash. However, equally important is the access that the enterprise has to borrowing. A company may have a deficit of liquid assets as compared to its short-term liabilities, but if it has access to sufficient borrowing facilities it will still be able to meet its short-term liabilities. Thus a vital piece of information for people trying to assess the liquidity/solvency of an enterprise is information about borrowing facilities. Unfortunately, such information is not normally disclosed in the annual financial statements of enterprises.

There is a great deal of mythology regarding what are acceptable values for the current and liquid ratios of enterprises. Many commentators suggest that a company should have a current ratio with a value between 1 and 2, and that companies with liquid ratios of less than 1 are facing liquidity problems. Such views fail to take into account the different circumstances which companies face and the different patterns of cash flow persisting in different commercial sectors. Thus, for example, it is quite normal for successful retailers to have liquid ratios of less than 1 because their strong positive cash flows ensure their solvency. Similarly, they fail to take into account the fact that investment in current/liquid assets by a company should be evaluated in the same way as any other investment, i.e. in terms of the returns that are generated. While large cash balances may ensure solvency, they may not be generating much profit for shareholders. Too large a cash balance may indicate that management is not using the resources available to it effectively. It may even indicate that the business is in decline. If a business's sales are declining, then, at least in the short term, its cash resources may increase. This is the result of its receiving cash from previous credit customers while not having to pay out cash to suppliers for materials. A company's cash position needs to be assessed in relation to its overall pattern of trade, rather than independently of it.

While the current and liquid ratios focus on the overall liquidity and solvency of the enterprise, there is another group of financial ratios which look in more detail at individual short-term assets and liabilities. These ratios are concerned with the specifics of working-capital management. All of these ratios compare the 'stock' of a particular category of current asset or liability with the flows of costs or revenues associated with that asset or liability. Thus debtors are compared with the credit sales which lead to the creation of debtors, and inventories are compared with cost of sales. There are two different ways of presenting these ratios. They can be presented as turnover rates, i.e. the number of times a particular class of asset/liability turns over each year. Alternatively, they can be presented in terms of the number of days' activity the 'stock' of the particular asset or liability represents. These different presentations will be illustrated, using the example of Motors, for the most usually calculated ratios, which are:

- **Stock turnover**: this ratio compares the amount that a company has invested in inventories with the cost of sales which these inventories support. The money which a company invests in inventories is not available for other purposes; it is money which is 'tied up', and in general companies would prefer to have as little money 'tied up' in inventories as possible. Chapter 17 discusses in more detail the reasons why companies hold inventories. For the present, it is sufficient to recognise that it is generally accepted that efficient companies have lower levels of inventory relative to their cost of sales than do inefficient companies. Thus a high stock turnover rate (or low stock turnover period) will usually be regarded as a sign of good management. Stock turnover rate is calculated as:

$$\frac{\text{Cost of sales}}{\text{Stock}} \qquad (7.10)$$

Stock turnover period is calculated as:

$$\frac{\text{Stock}}{\text{Cost of sales}} \times 365 \text{ (assuming 365 days in a financial year)} \qquad (7.11)$$

Both of these ratios combine a flow (cost of sales) with a position (stock), and as such are dependent on the choice of position that is made (opening stock, closing stock or average stock). As indicated earlier, for the purposes of simplicity we will use the closing value for illustration. However, the implications of doing this need to be recognised. If the closing value is in any way atypical the resultant ratio may give an inappropriate portrayal of performance. It is widely accepted that some companies choose their financial year-ends to reflect points in time when their stock levels are low. Thus many retailers have financial periods ending on 31 January, i.e. after the busy Christmas periods and the January sales. In the case of Motors the stock turnover periods are:

$$19X7: \quad \frac{290\,000}{1\,382\,000} \times 365 = 76.59 \text{ days}$$

$$19X6: \quad \frac{155\,000}{1\,950\,000} \times 365 = 35.92 \text{ days}$$

There has been a dramatic increase in Motor's stock turnover period. Prima facie, this indicates that Motors has a major problem and has lost control of its stock levels. This could well be the case. However, the stock turnover period ratio simply tells us that there has been a change. It does not tell us the reason for the change. It might be that management has lost control of its stocks. Equally, the increase might be the result of deliberate management policies, such as stocking up to enable them to meet a large customer order due for delivery shortly after the financial year-end or the result of a large purchase made shortly before the year-end at low prices. The ratio simply tells us that there has been a change in the relationship between inventories and cost of sales, and therefore indicates that users should ask why this change has taken place. It does not, and cannot, tell users whether this change represents good or bad performance. Unfortunately, all too often analysts react to the change without further investigation and regard an increase in stock turnover period as being a negative performance indicator.

■ **Debtor turnover**: this ratio links the value of debtors with the credit sales that gave rise to these debtors. Companies would prefer to sell goods and services for cash rather than on credit, as by doing so they avoid the risk of bad debts and do not have to finance their customers' purchases. Unfortunately for them, credit sales are a well-established fact of life in the world of commerce and industry. Companies which insist on cash-only sales are likely to sell less than those which offer their customers credit facilities, and therefore lose the profit that they could have made on these credit sales. However, granting credit to customers has a cost – the opportunity cost of the cash resources tied up in financing debtors, apart from the risk of non-payment by customers. When they offer customers credit facilities companies will normally seek to obtain settlement as soon as possible. The debtor turnover ratios provide an indication of how successful they are in this respect. As with stock turnover, there are two versions of these ratios – the debtor turnover rate and the debtor turnover period. Debtor turnover rate is calculated as:

$$\frac{\text{Credit sales}}{\text{Debtors}} \qquad (7.12)$$

Debtor turnover period is calculated as:

$$\frac{\text{Debtors}}{\text{Credit sales}} \times 365 \quad \text{(assuming 365 days in a financial year)} \qquad (7.13)$$

As with stock turnover, debtor turnover involves a comparison between a flow (credit sales) and a position (debtors), and poses the same issues regarding how typical the position value is. For example, a large credit sale shortly before the year-end could distort the value of the ratio. A further difficulty is that corporate financial statements do not normally disclose the value of credit sales; instead, they simply disclose the value of total sales. This means that external analysts can base their calculations of debtor turnover only on the total sales figure, and that the computation is susceptible to any changes in the balance between cash and credit sales. Management, of course, has access to the necessary information to compute the ratio more precisely. In practice, some companies analyse their debtor turnover in rather more detail, for example by business sectors or customer groups, because they believe such analyses improve the quality of their decision taking.

In the case of Motors the debtor turnover for the two years is as shown below, assuming that all sales were in fact credit sales because of a lack of information regarding the balance between credit and cash sales.

$$\text{19X7:} \quad \frac{130\ 000}{1\ 700\ 000} \times 365 = 27.91 \text{ days}$$

$$\text{19X6:} \quad \frac{75\ 000}{1\ 950\ 000} \times 365 = 14.04 \text{ days}$$

The period of credit being taken, on average, by Motors customers has nearly doubled, and, prima facie, this is a bad sign, perhaps indicating that the management of Motors has lost control of its debtor position or that it is having to offer extended credit to secure business. Taken together with the earlier query about why Motors is selling on credit in the first place, this suggests that a prospective purchaser should raise a number of questions about its credit policies and credit management. Chapter 17 looks into credit-management issues in more detail.

■ **Creditor turnover**: this ratio links the value of creditors with the amount of goods and services that a business is purchasing on credit terms. It suffers from exactly the same problems as any other financial ratio which links a flow (purchases) with a position (creditors) and, accordingly, needs to be viewed with some caution. A commonly held view is that creditors provide a source of free finance to a business and that payments to creditors should be deferred as long as practicable, suggesting that creditor turnover periods should be extended rather than reduced. This view ignores the value of any cash-settlement discounts that may be offered by the supplier. As is demonstrated in Chapter 17, such cash-settlement discounts can in fact be very valuable. Chapter 17 also discusses the fact that the speed with which creditors are paid is only one element in the relationships that a business has with its suppliers. Other elements include the prices paid for goods and services, the quality of these goods and services, and the willingness of the supplier to meet the precise requirements of the business. Excessive delay of payment to suppliers might lead to them ceasing to value the business being offered, and to a reduction in the general terms of trade which they are prepared to offer, as well as to the loss of cash-settlement discounts.

Motors provides an example of the difficulties faced by external users of financial statements in evaluating the credit management of companies. As is usually the case, no figures are provided for purchases by the business on credit terms. Accordingly, the ratios shown below are based on the (rather heroic) assumption that the cost of sales and other costs shown in the summary financial statements represent credit purchases.

$$19X7: \quad \frac{235\,000}{1\,382\,000 + 201\,000} \times 365 = 54.18 \text{ days}$$

$$19X6: \quad \frac{130\,000}{1\,575\,000 + 225\,000} \times 365 = 26.36 \text{ days}$$

This indicates that the period of credit that Motors is taking from its suppliers has more than doubled. This is a significant change and a potential purchaser would need to investigate the reasons for the change thoroughly. If it is the case that the change is a result of the business' inability to generate sufficient cash inflows to match its previous pattern of paying suppliers this would be very worrying, both as regards its ability to meet its liabilities and as regards its future terms of trade with its suppliers. While a company's ability to meet its short-term liabilities will be significantly influenced by its short-term working-capital management, it will also reflect its long-term capital structure.

Financing ratios

The principal focus of these indicators is financial risk, that is, the risk to those associated with the company which derives from the financial structure of the company, and, in particular, the risk introduced by a capital structure which involves debt and other forms of capital having preferential rights as compared to equity. The prior claims of such capital, as regards both its annual servicing and its ultimate capital repayment, perhaps on a secured basis, have significant risk implications for the company as a whole and for the different classes of capital providers. There is a substantial body of research into, and literature regarding, the implications of capital structure for a company and its participants. Samuels *et al.* (1995) provide a useful overview of this area. Broadly speaking, debt capital is cheaper than equity capital because it enjoys greater security, as regards its entitlement both to annual interest payments (which must be met before any dividend can be paid to shareholders) and to the ultimate repayment of the capital (which must be repaid before any distribution of capital is made to shareholders). However, the larger the proportion of these prior claims of debt holders, the more risky is the investment of the equity holders, as regards their entitlement both to a share of the business's income and to repayment of their capital. There are two financial ratios that attempt to measure this risk; one focuses on the capital values of debt and equity (the balance-sheet gearing ratio) and the other focuses on the income entitlements (the income gearing ratio). These ratios are sometimes referred to as leverage ratios rather than gearing ratios.

■ **Balance-sheet gearing ratio**: there are a number of different versions of this ratio, some using financial statement values of debt and equity and some using capital market values. However, the principal is the same – a focus on the relative proportions of debt and equity capital. A common version of this ratio is:

$$\frac{\text{Debt capital}}{\text{Debt capital + equity capital}} \times 100 \qquad (7.14)$$

This ratio provides a measure, albeit a fairly simplistic one, of the relative claims of debt holders and equity holders against the assets of the company. The higher the proportion of debt holders claims, with their preferential status, the more risky the shareholder claims become. In fact, if the debt holder claims become sufficiently large they themselves start to become more risky. Thus the ratio in this form is a fairly crude indicator of financial risk. This crudity becomes even more apparent with the recognition of the range of debt instruments that companies can issue. These include mortgages, floating-charge debentures, convertible loan stock and various types of preference shares. The situation is further complicated by the fact that different commercial sectors commonly have different patterns of capital structure. What might be an acceptable capital structure for a property company with a strong asset base might be totally unacceptable for a company operating in the service sector with a strong but volatile cash flow. The capital market tends to have quite strong views regarding acceptable levels of gearing in different sectors, and enterprises which exceed these levels may well find their share values being significantly downgraded.

In the case of Motors this balance-sheet ratio reveals the following:

$$19X7: \quad \frac{100\,000}{100\,000 + 250\,000} \times 100 = 28.57\%$$

$$19X6: \quad \frac{150\,000}{150\,000 + 212\,000} \times 100 = 41.44\%$$

This indicates that there has been a sharp decline in the proportion that debt finance provides in the overall long-term financing of Motors. However, this is primarily the result of the repayment by the company of £50 000 of such finance and this needs to be taken into account in the overall assessment of Motor's financial position, especially given the decline in its short-term liquidity which was discussed earlier.

Although this ratio provides a useful indicator of one aspect of it, financial risk, it does not cover an equally, and perhaps more important aspect of such risk, the terms on such prior claim finance has been made available, including its maturity or repayment dates. Particular attention needs to be paid to possible exposure of an enterprise to short-term claims for the repayment of such finance and to whether or not it could fund such repayments, either out of its own funds or by access to other lines of credit. The Companies Acts require quite extensive disclosure in relation to prior-claim finance. However, this disclosure is most normally contained in the notes to the accounts, a part of the annual report which research has shown to be read by the fewest people.

A related issue is the extent of the company's borrowing powers. It is normal for a company's Articles of Association to empower the directors to borrow money and pledge the company's assets as security for such borrowing. However, it is rare for this authority to be unfettered. Limits are normally placed on the amount of the borrowing, and these limits are frequently expressed in terms of a proportion of the company's net assets or equity. Debenture trust deeds often place similar restrictions on borrowing powers. Thus the balance-sheet gearing ratio, when looked at in conjunction with these sources, provides a useful indicator of the extent to which the company is within its authorised borrowing limits.

■ **Income gearing ratio**: this ratio compares the amount of preferential charges on corporate income to the amount of that income. The greater the proportion of these prior charges, the more the residual (equity holders') share of corporate income is at risk. Relatively small declines in overall income can lead to much greater declines in the income attributable to shareholders. The ratio is normally calculated as follows:

$$\frac{\text{Interest and other prior charges on income}}{\text{Operating profit}} \times 100 \qquad (7.15)$$

In the case of Motors, assuming an interest rate of 10% per annum on the long-term debt, the income gearing ratios for the two years for which financial information is available are:

$$19X7: \quad \frac{10\,000}{117\,000 + 10\,000} \times 100 = 7.87\%$$

$$19X6: \quad \frac{15\,000}{150\,000 + 15\,000} \times 100 = 9.09\%$$

This indicates that the proportion that prior-claim debt charges have on corporate income has declined. This would normally be regarded as a good thing from the point of view of the shareholders as it makes their share of corporate income more secure. However, security is not everything. Investment in the equity capital of companies is essentially a risk investment. Investors accept this risk in the hope/expectation that they will receive a return which will compensate them for taking this risk. Financial ratios need to measure these potential returns.

Investment performance ratios

This group of ratios concentrates on assessing investment performance from the perspective of the equity holder. They are directly concerned with security of the dividends payable to shareholders, and the relationship between the price that a shareholder pays to acquire shares in an enterprise and the earnings and dividends attributable to the holding of such shares. The most commonly computed ratios in this area are:

■ **Earnings per share**: this ratio measures the potential benefit that shareholders derive from the profitability of the company in which they have invested, irrespective of the extent to which such profits have been reflected in dividend distributions. As such, it is a key indicator of corporate performance from a shareholder perspective and is widely quoted in the financial press, at least as regards listed companies. It is computed by:

$$\frac{\text{Earnings attributable to shareholders (profit after taxation)}}{\text{Number of shares in issue}} \qquad (7.16)$$

There are a number of technical issues associated with the computation of earnings per share in practice, which are mainly caused by the sometimes complex financial instruments issued by companies. However, the focus is clear – identifying the financial performance of a company as regards an individual shareholder. In the relatively straightforward case of Motors the earnings per share are:

$$19X7: \quad \frac{74\,000}{150\,000} = \text{£}0.49 \text{ per share}$$

$$19X6: \quad \frac{103\,000}{150\,000} = \text{£}0.69 \text{ per share}$$

This indicates that, as regards shareholders, the overall financial performance of Motors was worse in 19X7 than 19X6 to quite a significant extent. This reflects the decline in sales revenue that was discussed earlier. However, earnings per share on its own do not reflect the benefit/cost ratio from investment in a company. To achieve this, it is necessary to link the earnings attributable to owning a share with the cost of purchasing a share.

■ **Price–earnings ratio**: this ratio compares the benefits derived (at least potentially) from owning a share with the cost of purchasing such a share. It is calculated as:

$$\frac{\text{Market price of a share}}{\text{Earnings per share}} \qquad (17.17)$$

This ratio compares the earnings per share with the market price of a share. As such, it compares directly the profit that is generated for equity shareholders with the price that currently has to be paid to participate in those profits. It provides a very clear indication of the value that the capital market places on those earnings and is prepared to pay for participation. It reflects the capital market's assessment of both the amount and the risk of these earnings, albeit subject to overall market and economic considerations. In view of this, it is a ratio which is regularly calculated and reported in the financial press, and is frequently invoked in takeover negotiations and the issue of new equity capital. However, it must be noted again that the comparison is between past earning performance and current market prices. There is no guarantee that this past performance will be repeated in the future, and yet it is future earnings in which a new investor will participate. Past earnings are being used as a surrogate for future earnings.

■ **Dividend cover**: this ratio focuses on the security of the current rates of dividends, and by doing so provides a measure of the likelihood of those dividends being maintained in the future. It does this by measuring the proportion that current rates of dividends constitute of the profits from which such dividends can be declared without drawing on retained profits. The higher the ratio, the more profits could decline without dividends being affected. This is particularly important in the light of the widely held view that the capital market places a very high premium on companies that maintain a steady, preferably expanding, rate of dividend payments rather than companies whose dividend rates fluctuate. In the case of Motors the dividend cover ratios are:

$$19X7: \quad \frac{74\,000}{36\,000} = 2.06$$

$$19X6: \quad \frac{103\,000}{36\,000} = 2.86$$

Motors has been able to maintain its rate of dividend to shareholders despite a fall in post-tax profits from £103 000 to £74 000. However, the dividend payment is now only covered by profits by a factor of 2.06 rather than the 2.86 of the previous year. A further similar decline in profit means that the company would be unable to maintain its dividend rate without recourse to profits retained from earlier years.

■ **Dividend yield**: in many ways this is the acid test of corporate financial performance from an investors point of view. It is calculated as:

$$\frac{\text{Dividend per share}}{\text{Market price of a share}} \times 100 \qquad (17.18)$$

In today's financial markets, an investor has a wide range of available investment opportunities and will want to assess the relative merits of these different opportunities. An important element in such an assessment will be the relative yields to be derived from different investment opportunities in the light of the relative risks involved, and this is where the dividend yield ratio comes into its own. It compares the amount of the dividend per share with the market price of a share and provides a direct measure of the return on investment in the shares of an enterprise.

However, a note of caution must be sounded. The dividends in the numerator are historic dividends. They are the dividends that have been paid in the past, and not necessarily those future dividends which will be paid and are the real basis of a return on investment. Similarly, it must be recognised that stock-market prices can be very volatile, being influenced by many factors, far from all of which have anything to do with the performance of an individual enterprise. Thus, while the ratio attempts to address something of crucial importance to an investor, it has to do so using past data on dividends in relation to what might be a rapidly changing market price.

A further note of caution is that the dividend yield ratio ignores the possibility of capital appreciation resulting from increases in the market value of a company's shares. The price earnings ratio attempts, in part, to rectify this by reflecting the fact that not all of an enterprise's profits are necessarily distributed as dividends. Some will almost certainly be retained and reinvested to secure future profits. A shareholder is, at least in theory, entitled to a share of both these retained profits and the future profits arising from reinvestment. The latter may, of course, be highly speculative. These will be important elements in the capital market's attitude to a company and the resultant market price of its shares.

Conclusions

As the foregoing indicates, a wide range of financial ratios can be calculated from the financial statements of an enterprise – even more if other sources of data are utilised as well. Such ratios can be of enormous help in gaining a fuller appreciation of an enterprise's financial performance. However, it is all too easy to calculate and use such ratios in a simplistic and trivial way. The ratios cannot be better than the information on which they are based – in the main, financial statements based on traditional historical-cost concepts. While financial ratios do provide a useful structure for the interpretation of information contained in financial statements, they do not and cannot provide a system for the assessment of the performance of companies and management. This is because, while they can highlight changes in financial performance, they cannot identify the reasons for these changes and it is the reasons that are important. Instead, financial ratio analysis helps users of financial statements to identify the changes that have taken place and to ask more focused questions about such changes.

The data contained in the annual financial statements of enterprises are an important source of information for stakeholders. The technique of ratio analysis enables more effective use to be made of this information. It focuses on the relationships between key items of information, enabling important linkages to be established and analysis of trends to be undertaken. Care must be taken to ensure that ratios are not over-interpreted, and it must be recognised that the ratios depend on the reliability of the information contained in the underlying financial statements. The main areas where ratios can be of use are assessing and analysing an enterprise's:

- profitability;
- profit;
- liquidity and working capital;
- financial structure;
- performance as an investment.

Commentary Ltd: Draft balance sheet as at 31 December 1997

	1997		1996	
	£000	£000	£000	£000
Fixed assets:				
Freehold premises at cost		450		450
Motor vehicles: cost	300		300	
depreciation	180		120	
		120		180
		570		630
Current assets:				
Stocks	260		180	
Debtors	160		120	
	420		300	
Current liabilities:				
Creditors	120		140	
Bank overdraft	100		50	
	220		190	
Net current assets		200		110
Net assets		770		740
Shareholders' interests:				
Share capital (£1 shares)		400		400
Retained profits		170		140
		570		540
Long-term liabilities:				
12% debentures		200		200
		770		740

Commentary Ltd: Draft profit and loss account – year to 31 December 1997

	1997		1996	
	£000	£000	£000	£000
Turnover		1 050		850
Cost of sales		710		580
Gross profit		340		270
Distribution expenses	125		105	
Administration expenses	81		66	
Debenture interest	24		24	
		230		195
Profit before taxation		110		75
Taxation		50		35
Profit after taxation		60		40
Dividend		30		25
Retained profit for year		30		15

Note: Distribution and administration expenses incorporate depreciation charges amounting to £60 000 (1996: £50 000).

Further reading

Holmes and Sugden (1994) provide an analysis of how to interpret the information contained in published accounts, as do Alexander and Britton (1996), albeit in less detail. Griffiths (1995) and Smith (1996) show how to avoid a number of pitfalls in the interpretation of published financial statements.

Questions and exercises

1 The draft accounts for Commentary Ltd for the year ended 31 December 1997 are shown on the previous page.

When these draft accounts were laid before the board of directors (none of whom has had any training in accounting) the following points and questions were raised by board members. Reply to each of these points in clear, simple terms, avoiding the use of unexplained jargon. Where appropriate, support your replies with calculations.

(a) 'It doesn't seem to do us much good to make profits; our cash position seems to go from worse to worse.'

(b) 'Why are our premises shown in the balance sheet at £450 000. It would cost us at least £1 000 000 to buy premises like ours today and we could easily sell them for that amount.'

(c) 'It is ridiculous to describe our motor vehicles as fixed assets. I never saw anything less fixed than our motor vehicles.'

(d) 'There is something wrong with the depreciation. For a start the figures in the balance sheet don't agree with the profit and loss account. Also, I am sure that we are not providing enough depreciation to enable us to replace our vehicles at today's prices.'

(e) 'We seem to have let control over our debtors and stocks slip, so that the amount we have tied up in these items has increased alarmingly. Is there any simple way of measuring how seriously we have strayed from our previous pattern?'

(f) 'What is our rate of return on capital employed? Does it make sense to compare that figure with those of other companies as a test of our performance?'

(g) 'I am told that financial analysts judge a company on its earnings per share. What is this figure for Commentary and what does it mean?'

2 You are the accountant of a small family company called Mayday, and you have just prepared the draft accounts for the year ended 31 August 1997, which are shown on the following page.

When you present these draft accounts to the board of directors for approval, Josiah Mayday, one of the directors, who has recently returned from an extensive polar exploration trip, asks you the following questions:

(a) 'This is a well-established business with loyal staff and loyal customers. This is in part demonstrated by the increase in sales during the year to our existing customers. The business enjoys an enormous amount of goodwill – from our customers, our staff and the local community. This might almost be our major asset. Why is this asset not reflected in the accounts?'

Mayday Ltd: Draft balance sheet as at 31 August 1997

	1997		1996	
	£000	£000	£000	£000
Fixed assets:				
Freehold premises:				
Cost	600		600	
Accumulated depreciation	200	400	188	412
Equipment:				
Cost	640		460	
Accumulated depreciation	300	340	320	140
		740		552
Current assets:				
Stock	370		290	
Debtors	410		320	
Cash	20		60	
	800		670	
Current liabilities:				
Creditors	620		560	
Net current assets		180		110
10% debentures		(200)		–
		720		662
Share capital (£1 shares)		400		400
Retained profits		320		262
		720		662

Mayday Ltd: Draft profit and loss account – year ended 31 August 1997

	1997	1996
	£000	£000
Sales	2 400	1 980
Cost of sales	1 900	1 600
Gross profit	500	380
Other costs	170	160
Net profit	330	220
Taxation	110	80
Profit after taxation	220	140
Dividends	162	130
Retained profit	58	10

Concentration Ltd: Balance sheet as at 31 December 1997

	1997		1996	
	£000	£000	£000	£000
Fixed assets:				
Land and buildings				
Cost	550		520	
Accumulated depreciation	90	460	80	440
Machinery				
Cost	1 340		1 120	
Accumulated depreciation	750	590	580	540
		1 050		980
Current assets:				
Stocks	980		830	
Debtors	570		650	
Cash	40		120	
	1 590		1 600	
Current liabilities:				
Creditors	358		310	
Net current assets		1 232		1 290
Net assets		2 282		2 270
Share capital (£1 shares)		1 200		1 200
Retained profits		282		270
		1 482		1 470
10% debentures		800		800
		2 282		2 270

Concentration Ltd: Profit and loss account – year to 31 December 1997

	1997		1996	
	£000s	£000s	£000s	£000s
Turnover		3 200		2 200
Cost of sales		2 590		1 610
Gross profit		610		590
Distribution expenses	320		260	
Administration expenses	170		190	
		490		450
Profit before taxation		120		140
Taxation		48		56
Profit after taxation		72		84
Dividend		60		90
Retained profit for year		12		(6)

Note: Included in the distribution and administration expenses is the amount of £180 000 (1996: £110 000) for depreciation charges.

(b) 'I don't understand all this accounting jargon about depreciation and fixed assets. I knew the accounts would confuse me, except as regards our freehold property, where I knew nothing had changed. That is why I asked you to tell me in advance of this meeting how much we had spent on acquiring new fixed assets, how much we had sold old assets for, and how much depreciation we had charged this year on our assets. You told me that we had spent £350 000 on new fixed assets, had sold old assets for £30 000 (and made a loss on the sale) and had charged depreciation of £60 000 during the year. This makes a nonsense of your draft accounts. If we charged £60 000 of depreciation during the year, how can the accumulated depreciation on our fixed assets, other than freehold property, have gone down?'

(c) 'As you know, I depend on the dividends on my shares for my income. I was against issuing the debentures that you advised us to issue. I am sure this makes my income more risky. Is there any way I can measure this increased risk?'

(d) 'On top of this, the money we are owed by our customers has gone up by nearly 30% over the year, and this in a time of recession. You must have lost control over the situation. What are you going to do about it?'

(e) 'All in all, I think I should sell my shares. I have been talking to my stockbroker and he tells me that companies like ours have a price–earnings ratio of about 15 to 1. What does this mean, and what does it indicate about the price I should sell my shares for?'

Provide Mr Josiah Mayday with answers to his questions, avoiding the use of technical jargon wherever possible.

3   The balance sheet and profit and loss account of Concentration Ltd for the years ending 31 December 1996 and 1997 are shown above.

A friend of yours who has little knowledge of accounting has asked you to comment on the company's performance as revealed by the above accounts, with particular reference to the use of accounting ratios, as he would like to know more about them.

4   Identify from the perspective of a potential investor the principal areas regarding which s/he would like to have information to help him/her assess whether or not to invest in the shares of a publicly listed company. Comment on the extent to which the annual financial statements of companies provide a source of such information.

5   What are the principal advantages and dangers of using ratio analysis to interpret the information contained in a company's annual financial statements?

6   You are the corporate loans officer in a high-street branch of a bank. You have to decide on whether or not to make advances to corporate organisations. Jason's Ltd is a well-established fashion store in Borchester and its directors have approached you with a view to your bank granting them loan facilities. What information would you ask them to provide to help you assess the creditworthiness of the company and what sort of analysis would you carry out on this information?

7   'Ratios on their own are fairly useless – they only become useful when they are compared with something.' What are the difficulties that might be encountered in making such comparisons by:

(a) a company's management;

(b) a shareholder;

(c) a banker.

8 'There can be problems with using return on capital employed (ROCE) as a measure of the economic performance of many companies. In fact, ROCE based on historic-cost financial statements will typically overstate such performance.' Do you agree with this statement? Give reasons for your answer.

9 Ratio analysis can combine figures derived from a company's financial statements with figures from other sources (e.g. the price–earnings ratio). List ratios which do this and might usefully be used for analysing the financial performance of:

(a) an airline;

(b) a chain of retail stores;

(c) a high-technology manufacturing company.

10 'Traditional financial ratios are of more use to management than to external stakeholders when it comes to assessing business performance.' Do you agree with this statement? If so, why? If not, why not?

8 Comparative international financial reporting

Objectives

So far we have concentrated on accounting and financial reporting in the UK, although occasional reference has been made to the work of the IASC and other international accounting bodies. In this chapter we look at financial reporting in other countries and ask how their practices differ from those in the UK. In the light of the answer to this question we then examine a number of related issues:

■ Why have these differences arisen?
■ What are the implications of these differences for the management of commercial enterprises, particularly multinational enterprises?
■ What efforts, if any, are being made to reconcile these differences and how successful are they?

Financial reporting in different countries

Accounting is one of the areas in which international law does not exist, except to some extent within the EU. Each country has its own system of statutory and other regulation of financial reporting. There are approximately 180 different countries represented at the United Nations and it would not be practical to examine the structure of financial reporting in each of those countries. A number of researchers (see Nobes and Parker 1995: ch. 4) have examined core differences and similarities between financial reporting systems in different countries and have proposed classification schemes for these systems. In this chapter we focus primarily on a *reportage* of these differences and their implications. Readers interested in a more detailed analysis of international financial reporting differences should look at specialist texts such as Nobes and Parker (1995) and Alexander and Nobes (1994). However, as Nobes and Parker point out, any review of international financial reporting is at best a 'snapshot' of a point in time. Financial reporting, and its regulation (both nationally and internationally), is a 'moving feast'.

Before proceeding further it would be helpful to obtain some insight into the impact of these differences. In 1989 Touche Ross & Co. (Simmonds and Azières 1989) illustrated the diversity of financial accounting practice within Europe with a case study which applied the accounting practices of different countries to a series

Table 8.1 Profit sensitivity in different European countries

Millions of Ecus	B	D	E	F	I	NL	UK
Maximum achievable	193	140	192	160	193	156	194
Most likely	135	133	131	149	174	140	192
Minimum achievable	90	27	121	121	167	76	171

Country codes: B = Belgium; D = Germany; E = Eire; F = France; I = Italy; NL = Netherlands;
UK = United Kingdom.
Source: Simmonds and Azières (1989: 36).

of transactions with a view to identifying for each country the most likely, the maximum achievable and the minimum achievable financial results. Table 8.1 summarises the results of this case study.

As can be seen from Table 8.1, there are significant differences between the countries as to both the level of profit achieved by applying the extremes of permitted financial reporting practice in the different countries and the variability of this profit. Similar variations apply if, for example, the financial statements of companies are prepared under US as opposed to UK financial reporting principles – a standard practice for companies whose shares are listed on both the London and New York Stock Exchanges. Thus, the Reuters Holdings plc accounts for the year ended 31 December 1996 reveal (pp. 75–7) that profit for the year in accordance with UK principles was £491 million, but in accordance with US principles was only £440 million. Similarly, in accordance with UK principles the capital employed was £1260 million, but when measured in accordance with US principles was £1561 million. Ernst & Young (1992) provide many other examples of significant differences between financial statements prepared under UK and US accounting principles. The problem is compounded when financial statements prepared under other regimes are considered, as is inevitably the case when companies' shares are listed on a number of different stock exchanges. With the development of globalised financial markets this is becoming increasingly prevalent. Table 8.2 shows the number of non-domestic companies listed on the world's principal stock exchanges. Table 8.3 further illustrates the internationalisation of capital markets by identifying the ten largest non-domestic companies (by value of shares traded and by total equity value) listed on the London Stock Exchange.

The implications of differing financial reporting practices

It is commonly accepted that a company's annual financial statements are an important source of information (albeit far from the only one) underpinning the decision taking of investors in the shares of listed companies and providing 'stewardship' information regarding the discharge of their duties by directors. The existence of two (or more) different sets of financial statements for the same company for the same financial period will, at best, introduce some 'noise' into the information value of the financial statements. It could even lead to significant misunderstanding of the information and poor decision taking by investors.

The diversity of financial reporting regulation and accounting principles also causes problems for companies which operate on a transnational basis and which raise finance

Table 8.2 Non-domestic companies listed on leading stock exchanges

Exchange	No. of non-domestic companies listed
Amsterdam	216
Brussels	146
London	533
Luxembourg	224
Nasdaq	416
New York	305
Singapore	187
Switzerland	223

Source: Extracted from London Stock Exchange (1997: 37).
Note: Nasdaq = National Association of Securities Dealers Automated Quotations.

Table 8.3 The ten largest non-domestic companies listed on the London Stock Exchange

Company	Country of incorporation
By trading activity during 1996:	
Royal Dutch Petroleum Co. NV	Netherlands
Société Elf Aquitaine SA	France
Astra AB	Sweden
ENI	Italy
VEBA AG	Germany
Roche Holding AG	Switzerland
Total	France
Siemens AG	Germany
Unilever NV	Netherlands
Daimler-Benz AG	Germany
By equity market value at 31 December 1996:	
General Electric Co. Inc.	USA
Exxon Corporation	USA
Nippon Telegraph & Telephone Corporation	Japan
Toyota Motor Corporation	Japan
Bank of Tokyo Mitsubishi	Japan
Royal Dutch Petroleum Co. NV	Netherlands
International Business Machines Corp.	USA
Proctor & Gamble Co.	USA
Coca-Cola Co.	USA
Du Pont (E.I.) De Nemours & Co.	USA

Source: Extracted from London Stock Exchange (1997: 51, 54).

across frontiers. At the very least, they will incur additional 'compliance' costs in meeting the requirements of different regulatory and reporting regimes. Thus a holding company seeking to prepare consolidated accounts for itself and its worldwide affiliates will not simply be able to aggregate its own and the statutory accounts of the affiliates, making the normal consolidation adjustments after translating the foreign currencies into its domestic currency. It will require that the financial statements of the affiliates be restated using the domestic accounting principles of its country of incorporation. Frequently, this process will work the other way round – the financial statements required for consolidation will be the first to be prepared, followed by recalculation using local accounting principles for the purposes of complying with local legislation. If such a company has listings on other than its domestic stock exchange further restatements may be required. However the process is carried out the cost could be substantial. Problems may also arise with cross-border acquisitions – a company will not be able to rely on published financial information to assess potential acquisitions. Similar problems may arise with establishing and managing international joint ventures, with assessing the performance of operating units, and with the transfer of finance and accounting staff between units. The existence of divergent accounting principles can also cause problems for governments, their regulatory agencies and taxation authorities in their dealings with multinational and transnational enterprises.

The reasons why different financial reporting principles have emerged

Why have the differences commented on above arisen? In essence, the answer to this question relates to the differing ways in which countries have originated and developed their systems. Some of the more important aspects in this respect include:

■ **Sources of finance**: the core issue here is the extent to which equity capital in companies is provided (owned) by third parties who do not have any privileged access to information about the affairs of the company – the typical external shareholder. In such circumstances the annual financial statements of companies are a crucial source of information to these providers of finance, and there is likely to be pressure to ensure that these statements provide information helpful to them in making assessments about the economic performance and prospects of the company. Historically, this has been the case in countries such as the UK and the USA, with their long-established and well-developed stock exchanges. On the other hand, there are countries where the pattern of share ownership is different. Thus, for example, in Germany the major commercial banks not only provide companies with debt finance, but are also significant owners of equity capital. In some countries, such as Japan, there are significant patterns of cross-shareholding between companies and banks. In other countries it is the state which owns the equity capital (although this has become less common in recent years with the reconstruction of a number of previously communist economies and the 'privatisation' drive elsewhere). In yet other countries major commercial companies are essentially family-owned. In all these cases the shareholders have close relationships with companies and, as a result, access to 'inside' information about corporate affairs. In these circumstances the need for published financial statements to help shareholders form assessments about companies' state of affairs is less pressing. Instead, the emphasis has been on the preparation of financial statements for governmental purposes such as taxation. This is not to say that there is no need for financial statements in the same sense as in the UK or the USA – particularly as the stock exchanges in these various countries have become more important sources of finance for companies – rather, that the historic emphasis has been different.

■ **Legal systems**: in Chapter 4 we identified that, certainly within the UK, the two main sources of regulation on the preparation and publication of financial statements have been statute law (the Companies Acts) and the accounting profession.

In all other countries law is also an important element in the regulation of financial reporting. However, there are a number of different systems of law. Two of these are the Anglo-Saxon common-law tradition and the Roman law tradition. The first restricts the role of statute law and places great emphasis on the role of the courts interpreting the relatively limited amount of statute law, which is thus supplemented by a great deal of case law and the development of precedents, albeit ones that are not necessarily binding. The second places a great deal of emphasis on the codification of the law by the government (statute law) and considerably less on case law. In countries which follow a common-law tradition (the UK, the USA, Australia and others) there is limited amount of detailed statutory regulation of financial reporting. In countries with a Roman law tradition (France, Germany, Spain and others) – or with traditions which, while not being derived from Roman law, also place a great deal of emphasis on statutory regulation – the reverse is the case. The regulation of company financial reporting is largely seen as an extension of (or is directly incorporated in) company-related statute law. Such systems, as for example in France, Spain or the former communist countries of Eastern Europe, typically have very detailed charts of account with which companies are expected to comply (e.g. the French *plan comptable général*).

■ **Taxation systems**: the key issue here is the extent to which taxation legislation dictates the treatment of items in a company's financial statements; that is, is there an identity between taxation rules and accounting rules? In general, the more that a country's accounting rules are codified in law, the closer the identity between these rules and the taxation rules. On the other hand, there are countries where the regulation of financial reporting and the administration of corporate taxation are clearly distinct activities. In these circumstances the core objective of the financial statements is perceived as being the provision of useful information to stakeholders; that of facilitating the computation of taxation liabilities is secondary. In such circumstances, as we saw in Chapter 5, the reported profit is simply the starting point in the computation of taxation, with a number of adjustments being necessary to convert 'accounting' profit to 'taxable' profit.

■ **Role of the accounting profession**: as we saw in Chapter 4, within the UK the accounting profession has had a significant and proactive role to play in the development of accounting regulation. The same has been true, albeit in different ways, in a number of other countries, such as Australia and the USA. In many other countries, particularly those having more detailed statutory regulation of financial reporting, the influence of the accounting profession has been much less, with the emphasis being primarily on the implementation of statutory regulation.

There are undoubtedly other economic, cultural and political factors that have led to differences in financial reporting and its regulation across countries. The above are simply those commonly regarded as the most influential. However, it is important to recognise that these factors are not static, and as they change so financial reporting changes, albeit sometimes rather slowly. Thus, the implementation of the EU company law Directives has moved financial reporting in the UK somewhat closer to the codified system prevalent throughout the rest of Europe, while the development of stock exchanges has moved financial reporting in a number of other European countries some way towards Anglo-American practice.

The principal areas of difference in financial reporting

So far we have stated that there are differences in financial reporting across countries but have not identified in any detail what these differences are. This we will now do. The principal areas where there are significant differences in the financial reporting systems of different countries include:

- **Fixed assets**: in Chapter 2 we saw that a fixed asset is an asset owned by an entity which it intends to use in its operations for the long term. Fixed assets can be tangible or intangible. Virtually throughout the world, the starting point for accounting for tangible fixed assets is original (historic) cost, from which depreciation is deducted to arrive at net book value (carrying value). Diversity of practice comes in the extent to which countries permit subsequent adjustment (revaluation) of this original cost. In North America such revaluation almost never takes place. Nor is it permitted in Japan. In the UK revaluations are quite common with regard to land and buildings but much less common with regard to other fixed assets. In some countries such revaluations are not normal practice but have been permitted under exceptional inflationary circumstances (e.g. Germany in the 1920s and France in the 1970s). In other countries which have suffered from persistent inflation, for example in Latin America, revaluation of fixed assets, often based on indexation rather than revaluation, is almost standard practice.

  There are also differences regarding the treatment of intangible assets, even disregarding goodwill arising on consolidation, which we discuss later. In a number of continental countries companies are permitted to capitalise their formation expenses and to amortise them over a number of years. This is true of Japan, but such capitalisation is not permitted in the UK or the USA. Practice also differs with regard to expenditure on research and development. In the USA all expenditure on research and development (other than that which creates long-lived physical assets) is immediately expensed; in the UK and a number of other countries, such as Japan, development expenditure may be capitalised (and subsequently amortised) if it is expected that it will lead to a viable commercial product; in other countries, such as France and Spain, research as well as development expenditure is sometimes capitalised. In the UK a number of companies have in recent years included in their balance sheets values for the brand names which they have developed, as well as other intangible assets such as publishing rights and publication titles. This is also permitted in a number of other countries, such as France and the Netherlands, but is a practice which is far from universal.

- **Depreciation policies**: as we saw in Chapter 2, depreciation is the means via which the cost (net of any anticipated salvage value) of a fixed asset is allocated to the financial periods comprising the anticipated life of the asset. We also saw that there are a number of different methods of calculating depreciation, including time-based methods (such as the straight-line and reducing-balance methods) and usage-based methods. A major difference between countries regarding depreciation is the extent to which there is an identity between accounting regulation and taxation regulation. In some countries (as mentioned above) there is a close relationship between the depreciation allowed for taxation purposes and that reported in the financial statements. This applies both to the method of computing the depreciation and to the asset lives that are used in the computation. Examples of such countries are France, Germany and Japan. In other countries, such as the UK, the USA and the Netherlands, there is no such close relationship, which leads to the possibility of 'timing differences' (see Chapter 5) between the charging of depreciation for financial and taxation purposes.

■ **Accounting for leases**: in a number of countries which emphasise the economic substance as opposed to the legal form of transactions (see Chapter 2), for example the UK, assets which are the subject of finance leases are capitalised. In others, such as Germany, Italy and Japan, they are not.

■ **Group accounts**: as discussed in Chapter 4, group accounts are the accounts which aggregate the financial statements of the parent (holding) company with those of its subsidiary companies and associated companies. They are prepared to present aggregated information about an economic entity (the 'group') as opposed to information about each of the separate legal entities (the companies) which comprise the group. The main areas of variation between countries regarding the preparation of group accounts are the extent to which such accounts are legally required and the specification of exactly what comprises a group for this purpose. Historically, these have been areas where there have been major differences between countries. However, within Europe the Seventh Directive has sought to harmonise financial reporting practice, although some countries proved rather tardy in implementing this Directive. The principal issue which the Directive addressed was the definition of a subsidiary company for the purpose of the preparation of group accounts. Prior to the Directive not all EU countries required the preparation of group accounts and there were differences in the specification of what were to be regarded as subsidiary companies. The approach that the Directive adopted was one in which control was to be the determining factor in whether an entity should be included in the group accounts as a subsidiary (and the Directive identified a number of different factors which would indicate control) as opposed to ownership (of 50%+ of the share capital), which had previously been the determining factor in a number of regimes.

The most common basis of preparing group accounts is the 'acquisition' method, in which the assumption is that one company has acquired/'taken-over' another company. However, business combinations may also take place via a 'merger', in which previously separate entities combine ('pool their interests') as opposed to one entity 'taking the other over'. In such circumstances it might be more appropriate to use a different method of group accounting, which is usually referred to as 'merger (pooling of interest) accounting' – one important element of this is that it does not lead to the creation in the financial statements of 'goodwill arising on consolidation' (see below). One other aspect of group accounts that needs to be recognised is that situations might arise in which one company (A), while not being able to control another (B) (i.e. there is not a parent–subsidiary relationship), is still able to exercise significant influence over company B. In such circumstances some financial reporting regimes require that company B be incorporated in the group accounts of company A as an *associated company* using the *equity* method, rather than simply as a trade investment. As the foregoing indicates, the preparation of group accounts is a highly technical area of accounting, and as such is beyond the scope of this book – readers seeking more detailed technical information about the preparation of group accounts are advised to look at a specialist text such as P. A. Taylor (1996).

Given its complexity, it is hardly surprising that group accounting provides considerable scope for international differences. Merger accounting is virtually unknown in Europe other than in the UK, and then only rarely. However, it is rather more common in the USA. In Canada, the UK and the USA, as well as some other European countries, such as Germany, equity accounting is required for associated companies. In a number of other countries there is no similar requirement. Group accounts do in fact represent one of the (apparent) success stories for the 'harmonisation' of financial reporting. There is much more common practice now than there was some years ago, at least as regards the need for group accounts and what entities should be included in them. In this the work of the Commission of the European Union, the JSAC and the globalisation of financial markets has been very influential. However, differences still remain, as described below.

- **Goodwill arising on consolidation**: this is a feature of the acquisition method of preparing group (consolidated) accounts which involves (in the preparation of the consolidated balance sheet) the substitution of the assets and liabilities of the subsidiary companies for the original amount of the investments of the parent company in those subsidiaries (as shown in the parent company's balance sheet). Part of this process involves distinguishing between increases in the net assets of subsidiaries since their acquisition by the parent company (undistributed post-acquisition profits) and differences between their value on the date of acquisition and the amount that the parent company paid to acquire them (by purchasing the shares in the subsidiary company). The situation can be made more complicated where a parent company does not own 100% of a subsidiary company (i.e. where there are *minority interests*).

  However, the issue remains the same – how to account for any difference between the financial-statement 'carrying value' of the net assets of a subsidiary as at the date of the acquisition and the price the parent company paid to acquire control of these net assets. Where this price is greater than the 'carrying value' the difference is called goodwill on consolidation and would, historically, have been shown as an asset in the consolidated balance sheet, thereby ensuring that it balanced. The question that then arises is how long this 'asset' should remain on the balance sheet, and this is one area in which financial reporting differences arise. Another area of difference is how this goodwill is to be calculated. An approach adopted by a number of countries (including the UK) is what is often called 'fair-value' accounting. Under this approach the individual assets and liabilities of the subsidiary are restated to their 'fair value' as at the date of acquisition ('fair value' in this context effectively means current market value). Goodwill is then calculated based on the difference between the acquisition cost and the restated 'fair value' of the net assets acquired. In other countries 'fair-value' consolidation is not practised and goodwill is calculated by reference to the balance-sheet carrying value of the net assets as at the date of acquisition. Practice with regard to the subsequent treatment of goodwill on consolidation is even more varied: in some countries (e.g. the UK and the Netherlands) normal practice is to write this goodwill off against reserves immediately; in others it is to capitalise it and then to amortise it over a number of years (ranging from 1–5 in Japan, to 5 in Spain and up to 40 in France).

- **The valuation of inventories**: the general principle prevailing in the valuation of inventories in financial statements is the 'lower of cost and market value principle', discussed in Chapter 2. Differences, however, arise in the way that 'cost' and 'market value' are interpreted in different countries. Thus in some countries, such as the UK and France, the LIFO basis of measuring cost is not normally permitted. In other countries, for example Germany and the Netherlands, LIFO is permitted and is used by some companies. In other countries, such as the USA, LIFO is a common method of valuing inventories. Some countries, such as the UK, interpret 'market value' as meaning net realisable value, while others, such as Germany and the USA, permit the use of replacement cost where this is lower than net realisable value.

■ **Deferred taxation**: this arises only where there are material timing differences between the recognition of items for financial reporting and taxation purposes. As such it is not a common element in financial statements where there is a close relationship between the regulation of financial statements and taxation regulations, e.g. in Belgium and France. As Chapter 5 indicates, there are two main approaches to accounting for deferred taxation: the liability method and the deferral method. The liability method of accounting is used in countries such as Germany and the USA. The deferral method is used in Canada, while Singapore permits both methods.

■ **Foreign-currency translation**: this relates principally to the need for a multi-national holding company to translate the financial statements of its foreign affiliates into its domestic currency for the purpose of preparing consolidated accounts. In principle, this is a straightforward task – these financial statements should be translated at the exchange rates prevailing at the end of the relevant financial period (the so-called 'closing rate') and this is a common practice as regards balance sheets. However, unlike the balance sheet, the profit and loss account and cash-flow statement are flow statements covering a period of time rather than a point in time. Accordingly, it might seem sensible to translate these statements at an 'average rate' for the financial period. Many countries, including the USA and most continental countries, require the use of this method. Another method, 'the temporal method', is permitted in some countries such as Germany and Japan. In the temporal method some of the items in the profit and loss account (most notably those relating to fixed assets such as the depreciation charge) are translated at historic exchange rates.

In addition to the foregoing, other areas of difference in financial-statement preparation exist across different countries. For example, some countries permit (require) financial statements which are prepared on a current-cost or other basis which allows for changing price levels; allow for dual-standard reporting (e.g. separate financial statements to ensure compliance with both domestic and international accounting standards); require statutory non-distributable reserves (often as a fixed proportion of share capital or annual profit); identify unusual items (whether revenues or costs) separately in the profit and loss account; and differentiate between the levels of disclosure required for companies of different sizes and patterns of ownership. There is enormous diversity in financial reporting practice, with all the potentially negative consequences discussed earlier.

Harmonisation of financial reporting

In essence, the problems involved in financial reporting on an international basis are a macrocosm of the issues we looked at in the context of the UK in Chapters 3 and 4. It is a question of the interests, and the relative authority, of different groups. However, in this case one of these different groups is the individual nation-state involved. While the accounting profession (in the broadest sense) may intellectually subscribe to the value of ensuring comparable (common) financial reporting practice across a globe to facilitate multinational economic activity, individual governments may have a different, perhaps narrower, perspective closely linked to their perceptions of national identity and interest. This problem may be compounded by the extent to which the multinational perspective might be (or be perceived as) a western/Anglo-American (perhaps simply American) perspective and one which smacks of imperialism. On the other hand, there might be significant attractions to developing economies in what used to be called the 'Third World' and to those Eastern European countries which are transforming themselves from command to market economies in having access to an existing and well-developed set of financial reporting principles and practices (assuming such a thing existed). There is already considerable evidence that such countries are incorporating into their domestic legislation the pronouncements of bodies such as the IASC and the European Commission, although these pronouncements are not always entirely consistent.

Taken together, these concerns are part of the debate on whether financial reporting practices should be 'harmonised' or 'standardised'. 'Harmonisation' is frequently associated with the efforts of the Commission of the European Union to make financial reporting and company legislation more compatible and comparable within the EU, while 'standardisation' is often taken to imply a more *dirigiste* approach involving a narrow set of rules for the regulation of financial reporting and is frequently associated with the activities of the IASC. In practice, the comparison is something of a distinction without a difference as both approaches have similar objectives and both are characterised by permitting a degree of flexibility in financial reporting. A more practical difference is that the work of the Commission of the European Union has more statutory backing than that of the IASC.

The EU has utilised two main mechanisms for harmonisation: Regulations, which automatically become law, and Directives, which member countries are required to incorporate into their national laws. There been two draft Regulations, only one of which has been adopted (in 1985). This was concerned with a new form of cross-boundary joint-venture organisation for existing companies called a 'European Economic Interest Grouping'. The second draft Regulation concerning the introduction of a new type of pan-national EU company has, to date, been less successful and has not yet been adopted. There have been a number of Directives, which are summarised in Table 8.4. Although not always with great promptitude, the requirements of these Directives have been incorporated into the national law of EU member states. This process has been made easier by the fact that the Directives have sought to 'harmonise' rather than 'standardise'. Thus they allow for at least some flexibility to accommodate local circumstances, for example as regards reporting exemptions for small and medium-sized companies. Of these Directives, the ones with the clearest and most direct consequences for financial reporting were

Table 8.4 The EU Company Law Harmonisation Programme

Directives on company law	Drafts issued	Date adopted	Topic
First	1964	1968	*Ultra vires* rules
Second	1970, 1972	1976	Public companies
Third	1970, 1973 1975	1978	Mergers
Fourth	1971, 1974	1978	Format and rules of accounting
Fifth	1972, 1983		Structure, management and audit of companies
Sixth	1978	1982	De-mergers
Seventh	1976, 1978	1983	Consolidation accounting
Eighth	1978	1984	Auditors
Ninth			Links between public company groups
Tenth	1985		International mergers of public companies
Eleventh	1986	1989	Branch disclosures
Twelfth	1988	1989	Single-member companies
Thirteenth	1989		Takeovers
Vredeling	1980, 1983		Employee information and consultation

Source: Adapted from Alexander and Nobes (1994), with permission.

the Fourth Directive, which focused on the financial reporting per se, and the Seventh Directive, which dealt with group accounts. The requirements of these Directives were incorporated into UK law via the 1981 and 1989 Companies Acts, respectively, and they have similarly been incorporated into the laws of other member states, albeit with use being made of the flexibility in implementation which they afford. There is no doubt that the EU Directives have led to a more common approach to financial reporting within the EU.

However, it is important not to overstate the extent to which this commonality has led to standardisation at a detailed level. Equally, it is important to acknowledge the importance of other influences (e.g. multinational companies and the role of stock exchanges) in the emerging commonality. Differences, both of emphasis and of a more substantial nature, still persist, and a danger not to be underestimated is that of 'pseudo-harmonisation'. This occurs when the same terms (or at least their apparent equivalents in different languages) are used to describe accounting phenomena. A useful example of this is the concept of a 'true and fair view'. Alexander and Nobes (1994: 105) provide a table of the foreign-language equivalents of this phrase within the EU. They also emphasise (*ibid.*: 106) the differences in the ways in which the phrase is interpreted in practice in different countries. These range from the UK position, where a 'true and fair view' is the fundamental requirement for financial statements, even to the extent that it overrides compliance with other elements of company law if necessary (see Chapter 4), to others where, in essence, the phrase means little more than that the financial statements comply with relevant legislation. There is also a series of countries where there are intermediate positions.

The work of the EU Commission is an example of a legislative approach to the elimination of inter-country financial reporting differences, and one made possible by the particular legislative structure of the EU. On a broader front such an approach is not possible, and 'harmonisation'/standardisation' has largely had to rely on the efforts of the accounting profession. There are a number of different international groupings of accountants, many of which are working towards the harmonisation of financial reporting practices. The principal of these are:

- *IFAC*: the International Federation of Accountants was formed in the 1970s and built on earlier collaborations, having as its principal objective the development of a coordinated worldwide accountancy profession and the harmonisation of accounting standards.
- *IAPC*: the International Auditing Practices Committee is part of the IFAC and is responsible for the production of international auditing standards.
- *IASC*: the International Accounting Standards Committee was founded in 1973 by the professional accountancy bodies of nine major economies (including the UK) with the objective of developing international accounting standards and promoting their observance. It works closely with IFAC and has developed to a point where there are over eighty countries represented in its membership. It operates in a not dissimilar way to the ASB (and its predecessor the ASC) in the UK, i.e. issuing, on an agreed basis, accounting standards (in this case International Accounting Standards, IASs), which are preceded by Exposure Drafts. Within the UK the ASB has expressed its support for the work of IASC in its aims to harmonise international financial reporting and every FRS contains a section discussing how the contents of the FRS relate to any relevant IAS and state that in most cases compliance with an FRS will lead to compliance with relevant IASs. However, the ASB has also stated that where there is conflict the requirements of the FRS should take precedence (ASB 1993c). This illustrates a core problem with the international standardisation movement, which is discussed below.
- *FEE*: the Fédération des Experts Comptables Européens was formed in 1987 by the merger of two earlier organisations and is concerned with the coordination and harmonisation of accounting issues in Europe. As such it is potentially a potent voice in the development of financial reporting practices in Europe (assuming it can achieve internal agreement amongst its members).
- *IOSCO*: the International Organisation of Securities Commissions, while not an accountancy body, has a clear interest in promoting the harmonisation of financial reporting practice and since 1995 has had a cooperation agreement with the IASC for the development of a set of international accounting standards before the end of the century but there are concerns that this schedule might not be met. As a result the IASC's secretariat has recommended that it adopt US GAAP as the IAS for financial instruments. This is raising some concern that IASs may be becoming too influenced by US GAAP, to the detriment of their international acceptability (*Accountancy*, 13 October 1997, p. 13). The intention is that IOSCO will then formally endorse these standards and its members will require their observance by companies listed on their stock exchanges. The problem is that for this to be achieved the 'new' IASC standards will have to be less 'accommodating' of national differences than existing IASs. Even then, it is not clear that national stock exchanges will be able to override other domestic legislation.

This is the 'crunch' issue. There is a significant consensus that differing financial reporting standards are costly and a hindrance to the development of international trade and financial markets. However, the elimination of these differences would entail the sacrifice by countries, at least to some extent, of their historical rights to regulate the affairs of companies operating within their national boundaries. This would be a major sacrifice of national identity, and one which, for understandable reasons, a number of countries are reluctant to make. This means that the efforts of organisations such as the IASC may lack 'clout' insofar as, while they may be estimable, they may be unenforceable on a transnational basis, especially if they conflict with local regulation. The views of the ASB referred to earlier are illustrative of this tension between national perceptions and international aspirations, as is the debate about the role of US GAAP. However, it is to be hoped that the cooperation agreement between the IASC and IOSCO will bear at least some fruit.

Conclusions

For a variety of reasons, different financial reporting practices have evolved in different countries. These different practices reflect the differing national economic, social and political contexts of countries. The problem is that, increasingly, business is a transnational activity conducted across national boundaries with stakeholders in many different countries. Thus the challenge faced by accounting and entities preparing financial statements is that of responding to the domestic requirements of the countries in which they operate and at the same time presenting a coherent, and internationally comparable, view of their affairs which is acceptable to the various regimes in which they raise finance.

In this chapter we have identified the existence of differing financial reporting principles and practices in different countries. We have identified the principal reasons why these differences have arisen and the main areas of such difference. The implications of these differences have been discussed, as have the moves to remove them via a process of 'harmonisation/'standardisation' and the various bodies involved in this process. We have concluded that, while there is a consensus about the benefits of 'harmonisation', there is not a similar consensus about the means of achieving it.

Further reading

Alexander and Nobes (1994) examine differences in financial reporting with a focus on Europe, as do Simmonds and Azières (1989). Nobes and Parker (1995) do the same on a more global scale. Ernst & Young (1992) provide numerous examples of the impact of differing financial reporting practices. The European Accounting Review carries regular articles about financial reporting differences.

Questions and exercises

1 To what extent do you believe that differences in financial reporting in different countries are a function of:
   (a) differing national legal systems;
   (b) differing structures of corporate finance;
   (c) differing taxation regimes;
   (d) the relative power of the accountancy profession.

2 What are the implications of different national financial reporting requirements for the management of multinational enterprises? Give appropriate examples of these implications.

3 How does the thrust of the work of the IASC differ from that of the EU's Company Law Harmonisation Programme?

4 Review the principal differences in the way different countries require (permit) fixed assets to be accounted for in financial statements.

5 How influential are taxation requirements in determining the nature of financial reporting in different countries?

6 Clearly explain the different factors that are involved in defining a subsidiary company in the context of 'group accounts' and how they may differ in different jurisdictions.

7 What do you believe to be the major obstacles to the 'harmonisation'/'standardisation' of financial reporting practice.

8 Obtain the annual reports of:
   (a) a company listed on the London and New York Stock Exchanges;
   (b) a company listed on the London and Tokyo Stock Exchanges.
   How do these differ?

9 Summarise the principal differences between UK and US GAAP.

10 How successful do you think the ISAC will be achieving a set of IASs that will meet the requirements of the IOSCO. Why do you hold this view?

9 The organisational context of accounting

Objectives

This chapter marks a change in direction. Whereas the first part of this book has concentrated on aspects of financial accounting and financial reporting, the second part concentrates on internal accounting – accounting for managers, usually termed **management accounting**. In order to effect the transition, this chapter is concerned with the interface between accounting and the functions of management. It summarises the major differences between financial and management accounting, and discusses how management accounting can meet the information needs of management, recognising the behavioural foundations of management accounting.

Financial and management accounting

Both financial and management accounting deal with economic events. Each requires the quantification of the outcome of economic activity, and each is concerned with revenues and expenses, assets, liabilities and cash flows. The major differences between these two forms of accounting stem from the fact that they are intended for different audiences. Financial accounting is concerned with the provision of information to individuals and organisations external to the enterprise – investors, suppliers, lenders, government, etc. Its reports deal, in summary form, with the organisation as a whole. In financial accounting, costs are usually classified by the *object* or *subject* of the expense (salaries, materials, etc.), or perhaps by the *function* of the expense (cost of goods sold, administrative expenses, etc.) Managerial accounting, on the other hand, tends to use more sophisticated cost classifications, including ones based on the *behaviour* of costs (that is, differentiating between costs that change when activity levels vary and ones that do not change regardless of activity levels); the *controllability* of costs (differentiating between the managerial responsibilities for costs); and the *variability* of costs depending on the decisions that managers take. Unlike financial accounting, which provides general-purpose financial statements, management accounting provides reports which are specifically designed for a particular user or a particular decision – or at least it should be able to do so.

Financial accounting statements tend to concentrate almost exclusively on the results of past decisions, although their preparation does, inevitably, involve management having to make judgements about the future. Management accounting concentrates on what is likely to happen in the future, although this analysis of the future has, in large part, to be based on the past. Managerial accounting is intended to assist managers to make decisions, of whatever sort. Unfortunately, the information which managers ideally want for these decisions, i.e. information about the future, is not available. The best that accountants can do is to provide appropriate information about the past. This can be conflated with information about environmental changes to enable predictions of the future to be made, perhaps so as to provide the information that managers ideally want. As Dominiak and Louderback state:

> Managerial accounting has no restrictions such as the generally accepted accounting principles that govern financial accounting. For managerial purposes, relevance is the important concern, and the managerial accountant responds to specific information requirements. For example, market prices or replacement costs or some other measure will be used in a managerial accounting report if it will help the manager make a better decision. Such alternatives are not allowed usually in financial accounting.
>
> (Dominiak and Louderback 1988: 10)

Management accounting exists to serve managers in the differing functional areas of enterprises. These managers need financial information for planning and control purposes, including decision-making and performance evaluation. Management accounting obviously applies to business firms seeking to maximise profits and achieve other economic goals. It applies equally to public-sector bodies (agencies, hospitals and the like) and other not-for-profit organisations (such as charities and churches). These latter groups need to use their resources economically, efficiently and, above all, effectively.

Meeting the information needs of management

The most important functions of management are to plan and to control the activities of the enterprises they manage. The *planning function* is the process whereby goals are established and methods developed for achieving them. It includes the important process of operational *budgeting*, formal planning – the relationship between goals and the specific means of achieving them. Managers also have to have information to assist them in *decision-making*, often seen as a sub-function of planning. Decision-making can be short-term, for example deciding whether to sub-contract some work as a result of a skills shortage, or longer-term, for example deciding when to replace ageing plant and equipment.

The *control function* is the process of assessing whether the established goals are being achieved, and, if they are not, what can be done. Operational questions arise such as: what changes need to be made in order to achieve established goals? Should existing goals be revised? Implicit in the control process is *performance evaluation* – staff managers reviewing the performance of subordinate line managers.

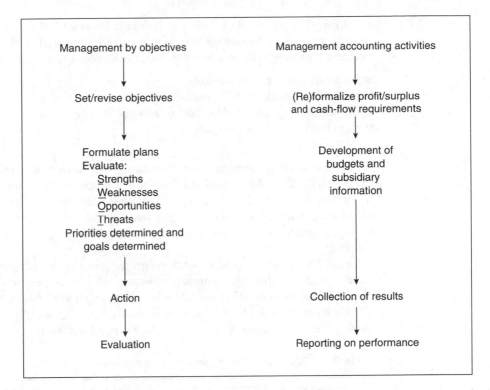

Figure 9.1
Management by
objectives and the
accounting
process.

Performance evaluation often includes the notion of *management by exception* – that is, highlighting areas of concern rather than necessarily providing too much information, much of which might simply indicate that most areas are in line with expectation. Figure 9.1 illustrates these managerial processes with the corresponding management accounting activities.

A critical issue for the management accountant is the way that information is presented. The question of the extent to which the format and content of management accounting reports influence the actions taken by managers is discussed at length in later chapters. For example, if the evaluation function is to succeed, the line manager being evaluated must know and accept the basis on which s/he is being evaluated. The information received by both the evaluator and the evaluatee must reflect and report on performance with respect to that basis. If the basis on which information is provided is not correct, this can lead to dysfunctional actions by line management. As an example, if a divisional manager were only to be assessed in terms of a return on capital employed it might be possible to 'fudge' this return in a period of economic downturn in order to give the impression that, despite difficult trading conditions, the division had achieved its target return. The problem is that by setting a performance measure expressed as a percentage return it is possible to manipulate the outcome when profits are down (a reduced numerator) by reducing the capital base (the denominator) on which the return is based. Chapter 16 considers this issue of performance evaluation further.

Information per se is of little use unless it influences the management decision-making process. Information needs to be communicated and acted upon. If the budgetary process is to be a success line management need to be motivated through:

- frequent contact about results;
- the use of results in performance appraisal;
- the use of departmental/section meetings;
- the creation of a 'game spirit'.

(Hofstede 1968: 247)

A major study of management accounting was undertaken by the AAA in 1972 (AAA 1972). This study outlined four core objectives of management accounting, which are summarised in Table 9.1. While these objectives reflect some of the priorities facing management accounting, inevitably they do not represent all the facets of the environment of management accounting. These are the subject of the ensuing chapters.

So far, little has been said about the objectives and goals of organisations. It is commonly assumed that the primary objective of private-sector enterprises is one of profit maximisation. However, this begs the question of what profit and when. An alternative statement of this objective, and one which is widely held within the capital markets, is that private-sector enterprises should act so as to maximise the value

Table 9.1   Objectives of management accounting

---

1 Management accounting should be related to the planning functions of the managers. This involves:
   - goal identification;
   - planning for optimal resource flows and their measurement.

2 Management accounting should be related to organizational problem areas. This includes:
   - relating the structure of the firm to its goals;
   - installing and maintaining an effective communication and reporting system;
   - measuring existing resource uses, discovering exceptional performance and identifying causal factors of such exceptions.

3. Management accounting should be related to the management control function. This includes:
   - determining economic characteristics of appropriate peformance areas which are significant in terms of overall goals;
   - helping to motivate desirable individual performances through a realistic communication of performance information in relation to goals;
   - highlighting performance measures indicating goal incongruity within identifiable performance and responsibility areas.

4 Management accounting should be related to operating systems management, by function, product, project or other segmentation of operations. This involves:
   - measurement of relevant cost input and/or revenue or statistical measures of outputs;
   - communication of appropriate data, of essentially economic character, to critical personnel on a timely basis.

---

of their shares. This is because share prices impute the future earnings stream of an enterprise and the accepted market assessment of the quality/riskiness of this earning stream. More specifically, the share price reflects the market's assessment of the quantity, quality and timing of the future cash flows that will be derived from the enterprise's operations. This approach gives clear guidance to management in its decision-making – it should seek to maximise the present worth of the enterprise's future cash flows; by doing this it will – assuming that the capital markets are efficient – maximise the value of its shares, thereby achieving the best results for shareholders.

What is the relationship between cash flows and profit? This can best be illustrated by considering an enterprise which has a finite life. Consider an enterprise which commenced operations on 1 January 19X0 and was wound up on 31 December 19X1. On 1 January 19X0 the owners of the enterprise subscribed £10 000 in share capital and on that date the enterprise purchased a machine costing £10 000. On the same date it rented this machine to a client on a two-year agreement at an annual rental of £6000. The enterprise forecast that the machine would have a market value of £4000 as at 31 December 19X1 and intended to use the straight-line basis for depreciation in the profit and loss account. Assuming all transactions are on a cash basis, the enterprise would show the following for its financial year ended 31 December 19X0:

	£
Rental income	6000
Depreciation (£10 000 – £4000) ÷ 2	3000
Profit	3000

Assuming that the forecast market value of the machine as at 31 December 19X1 is correct and that the machine is sold for this amount on that date, the profit and loss account for the year ending on that date would be the same as that shown above for the year ended 31 December 19X0, i.e. it would show a profit of £3000, and the position over the two years would be:

	19X0	*19X1*	*Total*
Rental income	6 000	6 000	12 000
Depreciation	3 000	3 000	6 000
Profit	3 000	3 000	6 000

The corresponding cash flows from the enterprise's perspective would be:

	19X0	*19X1*	*Total*
Received from investors	10 000		10 000
Paid for machine	(10 000)		(10 000)
Received from client	6 000	6 000	12 000
Received from sale of machine		4 000	4 000
	6 000	10 000	16 000

On its liquidation, the enterprise would be able to pay the investors £16 000, representing a cash gain of £6000 (£16 000 less the original investment of £10 000). That is, the total profit of £6000 shown above is exactly equal to the total cash gain to the investors. However, this profit has been apportioned, using the straight-line depreciation method, equally between the two years involved. This would not be the case if another method of depreciation, such as the reducing-balance method, was used (see Chapter 3 for the relevant formula). If this were done the profit and loss account would be:

	19X0 *£*	*19X1* *£*	*Total* *£*
Rental income	6 000	6 000	12 000
Depreciation	3 680	2 320	6 000
Profit	2 320	3 680	6 000

In this case the profit and loss accounts show a lower profit in the first year, and a higher one in the second year, although the *total* profit over the two years is the same and equals the total cash gain from the investors' perspective. Ultimately, the investors (shareholders) will be primarily concerned with this total cash gain (receiving it either directly via distributions or indirectly via its being imputed in the share price). Profit is nothing more than a performance measure which allocates this cash gain to individual account periods in an attempt to enable shareholders to assess how successfully the enterprise is pursuing the objective of increasing the cash (wealth) ultimately attributable to them. Different accounting bases (e.g. depreciation policies) will result in different allocations of this cash gain across accounting periods.

While this is a problem for financial accounting it should not be so for management/management accounting – here the focus should be clearly on cash flows and not on profit. Such a focus will ensure that management orients itself to what is the ultimate objective of private-sector enterprises – increasing shareholder wealth.

In the public sector the notion of maximisation of profit or share value is replaced by a requirement to keep costs to a minimum and to ensure the provision of services which represent value for money (see Chapter 6). In practice, business enterprises have a number of operational goals or effectiveness criteria which include 'maximising' or 'satisfying', profitability, market position, product leadership, throughput and productivity. The purposes of such goals range from the motivation of individuals, the recruitment of capital and other resources, the focusing of attention or direction, to the determination of a rationale or ideal for which the enterprise and the members aim. Since these purposes differ problems arise in operationalising them. It is beyond the scope of this book to examine in detail the issues that enterprises face in formulating and operationalising goals or objectives. Useful reviews of these issues can be found in work by Cyert and March (1963), Perrow (1970) and Simon (1957), as well as Freeman (1985), who raises the following questions:

- Should broad abstracts (such as good corporate citizenship) or specific goals (such as maximise market value) be used?

- How easy is the measurement of good performance? Broad abstracts are harder to measure than specific goals and therefore more difficult to build into a reward system.
- How congruent and consistent are the various goals (for instance good corporate citizenship v. market-value maximisation or short term v. long term)?
- How, and how quickly, do goals change?
- Are goals really determined by the organisation itself, or by its environment or by individuals within the organisation? In the first case the organisation has the power (in terms of competition, bargaining, absorption and coalition) to determine its own goals. In the second case the organisation has no power and so its goals are in direct response to its environment, requiring more cooperation and interaction. In the third case the goals are determined by the informal/formal coalition of its members' goals. Power is determined by dominant members, previous experience and commitments of individuals; bargaining and side payments through the internal and external political process.

If management accounting information is to be of use within the organisation it must be framed within a system that is appropriate to the specific circumstances in which an organisation finds itself. The aim of such information is to influence management behaviour towards the achievement of a particular goal or set of goals, 'the provision of information that will assist managers to guide their organisations in appropriate directions' (Emmanuel and Otley 1985: 68). The structure of an organisation is itself a potent form of control because by arranging people in a hierarchy with defined patterns of authority and responsibility it is possible to influence or even predetermine a great deal of their behaviour.

Over the decades, theorists have speculated about how organisations should be managed. This section concludes by reviewing three groups of management theories about the design of organisations. These are classical management theory, systems theory and decision-making theory.

Classical management theory

Three main strands can be identified within this category: scientific management, administrative theory and industrial psychology. Much of this work was developed and published before the 1950s. The scientific management school of thought was established by F. W. Taylor (1947). Taylor had an interesting career, rising from labourer to the position of chief engineer of a large US steel factory. He saw labour as simply a means of accomplishing mechanical tasks. There is a 'right way' or a 'wrong way' to accomplish activity. Motivation to perform a task the 'right way' was achieved solely by economic reward. Although Taylor was criticised for much of his approach, it is certainly true that his work has influenced many present-day techniques of work measurement and systems of payment, some aspects of the development of organisation and methods (O&M) analysis and standard costing (see Chapter 15). Administrative theory, based on the work of Henri Fayol (1949; originally published in French in 1914), is similar to the scientific school of thought but relates to administrative rather than physical work. Administrative theorists, as do scientific management theorists, believe that, regardless of the task, there is only one best way of organising it. The industrial-psychology school of thought had as its founding father E. Mayo (1933), who investigated the effects of social and work conditions, as well as individual factors, on worker productivity. While many have criticised the results of Mayo's research, he must be credited for having been the first to stimulate interest in the social environment of the workplace. His ideas spawned a series of work in the 1950s and 1960s (see Maslow 1954; Herzberg 1959; Likert 1961; McGregor 1960; Stedry 1960; Argyris 1964). For example, Stedry's work concluded that a moderately difficult budgeted standard of performance which was perceived by the budgetee as 'tight, yet attainable' motivates the best performance. Although Otley (1977) has criticised the experimental design of such work, this view nevertheless persists in nearly all management accounting texts.

Classical management theory seeks to find the 'best way' to organise, to manage or to motivate. As such its philosophy, at least implicitly, underpins much of the present-day approach to management accounting.

Systems theory

Systems theory seeks to study the activities undertaken within an organisation by reference to the context of the wider environment in which it is set. Emmanuel and Otley note that the basic premise of understanding organisational behaviour is that 'the organisation is profoundly affected by, and dependent upon, its environment and that its ultimate survival is determined by the degree to which it is able to adapt and accommodate itself to environmental contingencies' (Emmanuel and Otley 1985: 39). Writers such as Katz and Khan (1966) view the organisation as a social system; indeed, as a series of subsystems. Their approach is to guide organisational design towards integrating the activities of the different subsystems in order to, as a minimum, perpetuate the survival of the organisations. Some accounting researchers have been influenced by this approach to understanding organisational issues. However, little practical application has been offered to date. Despite this, systems theory has provided the base from which contingent benefits theory has been derived. The basic premise provided by a contingency framework is that the design of organisational structure is an important mechanism for achieving organisational control and that different structures are appropriate in different circumstances.

Decision-making theory

This third school of thought concentrates on organisational information flows and decision-making processes. As such, it combines elements of administrative theory, a human relations approach, systems theory and concepts of decision-making. The basic premise suggested by this theory is that of 'limited rationality'. Because individuals have limited powers of understanding and can only deal with limited amounts of information at any one time, they display limited rationality. This view implies that when seeking to solve a problem an individual will examine various options until the first acceptable solution is found, rather than continuing to search until the best or optimal solution is found. Such rationality implies that individuals tend to be 'satisfiers'. Translating this view to a management context means that managers tend to 'satisfy' and 'muddle through'. An improved knowledge of the human decision-making process, such as is provided by decision-making theory, has had a number of impacts on the ways that management accounting information is presented.

With this background to organisational theory design we are able to examine in more detail some of the behavioural foundations of management accounting.

Two alternative approaches to control-system design

Earlier we saw that internal accounting information is only useful if it assists managers in managing their organisation. This discussion was set against a recognition that many researchers have sought to further our understanding of the dynamics of organisational design. As Freeman states:

> To ensure that organisations meet their objectives, key decision-makers in these organisations need to understand and design appropriate control systems. Under different organisational settings cause/effect relationships become more uncertain, hence an optimal control system achieves its objectives by minimising information uncertainties.
>
> (Freeman 1985: 1)

We now consider the two alternative approaches to control-system design that feature most commonly in the literature on management accounting: the contingent benefits model that derives from the behavioural literature (referred to above) and the agency model that is described in the finance literature.

Otley states that the contingency approach to management accounting:

> is based on the premise that there is no universally appropriate accounting system which applies equally to all organisations in all circumstances. Rather, it is suggested that particular features of an appropriate accounting system will depend upon the specific circumstances in which an organisation finds itself.
>
> (Otley 1980: 413)

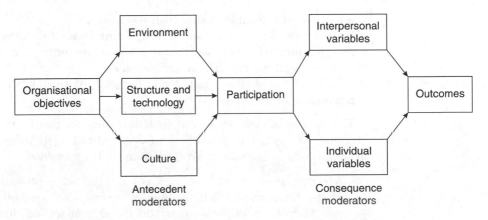

Figure 9.2
The Brownwell contingency model.

(*Source*: adapted from Freeman 1985)

Internal accounting control systems need, therefore, to be designed so as to achieve an optimum combination of these control variables. Several researchers have suggested models which help describe this process. For example, Brownell's (1982) model focuses on one particular control-system variable, participation, to assess in which 'situations' it is appropriate (see Figure 9.2).

The contingency literature has typically focused on two critical contextual variables which describe an organisation's contextual setting: *environment* and *technology*.

Environment

Clearly, the more dynamic an organisation, the more important it is for it to adapt quickly to change in order to survive. The more complicated the environment in which an organisation exists, the more complex will be the internal accounting system required to maintain control and the more uncertain will be the information flows it generates. Environmental factors can include:

- the competitive climate for a product/service;
- the economic climate (e.g. business cycle, role of government);
- the ecological climate (e.g. social/anti-social behaviour, pollution controls);
- the legal climate;
- the cultural climate;
- the demographic climate.

Technology

The less routine the production runs of an enterprise are or the less uniformity there is in its service provision, the less easy it will be to programme work jobs and, consequently, the less elaborate will be the technical features of the internal accounting system. More reliance will need to be placed on social controls such as those associated with the work of supervisors. As uncertainty increases because of environmental or technological complexity, better performance can only be achieved by structures which:

- are organic (or flexible) rather than mechanistic;
- include more interactive mechanisms, with increased differentiation;
- are decentralised, with structured lines of authority, and make use of more specialist staff, particularly as size increases;
- increasingly emphasise external, non-financial information (in addition to internal accounting information).

The agency model, which was first developed in the 1970s, follows traditional economic theory and it views the firm as a nexus of relationships among individuals making up the organisation. To quote one of its exponents:

> Agency theory research focuses on the optimal contractual relationships of the firm, where each member is assumed to be motivated solely by self interest. . . . In the agency model, one or more individuals (the principals) hire one or more persons (the agents) for the purpose of delegating

responsibilities to the latter. The rights and responsibilities of the members of the firm are specified in the firm's mutually agreed employment contracts. . . . In the agency model, the firm's employment contracts are optimal functions of the information supplied by the firm's managerial account information system. . . . Agency theory therefore provides a model from which uses of managerial accounting information can be derived and studied.

(Baimen 1985)

Under this approach, each individual makes decisions to maximise his/her total utility by equating the marginal utility from pecuniary (extrinsic) and non-pecuniary (intrinsic) rewards or consumption, given an available opportunity set. The agency perspective views the overriding organisational objective, irrespective of its specific business context, to be one of the maximising market value or wealth to the providers of capital. When applied to management, the thrust of the theory is the need to control management actions so that the decisions it takes do not diverge from the interests of the firm's owners. According to this view, for internal accounting to be effective it is important that the systems it deploys recognise the manager–shareholder relationship, the executive manager–line manager relationship and the manager–employee relationship. Given that there is one overriding organisational objective, proponents of agency theory argue that internal control systems, including internal accounting systems, are easier to model.

The contingency and the agency theory models have contrasting views on the hierarchical structure of organisations, even though they both strive to achieve the same outcome, effective organisational control. Of the two models, the behavioural (contingency) model is the more developed, both theoretically and empirically.

Why should managers need to understand the basic principles incorporated in each of these models? The reason is simple: many internal accounting systems are premised on the designer's particular views on how the organisation is or should be managed. If there is a general criticism of accountants by managers it is that, all too often, internal accounting systems do not really reflect the specific circumstances in which the organisation finds itself. Managers need to agree on the organisational structure that best suits their needs, and accountants need to 'tailor' accounting information requirements to that structure in order to provide relevant control information. Chapter 19 expands on this discussion by considering the accounting needs of strategic planning.

Accountability and control: a public-sector perspective

As stated above, in the public sector the notion of the maximisation of profit or share value is replaced by a requirement to keep costs to a minimum and to ensure that the provision of services represents value for money. A number of different accountability relationships have to be accommodated. To illustrate some of these complexities we consider some of the organisational contexts of accounting that exist in the NHS. Before continuing our discussion it is useful to summarise these and other implied accountabilities:

- professional disciplinary/occupational accountabilities;
- managerial accountabilities;
- interdepartmental accountabilities;
- purchaser accountabilities;
- financial/fiscal accountabilities;
- public/consumer accountabilities.

Each of these accountabilities requires a control system if it is to be real. The change from a hierarchy to a more market-based philosophy has altered the importance and pattern of these accountabilities. Professional accountabilities have virtually disappeared – except in the case of doctors – being replaced by managerial accountabilities in which individuals are accountable to general managers or managers from different disciplines. This can be traced to the introduction of general management in the 1980s.

In the case of doctors, accountabilities have changed with the introduction of a contract which specifies volume, cost and quality of services. Clinical decisions remain the province of the doctor. Although the rhetoric of clinical audit has produced many short-term projects and investigations, it would be inaccurate to suggest that there is yet a consistent pattern of clinical audit in the UK. Cost and volume contracts concern the type and levels of activity which can be undertaken, and clinicians must take account of the timing of their work load and their productivity. The accountability of the clinical director varies between providers and is often delegated in practice to the business manager, who, like the old administrator, has responsibility but very little power (or information?).

Interdepartmental accountability has been forced on service departments within provider units since they have no patients for whom they can charge. This raises questions of transfer charging to those departments which refer patients for investigations etc.

Purchaser accountability centres on the need to ensure that the services for which they contract provide value for money. This too creates the need for control systems; these are not actually directly provided by the purchaser but are subcontracted to the provider. It is the provider who draws up protocols, institutes clinical and internal audit control, and attempts to monitor patient outcome. Financial/fiscal accountabilities have remained materially unchanged since they are driven by the fixed revenue voted to the NHS and the Treasury's concern to control capital spending. All that the market has achieved is, linked to the need to ensure value for money, a division of financial accountability at the operational level.

Public accountability, previously seen as synonymous with political accountability, is largely discharged through the operation of the Patients' Charter (a set of activity indicators), the activity of the Community Health Council (a toothless watchdog), consultation between purchaser and the local community (limited in its application), and less so in terms of the national process. Politicians might have thought that with the introduction of *new public management* (NPM) they had managed to devolve this responsibility to chief executives and managers, but serious problems, as ever, inevitably still end up on their doorstep.

Accountability in the pre-market NHS left much to be desired, and the same could be said for the control systems that were in place. Some improvements have resulted in the current emphasis on the NPM philosophy, but more needs to be done to ensure that resources are used effectively. (For more on the background to this NPM philosophy, see Glynn and Perkins 1997). All control systems require objectives, measures or standards, a measurement process, interpretation of data, appropriate reporting lines and (where appropriate) management action at the appropriate level. Authors (e.g. Perkins 1996; Stacey 1993) often distinguish three types of control: feedback control, concurrent control and feedforward control. Feedback control is the more traditional from of control in the NHS. It is a slow-acting form of control, since the interpretation of data and subsequent action can take place well after the activity which is supposed to be controlled. End-of-period feedback on financial performance can do nothing for that period's performance. Management can only look to make improvements in the future. Likewise, studies of clinical outcome are of primary benefit to new generations of patients, not to the subjects of the study. The contracting process still, despite refinements, requires much ex-post reconciliation and adjustment to agree actual expenditure incurred within contract, to link expenditure to workload, and reconcile the timing and delivery of workload to that agreed in the contract.

Concurrent control operates through continual adjustment so that the management action is taken as soon as possible to prevent major deviations from planned courses of action before they occur. In some areas these types of system are being introduced, but generally to manage lower-order problems such as patient-flow management in clinics and outpatient departments. Feedforward control systems are required in situations of high risk and they are designed to try and 'control before the event'. For example, a radiotherapist may use a computer to simulate a treatment before the patient is treated in order to make the actual treatment as effective as possible and to avoid causing unnecessary tissue damage. However, few feedforward control systems exist to model patient flows and to measure, for example, the need for spare bed capacity. A well-voiced current concern within the NHS is the fact that the contracting process virtually eliminates spare capacity to deal with unanticipated demand. Effective control processes need, increasingly, to be more like concurrent or feedforward control processes, but this also implies a much greater emphasis on planning, which is in many respects a move away from market mechanisms. It also implies structured and integrated accountabilities in order to permit effective control systems to operate.

Conclusions

Management accounting exists to serve the needs of managers for information to assist them in discharging their planning, deciding and controlling responsibilities. The differing nature of enterprises, in both the private and public sectors, means that there is no single universally applicable system of management accounting. Instead, effective management accounting systems reflect their organisational context and the information needs of managers. There is no legal regulation of management accounting, unlike financial accounting. However, it does have an underpinning philosophy – it must be useful and cost-effective, and must provide information about the past, for control purposes, and about the future, for decision-making purposes.

This chapter has recognised that the two major roles of accounting – providing reports on financial performance for external shareholders (financial reporting) and assisting managers to manage more effectively (management accounting) – require different perspectives. The orientation of financial reporting is towards the past, with a focus on how much profit an enterprise has generated in a given financial period, and it operates in an increasingly regulated framework. Management accounting needs to have a future orientation, although this needs to be firmly grounded on reliable information about the past. Only by achieving this can it assist management in its various functions. Management accounting needs to reflect the environmental, technological and organisational contexts in which it exists, and to recognise that the focus of management should be the maximisation of the future cash flows which will derive from its decisions.

Further reading

There is a vast literature on the subject matter covered in this chapter. Hofstede's 1968 text is still a valuable read. The title, *The Game of Budget Control*, outlines well the theme of the book. Perkins (1996) is worth a read by those interested in public-sector issues. Argenti's text *Practical Corporate Planning* (1983) provides a useful general background to much of the discussion of this chapter.

Questions and exercises

1 Do you think that management accounting should be more tightly regulated? Should/could management accounting standards be set? Discuss.

2 Critically discuss, using examples, the relationship between cash and profit.

3 Why are cash and cash-flow analysis so fundamental to many of the techniques adopted by management accountants?

4 Stedry (1960) has concluded that a moderately difficult budgeted standard of performance which is perceived by the budgetee as 'tight, yet attainable' motivates the best performance. Do you agree? Why/why not?

5 'Traditionally, financial researchers have dealt almost exclusively with data that can be quantified in a predetermined way; in doing so, they have disregarded evidence on the psychological aspects of decision-making.' Discuss.

6 Of what value is 'agency theory' to our understanding of how individuals co-exist in an organisation?

7 Use Figure 9.1 to map out the key control systems within an organisation with which you are familiar. Do you consider that this organisation has a sound system of internal control?

8 To what extent do you think that internal management accounting reports have to be reconcilable with external financial statements?

9 What do you believe have been the dominant influences in the design of a management accounting system with which you are familiar?

10 To what extent is it fair to say that control and accountability in the public sector are more difficult to systematise given the conflicting interests of the various interested parties?

10 Cost concepts and measurements

Objectives

There are many individual concepts and measurements of 'cost', and sometimes these are confusing, or even conflicting. Different costs (or cost information) may be needed for financial accounting and external reporting, for forward planning for short-term as distinct from long-term decision-making, and for budgetary and other forms of management control. The objective of this chapter is to clarify this diversity as a background to the topic discussions in the chapters which follow.

Cost is a sacrifice through resource loss, consumption or transformation. The choice of cost concepts and measurements is affected by the type of decision or control situation, by the timespan with which we are concerned, by how identifiable or traceable is the cost data which is available, and by the type of production or other business (or public-service) activity that is being carried out. Here we have a particular concern for opportunity cost, fixed v. variable costs, direct v. indirect costs, and historical and absorption costs v. costs relevant for management planning, decisions and control.

Fundamental concepts

True cost

True cost is a statement or measurement of sacrifice. This sacrifice is the loss, consumption or surrender of resources, value, benefit or welfare. The purchase of goods involves the surrender of cash or the taking on of debt. Using raw materials in a factory involves the cost of consumption of the materials, although this cost is then transformed into new value in the production process (after allowing for any process waste, pilferage, etc.). Losing a watch involves cost in the form of the value of the loss, which could be measured by the original price of the watch or by the price of replacing it, according to the context of our concern or the decision facing us. Losing a briefcase may be viewed similarly, but if the briefcase was full of business or personal papers there will be more complex and intangible problems in assessing the total cost, or sacrifice, arising from this loss.

Opportunity cost

Opportunity cost is the measure of benefit forgone by using scarce resources to follow one option to the exclusion of the next-best option. Thus using a limited bank balance to buy a car may make it necessary to forgo a holiday; the opportunity cost is the forgone net satisfaction from the holiday. Using funds from trading profits to increase dividend payments may pre-empt the opportunity to purchase new, cost-saving machinery.

Opportunity cost is an important concept derived from economics. Opportunity costs are not routinely recorded in accounting records or reports. Rather, they arise in the mind, or on the back of an envelope, of the manager or decision-maker. They are often extremely important for good planning and decision-making, and the concept helps to emphasise that routine accounting information by itself seldom provides a sufficient basis for forward planning and decisions. Routine accounting records and reports provide information on past costs and revenues, but this is seldom a reliable predictor of the future as it takes no account of choice, uncertainty or risk.

Cash and accrual accounting

Simple accounting systems equate cost with cash expenditure. This is the basis of much governmental accounting because Parliament votes allocations of cash to specified public programmes and organisations, and the accounting task is to record and report the receipt and disbursement of authorised cash for the resources used. Small businesses may find it sufficient to keep their records wholly or mainly on a cash basis. And most of us, as private individuals, find it sufficient to operate our personal and housekeeping budgets on a cash basis. Cash costs, or cash-flow costs, are also sometimes known as outlay costs or as out-of-pocket expenses.

However, in the case of organisations, even governmental bodies where cash-flow accounting is adequate, or indeed required by law for financial accounting to fulfil parliamentary accountability, it has been increasingly recognised in recent years that the cash-flow basis is not sufficient for effective management accounting. For example, a hospital may buy X-ray film only once a year, so as to earn the maximum quantity discount. One year it buys in April (i.e. in the first month of the governmental financial year) and again in the following March. Perhaps then its stocks are sufficient not to need to reorder at all in the second financial year. On a cash-costs basis, it would show a double cost in the first year and no cost at all in the second year. This information would be greatly misleading for management control, so to support the cash accounting system it is important to introduce accrual accounting in the management accounts. In business firms, accrual accounting is used in both the financial accounts and the management accounts, and this may also soon become standard practice throughout the public sector.

Under an accrual accounting system the cash or debt outlay costs of resources which are not consumed at time of purchase are debited to asset accounts, e.g. for raw materials stocks, and these asset accounts are then credited or drawn down as the costs of materials consumed are recorded through the year. This is the basis for historical costing methods (see below), which link the financial and management accounting systems for corporate stewardship purposes.

Costs for different purposes

This chapter seeks to demonstrate that cost can be defined and measured in different ways. There is no single 'one correct way'. The most appropriate 'measure of cost is dependent upon the purpose for which it is required' (Parker 1984: 59). The three main purposes for which cost information is required are stewardship accounting, management control, and planning and decision-making. Stewardship accounting is accounting recording, and reporting for accountability and information for parties external to management: shareholders, creditors, regulators, tax collectors and, sometimes, employees and the general public.

The other two main purposes relate primarily to internal information for management, and they are interlinked. Management control is the function of measuring how well management plans and decisions are being achieved, and of providing guidance to any corrective action needed to improve the achievement of, or to amend, these targeted plans and decisions. Decision-making relates to specific problems, opportunities and new plans. In spite of being interlinked, these two main purposes for cost information often require different and distinctive cost concepts and measures to be used. A major reason for this is that cost-control information is concerned with the present and the recent past, while planning and decision-making information is concerned with the future, sometimes the short term and sometimes the long term. A complication is that many costs have a different significance, or a different measurement, according to the length of the time-horizon relevant to particular management decisions and planning activities. Short-term decisions are discussed in Chapter 11 and long-term decisions in Chapter 13.

Costs related to time and activity

Some business costs are constant or 'fixed' over a period of time, regardless of the volume of output or activity, while others will change with normal activity and can be described as 'variable'. In theory, over a long enough period of time, time-related fixed costs can be terminated, so that for the long term all costs may be considered as variable. But most cost analysis is concerned with business behaviour in the short term, both for management control and for decision-making, so that the separate identification and measurement of fixed costs and variable costs provide useful information.

Fixed costs

Fixed costs are those costs which are independent of the current level of activity and which are not expected to change in the short term, except for minor revisions for inflation, contract renewal, etc. As in most accounting measurement and reporting, the 'short term' for this purpose is usually taken to mean a period of one year ahead or the current financial and budget year of the firm. Examples of fixed costs include business rates, premises rental, equipment lease payments, and the salaries of permanent staff whose work is essential and unrelated to the level of short-term activity, e.g. the managing director, most accounting staff, security staff. Fixed costs are included in the 'overheads' of the business, but there are additional overheads (such as company car expenses) which are at least partly comprised of variable costs.

Fixed costs (FC) can be categorised into three main types:

1 Committed costs are costs deriving from ongoing legal or contractual obligations (e.g. rates, insurance premiums, rent, etc.) which typically could not be terminated short of winding up the business.
2 Managed costs include the salaries of staff essential to the continuance of current activity, together with other support costs of the organisation.
3 Programmed (or discretionary) fixed costs include the costs of services not directly linked to current operations or activity but which instead follow policy decisions to support corporate development. Examples include R&D, some personnel and training activities, and some marketing and promotional activities (e.g. sports and arts sponsorship).

Figure 10.1 illustrates these three types of fixed costs. Committed costs (CC) have a long time-horizon commitment, often for the life of the business. Managed costs (MC) have a shorter time-horizon, although frequently this is greater than a year unless it is upset by deep business recession. Programmed costs (PC), at least in theory, have the shortest time-horizon, being governed by the annual budget cycle for funding renewal; in practice, however, staffing and capital-spending programmes (e.g. in R&D) may make it difficult to cut even this category of fixed cost within as short a period as the next budget year. Programmed costs may also be termed discretionary costs. The distinctions between these three categories of fixed costs may be arbitrary to some extent, but (as can be seen in Figure 10.1) they help to illustrate that all fixed costs do not behave in the same way and that they can have widely different degrees of fixedness through time.

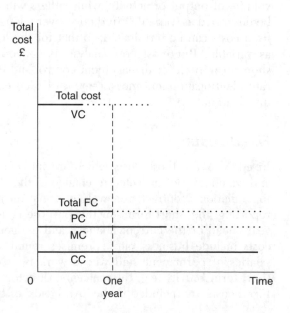

Figure 10.1
Fixed and variable costs related to time.

Variable costs

Variable costs comprise those costs which arise more or less in direct proportion to the level of activity, or the volume of output or of trading, occurring in the firm. The major variable costs are the payroll cost of employees working directly on operations and the costs of bought-in stocks used (whether raw materials, components or finished goods ready for resale). These are the 'prime costs' of the operations of a business, but, additionally, some overhead or indirect costs can be measured and controlled as variable costs because they are directly linked to operational activity; industrial examples include energy, supplies, lubricants and usage-linked equipment maintenance.

Figure 10.1 includes a line for variable cost (VC). Here it is assumed that activity remains at a constant level, so that total VC could, or should, also remain a constant over the short-term planning and budgeting cycle of a typical year. This assumption is usually unrealistic, with total VC changing through the year as activity levels change in response to seasonal, market and other influences.

Mixed costs

Some costs do not fit neatly into either the fixed-cost or variable-cost categories. These are the semi-fixed costs and semi-variable costs, collectively termed 'mixed costs'. Semi-fixed costs, also called 'step costs', are costs of a fixed or constant character which increase at intervals as activity rises: examples include the need to employ an additional supervisor or to lease an additional machine as output rises. Semi-variable costs are more subtle. At low outputs, labour may be inefficient, especially on new product runs where a 'learning curve' must be experienced before full efficiency is reached. At very high outputs stress, weariness, overcrowding and haste may increase waste and slow the production rate of both labour and machinery.

In Figure 10.2 we bring together the three kinds of time- and activity-related costs previously described. (FC1 indicates the fixed costs, VC1 the variable costs, and MC the mixed costs.) The figure shows the costs as solid lines over the normal range of activity and as dotted lines at the extremes of low and very high activity. An enterprise may have little or no experience of working outside the normal range of activity and therefore no firm evidence of what the costs would be. Another complication is that accountants find it awkward to track mixed costs in routine reporting and they prefer to estimate the semi-fixed costs as if they were fixed, at least over the normal range, and the semi-variable costs as if they were fully variable. The result of this is that the conventional cost–activity diagram does not show mixed costs but, instead, just the subdivision between fixed costs (FC2) and variable costs (VC2) on the basis **as if** these costs retained the same relationship throughout the entire activity range as they do within the normal range. It follows that conventional accounting estimates of the expected level of 'fixed + variable = total cost' at the extremes of the activity range may not be reliable. This may not be too important at very high levels of activity, where total costs should be well covered by revenue, but it could lead to critical misjudgements by a firm operating at low activity, e.g. during a recession, as regards the hidden 'variable' costs that may be incurred, and also as regards the potential for cutting some 'fixed' costs in the short term.

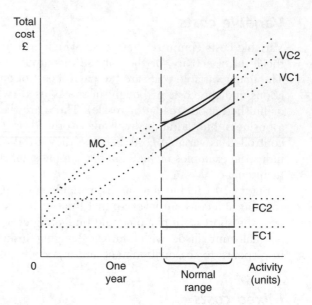

Figure 10.2
Total costs related
to activity.

Figures 10.1 and 10.2 show the subdivisions of **total costs** in relation to time or activity. But often it is more useful to study the behaviour of **unit costs** (i.e. costs per unit of activity, be this production, sales or service activity). This is illustrated in Figure 10.3. Once again, the costs are shown by solid lines over the normal range of activity and by dotted lines over the extreme ranges. Unit variable cost is assumed to be a constant value, at least over the normal range of activity. But fixed costs per unit fall as output increases. The same total values of FC2 and VC2 are used for Figure 10.3 as for Figure 10.2; the only difference is that they are displayed on the basis of cost per unit instead of total costs. Figure 10.3 confirms how unit cost falls as output rises, at least through to the upper end of the normal activity range, and this has important implications for the pricing decisions we shall consider in Chapter 12. Beyond the normal range of activity, for which staffing, equipment and space have been planned, there may arise significant extra semi-fixed and semi-variable costs (i.e. MC), which will need management review of output and pricing policy and decisions.

In Figure 10.3 the FC2 line shows the total of combined fixed and variable unit costs (after subsuming mixed costs). This can be termed 'total unit cost', 'full cost' or 'average unit cost' (ACR). ACR stands for 'average cost, rising', because cost calculations by accountants are usually based on the assumption of stable or rising activity levels. However, activity or output can fall as well as rise, and some of the variable costs and mixed costs can prove 'sticky' or slow in contracting on a downward movement of activity compared to their timing and rate of increase when the activity level is rising. This is a frequent cause of difficulty for firms during a recession or other cause of decline or contraction. This is illustrated in Figure 10.4 by the curve ACF (average cost, falling).

During periods of falling market activity, it is important for managers to be vigilant and keep variable and mixed costs under control so that they remain close to

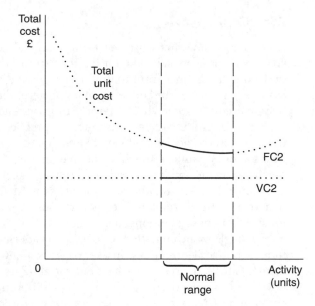

Figure 10.3
Unit costs related
to activity.

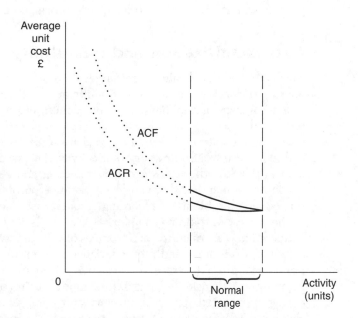

Figure 10.4
Average unit
costs with activity
changes.

the baseline represented by ACR. In practice, some managements may try to squeeze unit costs below ACR by pressing for higher productivity in variable costs, or by cutting out certain fixed costs. Here the programmed or discretionary costs such as staff training or R&D activity are most vulnerable, but drastic cuts in these policy areas of corporate activity can seriously weaken a firm's long-term capacity for revival and growth.

Marginal cost

Accountants sometimes use the term 'marginal cost' as synonymous with 'variable cost', perhaps especially when using the term in the context of decision-making and budgeting, as distinct from routine reporting and control. This can be confusing for readers who have studied economics, where the meaning and measurement of marginal cost is somewhat different. In economics marginal cost is defined as the extra cost of producing one extra unit. In practice this is usually the same, or nearly the same, as the accountant's unit variable cost. However, the economist assumes a continuous curvilinear function for marginal cost, so that the marginal cost of the second extra unit added, or deleted, is always slightly different from that of the first extra unit. In contrast, the accountant, as we have seen, assumes that variable or marginal unit cost remains a constant across a normal range of activity. Of course, for most business decisions, one is not working in the context of making or selling only a single extra unit. Rather, one is considering some larger number of units to fulfil a contract, enter a new market or stock a new branch, etc. For decision-making in such situations, one must look out for all costs which may change, including any new fixed or mixed costs. This involves differential cost analysis, which we shall consider in Chapter 11. But first we must consider some of the terminology and problems of identifying and tracing cost information.

Cost identification and traceability

Cost is the sacrificed value of resources used or consumed. This value comprises the physical quantity of resources used multiplied by the unit 'prices' of those resources. The accountant usually has access to accurate information on resource prices, from invoice files, payroll records, etc. But accountants must depend upon managers for providing accurate information on what resources are used, in what quantity, when, and to achieve what output or other activity. The accountant usually will provide, or help to develop, the necessary data collection and recording systems. Where work is non-uniform and/or there are many separate outputs drawing on common support services, the problems of recording resource use data accurately and tracing them to the correct output are complex.

Recording the quantity of resources used, and when, is fairly straightforward, although it is tedious and requires vigilance to ensure continuing accuracy. The big problem is often to trace the resource usage to a specific output (required for planning and decision-making information) and to the accountability of a specific manager (required for the budgetary and management control discussed in later chapters). To achieve this traceability of costs we need to introduce some additional concepts for classifying costs and handling cost information.

Direct costs

Direct costs are costs which can be accurately traced to specific activities, outputs, contracts or decisions (or, in control accounting, to budgetary accountability). The most obvious direct costs are the costs of labour and materials directly used in a specific activity to provide a specific output; these costs are known as 'direct labour' and 'direct material', and added together they are called 'prime cost'. Sometimes equipment use and some support services are so specific or committed to just one purpose that their costs also can be included as traceable direct costs.

Indirect costs

Indirect costs comprise all costs and expenses which are not directly traced to specific products, activities or outputs. Common examples include heating and lighting, consumable supplies, equipment and buildings maintenance, and all central services. In practice the demarcation between direct and indirect cost is as much a matter of convenience and of whether or not more precise information is worth the expense of providing it, as it is a matter of inherent nature. For example, in universities and many other organisations telephone use was treated as a general overhead expense and was not divided among departments. Then an attempt was made to estimate telephone use for recharge to departmental costs and budgets. However, the latter estimates were too tenuous or uncertain to carry conviction for enforcing cost control and reduction. So the final stage, when cost-effective technology became available, was to install expensive telephone logging equipment, so that the use, and cost of use, of every separate telephone extension could be recorded and then be recharged as an accountable direct cost to the user departments. Where telephone use cost fell by more than the annualised cost of new equipment and the monitoring and book-keeping involved, then, clearly, converting an indirect cost into a direct cost could prove worthwhile. The detailed metering of energy consumption, especially in factories, provides another example where traditional treatment as an indirect cost can usefully be reorganised to permit recording and charging as a direct cost. In contrast, in a factory producing furniture where pots of glue stand ready beside the work-benches it probably will not be worth the 'cost of costing' to set up a control procedure to allow glue consumption to be charged as a direct cost to each unit or batch of product completed.

Overhead and period costs

The strict definition of 'overhead' or 'overhead costs' is that this comprises all expenses not charged to output as direct costs (sometimes just direct labour and direct material). More generally, it is widely held that some indirect costs can be traced and estimated sufficiently accurately to be usefully charged to products, activities or at least their host departments, and that we should restrict the use of the term 'overhead' to those expenses which are remote from productive activities and remote from any effective control or accountability by the managers of those activities. Examples include rent, rates and the costs of head office and central services.

Product costs, both direct and indirect, are carried forward into completed stock/inventory value and should not be recharged against corporate profit and loss until the year in which they are sold. In contrast, the general overheads defined above relate more to keeping the business in being than to specific products or production levels. In this context they are termed 'period costs' and should be charged to corporate profit and loss in the year in which they are incurred. This latter group of costs includes the expenses of promotion, distribution and sales, which are normally very remote from production activity, outputs and costs.

Common costs and joint costs

Common costs are defined as 'costs of facilities and services shared by a number of departments' (Parker 1984: 39). Such facilities and services may include a development department, engineering workshops, drawing office, maintenance department, as well as central services such as personnel and training. The use of the term 'common costs' tends to imply that these costs will be treated as overheads, but often they are best charged to user departments as indirect costs, or even as direct costs where a direct linkage can be traced between specific service provision and specific production runs or batches.

Joint costs must not be confused with common costs. Whereas the latter relate to services which back up the production process, joint costs are the specific costs of production itself. They are the costs of shared resources of material, labour, energy, etc. entering into a production process or series of processes from which emerge two or more saleable products (though these may be saleable only after further, separate processing or after being combined with other product components). The outputs of joint-costs production are known as 'joint products' if each is of significant sales value. Joint products of limited sales value are termed 'by-products', but the distinction is often arbitrary. Classic examples of joint-product situations include petroleum refineries and petrochemicals, and meat processing (meat, tallow, offal, leather, etc.).

Given the nature of the joint-products production process, it is usually impossible to measure and validate a unique cost for each of the joint products and by-products. The problem is compounded if varying the proportion of the inputs or details of joint processing can result in different proportions of volume output of the separate joint products, as in the case of oil refining. The problem is most acute when accountants need defensible costs to use in cost of sales and profit and loss calculations, and in stock/inventory valuation. Here there are several alternative approaches to cost allocation and valuation, of concern mainly to the professional accountant and explained in detail in specialist texts such as that by Drury (1996). Fortunately, the above accounting allocation and valuation problems are not usually important in the control of joint processes, for which physical performance measures and targets can often be used, or in the decision-making process, where the main objective will be to maximise the excess of combined sales of all the joint products over and above their combined joint (and separate) costs.

Historical, absorption and variable costing

So far, this chapter has concentrated on concepts and measures of cost which may be relevant for studying problems of planning, decision-making or control. These costs are often not immediately available from the firm's accounts but instead may have to be estimated or derived from other sources. Once relevant and accurate data is to hand, cost analysis can often be done on the back of an envelope or, better, on a good PC spreadsheet package. In contrast, there is one form of cost information which is usually readily available from the ongoing accounts or accounting records of the firm. This comprises the 'historical costs' of the enterprise, covering past (i.e. historical) resource purchases, stockholding, use and conversion into outputs.

The main reason for the historical-cost records is to provide a link with the financial accounting system of the firm. These records feed in information needed for periodic determination of profit and loss and of the balance-sheet values of stocks of materials (including components, parts and supplies), work-in-progress and finished goods. In principle this need applies to all kinds of businesses. In practice the accounting may be relatively simpler for service businesses which produce no physical product and thus have no physical work-in-progress or finished goods stock. Retailers and wholesalers, by definition, have no physical product-conversion processes or work-in-progress, although they do usually carry finished stocks. It is in production businesses where the full complexity of historical costing arises; here the method of charging and recharging production costs is known as 'absorption costing', and this is explained below. An alternative approach termed 'variable costing' is then compared with absorption costing in an illustrative example, helping to point up some of the weaknesses of historical costing.

Types of production and costing

There are three main types of production. **Job (or one-off) production** is where a single unit of a given specification is made at any one time. Examples include individual ships, bridges, hospitals and power-station generators. Job production is normally to customer's order and not for stock. **Batch (or intermittent) production** is where a predetermined number of units are produced at one time, either for stock or to fill a specific customer order. Often the production is on multi-purpose plant, so that time and cost control must allow for 'set-up time' in the changeover from one batch run to another. The third type of production is **flow (or continuous) production**. This can be a production or assembly line always making the same product. However, more usually it is a flow-line process plant typically producing petroleum or other chemical or mineral products on a continuous basis.

Historical costing, and also costing information for management control, varies somewhat according to the type of production. Job costing and batch costing treat each job or batch as a separate cost unit or cost centre, whereas the process costing used in flow production is more concerned with average costs per unit of output and per unit of plant time. Where process production goes through distinct stages with separable costs it is usual to record the cost at each stage. The slightly different bookkeeping procedures for each type of production are illustrated in specialist costing textbooks.

Historical and absorption cost flow

Figure 10.5 is a highly simplified model or illustration of the flow of resource-use costs through production and into periodic profit and loss calculation. Rectangles are used to indicate balance-sheet accounts, while circles designate cost, expense and revenue accounts, and transactions. The numbers on Figure 10.5 denote the type of cost calculation being transferred. Direct costs of specific materials and labour (for

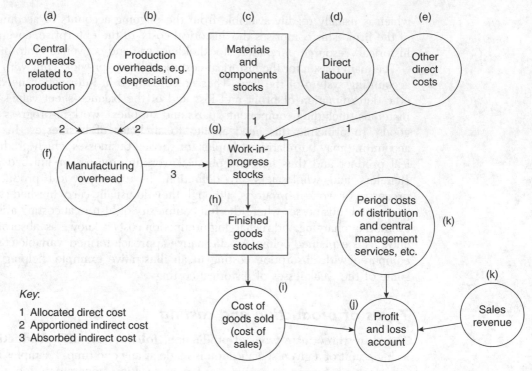

Figure 10.5
Historical
and absorp-
tion cost
flows.

Key:
1 Allocated direct cost
2 Apportioned indirect cost
3 Absorbed indirect cost

a known period of time) wholly committed to identified production can be charged
to production on a precise, verifiable basis, known as 'allocation'. While the costs of
production and other service departments may be direct and traceable when first
charged to the control accounts of these departments, their recharge of service
provided to benefit specific production jobs, batches, processes, etc. often involves
estimation and constitutes indirect cost. Such recharges are known as 'apportionment'. The final recharge of manufacturing overhead to the work-in-progress account
is termed 'absorption'; hence 'absorption costing', which will be contrasted with
'variable costing' below. The following paragraphs are keyed by letter to the rectangles and circles on Figure 10.5:

(a)   All central overheads could be recharged, as in (k), to profit and loss. But some
      central overheads (e.g. personnel and accounting) provide a definite benefit to
      manufacturing, which can be estimated and apportioned to manufacturing over-
      head for absorption. Sometimes, expenses such as heating, lighting and cleaning
      will be controlled and accounted for centrally instead of being separately
      measured and directly charged to production departments; these too can be
      apportioned.

(b)   Production department costs not directly traceable to production units, batches
      or runs need to be apportioned to manufacturing overhead for absorption.
      Often the production overheads are relatively small, but in job production – or
      where batches or processes are to comply with changing specifications or tight
      quality standards, etc. – large back-up costs of a drawing office, fitters, quality

inspectors, etc. may be involved. The depreciation cost of plant and machinery may be a major element of production overhead.

(c) Raw materials and components are traditionally stocked in secure stores and recorded in accounts as assets. They are then drawn out on requisitions (which should be closely monitored against waste and pilferage) and at that point become a direct charge to production. If the modern Japanese approach of just-in-time (JIT) delivery of components and other materials is adopted material inputs can be charged to production directly upon delivery and inspection.

(d) Labour time working on production is direct labour cost, to be allocated direct to production through the work-in-progress account, like direct materials. But direct workers will have time which is not directly productive, including sometimes maintenance, cleaning, fitting or inspection duties, or idle time because of delay in work flow or waiting for the completion of line reorganisation. These other activities should be separately recorded for charge to appropriate overhead accounts, which should be monitored for control. In practice, it is not always easy to ensure accurate time recording for this control.

(e) If there are resource costs additional to labour and materials directly traceable to production, these should preferably be charged to production as direct costs instead of being 'lumped in together' with production overheads. Examples include the lease costs of equipment specific to particular production, and energy costs if these are significant (as they are in many process industries) and are metered separately and accurately for direct matching with specific production jobs, batches or runs.

(f) Manufacturing overhead is used here as a control, or holding account, to bring together (on the debit side) all of the indirect or overhead costs/expenses apportioned to production (work-in-progress). On the credit side of the account will be entered the overhead absorption charges for the degree, or stages, of work completed. One cannot wait to know the final total of apportioned expenses, so one must estimate in advance what these expenses should amount to, or else one must set a target for them (see the discussion of standard costing in Chapter 15). One must also estimate the volume of production. In a multi-product situation one cannot realistically estimate accurately a unique overhead cost for each product, so the absorption recharging is normally based on linking cost absorption (or cost recovery into asset account values) to the particular input deemed to be most directly linked, or correlated, to the main causative influence on the level and/or variability of overhead costs. The absorption base chosen can be direct labour hours (or cost), direct material cost or machine hours (where the pace of production is largely governed by preset machine timings). If production workers effectively determine or fine-tune the production rate, direct labour hours are likely to be the best base for absorption charging. For example, assume that estimated manufacturing overhead for a period is £90 000, and estimated direct labour hours for the same period are estimated at 7500. The overhead absorption charge rate will be £12 per direct labour hour.

(g) The work-in-progress asset account is debited with all direct and indirect costs as work progresses. Subsidiary accounts/records segregate the costs of each separate job, batch or process until work is certified complete, at which time the relevant total costs will be transferred to the finished goods asset account.

(**h**) The finished goods asset account is debited with transfers from the work-in-progress account (unless the goods have been made to customer order, in which case they may instead be debited direct to the cost of goods sold account).

(**i**) All costs of output sold during a financial period are accumulated in the cost of goods sold (or cost of sales) account until periodic transfer to the profit and loss account.

(**j/k**) The profit and loss account also receives credits for sales revenues, and debits for all non-manufacturing period costs arising from the expenses of distribution, sales, promotion and central services. The residual balance in the account is the net profit or loss from trading/operations. Additional adjustments for interest and other financial corrections may be needed before establishing the final declared profit or loss.

Complications in historical absorption costing

It is easier to describe the general principle of the cost apportionment of production overheads and relevant general overheads (see (a) and (b) above) than it is to calculate these overhead costs fairly and reliably, at least when there is more than one department, line or process sharing the use of facilities and support services. For example, an obvious way to apportion costs such as rent, rates, insurance, heating and lighting, and buildings maintenance and depreciation is to base this on the floor area occupied (in square metres). However, this could be unfair to the extent that the age, condition, type of structure, height and insulation of different buildings can vary greatly. Other bases used include capital employed, number of employees using a facility, labour or machine hours of productive work or capacity, number of job orders handled. The key factor is to try to find the basis most closely correlated with the incidence of cost, and which is objectively and reliably measurable and recorded.

With the introduction of more capital-intensive production methods (including automated lines, robots) the proportion of direct labour and materials cost to total cost tends to fall, while the proportion of indirect cost for capital costs and for technical and other back-up services tends to rise. Put another way, the proportion of direct variable cost falls, while the proportion of fixed and indirect variable cost rises. This makes it all the more important to have an accurate understanding of support services and costs for realistic cost apportionment, as well as for the better management control of these often expensive services.

Another problem with support-service departments is that often they provide service to each other as well as to the direct-cost production departments. These are termed 'reciprocal services'. For example, a factory personnel department serves indirect staff in the stockroom, engineering workshops and other support departments, as well as the production operatives. Personnel department costs could be allocated direct to production, but it may be considered better for sensitive understanding and control of factory costs if the personnel overheads are distributed among all the relevant user departments and staff groups, for later recharge to production as part of the indirect overhead of these departments. Yet the personnel department also receives services from some of these user departments. Accountants have several methods for these cost redistributions, or inter-service cost transfers, including the use of simultaneous-equation solutions (see Drury 1996: 104–6).

A final problem to consider is the value to be placed upon materials when they are taken out of stores and charged into production. If specific materials (including components and parts) are ordered to fulfil a particular job order, then clearly their actual (i.e. invoice) cost should be charged to the direct costs of the relevant job. However, the more usual position for manufacturers, and indeed for retailers and wholesalers maintaining substantial base stocks of goods for resale, is for materials and other goods to have been bought in batches, often at different prices (owing to changes in market forces and inflation). Factory requisitions for production use on batch or process runs will seldom correspond to the exact quantities of materials purchased on particular orders (invoices). Also, if materials are of a standard, stock specification, will it always be easy to verify that particular order or delivery? Thus the physical identification of stock becomes detached from the identification of its true cost (or sacrifice value) when that stock is consigned into production. Accountants have three main methods of measuring this transfer of cost.

The first method assumes that the oldest stock received is the first used. It is called FIFO. Thus stock withdrawals will be charged at the oldest invoice price until the relevant quantity is exhausted, and then at the next oldest invoice price, and so on. FIFO is the favoured method in the UK. The obverse to FIFO is LIFO, which works on the basis of charging stock withdrawals first at the most recent invoice price until the relevant quantity is exhausted, and then at the next most recent invoice price, and so on. A compromise approach is to charge out stock withdrawals at the weighted-average price of stock on hand.

It may be argued that the true cost of consuming any resource which has a continuing economic use and value to the enterprise is its replacement cost. LIFO charging is an approximation to the use of replacement cost. Where FIFO charging for materials use has been followed, as is customary in the UK, the resultant total production cost figures will understate the 'real' cost of production, and these costs will not be sufficiently accurate or reliable for use in forward decision-making, at least during times of substantial inflation, market instability or significant technological change.

Variable costing v. absorption costing

Table 10.1 presents a simplified illustration of the differing figures for net profit and for closing stock (i.e. end-of-period finished goods stocks balance) that would arise from the use of historical absorption costing as contrasted to historical variable costing. The illustration is adapted from Drury (1996: 201–2), who goes into much more detail in evaluating the choice between the two costing methods than space permits here.

The variable costs comprise all direct product costs, plus variable indirect (or overhead) production costs. In the illustration we simply have the total of all of these combined. From the information given, the only basis we have for recharging (or recovering) the fixed indirect (or overhead) portions of production cost is to base this charge on each unit of output at the normal output level. Hence, £300 fixed costs at 150 units output yields a unit fixed cost of £2 per unit to be applied to each unit produced under the absorption costing system. When more than 150 units are produced there will be over-recovery of fixed costs (see period 5), and when fewer than 150 units are produced there will be under-recovery (see period 6). In contrast,

Table 10.1   A comparison of variable and absorption costing

The following information is available for periods 1–6 for a company which produces a single product:

	£
Unit selling price	10
Unit variable cost	6
Fixed costs for each period	300

Normal activity is expected to be 150 units per period and production and sales for each period are as follows:

	Period 1	Period 2	Period 3	Period 4	Period 5	Period 6
Units sold	150	120	180	150	140	160
Units produced	150	150	150	150	170	140

There were no opening stocks at the start of period 1 and the actual manufacturing fixed overhead incurred was £300 per period. We shall also assume that non-manufacturing overheads are £100 per period.

Variable costing statements

	Period 1 £	Period 2 £	Period 3 £	Period 4 £	Period 5 £	Period 6 £
Opening stock	–	–	180	–	–	180
Production cost	900	900	900	900	1 020	840
Closing stock	–	(180)	–	–	(180)	(60)
Cost of sales	900	720	1 080	900	840	960
Fixed costs	300	300	300	300	300	300
Total costs	1 200	1 020	1 380	1 200	1 140	1 260
Sales	1 500	1 200	1 800	1 500	1 400	1 600
Gross profit	300	180	420	300	260	340
Less non-manufacturing costs	100	100	100	100	100	100
Net profit	200	80	320	200	160	240

Absorption costing statements

	Period 1 £	Period 2 £	Period 3 £	Period 4 £	Period 5 £	Period 6 £
Opening stock	–	–	240	–	–	240
Production cost	1 200	1 200	1 200	1 200	1 360	1 120
Closing stock	–	(240)	–	–	(240)	(80)
Cost of sales	1 200	960	1 440	1 200	1 120	1 280
Adjustment for under/(over)-recovery of overhead	–	–	–	–	(40)	20
Total costs	1 200	960	1 440	1 200	1 080	1 300
Sales	1 500	1 200	1 800	1 500	1 400	1 600
Gross profit	300	240	360	300	320	300

Table 10.1 *continued*

Less non-manufacturing costs	100	100	100	100	100	100
Net profit	200	140	260	200	220	200

Source: adapted, with permission, from Colin Drury 1996: 201–2.

under variable costing the fixed production costs are not charged into production cost (or closing stock), but instead are charged below the line of cost of sales, as a period cost.

The data in Table 10.1 covers six periods. The periods could be weeks, months or years. Profit calculation for external reporting is usually yearly or half-yearly, but internal reporting for management control is frequently monthly. Where the periods covered are less than a full year there may be seasonal distortions to sales and/or production volumes.

The most obvious point of attention in contrasting the two statements is that the 'bottom-line' net profit is much more stable under absorption costing than under variable costing. This may represent an acceptable form of 'income smoothing' for external reporting, but it may not send the most useful signals to managers in internal reporting for management control as regards either the setting of production runs or the effort needed in sales promotion.

What absorption costing has done is to transfer into closing stock that portion of normal unit fixed cost charges which relates to all unsold production, inclusive of production in excess of the normal rate on which the unit fixed cost charge is based. In period 5 this amounts to £40 over-recovery in respect of production of 170 units compared to the normal 150 units. Now suppose instead that period 5 production had been 200 units, with the same sales of 140 units. In that case, closing stock value would have been £480, over-recovered overhead £100 and net profit £280. Readers should check these figures for themselves. The effect has been to increase net profit by relieving total costs for period 5 by a notional (unsold) product value of fixed-cost contributions carried forward in the end-of-period balance sheet in closing stock. In other words, under absorption costing it is open to production management to manipulate short-term net profit performance by producing goods in excess of current sales requirements. Eventually this distortion will cancel out, so where is the incentive to manipulate? If the periods are a full year, or even a half-year, there can always be hope that market changes, inflation, solving technical or efficiency problems in the production process, etc. will provide some relief to front-line managers' problems during the next period, so it could well be that some managers surrender to the temptation of this form of gamesmanship. The question remains open whether it is wise to use any accounting system, like absorption costing, which is so prone to yield misleading information and so open to manipulation.

The concerns expressed above regarding absorption cost accounting relate to its use in performance measurement and control. It may be even less relevant for management planning and decision-making, to be considered in Chapters 11–13.

Further problems in cost accounting

There are many technical and practical problems in cost and management accounting, often with conflicting views on how to deal with them which are beyond the scope of this book (but readers may consult a specialist text such as Drury 1996). However, before moving, in Chapters 11 and 12, to the use of cost and other accounting information in management decision-making, we will consider three particular problems of some importance: costing for services, depreciation costs and the transfer costs between organisational units.

Costing for services

Cost accounting developed originally mainly for application in factories, where hundreds or thousands of identical products are made under standardised work practices. At any one time, a factory worker or machine is usually involved with only a single product. It is therefore relatively easy to trace costs to that specific product. But in many service industries these characteristics do not apply. Sales clerks may sell any combination of hundreds of products in an hour. Bank clerks may process ten different kinds of service transactions in an hour. The work of solicitors, academics or doctors may be even more diffused, with some part of 'professional' activity not traceable to any specific 'product' or even customer, but, rather, committed to general professional learning or updating of skills and to organisational activity. So it becomes difficult to cost many kinds of service work accurately, at least without keeping detailed records of the use of time, which would interrupt the flow of work, or of customer contact and goodwill, and would not be worth the 'cost of costing'.

Responses to this problem vary widely but, in general, service costing aims to follow similar principles to factory costing where work is repetitive and tied to one service output, for example where clerks spend all day inputting into computers the details from cheques, bank slips, credit cards, mail-order forms, etc. The contrast in the work here to that of a secretary or personal assistant is obvious. Supermarket cashiers carry out repetitive duties of a single type also, but these are linked to an enormous variety of products passing through the till. For cost-efficiency measurement and control similar costing methods may be applied as for the clerks inputting into computers. Detailed tracing of the cashier costs to individual products or product lines may not be necessary for wider management control, where the emphasis may be on turnover and profitability per square foot or metre of display space. Here, cashier costs will be relatively small and relatively uniform across different products, so that fairly simple apportionments should suffice.

Where it is policy that a full range of products or services should be supplied, the emphasis in costing and cost analysis may not be on individual products or services, but, rather, on the performance of a managerial unit as a whole, whether this is a single department in a departmental store or each individual branch of a high-street bank.

Where services are non-standard and/or are performed by individuals working in isolation, prices are often charged on an hourly basis, whether for a solicitor or the call-out services of a breakdown engineer. It is assumed that the sum of all the hourly charges (plus any spare parts or extra expense charges) will cover not only the time of the specialist but also the indirect costs and overheads and the target profit margin. If profits turn out too low, manning levels and support costs – and prices if the market permits – will be re-examined, but seldom will this extend to accurate costing of the work of each individual specialist, the solicitor, engineer or whatever.

Following privatisation, most remaining public-sector organisations supply services rather than products, and typically these services are supplied free or at some arbitrary charge (e.g. NHS prescriptions) rather than being sold at cost or for a profit. The technical problems of costing services in the public sector are very similar to those in the private sector, but until recently even less attention was given to them. Partly, this was because there was less pressure and concern in the public services to maximise efficiency, with known funding from the public purse and no need for concern about survival. But it was also partly because Parliament itself had always made it clear that its main financial concern for public services was that they should not overspend their cash allocations and that money should be spent only on authorised activities. However, in recent years this has changed, and public-sector organisations are now expected to adopt best commercial practices in cost and management accounting and in budgetary control, insofar as this is practicable. Thus the civil service has been required to follow the Financial Management Initiative (FMI), with devolved budgetary and cost control accountability. The NHS is under pressure to cost accurately the hundreds of types of operations and other treatments it provides. The NHS has found it difficult to obtain accurate costings given the number and diversity of its treatments and the number of support services (e.g. X-ray and physiotherapy) used in widely different combinations for individual patients. It appears that the NHS's 'cost of costing' as required by government, with supporting computerisation to obtain resource use and cost information promptly and accurately, has been running at hundreds of millions of pounds per year and has raised doubts as to the value for money in the use of public funds (Henley *et al.*, 1992). The 1997 Labour Government has pledged to reduce NHS management costs, but how it will do so is not yet clear if accurate costing information is to be available.

In both the public and private sectors there appears to be much scope to develop new and better cost information and analysis. The new approach of activity-based costing (ABC), which is introduced in Chapter 11, may prove helpful in improving cost and management accounting for services.

Depreciation costs

Depreciation – that is, the annualised cost of the wearing out, using up, and/or obsolescence of a fixed asset, spread over the number of years during which economic benefit is obtained from the asset – is usually dealt with in accountancy primarily as a financial accounting topic (see Chapter 3). The purpose of depreciation accounting is to charge against profit and loss a sum sufficient to ensure that the financial capital of a business is retained intact (i.e. reinvested) so that it cannot be declared and distributed to shareholders as dividends, disguised as trading profits. However, in times of inflation it is not sufficient to retain just the annualised financial cost of depreciation, because the new replacement assets needed to retain economic earning power will usually cost more than the original assets. The traditional approach is to charge to production overheads just the annual depreciation on the original purchase price, on the historical absorption costing basis, ignoring inflation effects. Indeed, it would be difficult to do otherwise, given that the cost accounts are expected to reconcile with the financial accounts.

The effects of inflation can be shown in supplementary accounts, bringing in current-cost or replacement-cost valuations of assets and depreciation, together with other relevant adjustments. Many, if not most, accountants argue that current-cost accounts should not replace the historical-cost accounts, perhaps mainly on the grounds of the difficulty of assessing and auditing reliable replacement-cost figures. Technology changes, markets change, and often firms will not replace existing fixed assets with the same type or scale of assets, even if reliable current values can be established for the latter.

Thus it is normal for the routine historical-costing figures used for valuing the costs of production and the cost of goods sold (for use in the profit and loss account) to include depreciation only on the original cost. With major capital-intensive plant this practice can give quite misleading depreciation-cost figures, were these to be used in pricing policy and for other management decisions. This is simply one illustration of why routinely available historical or absorption costing figures may not be helpful to management; further illustrations are given in Chapter 11. In separate costing calculations, prepared specifically for use in pricing or other management decisions, it is of course possible at least to approximate the inflation-adjusted current cost of the use of fixed assets.

It is an interesting contrast to the private sector that the government has been requiring changes in the accounting of trading services run by central and local government, and of the NHS and some other public services, whereby their accounting, including their depreciation-cost charges, must be on a current-cost or replacement-cost basis. Initial (historical) fixed-asset values and depreciation charges are increased annually by reference to relevant building or equipment price indices, and land and buildings are to be revalued periodically by professional valuers to take account of changes in both market values and replacement costs. Current-cost depreciation has been encouraged in internal costings, the pricing of any external sales or internal-market sales (as in the NHS) and the annual financial accounts (Henley *et al.*, 1992).

Transfer of costs

This chapter, and Chapters 11 and 12, are written for the basic organisational case of the integrated firm with major planning and control decisions taken by a single manager or management team. This is broadly realistic for most small to medium-sized firms. However, as firms get larger, especially firms which diversify into more than one technology, product line or market, they may adopt decentralised organisational structures, typically identified as operating divisions but sometimes formed as subsidiary companies. Divisions or subsidiaries may trade with each other as well as with external markets; for example, one division may make castings both for external orders and to supply as components to another division or subsidiary. The spirit of decentralisation requires that intra-company trade should be at fair-market price, or at least a good cost-based estimate thereof, so that each unit of the company can be assessed on its profitability. This internal transfer of cost, often with some profit margin added and then called 'transfer pricing', does, however, give rise to many arguments, sometimes involving conflict between economic theory and organisational theory, and difficulties in cost measurement. Transfer pricing and divisional performance measurement have their own large literature (Emmanuel *et al.*, 1990) and the subject is discussed further in Chapter 16 of this book.

Conclusions

There are many concepts of cost and many ways of measuring cost. Further concepts and measures will be explained in Chapter 11. All this involves nuances of meaning, and considerable jargon. Here, the manager is at some disadvantage in communicating with the accountant to obtain the relevant cost information needed for effective control of current operations, and for forward planning and decision-making. There is a risk that busy accountants, if left to their own devices and stuck within their own four walls, will seek to answer management questions and requests by using cost information derived directly from their historical absorption-cost records, which are maintained primarily to feed production cost and value information into the financial accounting system.

It is essential for the accountant to be brought into the workplace and into open dialogue with managers so that the real needs of cost information for control, and for planning and decisions, can be established. Only then can the most relevant information be provided. Of the concepts explored in this chapter, perhaps the most valuable are opportunity cost and awareness of how some costs are dependent on volume, while other costs are governed more by other factors. Such other factors could include the passage of time, or the decisions or commitments of managers (sometimes by default rather than by conscious choice and decision) in creating and sustaining an ongoing core structure of costly service organisation and staffing, and of buildings, plant and equipment which may not always be adaptable to meet future needs and opportunities.

This chapter introduced the basic definitions, concepts and measures of business cost. These included opportunity cost, a measure of sacrifice, and the distinction between simple cash costs and the more complicated but accurate accrual costs. It explained how some costs vary with volume of activity, while other costs are largely independent of volume and are fixed during a period of time. Some costs combine variable and fixed elements, and of course over a long enough period of time all costs can be made variable (or at least avoidable) by management choice and action. The bases for identifying costs as fixed or variable, and as direct, indirect or overhead, were outlined.

The traditional ongoing system of cost recording and reporting in business, historical absorption costing, was explained, and some of its weaknesses for providing useful information to management were explored. Further weaknesses, together with alternative approaches to costing and cost analysis to provide better information for management decisions, will be explained in subsequent chapters.

Further reading

For a classic historical view of the issues, see Solomons (1952). For contemporary views and detail, see Drury (1996: Pt I; 1997: Pt II) or Horngren *et al.* (1994: ch. 11). The monthly *Management Accounting* is written mainly for professionals but also includes some good introductory articles on methods and current issues.

Questions and exercises

1 Define and explain 'opportunity cost', and explain also why opportunity cost is seldom mentioned or measured in routine cost measurement and reporting systems. Suggest how the opportunity-cost concept could be given explicit use or recognition in cost information for management.

2 'In the absence of inflation accounting or asset revaluation adjustments, cash accounting and accrual accounting should lead to the same total profit (or loss) over the lifetime of a business.' Explain why you agree or disagree with this statement. Does it matter which of these two systems we use for the purpose of providing information for management planning and control?

3 Draw a graph to display total unit cost related to activity (measured in volume of units produced or sold). Include in your costs variable costs, fixed costs and step-type (or semi-fixed) mixed costs. (NB graph paper need not be used for this question.) How far do you think the existence of mixed costs limits the usefulness of the conventional simplification of all costs into the two categories of fixed and variable?

4 It could be argued that total fixed costs broadly equate to total indirect costs, and that total variable costs broadly equate to total direct costs. Explain how and why the foregoing simple matching breaks down, and why it is important to use both of these two different cost-classification systems.

5 There is a choice in product costing between the absorption (or historical) costing method and the variable (or period) costing method. Speculate on the relative advantages and disadvantages of each of these two methods in respect of:
   (a) the valuation of finished stocks;
   (b) periodic profit or loss measurement;
   (c) control of production operations;
   (d) planning changes in product mix or volume.

6 How does depreciation cost for buildings and equipment differ in its nature and measurement from other production costs, and how might such differences affect the measurement and reporting of product costs for planning and control?

7 Bashers Ltd is a small metalworking business. For the month of September the total works overhead cost was £10 000. During that month only three jobs were worked on. All were started and completed within the month, and the following data is supplied:

	Job no. 1 £	Job no. 2 £	Job no. 3 £
Direct materials	5 000	2 000	1 000
Direct labour cost	7 500	5 000	500
Direct expenses	500	1 000	300
Prime cost	13 000	8 000	1 800
Direct labour hours	1 500	1 500	150
Machine hours	500	300	100

(a) Identify four different bases for calculating an overhead absorption rate for the work of the period, and calculate what the rate would be under each of the four bases.

(b) State whether the data and your results suggest which of the four bases is likely to be the most appropriate for use in this company? If so, explain why. If not, explain what additional information you would seek in order to choose the best overhead absorption basis.

8 The Elite Shoe Company manufactures two grades of shoes, A and B. Manufacturing costs for the year ended 31 March were:

	£000s
Direct materials	1000
Direct wages	560
Variable production overhead	140
Fixed production overhead	160
	1860

There was no work-in-progress at the beginning or end of the year. It is ascertained that:

(a) direct materials in grade A shoes cost twice as much as in grade B shoes (per pair);

(b) direct wages for grade B shoes were 60% of those for grade A shoes (per pair);

(c) fixed production overhead was the same per pair of A and B grade shoes, while variable production overhead was apportioned on the basis of direct wages;

(d) administration overhead for each grade of shoe was 50% of direct labour cost;

(e) selling cost was £1.75 per pair for each grade of shoe;

(f) production during the year was:
  ■ grade A, 40 000 pairs, of which 36 000 pairs were sold;
  ■ grade B, 120 000 pairs, of which 110 000 pairs were sold;

(g) factory prices were £25 per pair for grade A and £15 per pair for Grade B.

Assuming that all costs were exactly measured in the direct and indirect costs listed above, prepare a statement showing the total costs of production and sales for each grade of shoe; the unit costs and profit for each grade of shoe; and the balance sheet value of finished stocks at year-end.

9 Hi-tec Ltd is a small manufacturer of precision instruments. For the latest trading year its summary accounts, prepared on the absorption costing basis, are as follows:

	£000s
Opening stock	200
Prime cost	1400
Variable production overheads	200
Fixed production overheads	400
Less closing stock	(600)
Cost of sales	1600
Sales	2300
Gross profit	700
Variable admin and sales overheads	(150)
Fixed admin and sales overheads	(300)
Net profit	250

(a) Recast the above summary accounts using the alternative approach of variable costing. You will need to know that if the company had used variable costing in the previous year the opening stock balance at the beginning of the latest year would have been £150 000.

(b) Comparing the two sets of accounts, identify what inferences you can draw regarding the financial position of the company, and what advantages or disadvantages you see in the two alternative accounting and valuation approaches?

10 Machinations Ltd buys in steel strip for stores, and it machines this to a variety of specifications in batch runs to customer order and for holding a range of standard stock. We will look at its use of material and the flow of material cost to cost of sales. We are given the following information for the month of November (all figures are in £ million and relate solely to the materials component of each control account).

Opening materials	1000
Opening work-in-progress	1200
Materials purchased	2000
Cost of materials in finished goods sold and delivered	3000
Ending balances: materials	600
work-in-progress	1400
finished goods	700

(a) From the given information, calculate the values for materials requisitioned from stores to work-in-progress; for the material component of work-in-progress passed to finished goods; and for the opening balance of the finished goods account. (Hint: it may be helpful to link your calculations to the cost flows in Figure 10.5 and to use 'T' accounts and/or lay out your solution in tabular format.)

(b) Consider and then concisely suggest how you might deal in the cost-flow accounts with the following complications arising during November: the price of steel strip rose by 10% early in the month; a physical stock count at the end of the month showed £50 000 of strip to be missing from the materials store; and during the month 4% of steel strip in progress was wasted owing to machining errors (as against a normal wastage of 2%).

11 Accounting and short-term decisions

Objectives

Many business decisions involve both short-term and long-term implications, but for the purposes of analysis it is helpful to examine these separately. Short-term decisions are mainly concerned with making the most cost-effective and profitable use of existing resources, while long-term decisions typically revolve around the best use of new capital investment. This chapter concentrates on the understanding and use of accounting information which is most relevant to short-term decisions on the best choice of inputs, volumes of outputs and pricing.

We will also examine the decision-relevance of different types of cost information, in particular absorption costs, attributable costs, activity-based costs and differential costs. Methods of cost estimation are illustrated, and cost–volume–profit and contribution analysis are explained. Even though final decisions on production, marketing and pricing must be taken in the light of commercial strategy and market conditions, costing information can provide helpful guidance on product mix, volume and pricing.

Planning, control and decisions

Business planning looks forwards, sets objectives and targets, and develops detailed operational plans. The financial parts of these plans are termed 'budgets', and we will examine these in Chapter 14. Business control comprises monitoring and correcting current business performance in production and sales, and in cost-efficiency and profitability. Chapter 15 will discuss control in the particular context of standard costing and performance-variance analysis, while the chapter on budgeting explains how budgets link ongoing planning with control. Effective action to remedy control problems (e.g. inefficient use of labour or materials) requires decisions. Selecting, amending or updating plans and budgets requires decisions. More generally, rather like driving a car or steering a ship, there is a need in management for constant alertness, simultaneously implementing control, making choices, updating plans and generally adapting as optimally as possible in the current environment while moving towards agreed business goals. All this involves **making** decisions.

Whereas control is largely reactive, positive business management is mainly pro-active, making decisions concerned with change, choices, risk and uncertainty. Longer-term decisions usually involve the investment or disinvestment of capital, and we look at these in Chapter 13. Here we concentrate on short-term decisions, typically focused on what to make and sell, how to make it efficiently, and what price to seek or accept. Here cost information can be a valuable aid or it can be seriously misleading. We must have cost information which is relevant to each specific decision situation confronting us.

Relevant costs and costing systems

We have seen that routine, day-to-day cost recording and reporting systems are designed to meet the requirements of financial accounting – essentially to capture all historical costs of production activity and to allocate or apportion these fairly between the cost of goods sold and the cost of goods in unsold stock or inventory. The costing method usually employed is historical absorption costing, which was discussed in Chapter 10. This is normally based on the absorption of all production costs (i.e. costs incurred up to the point where goods are ready for sale), both fixed and variable. There is an alternative viewpoint that only variable costs (i.e. direct materials, direct labour, and direct or traceable variable overheads) should be charged to product costs, with the remaining overheads charged as period costs direct to current profit and loss, and thus not entering into finished stock or inventory values. However, it has been questioned whether or not either of these routine costing approaches provides the information which managers need to make decisions on sales and production strategies involving linked decisions on product mix and volume, sales and pricing policies, etc.

There has been continuing controversy regarding what alternative method of costing should be used for decision-making. Economists have argued their general case that rational firms should go on producing until marginal revenue falls to equal rising marginal cost. In other words, firms should ignore fixed costs and cut the prices of output as necessary to meet market conditions until the price for disposing of any extra output falls to equal the marginal costs of extra production. However, if this brings down the general price level firms may be unable to recover their fixed costs from the market. This tends to happen during recession and in export markets when a country is suffering high inflation without compensating exchange-rate adjustments; empirical observation suggests that following this guideline increases the risks of business failure and liquidation. Instead, there must be a much more fundamental and rigorous challenge of production methods and structures, and, indeed, of product designs and marketing.

Modern thinking (e.g. as reviewed in J.Y. Lee 1987) points out that as and where production becomes increasingly automated and computer controlled, and the production labour force shrinks in number but becomes more highly trained, 'white collar' and fixed in cost over time (ignoring major shakeouts during recession or reorganisation), the only major remaining variable cost is materials (including parts and components). Although there may be many exceptions in the older industries, the modern, growth, high-tech industries often, if not typically, operate with a high value-added cost and profit margin over and above the variable costs of their material inputs. Thus, it is argued, it will be very misleading to base volume, product mix and pricing decisions on an information system focused mainly on tracing and reporting variable (or marginal) costs.

Activity-based costing (ABC)

Recently some academics and consultants have been promoting an alternative system of production costing known as ABC. The initiative for this has come from the USA (Cooper and Kaplan 1988), where there has perhaps been greater awareness than in the UK regarding the survival need to improve manufacturing methods, structures and information systems in order to compete successfully in the world marketplace. Historically, the Anglo-American approach has been to concentrate cost control and information on direct labour (i.e. the people actually working hands-on in the production line or process plant). However, with increased automation in production occurring at the same time as the movement to more complicated and frequently changing product design, innovation and technical complexity, labour employment and the associated overhead costs related to space, equipment, training and IT support, etc. have often shifted greatly from the production line to the production planning and support services (including R&D). Given these changes, it has been argued that traditional historical absorption costing discloses misleading information both for control and for planning/decision-making.

ABC advocates do not claim that ABC systems routinely measure and report all the costing information which managers need for decisions, but nevertheless ABC information should prove more decision-relevant and help managers more often to identify problems and to ascertain what further information they will need to make decisions (e.g. using the differential costing approach described below). Absorption costing collects all production overheads into overhead department control accounts, and then it apportions this cost to production according to which of the main production indicators – machine hours, labour hours or materials used – appears to be the most reliable measure of productive work, i.e. achieved production volume. The ABC approach rejects the logic of this.

Under the ABC approach, the primary concern is for the study and understanding of each kind of support activity generating overhead costs. An activity-based costing system includes the following stages:

1 Identify the major activities supporting production (and the method can be extended to distribution as well).
2 Determine the 'cost driver' for each activity.
3 Set up an account (as a 'cost centre' or 'cost pool') to collect the costs of the activity.
4 Trace the cost of the separate activities through to individual products (i.e. to specific jobs, batches or process segments), using the cost-driver measures as indicators of the volume of each activity consumed on behalf of each individual product.

Activities may include design, purchasing, tooling, scheduling, set-up engineering, quality inspection. 'Cost driver' is a jargon term for the events, forces or transactions which cause or build up the total costs of the activities. 'Activities' may or may not match up closely with single departments as used in conventional factory overheads costing and budgeting. But clearly, cost drivers will often involve work, and therefore costs, from more than one traditional department. For example, a close study of resource consumption and cost may show that purchase orders often cause work in design and engineering, and in stores, stores inspection and accounts, as well as in the purchasing department proper. Careful tracking of the cost drivers may provide a much truer picture of the costs incurred by individual products than traditional absorption costing based on apportioning departmental costs. However, if factory budgetary control is based on departmental costs while production control is based on cost-driver-led activity costs there could be conflict and confusion in management control in the factory. One solution could be to reorganise factory management so that it is based on activity centres and flows rather than on traditional functional departments.

In its basic concept, ABC seems no more than common sense. However, it is being promoted, like most new systems, with a distinctive literature, its own jargon and detailed suggestions for implementation. All this is well explained by Drury (1996, 1997).

One situation where ABC advocates claim a clear advantage for their method is where a firm uses common production facilities to make the same or similar products for production orders and runs of widely differing quantities. It is alleged that traditional absorption costing will tend greatly to understate the true costs of small production quantities and overstate the true costs of large quantities. This is because traditional costing will average out all the support costs across all the units produced, whereas these costs are disproportionately caused by the small production orders and runs. This could lead to errors in pricing and depending on market forces, including the pricing behaviour of competitors, it could lead to the firm building up low-profit business at the expense of being priced out of high-volume, high-profit business.

Another situation where ABC information may be valuable is where the firm supplies various products making quite different levels of demand upon support services. Table 11.1 provides an example of this. The example is very much simplified, but the firm prints two kinds of publications: one is trade catalogues (A), including many photos and drawings, while the other is community magazines (B), comprising mainly simple typesetting but also a few drawings. It can be seen from the table that unit production costs for the two types of work can vary between the ABC method and the traditional absorption method by a material amount, in this case by more than the probable net profit margin on sales.

In summary, activity-based costing seeks to focus management attention on production overheads, and to trace these through to unit and order costs on a basis much more sensitive to the impact of support activities and costs, and the length of production runs, than is achieved through conventional absorption costing. ABC can be carried out as a one-off analysis study, or it can replace absorption costing as the routine ongoing recording and reporting system for production (or distribution) operations. We will look again at ABC, in greater detail, in Chapter 12.

Avoidable and attributable costs

'**Avoidable cost**' is a useful decision-relevant concept of cost. Avoidable costs are those costs which will be avoided, or saved, if a new project is not undertaken or,

Table 11.1 PrintPublish Ltd product costs 19XX

	Total costs	Absorption costs				ABC				Attributable costs			
		FC		VC		FC		VC		FC		VC	
		A	B	A	B	A	B	A	B	A	B	A	B
Materials (paper, covers, etc.)	300			100	200			100	200			100	200
Labour:													
Artwork, negotiation and set-ups	150	60	90			135	15			100	10		
Printing and binding (direct labour)	200			80	120			80	120			60	90
Supervision	50	20	30			25	25			10	10		
Premises (rent, rates, energy, etc.)	150	60	90			60	90			20	30		
Depreciation of equipment	100	40	60			40	60			30	10		
Accounts, purchasing and stores	60	24	36			30	30			10	10		
Central overheads (excluding marketing and distribution)	90	36	54			45	45			20	20		
Total FC and VC product costs		240	360			335	265			190	90		
Add VC to FC costs:	1100	180	320	180	320	180	320	180	320	160	290	160	290
Total production costs	1100	420	680			515	585			350	380		
Units produced (000s of items)	400	2000				400	2000			400	2000		
Average production cost per unit		£1.05	£0.34			£1.29	£0.29			£0.88	£0.19		

Costs in £000s

Notes:

FC = fixed costs; VC = variable costs.

The columns headed 'A' relate to trade-catalogue products; the columns headed 'B' relate to community-magazine products.

The table uses the simplifying assumptions that there is no beginning or ending inventory of unfinished work-in-progress, and that all indirect and overhead costs are wholly fixed costs

In the Absorption costs columns all indirect and overhead costs are recharged to products as a function of production-line activity, in this case proportional to direct labour cost.

In the ABC (activity-based costs) columns all indirect and overhead costs are charged to products (or product lines) by the use of cost drivers counting number of transactions, or use of activity time, relating to each product. For example, supervision cost is allocated by number of orders, set-ups and runs; artwork costs are allocated by the number of photos and other illustrations processed.

In the Attributable costs columns one can trace the indirect and overhead costs using either the absorption or the ABC approach, the key difference here being that the only costs charged to products will be those for resource use or expenditure which could be avoided or terminated if a product is discontinued (after a reasonable planning lead-time). This leaves the remaining overhead costs unallocated to products: instead they will be charged to profit and loss as 'period costs' together with the costs of distribution (i.e. promotion, marketing and physical distribution expenses).

It could be argued that the absorption unit costs are inaccurate and misleading for pricing and related decisions, while the ABC unit costs should come close to accuracy and relevance for long-term pricing and product-mix decisions. Attributable unit costs indicate minimum prices for continued production and sales unless and until a more profitable use for available resources is found.

more usually, if an existing product or activity is abandoned. This approach involves a critical study of overheads, as well as direct costs, to see where savings can be made or commitments avoided. It has some similarity to 'differential costing', which we consider in greater detail below. Applying the approach can make good use of the cost insights available from a rigorous activity-based costing system such as previously discussed.

'**Attributable cost**' is a structured approach to defining, collecting and using avoidable-cost data, put forward by Shillinglaw (1963). Here attributable cost is defined as the cost per unit which could be avoided, on average, if a function (or activity or product) were discontinued entirely without changing the supporting organisation structure. The assumption here is that the core of the organisation, and the related fixed or period costs, will continue. Any non-core function, or any product or commercial activity which could be separately abandoned, should be retained only if it generates more income than its attributable cost. Alternatively to abandonment, the approach can provide guidance on pricing policy, quantity discounts, delivery and customer service policies, etc.

Attributable costs clearly include all relevant direct variable costs, and also all traceable and avoidable variable overhead costs. They can include fixed costs which could be avoided given time for management planning and action. This involves unitising some fixed (i.e. period) costs to derive average unit (attributable) cost – which figure becomes the minimum price or revenue return to justify continuation of the product or activity. So, in a sense, this is a specific measurement of long-run marginal cost, although we include it in this chapter because it has application in the continuing (i.e. short-term) decision and performance review process, and because the method stops short of explicit consideration of the time-value of capital, the essence of the investment (or disinvestment) problems discussed in Chapter 13 on long-term decisions.

A simplified example of attributable costing is included in Table 11.1. It is assumed that there are just two separable elements to be costed, trade catalogues and community magazines as individual product lines. As should be expected, the average unit cost is less than under absorption costing or ABC, since core organisation costs have been excluded from allocation to products. Yet this attributable cost per unit is higher than unit marginal/variable cost, and it may be argued that it provides a more realistic minimum price for individual sales transactions or for keeping resources devoted to that product line instead of being disinvested. However, it tells us nothing about the opportunity costs, or the possibilities of other, more profitable lines or products.

In summary, absorption costing, activity-based costing and avoidable/attributable costing can all provide information that can be helpful for decision-making, as well as for performance monitoring and control. But since this information is based on existing activities and products, using past or historical data, the decision-relevance is limited to what could be described as the fine-tuning of the status quo. Ideally what we need is information relating to probable future costs and revenues, and to the choices of products, production or distribution methods, and markets. For this we need to employ 'differential analysis', but before discussing that approach we need to consider the problems of cost estimation and of cost–volume–profit analysis.

Cost estimation

Cost estimation is used when the information from routine costing systems – mainly designed for the financial accounting purposes of stock valuation and historical profit or loss determination, and/or designed for short-term cost-control use (see the discussion of standard costing in Chapter 15) – is not relevant for decisions on future action. Cost-estimation techniques have a particular concern for the separation of fixed (period) costs from variable (volume-related) costs. There are five main approaches: the engineering method, accounts inspection, visual fit, the high–low method and linear regression.

Given concern for the different total costs – and therefore different average unit costs – of production or supply at different volumes, it is often useful to study cost behaviour graphically. The relationship between fixed and variable costs can be summarised by the equation below:

$$Y = a + bX \tag{11.1}$$

where: Y = total costs;
X = volume of activity;
a = fixed costs;
b = unit variable cost.

Figure 11.1 illustrates the form of linear cost–volume relationships related to this equation. The practical problem, of course, is to obtain relevant and reliable measures and estimates of the values of a and b. Of the alternative techniques, the engineering method can and should be carried out as much as possible using data independent of the historical accounting system. The other four approaches normally derive their data from the historical records, so therefore they should always be challenged as to their robustness for use in forward decision-making. Even so, evidence of past cost performance offers some baseline of guidance (after adjustment for inflation) towards likely future experience.

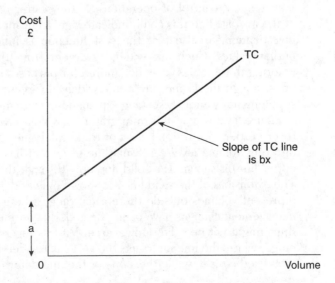

Figure 11.1
A linear
cost–volume
relationship.

Accounts inspection

The accountant can be asked to inspect the detail of the cost accounting records for specified products (or sales lines, markets, branches or services), to determine all the chargeable and relevant costs, to analyse these as between fixed and variable, and then to aggregate them to a determined total cost at a specified volume level. From this can be derived the average unit cost at that volume level. A cost determined in this way can vary considerably from the average unit cost routinely provided from an ongoing absorption costing system. However, it relies on subjective judgement in discriminating between fixed and variable costs and it may not give reliable guidance for the extrapolation of cost performance to alternative volume levels.

Repeating the accounts inspection analysis at times of differing volumes can provide a series of 'snapshots' of cost experience which can be analysed by the next three techniques below, possibly to yield a more sensitive and reliable feel for the relationship of fixed and variable costs to volume. These techniques can be applied also to data obtained directly from the routine cost absorption accounts. Both sets of data must be treated with some caution, partly because of the subjective nature of much of the data classification, partly because the effects of mixed costs may be sporadic and not directly detected, and partly because of the effects of inflation on performance results recorded at different times (although generally the inflation distortions can be corrected by appropriate index adjustments).

Visual fit

The 'visual-fit' technique involves entering on a graph, known as a 'scattergram', the historical values of total costs recorded (Ys) for different volumes experienced (Xs). A line is then drawn through the scatter of points so that it best weights their representation as a linear function of total cost to volume. If the scatter of points departs widely from the average line the results may be of limited validity, because of errors in the input cost data, random mixed costs which have not been identified or poor management control of operations. If the scatter of points is skewed at either end of the average line this could indicate significant mixed or step costs needing further investigation, or else that the cost function is inherently non-linear. In any case outlier values which are widely divergent from the average line (as determined ignoring those values) may be ignored for purposes of drawing the line of visual best fit, although these and any other widely divergent values could form the basis of supplementary enquiry seeking explanation of variation in management performance.

Figure 11.2 is a scattergram graph on which have been marked with crosses the recent experience of total costs of trade catalogues produced at PrintPublish Ltd, at different volume levels. A visual line of best fit has been entered. The line (i.e. the upper line) is shown as a solid line only through the range of volumes experienced. The extensions of the solid line are shown only as dotted lines, to emphasise that they represent volumes outside the normal range where, at least in the short term until management changes have been effected, the 'normal' fixed-to-variable cost relationships might not be valid. However, at least as regards the normal volume or activity range, where the line intersects the vertical axis determines the approximate value of total fixed costs a, while the slope of the line determines the unit variable cost b.

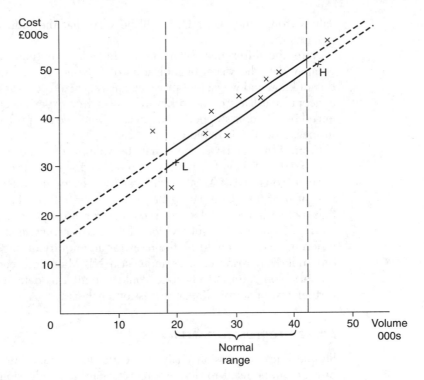

High–low method

An alternative simple method of fixed and variable cost estimation is known as the
high–low method. It also uses a scattergram and the same data as for the visual-fit
method. Again we use Figure 11.2 and the same data for illustration. This method
works by using the cost figures for the highest and lowest activity volume levels in
the data set used, and connecting these to determine the cost–fit line. If the highest
and lowest volume costs are markedly out of line with a linear function as a whole,
these outliers should be ignored in favour of cost points nearer to a linear function
but as close as possible to the extremes of the experienced volume range.

Following the above precepts, we have selected points H and L in Figure 11.2 to
give us what appears visually to be the most realistic cost–fit line between two
high–low volumes. Drawing the line, and again showing it dotted outside the range
of experienced or normal production volumes, we can determine the estimated fixed
costs from the intercept point on the vertical axis and the variable cost rate from the
slope of the line; or we can calculate these two costs arithmetically.

The data recorded in Figure 11.2 is taken from monthly cost reports during 19X0.
For month L the total costs are £30 000 for a volume of 20 000 units, and for month
H the total costs are £50 000 for a volume of 45 000 units. Taking our assumption
of linearity, which includes the assumption that all mixed or step costs become aver-
aged out over a larger volume, the increase in total costs between points L and H
is taken to consist wholly of variable costs. The increase is £20 000 for 25 000 units,
or £0.80 variable cost per unit. Returning to our basic cost equation, $Y = a + bX$,
this can be restated as $a = Y - bX$ to solve for fixed costs. From this, and taking our

values from either L or H, it will be seen that the indicated fixed cost is £14 000 per month.

Note the difference between the high–low method fixed costs of £14 000 as compared to the visual-fit indication of £18 000 per month. Which is correct? We do not know and we cannot prove an answer. Fixed costs at zero output are a notional concept, and fixed costs within our normal or experienced output range are influenced by mixed or stepped costs. In any event, we are probably more often interested in measuring the variable cost per unit.

From Table 11.1 we know that the volume of trade catalogues printed in 19X0 was 400 000. Taking the figures from our high–low solution, this would indicate total variable costs of £320 000, with total fixed costs of £168 000, giving a total overall cost of £488 000. Comparing these figures with Table 11.1 it appears that our total falls between the total costs recorded for absorption costing and activity-based costing. However, the subdivision of total cost as between fixed and variable is very different, and this could be the basis for an enquiry or engineering method study of the underlying resource uses and costs. (NB Many indirect and overhead costs may be variable.) Alternatively, one could submit the data in our scattergram to the further test of simple linear regression analysis.

Linear regression analysis

Simple linear regression analysis and the least-squares method of fitting a line of best fit can be used to derive a more scientific subdivision between fixed and variable cost than is possible by the visual-fit and high–low methods. The mechanics of the method are illustrated in detail in specialist management accounting texts such as those by Drury (1996) and Wilson and Chua (1993). With access to appropriate PC software, this mathematical solution may be the quickest as well as the most 'precise' solution available. We use the word 'precise' advisedly, rather than 'accurate' or 'true', because no mathematical solution can resolve abnormalities in the underlying data, whether arising from poor management control in the periods from which the data is drawn or from inherent mixed or stepped costs. Perhaps the best solution of all would be to have a computer graphics system on which the raw data and the least-squares regression solution are displayed, and where there is the further facility to generate visual best-fit lines for comparison with the regression solution. However, managerial experience of past events and awareness of the kinds of situations (e.g. particular volume levels or speeds of change to higher or lower volume levels) relevant to decisions pending may often be at least as significant in identifying relevant information as would be any mathematical or computer outputs applying 'precision' analysis to historical costs whose 'relevance' may be uncertain.

The engineering method

At its best, the 'engineering method' of cost estimation ignores historical costs, or else considers them only to the extent that they provide an alternative set of data for cross-checking the credibility of the data generated for the engineering-method exercise. The engineering method can be used not only for cost estimation for decision-making and planning, which is our present concern, but also for establishing accurate standard costs for use in management accounting control systems.

In spite of its name, the engineering method of cost estimation can be carried out by any accountant or manager with expert knowledge of the production or distribution processes involved. The method is especially appropriate when new products, processes or distribution channels are being introduced – with historical costs of little relevance – but it can also be used for periodic reviews of the continuing accuracy and credibility of the historical costing of continuing products, processes and distribution, perhaps on a three- to five-year cycle of rolling review.

The point of naming this method of cost estimation the 'engineering method' is that the critical skill needed is the ability to understand the technicalities of the production or distribution process involved, and to measure accurately the physical resources consumed from materials, labour and equipment. These physical measures of resource consumption, or real cost, can then be converted into money costs by the accountant multiplying the physical resource measures by their unit input prices. The method works best when the proportion of direct costs (including direct fixed costs as well as variable costs) is high relative to the indirect or overhead costs, because it will be obvious that the estimation and apportionment of the latter is a matter of 'expert opinion', with uncertainty, likely wide errors of judgement, and therefore the potential for unconscious or even wilful distortion of the apportionments in favour of the cost estimates the accountants or managers may be hoping for.

Time-and-motion studies and other careful study of work methods and flow are often important for the success of the engineering method, although these activities may require negotiation with trade unions or, at the least, tactful approaches to ensure the cooperation of workers, both from the general objective of sustaining plant morale and because uncooperative workers can lead to 'rubbish readings' in respect of work-study measurements of potential productivity.

The engineering method is especially appropriate where a change in products, production volumes, distribution methods, etc. is under consideration. It is also in this type of circumstance that differential costing, discussed in the next section, is most useful. The cost figures used in Table 11.2 are therefore obtained by using the engineering method.

Differential cost and revenue analysis

Differential analysis is the study of the results of changes in costs, or in revenues, arising from taking up one particular opportunity. It is a way of operationalising 'opportunity cost'. Even when one is studying only one specified new course of action there is the opportunity cost involved of otherwise doing nothing, just maintaining the status quo. Given that we are looking at change, at future possibilities, it follows that we should use future costs and revenues, not the historical figures obtainable from absorption costing records. Also, we should be using up-to-date information on current technology, attainable efficiency in production and distribution activities, and the current market prices of inputs; in short, the kind of information obtainable from good engineering-methods cost estimation.

Differential analysis can be used to study the effects of volume changes (downwards as well as upwards), the introduction of new products or other changes in the

Table 11.2 Absorption costs and differential costs compared – PrintPublish Ltd new product annual cost and profit or loss

	Absorption costs	Differential costs		
		Method A	Method B	Difference
	£	£	£	£
Annual fixed costs:				
Staff (to edit and obtain entries and orders)	60 000	50 000	60 000	10 000
Equipment leasing costs	10 000	10 000	20 000	10 000
Equipment maintenance contract	4 000	4 000	5 000	1 000
Premises costs	20 000	6 000	6 000	
Total fixed costs	94 000	70 000	91 000	21 000
Variable cost per unit:				
Direct materials	1.00	1.00	1.20	0.20
Direct labour (printing and binding, etc.)	5.00	5.00	3.00	(2.00)
Total unit variable cost	6.00	6.00	4.20	(1.80)
Estimated sales (10 000 units at £14.95)	149 500	149 500	149 500	
Less variable costs (10 000 units)	60 000	60 000	42 000	(18 000)
Contribution	89 500	89 500	107 500	18 000
Less annual fixed costs	94 000	70 000	91 000	21 000
Projected profit or (loss) on annual sales	(4 500)	19 500	16 500	(3 000)

product mix, or the introduction of new technology or change in the methods of distribution and marketing.

Often differential analysis will consist entirely, or almost entirely, of the cash-flow changes expected to result from a particular course of action. Non-cash accrual costs, notably depreciation, may be omitted either because they already exist and will not alter or because any needed new plant or equipment, or building space, can be leased or hired without long-term capital or contractual commitment. Existing capital and other costs which will not alter in amount in the decision situation we are studying can be ignored in the differential analysis. These costs are known as 'sunk costs'. But, of course, if old buildings or plant and equipment assets are made redundant by the new decision initiative these may have a cash resale or salvage value which should be taken into account in the differential analysis.

Differential analysis is primarily an approach for short-term decisions. Most long-term decisions involve the commitment of investment capital, and their assessment requires the use of the investment appraisal methods explained in Chapter 13. Even when formal investment appraisal is required, however, this will be based on careful cash-flow forecasts, which should be prepared on the same rigorous basis as the differential analysis described here.

It should be emphasised that in differential analysis we are studying all costs that change as a result of a particular decision. Thus if costs conventionally classified as 'fixed' in routine cost recording and reporting are expected to increase, or decrease, as a result of the specified decision situation it is as relevant to include in the differential analysis the amount of the change in fixed costs as the true variable costs.

Using differential cost analysis

Table 11.2 presents information for a business opportunity being considered by PrintPublish Ltd. Until now, in spite of its name, the company has worked only as a printer. Management seeks to expand, and is attracted by diversification into publishing to spread commercial risk and achieve hoped-for increases to value added. The proposition is to fill a market gap by publishing a good business directory for the company's region, South Anglia. Following an engineering-methods-type study, it has been established that there is sufficient space in the existing offices and workshops to house the new project, but new, specialised typesetting and printing equipment will be needed. The latter can be obtained on annual lease with all maintenance covered under annual contract. Based on the technical information supplied to him, the accountant has drawn up a summary of the costs which he considers should be properly chargeable to the new project. This is shown in the Absorption costs column of Table 11.2. Management estimates the sales potential of the directory at 10 000 copies per annum if it is priced at £14.95. On that volume, total revenue would be £149 500, as against total costs of £154 000, giving a loss of £4500 per annum. The chief executive is surprised, and he discusses with the accountant the basis of the costs used.

The discussion reveals that the accountant has included in the staff costs £10 000 of existing staff pay for time which he understands would be diverted to selling space in, and copies of, the new directory. However, he accepts that the extra work would largely be taking up slack and that none of this £10 000 would consist of extra cash cost. It also turns out that the £20 000 premises charge was mainly an allocation of existing overheads on a basis of estimated space to be used for the new product. Only £6000 of this charge was for additional out-of-pocket cash-flow costs. It thus appears that £24 000 of the product costs in the first column of Table 11.2 were simply bookkeeping reallocations and not true differential costs. Adjusting for this in the second column of Table 11.2 changes the projected loss to a projected differential profit of £19 500. Given that this profit would be achieved with no investment of company capital beyond working capital for work-in-progress and any stocks of unsold directories, this might be seen as a satisfactory return, at least for the first year. On the other hand, it is not an enormous profit margin for a product not sharing in the full recharge of corporate overheads, and this profit could be very sensitive to any shortfall in the predicted sales volume, especially as fixed costs comprise more than half the total costs on the predicted sales volume. We shall look at this uncertainty in more detail in the next section, on cost–volume–profit (CVP) analysis.

Subsequent to the above review, the technical director found a new desk-top publishing system which he thinks could give the firm better value in publishing the new directory. This allows us to show another application for differential costing, the case of comparing two mutually exclusive alternative means to meeting an agreed need.

In Table 11.2 the original proposal is shown as method A and the desk-top publishing alternative as method B. The fixed-cost figures entered have all been corrected for the differential-costing mistakes made in the data entered in the left-hand column. Looking at the differential costs between methods A and B, the total fixed costs for B are £21 000 greater than for A, but the variable cost per unit under method B is £1.80 less. At the expected production and sales level of 10 000 directories, method B will cost £3000 more, thus yielding £3000 less profit. But how will profits be affected if sales are significantly less than or greater than 10 000? This is one question that cost–volume–profit analysis helps to clarify, so we shall return to this example in the next section.

Cost–volume–profit analysis

In Chapter 10 we looked at the relationship of fixed and variable costs to changes in the volume of activity using graphical display. This was shown to be a helpful exercise, although one must be cautious about making judgements on the levels of costs at activity volumes which are outside the 'normal range' of operational experience. If data on sales revenue are included in the graphical analysis, in addition to data on costs, then the effect of changes in volume on profits can also be displayed and studied. Profits, of course, equal total revenue less total costs at any indicated level or volume of activity.

Break-even graph and profit graph

Figure 11.3 illustrates a conventional break-even graph. This takes its name from the critical volume level of sales at which total sales revenue and total costs chargeable against sales are exactly equal. Above break-even there is profit; below it there

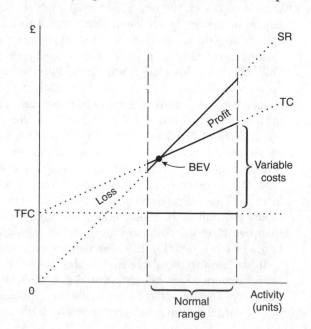

Figure 11.3
Break-even graph.
Note: For key to notation on graphs see Table 11.3.

is a loss. Critical interest should focus on the behaviour of both costs and revenue across the entire realistic range of operating volumes. The graph provides only a starting point for sensitive understanding. Especially when considering operating at volume levels near or outside the margins of the normal range, it becomes important to ask for specific cost-study information on how costs, especially fixed costs, could be controlled to maximise the benefit at any given revenue activity level.

Some managers prefer to focus just on the relationship between sales revenue volume and profit, and for them the relevant data in the break-even graph can be simplified to display as a profit graph (see Figure 11.4). This display loses the information on variable costs, which is made possible because of the assumption that variable cost per unit is constant and is a constant proportion of sales price, throughout at least the normal volume range. However, this is an assumption which should perhaps be kept visible and explicit, as in the break-even graph, if only so that managers are reminded to challenge the assumption from time to time, and to seek efficient means of reducing variable costs and thus further enhancing profits.

Contribution analysis

'Contribution' is defined as the excess of sales price over unit variable cost, or the excess of sales revenue over total variable costs (see Table 11.2). The concept and measurement of contribution can be applied when studying the pricing or marketing of individual products (including services, and retail and wholesale distribution), including the potential of new products and also reviews considering whether or not to drop existing products. It can additionally be used to study the overall performance of the firm. As volume increases from zero, all contribution is applied initially to recover fixed costs (and thus reduce loss) up to the break-even volume.

Beyond break-even all contribution received becomes profit. However, when seeking to expand sales beyond the existing or normal range it may be necessary to

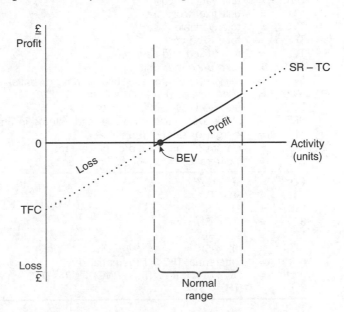

Figure 11.4
Profit graph.

spend disproportionate extra funds on marketing (including promotion, sales staff time, discounts, etc.), so that measurement of incremental contribution should be taken not from the graphs of the firm as a whole, but instead from one-off calculations using data (such as from engineering-method studies) explicitly tailored to the particular product(s) and market circumstances.

To illustrate some of the problems and methods of using CVP/break-even analysis and contribution analysis let us return to PrintPublish Ltd's pending decision whether or not to start a line in regional business directories and, if so, whether to produce these using method A or method B. The terminology and notation we will use for this are summarised in Table 11.3, together with the equations for key relationships of data. The data we will use is displayed in Table 11.2. The applications of the concepts and equations to the choice between method A and method B are summarised in Table 11.4.

Unit contribution and contribution ratio

Unit contribution, or sales price less unit variable cost, is shown in Table 11.4. Method B offers the prospect of an extra £1.80 per unit for every extra unit sold. This benefit will be reflected in the contribution ratio, 0.719 for B as against 0.599 for A, showing the proportional contributions to profits once the break-even point has been passed. But if sales fall below the break-even point, losses will be greater,

Table 11.3 Notation and equations for cost–volume–profit and differential analysis (see Table 11.4 and Figures 11.3, 11.4 and 11.5)

CU	=	contribution per unit sold at a given price
CT	=	contribution total for a given volume of sales
CR	=	contribution ratio or percentage to sales
UVC	=	unit variable cost
UFC	=	unit fixed cost
TVC	=	total variable cost
TFC	=	total fixed cost
TC	=	total (fixed and variable) costs
SP	=	sales price (per unit)
SR	=	sales revenue (for specified number of units)
SV	=	sales (revenue) volume, in units
BEV	=	break-even volume, in units
BEP	=	break-even price, for a specified volume in units
MS	=	margin of safety, in units
MSR	=	margin of safety ratio or percentage
IV	=	indifference volume (of sales in units)

CU	=	SP – UVC
CT	=	SR – TVC
CR	=	CU ÷ SP or CT ÷ SR
BEV	=	TFC ÷ CU
MS	=	SV – BEV
MSR	=	MS ÷ SV
IV	=	Differential TFC ÷ Differential UVC
Profit	=	SR – TC = SR – (TFC + TVC) = SR – (TFC + (SV)(UVC))
BEP	=	(TFC ÷ SV) + UVC

Table 11.4 Cost–volume–profit and differential-cost calculations for PrintPublish Ltd – proposal to produce and sell 10 000 directories at £14.95

		Method A	Method B
CU	=	£14.95 – £6.00 = £8.95	£14.95 – £4.20 = £10.75
CR	=	£8.95 ÷ £14.95 = 0.599	£10.75 ÷ £14.95 = 0.719
BEV	=	70 000 ÷ 8.95 = 7 821 units	91 000 ÷ £10.75 = 8 465 units
MS	=	10 000 – 7 821 = 2 179 units	10 000 – 8 465 = 1 535 units
MSR	=	2 179 ÷ 10 000 = 21.8%	1 535 ÷ 10 000 = 15.4%
IV	=	£21 000 ÷ £1.80 = 11 667 units (see Figure 11.4)	
BEP if sales, e.g., only 6 000 units		(70 000 ÷ 6 000) + £6.00 = £17.67	(£91 000 ÷ 6 000) + £4.20 = £19.37

Sensitivity at selected volumes	£ Profit	£ Profit
6 000 units	(16 300)	(26 500)
8 000	1 600	(5 000)
10 000	19 500	16 500
11 667	34 422	34 422
14 000	55 300	59 500
20 000	109 000	124 000

Note: For key to notation, see Table 11.3.

the higher the contribution ratio. This can be shown graphically, as in Figure 11.5, using data from Tables 11.2 and 11.4. Method A gives a break-even of 7821 units, compared to 8465 units for method B. The difference between break-even and a (realistic) sales volume is called the margin of safety: this is 2179 units (or 21.8%) for method A and 1535 units (or 15.4%) for method B. This suggests method B is higher risk.

One further test illustrated by Figure 11.4 is the 'indifference volume' (IV); that is, the volume at which total costs will be equal between the alternatives being compared, so that total profits will also be equal at that volume. In our example the IV is 11 667 units, well above the expected sales volume. Until sales volume reaches this level, profits will be less under method B than method A, but beyond this level they will be greater under method B.

Profit sensitivity analysis

'Sensitivity analysis' is not an analytical technique particular to accounting, but rather a general approach to subjecting operational data to testing to see what would or might be the likely outcomes resulting from a change in key variables affecting a decision. In our PrintPublish example we could test for differences in unit variable costs or in total fixed costs (including changes in the assumptions as regards including only incremental fixed costs or, alternatively, a proportional share of existing plus incremental fixed costs). For the present purpose of illustrating CVP analysis, however, it will suffice to show the effect on profits of different assumptions regarding the market sales volume. The results of this are shown at the bottom of Table 11.4. Method B will generate significantly greater profit at high sales volume,

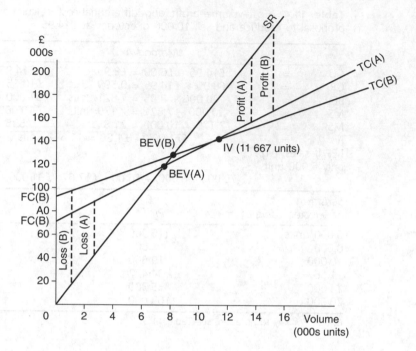

Figure 11.5
Frequency volume for alternative production methods (see Table 11.4).
Note: For key to notation on graphs, see Table 11.3

but also the trading loss will be much greater if there is a large shortfall in sales volume. The credibility of the sales forecast of 10 000 units should be re-examined. Even if credibility is confirmed uncertainly remains, and many, if not most, accountants would tend to recommend the risk-averse alternative of choosing method A, arguing that avoiding large losses is more important than gambling on larger but uncertain profits. Here, of course, is where managers rather than accountants must take the final decision – and the accountability!

One could also ask, what if a cautious or even realistic sales forecast were only 6000 units, what then would be the break-even price (BEP) for the new directory? Using the BEP equation from Table 11.3, we obtain the results shown near the bottom of Table 11.4; that is, the BEP would be £17.67 under method A and £19.37 under method B. Whichever method is chosen, and unless there is high credibility for the sales forecast of 10 000 units, a cautious approach would suggest that the price should perhaps be set higher than the £14.95 proposed, unless it is thought that the market will be price-resistant (including concern for any direct market competition from other publishers).

Limiting factors

In our PrintPublish example we have assumed that management has the time to take on the introduction and marketing of a new product range, that there was space and skill to undertake new production and that the extra production would be supplied on newly leased equipment. However, many decision situations will not be so straightforward. Indeed, for illustration, let us consider that in the PrintPublish example, while all the typesetting and printing will be done on new, leased equipment, the binding is to be done on the existing bindery production line. We shall have to accommodate all three of the company's products in the bindery: trade catalogues, community magazines and the new business directory. The bindery is nearing its maximum production capacity and new equipment cannot be leased but, instead, can only be purchased as a capital outlay, for which the company presently has no spare cash or any spare credit capacity (in the opinion of its bankers). It is therefore pertinent to ask, in view of this limited capacity (or limiting factor), how the firm should best use, or ration, its capacity to maximise total contribution and profits.

The relevant data is summarised in Table 11.5. The object of the analysis is to determine which product produces the highest contribution per unit of scarce resource, or limiting factor, consumed. In theory, the output of the product with the highest contribution per unit of limiting factor should be maximised until that product's market is saturated. In this example the optimal bindery product turns out to be the trade catalogues. The reason for this is probably that a high proportion of the cost and value in this product derives from the artwork and photo reproduction, while the binding costs are relatively small.

Limiting-factor analysis can be conducted at a more sophisticated level by the use of linear programming (see Wilson and Chua 1993). While this analysis may indeed lead to optimal product-mix decisions in the very short term – or during a recession or crisis, when new investment is barred by top-management policy decisions – it may be more constructive in typical circumstances for management to focus its energies on removing the limiting factor, rather than just accepting this and constraining its output and its ability to meet customer requirements. In PrintPublish, for example, the limiting-factor constraint might be removed simply by putting on an extra shift or half-shift in the bindery.

CVP in perspective

CVP, including contribution analysis and limiting-factor analysis, and preferably based on decision-relevant differential costs rather than historical absorption costs, offers powerful tools for short-term business decisions. These decisions include the

Table 11.5 PrintPublish Ltd limiting-factor analysis

	Trade catalogues	Community magazines	Business directories
Sales price per unit (SP)	£1.20	£0.40	£14.95
Less variable cost (VC)	0.45	0.16	4.20
Contribution per unit (CU)	£0.75	£0.24	£10.75
Divide by bindery time per unit (hours)	0.002	0.001	0.035
Contribution per bindery hour	£375.00	£240.00	£307.14
Limiting factor contribution ranking	1	3	2

solving of problems regarding pricing, new products, keeping or dropping existing products, production-mix and sales-mix planning, altering plant layouts and work flows, changing material-input mixes or process flows and output mixes, choices of distribution channels and promotional activities, and so on.

Nevertheless, the CVP and related analytical methods have their limitations. Their conclusions are no more reliable than the quality of the assumptions and parameters supplied by management, or the appropriateness of the physical resource use and cost data available to, or chosen by, the accountant. Both management and accountants need to communicate openly about their problems concerning objectives and data limitations in order to minimise the limitations and obtain the best decision-relevant advice.

Decisions on inputs and outputs

This chapter has been concerned with explaining the types of cost information and cost analysis which should prove helpful to management decision-making in specific circumstances. The key criterion, it is argued, is not precision or even accuracy, but relevance. Management science and production management textbooks abound with methods of analysis seeking to optimise the choice and use of inputs. The choices available relate to the use of alternative materials (e.g. steel v. aluminium tube), standard parts (for economy) v. tailor-made parts (for 'perfection' in design or performance); to questions of the substitution of higher-cost materials for labour costs involved in 'making do' with lower-cost, lower-grade materials; and to the merits of substituting capital-intensive methods of production for traditional, craft-skilled, high-cost, labour-intensive methods. The latter issue involves the 'time value of money' and the capital-investment decision considered in Chapter 13.

If non-relevant costs are fed into decision-making on production-input decisions such as the above examples 'rubbish' solutions will result. The manager must not just ask the accountant for the cost of a particular input, process or output. Rather, given that, as we have seen, there are many alternative measures of cost for any particular resource or activity, the manager must make clear to the accountant exactly what kind of decision-situation he needs decision-relevant cost information for.

The above examples typify the kinds of decision which should be taken before production begins, or perhaps even before there is a commitment to produce a particular product. There are other kinds of decision-situations which relate to ongoing management performance; these overlap between the topic areas of management planning and decisions, and management control. An example is the problem of determining what is the optimal stock to maintain of raw materials, parts and components, of work-in-progress, and of finished goods ready for sale and delivery. There is a well-established operations-research technique for solving this problem: the economic order quantity (EOQ) model, which is discussed in Chapter 17.

There is an approach, however, which could make the use of the EOQ redundant in many industries. This is the Japanese-inspired just-in-time (JIT) approach to disciplining both external suppliers and internal production lines to complete deliveries precisely on time to meet both production-line requirements for inputs and customer delivery requirements for outputs (J.Y. Lee 1987). In practice it will clearly be easier to apply the JIT approach to a plant with a limited range of regularly produced products, such as a bakery, than to a factory producing a thousand different lines of hardware, many in small quantities.

Conclusions

Routine costing systems provide information appropriate for valuing work-in-progress and stocks to meet financial accounting requirements, and also information useful in the day-to-day monitoring of shop-floor performance or in assisting budgetary control (especially in service organisations and the public sector).

However, the most important management decisions involve seeking out and assessing possible changes, in products or product mix, in technologies or production methods, and/or in markets or distribution methods. For these decision-situations routine cost accounting information is of little help, and management must demand relevant cost information and explain the nature of the decision-situation and choices under consideration to the accounting staff so that they can help provide relevant information and analysis.

For some decisions activity-based costs or attributable costs, unlike conventional absorption costs, may provide sufficiently relevant information. But where decisions involve the possibility of substantial changes in the volume or scale of operations, or in products or product mix, then ad hoc cost studies, often involving the so-called engineering method, and also more sophisticated analysis will be needed. Here the concepts and methods of cost estimation, differential costing, and contribution and cost–volume–profit analysis should be employed. Business and financial risk must also be considered, and where decision-situations involve significant capital outlays the 'time value of money' must additionally be brought into the decision process (this is discussed in Chapter 13).

This chapter has explained the cost concepts and forms of cost analysis which are useful to managers in making short-term decisions. It was necessary to consider some of the limitations of traditional absorption cost accounting, and how that approach might be modified and improved through activity-based-costing (ABC) and attributable-costing methods. At the heart of many business decisions is change – of product or product mix, or of technology or market. Assessing the consequences of change requires a clear separation of fixed or period costs, especially the core costs of the organisation, from the variable costs attributable to individual products (or services or markets) and to changes in their volume.

Methods of cost estimation for identifying fixed and variable costs were discussed. This led on to the concept of contribution and to methods of differential costing and cost–volume–profit analysis, including sensitivity and limiting-factor calculations.

Further reading

See Arnold and Turley (1996: chs 6–8) or Drury (1996: chs 9–11; 1997: chs 3–5). For an American approach, see Horngren *et al.* (1994: chs 3, 10, 11).

Questions and exercises

1 What is the concept of relevant cost, and what do you think may be the difficulties in applying it in practice?

2 **(a)** Why may any single given concept or measure of cost not be suitable equally for use in the separate exercises of planning, decision-making and control?

   (b) How does the time-horizon of forward planning and decisions affect the classification or measurement of costs?

3 Cost–volume–profit relationships can be studied by drawing a graph using the historical evidence from past months or years. Consider what factors sometimes might make this evidence unreliable as a predictor of future performance at increased or reduced volumes.

4 Briefly explain the principles and method of differential-cost analysis and suggest for what types of decision situations it may have the greatest advantage over analysis based on CVP (cost–volume–profit) studies derived from historical absorption costs.

5 'Attributable costing may be more relevant than either absorption costing or differential costing to many decisions involving marketing, pricing, and product-range and product-abandonment problems.' Explain why you agree or disagree with this statement.

6 Suppose that a particular cost simultaneously has (or at least might have) the characteristics of being controllable, traceable, avoidable, attributable, relevant, common (but not joint), volume-related and more suitable for allocation than apportionment. Concisely describe the character of the above cost without using the 'label' words used above. Also, can you suggest any examples of actual costs (or resource uses) which might fit this cost characterisation/description?

7 Dryways Ltd makes a single product, a dehumidifier. The price to wholesalers and direct to some large customers is normally £100. Recent years' sales have ranged between twenty thousand and thirty-five thousand units. Variable costs are currently £70 per unit and total fixed costs are £700 000.

   Draw one or more break-even or CVP graphs to display your findings (graph paper is helpful but not essential). You may find it useful to check your graph solutions by using some of the notation and equations in Table 11.3.

   (a) Determine the break-even volume under the company's existing pricing policy and price structure. Also determine at what volume profit will equal a 10% return on sales.

   (b) During a recession it is forecast that only 20 000 units can be sold at the normal price. However, it appears that up to a further 15 000 units could be sold through large mail-order distributors if the price were cut to £80.

(c) Alternatively to (b), the company could attempt to enlarge its normal market by reducing its normal price, as a result of product redesign to reduce material and labour costs, and of leasing new automated plant to further cut labour requirements. It is estimated that variable cost could be cut to £50 per unit but fixed costs would rise to £900 000. At what volume would management be indifferent between alternatives (c) and (a) or (c) and (b)?

(d) What other factors should be taken into account before a choice is made between alternatives and what additional information would you seek before making a decision?

8 Tork Ltd produces a single line of powered heavy-duty torque wrenches. Its budget profit and loss summary for a normal six months' trading is as follows:

	£000s	£000s
Sales (2400 units)		840
Direct labour	192	
Direct materials	180	
Variable production overhead	72	
Fixed production overhead	120	
Variable admin and sales overhead	36	
Fixed admin and sales overhead	96	
Total costs		696
Profit before tax		144

A foreign government has invited the firm to tender for a special order of 500 torque wrenches. The following additional information is supplied:

(i) The customer requires variations of product and delivery specifications whereby direct labour cost would be 12.5% above normal; direct material costs would be 20% above normal; sales overheads (transport) would cost £35 per unit more than usual; and special tooling costs of £10 000 would arise (and the tooling would have no certain value after completion of the special order).

(ii) The customer requires completion of the order within six months of confirmation of the order.

(iii) The firm does not want the investment risk of enlarging its premises, but present facilities can be used to produce up to 450 units per month. All units beyond 400 per month incur an overtime premium of £20 per unit.

You are required to:

(a) apply differential cost analysis to the special order;

(b) calculate the tender price which would leave the total company profits for six months unaltered; also calculate the tender price which would earn the same profit margin on sales as in the budget above, on the enlarged volume sold during the six months of the special order, and recalculate and show the six months' budget on this tender basis;

(c) comment on any simplifying assumptions you may have had to make in this exercise and on any other financial complications to be considered or any additional information needed before a final decision.

9 Information is supplied below on the year's accounting results for a division of Tinbrass Ltd supplying four hardware products.

Product	£000s A	£000s B	£000s C	£000s D
Sales revenue	180	120	60	100
Cost of purchases	80	60	40	90
Value added (sales less purchases)				
Value added (% of sales)				
Total historical absorption cost	150	105	55	96
Absorption net profit (margin)				
Absorption net profit to sales (%)				
Total transaction costs (ABC)	165	90	50	101
ABC net profit (margin)				
ABC net profit to sales (%)				
Total variable costs	140	80	40	93
Product contribution				
Product contribution ratio (%)				
Capital employed (estimated)	210	90	80	30
Capital turnover (ratio of sales to capital employed)				
Absorption-cost return on capital employed (ROCE)				
ABC return on capital employed				

You are required to:

(a) calculate the numbers to fill in the blanks left in the list above, and study the completed list for what you can learn or infer about the products and their cost, price and profit characteristics;

(b) assuming spare capacity, suggest which product(s) should be given the greatest sales promotion effort. What would you advise if, instead, the firm is at full capacity and the sales of one product can be increased only at the expense of another.

10 Ambridge Rusticks Ltd (ARL) is a cottage industry making a modest but growing profit from an expanding range of mainly wooden garden ornaments, including gnomes. A chain of garden centres has suggested the most popular line would sell better if it was additionally available in a shiny, easy-to-clean material, and they will contract to buy at least 10 000 in the first year at £5.30 per unit.

ARL finds it can make the product by either of two methods, plastic injection or a cheap 'ceramic' moulding process. ARL is averse to long-term risk and will only invest if an investment cash payback is probable within a year or so. They have obtained information on the outlay and operating costs for basic equipment for each of the two processes, including the data listed below.

	Plastic £	Ceramic £
Bulk price of raw materials (£s per kg)	0.40	0.10
Quantity of raw material (kg per unit)	3.00	7.00
Machine (and labour @ £8 per hour) hours per unit	0.10	0.20
Indirect labour, supplies and expenses (£s per unit)	0.40	0.70
Energy consumption (£s per unit)	0.10	0.50
Share of general overheads for 10 000 unit output (£s)	7 000	7 000
Capital outlay (NB to be depreciated on a unit basis, on an estimated 30 000 units-of-output working life, with nil salvage value) (£s)	40 000	20 000

You are required to:

(a) calculate unit costs and likely profitability from the contract available;

(b) apply sensitivity analysis for the possibilities that the initial contract might not be renewed, but equally additional products might be made at the same profit margins to absorb any underutilised time (NB the firm is committed to a 44-hour working week, 50 weeks per year);

(c) advise the company on whether or not to invest, on the choice of process, and on its use of costing methods for investment decisions.

12 Overheads, activity-based costs and pricing

Objectives

Problems with using routinely reported, historical cost accounting information have been mentioned in previous chapters. Some of the most important of these problems arise from the treatment of overheads in costings. This chapter reviews the overheads problem, possibly the largest single source of error in costings. It then considers the mechanics and advantages of activity-based costing (ABC) and its wider application in activity-based management (ABM) to consider how far this increasingly popular approach may resolve the overheads-measurement problem. One of the major uses of cost information, and of ABC/ABM, is setting and reviewing the prices of goods and services; the chapter explains this use and some limitations on the relevance of costs as determinants of prices.

Introduction

Accounting figures look precise, yet sometimes they are generated from processes that include estimates (e.g. of the rates of consumption of assets through depreciation or depletion) and assumptions (e.g. as regards the amount of 'benefit' or 'value' various end-products or services receive from central and departmental support activities and their costs). This chapter seeks to explore the particular problems of overhead costings, which will be contrasted between conventional absorption and the newer approaches being promoted as more relevant both for control and for management decisions. The currently most popular new approach, ABC, will be discussed in some detail. The chapter concludes by considering the use and limitations of costing information in decisions and periodic reviews of the pricing of goods and services.

Problems and change in management

In recent times it has been increasingly recognised that cost accounting, although moderately improved and also upgraded in status and role under the label of 'management accounting', has been failing to deliver the best or most relevant information for ongoing management planning, decisions and control. An important exposition of this recognition was made by Johnson and Kaplan (1987), whose arguments merit paraphrasing and then some further discussion of issues arising.

Through the nineteenth century financial accounting and cost accounting developed and operated largely independently of each other. Financial accounting developed to meet head-office, professional and audit requirements. Cost accounting developed to meet the requirements mainly of factory management and engineering. Cost figures were transferred at least annually from the cost accounts to the financial accounts, to obtain totals, or balances of, materials, work in progress, finished goods and goods sold for use in balance sheets and profit and loss statements.

By the early to mid-twentieth century, giant, vertically integrated and multi-divisional business organisations became important, with wider product ranges and a particular need to control and measure the performance of their separate divisions. ROI (return on investment; similar to ROCE) became a popular measure of divisional performance (as explained in detail in Chapter 16). ROI is essentially a *financial accounting* measure, orientated towards the performance criteria of the investment markets, whether for the corporate entity as a whole or for the individual divisions which, in an ideal world, should be at least notionally viable if floated in the investment markets as smaller, independent companies. Investment markets became more sophisticated and, amid the pressures from economic recessions and more rapid market and industrial change, increased emphasis was given to ROI and to the associated financial reporting of the constituent information feeding into ROI and into balance sheets.

As its importance grew, and as awareness of the scope for creative accounting spread, financial reporting came under increasing professional and government regulation. There were a number of reasons or justifications for the increased regulation, including improving the comparability of financial results between companies and reducing the scope for fraud. One area for potential fraud was the false statement of production costs, and the 'value' of stocks of material, work in progress and finished stocks. This helped to focus attention on product costs, and on simple and supposedly objective and easily verifiable measures of product costs. The traditional full-cost absorption cost accounting methods appeared to meet these criteria, and so the dominance of their use in cost and management accounting became confirmed in business practice, even though their usefulness for management planning, decision-making and control had already been challenged for some years by a minority of academics, accountants and managers. And at the same time, new information processing and business management techniques were emerging independently of accounting, not reflected in accounting information or always compatible or reconcilable with conventional accounting; hence the situation giving rise to Johnson and Kaplan's choice of theme and title: *Relevance Lost: The Rise and Fall of Management Accounting* (1987). They, of course, were not alone in seeing the need for reform of management accounting, but before suggesting particular reforms one should look more closely at the needs and uses for cost information, and the weaknesses of conventional cost accounting information for satisfying these needs and uses.

Uses for cost information

The following main uses or needs for cost information were found from one large survey of UK manufacturers (Bright *et al.*, 1992):

- for cost control   94%
- for product pricing   90%
- for investment evaluations   87%
- for management performance appraisal   77%
- for decisions on sourcing   67%
- for decisions on new products   67%

First, let us remind ourselves of the key characteristics of typical cost accounting systems. The entire organisation is subdivided into cost centres reflecting work of related character (typically by 'function'). Resource costs are classified by status as variable, fixed and (sometimes) mixed, and as resource acquisition or consumption is identified and reported (for labour, materials, purchases, etc.) the costed values of resources are charged to the cost centres as fixed or variable costs. As work progresses through its various stages costs are passed on from one cost centre to another, chargeable per unit of volume. What are clearly fixed costs at the initial cost centre, because of unitising and charging by volume, may come to be seen as variable costs in the decision-making of managers of cost centres later in the production cycle. The foregoing are the direct costs; additionally, indirect costs and at least some central overhead costs become allocated or apportioned to (i.e. added to) the unitised cost of production as the cycle progresses. At the end of the production process the final absorption cost per unit of production may appear to be largely variable, whereas in modern industrial (and other) businesses it has come to be recognised that in the short term most costs are largely fixed, except for materials and marginal overtime and casual labour. Whether costs are variable, fixed or mixed is of course a highly important classification base for costs, as we have seen in earlier chapters. Yet to state that a cost is variable does not definitely confirm whether it is direct, indirect or overhead in its inherent character, or in the way that its underlying real resources are managed or controlled.

Meeting needs for cost information

Referring back to the list of cost information needs or uses derived from the work of Bright *et al.* (1992), the most frequently recognised need was for information for use in cost control. Does conventional (absorption) costing provide really useful information for this purpose? Before answering, we must clarify what we mean by cost control. Do we mean observing/monitoring cost on the exception principle in case some significant deviation occurs which may merit probing and possible intervention? Do we mean exerting pressure continuously to squeeze/ratchet down costs (in real terms) to improve efficiency? Do we mean checking that costs have conformed to some predetermined target, standard or budget? Or do we mean studying costs selectively for aspects of process where tasks or other inputs may be re-engineered to achieve work needs by more cost-effective, often simpler, methods? All of these approaches to cost control may be found in practice, and all can reduce costs. However, exerting crude 'boss-pressure' to cut or ratchet down costs may arouse fear and resentment and undermine morale, so perhaps should not be done in a well-managed organisation. Again, the simple monitoring of current costs against historic (past) costs to look for deviation from trends is unscientific, given the implicit absence of any confirmation that historic costs represent efficient use of resources.

Of greater merit are the cost-control methods of comparing current costs against regularly updated target or 'standard costs' – with analysis and action on significant variances – and of selective studies of cost behaviour, which may be combined with 'standard costing'. As a major technique in its own right (usually, but not necessarily, combined with absorption costing), standard costing and the associated cost-variance analysis are considered in detail in Chapter 15, following discussion of budgetary control, which also can be closely linked to standard costing.

Returning to the need for cost-control information, conventional (absorption) costing can provide information of some use. It can show where aggregated costs (i.e. resource uses) are getting out of line with expectations based on historic cost or target standard cost. It can warn of the need for enquiry or corrective action, but it cannot always identify closely which resource uses are out of line or perhaps capable of significant improvement if analysed closely. The latter failure is partly because of the level of aggregation, partly because of unitising costs from earlier stages of the production cycle, and partly (and critically) because the approach focuses attention on the volume of units of production at every stage rather than on the work activities caused by the production process. Work activities of a direct and directly variable nature may be accurately captured by absorption costing, but the indirect costs and overheads can be wrongly costed by methods which absorb them solely on the most common absorption bases, such as direct labour hours or direct machine hours. To the extent, then, that simple absorption cost charging contains the built-in premise that all products receiving benefit from a pool of indirect support services or overhead expenditure receive that benefit in direct proportion to their share of direct labour or materials etc., it must follow that the cost distribution between the products is wrong. And if, and when, it occurs that figures for cost control are showing wrong total unit costs, and are not accurately tracing support activity and overhead costs and their contributions to different products, we must conclude that conventional cost information at least partly fails the needs of management for cost control.

Turning to the second need, information for product pricing, the above discussion may suggest an even greater weakness in conventional costing in its use for pricing than in its use for cost control. However, this critical conclusion must depend at least partly on the view that prices should closely reflect costs, and that the relative prices of different products forming part of a family of products should mirror their relative costs. This view will be discussed further in a later section of this chapter, on pricing. However, even if prices do not mirror relative costs, or if they cannot practically do so because prices are taken from the market, at the very least it is important to have accurate product costs to establish which products are most profitable and should therefore receive greatest strategic, marketing and promotional support to maximise their sales in search of maximum profits.

Regarding the third need, cost information for investment evaluation, this could, and indeed should, be a less important consideration when judging the merits of conventional costing. Why? Because, as suggested in the previous chapter, when one is considering new investment the relevant costs are not current full costs – whether based on absorption costing or otherwise – but, instead, the differential costs (that is, the net rise or fall in operating and overhead costs resulting from the new investment). The point was made that the differential costs may be best established by 'engineering studies', quite independently of reliance on routinely reported historic costs. Investment appraisals should be rigorous, and the relevant criteria and techniques for these are discussed in detail in Chapter 13, on longer-term decision-making.

As for the need for cost information for appraising management performance, the first point is that performance in meeting costs is only one of a number of criteria, by no means always sensibly the most important. The second point is that, if cost information is product-oriented and is wrong but consistently wrong in the same way, then little distortion in measuring managerial performance may result from using this data. On the other hand, if wrong costs are used, and if managers perceive the costs to be wrong or at least misleading, then the credibility and moral authority of using cost information in managerial appraisal are greatly weakened. If the main purposes of managerial appraisals are to help managers to improve their own performance and to increase managers' contributions to corporate economy and profitability, then the use of cost information linked to products by absorption costing may not be very helpful. Instead, we need data on costs classified in accordance with the concept of controllability (discussed in previous chapters), and based on the traceable costs of the separate activities supervised by the manager.

The last two needs for cost information, for decisions on sourcing (of contracted-out processing, support services, etc.) and for decisions on making and pricing new products (and how to make them), involve largely the same arguments and conclusions outlined previously for product pricing. If internal costs are wrong, then wrong decisions may be taken on whether or not to contract out, or excessive input prices may be tolerated.

This section has been highly critical of conventional absorption cost information. However, sometimes the product flow is sufficiently stable and homogeneous that any errors in product costs are too small to matter, and/or the extra expense involved in using an alternative, more complicated, costing system is not justified by any greater accuracy in product costs and in the analysis of indirect costs and overheads. But for other businesses, including many service businesses, there is a need for improved cost information, and ABC seems currently to be the most widely considered challenger to traditional absorption costing.

Activity-based costing

In the previous chapter ABC was briefly introduced to illustrate how the same total costs of a production (or service) organisation could be allocated in different amounts to individual products (and here of course the outputs of service organisations may be included as 'products') depending on the basis of allocation of indirect and overhead costs. Comparison among the conventional absorption method, ABC and attributable costing was shown in Table 11.1 and its notes.

We return again to ABC in more detail because of its importance. Its importance rests on the claim that ABC can solve most of the shortcomings of conventional costing (i.e. the absorption cost approach) explained in this and preceding chapters. Moreover, because it can be quite complicated and time-consuming to introduce ABC effectively, management consultancy firms have taken to ABC as a major service to promote, helping to generate more awareness of the method and perhaps some feeling among accountants and top management that ABC is a challenge they must tackle in order to be at the forefront in management information and techniques. The information generated by ABC can be used to help in a number of important management tasks; for this, the additional term 'activity-based management' (ABM) has been coined, and we will discuss this application of ABC later.

A further reason for the importance of ABC, in this book, is that business managers may become more directly involved in developing this new approach to cost information than has been necessary in the past with traditional absorption costing. The latter relied mainly on the physical volume of work documentation which managers undertook anyway for their own control purposes, combined with resource price information available direct from the accounting, purchasing and payroll records without taking up the time and attention of managers. But with ABC, in contrast, the more complex system of classifying and recording work activities within departments or cost centres does require, at least in the early stages of introduction and test-running of ABC, much more time and commitment from managers. In return, it is claimed, managers will obtain the reward of much useful new information to assist in controlling costs and in gaining awareness of how well their resources are being used to add customer value for the business.

But why now? Why has ABC come on to the scene only in the last five to ten years, after roughly a hundred years of use of absorption costing? Indeed, some academics and practitioners recognised the defects of absorption accounting many years ago, and at least thirty years ago some academics were teaching 'transactions cost analysis' (similar to ABC) as an improved method of tracing and apportioning overheads. The factors which have now made ABC of so much importance are arguably as follows:

- greater product (and 'production') diversification, straining the credibility of conventional costing to product level using volume-based absorption techniques;
- relative growth of indirect costs and overheads as product design and support services have become more complex and expensive, at the same time as many direct production activities have become relatively cheaper through mechanisation and simplification.
- growing concern for tighter cost control arising from tougher competition, especially from the Far East, together with rising awareness of (particularly) Japanese production control methods and their contribution to efficiency;
- perhaps crucially, the recent very large reductions in information gathering and processing costs (but note that while ABC may be economic to run as an established, ongoing system, the initial set-up costs will normally be quite high, and labour needs will be intensive and demanding).

ABC systems

Activity-based costing systems may be used in both industrial or service-type businesses. They are especially appropriate and useful where businesses operate with a relatively high proportion of indirect and overhead costs. NB hereafter, we shall just use the single term 'overheads' to include all costs which are not charged as direct costs to accounts at the level of individual products (or product 'lines' or 'families', where this level of aggregation is considered more relevant or practicable.) Under ABC, all direct costs are recorded and charged in the same way as under conventional absorption costing, although under ABC greater attention may be paid to accurate recording and subsequent analysis at the product level of account. The distinctive difference between conventional costing and ABC lies in the treatment of overheads. We have seen how, under conventional absorption costing, overheads are charged from departmental accounts to products on the basis of their relative share of the total of one or another of the direct cost measures, usually direct labour (hours or cost) or direct materials (cost). This conventional method contains the built-in presumption that all products consume overhead service resources (more or less) proportionally to their respective output volumes, measured by the aforesaid direct labour or direct materials consumption. This presumption is sometimes correct – and fairly frequently it may be somewhat inaccurate, but not so much that it leads to wrong managerial decisions – but often it may be widely inaccurate, and thus misleading for management decisions on product mix, pricing, and methods of work organisation and resource use.

Under ABC overheads are accumulated in 'activity cost pools' or 'activity cost centres' instead of, or in addition to, departmental accounts. There is a cost pool or cost centre for each 'activity' of significant size. There may be several significant overhead activities in any one department, or sometimes activities may involve inputs from more than one department. The overheads are then charged from the various activity cost pools (centres) to product-level accounts on a basis proportional to the usage of each activity by each product (or product line, family or other grouping).

But what are 'activities'? They are groupings of similar work (not performed as direct labour on products). Classic examples in production include machine set-ups, maintenance or inspections. Design and engineering, purchasing and procurement, materials handling, transport, operations accounting, payrolls, personnel and training are all support services which may decompose into a number of separate or specialised activities where the work, though broadly similar, may vary in detail, magnitude and therefore cost between one product and another. The whole point of the ABC exercise is to capture this variation in cost by product so that accurate relevant costs can be charged to each product.

Figure 12.1 illustrates the differences in cost flows and terminology between ABC and conventional absorption costing. Just to highlight the key differences, the illustration is simplified. In real life there might be ten or more departments, thousands of products and hundreds of activities – although for typical production situations Drury reports that 'between twenty and thirty activity centres tend to be the norm' (Drury 1996: 301). The point here is that if certain separable activities have very low total costs the 'cost of costing' may not justify separate accounting, as also in the case of more expensive related but separable activities, which in practice are found always to cost in (more or less) the same proportions as between different products. The most distinctive feature in Figure 12.1 is the dashed-arrow lines facing back from the products to the production-department cost centres in (a). This highlights the fact that the overhead absorption charges to products cannot be determined until

(a) Absorption costing system

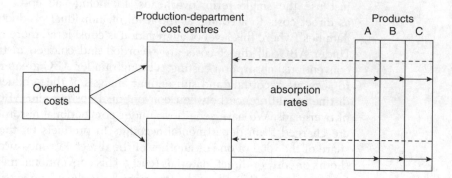

(b) Activity-based costing system

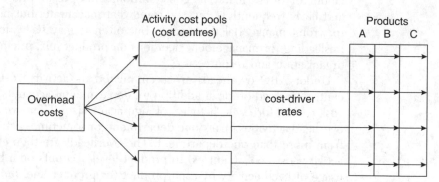

Figure 12.1
Product cost
assignment by
absorption costing
compared to
activity-based
costing.

information is fed back on the volume of direct labour, materials or machine time consumed for each product. In contrast, the ABC cost-driver rates are independent of the volume of workload in the direct production operations, but instead use recorded information on the time/resources used for each product within the activity cost centres/pools.

Stages in the application of ABC

The stages of ABC were noted in the previous chapter and we discuss them further here. (For greater detail, see Drury 1996: 300–2.)

Identifying major activities

Purchasing, production engineering or sales may be thought of as major activities, but for ABC purposes these usually represent too high a level of aggregation, probably organised as separate departments. So the actual work or tasks carried out must be studied, work flows plotted and links identified between interdependent tasks carried out in possibly separate departments. This process involves charting physical flows and hierarchical relationships of task activity, and some consultants have developed 'dictionaries' of activities. The disaggregation of tasks could be carried on *ad absurdum*; for example, it is possible to treat sticking bar-code labels on to documents before scanning the labels as a separate activity distinct from the complete label and scan activity. Indeed, this complete activity itself may usually be too low a level of disaggregation, although at the margin this may not be known until the fourth stage (below) is undertaken. An iterative process may be needed to shorten the final list of activity centres to include only those whose relative costs and differential impacts on product costs are material (i.e. significant).

When grouping tasks into activities, or when considering if particular activities should be treated as activity centres in their own right or merged with similarly behaving activity centres, it can be useful to classify activities according to their impact on, or relationship to, products. Cooper (1990) has suggested the following classification:

- **Unit-level activities:** these occur each time a unit of product or service is carried out or completed. Strictly, the costs of these activities qualify as direct costs, but if these activities are minor in total cost and/or carried out by staff from a service or support department they may be treated as overheads. Unit-level activity costs may occur at different rates for one product as compared to another; hence the need to assign costs by the ABC method rather than by conventional product–volume single absorption rates.
- **Batch-related activities:** these are activities whose costs arise only when new/ further 'batches' of product occur. Examples include machine or process set-ups, organising a delivery to a branch, arranging for a reprint or new edition of a textbook, etc. Whereas simple absorption costing would apportion batch costs evenly across all product units, ABC will correctly reflect the fact that batch-cost overheads per unit are higher for those products made in smaller or more frequent batches, or with more complex arrangements or specifications.
- **Product-sustaining activities:** these are activities which provide indirect but ongoing support to the production process, and which are not directly linked either to the volumes of separate products or to the number of 'batches' of product manufactured, distributed or supplied to customers. For example, in manufacturing the number of parts in a product or the number of parts-specification changes in a year may be indicative of the relative burdens placed by different products on these product-sustaining activities.
- **Facility-sustaining activities:** this category includes all remaining overheads of the production function, or of the marketing or other operational functions in the cases of distribution or service businesses. Examples include departmental or divisional administration, accounting, personnel, training, etc., together with (actual or notional) rent, business rates, energy and insurance, etc. Apportionment of these facilities overheads to individual products being necessarily arbitrary, it may often be preferable not to assign their costs to separate products by any method, but rather simply to deduct the lump-sum total of these overheads from the total operating margins or profit contributions from all products.

An alternative classification system has been suggested as follows:

- activities which add value for the customer (i.e. via the product);

- activities which add value to the business (i.e. its general capability to satisfy customers);
- essential sustaining activities (e.g. rents, rates, insurance, annual audits, etc.);
- all other activities, deemed to be non-value-adding and therefore preferably to be minimised or eliminated (material wastage, product or service rectification costs etc.).

It may be even harder to classify all costs under this second list than under the first, and some broad activities may include costs falling within more than one category. This could lead to a redefinition of the boundaries between specific activities (with an effect on determining which input costs will be charged to which activities).

Determining the 'cost driver' for each activity

A 'cost driver' is a quantified indicator, or measure, of the main workload of each activity. To be practical, the measurements of the cost driver need to be reasonably easy and economical to collect, and for ABC they must be clearly identifiable to specific products, product groups or customer orders. Thus, for the activity of purchasing, purchase ordering may seem the obvious cost driver. Number of orders placed could be the simplest cost driver for which to collect accurate information. However, orders may not be homogeneous, i.e. involving the same amounts and types of work. Some orders may involve telephoning, consultation with design or engineering staff, etc. and therefore impose a disproportionate workload. In such cases recording the time spent on purchase orders for each product may generate a much fairer cost driver than simply relying on counting the number of orders processed.

Establishing activity cost centres

Traditionally, departmental cost centres have been used:

1 to identify costs under the control and accountability of the departmental manager;
2 to link the foregoing with budgets and budgetary control of the departmental structure;
3 to 'hold' indirect and overhead costs until they are recharged (i.e. allocated or apportioned) to production or product-level cost centres by the absorption method.

Under ABC, while the existing departmental accounts could be retained for purposes 1 and 2, the particular concern is to fulfil purpose 3. This requires setting up activity cost centres (sometimes called 'cost pools') to collect and hold relevant costs until they are assigned to products by application of the cost drivers applied to the recorded level of activity. Some activity costs will clearly be specific (i.e. direct) to individual activity centres (e.g. the payroll of staff wholly employed in one activity), while other costs will include common overheads such as heating or space rent, which will have to be apportioned between activity centres.

If the potential of the information provided by ABC is fully exploited, then activity costs, at the levels both of the activity centre and of the individual products, will provide the main data for cost control. If one or more activity centres match up with the line- or functional-management responsibility of existing departmental budget holders, then the activity centres can also provide the main focus for budgets and budgetary control, so that the former departmental cost-centre accounts become redundant. Or where activities do not neatly match with former departmental responsibility boundaries there may be a case for reforming traditional departments, their boundaries and management roles to more closely reflect the product- and customer-oriented realities alleged to be highlighted by the use of ABC. Such wider issues of departmental and work orientation towards product and customer value added form part of the wider implementation of ABC through ABM (see below).

Assigning activity costs to products

Activity costs are recharged to product cost centres based on multiplying the relevant quantities of cost driver for each activity used for each product by the cost per item of cost driver for each activity. The cost rate per item of cost driver can be the current average cost, or it could be a (usually lower) target or standard cost based on studies carried out for budgeting or cost engineering purposes. If the latter, there may be a residual balance of unassigned cost in the activity cost centre at the end of the accounting period, comprising a variance representing the amount actual costs exceeded target or standard costs. In either case there may be a residual balance because actual volume achieved of some or all individual products was below the volume on which the original current average, target or standard cost per unit of product serviced was calculated and assigned in that accounting period.

Let us now consider an illustration which follows the stages of ABC as discussed above and as previously outlined in Figure 12.1 GreenWays supplies a range of timber sheds and summerhouses, a DIY self-assembly range of greenhouses, and an associated range of hardware and fittings. Some products it makes and others it buys in, but in this exercise we are only concerned with cost assignment to finished products actually sold. An ABC system is in use. For simplicity, 'products' have been combined into just three product lines, comprising sheds, greenhouses and hardware, and we will calculate costs for just one activity.

We are looking at the activity centre for Order Assembly and Packing, where two small teams work in linked activity to pick, assemble, package and pack orders to local agents and direct-sale DIY customers. The work situation is batch-related. As regards choice of cost driver, it was found that orders varied so much in size, mix and packing difficulty (e.g. glass for greenhouses) that the number of sales orders fulfilled would not give a fair reflection of cost. Instead, time sheets are kept, and hours of team time are recorded and used as the ABC cost driver. We have traced the costs which should be assigned to this activity centre. For this exercise we use the costs budgeted for the budgeted sales volumes for one month. We have combined costs for simplification, and the month's budget of costs comprises:

Payroll	£11 000
Packaging supplies	£8 000
Computer and other operation-sustaining services	£7 000
Rent, rates and other facility-sustaining overhead expenses	£10 000
Total	£36 000

To assign activity costs to products, we must first calculate the cost-driver rate and then apply this to the chosen cost-driver measure, activity labour hours. Total budgeted labour hours were 800, so the cost-driver rate was £45 per labour hour (i.e. £36 000/800 = £45 per labour hour). Budget and actual labour hours and labour costs (where the latter apply the budget driver rate to actual hours to determine chargeable activity cost) were as follows:

	Budget		*Actual*	
Products	*Hours*	*£*	*Hours*	*£*
Sheds	300	13 500	320	14 400
Greenhouses	300	13 500	250	11 250
Hardware	200	9 000	220	9 900
Total	800	36 000	790	35 550

The above figures allow identification of variances for each product line between budget and actual (except that the actual figures do not capture any actual input price and pay-rate variations). The total variance is £450, representing 10 hours underworking at a £45 per hour cost-driver rate. This small variance is not material. Any material variance should be subjected to analysis and enquiry – incorporating this with standard costing is explained in Chapter 15.

It may be of interest to compare the above cost-assignment results with the cost apportionments which would have resulted had a conventional absorption costing system been used instead, making possibly dubious assumptions that the activity centre defined for ABC exactly 'mapped' with a departmental centre under absorption costing, and that exactly the same costs had been traced or assigned to the two cost centres working under different systems. Under absorption cost the most relevant cost absorption basis for this service department would be direct materials value; in our example the direct materials included in budgeted sales were:

Sheds	£100 000
Greenhouses	£320 000
Hardware	£300 000
Total	£720 000

The absorption rate would have been 5% (£36 000 as a percentage of £720 000). The product apportionments would have been as follows: sheds, £5000; greenhouse, £16 000; and hardware, £15 000. These charges to the product ranges are substantially different from ABC, which is arguably generating more accurate and relevant cost figures. Combining figures from all activity centres might indicate differences in cost between the product ranges of such magnitude and impact on relative profitability as to lead management to a major review of its policies on product mix, pricing and promotion. Further recording of costs in the activity centres between sales to agents and sales direct to DIY customers could lead to a related review of policies as between these two market segments.

Activity-based (cost) management

Enthusiasts for ABC – including, of course, management consultants prospering from promoting and installing ABC systems for clients – have expanded their view beyond the original focus that ABC was worth undertaking even if only for the benefit of more accurate product-cost information, more detailed cost information on support activities and the opportunity for feedback from the product-cost implications of activity costs. It now involves an active search for cost-cutting among the activity costs. It has come to be argued that ABC information, both for its more detailed costing insights into the actual workloads and costs of activities, and for its more accurate product costs, provides decision-relevant information for a wider range of management issues. For this wider role we use the term 'activity-based cost management' or, more usually, just 'activity-based management' (ABM).

A survey among large companies by Innes and Mitchell (1995) found that 20% of respondents had adopted ABC, while a further 27% were considering adoption. The percentages of adopter companies reporting use of ABC information for various possible applications were as follows:

- for stock valuation   29%
- for product/service pricing   65%
- for output decisions   47%
- for cost reduction   88%
- for budgeting   59%
- for new product/service design   31%
- for customer profitability analysis   51%
- for performance measurement/improvement   67%
- for cost modelling   61%

We will briefly consider these possible applications of ABC/ABM.

It is realistic that ABC is not highly valued for stock valuation. Stock valuation is mainly a financial accounting problem, and it is the total value of stock (raw, in process and finished) which is of the essence. In normal conditions – where a firm is financially viable, balances of various kinds of stock remain reasonably stable and no stock is unsaleable – it is not normally material whether reasonably accurate total overhead costs are inaccurately or unfairly allocated *among* different products, as may happen under absorption costing. Total company balance-sheet values and net profit will not be greatly affected. That said, ABC should generate fairer stock values than absorption costing, and if the company's financial or trading status is not stable the extra accuracy could be important for managers, shareholders and creditors.

It is not surprising that ABC information is highly valued for product or service pricing. ABC is particularly concerned with the accurate recording and classification of overhead costs. Under modern technology and business conditions, the proportion of total costs comprising overheads has risen in many companies. It follows that ABC – or any system which is not itself overly expensive and bureaucratic, and which can better report and analyse the work of overhead activities, *and* also generate more accurate product costs – will assist in the better pricing of products and services. Similar reasoning pertains to linked analysis and decisions on product mix and output, on new product/service design, and on cost modelling.

Cost reduction is sought in any healthy organisation, although in modern British business it may be that there has been too much complacency about this during buoyant trading conditions, then too much arbitrary panic cost-cutting during recessions. ABC can clearly provide more accurate and precisely focused cost information on the work of overhead support activities. Related analysis of the work of activities to classify and evaluate specific activities' contributions to individual products and product lines should help to focus attention on the value-added benefits for customers and on whether added cost generates at least as much, and preferably more, added value. Classification systems for activities cited earlier in this chapter can help in identifying task areas for detailed enquiry into the need for work, its cost, and possible ways of achieving better efficiency, quality and/or cost reduction.

The survey results show substantial interest in using ABC in budgeting. The link to budgeting may occur directly or indirectly. Indirectly, the use of ABC in product costing, pricing, profitability, and output analysis and decisions will impact on budgets for overheads/activities as well as for direct costs, and production and sales programmes. More directly, and perhaps more controversially, budgeting by activity cost centres can replace budgeting by traditional functional departments such as purchasing or sales, including functional costs (such as payroll, heating, stationery, etc.) without any breakdown between activities or products. Traditional budgeting follows the traditional hierarchical management structure, with specialist managers for purchasing, sales, etc., and is intended to emphasise accountability and responsibility upwards through this hierarchical structure. If ABC is introduced there may be two or more activity centres per traditional department, and even some activity centres whose work spreads across two or more traditional departments. This is a conflict situation. It could be ameliorated by structuring activities arbitrarily so that they are defined wholly within existing departments, and by making the functional budget-holding manager's overall budget simply the sum total of the separate activities he/she supervises. More radically, but perhaps often with more long-term benefit, the logic of work and work flows revealed by the setting up of an ABC system should be used to provide the framework for a new organisational structure based on activity (cost) centres, with all the main overhead budgets directly interlinked with the activity costs.

Customer profitability analysis is not an automatic feature of ABC. However, making available more accurate product costs can clearly lead to more accurate and useful attributions of profit, whether by product line, technology, market, market segment, distribution channel or individual customer. If all goods or services are standard and supplied 'from stock' (of goods or of service labour on permanent standby), all the information needed from costing is contained in the routine ABC product costs. However, if bespoke goods or services are supplied – or if the production and distribution process is otherwise directly related to unique or differentiated specifications or product mixes for different market/customers – it will be important to trace the impact of this diversity on the activity costs themselves. This can be achieved, at the time of recording activity cost-driver information, by additionally noting and coding the relevant classifications of market/customer. In some cases it might be argued that certain activity costs should be excluded from recharge to product costs, but instead should be transferred to new-market or customer-control accounts, for later use in monitoring product–sale profitability to the individual markets or customers.

The survey showed a high level of interest in using ABC for performance measurement/improvement. This seems highly sensible whether one is dealing with the performance of products or markets, of particular activity services/centres or of the managers accountable for each of these. In the case of assessing managers' performance, however, attention should be given to separating general overheads from controllable costs before ABC (or other) performance measures are used as the basis for awarding managerial praise or blame, incentives or discipline.

The question is sometimes asked whether or not better results will be obtained for management by using ABC or by relying on the decision-related ad hoc costing studies and differential costing, etc. discussed in the preceding chapter? Ad hoc studies and differential analysis – or decision-relevant costing as it is sometimes called – are specific to circumstances which may involve assumptions of change in methods, products, markets, etc. which inevitably are not captured in a routine cost recording and reporting system based on ABC, on absorption costing or otherwise. However, ABC is more decision-relevant than absorption costing, and it can make information regularly and routinely available for many applications which differential costing and special cost studies might address. There is no reason why decision-relevant costing studies cannot be used simultaneously with ABC, drawing on the higher-quality costing data which a well-designed ABC system should provide.

In the next section we look at product and service pricing, and its link with costing information. A feedback from this link is 'target costing'. First one takes a price, whether from a market or from market research or other research to establish a viable selling price for a product or service. Then one deducts a target profit margin to establish allowable maximum product cost. The product must then be designed and engineered for production and marketing within this cost. While the importance of this approach is often attributable to Japan, and indeed the Japanese may have pursued it most rigorously, there can be little doubt that the approach has been followed since time immemorial, with many traders taking the price of widgets from the market then scheming how to cut their own costs enough to compete profitably. The Japanese simply formalised and promoted this approach more than others, including quality safeguards, as a method of continuously pushing forward operational improvement and cost reduction together with competitive products.

Pricing

The pricing of products (including services) is of interest to economists, marketing (and top) management and accountants. Broadly, economists provide background theory for optimal pricing behaviour, marketing specialists provide experience and ideas for exploiting markets with variations of pricing in combination with promotion and other non-price competition features; and accountants provide the cost information which often gives guidance on minimum acceptable prices, but seldom can predict the optimal price which will maximise corporate benefit. However, while in larger companies the accountant's role may usually be limited to supplying an important part of the information needed for pricing decisions and to warning against cutting prices below cost, the role may be greater in smaller companies, by default. That is, smaller companies may lack a proper marketing function, employing simply a sales staff lacking the time and expertise to obtain relevant information or to explore pricing alternatives. In such cases the accountant may become the office 'expert' on pricing, sometimes with the risk that price-setting will become too closely related to costs and fail to exploit market opportunities. Before discussing further the accountant's role and information for pricing, we will briefly consider the key points from economics and marketing which impinge on pricing and the choice of accounting information to assist effective pricing behaviour. Space does not permit detailed discussion of the economics and marketing viewpoints, but reference may be made to other courses of study or to specialist texts.

Economics and pricing

Investment, production and pricing are assumed to be governed by market competition, and by rational search for (preferably long-run) profit and wealth maximisation. In theory, competition ranges between nil and perfect, as follows:

- **Monopoly:** monopoly exists when there is a single supplier with nil competition. Either the product is unique or all existing and potential competitors are controlled or eliminated, or banned by law. Also, there must be no close substitutes. Thus piped water supplies (and waste-water sewerage systems) are usually as near to pure monopolies as exist; there are no close substitutes, and a combination of high capital entry costs and planning objections to digging up roads for duplicated pipe systems protect against competitor entry. Given this monopoly status, and to protect the public against price exploitation, private water industries operate under a price-regulatory system. Electricity, gas and rail services have also traditionally been monopolies, but in these cases there is more opportunity for product substitution, and partial competition has been introduced; yet, for the time being at least, basic prices remain regulated. Regulated pricing is a very specialised field, and we will not consider its great detail here.
- **Oligopoly:** this exists when there are a few large, rival sellers. Each seeks to protect its market share, so active competition by major price cuts risks retaliation and likely reduced profit margins for the small increase in market share. Prices, and certainly price changes, are likely to be closely related to underlying costs so long as competition permits. Active competition will often take forms which avoid changes to basic price structures, e.g. by special offers and promotions, non-price competition through quality or product-image promotions. Nevertheless, oligopolists are likely to be extremely sensitive to the relationship of costs to prices, and as it may not be easy to raise prices they will be extremely interested to search out cost reductions to widen margins.
- **Monopolistic competition:** here a large number of firms compete in a market, offering similar goods and services. An element of monopoly may exist through local geographical or distribution factors, or through effective product innovation. However, if such partial monopoly power is exploited by high prices it is likely that this will be only temporary, as competitors or new entrants deploy in the market. There will be a similar interest in the relationship between prices and costs, as in the case of oligopolists, and similar concern for cost-cutting.
- **Perfect competition:** a perfectly competitive market exists only when there is a very large number of suppliers and buyers, a homogeneous product, perfect infor-

mation on the product and market, no barriers to entry of new competitors, and no competitor large enough to alter the general market price solely as a result of its own pricing and other supply decisions. These conditions are extremely rigorous, so that in the real world it may be argued that perfect competition does not exist. Agricultural markets may once have been near perfect, but today governmental regulation, quotas, subsidies, etc. block this, certainly for most principal foodstuffs. The stock exchange may be as near to a perfect market as exists today, although on present standards of financial and commercial information disclosure one may argue that stock markets fail the test for lack of 'perfect information' available to both buyers and sellers. But although perfect competition may be purely theoretical, or certainly rare, there are many industries in which the level of competition is high. We can describe this as 'imperfect competition', embracing a spectrum of competitiveness between near-perfect competition and monopolistic competition, or perhaps even oligopoly. And we can seek guidelines for pricing, and for the use and relevance of cost information in pricing, which may have general relevance across this spectrum.

When seeking the optimal price of a product the economist looks at both the costs of supply and the level of demand. Under most market conditions where imperfect competition reigns, it is anticipated that lower prices will lead to larger sales. The measure of this relationship is known as the 'price elasticity of demand'. This is illustrated in Figure 12.2 for two products, AB and CD. AB has elastic demand because a small change in price leads to a substantial change in the quantity demanded. CD has inelastic demand because the quantity demanded changes much less for a given change in price. Type AB products may be non-essentials, substitutes may be available, or these products may not be very popular. Type CD products have the opposite characteristics. In real life the price–demand relationship is not likely to be linear and it may not even be representable by a continuous curve.

The economist uses cost and demand schedules, graphical analysis or differential calculus to demonstrate that the optimal price of a product is determined at that point of sales volume (i.e. demand) where falling marginal revenue (caused by price

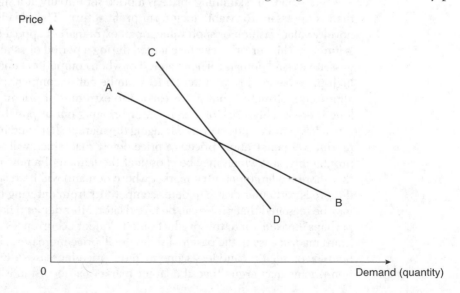

Figure 12.2
The price
elasticity of
demand.

reductions) just equals marginal cost. The optimal price maximises profit. Accountants and managers can accept the economist's theory, although the real-life determination of an optimum price is often difficult, owing to uncertainties over the true level of demand, competitors' behaviour, product substitution and even internal costs (if a substantial change in the volume or method of production or supply would be needed to adapt to substantially higher or lower levels of demand). We return to the demand-schedule approach to pricing in the section on accounting and pricing (pp. 273–5).

Marketing and pricing

The accountant sometimes sees it as a particular cultural and organisational problem that marketing and especially sales managers will be more focused on maximising sales volume or market share than on maximising profits. This may be exacerbated if staff performance appraisal and incentive systems are based solely on sales volume without regard to pricing and profit impacts. Should this problem become seriously dysfunctional it may of course be at least partially the accountant's fault for failing to keep senior marketing and sales managers fully informed as to the costs and profitability of different products, product lines, distributional arrangements, special promotions, etc. Traditional cost analysis and reporting have tended to focus mainly on the detail of production costs, but nowadays, and perhaps especially by adopting ABC methods, accountants should be able to provide much useful information to assist decision-making on prices, special offers, promotions, etc.

Aside from routine ongoing reporting of costs and profitability, accounting's main involvement with pricing decisions may be at the time when new products are introduced. Often new products are introduced at a price directly related to the prices of competitors already supplying similar or substitute products, or they are introduced on a full-cost plus normal margin basis. However, sometimes new products are introduced using the strategy of the 'creaming' or 'skimming' price, or the 'penetration' price (and it is the latter which especially worries the accountant).

A 'creaming' or 'skimming' price is a price set initially at a significantly higher level than is necessary for viable long-term profit return. The idea is that if a product has novelty value, fashion or snob value, or an extra market appeal to buyers while supply is limited, a higher price can be charged during a period of establishing market awareness, image and demand. Then, later, if or when competitors enter the market or initial high-price demand is saturated, prices can be cut to compete in a wider market. This approach is attractive, but if it is carried to extremes of pricing or maintained for too long there is a high risk of a competitor bringing out a (possibly better) product at a much lower price and severely damaging the market share and image of the 'skimming' product. A 'penetration' price is a price below that which will be viable for long-term profitability, and which may be chosen at the launch of a new product if it is thought that there is a large potential market whose demand will be responsive to low price or if there is particular desire to deter competitors from entering that product market. It may be reasoned that prices can be raised later, after demand has been established and perhaps 'hooked' on to this product (and frequent occurrences of inflation have sometimes made it easy in the past to disguise 'real' price increases, although the future may hold lower inflation and less scope to 'hide' price increases). Enthusiasts for penetration pricing may argue that, if a larger market can be established, cheaper means of mass production can be worked out later, to help widen margins without necessarily meaning large price increases. The accountant will be concerned that this latter enthusiasm may be misplaced, that competitors may enter the market with rival products designed to be viable at the existing low price, and that distributor and customer resistance may in fact make it difficult ever to move back to the original targeted long-term price and profit margins. One possible solution is to adopt target pricing and/or life-cycle pricing (discussed later in this chapter) and use these techniques to reduce the risk of underpricing new products.

Another area of potential conflict between marketing and accounting (and production) is with regard to product diversification and variety. Should the firm make/stock every size, colour or variety so as to fulfil every request from distributors or customers? Should a product line or family of products (whether defined by common technology or by common purchase/use by customers) attempt to meet all demand, even if some items in the range may sell so little that, after fair and accurate costing they sell at a loss? Marketing people like to maximise sales and customer satisfaction; accountants prefer all products to contribute profit. A balance has to be found.

Some years ago one firm which made a very wide range of types and sizes of bearings for industrial customers found it was encountering buyer complaints because some smaller bearings were priced higher than larger sizes of otherwise similar specification. Pricing had been set on a cost-plus basis, where unit cost for small volumes led to a higher price base than for certain popular sizes of larger bearings. The company devised a computer program incorporating weights for the various factors (size, material, finish, tolerances, etc.) which it deemed buyers would consider relevant to 'valuing' products. It then applied the formula to reconstructing its price list. It gave its new approach the title of 'product analysis pricing' (PAP). Few companies may go so far as to adopt a mechanistic solution such as PAP, but the underlying problem must be faced. Customer goodwill requires that pricing be seen as fair. If genuine interdependency of demand exists among products in a product line or family of products, then ideally we should evaluate them collectively for profit contribution to help determine the best level and relativity of prices. However, sometimes demand for certain products (or certain sizes, colours, etc.) falls very low, and no product-line or family-of-products argument should prevent the elimination of products which are failing to make at least some contribution to profits.

Accounting and pricing

Accountants typically have the role of bringing together information on sales forecasting and information on supply capacity to derive and evaluate estimates of operational profit (or loss) and cash flow. For new products and for periodic reviews of pricing policy, marketing (or perhaps external consultants) should provide a forecast or schedule of demand showing realistic estimates of sales demand at alternative prices within a feasible range (and the feasible range may be much wider for a completely new product than for the repositioning or repackaging of established products). The accountant can then expand the demand schedule with data on expected costs and profits. Table 12.1 shows an expanded schedule, taking the simplified case of a single product. Our task is to find the price which maximises profit while bearing in mind other factors mentioned in the preceding section. In theory,

Table 12.1 Demand, cost and profit schedule for a new product

Unit price £	Sales demand 000 units	Total sales revenue £000s	Marginal revenue £000s	Total costs £000s	Marginal cost £000s	Profit contribution £000s
15	30	450	–	400	–	50
14	35	490	40	420	20	70
13	40	520	30	440	20	80
12	45	540	20	460	20	80
11	50	550	10	520	60	30
10	55	550	0	540	20	10

the optimal price should be determined by that volume for which marginal revenue has fallen to equal marginal cost or at which total profit is maximised.

In Table 12.1 marginal revenue and marginal cost are equal at a price of £12 per unit. But profit at that level, £80 000, is also equalled at a price of £13. Here the problem is that our demand schedule is (realistically) measuring in full-pound pricing and in five-thousand-unit sales bands. Interpolation may suggest a true optimal price of £12.50, assuming sales of 42 500 units. But precise attainment of any theoretical optimum price (which has no higher probability than the demand forecasting on which it is based) may seldom happen. Given similar profit forecasts for different prices as in the Table 12.1 example, caution would normally advise setting the higher price (i.e. £13 in this example), partly to hedge against the risk of overoptimistic sales forecasts and partly because it is easier to adjust later by lowering prices than by raising prices. Also, in this example there is a substantial (step-cost) increase in total costs when volume exceeds 45 000 units, with a clear fall in total profits at the prices to achieve the high volumes. Such a step-cost might be caused by the extra cost of a second shift or by the cost of providing extra plant. Unless and until that step-cost can be ameliorated it may seem sensible to 'skim' a smaller market at a higher price. Sensitivity analysis for alternative permutations of price, demand and cost could be undertaken to gain a better feel for the possible consequences of any departures from the 'most probable' schedule.

The use of demand schedules may be most relevant for pricing new products – in this context, products which are inherently new or which at least are being differentiated into new market sectors or segments. The point is that there is no perfect competition, no existing market from which to take a price for entry. The study of the nearest competition or substitutes may give guidance. Market research may assist demand forecasting at different prices, but good research can be expensive and many, if not most, smaller firms will launch new products on the strength of their own experience and judgement rather than based on reliable research. Thus many demand schedules, even where they *are* prepared, will tend to be vague (and perhaps often overoptimistic) regarding the sales-volume estimates attached to particular prices.

The cost information matched alongside the sales-revenue forecasts will tend to be firmer, based usually on existing operational experience. However, one complication which makes demand–cost–profit schedules useful occurs even, or particularly, when the possible sales volumes are extremely uncertain. A wide range of production volumes could involve using different combinations of production facilities for different volumes, with different levels of variable cost and/or different types of capital plant and premises, thus altering the attributable fixed costs. In some cases, at least in the short run, it may be sensible to limit production so as fully to utilise any slack capacity or low-cost resources, and these circumstances could suggest a higher launch price than if large-scale facilities were committed from the beginning to that product. A new product will involve start-up costs. Even if there are no new research and development costs (perhaps because these have been previously charged as a general corporate overhead and will be recouped by future general overheads assigned against product sales) there will probably at least be prototype and engineering costs, and initial marketing and promotion costs.

Market v. cost-plus pricing

For existing products and for products which, although new to the firm, are direct competitors with other products already in the marketplace, prices will probably be 'taken' from the market. Where products are at all differentiated, prices of competing products may vary within a range determined by the quality image, special features or choice of distribution channels. But, broadly, the market will provide the price and the role of accounting will be to test the acceptability of that price against the relevant costs. This begs the question of what are the relevant costs.

The question of relevant costs arises also during periodic price reviews of all products or services offered by the firm. During periods of economic stability, technological progress and managerial efficiency gains may be able almost to balance input inflation so as to make it feasible to hold output prices more or less stable. However, prices do get squeezed by competition and management caution during recession, so that during periods of stability or prosperity everyone (including employees) considers that there is some 'catching up' to be done, and this may include (inflationary) output price increases over and above the rate of inflation. The firm will need to monitor the behaviour of competitors closely at such times, as well as during recession. Firms making bespoke products, or otherwise providing goods or services to customer order (as in the construction industry, for example) will experience even greater variability in the pricing margins between recession and prosperity.

In pricing reviews under any of these circumstances the key questions will be: (1) is price sufficient relative to profitability objectives, and (2), if not, and if costs cannot be reduced sufficiently through higher efficiency, how will the market, sales and future profitability react to any proposed price changes? Again, the supplementary question arises: what are the relevant costs to set against prices (i.e. against sales revenue)?

Historically, the most traditional basis for setting the prices of goods and services when market conditions permit, and for reviewing the offered prices as production, market or price-level circumstances change, is to measure or estimate the unit cost and then add a percentage mark-up to the cost. We now have two questions: which measure of cost is relevant to use, and how do we determine how much mark-up to add to the cost? The answers to the two questions are related.

Most accountants have an inherent preference for using full cost as the measure. Full cost, of course, includes all direct or variable costs traceable to the product. It also includes a fair share or apportionment of variable and fixed indirect costs and overheads. But while the latter can be restricted to production overheads; they can include marketing and distribution overheads as well; or they can additionally include their share of all central overheads (possibly including interest costs on borrowed capital, or even a notional interest charge on all capital employed). Although 'full costs' should strictly include a share of distribution and central overheads, practice does not always conform to this, and it is necessary in any particular firm to clarify the exact definition in use. Also, convention varies from industry to industry. Where front-line production/operations staff are empowered to quote prices to customers or clients it will be more likely that the cost used is the production/operating cost plus a mark-up. But does it matter which cost base is used?

A study by Drury *et al.* (1992) indicated that the three product-cost measures most 'often or always' used as the basis for cost-plus pricing were variable product cost (46%); total manufacturing cost, as used for stock valuation (58%); and total cost inclusive of fixed overheads (51%). Broadly, these same three popular cost measures have been used in Table 12.2 to illustrate how pricing mark-ups may be calculated. Data in the table are kept simplified; detail of direct labour and materials has been omitted, as also the subdivision of overheads between fixed and variable. There are columns for just two products, and for the company as a whole (or this could be the total for a product line or range for which internally consistent pricing mark-ups are desired). The build-up of product costs plus net profit margins is shown in the three left-hand columns, thus determining target prices (or sales revenue if applied to total costs for each product rather than just, as here, cost per unit).

Table 12.2 Calculating profit mark-ups and their effects on prices

	Product A costs £	Product B costs £	Company total costs £	Pricing mark-up %	Product A price £	Product B price £	total sales £
Variable production cost	10.00	20.00	30.00	30/30 = 100%	20.00	40.00	60.00
Production overheads	4.00	6.00	10.00				
Total production costs	14.00	26.00	40.00	20/40 = 50%	21.00	39.00	60.00
Marketing and central overheads	4.00	6.00	10.00				
Total cost	18.00	32.00	50.00	10/50 = 20%	21.60	38.40	60.00
Target profit margin (mark-up) 20%	3.60	6.40	10.00				
Target sales/price	21.60	38.40	60.00				

The fourth column of Table 12.2 calculates the mark-up for each of the three cost measures. Separately for each measure, the mark-up is determined as the percentage value of the difference between the value of that cost measure and the target sales/price, divided by the value of that cost measure. The three mark-ups calculated are then applied in the subsequent two columns to determine what the price of each product would be if each of the three cost measures were used. It will be seen that although the total sales value remains constant the prices of products A and B vary according to which cost measure is used for the mark-up. This is because the different components of total cost do not remain constant proportionally between the two products. The relevant marketing and overhead costs do not impinge in equal proportion on the two products (and this is a feature even more likely under ABC than under absorption costing). In this example the price differences are not great, so they may not matter except in a very price-competitive market where dominant competitors use the same measure (whichever it may be); in such a case one competitor using a different measure to determine mark-ups may appear noticeably out of line, with some prices low and some high.

Which cost base for pricing?

By now it must be clear that ABC should provide truer, fairer measures of total costs inclusive of overheads than will conventional absorption costing, which is still probably the most widely used system. However, problems could arise if the logic of ABC-based cost-plus pricing is applied in a price-competitive market (e.g. building materials or automotive parts) where competitors are mainly still using absorption cost-plus pricing. In logic, the firm using ABC will probably raise some prices and lower others, seeking the same fair contribution return after overheads from all products. The result in the marketplace could be that buyers 'cherry pick', buying the products on which prices have been cut while not buying the products on which prices have been raised. The practical compromise may be to change the price structure only gradually, to lower existing prices only partially unless one is sure of major competitive advantage, and to raise prices significantly only after taking a view that those products' profitability is so low that one will not mind if demand falls so low that the products are dropped from the line (and if one is not worried that failing to offer a full line will harm overall sales profitability). In other words, what is perceived to be a fair price, and a price which moves goods and services, is more likely to be decided by the buyer in the market than by the cost accountant in the seller's back office.

For periodic reviews of prices of ongoing products or services, especially where hundreds or more of different 'products' are offered, the expense of demand forecasting, detailed cost analysis, etc. on a product-by-product basis will rule out complex analysis. Price adjustments will be made on some formulaic basis, either linked to routinely available (absorption or ABC) costs or linked to data on how well separate products are selling and intuitive feelings regarding likely market response to price increases. For decisions on major new products, much more sophisticated analysis is justified.

To a degree all goods produced in industry or stocked and sold in wholesale and retail trades are 'joint products', in that they share many common costs from the overheads of management, space, equipment, support staff, etc. Conventional absorption costing, or indeed activity-based costing, will provide a baseline of unit cost which traditionally would be taken as the starting point for setting target prices. This cost data will determine the *relative prices* of the different goods offered for sale. For industries with truly 'joint' products where the separate products emerge from common raw materials and largely common processing (e.g. meat processing or oil refining), accountants have developed mechanistic cost or value allocation procedures for measuring product cost for the purposes of stock valuation and profit and loss determination (Drury 1996). However, these costs are often almost useless for guidance on pricing. The state of relative market demand and product 'value' may differ widely between the separate markets for different joint products (and by-products). Therefore the pricing policy of the firm must not focus on individual products in isolation but, instead, should concentrate on maximising the total revenue in excess of total costs, including not just joint costs but also the separate costs of all products beyond the stage of joint processing. In other words, what is needed is a form of analysis to maximise total contribution from all joint products (after allowing for any separate processing costs). This analysis can be expedited with the help of appropriate computer software.

Target pricing and life-cycle pricing

For major new products, especially products requiring substantial capital investment, it is obvious that more thorough analysis of pricing (and of all costs related to that pricing) should be undertaken than would be feasible during periodic pricing reviews of an ongoing product range. Target costing has previously been mentioned; this is effectively a derivative of target pricing. That is, the firm does market research, assesses its technology and capabilities, and selects a product (or service) to provide. Market and other research will have indicated a particular price for a forecast share of demand in the target market, or a range of prices based on feature/quality variations or on alternative distribution/promotional arrangements if these still remain open for final decision. Once a final choice or manageable shortlist of specifications and price(s) is agreed, target profit margins and relevant overhead charges will be deducted to obtain target direct cost. The work needed on the product at each stage of design, engineering, production and supply will then be assessed and costed to establish direct cost. If the forecast direct cost exceeds target cost this could be a signal to abandon a product proposal or to risk setting a higher price. But in the high-tech mass-market industries of Japan, where this target-pricing approach appears to have been most consistently used, there seems to be the presumption of continuous product innovation and continuous improvement in production method so that it is presumed additionally that reasonable market-related prices can be met, and will be met, by redesign and re-engineering if necessary. Although there are obviously important cultural differences between Japan and western countries, it seems likely, even in this case, that the formal adoption of target pricing and costing with strong top-management support can make an important contribution to improved efficiency, competitiveness and profitability. Target pricing and target costing are most relevant for a firm with a range of products sharing existing production technologies and facilities. Often a 'new' product will in one sense be no more than a 'new model' replacing a product now obsolete in market terms and being phased out of production. The new product may simply 'slot in' to the production process after only minor or evolutionary change. The introduction of such products, then, may not involve any major new capital investment or new financial risks, although of course every new business commitment does carry opportunity cost – that is, the possibility, whether recognised or just ignored by default, that resources could alternatively be committed to a more profitable use.

Sometimes new products will require major new capital investment and/or longer-term commitments in the form of ongoing new distributional networks, service networks, promotional campaigns (including, for example, ongoing sports sponsorships), etc. Sometimes products will be forecast to start slowly in the market, building up later, peaking and eventually tailing away because of technical or fashion obsolescence until they are replaced. Similarly, initial production costs may be capable of future reduction after a 'learning curve' of experience and as a result of future reviews of methods and resource use. Activity analysis and challenge of overhead activities, assisted by ABC or by other decision-relevant accounting approaches, may enable future reduction of overheads. All these factors, combined, could lead to higher profits after the launch period, or else sometimes lower profits if markets are highly price–cost competitive and competitors are going through similar processes.

Many products will have a finite life-cycle before market obsolescence forces abandonment or replacement. In some modern high-tech industries these life-cycles will be fairly short and perhaps fairly predictable (since they result in part from pre-programmed forward planning and behaviour in rival firms more or less equally adapted to the market). (Product) life-cycle costing has been extensively discussed in the USA (Horngren *et al.* 1994). It involves forecasting all the factors discussed above for the expected future life of a product (or, say, for a period of at least five to ten years, beyond which the level of uncertainty may become too great and the level of financial significance to today's investment decision too small). With future revenue also forecasted, a future profit forecast may be derived for the life-cycle. Sensitivity analysis may be employed to assess the marginal impact on life-cycle profitability of alternative scenarios of cost-efficiency and, more critically and with greater uncertainty, of competitor behaviour, prices, and market share and conditions. Combining all this with the essence of target costing may then lead to the notion of life-cycle budgeting; that is, of setting down firm targets on cost, volume, market share, price and profitability for the full life-cycle (or at least the aforesaid five to ten years). Once life-cycle budgeting and/or costing are undertaken, it has been further suggested that all accounting data for the product should be kept on record during the life-cycle, so that life-cycle auditing can be performed at or near the end of the cycle to provide a learning experience for the company's future development.

To be complete, the costs included in the life-cycle costing and budgeting will need to take account of the timing, amounts and costs of capital employed. Accounting costs are usually recorded by accrual accounting, including the non-cash cost of depreciation on the real assets provided by past investment. But over a product's life-cycle, with initial or replacement capital-investment outlays, all accrual costs tend to become proxied by cash flows, and it is (future) cash flows which are of particular importance to the investment decision. These decisions, cash flow, capital budgeting and investment appraisal, are the subjects covered in Chapter 13.

Conclusions

There is no doubt that overheads, especially if broadly defined to include all 'indirect costs', have become a higher proportion of total costs in many businesses, and therefore all the more important to understand, measure and control. This applies especially to businesses with multiple products, multiple technologies, customised product specifications, and/or necessarily high R&D expenditures. When choosing product mix, or when setting or negotiating prices, it is obviously important to have accurate knowledge of product costs.

It has been argued that ABC provides more accurate tracing and allocation of costs to products than does traditional absorption costing. This argument is probably correct. There are just two main problems. First, ABC is a more expensive costing system, and is much more intrusive and demanding on management time, particularly in the first two or three years of designing, installing, testing and debugging the system. Second, if the full concept of ABC is implemented the cost collection process (and any control procedures or performance sanctions) may cut across existing departmental structures and therefore risk causing conflict with established departmental management authority and accountability, and with the working of traditional budgeting – which is, of course, in essence a resource-rationing and control system normally closely linked to the established departmental management structure (e.g. the organisation chart). This conflict may be the main underlying reason why many businesses which have experimented with ABC have not been fully satisfied. Resolving this conflict may be of the essence in determining whether ABC/ABM systems continue to become more widely used, or whether some new 'flavour of the month' will be proposed as a further improvement to costing for management decisions, while at the same time being fully compatible with the needs of management organisation, responsibility, accountability and financial control.

This chapter reviewed the weakness of traditional absorption costing. Decision-relevant costing methods such as differential cost analysis may overcome the main weaknesses, but they are normally provided only in special studies and are not available for ongoing cost control or for quick reference when cost information is needed for management decisions on product mix, pricing and volume. ABC is an ongoing costing system which may offer significantly improved information. The characteristics of ABC needed for it to provide accurate and relevant information were considered in some detail. The uses and limitations of cost information for determining and reviewing prices were explained, and two possible future developments were introduced: target pricing and life-cycle pricing.

Further reading

For a more detailed treatment of topics in this chapter, especially as regards theoretical proofs and methodology, readers may consult specialist texts, especially those by Drury (1996), for a UK view, and Horngren *et al.* (1994), for a USA view. For a treatment which is more detailed in respect of the organisational and behavioural context in which costs are used in management control, see Emmanuel *et al.* (1990).

Questions and exercises

1 Although, strictly, 'overheads' is a narrower concept or classification than 'indirect costs', the label of overheads has come to be applied to almost all costs not charged as direct costs to marketable end-products or end-services. Concisely, suggest possible reasons for this, and also discuss why accounting for overheads has attracted increasing concern and importance in recent years.

2 Concisely outline the distinctive features of ABC and explain its main differences from absorption costing.

3 It has been alleged that the use of ABC should result in end-product costings which are fairer, truer and more useful to management than traditional costing methods. Critically assess this statement and briefly speculate on how far ABC costs may also be more 'decision-relevant'.

4 List and briefly describe the several steps/stages of change/innovation which would be needed when installing and operationalising a new ABC system in a company using traditional cost accounting. Include managerial/organisational steps/stages as well as those concerned with technical accounting innovation.

5 What types/measures of accounting information should the marketing manager be provided with in connection with (a) pricing new products and (b) conducting annual price reviews of all products? Does the nature of the firm's markets/marketing affect your answer to this question and, if so, how?

6 Why are pricing decisions more difficult for firms with multiple products than for firms with single products? Also, to the extent that prices are based on or related to costs, can you suggest any one concept or measure of cost that is generally most relevant to pricing decisions? Explain this viewpoint.

7 Manor Conservatories plc (MCP) aspires to make, market and install high-quality conservatories, although the company is better known for its high-pressure salesmen. The company is organised into two main 'divisions', the product division, which manufactures and pre-assembles conservatories, and the customer services division, which embraces marketing, design, selling, site work, delivery and on-site assembly.

Each division records its separate direct costs and each is a major overheads cost centre, both for budgeting and for cost control. The production division is capital-intensive, highly mechanised and charges/recovers its overheads on a machine-hour basis (the current rate being £14 per hour). Customer services is labour-intensive and charges/recovers overheads on a direct-labour-hour basis (£11 per hour).

Although made up from a range of standard design features, each conservatory is tailored to individual customers' requirements (and differing site conditions). Therefore each conservatory contract is treated as a separate product and a separate 'profit centre'. Below is the information concerning one four-week control period; for simplicity, there are only three contracts and it is assumed that these contracts were all started and completed within the given four-week period. Contract details are as follows:

	Contract 2175		Contract 2176		Contract 2177	
	Production	Customer Services	Production	Customer Services	Production	Customer Services
Labour hours	200	200	400	500	150	200
Machine hours	500		800		600	
Labour cost (£s)	2 400	2 000	4 800	5 000	1 800	2 000
Materials cost (£s)	10 000	1 200	18 000	2400	9 000	1 400

The overhead costs recorded in the control accounts of the production division and the customer services division for the above period were £33 000 and £10 500, respectively.

(a) Calculate the overheads allocated to each of the three contracts and the total cost for each contract.

(b) Do you see any advantage in the company having used direct labour hours as the basis for overheads allocation rather than direct labour costs?

(c) Compare the total overheads allocated against the amounts of actual overheads recorded in control accounts and briefly suggest the possible cause(s) of any differences.

(d) From the limited information available, is there anything to suggest that a change of overheads accounting to the ABC system might be beneficial?

8 Aus Wings Ltd (AWL) supplies long-haul holidays, especially to and from Australasia. It arranges tailor-made travel, but mainly operates organised package tours with tour leaders. It markets tours under two separate brand names, the two being slightly differentiated in price and content. One brand name is marketed solely through travel agents, while the other brand name is marketed exclusively through advertising and direct mail. Each holiday tour is managed as a profit centre, as are the two brands at a higher level of aggregation.

AWL is organised into three main departments, which are the principal cost and budget centres for all direct costs, advertising and promotions. Marketing is responsible for market research, advertising and promotions, direct mail, telephone and agency bookings, and customer services. Operations researches, plans and organises travel and tour itineraries and facilities, and recruits and supervises tour leaders. Administration provides computer, clerical, accounting, foreign-exchange, insurance and other services to, or through, the other two departments.

Administration is not charged direct to profit centres, but instead to the other two departments. Here, routine services are charged monthly, based on the achieved volume percentage of the agreed annual budget; extra or special services are charged at estimated full cost. All overhead recharges to the profit centres arise from the other two departments; they are calculated on the basis of distribution to tour/brand profit centres in proportion to the monthly share of total bookings revenue achieved by each separate tour. The only direct costs charged or recharged to profit centres comprise the airline and other travel and accommodation expenses, and the pay and expenses of the tour leaders incurred for each tour.

While the external auditors see no problem affecting profit determination for the company as a whole, they have criticised the present overhead accounting arrangements as possibly giving rise to misleading information for internal management and have suggested the company introduces ABC systems.

(a) Write a concise report explaining (i) all the likely weaknesses of the present system of overhead allocation, relevant to management needs and (ii) the probable advantages and/or disadvantages of a change to using ABC.

(b) Outline the sequence of steps/actions you would undertake in order to install, operate and benefit from a new ABC system, bearing in mind managerial and behavioural issues as well as technical accounting requirements.

9 Chippers Ltd trades under the motto 'Anything with chips', and it supplies a wide range of electronic components to the automotive and other industries. It works to the designs of both its own staff and major customers. It does not carry out any basic manufacture, but instead buys all its parts and sundries from specialist manufacturers, often from low-cost overseas sources. All incoming parts are tested to high standards, and Chippers is proud of the quality and inspection standards of its own main work, which is the precision assembly of electronic components and systems as finished products.

Chippers has four main departments: assembly, marketing, administration and design. The purchasing function is located within the assembly department, but for quality-control reasons the design department is responsible for the technical specification in purchase orders, for listing approved suppliers, and for quality inspection and testing of incoming purchases (and of completed assembly work). The assembly department is responsible for stock availability and storage, and it controls the timing and quantities for purchase orders (and for assembly production orders).

Chippers has used an absorption costing system to assign overheads (together with direct costs) to profit-contribution accounts for each final product. It is now considering changing to an ABC system.

The chief executive has asked you to prepare a concise report

(a) to show a comparison of the cost allocations as between absorption costing and ABC;

(b) to comment on any differences and why the figures under one or the other system may be more true or more helpful to management;

(c) to explain briefly whether your findings have any implications for Chipper's pricing policies (where it is a price maker) or for its willingness to accept orders (where it is a price taker).

Data for the company, for the latest month are given below; for simplicity, only few overheads and just two products are included. You may assume that these are representative (and you may make additional assumptions, provided that you make these explicit).

Overhead	*Absorption basis*	*Cost in month £*	*Hours of ABC time*
Purchasing	Materials value	£1 000 000 30 000	1 200
Production control	Direct labour hours	100 000 18 000	800
Inspection and testing	Materials value	£1 000 000 15 000	400
Design services	Direct labour hours	100 000 25 000	500

Preliminary enquiry finds that numbers of transactions will not provide a useful ABC cost driver, but that recording service activity time traceable to each product (and reallocating all general-service office time in proportion to each product) should produce a fair cost driver. ABC-relevant chargeable time and absorption values are given below for two products for the month under study:

	Product A	Product B
Value of material issued to product	£100 000	£50 000
Direct labour hours in assembly department	15 000	5 000
Overhead activity for each product:		
Purchasing	100	80
Production control	110	70
Inspection and testing	40	30
Design services	20	6

Hint: first calculate the cost/absorption-driver rates for the two methods and then apply the two sets of recharging rates to each product for interpretation and any comparisons possibly relevant to your report.

10 Cozee Bedrooms Ltd sells complete bedroom remake packages, comprising bought-in furniture, fabrics, wallpapers, etc., customised and installed within a range of choices in each package. There are four standard, fixed-price packages: Countess, the cheapest, Duchess, Princess and Empress. You are the company manager and your accountant has just informed you that in his/her opinion the Countess package should be discontinued because it is making a loss. He/she has given you the following updated figures for the Countess:

	£	£
Countess package fixed price per sale		1 995
Less average costs per package completed:		
Purchases of beds and other furniture and fittings	850	
Purchases of fabric and decorative materials	250	
Direct labour to customise, make up and install	350	
Overheads	650	2 100
Loss on each Countess sale		(105)

You are surprised by the loss and by the overheads charge as you know that, company-wide, the overheads are a little under 25% of sales revenue. You ask the accountant for an overheads breakdown. The accountant is surprised in his/her turn and perhaps a little peeved. He/she suggests that the overheads appear proportionately larger on the Countess only because the furniture and other materials used in the package are so relatively cheap. He/she supplies the following breakdown of estimated Countess overheads:

	£
Selling expenses (the same average cost as calculated for all four product packages on number of sales completed)	230
Workshop (indirect) labour (for customising furniture, making up curtains, etc., based on average of sampled job sheets)	120
Energy, rent, rates and other premises costs (apportioned on a basis proportional to direct labour)	110
Transport (apportioned on a basis proportional to direct labour)	100
Administration (apportioned on the basis of total Countess revenue as a proportion of total company sales revenue, per unit)	90
Total overheads per Countess sale	650

(a) On the evidence available, would you discontinue or retain the Countess sales package? What are the arguments for and against?

(b) Briefly assess the decision-relevance of each of the five overhead categories and the cost allocation or apportionment bases used.

(c) What further accounting and/or other information would you wish to have in the real world before making a final decision on the Countess package?

13 Accounting and longer-term decision-making

Objectives

This chapter looks at the contribution that can be made to effective long-term decision-making by capital budgeting techniques and contrasts the effectiveness of discounting and non-discounting techniques in this respect. The taxation implications of capital investment are reviewed, as are the benefits that can be derived from the post-completion audits of capital projects.

The background to capital budgeting

In Chapter 9 we saw that the principal financial objective of management in the private sector is to maximise the overall value of the company. In practical terms this equates to the maximisation, over time, of dividend payments to shareholders. The more successful the company is in generating cash inflows, the greater the productive investments that it can undertake. This, in turn, should lead to the prospect of increased dividend payments in the future and a rise in share price.

Investment appraisal is equally important in the public sector, even though some have argued that it is inappropriate as the majority of public-sector investments do not produce commercially sold outputs. This view is quite wrong. Outputs can sometimes be valued even when they are not sold commercially; investment appraisals where such values are regarded as very important (such as the siting of an airport/hospital or the routing of a bypass) are called 'cost–benefit analysis' (CBA). Even if outputs cannot be satisfactorily valued, investment appraisal can still show the cheapest way of providing a given level of output; this is called 'cost-effectiveness analysis' (CEA).

This chapter is principally devoted to the use of discounted cash-flow (DCF) techniques for the proper evaluation of potential investments. It is a technical chapter that describes criteria to be used in assessing whether an investment is worth undertaking; assessing which mutually exclusive project is to be preferred in ranking the acceptability of projects when investment funds are limited; and deciding when the economic life of a project has come to an end. However, it needs to be stressed that the process of evaluation, as described in this chapter, is but one stage in the overall process of deciding whether or not to undertake a particular project. Pinches (1982) warns against focusing too much attention on the selection phase of this process to the exclusion of the identification, development and control phases. Simon (1960) and Ansoff (1968) both provide useful insights into the general framework of decision theory.

In the first section of the chapter we briefly consider non-discounting appraisal techniques. The subsequent section considers the principles associated with discounted cash-flow techniques and concludes that, of the two methods discussed, the net present value (NPV) method is theoretically superior to the internal rate of return (IRR) method. The next section continues the discussion by demonstrating that in many practical situations the NPV approach is also practically superior to the IRR approach. The impact of taxation on investment appraisal is discussed in the subsequent section. We then consider investment appraisal in the public sector before looking at empirical evidence about the application of these various techniques in practice and setting out a framework for the establishment of post-completion audits of capital projects. The final section reviews the main themes of the chapter and provides a brief guide to further reading on this important area. This chapter builds on the principles set out in Chapter 11 to consider decision making in circumstances when it may take some years to assess whether funds have been prudently invested.

Non-discounting appraisal techniques

Though the concern of this chapter is with the net cash flows generated by alternative projects over time, we start by briefly discussing two traditional, non-discounting appraisal techniques as, historically, they have been commonly used in business. The two techniques are the accounting rate of return (or return on capital employed), introduced in Chapter 7, and the payback method.

Accounting rate of return

Accounting rate of return (ARR) is also referred to as the return on investment (ROI). There are many ways in which this measure can be derived, its base form being the ratio of some measure of accounting profit to a corresponding measure of capital outlay. One of the more common ways of deriving this ratio for decision-making is to calculate a project's average profit after depreciation, but before any allowance for taxation, and divide this by the average capital employed during the life of the project. If significant, it would also be usual practice to include in capital employed any increases in working capital required should the project be accepted. Let us consider a simple example: a project requires an initial capital outlay of £500 000 and has a life of five years, at the end of which it can be sold as scrap for £50 000. The expected annual profits over this period for the project are:

Year	£
1	40 000
2	100 000
3	160 000
4	120 000
5	30 000

(a) Average annual profit:
$$\frac{(40\ 000\ +\ 100\ 000\ +\ 160\ 000\ +\ 120\ 000\ +\ 30\ 000)}{5} = £90\ 000$$

(b) Average capital employed:
$$\frac{£500\ 000\ -\ £50\ 000}{2} = £225\ 000$$

(c) Accounting rate of return (ARR):
$$\frac{£90\ 000}{£225\ 000} \times 100\% = 40\%$$

Note that the denominators for the first two stages of this calculation were 5 and 2, respectively. In (a) 5 was used to give the average annual profit, while in (b) 2 was used to give the simple average of capital deployed throughout the entire five-year life of the project.

Once the ARR has been determined a simple accept/reject decision is then made on the basis of the percentage return achieved. Providing the ARR, which in this case was 40%, exceeds some predetermined 'target' rate of return, the project is accepted; otherwise it is rejected. In the case of competing projects the decision rule is to accept the one with the higher accounting rate of return, provided that it is larger than the target rate.

The advantages of this technique are its ease of calculation, the fact that it considers the accounting profit flows throughout the life of the project, and the fact that it produces a percentage rate of return which is a ratio commonly used by market analysts and others when measuring the profitability of a company. The disadvantages do, however, outweigh these advantages. As alluded to earlier, there is no standard measure of capital employed or profit. Since this is an accounting ratio, non-cash items such as depreciation are included. The production of a ratio in percentage terms fails to reflect the absolute size of investment and, although the whole life of individual projects are considered, this method fails to distinguish between the differing lives of mutually exclusive projects. Finally, and most fundamentally, the ARR method ignores the *timing* of the earnings streams of projects. An illustration of this is provided in Table 13.1 which compares two projects and having a five-year life, and requiring an initial investment of £200 000 with an anticipated scrap value of £0.

The payback method

The second commonly used non-discounting appraisal technique is the payback method. Strictly speaking, this method is more of a liquidity measure than a profitability measure. Recall the importance of all organisations remaining 'liquid' in cash terms (see Chapter 7). As with the ARR, the payback calculation is simple but it concentrates on cash flows and not accounting measures. Individual projects are accepted provided that they 'pay back' within a specified target period, while mutually exclusive projects are ranked by speed of repayment. Let us consider two further projects, C and D:

Table 13.1 Illustration of accounting rate of returns

Year	Project A	Project B
1	£10 000	£50 000
2	£20 000	£40 000
3	£30 000	£30 000
4	£40 000	£20 000
5	£50 000	£10 000

Which project is preferred?
The result with the ARR is inconclusive:

Average annual profit	£30 000	£30 000
Average capital employed	£100 000	£100 000
ARR	30%	30%

Both projects have the same ARR, although the earnings of project B arise earlier than those of project A. Most people would prefer project B on this basis, although ARR fails to distinguish between them.

	Project C £	Project D £
Initial investment (t_0)	– 20 000	– 20 000
Net cash flows each year:		
1(t_1)	+ 12 000	+ 8 000
2(t_2)	+ 8 000	+ 8 000
3(t_3)	+ 8 640	+ 4 000
4(t_4)		+ 8 000
5(t_5)		+ 6 000

For ease of expression, initial investments are denoted as being made at time t_0. Thereafter cash flows are taken at the end of each year, commencing at t_1. Investments and net negative cash flows are denoted by a negative (–) sign, while net positive cash flows are denoted by a positive (+) sign. This notation will be used throughout the remainder of this chapter. If the target cut-off payback period was three years both projects would be acceptable. If, however, projects C and D were mutually exclusive, project C would be preferred to project D since its payback period is two years compared to D's three-year period, despite D's larger net cash-flow surplus.

The payback method can also be discredited because it fails to take account of any cash flows arising after the payback period and, like the ARR, it ignores the time value of money. A variation of the payback method is the discounted payback method, based on the principles set out below. While this method is an improvement, in that it discounts cash flows in calculating the payback period, it still ignores cash flows arising thereafter.

The theory behind discounted cash-flow appraisal techniques

For many private-sector managers the overall corporate goal of maximising the value of the firm may initially appear vague. We begin this section by examining a normative model which, under a series of restrictive assumptions about the real world, illustrates the microeconomic theory underpinning the principles of investment appraisal. It is based on a two-period graphical analysis, first suggested by Hirshleifer (1958), which adopts the principles laid down by Fisher's (1907, 1930) work on the theory of interest.

Broadly, two categories of investment opportunities are available to firms: to invest in the external capital market or to invest in internal productive opportunities. It could, of course, be argued that if no productive opportunities are available the firm should repay its funds to its shareholders and allow them either to deal directly with the capital market or to reinvest in other firms. With respect to investment in internal productive opportunities, this means investment in a range of tangible assets such as buildings, plant and machinery, or in intangible assets such as patents and licences. Productive opportunities are clearly more attractive than investing in the capital market if they provide a greater return.

The theory outlined by Hirschleifer (1958) is presented by means of a simplified numerical example. Let us assume that a firm has recently been established with a share capital of £1 million (distributed as £1 nominal-value ordinary shares). The firm is also able to borrow, or lend, on the capital market at a rate of 15% per annum. Various other assumptions have been made to produce Figure 13.1. Figure 13.1(a) explains the structure of the graph, while Figure 13.1(b) records the transactions in terms of pounds.

Having studied the parameters of the graph presented in Figure 13.1(a), examine the results presented in Figure 13.1(b). The management has £1 million to invest. Its first task is to decide on which productive opportunities to undertake. From the graph it can be seen that £0.5 million invested in productive opportunities at t_0 will yield £0.94 million at t_1. All productive opportunities, as stated in Figure 13.1(a), lie along a concave curve, ranked in terms of their return, beginning with the largest return. Investing in productive opportunities beyond point I_0 is unwise as the returns offered are less than those available on the capital market. The firm should therefore invest the balance of its funds, £0.5m, in the market at 15% to earn £0.575 million at the end of the period t_1. This strategy of investing half of the available funds internally on productive opportunities and half externally on the capital market returns a total of £1.515 million to the firm at t_1. Under the efficient-markets hypothesis (EMH) the current value of the company, at t_0, will rise from £1 million to £1.317 million, i.e. the future value available to the firm of £1.515 million discounted at the external capital market opportunity cost of 15%:

$$\frac{£1.515m}{1.15} = £1.317m$$

At this point, two issues need to be noted. The EMH states, in broad terms, that the current value of the firm will rise once the market becomes aware of the investment and financing strategies adopted by the firm. The EMH is further discussed in the 'Glossary of accounting terms' at the end of this book (pp. 439–61). The use of the term 'external capital market opportunity cost' follows on from the discussion in Chapter 11. Recall that the definition of an opportunity cost is 'the cost of the best opportunity forgone', and the opportunity forgone by investing in internal productive opportunities is that available from lending in the external capital market.

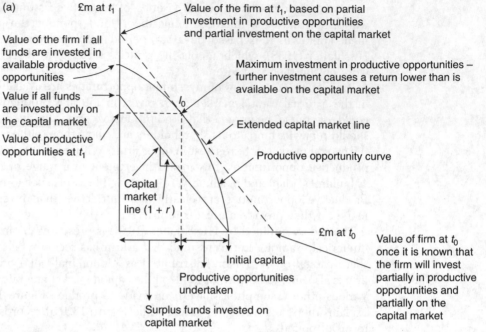

Note that:

The downward sloping line of the capital market line represents the rate of exchange $(1 + r)$ on the capital market, where r denotes the rate of interest over this period.

Productive investment opportunities are represented as a concave investment opportunity line. Each productive opportunity is ranked in terms of its return, commencing with that which offers the largest return, thus:

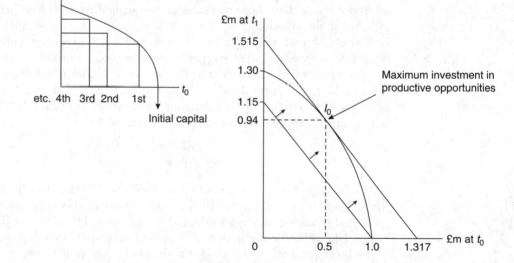

Figure 13.1
(a) Illustration of a two-period investment decision.
(b) Illustration of a two-period investment decision (continued).

This illustration demonstrates what has become known in the finance literature as the *separation theorem* (Tobin 1958). It is a theorem that has two propositions:

1 Management should invest in all productive opportunities that yield a return greater than that available on the capital market.
2 Shareholders should borrow or lend on the capital market to produce the cash flows that meet their own individual needs.

The market value of the firm today (at t_0) is £1.317 million. The shares issued at a nominal value of £1 therefore have a market value of £1.317. Examine Figure 13.1(b) again. It is drawn to scale. Is there any alternative strategy to be followed? We think not. The shareholders could sell all/some of their shares for an immediate capital gain, or they could stay with the firm and receive a dividend at t_1 from the profits that the firm decides to distribute and increased capital gains as the remaining funds are reinvested in further productive opportunities. The nature of this scenario is that the firm's management seeks to ensure the best interests of its shareholders. This investment strategy is one that serves all their interests.

The foregoing analysis assumed that borrowing and lending rates on the capital market were equal. As we know, in reality borrowing rates in the market are higher than lending rates. Management must still decide on the optimal selection of productive opportunities. Productive opportunities should first be selected by reference to the (higher) borrowing rate. If available funds are insufficient to accept all available opportunities, then additional funds can be borrowed, as productive opportunities will produce returns more than sufficient to cover the cost of borrowing. If, however, the firm has surplus funds available after this exercise, management should then evaluate all remaining opportunities at the lending rate, as these additional productive projects will earn a return greater than is available on the market.

This two-period analysis can be further developed to accommodate longer time horizons. In fact, it is the theoretical basis on which the NPV discounted cash-flow approach to investment appraisal depends. As Bromwich states:

> a project with a positive net present value covers the opportunity cost of both internal and external funds. Its acceptance, therefore, makes the shareholders better off. Looking at it another way, the net present value of the project is the price at which the firm (and its shareholders) could sell the opportunity to undertake the project to someone else and be no worse off.
>
> (Bromwich 1976: 7)

As is stated above, this approach is normative, based on how rational managers and shareholders (investors) should act given the stated assumptions. It presents a logical structure for the management of the financial affairs of enterprises and a link to the pragmatic business environment that operates in the real world. Thus financial theory lays a foundation for sound corporate financial management. To this it is necessary to add the constraints of the present-day business environment as provided by government fiscal policy, financial institutions, legislation and practice. Further support for this theoretical approach to financial management is supplied by the Companies Acts, which state that directors of companies are expected to run them in the best interests of the shareholders.

In a multi-period situation NPV can be found by the following expression:

$$\text{NPV} = \frac{Cf_1}{(1+r)^1} + \frac{Cf_2}{(1+r)^2} + \frac{Cf_3}{(1+r)^3} + \ldots + \frac{Cf_n}{(1+r)^n} - Inv_0 \quad (13.1)$$

or:

$$\text{NPV} = \sum_{t=1}^{t=n} \frac{Cf_t}{(1+r)^t} - Inv_0 \quad (13.2)$$

where: Cf_t = the net cash flow at the end of year t;
Inv_0 = the initial investment outlay at $t = 0$;
r = the discount rate based on the opportunity cost of capital;
n = the project's expected life-cycle.

The NPV imputes a known discount rate, which is based on the market-determined opportunity cost of capital. Projects that have a positive NPV using this approach are accepted. The net cash flow for each year is expressed in present value terms by dividing by $(1 + r)^t$ as appropriate. The following illustration represents the present-value factors for a discount rate of 10%.

$$\frac{1}{(1+r)} = \frac{1}{(1.1)} = 0.909$$

$$\frac{1}{(1+r)^2} = \frac{1}{(1.1)^2} = 0.826$$

$$\frac{1}{(1+r)^3} = \frac{1}{(1.1)^3} = 0.751$$

$$\frac{1}{(1+r)^4} = \frac{1}{(1.1)^4} = 0.683$$

$$\frac{1}{(1+r)^5} = \frac{1}{(1.1)^5} = 0.621$$

In simple terms, a return of £100 in five years' time is today worth £62.10 at a market opportunity cost of 10% per annum. This is simply the application of compound interest in reverse, since £62.10 invested today at 10% per annum would yield £100 in five years' time.

At this point it might be useful to reconsider the cash flows associated with projects C and D, introduced earlier. Let us assume that the relevant opportunity cost of capital is 10%. This would probably, in practice, be based on some weighted-average cost of capital (see Appendix 13.A). The relevant calculations for C and D are now:

	Project C			*Project D*		
	£	PVF (10%)	PV (£)	£	PVF (10%)	PV (£)
t_0	−20 000	1.000	−20 000	−20 000	1.000	−20 000
t_1	+12 000	0.909	+10 908	+8 000	0.909	+7 272
t_2	+8 000	0.826	+6 608	+8 000	0.826	+6 608
t_3	+8 640	0.751	+6 489	+4 000	0.751	+3 004
t_4				+8 000	0.683	+5 464
t_5				+6 000	0.621	+3 726
		NPV	£+4 005		NPV	£+6 074

(PVF = present value factor; PV = present value.)

Both projects have positive NPVs, but if they were mutually exclusive project D would be preferred. This is the reverse situation to the advice given by the payback method. The difference between these two methods is that the NPV approach takes into account those cash flows arising after the payback cut-off period and also considers the time value of the funds so invested.

Appendix 13.B introduces the reader to two tables; one provides present-value factors and one provides cumulative present-value factors. Both tables greatly facilitate calculations of the NPV. The relevant figures are provided at yearly intervals since this coincides with the usual convention that all costs occurring during a year are accumulated and discounted at the year-end. In practice it is possible to have other values at shorter intervals if this is deemed useful. In financial leasing, for example, monthly and quarterly rates are often used.

The second discounted cash-flow technique is the IRR method. This technique calculates the discount rate which equates the present value of future cash flows to the cost of the initial investment, i.e. which equates all the cash flows associated with a project to a net present value of zero. Providing that the IRR for a project exceeds a known predetermined hurdle rate the project is accepted, in the absence of limits to the supply of capital (known as 'capital rationing'; see below). Often the hurdle rate set is the opportunity cost of capital. The IRR can be found by solving for i in the following expression:

$$Inv_0 = \frac{Cf_1}{(1 + i)^1} + \frac{Cf_2}{(1 + i)^2} + \frac{Cf_3}{(1 + i)^3} + \ldots + \frac{Cf_n}{(1 + i)^n} \tag{13.3}$$

or:

$$Inv_0 = \sum_{t = 1}^{t = n} \frac{Cf_t}{(1 + i)^t} - Inv_0 \tag{13.4}$$

where: Cf_t = the net cash flow at the end of year t;
Inv_0 = the initial investment outlay at $t = 0$;
n = the project's expected life-span;
i = the discount rate that equates the sum of future cash flows to the INV_0.

While the calculation of IRRs may call for the solution of complex polynomial equations, there are several computer software packages that can expedite their solution. An alternative approach, which provides a good approximation of a project's IRR, can be found by using the mathematical technique of linear interpolation. We can calculate the IRR for project C by means of linear interpolation as follows:

(a) let $i = 20\%$

	£	PVF (20%)	PV (£)
t_0	−20 000	1.000	−20 000
t_1	+12 000	0.833	+9 996
t_2	+8 000	0.694	+5 552
t_3	+8 640	0.579	+5 003
		NPV	£+551

This result indicates an IRR greater than 20%.

(b) let $i = 25\%$

	£	PVF (25%)	PV (£)
t_0	−20 000	1.000	−20 000
t_1	+12 000	0.800	+9 600
t_2	+8 000	0.640	+5 120
t_3	+8 640	0.512	+4 424
		NPV	£−856

This result indicates an IRR less than 25%.

With these two results we can now interpolate to find the exact value:

$$0.20 + \frac{551}{551 + 856} \times (0.25 - 0.20) = 0.22, \text{ or } 22\%.$$

We can now test the 'soundness' of our approximation by letting $i = 22\%$:

	£	PVF (22%)	PV (£)
t_0	−20 000	1.000	−20 000
t_1	+12 000	0.820	+9 840
t_2	+8 000	0.672	+5 376
t_3	+8 640	0.551	+4 761
		NPV	£−23

Only a small rounding difference of £23 is left.

Readers can confirm their familiarity with the technique of linear interpolation by calculating the IRR for project C. The result should also work out at 22%, meaning that if these two projects were mutually exclusive management might be indifferent between them. It could be argued that marginal preference be given to project B, since it has the shorter life-cycle, and because the further into the future we go, the more difficult it is to forecast cash flows with relative precision.

While it is true that usually the NPV and IRR approaches produce the same recommendation, there are important occasions when these two approaches can provide conflicting advice. Bromwich states that 'knowledge of a project's internal rate of return is neither necessary nor sufficient for optimal investment decisions' (Bromwich 1976: 87). On its own the IRR of a project gives no information about either a project's present value or the effect of its acceptance on the value of the firm. Whereas the NPV provides an absolute value, the IRR does not. The above consideration of projects C and D is a case in point. While the NPV approach favours project D, with an absolute value of £6074, the IRR approach was indifferent between the two.

We can summarise our discussion on the NPV and IRR techniques as follows:

■ The NPV rule is sufficient in itself, whereas the IRR rule does not make economic sense – knowledge of a project's IRR is neither necessary nor sufficient for optimal decisions.

- IRR on its own gives no information about either a project's present value – an absolute measure – or the effect of its acceptance on shareholder's wealth.
- Both techniques have different reinvestment assumptions. Implicit in the NPV rule is that any positive cash flows occurring during the project's life can be reinvested at a rate of interest equal to that used as the discount rate. By contrast, the IRR decision rule assumes that the cash flows resulting during the life-cycle of a project have an opportunity cost equal to the IRR that generated them. The theoretical basis for the NPV approach is that the discount rate used is determined by the capital market. No such theoretical basis exists for the IRR approach. Can we really suppose that surplus cash flows arising from one investment will earn the same IRR in the next investment?

Refer to Table 13.2, which illustrates that notion of opportunity cost associated with the NPV.

Practical issues surrounding the application of the NPV and IRR appraisal techniques

In this section we consider technical issues surrounding the application of the NPV and IRR techniques. In each instance we demonstrate that the NPV technique is, in practice, the preferred technique. Our discussion continues under the following headings:

Mutually exclusive investments

As is stated above, it is often the case that capital resources are limited and that competing projects are therefore mutually exclusive. For example, if a construction

Table 13.2 Comparison of net present value and net terminal sum

Consider a project that requires an initial investment of £1 000 and returns net cash inflows in each of the subsequent three years. The relevant opportunity cost of capital can be assumed as 10%. The NPV of this project is £492. There is a net terminal surplus (NTS) of £655, being the increase in value over and above the opportunity given up in the capital market of £331. The relevant figures are set out below.

	Cash flows	Interest received on surpluses reinvested at 10%		Terminal value	DCF (10%)	PV
		Year 2	Year 3			
t_0	(1 000)			(1 000)	1.000	(1 000)
t_1	600	60	66	726	0.909	545
t_2	600		60	660	0.826	496
t_3	600			600	0.751	451
	Net terminal value			986	NPV	492 *
	less opportunity cost of capital					
	1 000 at 10% for 3 years			331		
			NTS	655		

Note: *The NPV of the NTS is £655 × 0.751 = £492, allowing for rounding differences in the calculations.

company had a particular development site various development options might be available but only one proposal could ultimately be undertaken. These proposals are therefore mutually exclusive. Consider two mutually exclusive projects, E and F, with the following pattern of cash flows:

	t_0	t_1	t_2	t_3	NPV (10%)	IRR
Project E	£(1 000)	475	475	475	181	20%
Project F	£(500)	256	256	256	137	25%

Whereas the NPV approach favours project E, the IRR approach favours project F. Some authors, for example Levy and Sarnatt (1986), suggest that this conflict in advice can be solved using the 'incremental yield approach'; that is, by evaluating the incremental project, in this case E – F. The resultant cash flows are:

	t_0	t_1	t_2	t_3	NPV (10%)	IRR
Project (E – F)	£(500)	219	219	219	44	15%

If, as in the case in point, the incremental project produces a positive net present value and an IRR greater than the opportunity cost of capital (here 10%) the larger project, project E, should be accepted. The Levy and Sarnatt (1986) approach ignores the unrealistic reinvestment assumption implicit in the IRR approach. Further, as we need to calculate the opportunity cost of capital in order to assess the incremental project, why not simply use the NPV approach in the first place?

Multiple rates of return

The IRR approach is unable to provide solutions to those potential projects that have unconventional cash flows. In such situations an IRR may not exist, or, if it does, it may not be unique. Such situations could occur, for example, when a project has an expansion option phased into it which could lead to an overall net cash outflow a few years into the life of the project, before potential (and increased) cash flows resume. Another example occurs in the extractive industry when net cash outflows occur at the end of a project's life, due to landscaping and other rectification costs incurred to restore the environment. Levy and Sarnatt (1986: 87) provide an illustration of a non-conventional cash flow that has no IRR. The numbers are $t_0 = +£100$, $t_1 = -£200$ and $t_2 = +£150$. Rather than waste time in calculations, we can accept their assertion that no solution is to be found. Interestingly this sequence of cash flows, if discounted at 10%, produces a positive NPV. An alternative sequence of $t_0 = -£20\,000$, $t_1 = +£51\,000$ and $t_2 = -£31\,500$ produces two IRRs, 5% and 50%. Bromwich (1976: 103) provides further analysis and discussion of this phenomenon. Suffice it to say, for our purposes, that where multiple rates of return exist there are no mathematical or economic grounds for specifying any one IRR over another.

Timing of cash flows

Consider two further projects, G and H, with the following patterns of cash flows:

	t_0	t_1	t_2	*NPV*	*IRR*
Project G	£(1 000)	1 000	200	76	16.67%
Project H	£(1 000)	200	1 100	95	15.42%

Here again we have conflicting advice, with the NPV approach favouring project H, when a 10% discount factor is used, and the IRR approach favouring project G. This case is different to that illustrated by projects E and F, in that this conflict in advice cannot be resolved via incremental analysis since both projects require the same capital outlay. The problem here lies with the underlying reinvestment assumptions between the NPV and IRR approaches and the differences in the timing of the receipt of the post-investment cash flows that result. This problem is illustrated in Figure 13.2. The curves associated with both projects approximate the net present values at different rates of interest. The NPV rule would advise project H if the firm's cost of capital is below 13% and project G if it is higher. As the opportunity cost of capital is less than 13%, project H is to be preferred.

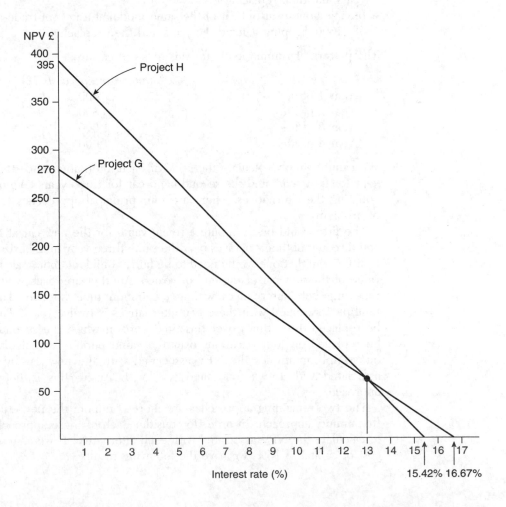

Figure 13.2
Comparison of
NPV and IRR.

Uneven project lives

One final problem with the IRR approach is that it is impossible to use it when projects have different lives (see Cooke and Glynn 1981). Typically, asset replacement decisions fall into this category of appraisal. Plant and machinery, for example, cannot be kept indefinitely; as their age increases so do their operating and maintenance costs, while their residual value declines. Management needs to decide when to replace an existing machine with a new one and also to have some notion of the expected optimal life of its replacement. Not only capital outlay costs need to be considered, but also any difference that arises in working capital requirements between operating and maintaining current equipment compared to using replacement technology. The concern of such calculations is therefore to determine the 'economic life' of an asset rather than its physical life.

Consider the everyday problem of having to replace a car. Let us consider, for simplicity, that our choice is between the two propositions:

- buying a new car at a net (of trade-in allowance) cost of £2000, keeping it for four years and then replacing it;
- buying a one-year-old car of the same model at a net (of trade-in allowance) cost of £1600, keeping it for three years and then replacing it.

The pattern of running costs for this make of car are:

	Annual running costs (£)
Year 1 of life	600
Year 2 of life	800
Year 3 of life	1 000
Year 4 of life	1 600

We cannot simply calculate the NPV of each alternative since the new car will be kept for four years and the second-hand car for three years. We need some way of equating the alternatives. There are four principal approaches to solving this sort of problem.

The first would be to impute a resale value for the new car at the end of year 3 and discount both alternatives over the same three-year time horizon. This approach is difficult in that one would need to be fairly confident about calculating the market value of the new car at the end of year 3. Another approach would be to consider repeating both alternatives within a common time horizon. The least common multiple associated with these two alternatives is twelve years. The new car would be replaced three times over this time horizon whilst the second-hand car would be replaced on four occasions over the same period. To calculate this approach one simply multiplies the NPV associated with the new car by 3, and the NPV associated with the second-hand car by 4. Again, this is not a very practical approach.

The two remaining approaches are more common: the perpetuity approach and the annuity approach. In order to consider each of these approaches we need first to calculate the NPV associated with each alternative. If we assume an opportunity cost of capital of 15%, we have the following results:

	PV New car (£)	PV Second-hand car (£)
t_0	−2 000	−1 600
t_1	−600	−800
t_2	−800	−1 000
t_3	−1 000	−1 600
t_4	−1 600	–
NPV (15%)	−4 699	−4 104

With the perpetuity approach we assume a chain of replacements starting now and taking place every three or four years. The present value of the four-year replacement cycle of the new car is:

$$\frac{£ -4\ 699}{(1 - 0.5718)} = £ -10\ 974$$

The present value associated with the three-year replacement cycle of the second-hand car is:

$$\frac{£ -4\ 104}{(1 - 0.6575)} = £ -11\ 982$$

By this approach we have determined that an investment outlay of £10 974 is required in order to buy a new car, run it for four years and then replace it. The sum of £10 974, if invested at 15%, would provide sufficient funds to meet the annual cash outflows identified above. In similar fashion an investment outlay of £11 982 is required in order to buy and run the second-hand car. Therefore it is prudent to buy the new car.

The annuity approach is to calculate the annual equivalent cost of operating either choice. We have found in practice that it is this approach that managers most readily understand. The relevant calculations are:

New car: $$\frac{£ -4\ 699}{2.855} = £ -1\ 646$$

Second-hand car: $$\frac{£ -4\ 104}{2.283} = £ -1\ 798$$

The denominators are cumulative net present-value factors from Appendix 13.B. Again, the new-car alternative is preferred as it has the lowest annual equivalent cost.

In summary we are able to point to four practical problems associated with the IRR approach:

- It can give different advice due to the time pattern of cash flows (i.e. the time crossing of present values).
- Problems can arise due to multiple roots.
- It has a different (unrealistic) reinvestment assumption which assumes intermediate cash flows can earn a return equal to the project's IRR.
- It cannot be applied to problems associated with different economic life-cycles.

Risk and uncertainty

Having demonstrated that the NPV is the preferred technique for investment appraisal, we have to recognise that the future is not certain. The techniques that firms use to evaluate risks range from traditional methods such as simulation and sensitivity analysis through to market-oriented techniques such as the capital asset pricing model (CAPM). In some instances even cruder approaches have been adopted, such as simply increasing the discount factor by an amount as a 'hedge' against future uncertainties. This latter approach has little merit since it unrealistically presupposes that risk is compounded over time.

The advantage of simulation analysis is that it compels project planners to review carefully the key relationships that affect the projected cash flows. Brearley and Myers (1991) consider that model-building leads to a deeper understanding of the project. Particular simulation techniques such as Monte Carlo simulation analysis require the construction of probability distributions for each factor that influences the capital-investment decision. Sensitivity analysis enables managers to assess how responsive the NPV is to changes in the variables which are used to calculate it. This approach requires that the NPVs are calculated under alternative assumptions to determine how sensitive they are to changing conditions; that is, it indicates why a project might fail. Drury (1996) provides useful illustrations of these techniques but it should be noted that these techniques rely on discounting the cash flows at a risk-free rate.

The CAPM, although still not widely used, has become one well-recognised technique that provides a risk-adjusted discount rate based on the principles of portfolio analysis. Risk is measured by a beta factor, which measures the sensitivity of the return on a quoted share with the movement of the market as a whole. The values of betas for all UK quoted companies are published by the London Business School and Datastream. These values are used in a formula developed by Sharpe (1964):

$$Erj = rf + \beta j \ (Erm - rf) \tag{13.5}$$

where: *Erj*   = the expected return of the share;
        rf   = a risk-free return (typically equated to the return on government bonds);
        Erm   = the expected return on the market as a whole;
        (Erm − rf) = the market premium;
        βj   = the risk of the share *j* relative to the market index.

For a fuller discussion of the application of this technique, see Collier *et al.* (1988)

In concluding this section, brief mention should be made of how the impact of *inflation* should be taken into account. Two basic approaches can be adopted. First, a market-determined discount rate can be used to discount inflation-adjusted cash flows. These cash flows should not be revised in line with a general index of inflation; rather, specific inputs should be uprated using specific indices. The second alternative, though less practical, is to exclude the impact of inflation from the discount rate and discount what economists term 'real' cash flows.

Taxation and investment appraisal

So far in our discussion we have ignored the impact of taxation. With Chapter 5 as a background, we can now consider how taxation can be incorporated into NPV calculations. The approach to adopt is fairly straightforward; it is to incorporate the impact of taxation into the incremental cash flows arising from the investment and to discount the resultant net cash flows by a net-of-tax discount rate. The discount rate should reflect the tax advantage of the deductibility of debt interest. This process is illustrated by the example of Strathmore plc.

Strathmore plc is considering whether to purchase some additional machinery that will cost £250 000 and should contribute additional cash flows of £125 000 per annum for four years. The net-of-tax cost of capital is 10% per annum and corporation tax is at the rate of 33%. The machinery is eligible for 25% annual writing-down allowances. It is anticipated that the machinery can be sold at the end of year 4 at its written-down value for taxation purposes.

Table 13.3 contains the necessary calculations. Remember from Chapter 5 that depreciation is not a cash flow and should not appear in the calculation. In Section A the writing-down allowances are calculated. In Section B we can see the additional corporation-tax liability that arises from the anticipated incremental cash flows. In Section C the net present value is calculated, but note the timing of the tax payments. Tax payments have been assumed to be payable in the year following the receipt of the additional cash flows. As there is a net present value of £127 948 this project should be accepted. Recall from Chapter 5 that had the machinery been projected to be sold for a figure greater than its written-down value a 'balancing charge' would have had to have been included in the calculation to recoup excess capital allowances.

Investment appraisal in the public sector

The rationale behind the use of the NPV approach in the private sector is accepted by government as being exactly analogous to that in the public sector. This is because 'jam today is worth more than jam tomorrow' (HM Treasury 1984: 14) since, just as in the private sector, 'more weight is given to earlier than to later cost and benefits' (*ibid.*). The discount rate for use in the public sector is commonly referred to as the test discount rate (TDR). The TDR was introduced in the early 1960s as a means of promoting consistent investment appraisal by nationalised industries. Its use subsequently spread to other areas of the public sector. Since 1978 (Cmnd. 7131) the discount rates used by nationalised industries have not been set centrally but have been a matter of individual consultation between each industry and its sponsoring department. Typically, public-sector capital appraisals are expected to be based on the basis of *real cash flows* using a *real discount rate*, which, at the time of writing, is set at 6%.

In many instances public-sector capital projects are similar in character to those carried out in the private sector. Often, though, the emphasis is on cost-effectiveness rather than overall profit maximisation. On occasions social costs and benefits may be incorporated into the calculation. Consider the building of a hospital. With respect to its location, social benefits could arise in terms of the time saved in travelling by

Table 13.3 Illustration of taxation in investment appraisal

A	End of year	Writing-down allowance (25%)		Written-down value carried forward
	£	£	£	
	0	0		250 000
	1	62 500	(25% × 250 000)	187 500
	2	46 875	(25% × 187 500)	140 625
	3	35 156	(25% × 140 625)	105 469
	4	26 367	(25% × 105 469)	79 102

B		Year 1	Year 2	Year 3	Year 4
		£	£	£	£
Incremental cash flows		125 000	125 000	125 000	125 000
less writing down allowance		62 500	46 875	35 156	26 367
Incremental cash flows subject to taxation		62 500	78 125	89 844	98 633
Incremental tax (31%)		19 375	24 219	27 852	30 576

C	Year	Cash flow	Taxation	Net cash flow	Discount factor	Present value
		£	£	£	£	£
	0	−250 000	0	−250 000	1.000	−250 000
	1	+125 000	0	+125 000	0.909	+113 625
	2	+125 000	−19 375	+105 625	0.826	+87 246
	3	+125 000	−24 219	+100 781	0.751	+75 686
	4	+125 000	−27 852	+97 148	0.683	+66 352
		+79 102 [a]		+79 102	0.683	+54 027
	5	0	−30 576	−30 576	0.621	−18 988
				Net present value		£+127 948

Note: [a] Projected sale of machinery at the written-down value for tax purposes. All calculations are rounded to the nearest whole £1.

out-patients (particularly emergency cases) and visitors. Conversely, social costs can arise in addition to the direct cash outlays associated with the construction of the project. As Glynn states:

> The accountant engaged in a CBA project is not, in essence then, asking a different sort of question from that being asked by the accountant of a private firm. Rather, the same sort of question is being asked about a wider group of people – who comprise society – and is being asked more searchingly.
>
> (Glynn 1987: 88)

Mishan (1971) provides several examples of the application of CBA to public-sector capital investment.

Project appraisal in practice

This chapter has concentrated on the preferred approach to project appraisal – the net present-value approach. In practice this approach has been slow in gaining popularity and, when used, has often been used in conjunction with one of the other approaches referred to earlier. Why is this? Traditionally, British management has not seriously considered the importance of investment appraisal, or else it has paid too close attention to short-term measures rather than taking an economic approach. The ARR is used, as stated, because it is a simple technique; second, it is similar to the accounting ratios used by market analysts, and it has to be recognised that (as discussed in Chapter 7) financial accounting communicates important information externally and some managements may feel that it is important to undertake projects that confer 'relevant' information to the market. This, we would argue, is far too short-sighted. Accounting cannot supplant the long-term need of companies to generate surplus cash flows. Likewise, the payback approach may be used when funds are in limited supply or as a crude measure of risk. However, such an approach is not a maximising one; it is an optimising one, given limited funds for investment.

Several surveys have been carried out regarding the capital budgeting practices of private firms and public-sector bodies. Surveys by Pike and Wolfe (1988), McIntyre and Coulthurst (1986), and Drury *et al.* (1992) show that, despite earlier criticisms, the payback method is the appraisal technique most frequently used by firms. However, many firms in these surveys did appear to use a combination of the evaluation methods discussed in this chapter. Despite its theoretical and practical drawbacks, the IRR is still preferred to the NPV in many firms. In discussing these results, Drury considers that 'financial measures of performance evaluation place undue emphasis on the short term and may not be consistent with DCF decision-making models' (Drury 1996: 402). Lapsley (1986) reports research which shows that in the public sector a number of investment appraisal techniques are used, despite the government's preference for the NPV technique.

In concluding this section it is apt to return briefly to an issue raised earlier, that of 'capital rationing'. Capital rationing, a restriction on the funds available for reinvestment, quite often exists in organisations. Capital rationing may apply only in a particular year (single-period rationing) or there may be a limit on funds over several years (multi-period rationing). In the case of single-period capital rationing the preferred approach is to rank competing projects in terms of the NPV contribution per £1 of outlay. This is easily done by dividing a project's NPV by the initial investment sum. In situations of multi-period capital rationing mathematical programming needs to be employed. Carsberg (1969) provides a useful introduction to mathematical programming, while Mepham (1980) provides a guide to the detailed application of linear and matrix algebra.

Post-completion audits of capital projects

Once a decision has been made to undertake a particular project it is sound management practice to compare the actual results with those forecast in the investment appraisal. Important questions need to be asked; for example, was capital expenditure as budgeted? Were anticipated costs and benefits as anticipated? Despite the uniqueness of many projects, a 'post-completion audit' can provide important information for management. As Drury states, 'a record of past performance and mistakes is one way of improving future performance and ensuring that fewer mistakes are made' (Drury 1996: 444). Pike and Wolfe (1988) found that ex-post monitoring of capital investment decisions operates in almost all the major UK companies. Lapsley

(1986) reported that 47% of public-sector organisations conducted post-completion audits.

> The objective of capital budgeting is, in the private sector, to maximise share-holders' wealth. In the public sector the objective is to undertake cost-effective projects. Of the four techniques reviewed, the NPV approach is regarded as being both theoretically and technically superior. The other three techniques, despite their frequent use in practice, are theoretically unsound.

Further reading

For those wishing for further illustrative examples of project appraisals we would suggest Drury (1996) and Lumby (1991). Both texts are popular with students and are regularly updated. Another useful text is that by Butler (1993), which is based upon a study of strategic investment decisions in a wide range of UK and international companies. The authors examine these decisions from the perspective of organisational decision-making theory and find that investments are made not only by the application of formal quantitative procedures but also involve the more qualitative processes of judgement, negotiation and inspiration.

Questions and exercises

1 The board of directors of Porterhouse Plc is considering whether or not to launch a new product which has been subject to extensive research and development. It is expected that this new product will have a market life of ten years, with sales running at 40 000 units annually at a unit selling price of £90. The expected unit costs of the new product are:

	£
Direct materials	28
Direct labour	12
Manufacturing overheads	22
Selling and administrative costs	12
Total unit costs	£74

To manufacture this new product will require an immediate investment in plant and machinery of £2 million. The anticipated scrap value of this equipment will be £100 000. In addition to the investment in plant and machinery, it is expected that the company will need to increase its working-capital investment by £1.8 million because of the increased levels of stock and debtors associated with the new product.

The manufacturing overheads include an allocation of existing costs to the new product of £300 000 but make no allowance for depreciation. The remaining manufacturing costs are variable.

The selling and administrative costs represent an allocation of the company's overall costs in these areas to the new product on the basis of anticipated sales value. Included in these overall costs is the £4 per unit sales commission which will be payable to sales agents who will be responsible for the sales of the new product. This commission is the only incremental selling and administrative cost likely to be associated with the new product. After reviewing the above details the managing director says:

> We have already spent £1 million on research and development for this product, and we are now being asked to invest £3.8 million further in its production. This would bring our total investment to £4.8 million, and for what? On the information we have it is only going to generate an annual profit of £640 000 before taxation. Remember that corporation tax will swallow up one-third of this profit. This is a rate of return of just under 9%, as compared with our cost of capital of 15%. In my view, every product should pay its own way, cover its own costs and give us a decent return. This one will not, so we should not go ahead with it. We should write off the research and development to experience and learn from our mistake. Do you all agree?

Respond in clear, non-technical language to the managing director's statement, saying whether or not you agree with his analysis and recommendation.

2 The directors of Dobson Ltd are considering whether to accept one of two mutually exclusive projects and, if so, which one to accept. Each project involves an immediate outlay of £1 million, and the estimates of the subsequent cash inflows are as follows:

	Project A £	Project B £
Net cash inflow at the end of:		
Year 1	800 000	100 000
Year 2	500 000	300 000
Year 3	300 000	1 500 000

The directors of Dobson Ltd do not expect capital or any other resource to be in short supply during the next three years, and taxation can be ignored.

(a) Prepare a graph to show the functional relationship between the net present value and the discount rate for the two projects.

(b) Use the graph to estimate the internal rate of return of each project.

(c) On the basis of the information given, advise which project to accept if the cost of capital is (i) 10% and (ii) 20%.

(d) Describe briefly any additional information that you think would be useful in choosing between the projects.

3 The Midshire Community Trust is considering establishing its own pathology services facility, for which it currently contracts with the St Bottomley Hospital Trust. Midshire's board of management believes not only that establishing its own facilities will lead to a cheaper and more efficient service, but that additional income could be earned by offering its own service to other health-service trusts

and GP fundholders. You have been asked to prepare a brief report for a forthcoming board meeting which should appraise the two alternatives of negotiating a new three-year contract with St Bottomley and establishing this facility in-house. The finance director has provided you with the following information:

(i) The capital cost of establishing a pathology laboratory for Midshire would be £250 000, and the estimated total annual running costs for the first three years are estimated, respectively, at £650 000, £750 000 and £800 000.

(ii) The annual charges for pathology services proposed by St Bottomley's for the next three years are, respectively, £750 000, £850 000 and £900 000.

(iii) If the new pathology laboratory is built it will be built on land owned by Midshire that is currently rented out to a road-haulage contractor for warehousing at an annual rent of £15 000.

(iv) If Midshire has mis-estimated the success of establishing its own facility it ought to be able to sell it off on a 99-year lease for £100 000 at the end of three years.

She has further suggested that you use 6% as an appropriate discount factor, but you are concerned that 12% seems more like a return at which money might be borrowed from a bank or other financial lender.

Prepare a brief report for the board of management of the Midshire Community Trust which clearly outlines the financial feasibility of establishing an in-house pathology service. Be sure to state any assumptions that you have made and to raise any additional considerations not covered in your calculations that you feel the board should consider. Attach your calculations as an appendix to your report. Any implications regarding taxation should be ignored.

4 Your friend, who is the senior engineer of a local factory, Jackson Limited, is seeking your advice on the replacement of some machinery. He states, 'At a recent seminar I learned that it is the economic life of an asset that is important and not its physical life. I really am somewhat confused about this concept. How does it apply to my company's circumstances?'

He says that the machines the company is currently using could be sold now for £30 000 each and estimates that in a year's time they would realise £15 000 each; in two years' time, £6000 each. He also estimates that each machine's operating costs would be:

Year 1	£40 000
Year 2	£60 000

The replacement machines that he is considering have a purchase price of £120 000 each and he estimates that their operating costs (including any adjustments to working-capital requirements) would be:

Year 1	£24 000
Year 2	£30 000
Year 3	£34 000
Year 4	£39 000
Year 5	£45 000
Year 6	£59 000

These new machines are expected to have a residual (net resale) value of £60 000 at the end of one year; £36 000 at the end of two years; £32 000 at the end of three years; £22 000 at the end of four years; £16 000 at the end of five years; and £12 000 at the end of six years.

The cost of capital is 12% per annum.

Using the information given above, advise whether the present series of machines should be replaced by more modern machinery. In your analysis, be sure to explain why it is the economic life of a machine that is important rather than its operational life.

5 'The main reason that many firms choose not to use the discounted cash-flow approach to investment appraisal is the unreality of the assumptions underlying the relevant theory.' Discuss.

6 The rationale behind the use of the net present-value approach to project appraisal in the public sector is accepted by government as being exactly analogous to the private sector. Explain this rationale and consider any contentious issues that arise when applying this technique in practice.

7 Empirical studies suggest that there are major differences between current theories of investment appraisal and the methods which both private- and public-sector organisations actually use in evaluating long-term investments. Why is this so and what can be done to improve the financial management aspects of long-term decision-making?

8 Accounting rate of return and payback are widely used by firms in the capital-investment process. Suggest reasons for their widespread use. Do you agree with these reasons?

9 Outline how risk might be taken into consideration when using the net present-value approach to project appraisal.

10 Explain how the impact of taxation is incorporated into investment-appraisal decisions. Indicate the effects which a lack of taxable profits may have on investment decisions and comment on the main possibilities open to a firm to overcome such effects.

Appendix 13.A: Calculating the opportunity cost of capital

The opportunity cost of capital used in capital budgeting is, for most private-sector organisations, based on the organisation's weighted-average cost of capital. The calculation of this rate can be complex and the purpose of this appendix is to provide readers with a brief introduction to the topic.

In the private sector we will assume, for simplicity, that there are only two sources of funds: equity capital and debt finance. The suppliers of debt finance receive their return by way of fixed interest payments, while those that supply equity funds have claims over the residual funds which remain after all other payments (including interest payments) have been made. Typically, equity investors receive annual dividends and they can also sell their shares should they wish to liquidate their investment; the market price of these shares is a reflection of their expected future earnings. Supplying debt finance is less risky than supplying equity finance, and so investors will demand a lower rate of return on a firm's debt securities than on its equity securities. Additionally, the cost of debt finance is made even cheaper because debt-interest payments are a tax-deductible expense. The overall cost of capital for a firm is the weighted average of these two sources of finance and is calculated as follows:

$$WACC = [Ke \times E/V] + [Kd\,(1 - C) \times D/V] \qquad (13.A.1)$$

where: $WACC$ = weighted-average cost of capital;
Ke = cost of equity capital;
Kd = cost of debt;
E = market value of equity capital;
D = market value of debt capital;
V = total market capital value;
C = the corporation tax rate.

The cost of each source of funds is a function of three components:

1 **The time preference rate**: this is the rate of return investors would require from a riskless investment when no changes in future prices are expected. Economists would describe this rate as that required in order to forgo current consumption.
2 **The expected rate of inflation**: the higher the rate of inflation, the lower the real value of the expected future returns, and hence the higher the rate of return investors will require.
3 **The riskiness of the investment**: investors are assumed to be risk-averse, and therefore the required rate of return they require will increase with the perceived riskiness of an investment.

The appropriate values of the cost of equity and debt finance are the current required returns from these securities as they represent the opportunity cost of utilising such funds. The current overall return, or weighted-average cost, is equal to the discount rate used in the evaluation of the firm's projects.

For further discussion on how to measure a firm's cost of capital, see Collier *et al.* (1988).

Appendix 13.B: Present value factors

Table13.B.1   The table gives the present value of a single payment received in *n* years in the future discounted at *x*% per year. For example, with a discount rate of 7% a single payment of £1 in six years time has a present value of £0.6663 or 66.63p. (Reproduced from Drury, 1992).

Years	1%	2%	3%	4%	5%	6%	7%	8%	9%	10%
1	0.9901	0.9804	0.9709	0.9615	0.9524	0.9434	0.9346	0.9259	0.9174	0.9091
2	0.9803	0.9612	0.9426	0.9426	0.9070	0.8900	0.8734	0.8573	0.8417	0.8264
3	0.9706	0.9423	0.9151	0.8890	0.8638	0.8396	0.8163	0.7938	0.7722	0.7513
4	0.9610	0.9238	0.885	0.8548	0.8227	0.7921	0.7629	0.7350	0.7084	0.6830
5	0.9515	0.9057	0.8626	0.8219	0.7835	0.7473	0.7130	0.6806	0.6499	0.6209
6	0.9420	0.8880	0.8375	0.7903	0.7462	0.7050	0.6663	0.6302	0.5963	0.5645
7	0.9327	0.8706	0.8131	0.7599	0.7107	0.6651	0.6227	0.5835	0.5470	0.5132
8	0.9235	0.8535	0.7894	0.7307	0.6768	0.6274	0.5820	0.5403	0.5019	0.4665
9	0.9143	0.8368	0.7664	0.7026	0.6446	0.5919	0.5439	0.5002	0.4604	0.4241
10	0.9053	0.8203	0.7441	0.6756	0.6139	0.5584	0.5083	0.4632	0.4224	0.3855
11	0.8963	0.8043	0.7224	0.6496	0.5847	0.5268	0.4751	0.4289	0.3875	0.3505
12	0.8874	0.7885	0.7014	0.6246	0.5568	0.4970	0.4440	0.3971	0.3555	0.3186
13	0.8787	0.7730	0.6810	0.6006	0.5303	0.4688	0.4150	0.3677	0.3262	0.2897
14	0.8700	0.7579	0.6611	0.5775	0.5051	0.4423	0.3878	0.3405	0.2992	0.2633
15	0.8613	0.7430	0.6419	0.5553	0.4810	0.4173	0.3624	0.3152	0.2745	0.2394
16	0.8528	0.7284	0.6323	0.5339	0.4581	0.3936	0.3387	0.2919	0.2519	0.2176
17	0.8444	0.7142	0.6050	0.5134	0.4363	0.3714	0.3166	0.2703	0.2311	0.1978
18	0.8360	0.7002	0.5874	0.4936	0.4155	0.3503	0.2959	0.2502	0.2120	0.1799
19	0.8277	0.6864	0.5703	0.4746	0.3957	0.3305	0.2765	0.2317	0.1945	0.1635
20	0.8195	0.6730	0.5537	0.4564	0.3769	0.3118	0.2584	0.2145	0.1784	0.1486
21	0.8114	0.6598	0.5375	0.4388	0.3589	0.2942	0.2415	0.1987	0.1637	0.1351
22	0.8034	0.6468	0.5219	0.4220	0.3418	0.2775	0.2257	0.1839	0.1502	0.1228
23	0.7954	0.6342	0.5067	0.4057	0.3256	0.2618	0.2109	0.1703	0.1378	0.1117
24	0.7876	0.6217	0.4919	0.3901	0.3101	0.2470	0.1971	0.1577	0.1264	0.1015
25	0.7798	0.6095	0.4776	0.3751	0.2953	0.2330	0.1842	0.1460	0.1160	0.0923
26	0.7720	0.5976	0.4637	0.3607	0.2812	0.2198	0.1722	0.1352	0.1064	0.0839
27	0.7644	0.5859	0.4502	0.3468	0.2678	0.2074	0.1609	0.1252	0.0976	0.0763
28	0.7568	0.5744	0.4371	0.3335	0.2551	0.1956	0.1504	0.1159	0.0895	0.0693
29	0.7493	0.5631	0.4243	0.3207	0.2429	0.1846	0.1406	0.1073	0.0822	0.0630
30	0.7419	0.5521	0.4120	0.3083	0.2314	0.1741	0.1314	0.0994	0.0754	0.0573
35	0.7059	0.5000	0.3554	0.2534	0.1813	0.1301	0.0937	0.0676	0.0490	0.0356
40	0.6717	0.4529	0.3066	0.2083	0.1420	0.0972	0.0668	0.0460	0.0318	0.0221
45	0.6391	0.4102	0.2644	0.1712	0.1113	0.0727	0.0476	0.0313	0.0207	0.0137
50	0.6080	0.3715	0.2281	0.1407	0.0872	0.0543	0.0339	0.0213	0.0134	0.0085

Table13.B.1 *cont.*

11%	12%	13%	14%	15%	16%	17%	18%	19%	20%	Years
0.9009	0.8929	0.8850	0.8772	0.8696	0.8621	0.8547	0.8475	0.8403	0.8333	1
0.8116	0.7972	0.7831	0.7695	0.7561	0.7432	0.7305	0.7182	0.7062	0.6944	2
0.7312	0.7118	0.6931	0.6750	0.6575	0.6407	0.6244	0.6086	0.5934	0.5787	3
0.6587	0.6355	0.6133	0.5921	0.5718	0.5523	0.5337	0.5158	0.4987	0.4823	4
0.5935	0.5674	0.5428	0.5194	0.4972	0.4761	0.4561	0.4371	0.4190	0.4019	5
0.5346	0.5066	0.4803	0.4556	0.4323	0.4104	0.3898	0.3704	0.3521	0.3349	6
0.4817	0.4523	0.4251	0.3996	0.3759	0.3538	0.3332	0.3139	0.2959	0.2791	7
0.4339	0.4039	0.3762	0.3506	0.3269	0.3050	0.2848	0.2660	0.2487	0.2326	8
0.3909	0.3606	0.3329	0.3075	0.2843	0.2630	0.2434	0.2225	0.2090	0.1938	9
0.3522	0.3220	0.2946	0.2697	0.2472	0.2267	0.2080	0.1911	0.1756	0.1615	10
0.3173	0.2875	0.2607	0.2366	0.2149	0.1954	0.1778	0.1619	0.1476	0.1346	11
0.2858	0.2567	0.2307	0.2076	0.1869	0.1685	0.1520	0.1372	0.1240	0.1122	12
0.2575	0.2292	0.2042	0.1821	0.1625	0.1452	0.1299	0.1163	0.1042	0.0935	13
0.2320	0.2046	0.1807	0.1597	0.1413	0.1252	0.1110	0.0985	0.0876	0.0779	14
0.2090	0.1827	0.1599	0.1401	0.1229	0.1079	0.0949	0.0835	0.0736	0.0649	15
0.1883	0.1631	0.1415	0.1229	0.1069	0.0930	0.0811	0.0708	0.0618	0.0541	16
0.1696	0.1456	0.1252	0.1078	0.0929	0.0802	0.0693	0.0600	0.0520	0.0451	17
0.1528	0.1300	0.1108	0.0946	0.0808	0.0691	0.0592	0.0508	0.0437	0.0376	18
0.1377	0.1161	0.0981	0.0829	0.0703	0.0596	0.0506	0.0431	0.0367	0.0313	19
0.1240	0.1037	0.0868	0.0728	0.0611	0.0514	0.0433	0.0365	0.0308	0.0261	20
0.1117	0.0926	0.0768	0.0638	0.0531	0.0443	0.0370	0.0309	0.0259	0.0217	21
0.1007	0.0826	0.0680	0.0560	0.0462	0.0382	0.0316	0.0262	0.0218	0.0181	22
0.0907	0.0738	0.0601	0.0491	0.0402	0.0329	0.0270	0.0222	0.0183	0.0151	23
0.0817	0.0659	0.0532	0.0431	0.0349	0.0284	0.0231	0.0188	0.0154	0.0126	24
0.0736	0.0588	0.0471	0.0378	0.0304	0.0245	0.0197	0.0160	0.0129	0.0105	25
0.0663	0.0525	0.0417	0.0331	0.0264	0.0211	0.0169	0.0135	0.0109	0.0087	26
0.0597	0.0469	0.0369	0.0291	0.0230	0.0182	0.0144	0.0115	0.0091	0.0073	27
0.0538	0.0419	0.0326	0.0255	0.0200	0.0157	0.0123	0.0097	0.0077	0.0061	28
0.0485	0.0374	0.0289	0.0224	0.0174	0.0135	0.0105	0.0082	0.0064	0.0051	29
0.0437	0.0334	0.0256	0.0194	0.0151	0.0116	0.0090	0.0070	0.0054	0.0042	30
0.0259	0.0189	0.0139	0.0102	0.0075	0.0055	0.0041	0.0030	0.0023	0.0017	35
0.0154	0.0107	0.0075	0.0053	0.0037	0.0026	0.0019	0.0013	0.0010	0.0007	40
0.0091	0.0061	0.0041	0.0027	0.0019	0.0013	0.0009	0.0006	0.0004	0.0003	45
0.0054	0.0035	0.0022	0.0014	0.0009	0.0006	0.0004	0.0003	0.0002	0.0001	50

Table 13.B.2   The table gives the present value of n annual payments of £1 received for the next *n* years with a constant discount of *x*% per year. For example, with a discount rate of 7% and with 6 annual payments of £1, the present value is £4.767. (Reproduced from Drury, 1992.)

Years 0 to:	1%	2%	3%	4%	5%	6%	7%	8%	9%	10%
1	0.990	0.980	0.971	0.962	0.952	0.943	0.935	0.926	0.917	0.909
2	1.970	1.942	1.913	1.886	1.859	1.833	1.808	1.783	1.759	1.736
3	2.941	2.884	2.829	2.775	2.723	2.673	2.624	2.577	2.531	2.487
4	3.902	3.080	3.717	3.630	3.546	3.465	3.387	3.312	3.240	3.170
5	4.853	4.713	4.580	4.452	4.329	4.212	4.100	3.993	3.890	3.791
6	5.795	5.061	5.417	5.242	5.076	4.917	4.767	4.623	4.486	4.355
7	6.728	6.472	6.230	6.002	5.786	5.582	5.389	5.206	5.033	4.868
8	7.652	7.352	7.020	6.733	6.463	6.210	5.971	5.747	5.535	5.335
9	8.566	8.162	7.786	7.435	7.108	6.802	6.515	6.247	5.995	5.759
10	9.471	8.983	8.530	8.111	7.722	7.360	7.024	6.710	6.418	6.145
11	10.368	9.787	9.253	8.760	8.306	7.887	7.499	7.139	6.805	6.495
12	11.255	10.575	9.954	9.385	8.863	8.384	7.943	7.536	7.161	6.814
13	12.134	11.348	10.635	9.986	9.394	8.853	8.358	7.904	7.487	7.103
14	13.004	12.106	11.296	10.563	9.899	9.295	8.745	8.244	7.786	7.367
15	13.865	12.849	11.938	11.118	10.380	9.712	9.108	8.559	8.061	7.606
16	14.718	13.578	12.561	11.652	10.838	10.106	9.447	8.851	8.313	7.824
17	15.562	14.292	13.166	12.166	11.274	10.427	9.763	9.122	8.544	8.022
18	16.398	14.992	13.754	12.659	11.690	10.828	10.059	9.372	8.756	8.201
19	17.226	15.678	14.324	13.134	12.085	11.158	10.336	9.604	8.950	8.365
20	18.046	16.351	14.877	13.590	12.462	11.470	10.594	9.818	9.129	8.514
21	18.857	17.011	15.415	14.029	12.821	11.764	10.836	10.017	9.292	8.649
22	19.660	17.658	15.937	14.451	13.163	12.042	11.061	10.201	9.442	8.772
23	20.456	18.292	16.444	14.857	13.489	12.303	11.272	10.371	9.580	8.883
24	21.243	18.914	16.939	15.247	13.799	12.550	11.469	10.529	9.707	9.985
25	22.023	19.523	17.413	15.622	14.094	12.783	11.654	10.675	9.823	9.077
26	22.795	20.121	17.877	15.983	13.375	13.003	11.826	10.810	9.929	9.161
27	23.560	20.707	18.327	16.330	14.643	13.211	11.987	10.935	10.027	9.237
28	24.316	21.281	18.764	16.663	13.898	13.406	12.137	11.051	10.116	9.307
29	25.066	21.844	19.188	16.984	15.141	13.591	12.278	11.158	10.198	9.307
30	25.808	22.396	19.600	17.292	15.372	13.765	12.409	11.258	10.274	9.427
35	29.409	24.999	21.487	18.665	16.374	14.498	12.948	11.655	10.567	9.644
40	32.835	27.355	23.115	19.793	17.159	15.046	13.332	11.925	10.575	9.779
45	36.095	29.490	24.519	20.720	17.774	15.456	13.606	12.108	10.881	9.863
50	39.196	31.424	25.730	21.482	18.256	15.762	13.801	12.233	10.962	9.915

Table13.B.2 *cont.*

11%	12%	13%	14%	15%	16%	17%	18%	19%	20%	Years 0 to:
0.901	0.893	0.885	0.877	0.870	0.862	0.855	0.847	0.840	0.833	1
1.713	1.690	1.668	1.647	1.626	1.605	1.585	1.566	1.547	1.528	2
2.444	2.402	2.361	2.322	2.283	2.246	2.210	2.174	2.140	2.106	3
3.102	3.037	2.974	2.914	2.855	2.798	2.743	2.690	2.639	2.589	4
3.696	3.605	3.517	3.433	3.352	3.274	3.199	3.127	3.058	2.991	5
4.231	4.111	3.998	3.889	3.784	3.685	3.589	3.498	3.410	3.326	6
4.712	4.564	4.423	4.288	4.160	4.039	3.922	3.812	3.706	3.605	7
5.146	4.968	4.799	4.639	4.487	4.344	4.207	4.078	3.954	3.837	8
5.537	5.328	5.132	4.946	4.772	4.607	4.451	4.303	4.163	4.031	9
5.889	5.650	5.426	5.216	5.019	4.833	4.659	4.494	4.339	4.192	10
6.207	5.938	5.687	5.453	5.234	5.029	4.836	4.656	4.486	4.327	11
6.492	6.194	5.918	5.660	5.421	5.197	4.988	4.793	4.611	4.439	12
6.750	6.424	6.122	5.842	5.583	5.342	5.118	4.910	4.715	4.533	13
6.982	6.628	6.302	6.002	5.724	5.468	5.229	5.008	4.802	4.611	14
7.191	6.811	6.462	6.142	5.847	5.575	5.324	5.092	4.876	4.675	15
7.379	6.974	6.604	6.265	5.954	5.668	5.405	5.162	4.938	4.730	16
7.549	7.120	6.729	6.373	6.047	5.749	5.475	5.222	4.990	4.775	17
7.702	7.250	6.840	6.467	6.128	5.818	5.534	5.273	5.033	4.812	18
7.839	7.366	6.938	6.550	6.198	5.877	5.584	5.316	5.070	4.843	19
7.963	7.469	7.025	6.623	6.259	5.929	5.628	5.353	5.101	4.870	20
8.075	7.562	7.102	6.687	6.312	5.973	5.665	5.384	5.127	4.891	21
8.176	7.645	7.170	6.743	6.359	6.011	5.696	5.410	5.149	4.909	22
8.266	7.718	7.230	6.792	6.399	6.044	5.723	5.432	5.167	4.925	23
8.348	7.784	7.283	6.835	6.434	6.073	5.746	5.451	5.182	4.937	24
8.422	7.843	7.330	6.873	6.464	6.097	5.766	5.467	5.195	4.948	25
8.488	7.896	7.372	6.906	6.491	6.118	5.783	5.480	5.206	4.956	26
8.548	7.943	7.409	6.935	6.514	6.136	5.798	5.492	5.215	4.964	27
8.602	7.984	7.441	6.961	6.534	6.152	5.810	5.502	5.223	4.970	28
8.650	8.022	7.470	6.983	6.551	6.166	5.820	5.510	5.229	4.975	29
8.694	8.055	7.496	7.003	6.566	6.177	5.829	5.517	5.235	4.979	30
8.855	8.176	7.586	7.070	6.617	6.215	5.858	5.539	5.251	4.992	35
8.951	8.244	7.634	7.105	6.642	6.233	5.871	5.548	5.258	4.997	40
9.008	8.283	7.661	7.123	6.654	6.242	5.877	5.552	5.261	4.999	45
0.042	8.304	7.675	7.133	6.661	6.246	5.880	5.554	5.262	4.999	50

14 Budgetary planning and control

Objectives

Budgets are financial plans. Checking performance against plans assists managerial control. Since budgets are normally identified with accountable managers, budgeting is sometimes described as **responsibility accounting**. Good budgeting is especially important where outputs are diverse, or non-standard, as in a factory R&D department, an advertising agency or, within the public sector, a school, hospital or social services department.

This chapter explains how budgets link financial accountability with the management organisation structure, how they are constructed, and how follow-up reporting and corrective action is needed. Some budgets are 'fixed' for the year, and some need to be 'flexible' to allow spending to reflect achieved activity volumes and costs. The budget cycle and timetable are explained, and the components of the 'master budget', which shadows the annual financial accounts of the organisation, are examined. The behavioural problems in achieving effective budgeting are considered, together with some specialised applications of budgeting, including both private- and public-sector service organisations, budgeting for capital, and the management-by-objectives (MBO) approach to stimulating improvement in management performance.

The nature of budgeting

Budgeting is any formalised system of forecasting, planning, monitoring and controlling the use of resources. Budgets can be prepared in physical units of inputs, outputs or sales, but normally this is followed by 'pricing' each unit in order to express the final budgets and budget reports in financial terms.

Sometimes budgets are set in the first instance in financial terms, providing limits to spending and leaving it to managers to determine subsequently how to subdivide the monetary resource allocation among different physical resources, comprising employees, premises, equipment, etc. This latter alternative applies especially to budgeting in the public sector.

The term 'budget' derives from the public sector. A 'bougette' (*OED*; from the French) is a small leather bag or case. At least by 1733 (*OED*), and probably earlier, the chancellor of the exchequer would bring his proposals for collecting and spending public revenues to Parliament in a bougette. Opening his bag and revealing his proposal papers led to the expression 'to open the budget', a tradition carried on to this day with the familiar red dispatch box.

Given that public spending involves the allocation of finite funds from taxation (and sometimes, more controversially, from government borrowing), it is natural that budgets for public services are set as limits to spending. Thus 'control' will be exercised as much by prohibition of overspending as by any later review of the wisdom of how funds were spent or of the results achieved. Although budgetary practice in the public sector is today coming closer to that in the private sector, there remain some distinctive problems and features, to which we return later in the chapter.

In private business the firm's spending and commitments must be responsive to changes in the marketplace, as well as to longer-term objectives of business development. Budgetary planning and control are typically more complex in the business firm than in government, so we shall take business budgeting as our general model in the chapter. Emmanuel *et al.* (1990) have suggested five main functions or roles for budgets:

- a system of authorisation;
- a means of forecasting and planning;
- a channel of communication and coordination;
- a motivational device;
- a means of performance evaluation and control, as well as of providing a basis for decision making.

These functions will arise for discussion in different contexts through the present chapter. First, let us clarify the meanings of certain words as they will be used in the discussion of budgeting. Some of these words have alternative meanings or nuances in other contexts; it is just unfortunate that the terminology, or jargon, of accounting is composed largely of words with everyday meanings!

- **Estimates** are approximations of what might happen under specified assumptions. Often one will specify alternative or multiple assumptions. This can be a form of search or even sensitivity analysis to help focus choice.
- **Forecasts** are predictions of what will happen under a chosen alternative set of assumptions or, occasionally, of what would happen under alternative assumptions. Forecasts, like estimates, are often linked with the study of uncertainty, and uncertainty is usually greatest when studying markets, likely sales, technological change and political environments (e.g. interest rates, exchange rates, the trade policies of foreign governments). It is often useful to have independent outside experts as advisers on key issues of forecasting, and market research is often used to help with the making of predictions.
- **Plans** are the details of intended future operations which, once agreed or approved, form commitments to future action. However, there should be known channels and procedures for reviewing, updating and revising any plans which are made.
- **Budgets** are a specialised type of plans, usually in financial rather than physical resource terms. Budgets link together all the parts of the organisation, in the common denominator of cost and revenue flows, and their interdependencies.

Managers who accept and administer budgets are called 'budget holders'. Budget holding is a major managerial responsibility. The accounting and reporting procedures developed for budgets are often called **responsibility accounting**. This is linked with agency theory. An agency relationship involves an actual or implicit contract under which one or more persons (i.e. the principals) engage another person (i.e. the agent) to provide some service or function on their behalf, with some degree of delegated powers in carrying out that service or function. Agency costs can arise because the agent may not always act in the best interests of the principal(s) – in this case the business organisation and its official objectives, plans and budgets. Failure to act in the best interests of the organisation can result from lack of experience, bad luck, slackness or conflict of interests. The latter two causes are behavioural problems which we consider later in the chapter. First, we consider the normative model of how budgeting should work in an ideal situation with goal congruence and with the budgets providing a kind of financial mirror-image to the formal organisation structure and objectives of the enterprise.

Budget organisation

Managerial responsibility is the role situation of exercising authority over specified and often limited resources to be used in pursuit of agreed organisational goals, with accountability for the results. Accountability involves disclosure of performance, for evaluation and performance appraisal, and for any rewards or penalties that might result. Budgeting is a financial information system which exists to:

■ help managers reach their goals and discharge their responsibilities;
■ make managers fairly accountable for their performance.

Achieving these objectives requires that budgeting should be relevant, accurate, and prompt in reporting any performance problems and assisting with explaining their cause. We shall return to these aspects later. The key point for the moment is to highlight that, given the description of budgeting set out above, it should be clear that budgets should reflect the organisation chart/structure of the firm (or public-sector body) – and therefore be a mirror-image.

Budget centres

An organisation chart is pyramidal, and the chart of budgets must reflect this (see Figure 14.1). Major accounts for bringing together the costs, revenues, etc. associated with a particular activity, product or service, or with the area of responsibility of a particular manager are termed 'centres' (and this term combines both the focus of managerial accountability and the gathering of relevant financial information). Let us illustrate this by reference to the four levels of budget accountability in Figure 14.1.

■ **Investment centre**: level A, at the top of the organisation, is where the budget holder is responsible for capital investments and the rate of return earned on capital, as well as for the supporting pyramid of profit or loss comprising the total revenues less total costs. This budget holder would be the chief executive of the company, a subsidiary company, or a division organised on the basis of delegated

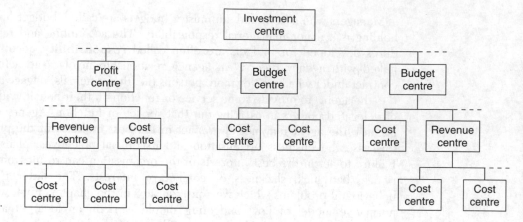

Figure 14.1
A pyramid of
budget centres.

or decentralised control over and accountability for the level of investment and the rate of return earned.

■ **Profit centre**: shown at level B, the profit-centre budget holder will typically be a general manager in charge of a department or division, with responsibility for both revenue-earning and cost-incurring activities. Sometimes he/she could be a 'brand manager' or 'product-line manager' with only notional real control over resources, but with responsibility for planning and coordinating the marketing (and sometimes the production) requirements for a particular brand or product line. Below the level of a divisional general manager, a budget holder's control over fixed costs or overheads and their apportionment or absorption between different activities, outputs or organisational units may be weak, so that it could be quite unfair to try to hold the manager accountable for precise measures of profit. Here it would be better to designate a 'contribution-centre' budget, based on the excess of revenues over variable or attributable costs; and here the manager's objective is simply to maximise contribution.

■ **Budget centre**: in the wider sense, all financial information accounts centres are 'budget centres', assuming they are used for financial planning, monitoring and control, and not just for collecting data for historical accounts. However, the term is used here in the narrower sense, in level B, to identify budgets which are normally 'fixed' in maximum spending limits (see below); examples include R&D, personnel, finance, public relations, etc.

■ **Revenue centre**: revenue centres are shown at level C. These show sales or other income as compared to budgeted targets for revenue. Revenue budget holders could be general managers, marketing managers, sales managers or brand managers.

■ **Cost centre**: cost centres, shown at both level C and level D, are the basic collection accounts for recorded costs, whether related to activity (i.e. inputs), outputs or authorised spending against fixed budgets. Thus a budget-centre manager may have a number of cost-centre budgets beneath his/her overall budget; for example, a public relations manager may have separate cost budgets for conference expenses, for printing, and for departmental staff and expenses. A manager whose primary role is as a revenue budget holder may also have cost budgets; for example, a sales or brands manager may hold the advertising and promotions expense budgets for relevant brands, products or markets. A manager whose primary role is as a cost-centre budget holder may also hold subsidiary cost budgets; for example, a warehouse manager whose overall budget is for stock-handling costs may have subsidiary budgets for premises and equipment maintenance.

Budgets and decentralisation

Good budgetary planning and control facilitate the decentralisation of corporate organisational structure where this is desired. Decentralisation can take various forms, based on geographical units, markets served, products or technologies, or simply parallel and competing enterprises. There are many ramifications – the subject matter of business organisation textbooks – but for our purposes the key point is that an essential prerequisite of decentralisation, devolution and the delegation of effective operational authority and responsibility to subordinate units (be these known as departments, divisions or subsidiary companies) is that central management has access to high-quality and timely management information in order to monitor performance, and to be able to intervene and take corrective action in the case of serious failure or major deviation from agreed strategies and plans. The budgeting system can and should provide this information.

It is a task for top-management policy-making to decide the degree to which decentralisation and authority delegation should be employed. Thus, for example, a division could be run as an investment centre, with divisional management empowered to take the lead in capital-investment planning and decisions, and to be held accountable for the return on capital achieved. Alternatively, the same division could be run as just a profit centre, with investment decisions retained at central-management level and the divisional manager held accountable only for optimising profit, or profit contribution, from the use of the capital assets he/she is provided with. Divisionalisation is further discussed in Chapter 16. Similarly, at lower management levels the more accurate, detailed and timely the budgetary reporting system is, the greater will be the degree of decision-taking authority which may safely be delegated. The degree is a matter of top-management choice.

Budgeting based on costing

Revenue budgets are based on targets and forecasts of sales volume and prices, and they are inevitably subject to the vagaries of the marketplace. But most budgets are for costs and expenses, and here management has greater control. Budgets are built upon forecast costs at specific volumes of activity, and subsequent budgetary performance reports compare these budgets with the outturn derived from actual costs at actual volumes of activity. So cost information forms the 'building blocks' both for realistic budgets and for accurate budgetary performance reports. It follows that it is impossible to have a high-quality budgetary planning and control system unless the organisation's costing methods and systems, as discussed in previous chapters, are also of a high degree of relevance and accuracy, with data available promptly. And the quality of costing data, in its turn, is dependent not just or even mainly on the work of accounting in 'pricing' units of inputs or activity, but rather on the relevance and accuracy of the departmental recording, both of the use of physical resource inputs and of the outputs achieved.

The budget cycle and administration

This section explains the time-cycle of budgeting, the form of control which budgeting can provide, and some of the administrative arrangements for effective budget planning and control.

The time-cycle of budget planning and control

Most budgets are managed on an annual basis to coincide with the corporate financial year. But for each year's budgets planning must begin in the preceding year, while the annual end-of-year 'postmortem' review and final corrective action can extend well into the following year. This cycle of planning and control is summarised in Table 14.1. The table is simplified in that it shows only the activity related to one year's budgets, year 2 in the example. In practice, work is going on simultaneously on the adjoining years' budget planning and control follow-through.

In year 1, the year preceding our illustrative budget, preparatory work is needed before individual budgets can be drawn up. The detail and thoroughness of this preparatory work vary greatly between organisations, but, in general, the larger and more complex the organisation, the greater the degree to which it is decentralised; and the more dynamic the markets in which it operates, the more important it is that the preparatory work is comprehensive. This may begin in the middle of the financial year, or even earlier, commencing from the completion of the control postmortem on the previous year's performance.

The work in year 1 should comprise a strategic review of the firm's markets, capacity, technology, capital-investment programme and objectives. From this review initial budget guidelines should emerge for use by the budget staff in helping managers draft individual budgets. These draft budgets are then combined into an

Table 14.1 The time-cycle of budget planning and control

Time	Budgeting	Control
Year 1	Strategic review Set budget guidelines Draft individual budgets Assemble master budget Adjust or reiterate until all budgets are optimal	
Year 2	Collect cost, revenue, etc. data by budget centre and prepare progress reports for managers, including variance analysis	Reports and variance analysis flag problems for corrective action Budget staff and higher management follow up major budget problems
Year 3		Postmortem analysis of prior budget year, with feedback into the next strategic review

overall master budget (see below) to see if the 'sum of the parts' really adds up to fulfilment of the corporate objectives. If it does not, individual budgets must be revised, iteratively, and/or the corporate objectives and strategy must be amended, until an optimal but realistic set of budgets is obtained and agreed. This budget planning sequence can take several months, and it should be completed at least a month or two before the start of the new budget year so that managers have lead-time to organise for implementation. In the public sector there is an occasional complaint because budgets are not always finally determined before the start of the new budget year, owing to late notification by government of the allowed total funding or to other delays in the resource-allocation decision process.

Moving to year 2 cost accountants and budget staff work to collect all relevant cost (or revenue) data, usually bringing these together in monthly summaries or budget-performance reports (see below), to be made available promptly to each budget holder. As is summarised in the Control column of Table 14.1, the monthly budget reports are intended to be studied by managers for evidence as to how well they are achieving budget plans/targets. To assist in this, differences between budgeted and actual costs/revenues are usually printed out in separate report columns. These differences are termed 'budget variances'; variance accounting is illustrated in detail in the next chapter in the specific context of standard costing, a costing approach often used in combination with budgeting to improve the quality of reporting and control information. Budget staff should be available to answer budget holders' queries regarding any budget results they do not understand, and the budget staff should themselves take the initiative to work with management budget holders to find the causes of significant unfavourable variances and to take corrective action (which could include amending the budget should this be found to have been genuinely unrealistic).

At the start of year 3 all the individual budgets, together with the overall master budget, should be subjected to a close review. Sometimes this may be linked with the annual performance reviews or assessments of managers, although, clearly, budgetary performance forms only one part of a much wider range of assessment criteria. But always this annual review, or postmortem on the previous year, should be used positively to provide feedback of information and insight to assist the monitoring of current budgets and the preparation of the next strategic review.

Feedback and feedforward control

Planning and control may be likened to two sides of the same coin. They should match, in size and worth. That is, assuming our plan is optimal given the state of knowledge and uncertainty, our object with control systems is to ensure that performance matches or achieves the plan. Broadly, two main control concepts or types of control systems are identified and developed in the literature (Emmanuel *et al.* 1990; Wilson and Chua 1993): feedback control and feedforward control.

Feedback is the traditional control system, historically associated with budgeting. Performance would be recorded, accumulated on file and then assembled in reports to managers, typically monthly but sometimes more frequently. If reported performance showed unfavourable variances from plan, corrective action would be taken.

Feedforward is the more modern approach to control systems. The object is to control performance in real time, as it happens; or, even better, to achieve control through prediction and anticipation of what action is needed to achieve plans or other targets or criteria of good performance. Modern technology of instrumentation and computer control makes the feedforward approach feasible and valuable in many productive operations, for example helping to eliminate rejects and waste in production lines by sensing machine deviation from set specification. This leads either to machines correcting themselves or at least to the production line stopping if human corrective intervention is needed. Real-time control has other applications also, such as in the stock-control, distribution and ordering arrangements for supermarket chains. Feedforward control is usually applied using physical resource measures rather than cost data. In such situations the budget objectives are sought through optimising control of the physical surrogates for financial targets. Periodic budget reports may become less important, or certainly less urgent or critical in their control role, but will remain essential for monitoring to check that the performance of individual operations and departments, when expressed in money terms for combination with other activities in the overall master budgets, is on course to meet the financial targets and objectives of the enterprise as a whole.

The principle of feedforward control is important, and management should seek to implement feedforward control whenever it is feasible and cost-effective, especially the aspects of anticipation and prediction to avoid problems or unfavourable deviations from plan before they begin to bite. Nevertheless, there remain many areas of activity where automatic feedforward control systems cannot be used (as yet) and where traditional budgetary control feedback reporting systems remain the major form of financial control. These areas are typically where work is not routine or standardised, or where work cannot be planned in detail in advance but must evolve under management discretion stage by stage. Examples here include much of the work of commercial marketing and R&D, many professional services, university research projects, and much of the work of the social services and the NHS.

Feedforward control is but one example of the expanding ways in which information technology (IT) is contributing to improved budgeting and financial management. Other examples include financial modelling, analysis for risk and uncertainty or probability, and the general ability to employ sensitivity analysis in financial and budgetary planning. In a budgeting context, sensitivity analysis involves the quantification of a wide range of different permutations of production mix, costs, prices and marketing mix in search of the most favourable of profitable prospects.

Budget administration

In many large organisations a specialist budget director is appointed, reporting to the finance director or controller. In smaller organisations the role may be combined with that of the chief management accountant. Again, larger organisations are likely to have a budget committee comprised of senior executives to review financial strategy, set budget guidelines, study main budget proposals, review and approve main budgets and the master budget, adjudicate any disputes between budget holders and budget staff, and generally monitor the effectiveness of the budgetary planning and control system.

Organisations of any size will provide budget manuals giving detailed instructions on the layout of budgets, what to include and where, the routines to be followed, and the coding system for matching resource use and costs (or revenues) with the specific inputs, activities, outputs, items of stock, items of sales, or organisational units and activities whose budgets should be charged (or credited). Good design of the coding system is of the highest importance, both so that it is comprehensible to the clerks and other workers who have to enter activity data by code, and so that the data can be manipulated by computer into all the various combinations of cost, budget and revenue analysis reports which may be required.

A key issue in budget administration is whether budgets should be drafted by budget or accounting staff, and then discussed with budget-holding managers and amended as necessary, or whether budget holders should be given a blank budget form, together with copies of current budget guidelines and last year's budget for reference, and be told to get on with drafting their own budgets. Opinions differ. Practice differs. The nature of the business and the culture of the organisation are important factors in how to proceed on this. There are also important behavioural factors to consider in budgetary planning and control, which will be discussed in a separate section later in this chapter.

An important aspect of budget administration is the arrangements for amending or updating budgets if and when circumstances change during the budget year. There should be clear procedures for amending budgets – or making budget revisions, as they are often called, especially in the public sector. One form of amendment may involve not change in the total budget, but rather the switching of planned expenditure from one budget heading (or resource category) to another. Budget rules in the business world may often give managers substantial discretion as regards switching, whereas the tradition in the public service sector has been to set tight rules (here a particular term, 'virement', is used to identify the process of switching funds from one budget heading to another).

Budgets and budget reports

Budgets are required for every element of cost, expense and revenue for all the financial flows represented in the periodic operational profit and loss accounts or income statements. They are also required for all the asset and liability categories represented in the balance sheet. There are also budgets which link these two sets, perhaps most importantly the purchases budget, which effectively authorises expenditure on materials, parts and components for production or on finished goods for distribution. The purchases budget is extremely important, because it must meet the needs of sales plans (and thus of production plans in manufacturing businesses), yet also be reconciled with the firm's cash position and overall credit and working-capital plans and limits.

Operational budgets

We set out below a list of the main budgets, or control budgets, for a typical manufacturing firm. It must be remembered that supporting each of these main or control budgets there will be separate subordinate budgets for each cost or revenue category

– or centre – which is of sufficient importance to be managed as a budget centre in its own right, with a designated and accountable manager as budget holder.

- **Sales budget**: this might be subdivided or segmented in one or more of the following ways: product, area, brands, class of customer, exports, divisions, branches, etc.
- **Production budget**: this might be subdivided by plant or technology, and/or match the subdivisions in the sales budget. Both the production and sales budgets may be set out in physical volume terms as well as money costs and revenues.
- **Purchase budget**: this links the forecast requirements of sales and production, with other interlinkages mentioned in the preceding paragraph.
- **Personnel budget** (sometimes called the labour budget or manpower budget): this may classify requirements by skills, grades or types of labour. Supporting expense budgets may cover recruitment, training, welfare and redundancy.
- **Marketing budget**: this is linked to the sales budget, and includes the expenses of marketing planning and administration, advertising and promotion (including sponsorships of sporting and cultural activities).
- **Capital budget**: this shows the amount and timing of approved major capital (fixed assets) expenditure over the budget year. Minor plant, equipment and vehicle expenditure may be included in other operational budgets, especially for production.
- **Cash budget**: this summarises all cash receipts and disbursements arising from trading, and also often includes cash flows arising from the capital budget and any new funding. Seasonal and other factors may result in periods of negative cash balances; these must be reconciled to overdraft limits and other borrowing arrangements. At other times there may be cash surpluses in excess of operational requirements, and how these should be invested profitably but safely in the short term needs to be planned.
- **Budgeted working capital or sources and application of funds statements**: these link with financing plans and the cash budget, as well as with the budgeted profit and loss and balance sheet (see below).
- **Budgeted profit and loss or income statement**: this draws together all revenue, cost and expense budget totals to derive the budgeted, or expected, profit and loss for the (usually) annual budget period.
- **Budgeted balance sheet**: this draws together the effects of all the above budgets on the expected end-of-period values of the firm's assets, liabilities and residual capital balances.

The master budget

The term 'master budget' is used in two ways. Usually, it designates the key budgets at the top of the pyramid of budget planning – for profit and loss and the balance sheet – which must be approved by top management before all the subsidiary budgets can be accepted as firm and approved. If these key budgets are not acceptable – or indeed if the cash or working-capital budgets are not viable or are too risky – the entire budget planning process may have to be reiterated until the impact on the master budget becomes acceptable. There is, of course, the risk of junior managers 'fudging' some budgets against their realistic expectations or intuitive judgement in order to accommodate this reiteration exercise.

Once agreed, the above master budget becomes a firm plan and commitment for management. By extension, the term 'master budget' is sometimes used to identify the final, agreed form of each and every subordinate budget as well. In this context, all such master budgets are apparently 'fixed' in character; we shall consider the differences between 'fixed' and 'flexible' budgets further below.

Budget reports

Main budgets are usually made on an annual basis, but normally subdivided by months (or sometimes into thirteen four-week periods to facilitate inter-period comparisons). Monthly or four-weekly periods are the traditional intervals for which to issue budgetary control progress reports. However, for some budgets thought critical at particular stages of business – often cash budgets – reports may be issued more frequently, and with modern computer systems it will become increasingly common for managers to check their budget positions at any time between the formal reporting and review dates.

Table 14.2 provides a simplified example of a monthly production-department budget report. The budgets agreed before the start of the year, or with any approved amendments, are shown for the current month and for the year to date for each main category or cost centre within the budget. Against each budget are set the actual costs charged to the cost centres for the periods concerned, and the differences between these two figures are then displayed in the variance columns.

Supporting each of the main budget cost centres there may be a whole series of subordinate cost centres with supporting detail. Direct materials, for example, may be supported by separate cost accounts for each major item or type of material, part and component used. Often many more cost categories will be shown than in our example, but there is a view that many managers are too busy to be able to scrutinise detailed budgets properly, and that it is preferable that summary budget reports should be restricted to such detail as can be displayed on a single sheet.

Table 14.2 Production-department budget report

Department Q – month 3							
Current month			*Costs*	*Code*	*Year to date*		
Budget	*Actual*	*Variance*			*Budget*	*Actual*	*Variance*
£48 000	£46 400	£1 600	Direct materials	801	£144 000	£145 400	£–1 400
18 000	18 800	–800	Direct labour	802	54 000	56 200	–2 200
10 000	10 000		Fixed overheads	803	30 000	30 000	
6 000	6 300	–300	Variable overheads	804	18 000	18 600	–600
£82 000	£81 500	£500	Totals		£246 000	£250 200	–£4 200
4 000	3 800	–200	Units produced		12 000	11 500	–500
£20.50	£21.45	–£0.95	Unit production cost		£20.50	£21.76	–£1.26

Note: Minus signs indicate unfavourable variances.

There are two important simplifying assumptions in Table 14.2. First, it has been assumed that the budget is identical for each month, implying a continuously stable rate of production, and thus probably of sales. Often, though, seasonal patterns of demand, planned promotion or product innovation, or forecast expansion or contraction of markets, as well as closures for holidays or plant overhaul or replacement, will result in variations in planned output and authorised budget from month to month. Second, our example shows actual fixed overheads as identical to budget. In real life this will happen sometimes, but not always. Whether it happens or not, there is a school of thought which holds that where fixed overheads are not under the control of the budget holder variances arising should not be included in that budget holder's report (possibly distorting or at least confusing his/her accountable performance). Proponents of this viewpoint would prefer to see the fixed overhead variances carried to a separate account for which top management would be accountable. Of course, proponents of variable costing or contribution costing would anyway wish to see fixed overheads wholly excluded from the production budget and unit-cost calculations, on the grounds discussed in previous chapters.

The variance figures in Table 14.2 are net variances, and supplementary analysis may be needed to explain their full causes and significance. Take the apparently favourable variance of £1600 on direct materials. Yet output was down 200 units, or 5%, on budget. Prima facie, direct-materials cost should also have fallen by 5%, or £2400. Thus the budget holder has actually incurred materials costs £800 greater than expected, an unfavourable variance. This may have been caused by wastage owing to poor quality of material or to production errors, or it may be due to higher material prices than forecast when the budget was set. Ad hoc enquiry or supplementary analysis can explain the true nature of, and accountability for, the overall net variance. However, our first distortion, owing to the deviation in production volume, can be resolved by using the flexible budgeting approach described below in place of fixed budgets. And the second distortion, or uncertainty as to the cause(s) of the remaining variance, may be more easily explained by linking budgetary reporting with the routine use of standard costing and standard cost-variance analysis, as explained in Chapter 15.

Flexible budgeting

True fixed budgets set out absolute limits to expenditure, although sometimes these can be amended to allow for the effects of inflation on input costs beyond the control of the budget holder. Fixed budgets are used in the private sector when there is no direct linkage between expenditure and (at least short-term) market performance. This applies to many administrative costs, and to what are known as 'policy costs', including outlays on R&D and some parts of outlays on marketing, market research, promotion, sponsorship and public relations.

Most public-sector budgets are fixed budgets, since they represent maximum expenditure allocations from central or local government. Prior to 1976 many of these fixed budgets were automatically uplifted for inflation as the budget year progressed, funded by supplementary votes in Parliament. From 1976 the 'cash-limits' system was introduced, whereby initial budgets were fixed to include forecast inflation, with, normally, no subsequent uplift allowed. However, the governmental allowances for inflation were often 'wishful thinking' underestimates of the actual inflation, so that public-sector funding has been constricted in 'real terms'; that is, in the purchasing power for real resources which government cash limits have covered.

Where production or selling activity is demand-led or market-led budgets should be flexible to reflect the levels of expenditure (and revenue) needed to cover the volume of activity meeting demand. Even in demand-led circumstances one could use fixed budgets, but they would never give realistic guidance on expenditure. There would often be large variances, which would have to be analysed to establish what part of the variances were caused by volume changes from the baseline used for the fixed budgets, as distinct from variances for efficiency and the prices of resource inputs.

Flexible budgets are illustrated in Table 14.3. Section A shows a basic or traditional form of flexible budgeting. Here it is assumed that both direct materials and direct labour are fully variable, i.e. that direct material and labour cost is a linear function, with a constant cost per unit regardless of the volume level. However, as discussed in previous chapters, this is an unrealistic assumption, at least in the short term when management may be unable to reduce the workforce quickly, or indeed to recruit and train new workers quickly. There may also be inherent technical features of the production process which cause step-costs (i.e. semi-fixed or semi-variable costs) in the use of direct labour at different production volumes. In Table 14.3 it is assumed that 10 000 units constitute the standard output for the budget period and that if a single fixed budget were used this would be the middle column in Section A.

Table 14.3 Flexible budgets of production department

	8 000 units £000	10 000 units £000	12 000 units £000
A Traditional allocation:			
Fixed overheads	80	80	80
Direct material (£10 per unit)	80	100	120
Direct labour (£8 per unit)	64	80	96
Variable overheads (£4 per unit)	32	40	48
Total cost	£256	£300	£344
Unit cost	£32	£30	£28.67
B Alternative allocation:			
Fixed overheads	80	80	80
Direct material (£10 per unit)	80	100	120
Direct labour			
core/fixed (7–14 000 units)	60	60	60
variable (0–11 000 units; £2 per unit)	16	20	22
variable (11 000+ units; £4 per unit)	–	–	4
Variable overheads (£4 per unit)	32	40	48
Total cost	£268	£300	£334
Unit cost	£33.50	£30	£27.83

Flexible budgets calculate the expected cost (or revenue) at alternative, relevant volume levels. Monthly or other periodic budget reports can show the precise combination of fixed costs plus aggregate unit variable costs for the actual volume achieved. The type of multiple-column, alternative-volume layout shown in Figure 14.3 would be prepared before the start of the year to give managers guidance in short-term planning of resources and expenditure. The flexible budgeting process also allows calculation of the unit production costs that are expected at each volume, which should provide helpful information for marketing decisions on product pricing.

Section B of Table 14.3 illustrates the alternative of recognising that, while direct materials may be a fully variable cost, direct labour usually is not fully variable. Analysis of production can determine a core of staff needed for essential skills and for minimum manning of separate workstations, which defines the minimum workforce for continuing, efficient operations. This part of labour cost can then be seen for budgetary purposes as a fixed cost (as shown in Table 14.3). There then follows a more genuinely variable element of labour cost, comprising the result of marginal expansion or contraction of the labour force, ordinary overtime, use of casual labour, etc. Finally, beyond a certain volume (11 000 units in our illustration) excess overtime and/or subcontracting out part of the work will cause short-term unit variable cost to rise for the 'excess' production.

It is interesting to note the differences in unit costs disclosed by the two approaches to flexible budgeting in Table 14.3. These differences reflect the economies of scale from higher outputs made evident by departing from a simplistic assumption that direct labour is a fully variable cost (and this is an insight which may be obtained also from ABC, discussed previously). Even so, the differences in unit costs disclosed between the two approaches may not be so great as to alter company pricing and production plans in most business situations. In contrast, the differences in expected expenditure on production between the alternatives – e.g. showing that total production cost would be expected to be £12 000 higher at 8000 units, but £10 000 lower at 12 000 units – are quite substantial sums of expenditure in the context of budgetary reporting, accountability and control. At the lower volume level the budget holding manager might be wrongly accused of inefficiency or overspending, while at the higher volume level a flexible budget based simplistically on the approach in section A of the table could serve to conceal ineffficiency. It is of the essence that budgets and budgetary-control reports must be relevant, realistic, accurate and fair if they are to be effective aids to management. Where they fail to meet these requirements, as often happens, budget holders will resist the discipline of the budgets and engage in counterproductive behaviour. This will be considered further in the next section.

Budgets and behaviour

There used to be two sets of convenient assumptions about accounting information and its use, including budget planning and control. The first assumption was that accounting and budgeting normally provided information which was objective, accurate and relevant, and which all managers should accept as rational guidance for positive action in the corporate interest. The second assumption was that all managers (and indeed all accountants) shared goal congruence in the corporate interest and would prepare and use budget information solely, or at least mainly, to that end. We now know that both assumptions are often wrong.

There is not space here to go into behavioural issues in detail, but much of the mainstream literature on business organisation and organisational behaviour applies. The classic organisational study of the behavioural problems of budgeting is by Hofstede (1968). Lowe and Machin (1983) provide excellent coverage of the problems of accounting and budgetary control combined with wider issues of managerial control. Emmanuel *et al*. (1990) develop a comprehensive overall review of the role and use of accounting in management control.

Behavioural problems

Among the key problems identified by the authors mentioned above are:

1 **Budget slack**: where managers propose their own budgets, or even where they simply feed in non-financial resource data to a budget officer or accountant to draft the formal budgets, there is a great temptation for managers to overstate their resource needs. This could be to provide a safety margin against uncertainty and/or to secure some spare funding which they may later be able to divert to a spending interest which would not obtain approval if disclosed in advance at the budget planning and review stage (e.g. to pay for some extra equipment, maintenance or travel). This is a natural human reaction: even as individuals within a family discussing our budgets, we may, for example, exaggerate the amount we expect to need to service the car in the year ahead, hoping for some slack which could be diverted to buying golf clubs, or to extra visits to the theatre or pub!

　　The temptation to budget holders to build slack into their budgets will be greatest where one or more of the following circumstances apply:
   - There is great pressure (and possible sanctions) not to overspend budgets, sometimes even when the operational situation has changed from that which was planned or expected. This can happen if fixed budgets are used when operational conditions would be more realistically reflected by flexible budgets. Of course, in the public sector the use of fixed budgets may often be unavoidable given public spending (cash) limits.
   - There is no efficient machinery for review, updating or amendment of budgets after the start of the budget year.
   - The budget controller or senior management is concerned only with compliance with total budget limits, and if the latter are achieved there is no enquiry into the detail of spending from the budget.
   - Budget holders are dealt with individually, in isolation, so that budgeting is seen as a game between the individual and the corporate bureaucracy. The alternative is to develop 'team budgeting', a consensual approach to resource planning, and a climate of interdependence and shared responsibility. Unfortunately, this is time-consuming and requires skilful leadership.
2 **Pumping**: 'pumping' occurs if one manager passes on a cost from his/her own budget to another manager's budget. This is most likely to occur between production departments or divisions where there is process or sequential work flow and multiple products. For example, if a budget holder has several jobs or batches of

work on hand and knows the costings are more generous on some than on others he/she may depart from the optimal production timetable and produce more than is currently needed of the products on which he/she knows the input-cost budget can be beaten. This leaves the next department with a currently unwanted stock charge, not to mention possible congestion from storing the extra stock until it is needed and possible shortages of other stock.

3 **Overreaction**: in some organisations, 'achieving the budget' has been given a degree of preeminence in assessing managerial performance possibly beyond its true importance, and often beyond the relevance and credibility of the data included in budget charges (especially where a high proportion of the charges are indirect or for overheads or result from decisions taken elsewhere in the organisation). The problem is compounded if budget achievement is used as a key factor in performance reviews or in performance-related pay.

Some budget holders may expend precious time trying to find faults or errors in their budgets (and, if they succeed, this, while constructive in one sense, will also serve to further reduce morale and confidence in the 'management information system', of which budgeting is meant to be a major component). Other budget holders may fall back on devious excuses, or simply seek to ignore the problem. None of this contributes to better management.

Effective budgeting and management by objectives (MBO)

It is easier to specify the conditions for effective budgeting as an information aid and tool for good management than it is to achieve them. The first need is for good management leadership from the top, with an open willingness to discuss choices, problems and objectives with the lower tiers of managers who are the operational budget holders. The second need is for accurate, relevant and timely information on resource use and on who is properly accountable for that use. Here first-class computer support is essential and the objective should be to provide managers with terminals and systems allowing budget holders to monitor regularly their resource use, commitments, costs (and revenues, where relevant). The third need is for budget staff who interact frequently, openly and constructively with budget holders to assist understanding, facilitate team-working and goal congruence, and sort out any budget uncertainties or conflicts quickly and fairly.

Top down or bottom up?

There are two basic approaches to the preparation of budgets for individual managers. The top-down approach involves the budget officer or accountant in preparing a draft budget for each manager, drawing on his/her knowledge of agreed strategic plans, forecasts of sales and production, etc. for the coming year or other budget period. Many budgets interact; that is, their resource use and output assumptions are interdependent, so these must be reconciled as consistent. The budget officer circulates the draft budgets to managers and should then follow through by discussing and explaining the draft with each manager to obtain his/her agreement that this is a feasible plan for which he/she accepts responsibility – or else to clarify what changes in the draft he/she needs or seeks before giving commitment to the budget.

The bottom-up approach operates by the budget officer providing the manager with a budget form with money figures not yet entered, together with a copy of last year's budget, and a summary of relevant strategic and forecast factors. The manager may then be left to work up the budget on his/her own, or the manager can do this with the budget officer in attendance for supplementary information or advice. In theory, this bottom-up approach should introduce greater realism, accuracy and commitment into the budget. In practice, budgeting will often take place as some mixture of or compromise between the two approaches.

Budgets for managers will have to be approved by their senior managers. Often this may involve only nominal or cursory attention from the senior manager, in conjunction with the budget officer. However, for budgets to be taken seriously, with full commitment at each management level, it can be argued that each manager should agree and accept his/her budget in the presence of the senior manager after appropriate discussion of any uncertainties, with the advice of the budget officer in attendance. This three-way commitment is often recommended for use in MBO systems.

Management by objectives (MBO)

Budget systems are concerned with the totality of cost, expenditure or revenue for a specified budget centre or budget holder. It is not easy to focus budgetary control on one management issue in isolation for concentrated attention. Also, while in theory budgets can be expressed in physical units rather than money measurements, in practice nearly all managerial budgets are financial. Thus to supplement budgeting it is useful to have a technique widely known as MBO.

MBO involves setting individual managers one or more operational objectives for which to seek measurable improvement over a period, typically of six to twelve months. For example, improving staff morale may be a worthy objective, but improvement could be difficult to measure objectively. In contrast, labour/staff turnover is measurable, or quantifiable, and it could serve as a partial surrogate for 'morale'. Moreover, while high labour turnover clearly incurs costs – in severance, temporary manpower shortages, recruitment and training – these costs are not clearly isolated in departmental budgets, so that management attention is not focused on the underlying problem. But an MBO exercise can focus on the problem. The manager can be set the specific objective of reducing his department's labour turnover by 20%, or whatever, over the budget year or some shorter period.

Conventional guidelines for MBO systems recommend that just one important objective, or one problem inhibiting achievement of objectives, should be tackled by a manager at any one point in time. There should be an MBO officer, who could be, but need not be, the budget officer or accountant, and who is held responsible by higher management for running and reporting on the MBO projects. The objective or problem for improvement must be quantifiable, and progress in the MBO task must be measured and reported periodically. At intervals, or certainly at the end of the MBO assignment, the MBO officer should meet with the manager and with his superior to review and evaluate progress and to consider what the next-stage MBO assignment should be. Thus the model for running an effective MBO system is very similar to that discussed previously for effective budgetary-planning and control systems. That is, effective commitment and discipline in achieving budgetary and other corporate objectives is very dependent upon personal accountability and responsibility between each manager and his superior, with the role of the MBO/ budget officer or accountant being that of facilitator, providing timely information and technical advice as needed.

Budgeting in the public sector

Historically, public-sector budgeting has been dominated by the need to account to Parliament, and later to local government, for the expenditure and use of the **cash spending** authorised by governments. Budgets solely or mainly to allocate and control cash are technically simple. The intellectually interesting input has come at the budget-planning stage from the economists and the politicians. However, in recent years the public sector has been forced to change, starting even before the arrival of Mrs Thatcher's government.

The 1974 reorganisations of local government and the NHS marked the beginning of major change. In 1974 the new regional water authorities were formed from services previously under local-government control, and these new water authorities were enjoined to adopt commercial financial and budgetary practices, and to keep and report their financial accounts under 'best commercial practice'. The NHS was told to improve its costing and budgeting systems, although progress was slow. After 1979 the process of change accelerated. The introduction of the 'internal market' in health care, and of the NHS Trusts, forced the NHS to move largely to commercial accounting methods, even though it remained the case that the underlying cost information on the enormous number of diverse services provided did not yet enable highly accurate costings for budgetary management to be effected at the disaggregated level of the workload of individual hospital doctors, or even of teams of doctors working together in 'specialties' (e.g. orthopaedics) (see Perrin 1988). However, cost information for budgeting and control continued to improve gradually in the NHS, and even though the 1997 Labour government undertook to dismantle the NHS 'internal market' – based on individual Health Trusts acting as separate profit and investment centres and 'selling' their services to health authorities and GPs – it seems likely that continuing shortages of funding will mean that costing and budgeting systems will continue to be developed and to be used ever more rigorously in the NHS, as also in other cash-limited public services.

Table 14.4 illustrates a form of budget report for an NHS hospital specialty or 'team'. Although based on a public service, the report illustrates features which could be applied equally in the private sector, especially for a service department inside a larger enterprise where the department works to a fixed budget and does not market its output outside that enterprise. First, the section captions are 'user-friendly' and avoid accounting jargon. Second, the budget costs are classified logically to reflect the degrees of financial accountability expected from the team or its leader. The first item, medical salaries, is the only cost wholly controlled by the team. The second category includes the volume-related or variable direct costs of other resources used at the team's discretion. The subtotals that follow this indicate the budget expenditure for which the team has primary accountability (even though it has no control over the

Table 14.4 Budget report for surgical team

Current month				Expense codes	Year to date		
Budget £	Actual £	Variance £		*Staff costs controlled by team*	Budget £	Actual £	Variance £
10 998	10 697	−301	800	Medical staff costs	54 990	53 166	−1 024
				Other expenses controlled by team			
12 499	12 014	−485	809	Prescribed drugs	62 495	58 712	−3 783
290	248	−42	811	Histopathology – consumables	1 450	1 193	−257
7 697	9 016	1 319	820	Radiology –consumables	40 837	44 808	3 971
7 283	7 892	609	821	Operating theatre – consumables	36 415	38 878	2 463
38 767	39 867	1 100		Total costs controlled by team	197 187	196 757	570
				Costs influenced by team			
4 166	5 152	986	840	Ward – consumables	20 830	22 584	1 754
83	149	66	841	Outpatient – consumables	415	495	80
11 572	10 983	−589	845	Ward – overheads	57 860	58 592	732
41	193	152	846	Outpatient – overheads	205	452	247
1 565	1 782	217	849	Pharmacy – overheads	7 825	8 571	746
833	814	−19	851	Histopathology – overheads	4 165	4 046	−119
8 208	7 932	−276	857	Operating theatre overheads	41 040	40 643	−397
4 107	4 182	75	868	ECG – overheads	20 535	21 916	1 381
15 485	15 654	169	880	Physiotherapy–hydrotherapy	77 425	75 296	−2 129
46 060	46 841	781		Total costs influenced by team	230 300	232 595	2 295
				General services overheads			
2 499	2 261	−238	890	Unit administration	12 495	11 236	−1 259
973	1 028	55	891	Catering	4 865	5 386	521
1 219	817	−402	892	Domestic	6 095	3 932	−2 163
832	946	114	894	Linen/laundry	4 160	4 701	541
7 499	6 753	−746	896	Estate management	37 495	35 388	−2 107
13 022	11 805	−1 217		Total general services overheads	65 110	60 643	−4 467
97 849	98 513	664		Total costs for team	491 597	489 995	−1 602
				Memorandum statistics			
857	878	21	900	Inpatients – days	4 285	4 382	97
148	193	45	903	Outpatients – attendances	740	849	109
499	296	−203	914	Histopathology – tests	2 495	2 650	155
473	682	209	937	Radiology – tests	2 801	3 690	889
599	634	35	940	Operating theatre – hours	2 995	3 286	291

Source: draft for a report, with simulated cost figures, from a Clinical Accountability, Service Planning and Evaluation Project at a London hospital, by permission.
Note: ECG = electrocardiograph.

ordering or pricing of the drugs and consumables listed). The third category combines some variable costs over which the team does not have primary control (e.g. ward consumables controlled by nurses) and the fixed costs or overheads (including salary allocations) of other service departments on which the team draws; these together comprise the indirect costs, in this case being outside the accountability of the team but subject to the influence of the team's behaviour, in that, in the longer term, planning and joint agreements with the team could serve to alter the staffing establishment and fixed costs. The last category comprises central overheads entirely outside team accountability or influence. Finally, the report concludes with selected workload statistics which may roughly correlate with service output and which serve as a kind of surrogate for a marketed output.

Overall, the distinctive features of public-sector accounting – and thus of budgeting, which is essentially the forward-looking mirror-image of (cost and management) accounting – have become blurred or diluted. Commercial systems of accounting and budgeting are likely to be encouraged even under a Labour government. However, there are two post-war developments in public-sector budgeting which have had some wider impact. These are PPBS and ZBB.

Planning, programming and budgeting system (PPBS)

PPBS is a method of planning, resource allocation and budgeting originally developed in the USA, in the Department of Defense during the cold war. Nowadays, the approach is more generally known as programme budgeting. Programmes are targeted on objectives, outcomes or output for specified groups of clients or beneficiaries (or customers). Thus, a government may decide to target the 'elderly' as a specific group to receive maximised benefit within the resources available. A national programme of benefit or care for the elderly will involve resource use (and budgets) in the NHS, social security, local social services, and voluntary and private-sector elderly care homes. Coordinating such disparate bodies is almost impossible in the real world of politics and management competition. Even taking the much more limited objective of a programme budget for the elderly *within* the NHS, there remain major problems.

Elderly people are treated within the NHS geriatric services but they also form the largest group of patients in most other NHS specialties and in NHS community-care facilities. They also comprise the largest group taking up the time and resources of NHS family doctors. All these budget holders are on different lines of resource funding, detailed planning and managerial accountability. Effective operational budgeting depends on clear accountability to one manager, or at least to one organisational source of control and discipline. Thus programme budgeting (PB) fails the test of being an effective operational budgeting system. However, the PB, or PPBS, approach is important in that it involves separate organisations joining together in the generalised **planning** of the distribution, use and target objectives of public resources, even though it can not be applied effectively in the detailed administration of budgetary **control**. There may be few opportunities for the application of PB/PPBS in the private business sector, but sometimes the concept can be applied, as for example in overviewing the planning and budget funding of a new product, combining R&D, pilot production and market testing, and the main product launch and its promotion.

Zero-base budgeting (ZBB)

Again of American origin, ZBB is a technique designed to escape from the traditional approach to public-sector budgeting, incremental budgeting. Incremental budgeting is found also, all too frequently, in the private business sector. It involves the assumption by managers that last year's budget, plus adjustment for inflation, provides the baseline for negotiating the next year's budget. That is, it is assumed that the budget planning debate is concerned largely with how much extra or incremental funding the budget holder can get and how it should be applied. ZBB challenges this assumption.

ZBB operates on the basis that a manager should justify all expenditure in order to get his/her budget renewed. To do this is difficult unless one can somehow relate expenditure to the outputs, outcomes or benefits obtained for service objectives or client groups. To this end, the ZBB approach requires that managers allocate their resources and expenditure between separate 'decision packages', on the assumption that if a particular decision package is not yielding benefits greater than its cost it could be deleted from future budget funding. Obvious problems here are the apportionment of common or joint costs among the decision packages on a basis which is realistic as regards what could be saved if specific service activities were to be withdrawn, and also the degree of job security and narrowly specific (professional) skill training of public employees. Also there is the intractable problem of evaluating the benefits obtained from using resources in each decision package. In theory, this could be achieved using the economist's method of cost–benefit analysis (CBA), but in practice the priorities, prejudices and current 'fashions' of politicians and senior management will usually prevail.

No British public body has ever formally adopted ZBB as a routine resource-allocation system. The system requires a large investment of the time of senior management, accounting and other expert staff and consultants, so doubters challenge whether it is cost-effective. Annual repetition of the ZBB exercise would cover the same ground again and again, and budget holders would become increasingly 'street-wise' in structuring and defending their decision packages so as to make cuts unlikely. However, discussions with many senior public-sector accountants show that they are attracted by the ZBB approach as a concept, and that they have been influenced by it in the way they negotiate with budget holders. Perhaps the nearest equivalent to ZBB in the private business sector is when firms, during recession or other times of crisis, embark on major cost-cutting exercises to scale down or eliminate staff activities deemed to be of low marginal benefit to (at least short-term) commercial operations.

Budgeting in service organisations

Manufacturers, farmers, wholesalers and retailers supply products. Most of the examples of costing and budgeting in this book are based on products or production activities. Supplying products is a 'service'. By the term 'service organisations' we mean more specifically those organisations whose outputs are not tangible, physical products. Service organisations typically are labour-intensive; they apply specific labour skills to the particular requirements or problems of individual clients or customers. The police, universities and NHS hospitals are service organisations, as are stockbrokers, advertising agencies and hairdressers. The question is whether there are distinctive features of service organisations, compared with product-based organisations, which need different kinds of budgetary (and/or costing) planning and control systems.

Arguably, however, the main distinction between organisations for budgetary and costing purposes is not whether they are product-based or service-based or whether they are in the public sector or the private sector, but rather whether they are trading in a genuine market or, instead, supplying a free or subsidised service or other output for which the market is not providing an independent validation of value. In the NHS, where an internal-market separation of healthcare 'purchasers' (i.e. health authorities and general practitioners with fundholder budgets) from healthcare 'providers' (e.g. NHS Trusts and directly managed hospitals) was introduced with the discipline of notional 'market' prices for specified services, no clear success was demonstrated in replicating 'genuine market' behaviour. There remains the major problem, in the NHS as in many private-sector service businesses, that the outputs marketed are diverse, while many of the resource inputs are in the form of common costs or joint costs, so that direct linkage between expenditure budgets and market performance is tenuous. This is an area awaiting new research and information-systems development. Included within this may be the extension of ABC or standard costing and variance analysis, as discussed in Chapter 15, to wider application in service businesses.

Capital budgeting

The capital budget was mentioned briefly earlier in this chapter. Capital budgeting is a major topic in its own right. It involves most of the characteristics and problems outlined in this chapter. It comprises the search for capital-investment opportunities, the evaluation of alternative investments, the planning of investment programmes (including linking the timing of finance with the timing of capital-expenditure payments), control of the implementation of capital programmes, and postmortem audits or reviews of the success of individual programmes. Of these five stages, it is the evaluation stage which attracts the most attention in textbooks (see Chapter 13, on longer-term decisions), probably because of the analytical interest involved in discounting for the time-value of money and in the associated analysis for risk and uncertainty.

It has been argued, however, that it is the first stage, the search for opportunities (i.e. new technologies, products and markets), which is most often neglected and which may be the weakest link in the decision-making chain. It is also very likely that the evaluation and decision variables for investment (e.g. cost estimates for new products and for capital developments, and marketing, sales and price forecasts) are often estimated too roughly, too optimistically, and without adequate market research and professional advice. These are, of course, areas of action and responsibility for management, not the accountant. The accountant can calculate discounted cash flows and risk analysis with computer programmes but cannot supply most of the forecast data. And, to paraphrase: garbage data in, garbage solutions out. Capital budgeting deserves better than this; it is crucial to the firm's survival and growth.

Conclusions

Some of the comments above concerning capital budgeting apply similarly, if not always so critically, to annual cost and revenue budgeting, as discussed more generally in this chapter. The mechanics of preparing budgets and budget reports can be tedious, like the time managers may have to spend in committees planning or reviewing budgets. But budget mechanics are of secondary importance compared to two other aspects. First, in the budget-planning stage are the alternative uses of resources fully explored and rigorously assessed with realistic estimates of efficiency, cost and related revenue? Second, are the organisational culture and climate and management leadership properly developed to make use of budget systems and information as a powerful tool of management planning, coordination and control?

For effective budgeting, managers must be able to see their budgets, not as some sort of independent fiefdom, but, rather, as a piece in the jigsaw of the organisation as a whole. Debate about issues raised by budget planning and control should be as open and wide as possible, and this may be assisted if top management makes it clear that rigidly following budgets and achieving them is not directly linked to pay and promotion. There must be discipline in budgeting, but, beyond that, it should be primarily a system to aid managerial learning, choosing and improvement.

Budgets are plans, usually expressed in money terms. Once agreed, they are also used for coordination and control. Budgets should mirror the structure of the organisation and provide accountability covering all of its resources and activities. There are different kinds of budgets and budget centres, for investment, profit, sales or revenue, and costs and expenses. Most budgets are for costs, generally derived from the historical cost accrual accounting system, but sometimes (especially in the public sector) they are based on cash expenditure. Performance against budgets should be monitored at least monthly, with progress reports supplied promptly and significant variances checked out for any corrective action which may be needed. Many budgets are fixed, but flexible budgeting is better when output or sales fluctuate with market demand.

Budgets can be seen as a straitjacket on managers, but the ideal is for them to be seen as a self-help information system for managers' use to improve the management of their own responsibilities and their coordination with other parts of the organisation. In reality, however, there are important behavioural problems associated with budgeting, notably the temptation to build in 'budgetary slack' and the failure to undertake adequate budgetary planning, which leads to managers blaming poor performance on failings or unfairness in the budgets. Nevertheless, budgeting is necessary and relevant in all types of organisation – industrial, retail and service – and it is especially prominent for activities (such as many public services) where total expenditure is strictly limited.

Further reading

For classical insights into the behavioural and organisational contexts and problems of budgeting, see Argyris (1964) and Hofstede (1968). For greater detail on the structure of budgets and budget reports, see Arnold and Turley (1996: chs 15, 16) or Drury (1996: chs 17, 21; 1997: chs 10, 14). For a comprehensive view of budgeting and control in all their contexts, see Emmanuel *et al.* (1990).

Questions and exercises

1 Metalfab Ltd has adopted a budgetary system in which budget centres are charged only with direct or indirect costs which their budget holders can control or strongly influence. The information below is for use in a flexible budget for the supervisor of Metalfab's machine shop:

(i) Work is machine paced and capacity is limited by the available machine time. There are twelve machines, each needing one operator. The standard workweek is forty hours, with a maximum of fourteen hours of overtime available. The factory works a 48-week year and budgets are based on four-week periods of 'months'. Bank holidays are ignored.

(ii) There are twelve operators, plus the supervisor. Eight operators and the supervisor work full time, while four operators are 'casual' and work only as required. All operators cost £7 per hour, inclusive of national insurance and other payroll-linked expenses, or £9 on overtime. The supervisor costs £10 per hour, or £12 on overtime.

(iii) Normal working is 85% productive time and 15% for set-ups, maintenance and stopped time. Non-productive labour time is recorded and charged to budget as a separate cost category and is monitored for control. The same hourly charge rates are used for both productive and non-productive time.

(iv) Heating and lighting averages £80 per week over the year.

(v) Power costs £0.50 per productive machine hour.

(vi) Breakdown and repair costs average £0.60 per productive machine hour.

(vii) Lubricants and sundries cost £0.40 per productive machine hour.

(viii) Depreciation charges are £35 000 for the year.

(ix) Materials wastage and spoilage varies, but experience suggests the equivalent of £2 per productive machine hour as a realistic target. All wastage and spoilage are costed and charged against budget.

(x) Materials costs (other than wastage and spoilage) are not charged to the machine-shop budget. Instead, these are charged to the budget of the head of purchasing and production scheduling on the grounds that this is where control and responsibility resides. In addition, materials costs, machine shop and other service department costs are all charged to individual job sheets, whose total for open jobs is summarised in the work in progress control account.

(xi) The machine-shop budget uses productive machine hours as its activity unit for flexing the budget. The activity range to be considered is that between 1000 and 2000 productive machine hours per four-week budget period.

You are required to:

(a) make the necessary calculations and draft a four-week flexible budget for Metalfab's machine shop, spanning the activity range given above;

(b) comment on any shortages or weaknesses in the available information, and/or comment on any further improvements you might envisage for the effective budget management and control of the machine shop.

2 Hustlers Ltd operates a chain of high-street shops. Each shop is managed as a

profit centre and is annually assigned a set of fixed budgets covering costs and expenses, and sales. The budget targets are set very tight to provide a challenge to shop managers and also to try to exert pressure towards higher corporate profits. The budgets of all shops are tightened by the same proportional amounts. The finance director is new and takes personal control of the shop budgets. To researchers he confides that he does not expect many shop managers to meet their budgets but that it is essential to keep up the pressure on shops at all times. He produces a copy of a letter he has just sent to one shop manager. It reads as follows:

Dear . . .
I have just gone through the latest monthly budget reports for shops in your region. Your performance is about the worst.

I hope you appreciate that this cannot go on. If next month's report is as bad as this, I will have to call you to head office to make the position clear.

I am sure by now you understand that in this company, the only thing that matters is the bottom line, the net profit.
Yours faithfully

You are required to provide answers to the following questions:
(a) What possible weaknesses in organisation behaviour and management leadership does the above information suggest?
(b) How do you think the company should have gone about assisting and motivating the shop managers to improve their budgetary performance (and thus their overall performance)?
(c) What, if any, other weaknesses or omissions do you see in the company's budget system or administrative arrangements which might be remedied to improve the effectiveness of budgetary planning and control for both budget holders and higher management?

3 Chememulsions Ltd makes three domestic cleaning products for distribution through supermarkets and shops. The following data have been prepared in connection with the marketing director's annual presentation of the advertising and promotion budget requests. 'Profits' and 'losses' are shown below at values *before* charging expenditure on advertising and promotion (A&P); all figures are in thousands of pounds.

A&P is a fixed budget which must be renegotiated annually and needs justification by evidence of results achieved.

| Date | SKWEEZ Detergent | | | PHOAMY Detergent | | | SACHET Car Wash | | |
	Sales	Profit	A&P	Sales	Profit	A&P	Sales	Profit	A&P
19X1	500	100	20	500	50	40	–	–	–
19X2	450	80	20	560	68	50	–	–	–
19X3	420	68	20	600	80	56	–	–	–
19X4	400	80	20	700	110	60	40	(12)	10
19X5	410	84	25	750	125	70	100	0	12
19X6	320	48	25	710	113	75	150	10	15
Budget 19X7	310	50	30	800	140	71	250	30	20

Evaluate the given data, state any conclusions and/or implications that may derive from your analysis, and state what further data the budget controller should request or what enquiries he/she should make. Assume that sales prices per unit and total fixed costs have not changed over the time-span under review.

4 As a consultant you have been assigned to a budget project at Tweedshire Council (TC), which is too short-staffed to cover the introduction of improved budgets in all council services. Your project includes preparing a new budget for the next year for Tweedshire Libraries (TL). TL have had a single, cash-limited, departmental budget. Nine months into the current year it is forecast that the year's budget will probably just be met, albeit only by postponing some orders for books, equipment and maintenance. The budgeted costs for the year were as follows:

	£
Staff costs (full and part time and casual)	250 000
Purchases of books and periodicals, new bindings, etc.	125 000
Purchases of CDs, records, tapes, software, etc.	60 000
Furnishings, fittings and equipment (FFE) including computers	70 000
Rent charge by TC for premises used	50 000
Maintenance of premises and of FFE (and energy costs)	40 000

The control budget is on a cash basis. Pending actual transfer to accrual accounting, depreciation (covering all assets other than premises) is shown as a footnote to the budget. For the current year, depreciation was set at 20%, on estimated year-end historical-cost asset values of £600 000.

The improved budget for next year is to reflect new operational objectives assigned to TL management. Books and periodicals are to operate as a cost centre, fully funded (NB fines and charges, being negligible, can be ignored). Services relating to CDs, records, tapes, software and public use of computers, etc. are to operate as a contribution centre (and, at the least, to break even; partly so as not to provide unfair competition to local private businesses); target revenue for these services next year is to be set at 10% above budget costs (with any profit contribution to be divided equally between TC general funds and TL funds for carry-forward for extra spending in the following year).

Next year's total budget will be the same as for the current year, except for uplift of 3% in line with the general inflation forecast. However, average hourly pay is expected to increase by 5%, and to cover for this staff hours will be cut by 1%, and purchases of books and periodicals will be cut by 2%. All other cost categories are expected to rise in line with general inflation. The proportions of budget headings chargeable to the new contribution centre are forecast to be as follows:

Staff	40%
FFE spending	60%
Rent and maintenance (proportional to space)	30%

You are required to draft a budget for TL for next year. The budget statements should be constructed with user-friendly captions, and should reflect controllability and operational objectives.

5 If budgets are to match or mirror organisation structure, what characteristics of organisation (e.g. of authority and responsibility relationships, etc.) should help decide the types and levels of budget centre, and the types of resource accountability to be included therein.

6 Briefly list and explain the features of an effective system of budgetary performance and reporting *and* control.

7 Flexible budgets need more sophisticated management and cost information than do fixed budgets. Why is this so, and what are the implications for the choice of costing methods?

8 'The weakest link in any system of budgetary planning and control is human behaviour.' Defend or refute this statement with reasoned argument.

9 Both the top-down and bottom-up approaches to budgetary planning have good arguments in their favour. What may these arguments be, and how should the choice of approach be decided?

10 It has been noted that a precondition of good budget planning and control is a good cost information system. It has also been noted that in the public sector cost information is often poor, yet public-sector budgets are given a very important status in management and in assessing managers' performance. How do you explain this apparent paradox? What courses of action might be followed to remove or avoid this paradox?

15 Accounting as a control system

Objectives

This chapter concentrates on the ways in which accounting can contribute to enhancing control within the enterprise. The chapter begins with an examination of the key considerations that need to be taken into account if an organisation is to implement an effective internal control system, particularly with respect to the accounting aspects of that system. We then discuss a major accounting control technique known as standard costing or variance analysis. This discussion builds upon the introduction to flexible budgeting provided in Chapter 14. Within the broader framework of management control we need also to appreciate that not all controls are quantitative controls and that, indeed, not all quantitative controls are accounting controls. Variance analysis is not always appropriate, and in certain instances in the public sector the budgetary control framework may be supplemented by the use of performance indicators, some of which may have an economic value but may, if necessary, include related issues such as the output, efficiency or effectiveness of a particular management strategy.

Background to budgets

In Chapter 14 the overall structure of budgetary control was introduced, and emphasis was placed on the many roles that budgets can be called upon to play within enterprises and on the fact that these roles are not always compatible. In this chapter we take this discussion further. We discuss the need for overall organisational control and the role that budgets play therein. Important though budgets are, they need to be supplemented in order for effective management control to be obtained. Often this is achieved in the private sector by means of variance analysis – the investigation of differences between the budget and actual performance. The approach which should be adopted is one that clearly distinguishes between planning and operational variances. This is important since in most large organisations different managers are responsible for planning and operational activities. Increasingly, budgets in the public sector are supplemented by performance indicators that are designed to demonstrate the accountability of management, not just in terms of financial compliance, but in terms of the economy, efficiency and effectiveness with which their services were delivered. These three 'E's are often grouped under the general term of 'value for money', previously introduced in Chapter 6.

We discuss both variance analysis, also referred to as standard costing, and the developing trend for operational performance indicators. Though these developments have their origins in different sectors, variance analysis is increasingly being adopted in the public sector and performance indicators are being adopted in non-manufacturing enterprises in the private sector.

The need for effective internal control

The essence of accounting control is feedback, the comparison of actual performance with planned performance. Techniques such as flexible budgets, standard costs and performance indicators are major attention-directing techniques for future planning and day-to-day operational control. They form part of the overall internal control system of an organisation, which operate at three basic levels (De Paula and Attwood 1982):

- management controls;
- organisational controls and segregation of duties;
- accounting controls.

A key feature of any system of effective internal control is that senior management should systematically review the organisation's financial operations and production/service delivery levels at regular and frequent meetings, aided by periodic financial statements, operational summaries, statistical and other appropriate information. In addition to regular reviews, management may also institute special reviews which constitute another, perhaps more strategic, instrument of control. In many large organisations a key feature of an effective internal control system is often the internal audit department. Principally concerned with accounting controls, the internal audit staff have the task of assuring management of the efficient and effective design and operation of internal checks within the financial and management accounting systems.

Organisations should have hierarchy charts or similar mechanisms that clearly show the extent to which authority and responsibility have been appropriately allocated in a clear reporting structure. If this is done, accountabilities and individual responsibilities are less likely to be confused. Accounting controls should ensure that transactions have been:

- authorised and approved;
- correctly recorded;
- appropriately reported.

A good *responsibility accounting* system should report only on factors that management can control. Thus non-controllable costs either should not appear in performance reports or should be carefully segregated so as not to form part of the evaluation of a manager. As Dominiak and Louderback state:

> Most of the major problems in developing an effective responsibility accounting system are behavioural. Managers must trust the reporting

system; they must believe that it accurately depicts their performances. Managers must also believe that the system is fair. Accordingly, the evaluation system should use performance evaluation criteria that are under the control of the managers. But if the system is to perform its function for the company as a whole, the feedback provided, and the criteria used for, evaluating the managers should also motivate them to act in such a way as to advance the overall goals of the firm.

(Dominiak and Louderback 1988: 362)

Organisational structures influence reporting systems. This is because different organisational structures result in different groupings of management responsibilities. For example, in a divisionalised company the marketing activity may be devolved to individual operating divisions or it may remain a main board responsibility.

Within the broader framework of management control it must be appreciated that not all controls are quantitative controls and not all quantitative controls are accounting controls. Amey and Egginton (1975) point out that the latter, when coupled with planning, are the most important subset if they are effective and operate to increase efficiency. They suggest that the major control devices used within an organisation 'constitute a continuum', ranging from tight to loose control, depending upon the amenability to control of the activities in question. Feedback controls can be listed or ranked in descending order of degree of control, as illustrated below:

- **automatic**: for example mechanical systems, such as a steam valve, or electronic devices for measuring tolerances etc.;
- **statistical**: for example quality-control and consumer surveys;
- **technical standards:** for example the minimum composition of base metals in an alloy or staffing requirements in an NHS clinic;
- **performance standards**: for example output per hour or, in the public sector, numbers of unemployed youths obtaining employment after receiving training;
- **via resource allocation**: for example research and development or training budgets;
- **profitability measures**: for example departmental contribution;
- **investment-centre measures**: for example divisional return on investment (discussed in Chapter 16).

The continuum relates both to the degree of control that can be exercised and the degree of responsibility delegated:

As a very broad generalisation it might be said that as firms succeed in moving more activities and problems towards the 'tightly controlled' end of the spectrum there is a tendency for new 'loosely controllable' activities to appear at the other end, such things as multinational activities, diversification, and more complex technologies which are only partially understood by top management.

(Amey and Egginton 1975: 392)

The two principal accounting control techniques are known as budgetary control and standard costing/variance analysis. Budgets were discussed in Chapter 14; in the next section we discuss how flexible budgets form the basis from which variances can be analysed. This process involves determining internal standards of performance and feeding back to those concerned comparisons of their actual results with these predetermined targets or norms. In budgetary control and standard costing as normally practised the boundary of control is co-extensive with the boundaries of the firm.

Organisational management-control structures can, in general terms, be characterised as **centralised** or **decentralised**, depending on the extent of responsibilities delegated to individual managers. Managers who have a good deal of authority and can take a number of key decisions – such as pricing and production levels and even, perhaps, investment decisions – without the approval of higher levels of management tend to belong to decentralised organisations. Whereas managers who have little scope to act on their own initiative tend to belong to centralised organisations. As mentioned above, we consider the question of decentralisation and its associated control problems in Chapter 16.

All too often, organisations establish management accounting control systems that violate the principle of devolved management controllability because there is an over-riding desire by senior board members to concentrate their attention on making calculations of and drawing attention to the **full cost** of an activity provided by a production or service department. In part, this is because of the need to evaluate the performance of the division as well as that of the manager. Recall that full cost represents a combination of costs that are both directly traceable to the activity under consideration and indirectly apportioned to it, based on some 'fair share' of apportioned/absorbed costs from elsewhere in the organisation. Whatever the plan for segmenting an organisation for reporting purposes, individual managers should be held responsible only for that which they can control. If this is not the case managers will, naturally enough, tend to act in their own interests, and this may be dysfunctional for the organisation as a whole.

Variance analysis

In most manufacturing enterprises standard cost, i.e. the costs per unit of activity, forms part of the basis on which the overall budget is constructed. Standard costs should represent anticipated target costs and are based on either historical records or, preferably, **engineered** standards. Engineered standards involve the collection of a great deal of information about a product's technical specification, ideal production pattern and so on. Standard costs based on historical records assume or imply a level of operational efficiency which may not have occurred. Drury (1996: 548) points out that standards are normally classified into three broad categories:

- basic standard costs;
- ideal standards;
- currently attainable standards.

Basic standard costs tend to be left unchanged over long periods and to be used as a planning tool for plotting trends in efficiency. Ideal standards represent the minimum operational costs expected under the most efficient production conditions. In practice, ideal standards are rarely used since management can be demotivated if asked to achieve what are virtually unobtainable results in practice. Currently attainable standards are the most commonly used form of standards, and represent difficult targets but ones that ought to be capable of achievement by management. Standards are only of use if they motivate the desired behaviour by management. It is therefore important that management is fully involved in the standard-setting process, along with management accountants and supported by the technical expertise of production engineers, operations researchers and so on.

A standard cost is produced by the multiple of a unit(s) of productive input (materials, labour or overhead) and unit costs or rates. Once calculated, standard costs can be utilised to compare planned with actual performance. The core model for all productive variance analysis is based on the following set of expressions:

1 Standard cost (SC) = Standard price (SP) × Standard quantity (SQ)
2 Actual cost (AC) = Actual price (AP) × Actual quantity (AQ)
3 Total variance = (SP × SQ) − (AP × AQ)
4 Price/rate variance = (SP − AP) × AQ
5 Quantity variance = (SQ − AQ) × SP

To understand the application of expressions 3–5 let us consider the following example. Elexitron Digital Instruments PLC manufactures a particular product that requires four printed circuit boards at a cost of £5 each, a total of £20 per unit manufactured. When it came to evaluate actual production costs it found that the particular circuit boards specified were in short supply and that it had been necessary to substitute the circuit boards with an alternative of lesser specification. In practice this meant using five of the inferior circuit boards, at a cost of £4.50 each, i.e. a total cost of £22.50.

This variance can be analysed as follows:

3 Total variance = £20 − £22.50 = £2.50 (unfavourable)
4 Price/rate variance = (£5 − £4.50) × 5 = £2.50 (favourable)
5 Quantity variance = (4 − 5) × £5 = £5.00 (unfavourable)

Several issues are highlighted by this basic illustration:

- The analysis of the total variance recognises that, inevitably, different managers have different areas of responsibility. Typically, as regards materials the purchasing function is a separate function from the production function. As regards labour the personnel department would be responsible for the relevant pay rates but line management would be responsible for the deployment of the mix of staff available to them, including the use of overtime.
- In most computerised standard costing systems, the price (for materials) and the rate (for labour) variances would be calculated first. This makes sense, since to be of use variances should be produced in as timely a way as possible. If one considers material, it is more relevant to calculate the price variance at the time of acquisition. The materials are then entered to stock at the standard price and charged out to production at the standard price. Subsequently, when production has taken place, the quantity variance can be calculated.
- The variances above have been termed either favourable or unfavourable. These terms are used *only* to denote the direction of the variance. Other texts may use

alternative terminology but all point out that it is the analysis of the variance that is important.

■ Some variances can be further subdivided. For example, the quantity variance could, if appropriate, be further subdivided into a yield and a mix variance. Such subdivision depends on the individual circumstances of particular enterprises. A yield/mix division would, for example, be an appropriate subclassification in the chemical or plastics industry.

■ Many books favour a long list of formulae for variances. For managers we think this is unnecessary; instead, they should be conversant with the principles of variance analysis so as to be able to define the type of information that they expect their management accountant to prepare for them. Table 15.1 lists the relevant expressions for the production variances used in this text. There are two points to note: first, the expressions for labour, material and variable overheads all follow the same pattern; second, fixed overheads are classified only as expenditure variances. This is because we do not see the relevance of further disaggregating these items of expenditure. Other texts do disaggregate fixed overheads. We discuss this issue again later in the chapter.

Standard costing can be implemented only in organisations which already have a sound budgetary-control system. When preparing variances it is not sufficient simply to compare the original budget with actual results. To do so would produce variances that muddled both planning and operating variances, and though the figures produced could be reconciled they would produce relatively meaningless figures by which to manage. In order to compute meaningful operational variances budgets must be flexed to reflect the actual level of activity achieved in a period. This is necessary if we are to look at operational performance on a comparative basis. It could be, for example, that a firm had planned to produce 1000 items per month but in fact, due to the high demand for its product, production was 20% higher, at 1200 units per month. Simply comparing the original budget with actual performance would produce

Table 15.1 Operational production variances

Labour:	Total	(Standard hours × Standard rate) − (Actual hours × Actual rate) $(SH \times SR) - (AH \times AR)$
	Rate	(Standard rate − Actual rate) × Actual hours $(SR - AR) \times AH$
	Efficiency	(Standard hours − Actual hours) × Standard rate $(SH - AH) \times SR$
Materials:	Total	(Standard price × Standard quantity) − (Actual price × Actual quantity) $(SP \times SQ) - (AP \times AQ)$
	Price	(Standard price − Actual price) × Actual quantity $(SP - AP) \times AQ$
	Quantity	(Standard quantity − Actual quantity) × Standard price $(SQ - AQ) \times SP$
Variable overheads:	As per the three labour expressions above	
Fixed overheads:	Total	Actual fixed overheads − Budgeted fixed overheads $AFO - BFO$
	Expenditure	$AFO - BFO$

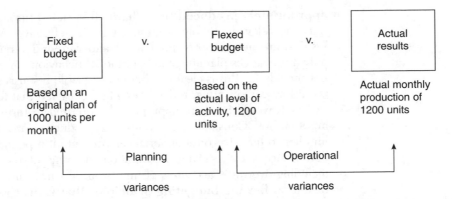

Figure 15.1

a string of unfavourable variances and little attention would be paid to the efficiency of actual production since everyone would expect actual performance to produce these slightly absurd results. The question, in reviewing actual production, is how well production management has done relative to the standards expected of it. We need, therefore, to compare the fixed budget with a flexed budget. This will identify planning variances at standard cost, and then by comparing the flexed budget with actual results we can compute operational variances (see Figure 15.1).

As explained above, the purpose of this chapter is to introduce managers to the basic constructions of variance analysis. That is why, for simplicity, we have flexed the fixed budget using the original standard costs. In practice, standard costs would of course be periodically updated and revised. This would mean that an analysis of the planning variances would not just identify, as outlined above, planning efficiency or quantity variances, but also allow for the preparation of planning-rate and price variances.

Purposes of variance analysis

Using the discussion to date, we can summarise the four principal purposes of variance analysis as being:

1 Comparison of actual performance with standard performance for a given level of activity. This can provide meaningful variances based on both value and volume changes that assist managers by:
   - providing control information on those aspects of activities where operations are not proceeding according to plan;
   - evaluating the performance of individual functions in the organisation (e.g. purchasing, production, service delivery, administration and so on);
   - providing information useful for future planning.
2 The production of periodic performance reports and variances on bases, which to be effective must be:
   - **behaviourally sound**: they should incorporate the notion of responsibility accounting and should 'map' the pattern of the firm's organisational structure. Variance analysis is of little use for budgetary control unless it 'fits' the organisational structure of each particular firm. As with other internal accounting systems, a classic failure is framing the reporting system around the external accounting reporting system.

■ **appropriately produced**: as we have often stated throughout the text, reports must be relevant, timely, accurate and cost-effective. Most variance analysis systems are not cheap to implement and run, and variance analysis is of use only if it changes planning and operational behaviour. A costly system that does not provide for this is clearly a drain on valuable resources, time and effort, and is entirely demotivating. Indeed, it could be argued that for some line managers variances would be more appropriately reported in terms of hours or units of input/output. Consider, for example, a production manager. Is it helpful to him/her to have to consider variances presented in pounds or would he/she be better served by receiving information in terms of the mix of labour hours, including overtime, and units of inputs/outputs in terms of kilograms, etc?

■ **based on flexible budgeting principles that reflect real levels of activity**.

3 The setting of standards to encourage managers to understand more fully the cost structures of those parts of the organisation that they manage, thereby enhancing their managerial effectiveness by:

■ saving valuable management time by identifying for their attention areas where planned performance is not being achieved;

■ facilitating management by exception, as many systems will only report significant variances rather than all variances – also, as discussed later, many variances are interrelated and the correction of one will often impact on others.

We are now in a position to consider a slightly more comprehensive illustration of variance analysis based on the principles so far outlined. Let us consider the problem of Fizzer plc. Fizzer plc manufactures and distributes an industrial bonding agent known as Bondlite, the standard direct costs per cylinder of which are:

Material	50 kg of A at 40p per kg
	100 kg of B at 50p per kg
Labour	5 hours at £1.80 per hour
Variable overheads	recovered on the basis of labour hours at a rate of 50p per hour

The budgeted monthly production/sales level is 750 cylinders and the selling price is £100 per cylinder. Budgeted fixed overheads of £5000 per month are anticipated. The following details relate to production in month 3, when 800 cylinders of Bondlite were produced and sold.:

	£
Sales	79 400
Materials used:	
A (44 000 kg)	16 720
B (75 200 kg)	39 104
Labour:	
3750 hours	7 125
Variable overheads	2 250
Fixed overheads	5 600
Total costs for month	70 799
Profit	8 601

George Snelling, the managing director, is surprised at the attitude of some of his colleagues, who see little to worry about as the actual profit generated was only about 3% below that anticipated when the original budget was set. Are these other managers being complacent?

An examination of the analysis presented in Table 15.2 shows that, in fact, compared to the standard for this level of production the profit is 12% below what would have been anticipated. But what of the individual line-item variances? Material A indicates a favourable price variance of £880 but an unfavourable quantity

Table 15.2   Fizzer plc – analysis of production variances

	Fixed monthly budget (750 cylinders) £	Flexed monthly budget (800 cylinders) £	Actual results for month (800 cylinders) £	Total operational variances £
Sales[1]	75 000	80 000	79 400	600 (U)
Material A[2]	15 000	16 000	16 720	720 (U)
Material B[3]	37 400	40 000	39 104	896 (F)
Labour[4]	6 750	7 200	7 125	75 (F)
Variable overheads[5]	1 875	2 000	2 250	250 (U)
Fixed overheads[6]	5 000	5 000	5 600	600 (U)
	66 125	70 200	70 799	599 (U)
Profit	8 875	9 800	8 601	1 199 (U)

Key: (U) = unfavourable operating variance (column 2 – column 3)
     (F) = favourable operating variance (column 2 – column 3)

1 Analysis of the sales variance is provided in Table 15.4.
2 Material A:
    Total variance: $(SQ \times SP) - (AQ \times AP)$ = £720 (U)
    Price variance: $(SP - AP) \times AQ$
               $(40p - 38p) \times 44\,000\,kg$ = £880 (F)
    Quantity $(SQ - AQ) \times SP$
               $(40\,000\,kg - 44\,000\,kg) \times 40p$ = £1 600 (U)
3 Material B:
    Total variance: $(SQ \times SP) - (AQ \times AP)$ = £896 (F)
    Price variance: $(SP - AP) \times AQ$
               $(50p - 52p) \times 75\,200\,kg$ = £1 504 (U)
    Quantity: $(SQ - AQ) \times SP$
               $(80\,000\,kg - 75\,200\,kg) \times 50p$ = £2 400 (F)
4 Labour:
    Total variance: $(SH \times SR) - (AH \times AR)$ = £75 (F)
    Rate: $(SR - AR) \times AH$
               $(£1.80 - £1.90) \times 3\,750\,hours$ = £375 (U)
    Efficiency: $(SH - AH) \times SR$
               $(4\,000\,hours - 3\,750\,hours) \times £1.80$ = £450 (F)
5 Variable overheads:
    Total variance: $(SH \times SR) - (AH \times AR)$ = £250 (U)
    Rate: $(SR - AR) \times AH$
               $(50p - 60p) \times 3\,750\,hours$ = £375 (U)
    Efficiency: $(SH - AH) \times SR$
               $(4\,000\,hours - 3\,750\,hours) \times 50p$ = £125 (F)
6 Fixed overheads: *Note*: not flexed due to change in activity; the £600 (U) variance is solely due to expenditure.

variance of £1600. Why? There are several possible reasons. One could be that an inferior quality was purchased which meant a lower price, but that a larger quantity was needed. Perhaps an opposite explanation could be given for material B. Is the labour variance worth investigating? After all, the total is only £75 favourable. However, this variance is the net of an unfavourable rate variance of £375 and a favourable efficiency variance of £450. What caused this? Was this due to an under-estimation at the time the original budget was set of the pay scales for labour, countered by too lax an estimation of the labour hours required? Alternatively, did the hourly rate paid constitute an incentive that resulted in better than standard productivity? The principal difference with the variable overheads seems to have been an underestimation of the hourly recovery rate. The variable overhead efficiency variance is, for obvious reasons, in line with the labour efficiency variance.

The fixed overhead adverse expenditure variance was £600. Note that this was not flexed. If the cost accounting system used in the organisation was based on absorption-costing principles (see Chapter 10) this expenditure heading might have been flexed. However, our view is that, although this can be done and expenditure and efficiency variances produced, little practical information is achieved, other than that the computation produces an over- or under-recovery of expenditure. In our opinion, it is of no practical use to calculate variances unless they actually provide meaningful information on which management can act. The reality is that the budget for fixed overheads was understated, and it is this that requires investigation.

The reasons given for the variances of Fizzer plc are only speculative. In practice, variances indicate only of which manager enquiries should be made. This example has been constructed simply to demonstrate that, although, overall, the target profit was close to that expected, this result is far from satisfactory and further investigation is indeed called for. However, the need to investigate variances is not always self-evident. While the accounting system will quantify the size and classification of a variance, management should be concerned about the cause as well as the size. Clearly, in an 'on-line' situation managers need to weigh up the costs and benefits of further investigation but should not base such decisions simply on whether a variance is favourable or unfavourable. To help with this, some standard costing systems use statistical techniques, often derived from the techniques of engineering quality-control analysis.

So far in this discussion, we have not commented on sales variances. The principles on which they are based are similar to those of production variances except that actual sales margins are determined based on the original budgeted margins. This is only equitable since the sales function would typically be expected to achieve a budgeted profit or contribution margin and it is not their responsibility if production costs were more or less than was budgeted for. Table 15.3 provides the relevant expressions for the calculation of sales margin variances and a simplified illustration, and Table 15.4 provides the analysis of the Fizzer plc sales variance. Note that, as presented, the overall operational sales variance will be due to differences in the sales price obtained.

The exercises at the end of this chapter provide further illustrations of variance analysis. Note that the analysis of these questions can be based on either an absorption or a contribution-based cost accounting system. Given the earlier discussion in Chapter 10, and examining the illustrations at the end of this chapter, readers should appreciate that whichever system is in operation the basic technique for the analysis of variances remains unchanged. For sales variances the difference between the

Table 15.3 Sales margin variances – general expression and illustration

Sales margin variance analysis assumes that all production costs are at standard. This is sensible since the sales activity of an organisation is relatively independent of production or service activities. By convention, therefore, sales variance analysis assumes that the cost price of all units sold is at standard cost; the actual costs do not enter the analysis at all.

Total sales margin variance	(Actual sales – Standard cost of sales) – (Budgeted sales – Standard cost of sales)
	(AS – SCS) – (BS – SCS)
Sales margin price variance	*either* (Actual margin per unit – Standard margin per unit) × Actual sales units
	(AMU –SMU) × ASU
	or* (Actual sales price – Standard sales price) × Actual sales units
	(ASP –SSP) × ASU
Sales quantity	(Actual sales variance – Budgeted sales variance) × Standard margin per unit
	(ASU – BSU) × SMU

Note: It is possible to further subdivide the sales quantity variance into miscellaneous and yield variances. This would be necessary only in certain instances, such as in the chemical industry.
* Both formulae give the same result; this is because the AMU is derived by deducting the standard cost of sales from the actual sales price and this is a constant term because the SMU also uses this value.

Table 15.4 Fizzer plc – analysis of sales margin variances*

Total sales margin variance	(AS – SCS) – (BS – SCS)
	(£79 400 – £70 200) – (£75 000 – £66 125)
	£9 200 – £8 875
	£325 (F)
Sales margin price variance	*either* (AMU – SMU) × ASU
	(£17.75 – £18.50) × 800
	£600 (U)
	or (ASP – SSP) × ASU
	(£99.25 – £100) × 800
	£600 (U)

(ASP = £79 400 ÷ 800 units = £99.25; AMU = £99.25 – £81.50 = £17.75; SMU = £100 – £81.50 = £18.50, where £81.50 is the standard cost per unit before fixed costs.)

Sales quantity variance	(ASU – BSU) × SMU
	(800 – 750) × £18.50
	£925 (F)

*Note: In Table 15.2 the sales variance shown was £600(U); this is because under this approach to flexible budgeting we are comparing actual sales with a budget which is flexed relative to actual sales activity. The full analysis is provided here.

actual profit/contribution margin and the budget profit/contribution margin under both approaches is the same, since the fixed-cost element is a common term for the determination of both the budgeted and the actual profit margins. These exercises also include a public-sector illustration, St Margaret's Hospital. Though it is a relatively simple example, it highlights that several possible applications of this approach to variance analysis are available in the public sector.

To conclude this section, we can say that there are probably four major causes of variances:

- inefficient operations;
- incorrect original plans and specifications;
- poor communication of standards and budgetary goals;
- failure to take interdependencies into account when setting standards and preparing a budget.

With respect to inefficient operations we would want to know whether the variance was controllable by management and, if so, whether its cause could be identified. Often, as previously stated, variances can be the result of interdependencies. For example, as illustrated above, when variable overheads are based on a labour-hour recovery rate, was adverse performance in one productive department the result of bad management in that department or a technical fault in another department? It could be that because a particular job arrived behind schedule in one department overtime had to be worked. The reason for the delay could have been poor scheduling earlier in the production cycle or, perhaps, an earlier machine failure. For planning, we need information on market-effect changes and we would need to know if variances are persistent in order to determine whether our overall long-term plan needs changing. Also, importantly, we need feedback from those responsible for planning, since it takes much longer to rectify planning failures than operational failures.

Performance indicators

Although the concern with economy, efficiency and effectiveness (the three Es) is not new to the British government, its emphasis was given a boost following the public-sector crisis of the mid-1970s and the return of the Conservative Party to government in 1979. A series of reforms gave pre-eminence to the gospel of the new public management in central government; the efficiency movement began with the Rayner scrutinies and was followed by the Financial Management Initiative (FMI), with its emphasis on accountable management and information systems, and the more recent development of executive agencies, each with its service and resource targets. Local government, the NHS and other parts of the public sector have not been immune. Indeed, they have often been at the forefront of developments, including the Citizens' Charter movement, which reflect the increasing concern, not just with the economical management of resources, but also with the efficiency and effectiveness of service delivery.

Public-sector organisations have to operate in a strict financial climate that includes the use of cash limits, cash planning and the development of performance indicators intended to demonstrate whether the public at large receives value for money from the services provided. The use of performance indicators is seen as a vital part of internal control, and they are also used in annual reports as an important supplement to financial information. As Glynn states, 'Accountability in the public sector occurs when both politicians and the public at large are assured that public funds are being spent *efficiently*, *economically* and on programmes that are *effective*' (Glynn 1985: 18). Performance indicators are concerned with demonstrating that services are provided efficiently and that the output from any activity/service is achieving the desired results.

Efficiency indicators refer to the productive use of resources. In order to produce such measures managers need to be able to identify and measure both programme outputs and programme inputs. In order to define suitable efficiency measures it is necessary to assess five factors:

- the suitable delineation of individual departmental or programme goals to all levels of the organisation;
- the adequacy of controls and systems used by management in monitoring and measuring both the efficiency and the level of service they offer;
- the level of efficiency currently attained, as well as measures of comparable results (if available);
- the efforts taken to improve methods of operation in order to improve efficiency;
- whether efficiency measures are feasible and, if not, the reasons why.

The term 'efficiency' is often wrongly confused with the term 'productivity'. Productivity is simply the ratio between output and input, whereas efficiency is the relationship of actual output/input (productivity) to a performance standard. Efficiency can be measured in terms of a rate of return of production, the work content measured over time, or the unit cost of an output. Consider the following example (based on Glynn 1985) in relation to the dispensing of prescriptions by a hospital pharmacy.

A hospital employs two pharmacists who each work a 35-hour week. The *standard rate of production* is six prescriptions/hour; which in terms of *work content in time* is ten minutes/prescription. Each pharmacist is paid £8.40 per hour, so that the *unit cost per prescription* is £1.40. Statistics show that, on average, 924 prescriptions are dispensed each month. Efficiency can be measured as follows:

$$\frac{\text{Actual rate per hour}}{\text{Standard rate per hour}} = \frac{6.60}{6} \times 100 = 110\%$$

$$\frac{\text{Standard time (minutes)/prescription}}{\text{Actual time (minutes)/prescription}} = \frac{10}{9.09} \times 100 = 110\%$$

$$\frac{\text{Standard cost (£)/prescription}}{\text{Actual cost (£)/prescription}} = \frac{£1.40}{£1.27} \times 100 = 110\%$$

Various points arise from this example. In comparing actual costs with standard costs, management should first consider the economy of operations. Efficiency measures are only possible when outputs can be separated from each other and possess uniform characteristics. A repetitive process, as in our example, meets these criteria. There are instances when efficiency measures are either not practicable or not possible. Consider the potential difficulties associated with attempting to measure the efficiency of a community policing programme. Though tasks may be clearly stated for the officers concerned (school visits, handling crime-prevention enquiries, maintaining and developing contacts with ethnic minorities, etc.), outputs, not necessarily being tangible, cannot be measured easily, if at all.

When an agreed standard of performance does not exist it might, in the first instance, be useful to compare present performance with some previous base period (e.g. the same month last year). Such a base output/input ratio is termed an historical standard or target. This assumes that past performance is an appropriate comparison for future performance; this may not always be so. For instance, if a new service is building up a client base one would naturally expect the efficiency ratio to improve over time. Hatry *et al.* (1979) provide a useful list of efficiency indicators, in six categories:

- comparisons over **time**;
- measurements compared between **geographical** areas;
- comparison of actual performance with **standards**, particularly in relation to standardised procedures;
- comparisons of actual performance with that **targeted** at the beginning of the year;
- comparisons with similar **private-sector** activities;
- **inter-authority** comparisons.

Clearly the purpose is not to measure efficiency for efficiency's sake – improving efficiency is the objective. By developing appropriate efficiency indicators management can contribute to improving efficiency and to determining the expected gains from suggested improvements. The 1981 Canadian Audit Guide (Canadian Government 1981: 5) discussed the importance of efficiency measures in the following terms:

> Standards and performance data are used for different purposes in various information and control systems. These are to:
> - demonstrate achievement of results by comparing performance data to standards, targets and goals;
> - plan operations and budget resource requirements by providing data for comparing present and proposed methods and procedures;
> - provide a rational basis for pricing goods and services (when charges are made);
> - make trade-off decisions between efficiency and the level of service; and
> - indicate to employees and supervisors what results are expected.

The key elements for management that arise from adopting efficiency measures are therefore:

1 An awareness of, and the determination to accomplish, programme goals in the most economical and efficient manner.
2 The need to plan operations as efficiently as possible for a given level of resources (or budgeted level of income if a statutory authority is expected largely to generate its own income).
3 The need to have a structured organisation whose administration should follow prescribed work measures and procedures in order to avoid duplication of effort, unnecessary tasks, idle time, etc.
4 The provision of work instructions, in sufficient detail, to employees who are suitably qualified and trained for the duties they are required to perform.

As the report of the Layfield Committee states, 'the best way of promoting efficiency and securing value for money by external means is through the dissemination of comprehensive but intelligible information on the methods employed by local authorities and the results they achieve' (Layfield Committee 1976: 95).

By contrast to measuring efficiency, the notion of effectiveness is probably the most important yet least precise element of the three Es. Consider the following definitions:

> [Effectiveness is] The extent to which the objectives of a policy are achieved. The most effective policy is one which achieves all its objectives.
>
> (Treasury 1988: 28)

> Effectiveness means providing the right services to enable the local authority to implement its policies and objectives.
>
> (Audit Commission 1986: 8)

> Ensuring that the output from any given activity is achieving the desired result.
>
> (Price Waterhouse 1990: 4)

The definitions contain a variety of terms and implications but share a common view of effectiveness: it is a *value* given to the relationship between an activity and its effects. Glynn *et al.* (1992) believe that there is something of a conventional wisdom about what different effectiveness measures can be. These can be measured in terms of:

- outputs – units of goods or services produced;
- outcomes – externalities to the activities themselves;
- impacts – the ultimate policy effects of a programme, project or policy.

Of these three measures, outputs are the most easily measured. Output performance indicators relate to the direct products of management processes, such as numbers of young persons on training schemes, housing units built, etc. Outcomes represent direct and measurable consequences of an activity, for example the proportion of training scheme recipients obtaining vocational qualifications or employment and the reduction in homelessness. Impacts are much harder to report in terms of performance indicators since impacts tend to be associated with the more abstract notion of 'quality of life'; that is, the broader impact of training schemes and crime-prevention campaigns on the quality of life of citizens.

The production of performance indicators is a relatively new concept, albeit one increasingly used since the late 1980s. Performance indicators are quantitative expressions of various characteristics or consequences of an activity (see Jackson and Palmer 1989). Indicators are, as the word implies, *indicative* of performance, and are thus attempts to portray the achievements of an activity where actual outputs or impacts are difficult to measure. There are essentially two classes of effectiveness indicators: absolute indicators, which report volume or incidence (e.g. numbers of university graduates obtaining first-class degrees), and indices, which report relative achievements (e.g. percentage of university graduates with first-class degrees). Both classes focus on descriptions of aggregate activities. Thus their function is primarily descriptive, but they may, in a limited way, also address normative and prescriptive questions. They are unlikely, however, to provide explanations of what they reveal and they do not always measure effectiveness directly. Nevertheless, they often have to be used as proxies for effectiveness, because it is difficult to identify and measure outcomes and impacts themselves.

Although this section of the chapter has dealt with public-sector issues, it should be obvious to the reader that in service-sector industries the development of performance indicators is probably more to be commended than the development of flexible budgets and detailed variance analysis.

Conclusions

Management has a need for control information to help evaluate performance against budgets, standards and targets. A common accounting technique for the provision of such information is that of standard costing. When combined with flexible budgeting, a standard costing approach enables the identification of planning variances (focusing on the impact of a differing actual level of activity from that originally budgeted for) and operational variances (focusing on the extent to which actual operational performance met the standards – targets – underpinning the budgetary process). However, this analysis has a strong financial orientation. As such, it may well require supplementation by (integration with) non-financial performance measures if effective control is to be achieved.

This chapter has considered the contribution which accounting can make to management control. The first half of the chapter sought to develop the foundations of budgetary control introduced in Chapter 14. The second half of the chapter recognised that in many instances most notably in the public sector, budgetary information needs to be supplemented by the development of performance indicators, which should assist management in monitoring and reporting on the efficiency and effectiveness of programmes. The end of chapter exercises illustrate further the production and analysis of budgetary variances. Various questions are also asked to test whether you are familiar with the basic methodology required to produce performance indicators.

Further reading

Drury (1996) provides ample illustrations of more applied approaches to variance analysis/standard costing. Hofstede's (1968) classic work is also a useful read with regard to the behavioural aspects of accounting control systems. This is an area where readers should also refer to relevant journals, which include the *Journal of Business, Journal of Business, Finance and Accounting, Accounting and Business Research* and *Accounting, Organisations and Society*.

Questions and exercises

1 Eastbrook Plc manufactures a revolutionary insulating material which is marketed under the brand name Cosiwrap for £5.40 per roll. Originally, the company had planned to manufacture 100 000 rolls per month on the basis of a standard marginal unit cost computed as follows:

	£
Material A (2 kg @ 40p)	0.80
Material B (2 kg @ 50p)	1.00
Material C (4 kg @ 30p)	1.20
	3.00
Labour (15 minutes)	0.75
Variable expenses	0.25
	4.00

Fixed expenses were estimated at £80 000 per month.

Unfortunately for Eastbrook, there has been severe market competition for insulating material and the actual results for the last month were:

Production and sales (rolls)	80 000
Sales	£392 000
Material A 128 000 kg	57 600
Material B 256 000 kg	115 200
Material C 256 000 kg	76 800
Labour (16 000 hours)	54 400
Variable expenses	18 400
Fixed expenses	82 000
	404 000
Loss	12 400

Although the managing director is aware that his product has many competitors and that there have been problems with the supply of materials, he is amazed by the company's poor performance. Thus he has asked you to prepare a short report:

(a) that reconciles actual and planned performance by analysing all important variables;

(b) that provides a commentary on the results for the month.

2 Musicality plc manufactures cassette players and sells them to the major consumer-goods retailers, who market them under their own brand names. It works closely with this relatively small number of major customers and operates a just-in-time (JIT) inventory-management system, holding no stocks of raw materials,

work-in-progress or finished goods. In addition, the company operates a standard costing system. The standard costing information for the product is:

	£
Unit selling price	60.00
Direct materials (1 assembly kit @ £12.00)	12.00
Direct labour (2 hours @ £9.00 per hour)	18.00
Variable overheads (@ £4.00 per labour hour)	8.00
Fixed overhead recovery*	12.00
Total unit cost	50.00
Unit profit	10.00

(*The annual budget for these costs totals £480 000 and this is allocated to product units on the basis of a forecast annual production of 40 000 units.)

Musicality's budget for May 1998 estimated that it would sell 4000 units during the month. In fact, its accounting records reveal the following information:

Sales	4 200 units @ £61.00 per unit
Direct material purchases	4 400 kits @ £11.50 per kit
Direct labour	7 400 hours @ £9.50 per hour
Variable overhead expenditure	£32 560
Fixed costs expenditure	£41 000

Prepare a report for Musicality's management which:
(a) shows the original budgeted profit for the month;
(b) shows the actual profit for the month;
(c) reconciles any difference between (a) and (b) above, showing the impact of any:
    (i) planning variances;
    (ii) operating variances.
(d) comments on the managerial implications of the financial information contained in the report.

3 In 1997 the St Margaret's Hospital Trust started promoting its new Sports Injuries Clinic. The clinic specialises in the treatment of athletic injuries. The budgeted and actual financial data relating to the three months ending December 1997 are as follows:

	Budget		Actual	
	£	£	£	£
Fee income		75 000		82 500
Physiotherapists' salaries	25 000		27 500	
Bought-in services from other departments	12 500		14 950	
Clinical facilities	28 750	66 250	30 000	72 450
Surplus		£8 750		£10 050

The following additional information is available:

(i) The actual unit fee of £75 was the same as that budgeted.

(ii) X-rays and other bought-in services are paid for on a unit-cost basis. Overall, the unit manager, Mrs T, states that usage of these services was 15% higher than budgeted and that the unit price was, on average, 4% higher than budgeted.

(iii) Sessional physiotherapists' time was at the volume budgeted. However, the budget had only allowed for a 5% pay rise from 1 October, whereas the actual pay rise was 10%, compared with a national average of 8%.

(iv) Clinic facilities represent allocated costs incurred by the clinic. These include a secretary/receptionist and a full-time staff nurse. It was expected that this charge would also be sufficient to cover other establishment costs.

Prepare a short report for the finance officer in a form that most clearly sets out an analysis of variances between budgeted and actual results. In this report also include recommendations on how this information might more usefully be presented in the future.

4 Adhesives plc manufactures industrial adhesives. Shown below is the standard prime cost of a tube of adhesive, which is the only product manufactured in one department of the company.

	£ per tube	£ per tube
Materials:		
Powder	1.50	
Chemical	0.60	
Tube	0.30	2.40
Labour		1.80
		4.20

The standard material allowance for each tube of adhesive is 2 kg of powder, 0.25 litres of chemical and one tube. The standard wage rate is £4.50 per hour.

During the previous month 4500 tubes of adhesive were manufactured. There was no work-in-progress at the start or the end of the month, and the receipts and issues of materials during the month were:

	Powder (kg)	Chemicals (litres)	Tubes
Opening stock	1 500	200	100
Purchases	10 000 at 70p	600 at £2.30	200 at 40p
		600 at £2.50	5 000 at 30p
Issues	9 800	1 050	4 520

The above materials are used exclusively in the production of adhesive and it is the policy of the company to calculate any price variances when the materials are purchased.

The direct employees of the department worked a total of 2050 hours during the month and earned gross wages of £8910.

Prepare a statement showing the operating variances for the department and comment on possible causes for these variances.

5 Outline what you consider to be the main features of an accounting control system.

6 Discuss the advantages of flexible budgeting when it comes to preparing performance reports.

7 'Because of its emphasis on comparison between the actual results and the original plans, the traditional standard costing system does not yield useful information for decision-making.' Discuss.

8 'Standard costing and variance analysis are only of limited importance to the NHS.' Critically discuss this statement.

9 Outline what you understand by the terms:

   (a) economy;

   (b) efficiency;

   (c) effectiveness.

   Within a context with which you are familiar, illustrate your understanding of these terms by defining three performance indicators for each.

10 'The effectiveness of a government activity may be conceptualised as encompassing outputs, outcomes and impacts.' How easy is it in practice to measure effectiveness? In your answer be clear to distinguish between the terms 'output', 'outcome' and 'impact'.

16 Internal performance evaluation and transfer pricing

Objectives

This chapter is concerned with responsibility accounting, with particular reference to divisionalised organisations. Within such organisations the management-control process is important in ensuring that overall goal congruence is achieved while at the same time promoting and maintaining divisional autonomy. All too often organisations institute performance criteria for managers which evaluate short-term performance at the expense of longer-term objectives.

We will examine the arguments for and against a divisionalised organisational structure. Depending on the type of divisional structure adopted, certain performance measures are either more or less appropriate. The responsibility accounting system must parallel the structure of the organisation. This structure depends on the nature of the organisation's operations and on the attitudes and management styles of its senior management. The reporting segments of this type of responsibility accounting system may be cost centres, profit centres (either natural or artificial) or investment centres.

We will examine each of these segments and analyse what may be appropriate performance measures. We will also discuss issues relating to internal transfer prices – the selling prices established for trading between artificial profit centres – as problems may arise if the bases on which these prices are determined either motivate or demotivate the managers concerned.

Divisionalisation

If managers are to be held accountable for their performance they must have clearly defined areas of responsibility – activities over which they can exercise control. Such defined areas of responsibility are to be found in any decentralised organisation. At its simplest this can be a functional department or cost centre where financial accountability is achieved by keeping expenditure within agreed budget limits. In highly decentralised organisations operational units may well be termed 'divisions'. Within a divisionalised organisation there is usually an additional element to a manager's financial accountability, i.e. the concept of delegated profit responsibility. As Solomons states:

> A division has been defined as a company unit headed by a person fully responsible for the profitability of its operations, including planning, production, financial and accounting activities, and which usually, although not always, has its own sales force. The division may be a unit of the parent company or it may be a wholly or partially owned subsidiary.
>
> (Solomons 1983: 3)

Divisional management responsibility covers not only how operations should be carried out but also, within prescribed limits, what those operations should be. This discretion will cover such areas as what products or services to sell and at what price; what manufacturing operations are to be performed within the division and what might be bought in from outside (including other companies/divisions within the group); and sales and research strategy. Divisions are often termed, for accounting control purposes, either profit or investment centres.

A profit centre can be either natural or artificial. A natural profit centre operates in external markets, whereas an artificial profit centre sells its output to other divisions within the organisation. It is also possible to have divisions that sell both externally and internally. The notion of artificial profit centres is becoming more popular, not just in industry, but also in the public sector. A local-authority direct-labour organisation is an example of an artificial profit centre (see Glynn 1993). Internal selling prices are usually termed transfer prices; these are discussed later in this chapter.

An investment centre is a division in which the divisional management controls not only revenues and costs but also investment. Rather than simply evaluating managers in terms of profit, it is more usual to evaluate the performance of investment centres in terms of a return on investment (ROI).

For profit centres to operate fully in the spirit set out by Solomons (above) it is preferable that divisional managers should have full (delegated) authority and control over the resources and decisions involved in divisional management. At the least, they should have primary influence (in the absence of ultimate control responsibility) over these resources and decisions. This is because of the guiding principle, based on our understanding of human behaviour, that managers can be held accountable effectively only for what they can realistically control. Where divisional managers are obliged to 'sell' goods to other divisions within the company at prices and volumes which they do not decide, or to use goods and services from other parts of the company at costs or input prices which they do not decide (or at least very strongly influence), the divisional (financial) autonomy is indeed artificial, and it may be preferable to plan, budget and assess performance on the basis of 'contribution centres' rather than profit centres. That is, contribution (as defined in earlier chapters) should be used to strike the bottom line on which divisional (managerial) performance is assessed. Below this line, head office can add in the further costs and revenues outside the control and accountability of divisional managers in order to derive a final net profit figure. This final net profit then represents the 'economic performance' of the division.

Economic performance is crucial to group-management strategic decisions affecting divisions, especially decisions on new investment, sale of the division or closure. Here, final net profit usually needs to be related to capital investment, in order for the profit return to be meaningfully compared with cost of capital, competitors and the opportunity costs of alternative investments. However, while it is important to calculate and report the return on investment centrally, it should not be used for managerial-performance control unless divisional managers have primary influence, even if not full control, over the level of divisional investment and its composition. As Dominiak and Louderback state:

> The choice of a type of responsibility centre for a particular activity (or group of activities) is unique to each firm. Such factors as size, industry, operating characteristics, and managerial philosophy influence organisational structure. . . . An important characteristic of good responsibility reporting is that its reports include only controllable costs. Whether or not a particular cost is controllable – and hence includable in the report to a particular manager – depends on the level of that manager in the hierarchy.
>
> (Dominiak and Louderback 1988: 360)

Having outlined what is meant by the term division, we come to the question of what advantages there are for an organisation that has a divisionalised structure. The answer is that seven key advantages are potentially to be obtained:

- Giving divisional managers autonomy with accountability should lead to them being better motivated. Research in the behavioural sciences suggests that individuals who are involved in the entire production process take more interest in their work and perform better than those who merely perform the same operation repeatedly. Similarly, a manager who is responsible for most operational aspects of a division may feel more in control of his/her performance than if he/she were responsible for only one core activity.
- Divisionalisation facilitates diversification. Many organisations operate in a number of markets or technologies and it is not possible for the central corporate management team to have detailed knowledge about the operational aspects of each division. For example, a pharmaceutical company could have a number of divisions, dealing with medicines, agricultural pesticides and so on. Each aspect of the organisation, represented by its operational divisions, has to develop products for what are essentially very different markets, each with their own particular business risks.
- Divisionalisation can reduce the need for complicated internal communications between the central corporate management team and the divisional managers. This, in turn, can lead to an improvement in the time taken over decisions and prevent a communications overload.
- Because divisional managers have an intimate knowledge of their division they are more likely to understand and be able to resolve issues affecting their division.
- Central corporate management will have more time to concentrate on overall corporate strategy and problem divisions, and management-by-exception principles can be applied.
- Performance measures can be produced which should lead to goal congruence between individual divisional managers and the organisation as a whole.
- Divisionalisation provides a training environment which enables future senior managers to 'cut their teeth' on smaller identifiable business units.

Decentralisation can also have its problems. The major and most worrying factor is that managers who operate in near autonomy may make decisions which harm the organisation as a whole. The challenge for central corporate management is to achieve overall goal congruence while at the same time promoting and maintaining divisional autonomy. There are a number of prerequisites for successful divisionalisation, and if these are not present problems will inevitably occur. They are:

■ Successful operating divisions need a sufficiently independent existence to make delegated profit responsibility a reality. Not all organisations can achieve this. Independence requires some clear organisational separateness of markets, of technology and/or of geographical location, as well as managerial structures and financial information systems supporting autonomy.

■ While key resources and decision areas must be delegated in order to achieve effective divisional performance, some common services may need to be centralised for economies of scale essential to overall optimum profitability. However, all such core common services must be responsive to divisional needs, and they must be 'charged for' at costs or internal prices which optimise corporate performance (see Transfer prices, pp. 372–8).

■ There should be an appropriate managerial-performance assessment and reward system, reflecting contributions to corporate as well as divisional profitability, and to other strategic objectives and performance criteria.

■ Divisional managers should be closely involved with the development of a sound participative budgetary system, and of internal relationships, information exchanges and transfer prices conducive to goal congruence.

■ There should be a recognised and supportive corporate culture which helps to foster unity within diversity.

■ No division should be able to increase its profits (or its return on capital) at the expense of reducing overall corporate profitability. This relates both to the management of internal service and trading relationships, and to the informational and motivational signals provided by the internal financial reporting (and budgeting) systems used to inform the allocation of resources between divisions and the assessment of divisional performance in annual reports (and in any more frequent interim progress reports from divisional to central management).

Internal financial reporting for divisionalised organisations

By convention, divisional managers tend to have their performance evaluated by measures that closely correspond to the organisation's overall financial reporting structure. The reasons for this are varied and include the following:

■ **Pressure on management**: professional investors tend to look for short-term financial profit performance, as this directly influences share market prices. Directors need to fulfil their accounting responsibilities under the Companies Acts, which are becoming increasingly onerous. Recall that many divisions may be corporate entities in their own right. Additionally, there is a need to produce regular periodic reports on accounting profits. For example, interim reports for

Stock Exchange purposes, profit and cash-flow forecasts for bankers and others, briefings for brokers, analysts, etc.

■ **Background of managers**: senior managers are increasingly aware of the need to use and relate to financial performance measures that are 'transferable' and understood by potential new employers. Rightly or wrongly, accounting profit is regarded as a universally transferable comparator of performance. It should also be remembered that many bonus schemes are also linked to accounting profit.

■ **Pressure from auditors**: auditors are always keen to see that financial accounts should be integrated with, or at least agree with, the management accounts. Aligned with this is the auditors' concern that a key aspect of internal control is that financial accounts should be positively traceable back to the accounting data base.

Return on investment

By far the most common measure used to evaluate divisional managers is the return on investment (ROI). This measure closely approximates the return on capital employed (ROCE), discussed in Chapter 7. ROI is the ratio of some measure of profit to some corresponding measure of divisional investment capital. Many UK companies use the following definition:

$$\text{ROI} = \frac{\text{Net profit}}{\text{Investment in net assets}} \times 100 \qquad (16.1)$$

This measure has the distinct advantage of assessing profit, not in isolation, but relative to a division's capital base. ROI therefore makes it possible to compare the efficiency of different-sized divisions by relating output (income/profit) to input (the capital investment base). As with the ROCE definition introduced earlier, the ROI measure can be restated as:

$$\text{ROI} = \frac{\text{Net profit}}{\text{Sales}} \times \frac{\text{Sales}}{\text{Investment in net assets}} \times 100 \qquad (16.2)$$

This subdivision helps to focus management's attention on the components of ROI. The first element of this revised expression focuses on the return-on-sales ratio; the second, on capital turnover. From this subdivision it is clear that an increase in sales, by itself, will not increase ROI because sales cancel out. But a decrease in investment, with other factors staying constant, will increase ROI. There is also scope for a manager to consider the impact on ROI of a decision that is expected to change two factors. For example, suppose that return on sales is currently 16% and that investment turnover is two times; ROI is therefore 32% (16% × 2). What is the likely impact on ROI if the manager considers changing the product mix to items with sales margins, say an average of 12%, which should increase capital turnover to three times? The outcome is that the ROI would rise to 36% (12% × 3).

The values of the components of ROI can often provide clues as to the kinds of strategies used by group management when they evaluate its different divisions or subsidiaries. Consider a retail company which operates both departmental and discount stores. Both kinds of store might earn the same ROI, but by adopting different strategies. Let us assume that the following information relates to two of the group's stores:

	The Debonair departmental store	*The Thrifty discount store*
Sales	£1000 000	£1200 000
Divisional profit	£120 000	£96 000
Divisional investment	£500 000	£400 000

The two ROI computations are:

$$\text{Debonair} = \frac{£120\,000}{£1\,000\,000} \times \frac{£1\,000\,000}{£500\,000} = 24\%$$

$$\text{Thrifty} = \frac{£96\,000}{£1\,200\,000} \times \frac{£1\,200\,000}{£400\,000} = 24\%$$

As can be seen, the Thrifty discount store, while producing a lower return on sales, obtains a higher sales volume for each pound invested.

Given that ROI is a ratio, it is important to ensure that the basis used for calculating the investment in net assets is compatible with the measure used for profit. In particular, if a 'controllable' measure is used for calculating profit, then a 'controllable' measure should be used for the measurement of net assets. Three alternative measures of net assets are net book value, gross book value and current value. Net book value creates a problem because the impact of depreciation is such that, for a given set of physical assets, a constant level of profit will produce, year by year, an increasing ROI. In difficult trading times divisional managers might be persuaded to keep assets beyond their useful economic life. A secondary problem is that assets are stated at historic values which do not measure their true opportunity value.

Gross book value removes the problem of depreciation but still relies on historical cost as a measure. Current value would produce a much more meaningful valuation of assets, if reliable figures could be obtained. However, as discussed in Chapter 3, there are a number of problems associated with the use of current values for accounting purposes. Even if current values were used for measuring a division's asset base we would still have the problem of historic-cost profit – ideally we would want to have both profit and asset base stated in current terms. However, given the rather sorry history of current-cost (value) accounting in the UK, this is likely to remain a pipe-dream.

There are two principal difficulties relating to divisional profit measures for ROI. The first difficulty relates to the situation of measuring revenues and costs when different divisions trade with each other. The (transfer) price at which this trade is carried out can have a significant impact on the profit of the divisions involved. As discussed in the next section, it is important to develop appropriate mechanisms for the setting and agreement of transfer prices. If this is not done and the (transfer) price is 'wrong', then:

- if volumes are large, relatively small changes in the transfer price can lead to big differences in the profits of the trading divisions;
- there can be significant impacts on the motivation of divisional managers, leading to a loss of some of the advantages of divisionalisation;

- the financial performance measures (e.g. ROI) may lead senior managers into thinking that divisions are more or less profitable than is really the case.

The second difficulty relates to the identification of the true costs of running a division. Two issues are particularly relevant:

- To what extent should a division be charged with a share of expenses (most commonly head-office/group expenses) the benefit of which are enjoyed by all parts of the company?
- There is a cost of capital associated with the net assets employed by the division. Should a financial charge be made for this?

Most divisional managers rapidly become aware of the potential flaws associated with the use of ROI to assess their performance. In order to prevent them exploiting the flexibility afforded by historic-cost accounting conventions, e.g. by exercising 'accounting judgement' with respect to items such as provision for doubtful debts and depreciation rates, group management needs to lay down explicit accounting rules and regulations. Nevertheless, the 'artful' divisional manager might seek to reduce discretionary expenditure, such as that on training and research and development. This is short-sighted and group management might seek to counter this by also instituting the use of non-financial (supplementary) performance measures; for example, with respect to training, an expectation that particular grades of staff should have a prescribed number of days' training each year. Divisional managers might also seek to adjust the asset base of their division by techniques of sale and lease-back and off-balance-sheet finance. Here again, group management may wish to exercise some general control on the degree of discretion afforded to divisional managers.

Despite the difficulties associated with using the historical-cost convention to measure ROI, we can summarise four main advantages of using ROI as a performance measure:

- It is a relative measure which reflects both the profit generated by the division and the resources (net assets) employed to generate those profits.
- It can be subdivided into a hierarchy of other measures and ratios which can be used to appraise divisional performance at a more detailed level if necessary.
- It mirrors a commonly used measure of overall corporate performance – ROCE – and as such can help develop goal congruence.
- It uses data compatible with those contained in the financial accounting data base and the external financial reports which a company needs to use.

Residual income

A second commonly used measure of divisional performance is residual income (RI). It is a measure of the amount of income that a division produces in excess of the **minimum desired** (sometimes called **target**) rate of return. This desired target rate of return is determined by group management since management has overall responsibility for the long-term financing strategy of the group. The target set is usually equal to or greater than the organisation's cost of capital. In general, RI is computed as follows:

$$\text{RI} = \text{Income} - (\text{Investment} \times \text{Target ROI}) \qquad (16.3)$$

The argument for using RI as a measure of divisional performance is that it measures the amount of profit that the division provides to the enterprise over and above the profit to be expected (the minimum required) for the amount invested. RI has an important advantage over ROI as a measure of divisional performance. It allows for the fact that a division with a higher ROI may be less valuable to the organisation as a whole than one with a lower ROI. Consider the following situation. Division A produces £400 000 profit on an investment of £2 000 000, an ROI of 20%. Division B earns a profit of £3 000 000 on an investment base of £20 000 000; ROI is 15%. The contributions of each division to the organisation as a whole will appear quite different depending on the desired ROI for the organisation. Let us consider two possible scenarios, ROI of 10% and ROI of 18%. The RIs for each division are calculated as follows.

| | *Scenario 1* | | *Scenario 2* | |
| | *Required ROI 10%* | | *Required ROI 18%* | |
	A	*B*	*A*	*B*
Investment base	£2 000 000	£20 000 000	£2 000 000	£20 000 000
Divisional profit	£400 000	£3 000 000	£400 000	£3 000 000
Desired minimum return (investment × minimum required return)	£200 000	£2 000 000	£360 000	£3 600 000
Residual income	£200 000	£1 000 000	£40 000	(£600 000)

As can be seen, if the minimum desired ROI is 10%, division B makes a greater contribution to the organisation than does division A, despite the fact that division B's ROI is lower. Division B is therefore the more valuable to the firm. However, if the minimum desired ROI is 18% this situation is dramatically reversed and division A is much more valuable to the organisation. As Dominiak and Louderback state:

> Generally speaking, using RI as the criterion for evaluating divisional performance, the division rated highest is the one with the greatest positive difference between profit and the minimum desired return. In some ways it is similar to the use of net present values (NPVs) as the criterion for evaluating capital expenditure. Under that criterion, the most desirable (valuable) capital project is the one with the highest net present value after discounting future returns at the cost of capital.
>
> (Dominiak and Louderback 1988: 410)

The above quotation links the RI approach both to evaluating current divisional performance and to making capital-expenditure decisions. The data in the above example of scenarios 1 and 2 was given in the context of past performance. If the RI is to be used to assess divisional economic performance data should be inclusive of all costs, and similarly with managerial performance (provided that all the costs included in arriving at divisional profit were controllable, or at least strongly influenced, by the divisional management). The same numbers could have been cited in a different context, future investment selection, where the 'investment base' represents forecast future capital outlays proposed, and the 'divisional profit' is the forecast profit from such new investment. The same RI figures would have been derived in this alternative context showing to us the changing attractiveness of new investment in the two divisions as the test rate of desired minimum return is altered. If divisions A and B have an absolute ability to obtain new capital from the centre each division will seek to invest up to the level of whatever target rate of RI (or of ROI) has been set for it. However, in the more usual situation of capital rationing at some stage affecting the corporate entity as a whole it is likely that an absolute right or ability to access new long-term capital cannot be granted to divisions. In this event corporate management must take responsibility for allocating capital, in order to optimise corporate profit. In severe cases of capital rationing it may be a misleading fiction to label divisions 'investment centres', and it may be fairer and more realistic to treat them as just profit centres (for assessing managerial performance, as distinct from economic performance).

Where divisions realistically can be managed as investment centres, and with largely delegated decision-making on investments, the RI approach will give decision signals consistent with corporate objectives, at least so long as:

1 net cash flows are constant year on year (where they are not the NPV test must always be used);
2 the minimum desired (or target) rate of return has been set at the optimal rate.

The optimal target rate of return can be described (but not always easily measured) as the opportunity rate of return on new capital for the best alternative investments allowing realistically for comparative risk. However, it has often been suggested that British management, suffering repeatedly form stop–go economics, volatile interest and exchange rates, etc., has become excessively risk averse, leading it too often to set unrealistically high target rates of return for investment. To illustrate, our example above was designed to show how the higher 18% target rate dramatically alters the apparent performance of the two divisions. However the 18% rate should not be used simply because it appears to offer a desirable 'motivational' target; it should be used only if it is the company's realistic risk-weighted opportunity return or its realistic marginal cost of capital (which should, in itself, include allowance for average corporate risk).

It has been suggested that the majority of divisionalised companies prefer to use ROI, rather than RI, as their primary indicator of divisional performance. This is understandable to the extent that managers think of ROI as the normal basis for assessing performance, especially as they wish to compare their performance against other (independent) businesses. Although the foregoing discussion suggests that the use of ROI is theoretically undesirable, it can be argued that in the common situation where divisions do not control their capital (or at least decisions on increments of capital) ROI leads to the same correct decision-signals as RI: this is because if the ROI is maximised on a given/fixed amount of capital the absolute return will itself also be maximised. However, even where ROI may be reliable for assessing the performance of divisional management operating de facto as a profit centre, central management may still need to look at RI for guidance on investment (or disinvestment) decisions.

It may be human nature to focus on a single performance variable – be this ROI, RI or any other – but also it may be wiser to draw attention to a wider range of performance measures. These include other financial indicators, including the financial ratios discussed in Chapter 7. They can include additionally a wide range of quantified indicators relating to the use of inputs or to achieved physical outputs. The public sector has pioneered a diversity of performance measures; the NHS, for example, has developed over 450 measures. Such a large number of measures may be excessive for strategic overview, but even in private businesses divisional reporting may usefully include additional selected measurements considered to be significant indicators of organisational health or performance. These might include some of the following:

- market share;
- sales turnover per employee;
- profit per employee;
- labour turnover rates;
- average labour remuneration;
- expenditure on staff training, and on research and development;
- number of customer complaints received.

Because calculating RI involves the same factors as those used in ROI above, similar questions arise about what elements and bases should or should not be included in computations, especially as regards asset valuation, depreciation and capital charges, and fair and relevant transfer prices and central services costs.

Transfer prices

As work progresses through an integrated organisation, the costs of the work flow in parallel, transferring from cost centre to cost centre. These costs could be called 'transfer costs'. But when the flow of work is between profit centres rather than mere cost centres and these profit centres are under more or less autonomous management often organised as corporate divisions, the transfer of costs is termed 'transfer prices' to reflect that some form of internal market exists within the overall enterprise. Moreover, these transfer prices in internal markets need not be the same amounts as simple historical-cost transfers, and in general they should normally be higher than that because otherwise the supplying division receives no revenue above cost to contribute to its own profits and viability, and thus no incentive to co-operate with the receiving division. On the other hand, if the receiving division is overcharged for internal supply it may be unable to compete in its end-product market, and the total corporate sales and profits will be reduced. The problem is to find a basis of transfer pricing which:

- optimises resource allocation and use for the total enterprise;
- does not undermine the autonomy of individual divisions nor result in an unfair or demotivating attribution of profits between them.

In the extreme case, all divisions are operationally self-contained and also can sell all their output to external customers at a prevailing market price. In this case interdivisional transfer pricing need not arise, although if for any reason any two of such divisions wished to trade with each other it should be obvious that transfer prices should be at the external market price – otherwise, total earnings of the corporate enterprise would be reduced. Even in this case, however, there may be central or common services shared by the operating divisions and charged for by transfer pricing (see below).

In the more general case, there is a degree of interdependence and internal trading between divisions. For example, one division may make castings and both sell its output into external markets and supply internally to another division of the company which uses the castings as a component in an end-product. If the castings sold externally and internally are of similar specification, and if the external market is 'reasonably perfect', once again the external market price will be the optimal transfer price internally. 'Reasonably perfect' markets require a number of competitors, active competition (i.e. not just a series of contractual, tied relationships at ad hoc bargained prices) and reasonably 'perfect information' (i.e. reliable information on prevailing market conditions). Frequently these conditions cannot be met, there is no stable, unequivocal 'market price', and so companies must consider alternative bases for transfer prices.

A further widely encountered case is where a large company is organised into divisions by function, so that there are one or more production divisions and one or more marketing/sales divisions. Here production divisions may sell exclusively to the internal marketing divisions, or at least sell mainly internally, simply 'flogging off' any periodic surplus capacity at the best bargaining price available. This periodic bargaining price will often have been struck on the basis of a short-term balance between demand and supply, and it may not itself be a realistic price to use in ongoing transfer pricing. Alternative information on a genuine market price may often be unavailable, so again one may need to turn to other methods to determine internal transfer prices between the divisions. Moreover, one may ask whether or not there is any real logic, or benefit, in having a divisional structure when some of the divisions are so internally dependent and inevitably are only artificial creations as 'autonomous profit centres'. The answer here appears to be that many top managements (and management consultants) feel that even artificial profit centres/divisions help to generate greater managerial motivation, to attract or hold better-calibre managers, and to encourage the constant search for efficiency, innovation, sales growth and diversification. The point is that the effect of any improvements or problems will show up more dramatically, and with more motivational impact, in profit-and-loss figures than when buried in aggregates or traditional cost or revenue information.

Economic theory teaches us that profit is maximised when volume reaches the point where (rising) marginal cost equals (falling) marginal revenue. Thus marginal cost is the key internal signal for corporate profit maximisation, and this is (theoretically) true whether the corporate business is integrated or divisionalised. It therefore follows that, ideally, each end-product division selling into external markets should be able to obtain internal supplies of goods and services at their marginal cost to the corporate entity. However, economic marginal cost changes with each volume change, and the exact value of marginal cost is often unknown – and accounting variable cost may be only a rough approximation. Moreover, transferring goods or services only at variable cost leaves the supplying division with no revenue to set against its fixed costs or to contribute to a profit; this is demotivating and goes against the spirit of divisional profit-centre accountability. Of course, where reasonably perfect external market prices exist for each division these can be used and will satisfy the theoretical requirements for optimisation, provided that savings of marketing and transport expense etc. are deducted from the external price used by the supplying division as its transfer price to the receiving division. The theoretical and practical complexities of transfer pricing are perhaps best explained in the classical work of Solomons (1965, 1983).

Given that, frequently, some divisions do not have genuine external markets or valid external market prices, and also that true marginal cost is frequently unknown or could only be used in a way that would demotivate the supplying divisions, let us consider the other methods used for setting transfer prices:

- **Cost-based prices**: many accountants seem to prefer to use full costs plus some small excess for profit contribution. For good discipline, budgeted or standard costs should be used in preference to actual outturn costs. However, full-cost-plus transfer pricing may not give the correct signals to the receiving division for its role in optimising corporate sales volume and profit. The alternative of variable-cost-plus transfer pricing is probably seldom used, if only because it undermines the supplying division's profit-centre status. Whatever cost-plus charging system is used, it runs the risk of including within its variable costs some element of central service costs and overheads which is actually a fixed cost in the overall context of the corporate group. Thus transferred variable costs could actually be significantly higher than the theoretical optimum marginal cost, resulting in suboptimisation.

- **Negotiated prices**: transfer prices can be negotiated between divisions to reach agreement or, failing agreement, they can be mediated by central management. There is a risk of transfer prices being determined more by the bargaining positions and skills of the negotiators than by rational economic information. Negotiators may introduce into the negotiating process estimates of true market price, various measures of costs and threats of turning to external suppliers. Of course, external suppliers in an imperfect market may be offering reduced 'penetration prices' which could later be raised if the company scrapped its internal supply and became dependent on the external suppliers. And where sensible agreement cannot be reached, so that mediation becomes involved or a central decision has to be imposed, the managerial autonomy and sense of personal responsibility of divisional managements are undermined.

- **Two-part-tariff prices**: this method charges divisions with receiving the budgeted or standard variable cost per unit of the intermediate good or service transferred, plus an annual 'block' charge (probably payable in monthly instalments) to cover approved fixed costs and a small margin for profit contribution. In effect, the block charge represents a form of contract whereby the receiving division undertakes responsibility for purchasing a given proportion of the supplying division's capacity in the year ahead. Central mediation will often be required. Supplying divisions will be free to seek external sales for surplus (i.e. uncontracted) capacity, but will be under moral pressure to supply additional units above contract if the receiving division encounters unexpectedly high (and profitable) sales opportunities. To discourage receiving divisions from the gamesmanship of understating future requirements (so as to minimise the block charge), the contract may impose extra charges for volumes above contract. For this method to work well there needs to be thorough advance planning of sales and of production resources as part of an integrated corporate budget, but arguably this is beneficial on balance and in spite of any interference with real or imagined divisional autonomy.

In conclusion, external market prices should be used if all divisions can sell all output in external markets. Aside from this rather limited case, and if viable profit centres and reasonable divisional autonomy are to be maintained, the two-part tariff could be the best method. But the latter involves extra effort and central mediation, so perhaps too often in the real world recourse is made to transfer pricing based on full-costs-plus or on negotiated estimates of fair market prices, even when either of these methods may well lead to suboptimal sales (and profit) performance for the divisions and for the corporate entity.

Before leaving this section, we should note one specialised situation where transfer pricing allegedly often departs from the above economic and operational criteria. This is in international trade, between divisions (typically organised locally as companies) supplying or receiving materials, components or finished products across national boundaries. Here, the overriding object may be to minimise total group taxation and to minimise the accumulation of profit-derived cash flows in countries with exchange controls preventing or delaying the outward transfer of profits or investment funds. Also, if transfer costs need in any way to come under regulation or audit for fairness in international trade, cost-based transfer prices will usually be the easiest to justify and document. This still begs the question of how far 'creative accounting' can alter systems of defining, measuring and charging costs within a plausible range of practices yet still carry conviction of reasonableness as well as 'objectivity' in justifying sometimes much higher transfer prices than would be considered optimal between divisions operating within a single country.

Transfer pricing for services

Corporate central services are not usually organised as separate 'divisions' and they need not even be designated as profit centres. They rarely trade externally, so seldom have the direct comparator of trading successfully at the current external market price. Even so, especially if they are large, costly or can easily be compared to external market prices and profits, they may be designated as divisions to enhance management motivation. Whatever the organisational name, these services generate costs which convention argues should be recharged to user divisions receiving benefit. However, if user divisions have no control or influence over service efficiency and no authority to seek alternative external suppliers there can be problems. Group management has an overall responsibility not to sanction transfer-pricing policies that provoke dysfunctional management behaviour by those operating at the divisional level. The case of Valleta Ltd illustrates this point.

Valleta Ltd has three operating divisions, X, Y and Z, and a transport division, T. Divisional managers are free to choose whether or not to use the company's own transport facilities, but T division has neither the marketing nor the administrative facilities to deal with customers outside the group.

T division has entered into an annual rental agreement with a hire company, under which ten vans are supplied to the division at a fixed rent of £2750 per week. If more vans are required, these can be hired at £50 per day. Other costs are expected to be £50 per vehicle per day up to ten vans and £150 per vehicle thereafter, plus fixed costs of £4560 per week. Divisions X, Y and Z have budgeted weekly requirements for vans during the next three months as follows:

	Monday	Tuesday	Wednesday	Thursday	Friday	Saturday	Total
X	5	5	5	4	4	3	26
Y	4	4	4	4	4	4	24
Z	1	3	3	1	1	1	10
	10	12	12	9	9	8	60

Actual requirements are often greater or less than budget. Divisions are charged £200 per vehicle per day at the end of each month for the vehicles which are actually used.

The management of Y division is considering whether to make an alternative arrangement outside the company, which would cost £3840 per week for a maximum of four vans per day, payable whether this number of vans was fully utilised or not. Should the management of Y be permitted to trade outside the company? What are the implications of the pricing policy adopted by T division? Clearly, a number of behavioural and economic consequences arise depending on the strategies adopted by each of the divisional management teams.

The first thing we can do is to construct T division's weekly budget in order to understand its charging policy:

		£
Fixed rent for 10 vans		2 750
Other fixed costs		4 560
		7 310
Four extra vans (Tuesday and Wednesday)		200
Other variable costs		
56 vans per week at £50		2 800
4 vans per week at £150		600
		10 910
Charges to X, Y and Z (60 @ £200)		12 000
Profit		1 090

It seems obvious that T division is charging the other three divisions on the basis of cost plus 10%. Questions need to be asked about this policy. Is this cost-plus policy in fact group policy or a policy established by the management of T division? As it stands, Y division would gain if it has the ability to accept the outside contract. The current charge to Y division by T division is £4800 (24 @ £200). The cost of external supply is £3840, a saving to Y division of £960 per week. However, whilst this may be advantageous to Y division it is not sensible from the overall group company point of view. There is, in fact, a net cost to the group because only certain of the costs currently incurred by T division can be avoided. Recall that T division has total weekly fixed costs of £7310. The cost to the group as a whole of T division accepting the outside contract can be calculated as follows:

	£
Savings by T division:	
Extra vans on Tuesday and Wednesday no longer needed	200
Other variable costs saved	
4 vans at £150	600
20 vans at £50	1 000
	1 800
Cost of external supply	3 840
Net additional cost to the group	2 040

This illustration highlights a not untypical situation where a divisional manager feels driven to obtain a particular service or product externally. Three options seem to arise from this illustration:

- Enquiry might establish that the prevailing market price for van use is well above the £3840 quoted to division Y by the outside supplier. This would suggest only a temporary cost-saving to division Y, which might have to pay more later; yet meanwhile the company's own fleet would have been cut back, with likely morale problems and fixed costs to be divided among a smaller number of vans. Therefore Y could be instructed not to contract with the outside supplier, although this would interfere with divisional autonomy,
- Alternatively, Y could be charged internally the same low price currently available from the external supplier, and T would then at least still receive some contribution above variable cost. However, this would create ill will with the other user divisions.
- Division T could be closed down, with all vans hired externally in future, on the presumption that T is uncompetitive. But first, however, the external price of £3840 needs validating as a sustainable ongoing price. Also, the fixed costs of £4560 charged to T need checking to discover how far these are controllable by T's manager and unavoidable to the group (e.g. allocation of rent for space in a large shared building) even if T division is closed down. These enquiries could lead to a conclusion that T should be retained but that fixed-cost charges should be reduced, with internal transfer prices reduced proportionally. This would alter T's status from a full profit centre to that of a controllable profit contribution centre, but, although departing from the classic divisional model of full costs and (notional) full autonomy, the result might actually be to increase the motivation and sense of accountability felt by the manager of T. The latter change could be combined with altering the transfer price into a two-part tariff, which would give user divisions a better understanding of the true cost of any incremental use of the van fleet.

With respect to the general problem of intercompany services, Solomons notes that most service departments are almost by definition, not market-oriented:

> There is, then, much to be said for a two-part tariff as a means of charging divisions for their services. The divisions should tend to demand services up to the point where the incremental value of the services equals the

incremental cost of providing them. Each division will bear its proportion of the service centre's fixed costs, but not in such a way as to affect its judgement as to how much of its services to take. Ideally, this should ensure that an optimal amount of services will be provided and used within the firm.

(Solomons 1983: 205)

Public-sector transfer pricing

The previous discussion has been set in a private business context. However, transfer pricing has become increasingly important in the public sector as well, not for its own sake, but as an inevitable consequence of the attempt to achieve greater efficiency in many parts of the public sector by introducing a business culture, subdividing work into operational profit centres, and therefore needing relevant costs for the inter-divisional supply of goods and (mainly) services. While the main objective may have been to encourage managerial efficiency by delegating focused responsibility and exacting tighter accountability, it appears that a secondary objective was to facilitate benchmarking and to test whether public services were viable for privatisation – or, if not, to consider contracting out those services if more economical.

The services given greatest attention for more accurate costing and setting fair (full-cost) transfer prices were initially those services where the work and skills were most closely comparable with the private sector, e.g. laundry, cleaning and catering in the NHS, and (building and maintenance) works services in local government. Interestingly, government has typically accepted the theoretical case (rejected in private business) that depreciation should be based on current costs rather than historical costs, while rejecting the theoretical case for variable-cost-plus or two-part-tariff transfer prices in favour of full-cost transfer prices often uplifted by target returns on assets employed (valued at net current replacement cost or value). Target rates of return have typically been at 5% or 6%; this may seem modest, but can be burdensome when based on realistic current values and when required to be included in internal price quotations sometimes judged in competition with private contractors completely free to offer prices on a marginal-cost-plus or market-penetration pricing basis.

Whereas in local authorities the use of transfer pricing has been mainly in the context of charging out central services at market prices or at full costs plus target ROCE, and intended to approximate to market prices, the NHS has used transfer prices more in the competing-divisions model, with the so-called internal market in healthcare delivery. Central NHS funding is allocated by demographic formula to local health authorities, who, de facto, act as purchasing divisions to buy or commission hospital and related services from local NHS Trusts, the latter acting as supply divisions. The geographically based trusts could also trade among themselves either to obtain extra specialised services or to take advantage of any transfer prices which may be below their own internal costs. In addition, some NHS funding was allocated direct to the budgets of many general practitioners (GPs) for the purpose of allowing them to 'shop around' among trusts (and private hospitals) so as to purchase the most cost-effective healthcare at the best prices on offer.

Its sponsors thought that the NHS internal market would lead to an active market in which NHS Trusts actively competed, both on price and quality (i.e. value for money), to attract and treat extra patients from other health authorities. In practice this was not widely achieved, at least outside the largest cities, where hospitals are reasonably close together. This may have been partly because of local loyalties; partly because of concern that long travel journeys have high ambulance costs and high social costs for patients (and for their families to visit hospitalised patients); and partly because the requirement to price services at full cost plus target ROCE was too inflexible to give much encouragement to relocate treatment from local hospitals. Thus the internal market in the NHS failed to develop into anything like a real or reasonable 'perfect' market in the commercial sense of developing active competition on the basis mainly of price or value for money. On the other hand, it did increase cost awareness, and intensify enquiry into the detail and nature of costs and the underlying resource use.

The Labour government has undertaken to make large cuts in the high management costs associated with the NHS internal market. However, the cost-cutting may not be easy or without loss of benefit, since a large proportion of the management costs have been spent on the new accounting and computerised management information systems needed for better cost control and resource management, regardless of whether or not any internal market continued to exist.

Conclusions

There is a deceptive simplicity in the application of financial performance measures such as profit or profitability in evaluating the performance of profit centres and divisions. As we have seen, this simplicity masks a number of real problems regarding the measures of profit and, for divisions, net investment. There is also the danger commented on by Johnson and Kaplan (1987) of an overemphasis on financial accounting based measures at the expense of more useful management information. However, such financially based measures are, unquestionably, widely used.

As organisations grow and their activities become more complex it may be more useful to decentralise decision-making as much as possible. One option is to create divisions which become, in effect, quasi-independent businesses. The managers of these divisions ought then to be evaluated on the basis of the effectiveness with which they deploy the assets in their charge. The test of effectiveness is not the absolute size of divisional income or profit.

The most frequently used test of effectiveness is ROI. However, as an overall measure of performance ROI has its problems. Some relate to the definition of the profit numerator and the capital denominator. Other problems can relate to the way in which divisional managers attempt to 'manipulate' accounting policies with respect to items such as depreciation, provisions and so on. The use of RI can overcome some, but not all, of these problems.

When divisions (or other forms of profit or investment centre, including in the public sector) trade internally it is necessary to establish internal (transfer) prices which, as fully as possible, both motivate managers and achieve optimum returns. If an external competitive market exists the optimal price would be the market price less any savings on internal trade. Failing near-perfect markets, theoretically optimal approaches such as marginal or opportunity cost would be best in terms of overall group returns. However, in practice these approaches are not widely accepted, so that it may be necessary to use techniques such as cost-plus or negotiated prices, or the two-part-tariff – but these alternatives may lead, from the overall group point of view, to suboptimal returns, and/or to some reduction of divisional autonomy and divisional management motivation and accountability.

Further reading

For the classic view of divisional performance and transfer pricing, see Solomons (1965, 1983). For alternative contemporary views, see Arnold and Turley (1996: ch. 18), Drury (1996: chs 26, 27; 1997: ch. 13). For the widest context of the topics, see Emmanuel *et al.* (1990). For an American view, see Horngren *et al.* (1994: chs 25, 26).

Questions and exercises

1 The manager of the Invicta Division of PFF plc has given you the following information related to budgeted operations for the coming year, 19X0:

Sales (100 000 units @ £50 each)	£5 000 000
Variable costs (@ £20 per unit)	2 000 000
Contribution (@ £30 per unit)	3 000 000
Fixed costs	1 200 000
Divisional profit	1 800 000
Divisional investment	£8 000 000

PFF has stated that the minimum desired return on investment (ROI) is 20%.
  (a) Determine Invicta's expected ROI and residual income (RI).
  (b) Invicta's management has just been approached by a new, potentially major, customer to sell an additional 10 000 units at £45 each. While unit variable costs are expected to remain unchanged, fixed costs would increase by £100 000. Additional investment of £500 000 would also be required to cover necessary extensions to productive capacity and additional working-capital requirements. If this order is accepted, what is the impact on Invicta's ROI and RI measures?
  (c) Of the total budgeted volume of 100 000 units, Invicta expects to sell 20 per cent to the Wessex Division of PFF plc. However, Invicta's management has been informed by Wessex that an external supplier is willing to supply them at £42 per unit. Unless Invicta agrees to match this price, Wessex will terminate its current agreement. If this happened Invicta would save £250 000 in fixed costs as a result of reducing its estimated production to 80 000 units.

If Invicta refuses to lower its internal transfer price to Wessex, evaluate what the impact would be for Invicta for Wessex and for PFF plc as a whole.

2 Carlton Plastics, a division of Harkness plc, has prepared the following profit plan for 19X1:

Sales	£2 500 000
Variable costs	1 250 000
Fixed costs	750 000
	2 000 000
Gross profit	500 000
Assets employed by the division	£2 000 000

The entire company has projected a rate of return of 15%. The cost of capital of the company is 12%.

The division is considering the following investment in new machinery for a new product line:

Cost of equipment	£100 000
Expected annual sales	£150 000
Variable costs	40% of sales
Annual fixed costs (including depreciation)	£70 000

Other divisions of Harkness plc have also submitted proposals for new projects that will provide a return on investment of approximately 15%.

(a) As a manager of Carlton, would you accept or reject the proposal?

(b) As a main board member of Harkness plc, would you want Carlton to accept or reject the proposal?

(c) What would you advise in order to avoid problems of this nature in the future?

3 Foolem plc is a large advertising and marketing promotions agency providing service outputs through television and other visual media. The agency has a cost of capital of 10%, but its target rate is a minimum 12%. Foolem has a divisional structure to incentivise management. Division A is biggest, sells only externally and is well known, with a good market share. It plans, organises and assembles promotional campaigns, and buys in specialist services both externally and from Division B. B is a technical support division with good skills and equipment for art and design, graphics and animations. B's sales are divided equally between Division A and a number of external customers. Both divisions sell externally on negotiated contract prices, as there are no list prices for their types of tailor-made services. Jobs are charged internally on the basis of the 'chargeable hours' of prime staff. Both divisions, especially B, are operating below the capacity of their space, equipment and management, allegedly because too often external contract quotations are too high priced.

Division C supplies usual central services but also has a Property Section controlling the firm's large London head office. Rent (proportional to average value of space allocated) is charged to A and B, like other central services, on the basis of block (fixed) charges negotiated on the annual budget.

£ million per annum (unless otherwise stated)	Division A	Division B	Division C Property	Other
External sales	200	40	–	–
Divisional variable costs	120	20	5	15
Depreciation transferred in (out)	5	10	(20)	5
Rent for space allocated per budget	20	40	–	10
Other central transfer service charges	10	10	–	–
Divisionally controlled fixed costs	20	10	–	20
Division-controlled capital employed	10	30	90	10
Chargeable hours of total sales time (000s)	200	200	–	–

The divisional variable costs of A include £40 million of internal sales from B, currently transferred at negotiated prices.

(a) Bearing in mind the company's circumstances, what alternative transfer prices might be considered for division B, and why?

(b) Show calculations for possible transfer prices for B based on (i) full-cost-plus, (ii) relevant-cost-plus and (iii) a two-part tariff.

(c) Briefly note any other issues, calculations or needs for further information.

4 From a management accounting perspective an organisation may determine its operational units to be classified as cost centres, profit centres or investment centres. Indeed, all three classifications might, as appropriate, be used by the one organisation. Explain each of these classifications and describe in which situation each is most appropriately adopted.

5 'The most suitable income figure for use in appraising the performance of divisional management, and also for use by divisional executives in guiding their decisions, is controllable residual income' (Solomons 1983: 83). Discuss.

6 (a) What are the main methods that are used to evaluate the performance of managers of divisionalised organisations?

(b) What are the main criteria that group management need to consider when establishing accounting control systems for evaluating the performance of their divisional colleagues?

7 Within any large and diversified organisation conflicts can arise between the aims of the group as a whole and the aspirations of individual divisional managers. What kinds of conflict might arise? How can the accounting function help resolve such conflicts?

8 Choose an organisation with which you are familiar and critically evaluate the accounting control mechanisms by which management's performance is evaluated. What, if any, recommendations would you make regarding the way in which management performance is evaluated?

9 'Accounting treatments of interdependence in multidivisional organisations must be as concerned with the behavioural effects of transfer prices as with their ability to secure possible solutions.' Discuss.

10 Set out in outline the questions you would investigate before giving advice to a large divisionalised enterprise as regards the basis or method(s) of transfer pricing which it should adopt.

17 Accounting and working-capital management

Objectives

In this chapter, we introduce the concept of working capital and explain why its effective management is important to the financial success of enterprises. We also look at the concept of the cash-conversion cycle, and see how the efficient management of this cycle involves careful attention being paid to the management of inventories, of debtors and of creditors. We discuss a number of techniques that can be employed for this purpose.

The meaning and importance of working capital

Working capital is the name given to the short-term resources (current assets) owned by an enterprise and the short-term funding (current liabilities) that it uses to support these resources. Typically, the value of the current assets of an enterprise will exceed the value of the current liabilities, leading to working-capital representing a net investment. As with any other investment, an enterprise should invest in working capital only insofar as such an investment will lead to positive returns greater than those that could be obtained from alternative forms of investment. Working capital can be analysed into four main constituent elements, as shown by the following equation:

$$\text{Working capital} = \text{Stock} + \text{Debtors} + \text{Cash} - \text{Creditors} \qquad (17.1)$$

Stock (inventories), debtors and cash are the normal components of current assets, and creditors represent current liabilities. Later in the chapter we will discuss the management of each of the different components of working capital in some detail, but before doing so we need to summarise briefly the reasons why enterprises choose to invest in the asset components of working capital and to use the liability component as a source of funding.

In the case of inventories we need to recognise that there are inventories of different types. One core distinction is that between production/sales-related inventories and service-related inventories. The former are directly related to the production/sales processes, while the latter are related to various overhead/support functions including items such as maintenance and office supplies. Production inventories include stocks of raw materials, work-in-progress and finished goods. If the enterprise did not invest in stocks of raw materials it would be entirely dependent on the timely delivery of materials from its suppliers to enable the production process to continue, although proponents of just-in-time (JIT) management would argue that this is exactly what an enterprise should seek to arrange with its suppliers. Work-in-progress represents inventories where the transformation to the final product has commenced but not yet been completed, and finished goods represent inventories which have been turned into the finished product but which have not yet been delivered to customers. They also include inventories purchased simply for resale, e.g. by a wholesaler or retailer. In all cases the investment in inventories is made to support the activities of the enterprise, whether they be production (e.g. raw materials), selling (finished goods) or support activities (e.g. maintenance stocks). The level of the inventory held in each case needs to be sufficient to ensure that the activity in question generates the necessary contribution to the overall profitability of the enterprise, but no more than that.

In the main, debtors are the result of an enterprise selling on credit terms to customers who have not, as yet, paid the amounts that they owe the enterprise as a result of these sales. However, they may also result from other forms of transactions such as the granting of short-term loans. Enterprises generally offer credit terms to their customers to secure sales that they might not otherwise have obtained. The extent and the terms of the credit that they offer to customers are a result of market-positioning decisions and will frequently be influenced by the customary practice of the industrial/commercial sector in which the enterprise operates. The balance to be struck here is one between the additional profits generated by extra sales and the costs of financing the resultant investment in debtors, and, of course, the potential cost of default by customers.

Enterprises need ready access to cash to enable them to find their day-to-day payment obligations and to deal with unexpected contingencies. However, maintaining liquid cash resources (including current bank accounts) means that these resources are not being used for alternative investments and are not generating the returns associated with these alternative investments. Such investments include not only productive investments but financial investments such as deposit accounts. Here, the balance that has to be struck is between the benefits of the liquidity, and flexibility, afforded by the holding of cash against the associated costs, in particular the opportunity costs of the foregone returns from alternative investments.

Creditors are the obverse of debtors. They represent the short-term funding that the enterprise has obtained. A major element here is likely to be the amounts owed to suppliers for purchases that the enterprise has made on credit terms, although creditors may also include short-term finance from lenders (e.g. bank overdrafts) and monies due to state agencies such as the Inland Revenue (for PAYE and national insurance) and HM Customs & Excise (for VAT). There may be a short period of time during which this credit appears costless, but there are often hidden costs, perhaps to do with the overall relationships with suppliers, which really need to be taken into account. Management needs to balance the costs of short-term funding, both apparent and hidden, against those of other types of funding and the returns generated from the investments made with the funds.

Based on the above summary, the core principles on which the management of working capital should be based are easily stated:

- Enterprises should invest in current assets so long as the return from such investment exceeds the cost of the capital used to fund such investments.
- Enterprises should make use of short-term funding so long as it has a lower cost than other sources of funding and can be used to make profitable investments after allowing for the cost of the funding.

However, the implementation of these principles in practice is normally rather more problematic. Most enterprises have well-defined procedures for the analysis and monitoring of investment in large-scale capital projects. These may include the use of discounted cash-flow analysis, or other techniques such as the payback method, for investment appraisal and will typically require a clear specification of the benefit to the enterprise of undertaking the investment. Clearly specified levels of authorisation, frequently involving senior management, will normally be required before an enterprise commits itself to undertaking an investment. This tends not to be the case with working capital. Even accepting that all organisations have internal control systems designed to prevent unauthorised expenditures, the same level of attention is not normally paid to investments in working capital. In part, this is because of the amounts involved in individual working-capital investments. While the overall investment in inventories or debtors may be significant, such investments are the outcome of many different individual decisions and transactions, each of which may in its own right appear to be relatively immaterial to the finances of the enterprise. Similarly, many different individuals in many different functions and at many different levels of seniority are likely to be involved in these decisions and transactions. The interests of all these individuals are likely to differ, and few of them will view working capital as an investment. Typically, they will be more concerned with operating within their expenditure and revenue budgets and with discharging their own responsibilities satisfactorily. Sales staff will focus on generating sales without regard to the costs of financing the resultant debtors; maintenance staff will want to ensure that they have a stock of spare parts sufficient to deal with any breakdowns; production staff will want to ensure that they have a sufficient stock of raw materials. There is great pressure to have more rather than less, and this can easily result in the investment in working capital becoming out of control, particularly in enterprises where individual budget holders are not charged with the cost of their department's investment in working capital. All too often, such costs are hidden costs and departmental managers have no incentive either to recognise or to minimise them.

To summarise, decisions which impact on the effectiveness of an enterprise's working-capital management are taken all the time, and at all levels of the organisation, by staff and managers who, all too often, are not aware of the financial impact of their decisions and are not held accountable for this impact.

The amount of an enterprise's investment in working capital will vary from enterprise to enterprise and from economic sector to economic sector. However, in most sectors/enterprises it will typically be of the order of 25–40% of net assets. Thus it represents a major investment and one which needs careful management attention, but, for the reasons described above, it does not always receive this attention – frequently to the ultimate cost of the enterprise. Management needs to determine clearly defined policies for the management of working capital and to ensure that all staff appreciate the importance of these policies for the financial well-being of the enterprise as part of their day-to-day decision taking. It needs to develop strategies for the implementation of these policies and mechanisms for the monitoring of this implementation. These policies need to be an integral part of their overall financing and financial-management strategies. In formulating these policies and strategies, regard needs to be had to the following:

■ The optimisation of investment in working capital involves issues of both efficiency and scale. For any given level of efficiency in the management of working capital, a change in the scale of activities of the enterprise will lead to a change in the quantum of the appropriate investment. If the level of business activity increases, then if there is no change in the level of efficiency the amount of investment will need to increase. Correspondingly, if the level of efficiency of working-capital management changes, then for any given level of business activity the investment in working capital will also change. In planning its working-capital management and the associated level of investment, management needs to consider both efficiency and level of activity. All too often, companies plan expansion without considering the consequences for their investment in working capital. In extreme cases, this can result in 'overtrading' (having insufficient funding to support the working-capital investment implicit in the higher level of activity), perhaps leading to insolvency.

■ The speed with which levels of investment in working capital can change with improvements or deteriorations in its management needs to be recognised. Working capital comprises short-term assets and liabilities. As such, its investment cycle is a short one and improvements in management will have a rapid impact. Correspondingly, so will deteriorations. The planning of working-capital management should involve the setting of performance targets, which are regularly monitored to detect any deterioration at an early stage so that corrective action can be taken and achievement of the benefits of improvements identified.

Working-capital management is an all too often neglected facet of financial management, but one which can have a major part to play in the overall financial viability and success of an enterprise. Enterprises need to develop and implement clearly defined working-capital management policies. In the remainder of this chapter we discuss the factors that need to be taken into account by management in identifying such strategies for the different components of working capital.

The flow of working capital

Effective working-capital management needs to reflect its dynamic nature and its individual components. The composition of working capital as a whole, and of its component elements, is constantly changing. This can be illustrated by considering the individual asset and liability categories:

■ **Inventories:** individual items of raw materials are purchased as the first step in the manufacture and ultimate sale of products. As these are used in the transformation process, they are converted first into work in progress and then into finished goods. To enable the transformation process to continue, these raw materials have to be replaced by fresh ones. Similarly, as the stock of finished goods is reduced by sales to customers it is constantly being replenished by the transformation of new raw materials or the purchase of new finished goods. The individual components of inventory are continually being diminished and replenished

- **Debtors:** individual debtors arise from sales on credit terms. However, they only exist as assets until the customer settles the debt. At this point they disappear and are replaced by another element of working capital – cash. In the meantime it is likely that further credit sales will have been made, resulting in the creation of new debtors.

- **Creditors:** individual creditors are created by individual purchases on credit terms or by other funding transactions. However, they remain as liabilities only until they are settled, resulting in a change to another component of working capital – cash. In the meantime it is likely that other credit purchase/funding transactions will have taken place, resulting in the creation of new creditors.

- **Cash:** cash and bank balances are constantly changing as a result of all the enterprise's payments and receipts. Many of these are associated with changes in other components of working capital (most notably debtors and creditors), although they are also associated with other events as well (e.g. new long-term funding, purchase of fixed assets, etc.)

The challenge facing management is that of controlling all the constantly changing individual items comprising working capital and thereby controlling working capital as a whole. There is a continual circulation of current assets through the business, and it is useful to think of this circulation in terms of the business cycle of the enterprise. This business cycle commences with the purchase of resource inputs, whether on cash or credit terms, and continues via the various transformation processes through the sale of the finished goods or services to the ultimate receipt of cash from the customer. This business cycle can be analysed into a number of component elements relating to the movements in the various elements of working capital. This is illustrated in Figure 17.1.

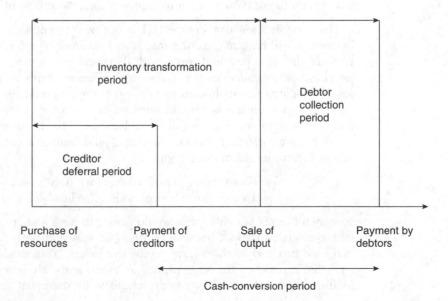

Figure 17.1
The working-capital cycle.

The cycle illustrated in Figure 17.1 demonstrates the linkages between the elements of working capital in the overall business cycle of the enterprise. The starting point is the purchase of the input resources, which is the commencement of two of the elements of the cycle (the inventory transformation period and the creditor deferral period). These elements of the cycle are:

- **Inventory transformation period:** this is the period of time from the purchase of the input resources (e.g. raw materials), through the transformation process (manufacturing and holding of finished product), to the point where the finished product is sold to the customer. This period will vary from sector to sector: it could be very short, particularly where the age of materials is an important factor (e.g. a restaurant which promotes itself on using only fresh produce, where the inventory conversion period might be less than twenty-four hours for much of the inventory); in the construction industry it might be several years before a construction project is completed. The end of the inventory transformation period (the sale of the finished goods) represents the commencement of the next element of the cycle.
- **Debtor collection period:** this is the period of time between the point of sale and the receipt of cash from the customer. In the case of cash sales this period will be effectively zero. In the case of credit sales it can be substantially longer, depending, at least in part, on the customary terms of trade in this particular industrial sector.
- **Creditor deferral period:** this is the period of time between the purchase of the resource inputs and the payment to the supplier. In the case of cash purchases it is effectively zero. In the case of credit purchases it may represent a substantial period of time. In the UK companies often take two to three months, or more, to pay their suppliers. The end of creditor deferral period, with the outflow of cash to the supplier, is the commencement of the final element of the working-capital cycle, the cash-conversion period. This represents the period of time between the outflow of cash to suppliers and the inflow of cash from customers.

The analysis shown in Figure 17.1 is obviously somewhat idealised. In real life, businesses will have many different sorts of inventory, with different transformation periods, different payment terms with its suppliers (ranging from cash purchase to purchase on extended credit terms) and different terms of sales to its customers (again ranging from cash sales to sales on deferred credit terms). However, it does focus attention on the key issues involved in managing working capital as a whole, and on the importance of the different elements of the cycle, thereby giving management a start towards effective working-capital management. An equation can be derived from the diagram in Figure 17.1:

$$\text{Cash-conversion period} = \text{Inventory transformation period} \\ + \text{Debtor collection period} - \text{Creditor deferral period} \qquad (17.2)$$

In general terms, an enterprise would prefer to have a shorter rather than a longer cash-conversion period, because by doing so it would be reducing the time that it had cash invested in short-term productive assets. This would enable it to use the cash that is freed up for other profitable investments. However, as we shall see later in the chapter, it would be overly simplistic to state that a core objective of the management of working capital must be the reduction of the cash-conversion period. While this must be an important objective, it must be tempered by the objectives relating to the reasons why inventory is held at all, why credit terms are given to customers and why credit is taken from suppliers. Effective working-capital management requires a conflation of these objectives with that of reducing, wherever possible, the cash-conversion period so as to maximise the overall profitability of the enterprise. In many ways, the essence of working-capital management is that of questioning why things happen – why do we hold the stocks we do or give/receive credit to business partners in the way we do? – and ensuring that the answers to these questions reflect the overall objectives of the enterprise.

Earlier we stated that an enterprise's working-capital requirements were a function of two things: – the effectiveness with which it managed its working capital and the scale of its operations. We can use equation (17.2) above to demonstrate this. Consider a business with the following characteristics:

- current annual sales of £288 000 with a gross margin of 50% (i.e. cost of sales of £144 000 per annum);
- an inventory transformation period of three months;
- a debtor collection period of 2.25 months;
- a creditor deferral period of 1.5 months.

The current working-capital requirements of such a business can be calculated as follows:

		£
Inventory	(£144 000 × 3)/12	36 000
Debtors	(£288 000 × 2.25)/12	54 000
Creditors	(£144 000 × 1.5)/12	(18 000)
		72 000

The impact of scale can be examined first. If the volume of activity were to increase by 10%, with no change in any of the other parameters, the working-capital requirements could be restated as:

		£
Inventory	(£144 000 × 1.1 × 3)/12	39 600
Debtors	(£288 000 × 1.1 × 2.25)/12	59 400
Creditors	(£144 000 × 1.1 × 1.5)/12	(19 800)
		79 200

Thus the overall working-capital requirement has risen by £7,200 (i.e. 10% of the original £72 000). The message is a clear and simple one. If the scale of the business (sales volume) increases and everything else remains the same (profit margins and working-capital conversion periods) a business will have to be able to finance an increase in working capital if it is to survive, and the proportion of this increase will be exactly the same as the proportion of the increase in business activity. Unfortunately, all too many businesses focus on growth – however it is measured (increases in sales revenue, increases in market share, etc.) – without recognising that such growth has a consequence for the amount of capital they require. This is particularly true of smaller businesses, which when organising their finances tend to concentrate on how the bigger individual items such as plant and machinery are to be financed. They tend to ignore the requirement to provide increasing amounts of finance for working capital as they expand, and may even grow beyond their ability to finance such increases. Technically, such growth beyond the ability to finance working-capital requirements is called 'over-trading', and it can, in extreme circumstances, lead to an inability to pay creditors and result in insolvency. Many are the profitable and growing businesses which are forced into insolvency because they did not plan and manage their working-capital requirements. One way out of this problem is to seek and obtain additional sources of finance. Another way is to improve, wherever possible given the prevailing terms of trade, the day-to-day management of working capital. This can also be illustrated using the above example.

We will continue to assume a sales growth of 10%, but in addition to this we will also now assume that the inventory conversion period is reduced by one week, that the debtor collection period is similarly reduced and that the creditor deferral period is increased by one week. In these circumstances the working-capital requirement becomes:

		£
Inventory	(£144 000 × 1.1 × 2.75)/12	36,300
Debtors	(£288 000 × 1.1 × 2)/12	52,800
Creditors	(£144 000 × 1.1 × 1.75)/12	(23,100)
		66 000

In this case the business has grown by 10% but, despite this, the amount it requires to invest in working capital has actually declined (from £72 000 to £66 000) because of the more effective working-capital management. This is obviously a constructed example, but it does illustrate the impact that attention to the management of working capital can have on a business's finances. Growth of 10% without any change in the effectiveness of working-capital management requires a commensurate growth in the financing of working capital, i.e. £7,200 (10%). It may be possible to achieve the same level of growth and at the same time reduce the investment in working capital by improving the effectiveness of working-capital management. The extent to which this is in fact possible will, of course, depend not just on management actions but also on the commercial circumstances in which management finds itself operating. However, it does suggest a focus for management's attention.

Inventory management

Earlier in this chapter we suggested that a prime motivation for a business to hold inventories was to enable it to service the needs of its production/transformation/sales processes, and thereby to meet the needs of its customers and to generate profit from so doing. If asked, most managers will advance this as the reason why they do in fact hold inventories. However, if the question is pursued further a number of different motives for holding inventory will start to emerge. The principal of these are:

■ **Transactions motive:** as described above, this relates to the holding of inventories in order to meet anticipated production/sales and service delivery requirements. It is, or should be, based on budgeted levels of production/sales and service delivery. However, all too often these requirements may not be clearly specified or managers may not trust the budget. This leads to a second motive for holding inventory.

■ **Precautionary motive:** here the managers involved do not want to be 'caught short'. They deliberately hold more inventory than the budgets and forecasts indicate that they need so that they can cope with any underestimates of demand that may have been made. Their aim is to avoid any loss of production/sales by ensuring that they have a margin of safety. The problem that this can, of course, cause is that different managers may have different estimates of the level of safety that they require and that these may lead, not just to an enterprise holding excessive stocks, but to it holding an uncoordinated pattern of stocks, leading to ineffectiveness. The precautionary motive is a perfectly reasonable motive for an enterprise to hold stocks beyond the level it forecasts that it needs. However, this needs to be done in a co-ordinated fashion.

■ **Speculative motive**: here the managers involved are speculating that there will be increases in the future prices of the items of stock, and that by buying now and holding in stock they will be able to save money, in terms of purchase prices. Again, this is a perfectly rational motive for holding stocks, provided that the costs of holding such stocks and any future price savings are taken into account. Unfortunately, all too often this is not the case, as the managers involved are not charged with the costs associated with holding the larger amount of stock.

■ **Budgetary motive**: this is a rather more difficult issue and relates to the issues discussed in Chapter 14 regarding the way in which an organisation implements its budgetary process. It is perhaps at its most pointed in the public sector, although it also applies to the private sector. A typical situation is one where a manager has a given expenditure budget for a financial period (year) to support a particular service/activity and, based on past experience, knows that if the budget is underspent it is likely that it will be reduced next year. Thus, ceteris paribus, the manager has an incentive to spend to the limit of the budget. One way that this can be done is to purchase more inventory (particularly if the budget is based on simple expenditure rather than a cost which reflects changes in inventory levels). Many managers feel that they gain in two ways by doing this. First, their expenditure is up to budget and this may help them in negotiating next year's budget. Second, the inventory that they have acquired will be available to support service provision next year and thereby provide them with something of a buffer against problems that they may encounter.

The amount of inventories that enterprises hold will depend in part on the nature of their activities (bakers will tend to hold less inventory than manufacturing companies) and in part on the scale of their activities (larger companies will tend to hold more inventory than smaller companies). It will also depend in part on the balance between the various motives for holding inventories outlined above, and in part on the attention that is devoted by management to inventory levels and the effectiveness of the policies that it implements for such management. In all cases the actual amount of inventory held will be the result of many different factors and of trade-offs between these factors. Ultimately, the determination of appropriate policies for the management of inventories requires some form of cost–benefit analysis (whether it be more or less sophisticated). Unfortunately, all too often the benefits (real or potential) are emphasised and the costs de-emphasised. We have already discussed some of the benefits of holding inventories, and these can be summarised as follows:

- Holding inventory reduces the uncertainty of operations. It enables a business to cope with unexpected demands either from customers (thereby avoiding the loss of potential sales) or from the production process itself.
- There is a possibility of obtaining discounts from suppliers for purchasing in bulk, thereby reducing the cost of materials.
- There is a possibility of purchasing in advance of anticipated price rises, thereby keeping costs lower than they might otherwise have been.
- Holding large levels of inventory may facilitate large production runs, thereby reducing the impact of set-up costs.

However, these benefits have costs associated with them, and not only may these costs be very significant, they may not be charged against the budgets of those who make the decisions regarding the levels of inventory that are to be held. Such costs are normally considered under two headings, the costs of acquiring the inventory and the costs of holding the inventory.

Frequently, these costs will be charged against the budgets of other managers, who may have little or no influence on stock-holding/purchasing decisions. In many ways, this problem is similar to that discussed in Chapter 15 regarding the use of standard costing and variance analysis and which managers should be held accountable for which variances. We can illustrate this by reviewing the costs associated with the acquisition and holding of inventories in a manufacturing company and considering in which managers' budgets these costs might actually accrue. Table 17.1 does this.

As can be seen from the table, many of the costs associated with the ordering and stockholding decisions of a particular department/function may never in fact be charged to that department/function. They will be borne by the budgets of other departments. However, as regards the enterprise as a whole, acquisition costs and holding costs will tend to move in different directions. Low levels of inventory imply that the enterprise will make frequent orders and, conversely, high levels of inven-

Table 17.1   Costs associated with holding inventories

Type of cost	Possibly charged to
Acquisition costs:	
Ordering costs	Purchasing-department budget
Handling costs	Stores budget
Holding costs:	
Opportunity costs of financing the inventories	General-finance budget
Obsolescence and deterioration	Stores budget
Insurance	General-finance budget
Labour and equipment costs	Stores budget
Administration costs	Stores budget

Source: adapted, with permission, from Coller *et al.* (1988)

tory imply that it will make fewer orders. Thus there is a trade-off to be made between the two types of costs. This leads to a concept called the economic order quantity (EOQ), which is that basis of inventory acquisition which minimises the combination of acquisition and holding costs. Assuming that the quantum of both these types of cost can be identified, that they are relatively constant, that there is no buffer stock (i.e. there is no defined minimum stock level above zero) and that there are no significant seasonal variations in the pattern of trade, there is a well-defined model for minimising these costs and determining the EOQ for any type of inventory. The notation for this model is:

C = carrying cost per unit of inventory;
S = sales volume;
O = cost of processing a purchase order;
Q = number of units of inventory per purchase order.

Given these assumptions, the total carrying cost of inventory is Average inventory level (in units) × Carrying cost per unit, or:

$$\frac{Q}{2} \times C \tag{17.3}$$

The total ordering cost is Sales volume (in units) ÷ Number of units per order × Cost per order, or

$$\frac{S}{Q} \times O \tag{17.4}$$

Therefore, summing equations (17.3) and (17.4), the total cost (of carrying and ordering) inventory is:

$$\text{Total cost} = ((Q/2) \times C) + (S/Q) \times O)) \tag{17.5}$$

If this equation is reorganised and differentiated with respect to Q, and the derivative set to 0, the value of Q which minimises the total inventory costs (the EOQ) is obtained, and this can be stated as:

$$\text{EOQ} = \sqrt{(2 \times S \times O)/C} \tag{17.6}$$

This EOQ model leads, as can be seen, to a classic square-root formula and is useful insofar as it prompts management to focus on important issues associated with inventory management. However, its practical utility is limited by the assumptions that it makes (e.g. as regards the constancy of ordering and holding costs and the pattern of inventory usage) and the fact that the necessary information may not be available. It is also a linear model. Operational researchers have developed numerous other models for inventory management which may prove more appropriate in particular cases. Moore (1976) provides a useful review of these. Despite this, the value of requiring management to ask themselves the right questions, even if they find them difficult to answer, should not be underestimated. It would also be impractical to expect management to focus to the same extent on all the different elements of inventory. A medium-sized manufacturing enterprise may hold several thousand different lines of inventory. To expect it to monitor and manage all these different lines of inventory to the same degree of detail would almost certainly be a waste of management time. Instead, management needs to concentrate on those areas of inventory where it can have the most impact on the overall financial performance of the enterprise.

One commonly used approach for this is that of 'usage value' combined with the Pareto relationship. Usage value is defined as follows:

$$\text{Usage value} = \text{Usage (in units)} \times \text{Cost (per unit)} \qquad (17.7)$$

Thus, usage value focuses directly on the amount of money that an enterprise is spending on the consumption of any given line of stock as part of its commercial activities. The Pareto relationship is a common pattern of the balance between the number of individual stock lines and their relative usage values. Table 17.2 illustrates a typical set of such relationships.

While the relationships portrayed in Table 17.2 might not apply in precise detail to the usage values in every individual enterprise, the message is a clear one. Something like 10% of the individual lines of stock will account for in the region of 60% of the usage value (the category A items). Careful attention to the management of these items is likely to be very rewarding. Conversely, the majority of the individual lines of stock (60%) will probably account for a rather small proportion of usage value (10%), and detailed management attention is likely to be correspondingly less rewarding. The use of the principles of the Pareto relationship will help management to focus its efforts where they are likely to be of most value.

In planning its inventory management policies an enterprise needs to have regard to issues other than simply identifying the EOQ. It also needs to have regard to other motives in relation to holding inventories. Of particular importance is the need to avoid running out of stock (avoiding a stock-out). Stock-outs fall into two main categories. One category is those that are the result of poor management planning and the second is those that result from the failure to purchase raw materials (finished goods in the case of wholesalers/retailers) in time to meet anticipated levels of activity. Good management should easily prevent stock-outs of this type, using three key concepts:

- **Usage rate**: this is simply the number of units of inventory required in any given period to meet production/sales requirements. This is often expressed as the number of units per day or per week.
- **Lead time**: this is the period of time needed to acquire new stocks from suppliers. It is likely to vary significantly from industry to industry, and perhaps from supplier to supplier. In some commercial sectors it could be as little as a few hours, while in other sectors such as the perfumery industry it could be as much as twelve months.

Table 17.2 The Pareto relationship

Stock category	Proportion of total usage value	Proportion of number of stock lines
A	60%	10%
B	30%	30%
C	10%	60%

- **Re-order level**: this is a function of the usage rate and the lead time, and is the stock level at which it is necessary to place a fresh purchase order so as to have new stock arriving before existing stocks are exhausted. For example, if a particular item of inventory has a usage rate of 1000 units per week and a lead time of two weeks, then it will be necessary to place a fresh purchase order whenever inventory levels decline to 2000 units. This should ensure that just as the existing stock (reorder level) of 2000 units is exhausted (i.e. after two weeks), the new supplies of inventory arrive (again after two weeks).

The strategy described is likely to be somewhat risky. However well management understands its business, and however well it budgets and plans it is doing so in a climate of uncertainty. This means that there is a danger that the plans and budgets may not reflect what actually happens. There may be a higher level of activity (usage) than anticipated or it may take longer to acquire the fresh inventories than management thought. These uncertainties need to be taken into account in determining inventory-management policies because of the financial consequences of potential stock-outs. The danger against which they need to guard is, in the case of finished goods stocks, that they may not have enough to meet customer demands, thereby losing sales and profit, and, in the case of raw materials stocks, that production will have to cease, leading to production problems and inefficiencies, and perhaps to lost sales. An approach commonly adopted to prevent this happening is the holding of buffer or safety stocks. These are stocks above those specifically required to meet planned activity levels and intended to provide a margin of safety against uncertainties.

There are a number of sophisticated techniques, largely derived from operational research, which are intended to help management decide on appropriate levels of safety stock and which are beyond the scope of this book. In the main, these techniques ask management to determine the financial costs of a stock-out and then use probability-based approaches to balance these against the financial costs of holding different levels of safety stock. While a number of organisations, particularly larger ones, do employ such techniques, many organisations adopt rather more pragmatic approaches. These approaches tend to be based on rather subjective assessments of the variability of the enterprise's pattern of trade and the nature of its relationships with its suppliers. However, at the core remain the key concepts of usage rates and lead-times.

In recent years much management literature has focused on the concept of JIT management. This is a management philosophy which requires that inventory should be available 'just in time' to meet the purpose for which it is required. It is a philosophy which seeks to minimise inventory levels, and therefore the costs and risks of holding inventories. It is frequently presented as an approach which was developed by successful Japanese companies, accounting, at least in part, for the competitive advantages that they appear to have enjoyed in recent years. To some extent, this is true and reflects the lack of attention that many UK companies paid to working-capital management up until the 1970s and 1980s, although there have been notable exceptions. The implementation of JIT requires that an enterprise establish very close relationships with its suppliers, involving rapid and effective communication of production planning and scheduling information. The motor-vehicle industry is often cited as an example of this: a car may start its way down the production line before its seats have been made, let alone delivered to the car manufacturer. At the time the seats need to be fitted, their supplier should have completed their manufacture and delivered them to the appropriate location. This is a rather extreme example, but one which encapsulates the core principles of JIT. The principal of these are:

- **reliability**: the manufacturer must be able to rely on supplies being delivered at the right time, to the right place, and at the right quality;
- **sharing of information**: the supplier must know what is expected at all times;
- **flexibility**: both the enterprise and its supplier must be able to respond to changes in the pattern of demand.

Suppliers in this context may be external or internal. The example of the motor industry used an external supplier. However, exactly the same principles apply to internal suppliers. Thus JIT principles apply both within and across organisations. In many ways, the successful implementation of JIT principles involves a blurring of organisational boundaries. In the case of external suppliers it depends on establishing and maintaining relationships between separate enterprises which are similar to those which should exist between units within the same enterprise. The financial benefits that can be obtained from the implementation of JIT principles are significant. However, such implementation carries a risk – that the 'partner' enterprise may fail to deliver. Thus adopting a JIT philosophy is not something which should be done lightly. It requires a very careful appraisal of the potential advantages and the capacity of the potential partner to meet the demands placed on it. (For a more detailed explanation of JIT, see Bailes and Kleinsorge 1992.)

Managing debtors

In broad terms, enterprises sell on credit to their customers, so as to generate higher levels of sales than they would otherwise have achieved and thereby increase their overall profitability. In deciding to do this, they need to balance the profit expected from the additional sales against the costs associated with having debtors. The principal of these costs are likely to be those of financing the investment in debtors (this will be a function of the anticipated level of debtors and the enterprise's cost of capital) and those associated with default by customers (i.e. uncollectable debts). Before offering credit to its customers an enterprise needs to be assured that this balance will be in its favour. Having said this, it needs to be recognised that the granting of credit to customers is a very pervasive feature of commercial activity in the UK and elsewhere. Accordingly, for most companies the question is not one of whether or not to offer credit to their customers; rather, it is one of how to maximise the benefits to be derived and minimise the costs associated with offering credit. To achieve this and thereby ensure the effective management of its debtors an enterprise needs to have a clearly defined credit policy, and this policy needs to cover a number of key aspects of debtor management.

The general terms on which it is prepared to grant credit

These terms will be dictated in part by the overall financial-management strategies of the enterprise and its ability to finance debtors without harming its overall financial soundness. It needs to plan the amount of debtors in the light of the other demands on its long- and short-term capital funding resources. However, decisions on this cannot be taken purely from an internal financial-management perspective. They also need to reflect the competitive environment within which the enterprise operates, and in particular the terms of credit that are being offered by its competitors. The terms of credit that an enterprise offers its customers are the interface between its financial management and its marketing management as part of its overall strategic decision taking process. As such they need to have regard to:

- **Linkages between credit terms and pricing policies**: an enterprise may be able to charge its customers higher prices than its competitors if it offers reasonably generous credit terms. Alternatively, it might decide to offer very restrictive credit terms but to price its products/services very competitively. Thus credit terms are an important part of the market positioning of an enterprise.

- **Custom and practice in the industrial/commercial sector**: as part of this market positioning an enterprise must have regard to what is normal practice within the sector in which it operates, and this can vary considerably. In this respect, regard needs to be had not just to the formal position but also to what actually happens. It is not at all uncommon for the formal (contractual) terms of credit to be thirty days after invoice date but for the actual period of credit being taken by customers to be nearer sixty or seventy days.

- **Cash-settlement discounts**: it is common practice in a number of sectors to offer customers a discount for prompt settlement. Thus, for example, an enterprise might offer customers thirty days' credit (from invoice date) but also offer a discount if the invoice is settled within seven days. Such a discount might be of the order of 2.5% of the invoice value. Again, this is part of the market positioning of the enterprise as, effectively, such discounts offer a price advantage to those customers who are able to settle their bills promptly. The financial consequences for the enterprise itself also need to be analysed. Suppose that a company has annual credit sales of £1 560 000 and that its average level of debtors is nine week's sales, despite the fact that its terms of trade are that customers are allowed only four weeks' credit. The company has to borrow money to finance the investment in debtors at an annual interest rate of 12% and is considering introducing a cash-settlement discount for customers who settle their invoices within seven days. It has estimated that this will lead to one-third of the customers taking advantage of the cash-settlement discount. Table 17.3 illustrates the likely financial impact of offering the cash settlement discount. In this case, there would appear not to be any benefit to the company in offering the cash-settlement discount – in fact there would be a net cost of £3400. In such circumstances the company would probably be better advised to concentrate on using other measures, such as tighter credit control, to reduce its average debtor collection period of nine weeks. However, as offering a cash-settlement discount is effectively offering a price reduction to those customers who settle their invoices promptly, it is possible that offering such a discount might lead to increased sales. If we assume that the company's gross profit margin is 25%, then if offering the discount led to an increase in sales (paid for within the discount period) of more than £13 600 (£3400/0.25), offering the discount would be financially advantageous.

Table 17.3 Appraisal of cash-settlement discount decision

Current average debtors (£1 560 000 × 9 ÷ 52)	£270 000
Forecast average debtors after offering the cash-settlement discount (£1 560 000 × 6 ÷ 52) + (1 560 000 ÷ (3 × 52))	190 000
Forecast reduction in debtors	80 000
Forecast saving in finance costs (£80 000 × 12%)	9 600
Cost of settlement discount (£1 560 000 × 0.025 ÷ 13)	13 000
Net cost of settlement discount (£13 000 – £10 800)	3 400

- **The likely/acceptable level of bad debts** and the potential impact of bad debts on the financial soundness of the enterprise: this will be a major element in determining the extent of the enhanced profitability to be obtained from offering credit terms and will be the result of the combination of a number of factors. Some sectors traditionally have a higher level of bad debts than others; enterprises with a large number of small debtors (e.g. departmental stores) are less at risk of financial failure resulting from a bad debt than those with a small number of high-value debtors (e.g. the construction industry); and the profit margins associated with credit sales.

Credit rating procedures

Having once determined its basic terms of credit, an enterprise then needs to install procedures aimed at identifying those potential credit customers to whom it is in fact prepared to offer credit. In essence, this involves making an assessment of the likelihood of the potential customer defaulting on the debt. Like many other aspects of management, this involves forecasting the future using information about the past and, as such, is inevitably risky. However, there is a wide range of potential sources of information that can, and should, be used in this context. These include:

- **Bank references**: enterprises should ask potential customers to supply a banker's reference. In practice, no bank is going to guarantee that a customer will settle its accounts. However, information about the present and the past state of its finances and the period of time it has been with its bankers can be informative in making a credit-rating assessment.
- **Company accounts**: reference should be made to the accounts of the potential customer for recent years. Analysis of these can help to detect trends in financial position and to appraise the position at the last balance-sheet date.
- **Trade references**: potential credit customers should be asked to supply references from suppliers who already supply them on credit terms. Again, these references should indicate the length of the trading relationship and how satisfactory the potential customer has been in adhering to credit terms.
- **Credit agencies**: these deal with both corporate organisations and individuals, and reference to them is virtually standard practice when dealing with consumer credit applications.

Use can also be made of 'informed trade gossip' and articles in trade journals and the wider press. However, at the end of the day a judgement has to be made. Is the customer to be granted credit, and, if so, how much and on what precise terms? The responsibility for such a decision will normally rest with the enterprise's credit controller, following guidelines laid down by senior management and, where large amounts are involved, having reference to senior finance-department staff. Once the judgement is made it is important that all interested parties are promptly notified. Principal amongst these interested parties are the customer, relevant sales staff and the credit-control department. A similar process needs to be gone through whenever a customer asks for a change in credit terms, whether it be a change in the credit limit or a change in settlement terms.

A credit management system

The essence of a credit-management system is that of ensuring that, as far as is practicable, all credit customers adhere to the terms of credit which were offered to them. A successful credit-management system will need to have regard to the following:

■ **Credit authorisation procedures**: the authorisation of credit terms for a customer is simply the first stage in an ongoing process. Thereafter, a procedure needs to be in place for the authorisation of individual credit sales transactions with the customer. An extreme example of this might be that any credit sale, of whatever value, needs specific authorisation, such authorisation normally come from a credit-control function within the enterprise. However, this might be felt to be unduly burdensome and therefore some upper limit might be placed for each customer on the amount of credit sales that can be made without seeking such specific authorisation. Sales below this value can proceed without seeking credit-control approval; sales above it require specific approval. Credit-authorisation procedures can often lead to tensions in enterprises. Sales staff are eager to secure sales (and perhaps earn commission), whereas credit-control staff are charged with ensuring that customers adhere to specified credit terms. It is important to ensure that credit-control staff are given, and are accepted as having, the power to refuse further credit to a customer unless and until the customer is adhering to the specified terms.

■ **Information systems**: the effective management of debtors requires that adequate information is available to all staff involved with customers, whether they be sales staff negotiating with the customer or credit-control staff monitoring the customers' credit performance. The core requirements of such a system are that it reflect, on a timely basis, the current credit terms being offered to a customer and how well that customer is adhering to those terms. This requires what is normally referred to as an 'ageing analysis' which analyses the amounts currently owed by a customer on the basis of how long they have been outstanding Typically, such an analysis would contain the information shown in Table 17.4.

The ageing analysis identifies, in aggregate terms, the amounts owed by the customer and for how long they have been outstanding. It enables a user to identify readily whether or not the customer is adhering to the agreed credit terms. In the example contained in Table 17.4 the customer is not adhering to the specified terms. While the total debt of £8490 is within the agreed credit limit of

Table 17.4 Debtor ageing analysis

Customer name:	Bloggs Engineering Ltd
Account no.:	0227635
Credit limit:	£10 000
Credit terms:	7 days settlement 2.5% discount, 30 days nett
1–30 days:	£3 400
31–60 days:	£4 200
61–90 days:	£0
90–120 days:	£0
over 120 days:	£890
Total	£8 490

£10 000, the settlement of amounts outstanding is not within the specified thirty-day limit: £4200 falls within the 31–60 day analysis, i.e. beyond the agreed thirty-day limit. Unfortunately, such a situation is all to common. Many credit customers will stretch their credit beyond the agreed terms. In some sectors, although it is never formally agreed, thirty days is taken to mean sixty days. In addition, a monthly ageing is something of a blunt instrument – it might be the case that this £4200 has been outstanding only for, say, 35 days and is likely to be settled shortly. A credit-control department would need to monitor the position closely. Thus, backing up an ageing analysis of the type illustrated in Table 17.4, an enterprise needs a more detailed analysis on an invoice-by-invoice basis.

In monitoring the behaviour of debtors an enterprise needs to pay careful attention to changes in the pattern of settlement by a credit customer. Some customers will always go beyond the agreed terms and settle their accounts after the due dates. If they are good customers in other respects – purchasing reasonable volumes of merchandise with good profit margins – then the enterprise might well be prepared informally to accept this. What would, however, be worrying is a situation where a customer who had previously settled accounts on time started not to do so. This might indicate that the customer was having cash-flow or other problems, and that the enterprise needs to take rapid action to collect the monies due to it and stop making further credit sales. An ageing analysis can also help to reveal disputes between customers and suppliers. In the case of Bloggs Engineering there is an amount of £890 which has been outstanding for over 120 days. Given that there is nothing outstanding in either the 61–90-day or 91–120-day categories, this would seen to indicate a problem. There may be a dispute about the delivery or quality of the goods, leading to Bloggs refusing to pay. Whatever the reason, the ageing analysis indicates that there is a problem which needs to be referred to the appropriate department, probably the sales department in the first instance.

The example in Table 17.4 relates to an individual customer. An enterprise will also require aggregate information on the ageing of its debtors. Such information will help its financial managers assess the overall efficacy of debtor-management policies and practices. However, if such information is to be useful, at both an aggregate and an individual customer level, it needs to be up to date. Timely processing and presentation of information are needed to ensure that management needs for decision taking are met. However, it goes further than this – the more rapidly a customer receives an invoice, the more rapidly it is likely to be settled, as many customers will settle their invoices in calendar order. Similarly, the more rapidly a customer's payment is recorded, the less likely it is that he/she will be refused credit, thereby avoiding the loss of goodwill and potential sales. As Figure 17.2 illustrates, there are a number of different stages in the debtor-management process, each of which needs to be performed on as timely a basis as possible.

As discussed earlier in this chapter, this process is likely to involve a number of different functions and staff within the enterprise: sales staff, credit-control staff, warehouse staff, invoice clerks, sales-ledger staff and cashiers. These staff will be involved in discharging their own responsibilities and providing information to enable others to discharge theirs, e.g. the cashier's staff informing the sales-ledger staff that cash has been received from a customer so that they can record this. The enterprise needs to ensure that all the individual functions and staff are aware

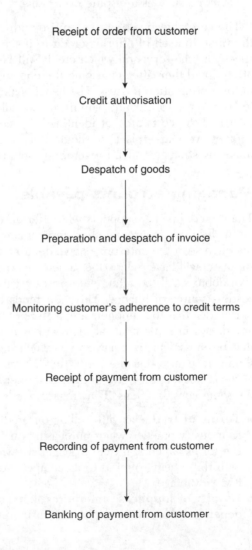

Receipt of order from customer

Credit authorisation

Despatch of goods

Preparation and despatch of invoice

Monitoring customer's adherence to credit terms

Receipt of payment from customer

Recording of payment from customer

Banking of payment from customer

Figure 17.2
Stages in the debtor management process.

of their interdependence, and of the importance of the rapid discharge of their functions and the transfer of information to others.

- **Debt collection procedures**: these follow on naturally from the other elements of the debtor-management system. They will, typically, comprise a series of increasingly purposeful steps towards the recovery of money from the customer. The first step could be a telephone call to the customer for a fairly informal reminder that a debt is overdue. After this, a series of letters is likely to be sent, at predetermined intervals. These would start with ones simply pointing out that the customer has overdue invoices, through to ones demanding payment and threatening, and then implementing, steps such as the cessation of supplies and court action. Normally these would emanate from the credit-control department. However, this department should not act independently. It needs to liaise closely with the marketing/sales department to enlist the help of the staff who may be in contact with the customer and to ensure that there are not valid reasons for non-payment, such as a dispute over delivery or quality.

The core objective of an enterprise with regard to debtors should be to optimise the value to itself of offering credit to its customers. Each of the three elements of specifying the terms on which credit will be offered, to which customers it will be offered and thereafter managing the ongoing credit relationships has a part to play in this optimisation process. The benefits and costs of these different elements need to be taken into account. Unfortunately, all too often the benefits are assumed to exist and the costs are not identified. While trade practice cannot be ignored in a competitive marketplace, it should not be accepted as 'holy writ', and alternative financing strategies such as factoring should always be considered.

Managing accounts payable

Trade creditors, i.e. suppliers who offer an enterprise supplies on credit terms, are often the major source of short-term finance for an enterprise. Such creditors are the obverse of the enterprise's own debtors, and it needs to be recognised that these suppliers will have exactly the same concerns as does the enterprise in managing its own debtors. All too often, enterprises regard trade credit as a readily available and costless source of finance. This view tends to lead to abuse of trade credit, rooted in the idea that the suppliers are keen to obtain business and that they will overlook any delays in settlement, at least within reason, because they do not want to lose that business. This is a naive view which needs to be guarded against. Enterprises should recognise that the credit they obtain from their suppliers is the counterpart of the credit that they give to their customers and needs to be managed using exactly the same considerations. Thus regard needs to be paid to the following:

- **Terms of trade**: as with selling on credit, an enterprise needs to pay attention to industry practice when purchasing on credit. By doing this, it will ensure that the terms which it is able to negotiate with its suppliers are at least comparable with those being offered to its competitors, thereby avoiding any loss of competitive advantage.
- **Loyalty of suppliers**: enterprises all too often fail to recognise the extent of their dependence on their suppliers, focusing instead on trade credit as a 'free' source

of finance. In part, this can be a reflection of the problem referred to earlier – different parts of an enterprise having different functional interests. The accountancy/finance department may focus on the deferral of payments to suppliers because of cash-flow considerations. The purchasing/production functions may focus on obtaining supplies of merchandise of appropriate quality and quantity at the appropriate time and at a competitive price. These focuses may conflict. If the finance department regularly delays payment to a supplier, this may make it much more difficult for the purchasing function to negotiate competitive prices. Suppliers will tend to favour those customers who kept to their credit terms in matters of preferential pricing and delivery. 'Trade gossip' will also spread information about enterprises which are 'poor payers', thereby making it more difficult for such enterprises to establish credit relationships with suppliers.

■ **Settlement discounts**: such discounts are a fairly common feature throughout the economy. However, many purchasers, particularly smaller enterprises, do not take advantage of them because of cash-flow considerations. Typically, such enterprises are undercapitalised and rely on the availability and flexibility offered by trade credit as an essential part of their financial management. However, obtaining finance by deciding not to take advantage of settlement discounts may be a very expensive approach. Consider the case of an enterprise which purchases goods from a supplier which offers credit terms, including a 2% cash-settlement discount for payment within ten days of the invoice date and thirty days nett. If the enterprise does not take advantage of this settlement discount it is financing that part of its business with the supplier in question at a very high effective annual interest rate. The annualised cost of the interest can be computed using the following formula:

$$\text{Cost} = \frac{\text{Discount \%}}{(100 - \text{Discount \%})} \times \frac{365}{(\text{Final due date} - \text{Discount period})} \quad (17.8)$$

Thus for the example of 2% for settlement within seven days:

$$\text{Cost} = \frac{2}{(100-2)} \times \frac{365}{(30-10)} = 44.56\% \quad (17.9)$$

Such an enterprise would be better off, if possible, obtaining an alternative form of finance and taking advantage of the settlement discount. While trade credit is fairly readily available, it has the disadvantage that it is essentially very short term in nature and easily withdrawn by suppliers, with potentially disastrous effects. It is also potentially very expensive. Enterprises would, in general, be better advised to seek more secure and cheaper forms of short-term finance. Possible sources of such finance are discussed in the next section.

As with debtors, an enterprise needs to pay careful attention to the recording of the amounts due to suppliers and to the management of the purchasing and payment procedures. Figure 17.3 illustrates the stages involved in this. Again, as with debtors, many different functions and staff are involved in the process, and the challenge which management faces is the integration of the different activities and decisions into a coherent framework which ensures that only duly authorised payments are made.

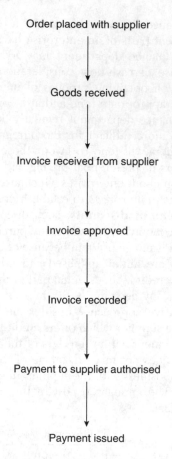

Figure 17.3
Stages in the
creditor-
management
process.

Order placed with supplier

Goods received

Invoice received from supplier

Invoice approved

Invoice recorded

Payment to supplier authorised

Payment issued

Management of cash

Earlier in this chapter we discussed the cash-transaction cycle and the management of inventories, debtors and creditors. Cash is the lifeblood of a commercial enterprise – without access to cash it will be unable to meet its liabilities or to engage in new and profitable ventures. At the same time, it needs to ensure that its cash resources are employed as efficiently as possible. This requires that an enterprise:

■ plan and monitor the flow of cash through the enterprise associated with its day-to-day activities – as we have seen this requires that policies be determined and implemented with regard to its management of inventories, debtors and creditors;
■ plan and monitor the sources of finance via which both its short- and longer-term activities are funded, having regard to its cash-flow position – of particular relevance to this chapter are the ways in which it does this regarding the use of short-term sources of finance.

There are a number of sources of short term finance, other than trade credit, available to a commercial enterprise. The principal of these are:

■ **Bank borrowing**: here the traditional method is that of the bank overdraft. Overdrafts have the advantage of flexibility, i.e. the enterprise has access to funds up to an agreed limit but does not have to use them if it does not need to. Thus, an enterprise has 'at least in theory' guaranteed access to finance, but only pays for that finance which it actually uses. However, the use of overdrafts has very considerable downside costs – the banks who provide such finance will typically look for security for their advances and charge premium interest rates. In addition, overdrafts are repayable on demand, thus exposing enterprises to the risk of its bankers foreclosing, as has been the case with many smaller enterprises in recent years, and they can be expensive in terms of bank charges.

- **Instalment credit**: there are a number of options here. In essence, all of them are aimed at enabling an enterprise to acquire an asset on deferred payment terms. Thus the principal orientation of instalment credit is towards the acquisition of fixed assets. The main types of instalment credit are leasing and hire purchase.

- **Financial instruments**: there are several types of these, but their essence is that they provide an enterprise with something which it can use to obtain cash in the financial markets. The most common sort of instrument is a 'bill of exchange', which effectively is a promissory note, normally issued by a customer, which an enterprise can sell on to a finance house at a discount and receive cash in exchange. The better the reputation of the customer and the nearer the due date of the bill, the greater the proportion of the face value of the bill that the enterprise will receive.

- **Factoring**: in essence, factoring involves an enterprise handing over its debtors to a factoring company. The factoring company pays the enterprise the face value of the debtors less a discount, and recoups this by collecting the debts. Factoring its debtors provides an enterprise with an immediate boost to its liquidity. There are several different methods of factoring, the principal distinctions involving the extent to which the factor has recourse to the enterprise (if the debts prove uncollectible) and the extent to which the factor takes over the administration of the enterprise's sales ledger (thereby saving the enterprise administrative costs). These differences will be reflected in the discount at which the factor accepts the debts. Historically, factoring has been thought of by many enterprises as being a slightly disreputable source of finance associated with negative images of debt collectors and companies having financial problems. However, it is a growing source of finance, particularly for smaller enterprises.

These different sources of finance have different advantages and disadvantages, including their availability, cost and flexibility. In deciding whether or not to use finance of this type, and to what extent, management needs to ensure that it is more relevant to the company's needs and cheaper than other, particularly longer-term, sources of finance. Whatever sources of finance an enterprise uses, it still needs to manage its day-to-day cash flows within the limits imposed by its finances. In particular, it needs to pay attention to the detailed management of the monies it receives from customers and other sources and the payments it makes to its suppliers. This requires clearly defined banking strategies, including the following:

- **Number and location of bank accounts**: maintaining a bank account has associated costs. A bank will seek – increasingly these days – to levy charges for the services it provides (apart from interest on any overdrawn balances) and these charges are likely to be higher for an enterprise which maintains a number of different bank accounts. A further factor is that of 'cleared balances'. Simply depositing a cheque from a customer into a bank account does not mean that the enterprise is credited with that amount. Only when the cheque has been 'cleared' by the customer's bankers will the enterprise finally receive credit for it. Typically, such clearance will take about three days. However, it may take longer if an enterprise deposits monies at a branch other than the one at which its account is maintained. This can be a particular problem for enterprises with a number of geographically dispersed sites. Such enterprises need to discuss the problem with their bankers and ensure that arrangements are made which reduce any delays in 'clearance' to a minimum.

- **Frequency of banking**: ideally, an enterprise should seek to deposit monies with its bank as soon as possible. Doing this will minimise the security risks of holding cash, help to reduce any interest charges on overdrawn accounts, and help to generate interest on interest-bearing accounts. However, the act of banking itself has costs. These include any transaction charge made by the bank and the enterprise's own administrative costs. These differing costs and risks need to be balanced in determining a policy dealing with the frequency of banking.
- **Use of cash and bank balances**: cash, including credit balances on current accounts, is an unproductive asset – it is not generating any return. Enterprises should use their cash resources in ways which do, in fact, generate returns while having regard to their liquidity requirements. Doing this successfully means that they should prepare cash-flow forecasts and monitor the outturn of these forecasts closely. By doing so, they can identify when they are likely to have cash surpluses and plan for the investment of such surpluses. A wide range of financial investment opportunities is available, ranging from the overnight money market to longer-term fixed interest accounts. Failing to do this can result in the enterprise incurring large opportunity costs in terms of forgone interest.

Conclusions

For many companies, particularly manufacturing ones, working capital (defined as current assets minus current liabilities) represents a major area of their activities. Many managers are constantly occupied in making decisions which affect the level of the investment in working capital. However, all too often these decisions are made with a narrow departmental/functional focus, lacking any strategic direction. The theory of managing an enterprise's investment in working capital is relatively straightforward (invest in short-term assets as long as they generate a return greater than the cost of capital, and use short-term sources of finance as long as they have a cost lower than other sources of capital) and a number of decision models are available to help managers achieve this. In practice, however, the management of working capital tends to be much more diffuse, involving numerous trade-offs, frequently based on rather ill-defined judgements.

In this chapter we have discussed the meaning of working capital and empha-sised that it reflects the short-term assets and funding of an enterprise. We have also emphasised the importance of its effective management to the financial well-being of the enterprise. The concept of the cash-conversion cycle was intro-duced, and based on this we then reviewed techniques that can be adopted to improve the management of the components of working capital, i.e.:

- inventory;
- debtors;
- creditors;
- cash.

Further reading

Samuels *et al.* (1995) provide a detailed analysis of a number of approaches to the management of working capital within the broader context of financial management. Hill and Sartoris (1995) focus entirely on short-term financial management, albeit in an American context. The monthly publication *Business Money Facts* provides useful information about the current availability and cost of a wide range of financial management opportunities.

Questions and exercises

1 Torment Ltd is a manufacturer of electronic components and is located in the countryside. All its sales are on credit terms and all its customers settle their accounts by cheque posted to Torment's premises. Because Torment is several miles from the nearest bank, its cashier banks the cheques received from customers on Friday lunchtimes after Friday's post has been opened.

A chief accountant has recently been appointed by Torment who has asked you, as cashier, to prepare a report for him reviewing its current banking policy. He has suggested that you consider three options:

(a) daily banking;

(b) banking twice per week (on Tuesdays and Fridays);

(c) continuing the existing banking practice.

You have collected the following data relating to Torment's receipts from customers and banking arrangements:

(i) Forecast receipts for the coming twelve months are £25 120 000.

(ii) The anticipated pattern of receipts is that they will be evenly spread throughout the year.

(iii) Typically, twice as much is received each Monday and Tuesday as is received on the other days of the week.

(iv) Torment makes extensive and continued use of its overdraft facility, for which the current interest rate is 10% per annum.

(v) Each visit to the bank and banking costs Torment £50.

Prepare the report requested by the chief accountant, comparing the three banking strategies.

2 At a recent board meeting of Merchant Trading plc an animated discussion took place about the company's trading prospects. While Harry Sleeze, the marketing director, was happy to state that 'our sales are up 25% on the previous year, therefore we are definitely in a healthy state and our shareholders ought to be well pleased with our efforts', the distribution director, Henrietta Ford, was more cautious, stating: 'What I don't understand is why I have finished goods staying in stock longer.' The finance director, Martina Bianca, stated: 'Profitability might well have gone up marginally on the increased volume of sales but, given that we are only just coming out of the recession, I pay greater attention to our liquidity.' George Giorgiou, the managing director, shares Bianca's concerns, stating: 'I agree. In last month's *Management Today* it stated that "all too often businesses fail to pay sufficient attention to their cash operating cycle".' The meeting ended with Bianca agreeing to make a short presentation on Merchant's cash operating problems at the next board meeting, in two week's time. However, Bianca is scheduled to take ten day's holiday and gives you the following information so that she can have a memorandum on her desk when she returns commenting on Merchant's cash operating cycle and outlining suggestions on how it might be improved.

	31 December 19X6 £000s	31 December 19X7 £000s
Stocks:		
raw materials	80	108
work-in-progress	56	72
finished goods	64	96
Purchases	384	520
Cost of goods sold	560	720
Sales	640	800
Debtors	128	192
Creditors	64	78

Prepare a memorandum for Martina Bianca and include as an appendix your calculations of the length of Merchant's cash operating cycle. Be sure to explain all terms used and, as requested, provide ideas on how Merchant's cash operating cycle might be improved.

3 Jason Ltd is a manufacturer of hardware which it sells on credit terms to wholesalers. Its current credit terms are thirty days nett, with no discount for prompt settlement. Currently the average period of credit taken by customers is seventy-three days.

The board of directors is considering introducing a 2.5% cash discount for customers who settle their invoices within seven days. The marketing director has estimated that this will lead to an increase in sales of 5% (from the current level of £2 million) and that these sales will generate the same gross profit margin (20%) as existing sales. He also estimates that 25% of customers would take advantage of the discount.

Jason currently operates using a substantial bank overdraft, on which it pays interest at a rate of 12%.

Write a report for the board assessing whether or not it would be financially advantageous to offer the discount.

4 Jakers Ltd is a small family company which was formed four years ago to manufacture and distribute via wholesalers and retailers a new novelty board game. Besides its founders, Jean and Jan Jakers, it has three other part-time employees involved with purchasing, despatch and invoicing. Its annual turnover is steady at about £600 000. The cost data for each game is:

Unit selling price	£36
Variable costs	£18
Fixed-costs apportionment	£6
	£24
Profit	£12

The current cost of capital of the company is 15% per annum.

The management of Jakers wants to expand its market penetration and believes that it can do this by offering their customers better credit terms. At present customers take, on average, thirty days to pay and all sales are on a credit basis. The company is considering three options as regards a new credit policy. These are:

	Option 1	Option 2	Option 3
Increase in average collection period (days)	10	20	30
Forecast increase in sales (£s)	30 000	45 000	50 000

To help finance this increased level of debtors, the company is also reconsidering its policy towards paying its raw materials suppliers. Raw materials account for £12 of the unit variable costs of the company's product. At present the company pays its suppliers at the end of a ten-day period after the invoice date to obtain a 2.5% settlement discount. It is considering delaying payment till the end of either a thirty- or a forty-five-day period after the invoice date, when it will pay the full amount of the invoice.

(a) Advise the company whether – and, if so, how – it is worth changing the terms of credit that it gives to its customers.

(b) Advise the company whether – and, if so, how – it is worth changing the way it pays its raw materials suppliers.

(c) Comment on any reservations you may have regarding the advice you have given at (a) and (b) above.

5 Outline the main reasons why many enterprises are unable to manage their working capital effectively.

6 Explain what is meant by 'overtrading' and what are its likely consequences for a business.

7 Analyse the principal motives a manufacturing company may have for holding high levels of stock.

8 Outline the principal elements of a successful credit-control system.

9 'Delaying payments to creditors may lead to short-term savings in a company's interest bill but a longer term cost-deterioration in its relationships with its suppliers.' Discuss.

10 It is often said that the availability of bank credit is more important to small and medium-sized firms than to large ones. Why might this be so?

18 Accounting for social responsibility and the environment

Objectives

Ever since the early 1980s there has been a growing concern to improve the level of social responsibility and environmental accounting in both the public and private sectors. While initial concerns tended to focus on issues such as the development of employee reports and value added statements, general social accounting disclosure has more recently focused on the reporting of environmental performance. At the same time, increasing emphasis has been placed on broader 'corporate governance' issues, particularly the roles and responsibilities of directors. Those who support greater social responsibility and environmental accounting by corporations see this in terms of a broader level of accountability owed to society as a whole, which should reveal the full impact of an enterprise's economic activities on a broader range of stakeholders.

This pressure for the development of a broader base of corporate accountability has arisen for various reasons. Incidents such as the Exxon Valdez oil spill and the Bhopal chemical leak received worldwide media attention. This has led to a number of national and international initiatives in reaction to this new climate of public opinion. In addition to initiatives undertaken by individual companies, organisations such as the CBI, the British Institute of Management and the Institute of Directors have launched a series of initiatives designed to promote greater managerial social responsibility. The Environmental Protection Act 1990 has also been recognised as an important step in implementing the 'polluter-pays' principle. Perhaps the most important accounting issue that arises as a result of this legislation is in terms of costing out new pollution-control methods under the legal obligation imposed to minimise waste production utilising what is called the 'best available technology not entailing excessive cost (BATNEEC) principle' (see Owen 1992).[1] At the same time, there is increasing concern about the responsibilities of corporations for their activities in 'third-world' countries (e.g. the use and remuneration of child labour) as part of the development of the ethical investment movement.

At the European Community level there has been the circulation of a draft Directive which has called for the compulsory environmental auditing of companies whose activities have a significant impact on the environment. There is also a resurgence of interest in the 'ethical behaviour' of businesses.

Introduction

Managers need to be well informed on the issues surrounding their organisation's broader social responsibilities. Touche Ross Management Consultants (1990) neatly sum up their attitude towards environmental issues in the title to their report: *Head in the Clouds or Head in the Sand*? Empirical evidence cited later in this chapter on the provision of information on social and environmental issues by UK companies tends to support the view that it is highly selective and largely public-relations-driven. Roberts (1992) has, for example, indicated that UK companies are generally failing to keep up with best European, most particularly German, practice. No wonder pressure groups such as Friends of the Earth have established the 'Green Con' award for companies making the most misleading claims. An oft-quoted defence by companies has been that greater social disclosure could harm the interests of their investors, but this is now being challenged as investors, both individual and institutional, also demand that such information be provided.

It is not only managers who are under attack for their failure to be more socially responsible. By 'focusing on issues of profit and efficiency whilst ignoring the social and environmental dimensions of organisational performance, conventional accounting techniques are heavily implicated in the current environmental mess we've got ourselves into' (Owen 1992: 22). This observation is not necessarily new. Writing sixty-five years ago, John Maynard Keynes (1933) observed that under 'the peculiar logic of accountancy' the men of the nineteenth century built slums rather than modern cities because slums paid more.

In this chapter we continue our discussion by first reviewing the nature of social responsibility accounting. We then go on, in turn, to discuss the impact of social responsibility and environmental issues on management accounting, external financial reporting and external audit.

What is social responsibility accounting?

Any discussion on social responsibility accounting raises the spectre of some hard and challenging issues for management. As Estes (1976, v) has observed:

- What is the worth of corporate 'social responsibility' activities such as aid to minority businesses, recycling programmes, energy conservation etc?
- Since social responsibility shows up in costs but not in revenues, how can the socially responsible corporation come out as good on the 'bottom line' as its irresponsible competitor? How can a company tell the story of its social contribution to the public?
- Will pollution-control laws, by driving productive corporations out of business, cost society more than they save?

Social responsibility accounting is about trying to provide answers to questions such as these. It can be defined as:

> The measurement and reporting of information on the impact that an organisation's activities are having on society as a whole. Such information may be used both internally and externally by management and as such extends beyond that traditionally prepared and reported upon.
>
> (Gray *et al.* 1987)

Management increasingly needs information on its organisation's social responsibilities. It may need it in order to respond to critical media attention or to present to a government agency. Public-interest groups, often referred to as pressure groups, continually lobby for greater social responsibility from corporations and this therefore has to be demonstrated. Such groups can range in diversity from consumer affairs organisations to environmental lobby groups and religious organisations. Concerns are raised about a diverse set of social issues which can cover such topics as the impact of corporate activity on the environment, ethical investment strategies, the treatment of ethnic and disadvantaged groups in society and abroad, community involvement and so on.

Often managers may not be entirely aware of the degree to which their organisation is in fact socially responsible, since much of this activity is devolved and not 'captured' centrally. While corporations are relatively well organised when it comes to deciding upon their reasons for general philanthropy – such as support of educational institutions or evaluating the benefits of its various human resource programmes – there is probably less appreciation of the 'social impact' arising more directly from the products and services that they provide. How much ethical effort and consequent financial resources are devoted to the completeness of product/service information (in terms of packaging, labelling and advertising)? Are electrical goods energy (and, if appropriate, water) efficient? To what degree do products contain biodegradable parts? Social responsibility accounting can take various forms, ranging from simple and relatively inexpensive systems through to highly complex and costly ones. Depending upon the organisation, the degree of social responsibility accounting can cover all/some of the following approaches:

- periodic informal reviews of social responsibility activities at localised management meetings;
- the preparation of cost estimates of the support of social programmes and activities;
- social impact analysis of the costs associated with the practice of socially undesirable activity (such as detrimental effects on the environment).

Practice varies as to the degree to which such information is reported externally. This can range from a couple of paragraphs outlining an organisation's 'attitudes' to its social responsibilities, largely devoid of related financial values, through to a very detailed outline of its responsibilities to society. However, as many researchers have observed, the selection and format of information reported is very much at the discretion of management and not in a regulated format as with the more traditional financial accounting information. As indicated earlier, the accounting profession has not entirely embraced the notion of social responsibility accounting. Jones (1990) conducted interviews with fifty-seven accountants working in six large manufacturing and merchanting firms, and elicited the overwhelming responses, in their view, profit is the prime, if not the only, goal of business and that social responsibilities were deserving of a very low level of priority.

The British Institute of Management has drawn up a charter for its members with respect to developing a policy for management and the environment (see Table 8.1). This policy promotes the ideas that 'good management of the environment is good management', and that management and reporting systems will have to be modified or developed to provide this newly demanded information (Lester 1992). The issue

Table 18.1 A policy for management and the environment

Management should:
■ Recognise its obligations to owners, employees, suppliers, customers, users, society and the environment
■ Appoint directors or managers with responsibilities that include environmental issues
■ Educate and train all employees in environmental excellence
■ Make the most effective use of all natural resources and safe energy sources for the benefit of the organisation and the overall public interest
■ Promote the use of sustainable resources and minimise the use of finite resources
■ Reduce the amount of waste, avoid harmful pollution and find ways of reprocessing or converting waste materials into useful products and safely disposing of the residue
■ Actively seek to restore and protect the biosphere
■ Reduce environmentally related risks
■ Market products, services and processes which create the minimum environmental damage
■ Be willing to exercise influence and skill for the benefit of the society within which the organisation operates
■ Ensure that all public communications are true and unambiguous, with full disclosure of environmental, health and safety issues
■ Develop economic and financial models, where appropriate, which include the full-cost compensation of damage or restoration to the environment

Source: Lester (1992: 44).

of social responsibility accounting is but part of a growing wider debate on the issue of corporate governance. As Carey notes:

> For most companies the days when their valuable assets were mainly in the form of bricks and mortar and plant and machinery, 'things which you could see and kick' are gone. Consequently, if the business community and the economy in general are to continue to enjoy sustainable growth we must pay far greater attention in the future to maintaining and developing our stock of human and natural assets than has traditionally been the case. If we are to be successful it is essential that environmental problems should not be seen in isolation but placed in the context of the wider debate on corporate governance.
>
> (Carey 1992: 87)

The impact of social responsibility and environmental issues on management accounting

In this section we consider how social responsibility factors and environmental factors can be incorporated into management accounting systems, with particular reference to investment appraisal and budgeting. Gray *et al* (1993) carried out a survey that suggested that less than 40% of large UK companies have any environmental factors built into their financial-investment appraisal process and less than 20% had environmental issues built into their budgeting systems. They also found that in only a minority of large companies are the accountants and accounting systems closely involved with central environmental questions as they relate to the company. One company which does this is the Body Shop. Burrit and Lehman (1995) discuss that company's evaluation of an investment appraisal of a wind farm for power generation. They conclude that 'environmental accountants can provide practical assistance . . . through the disclosure of qualitative, attention directing facets of investment decision-making as part of the accountability process' (Burrit and Lehman 1995: 170).

While individual organisations are now developing different forms of environmental performance targets, their integration with the traditional accounting systems is still somewhat rare. Table 18.2 provides one such illustration, a voluntary list of performance indicators adopted by the UK chemical industry.

So long as performance indicators are kept separate from the more traditional financial criteria the latter can always be expected to dominate when it comes to evaluating performance. One key issue of concern to organisations is that it is invariably far easier to identify social responsibility impact costs than it is to identify benefits (environmental, financial or otherwise). Mind you, this is not always the case, Ecotcc (1991) have reported that controlling pollution costs in the quarrying and cement and in the paper and pulp industries is reported as saving at least 7% gross costs. Coopers & Lybrand Deloitte have also reported that:

> Although there are many other pressures at the moment on businesses of all sizes, those companies that take the trouble to investigate their environmental performance, and then start to make improvements, will gain a significant long-term advantage over their less-aware competitors. Businesses which are slow off the mark are likely to find it increasingly difficult to market their products, dispose of waste, obtain insurance, attract finance, keep within a new and much enhanced legal framework and recruit and retain the best staff.
>
> (Coopers & Lybrand Deloitte 1990: 7)

Earlier we discussed the basic principles of investment appraisal and recognised that while, theoretically, there is one preferred basis, there are in practice a number

Table 18.2 Voluntary performance indicators adopted by the UK chemical industry

Health and safety
- fatalities
- non-fatal major accidents
- diseases
- accidents in relation to man-hours

Environment
- amount of 'special waste'
- discharges of 'red-list' substances
- site-specific data expressed in an 'environmental index'

Distribution
- number of transport incidents in relation to million tonne-miles

Energy
- energy consumption per tonne of product

Complaints
- number of complaints made by public and regulators

Source: adapted from KPMG European Environment Briefing Note (winter 1991/2). p. 11.

of practical considerations that also need to be considered. Similarly, there are a number of problems concerning the incorporation of environmental and other social responsibility issues into investment decisions. Remember too that investment decisions are not solely concerned with new venture opportunities; the majority of such decisions actually relate to day-to-day operational issues such as the replacement of plant and equipment or the decision to invest in a particular research and development project. As would have been apparent from our earlier discussions, investment techniques such as ARR and payback have a tendency to favour short-term, less risky investment opportunities. When one considers the prospect of additional social-impact costs and the fact that benefits might be longer-term rather than shorter-term in coming and even less tangible to measure, it is easy to appreciate that the more traditional investment-appraisal approaches have discouraged consideration of these issues. However, that is starting to change since environmental pressures (in the forms of legislation, technological development, societal attitudes, government regulations, etc.) now mean that management can no longer avoid such considerations. To this end, all organisations should always consider an environmental investment checklist such as that presented in Table 18.3.

Some organisations do take this response to environmental issues very seriously. An often-quoted example is that of Alcan, where all capital-expenditure proposals must include an environmental impact statement. Managers need to involve their accountants in such discussions; to do otherwise will lead to environmental considerations remaining marginalised.

When it comes to budgeting, Gray *et al.* (1993) found that less than 15% of accountants in large UK companies had any explicitly environmental factors built into their budgeting process and only another 4% had any plans to do so. Perhaps this is because a response to social responsibility accounting is not built into most organisations' appraisal systems. As Asher has aptly observed, there is a dilemma well known throughout management accounting:

> When managers see that their execution of socially responsible policies and programs is evaluated in promotional and compensation decisions, along with performance in meeting familiar profit, cost and productivity goals, they will believe and they will be motivated. For obvious and valid reasons middle managers concentrate their attention and skill on the accomplishment of performance objectives for which they know they are held responsible. They

Table 18.3 Ten-point checklist for more environmentally sensitive investment appraisal

1	Environmentally screen all investments
2	Reconsider costs
3	Reconsider benefits
4	Reconsider the criteria applied
5	Reconsider the possible options considered
6	Consider the opportunity costs
7	Reconsider the time horizon
8	Reconsider the discount rate
9	Consider the 'valuation of externalities'
10	Consider sustainable costs

Source: Gray *et al.* (1993: 160).

Table 18.4   Recommended action points

A management accountant, or indeed any other executive in a company, reading this report will quickly register possible action points. A checklist is set out below in the form of questions to be asked about any company. Some of them will not apply. For others, a positive response will be indicative of action already in hand. It is recommended that everyone should go through the questions after reading the report. There will be few cases where no possibilities to take positive steps emerge. Where action is indicated, it is vital that it is initiated.

In the context of your company ask the following questions – and ensure answers are forthcoming:

- Do we consistently monitor company practices and performance in terms of effects on the environment?
- Do we systematically check that all public references to the company are picked up, particularly those with environmental dimensions?
- Do we have a positive, proactive policy in respect of publicising positive environmental actions and policies?
- Are all our company vehicles currently run on lead-free fuel?
- For any that are not, can they be adjusted? If not, replacement should be considered.
- Is the presence of catalytic converters taken into account when setting our policy for purchase/leasing of company cars? Is it possible to retro-fit catalytic converters to any cars already in the fleet?
- How large is our electricity bill and how is it built up? What is the largest constituent?
- How can we make the use of lighting and heating more efficient without losses in its effectiveness?
- Is a combined heat and power scheme feasible for our factory or office block?
- Where and how soon can we set up schemes to recycle paper?
- What other materials do we use in quantities that are sufficient to initiate collection schemes? How about cans or glass?
- Do we already use recycled stationery or paper products? If so, what scope is there to extend the range? If recycled stationery is not in use, why not? Are we aware of the available range and quality of such recycled products?
- Do we know what environmental audits are about? If not, how soon can we obtain information, particularly copies of two basic publications? If we are familiar with such audits, when will we be undertaking one?

Source: CIMA (1990).

approve responsibility in terms of two familiar criteria. The first is what is measured and the second is what is rewarded.

(Asher 1980; quoted in Cheshire and Carlisle 1991: 54)

The message is obvious: not only must social impact and environmental criteria be seen to be explicitly recognised in post-evaluation management reviews, it must also form part of the performance reward system. Table 18.4 is from a Chartered Institute of Management Accountants 1990 research study and illustrates a useful list of action points for accountants and managers to consider in order to make their organisation more aware of a number of basic environmental issues.

The impact of social responsibility and environmental issues on external financial reporting

There have been numerous studies, both within the UK and elsewhere, that have reviewed the social responsibility and environmental disclosure policies of corporations and other forms of reporting entities. Guthrie and Parker (1989) undertook a comparative analysis of corporate social disclosure practices in the UK, the USA and Australia. The annual reports of the fifty largest listed companies in each country for the 1983 year were reviewed for evidence of disclosure relating to the environment, energy, human resources, products, community involvement and 'other'. The authors found that the mean corporate social disclosure in Australia (0.70 pages) was relatively low when compared to the USA (1.26 pages), while UK firms provided, on average, 0.89 pages of information. In relation to environmental disclosures, these authors found no company provided negative information about its activities. Within this survey it is perhaps worth saying a few more words about the UK data. Only two categories of information scored highly with UK companies, these being human resources (98%) and community involvement (96%). For other categories the scores were modest, with 14% for the environment, 10% for products and a miserly 2% for energy. The popularity of human resources and community involvement as disclosure categories is attributed by Guthrie and Parker (1989) to the fact that these were legal requirements. For example, companies must disclose information on numbers employed, remuneration and related benefits of dividends, etc.

Touche Ross Management Consultants (1990) conducted an in-depth survey into attitudes towards environmental issues on the part of thirty-two major UK companies. The survey indicated that, whereas more than half the companies studied claimed to devote some coverage, only a few dealt with the issues in any depth. As with the previous study, it was found that issues relating to human resources and community involvement rated far higher than those related to environmental issues. Gray *et al.* (1993) have summarised a number of general themes that have emerged from empirical research into the extent to which companies produce social responsibility information. This work is summarised in Table 18.5.

Roberts (1992) notes that the only European country with any specific disclosure requirements in the area of environmental impact is Norway. The Norwegian Enterprise Act 1989 requires corporations to include in the directors' report information on emission levels, contamination, and details of measures both planned and actually performed by the corporation with the objective of cleaning up the environment. Sadly, with few exceptions, the response of Norwegian corporations has been to

Table 18.5   Conclusions from UK business/environment surveys

1 A significant minority of companies still fail to recognise the environment as a major business factor
2 Not all companies recognise that the environment will increase in importance
3 Between 20% and 50% of companies do not have environmental responsibility at board level
4 About half of British companies still have no environmental policy
5 There is widespread doubt about and resistance to environmental disclosure
6 The majority of companies have not undertaken any environmental audit
7 The principal motivation for taking environmental issues seriously is equally divided between legislation and personal, social familial or public opinion
8 The primary areas of response are energy management, waste management, lead-free petrol and the use of recycled paper
9 Investment appraisal is still conducted without environmental criteria

Source: Gray *et al.* (1993: 35).

provide brief statements that all relevant legislation has been complied with rather than the disclosure of detailed quantitative information. While recognising that there are generally increasing levels of disclosure across Europe, she recognises that since environmental disclosure remains generally voluntary:

> This means that corporations have almost complete discretion in deciding what information to provide and the form that the disclosure should take. This gives them the opportunity to present their activities in the best possible light by the judicious choice of what information to disclose and the reporting format used.
>
> (Roberts 1992: 165)

Few companies, it seems, are brave enough to follow the policy of Norsk Hydro of Norway, which states: 'We believe that the public has a right to information, and there is nothing that we want to hide. If we have a problem, it is also in our interests that it is brought to full public view.'

Jupe (1994, 1997) looked at the annual reports of large listed UK companies and found that the majority of disclosures were in the non-statutory sections of the reports, but that there was an increasing trend of disclosure. However, he points out that these disclosures are selective, emphasising what might be seen as 'good' environmental performance, with a dearth of reports of failure. Again, most of the information disclosed is non-quantitative, and could be viewed as public-relations type information. However, some progress does seem to be being made, and this is demonstrated by analyses of the reports submitted for the annual ACCA Environmental Reporting Awards.

The impact of social responsibility and environmental issues on external audit

Despite a Gallup survey commissioned by Coopers and Lybrand in 1990 which suggested that 58% of financial directors felt it would be useful for their auditors to comment on how satisfactory their company's management information systems and processes were in respect of environmental issues, social audit largely remains the prerogative of consumer and other pressure groups. In the UK social audits have been carried out by, among others, the Consumers' Association, Social Audit Ltd and Counter Information Services.

Gray *et. al.* (1993) have reviewed the contributions of each of these three bodies. They note that commercial pressures in the late 1980s reduced the campaigning dimension of the Consumers' Association, leading it to focus narrowly upon product cost and efficiency. Social Audit Ltd's activities also faded in the 1980s but some of its earlier work can be found in *Social Audit Quarterly*. Counter Information Services was a radical group that referred to itself as a Marxist collective of journalists. Throughout the 1970s it targeted a number of prominent companies. For example, its report on Rio Tinto Zinc (RTZ) contained a number of serious observations, usually drawn from the *Ecologist* magazine, about the environmental performance of RTZ in general and one of its sites in particular.

Most commentators would agree that the 'social audit movement' is, was and remains a largely diffuse and intermittent activity undertaken by groups that come and go.

Conclusions

There is a growing interest in corporate social and environmental reporting, not just from the well-established pressure groups, and there is some evidence that larger companies, in particular, are responding to this. The difficulty remains that such responses are still largely voluntary and unquantified. There is also the ongoing debate about broader corporate governance issues and the rights to information of the various stakeholders associated with corporations. Thus, while the indications of change are at least positive, it would not do to be over-optimistic about the pace of such change. Perhaps changes in legislation are needed, in parallel with the development of explicit reporting standards for social and environmental reporting.

> For various reasons, managements need to pay far greater attention to the increasing importance of social responsibility and environmental accounting. Those who support these moves see them in terms of a broader level of accountability owed by organisations and those who manage them to society as a whole. The importance of this area of discussion is revisited in the final chapter as part of the growing wider debate on corporate governance.

Further reading

For those new to this area we would suggest three useful books. The first is Estes's classic work *Corporate Social Accounting* (1976). Although published in 1976, it provides an excellent overview of how social accounting has been and may be applied in corporations, whether profit-seeking or not for profit. Rob Gray *et al.*'s *Accounting for the Environment* was published in 1993 and remains a popularly quoted reference for environmental accounting issues. Finally we would suggest Dave Owen's *Green Reporting* (1992) as a text that provides the fundamental challenge to managers and accountants in the 1990s. It is a practical handbook that draws together the emerging issues in the environmental and social spheres, and addresses them in the context of that major medium of communication, the company report. Reference could also usefully be made to journals such as *Social and Environmental Reporting*.

Questions and exercises

1 For a company with which you are familiar, read the latest annual report and list as many references as you can to social responsibility issues. Consider whether these references are there purely because of legal requirements or because of other reasons.

2 Using the twelve points listed in Table 18.1, interview *either* (a) a small group of managers in the same organisation *or* (b) a cross-company group of managers to solicit their views to the issues raised. What is your response to their replies?

3 Using the approach adopted in Table 18.2, attempt to develop some environmental performance indicators for an industry you are familiar with. To whom would these be most useful and why?

4 To what extent do you agree with the quotation from Owen (1992: 22) included in the introduction to this chapter (see p. 412)? Can you give any examples to support or refute Owen's argument?

5 Suggest ways in which companies might be required to disclose greater information on environmental and other social responsibility performance, both in corporate annual reports and by any other forms of accountability you may consider useful.

6 One area of social responsibility covers employees, 'the human assets' of the enterprise. Discuss what issues of accountability and disclosure arise here, and what aspects of human assets might be routinely measured and reported (like other accounting information).

7 It has been suggested that companies report on environmental and social performance only when they have 'good news' to report. How might society ensure that there is full and objective reporting of such performance?

8 Some academics have suggested that 'human assets' (including aspects such as training and skilling) should be valued, or capitalised, and included in the financial balance sheet. Discuss the theoretical and practical arguments for and against this suggestion.

9 If you agree that most managers respond strongly only to performance objectives which they know about, which they understand, which are measurable and measured, and which affect their managerial performance assessment and rewards, then discuss how best to involve managers in achieving corporate environmental and other social responsibility objectives.

19 Strategic business accounting

Much of what has been written so far in the second half of this text has recognised that managers devote most of their energies to the planning and allocation of resources, and to motivating and controlling people in order to utilise those allocated resources to best effect. Senior management also finds itself involved in shaping and developing the strategic direction of the organisation as a whole.

In this final chapter we consider the importance of accounting in helping with the formulation and implementation of corporate strategy. In doing so, we will draw on some issues previously discussed, but re-emphasise their importance to strategy formulation. We will also introduce a few new accounting-focused issues and we will set our overall discussion against the on-going need for management to assess the organisation's strategic capability in a way that seeks always to 'add value'.

There are four sections to our discussion. First, we quickly summarise what some authors have termed the four generic approaches to strategy. Second, we consider the importance of accounting to helping shape the strategic direction of an organisation. We then discuss how management can assess the strategic direction of an organisation. This section is in many ways an *audit*, in the broadest sense of the term, which should assist managers in reconsidering the value of some of the discussion in earlier chapters. Finally, we review a number of recent developments in management accounting which, taken together, are sometimes dignified with the title of 'strategic management accounting'.

The four generic approaches to strategy formulation

In this section we seek to provide those not previously familiar with the literature on corporate strategy with a brief overview in order to place the remainder of our discussion in context. It is a section that summarises the explicit (normative) assumptions that underpin the four basic theories of strategy: classical, processual, evolutionary and systemic. For, as Whittington remind us:

> Theories are important. The contain our basic assumptions about key relationships in business life. They tell us what to look out for, what our first

steps should be and what to expect as a result of our actions. Saving us from having to go back to first principles at each stage, they are actually short cuts to action. Often these theories are not very explicit or very formal. Whether building from experience or from books, we all tend to have our own private assumptions about how things work, how to get things done.

(Whittington 1993: 10)

Each of the four theories to be discussed offers different views about our capacity as managers to think rationally and act effectively. It should be noted that they diverge widely in their implications for strategy formulation. Ultimately it is for each of us to finally decide which basic theory best aligns with our own experiences and needs.

The classical approach

Classicists see profitability as the key goal of any business, and rational planning as the means to achieve it. The economic framework on which this theory is based was mapped out in Chapter 13. It is a theory that states that management best serves the interest of *all* investors by undertaking all productive investment opportunities that yield a return greater than that available on the capital markets. Shareholders, in turn, borrow and lend on the capital markets to produce the cash flows that meet their own personal individual needs. In the 1960s authors such as Ansoff (1965), Chandler (1962) and Sloan (1963) wrote in support of the commitment to profit maximisation. Ansoff is credited with writing the first ever textbook on corporate strategy. He linked his strategic framework to a mix of military practice and normative economics. Chandler defined strategy as 'The determination of the basic, long-term goals and objectives of an enterprise, and the adoption of courses of action and the allocation of resources necessary for those goals' (Chandler 1962: 13). His is an approach that favours a top-down, planned and rational approach to strategy formulation. It is based on an historical analysis of the development of four large North American corporations.

Sloan, a former president of General Motors, stated that the strategic aim of business is to 'earn a return on capital, and if in any particular case the return in the long run is not satisfactory, the deficiency should be corrected or the activity abandoned' (Sloan 1963: 49). In over four decades with GM, Sloan helped pioneer the ROI criteria, the concept of divisionalised management structures and the separation of policy formulation from day-to-day operational management. More recently, other writers, such as Porter (1980) in his industry structure analysis, have continued to favour the classical approach to strategy formulation.

The evolutionary approach

Proponents of the evolutionary approach see the attainment of a strategic framework as a dangerous delusion. There is much less confidence in senior management's ability to plan and act in a rational manner. They expect markets to secure profit maximisation and managers to be rational optimisers in a 'law of the jungle' view of the business world where only the best performers survive. As Henderson, founder of the Boston Consulting Group, observes:

Classical economic theories of competition are so simplistic and sterile that they have been less contributions to understanding than obstacles. These theories postulate rational, self-interest behaviour by individuals who interact through market exchanges in a fixed and static legal system of property and contracts. . . . Darwin is probably a better guide to business competition than economists are.

(Henderson 1989: 143)

Hannan and Freeman (1988) support this proposition. They believe that the 'organisational selection process' is one that favours organisations with relatively inert structures, ones that cannot change their strategic direction and organisational structure at the same pace as their environments change. Williamson advises managers to seek always to be cost-effective and 'not to get distracted from the basics' (1991: 76). As Whittington (1993: 22) sums it up, the evolutionary advice is that it is better to let the environment do the strategy selection, not the managers.

The processual approach

Most processualists see strategy formulation as all about satisfying and settling for less than the optimal. They see the classicists as naive idealists, and though they share some common thinking with the evolutionists they are far less confident about the environment's ability to foster strategy selection.

To Cyert and March (1963) the notion of 'rational economic man' is a fiction; in practice, people are only 'boundedly rational'. By this they mean that managers are unable to handle more than a few factors at a time. Managers do not search unlimitedly for new information; rather, they are prone to accept the first satisfactory option that presents itself and they are easily biased by the information presented in support of that option. Organisations represent coalitions of individual managers, who each contribute their own personal objectives and value systems to the organisation. Managers bargain between themselves to arrive at a set of common goals more or less acceptable to them all. Bargaining involves compromise, which is just human nature. Strategic formulation is the result of 'political compromise' and has little to do with the concept of profit maximisation. Such an approach is by its very nature conservative, and hence is often slow to recognise the need for change, until some new 'dominant coalition' is recognised. Strategies represent ways in which managers attempt to simplify and bring order to the complex and chaotic daily environment in which our organisations exist.

Mintzberg (1987) proposes the metaphor of strategy as 'craft'. He likens the crafting of strategy to the potter who must use hands and mind together to shape the clay into a recognisable form. Crafting strategy is a continuous and adaptive process, with formation and implementation 'inextricably entangled'. Mintzberg argues that managers cannot be smart enough to think through strategy too far in advance. Managers should be honest with themselves and recognise that there is an inevitable logical incrementalism to the process, which will always involve a degree of experimentation and learning. Whittington summarises the views of the processualists when he states that:

> [to] focus on the imperfections of organisational and market processes yields at least four conceptions of strategy radically different from the classical

perspective: strategy may be a decision-making heuristic, a device to simplify reality into something managers can actually cope with; plans may just be managerial security blankets, providing reassurance as much as guidance; strategy may not precede action, but may only emerge retrospectively, once action has taken place; strategy is not just about carefully cultivating internal competencies. Many of the confident precepts of the Classicists are put into jeopardy; suddenly, it seems that goals are slippery and vague, long-term policy statements, vain delusions, and the separation of formulation from implementation a self-serving top management myth.

(Whittington 1993: 27)

Systemic theory

Unlike the evolutionary and processural theorists, systemic theorists do retain some faith in the capacity of management to plan forward and to act effectively in the best interests of their investors. The central tenet of systemic theory is that decision-makers are not simply detached, calculating individuals immersed in densely interwoven social systems. Granovetter (1985) suggests that behaviour that may appear irrational to the classicist may not appear so to systemic theorists, who believe that the performance of organisations differs according to the social and economic systems in which they are placed. This view is supported by Whitley (1991), who points out that different kinds of enterprise structure become feasible and successful in particular social contexts. Hu (1992) has illustrated, for example, how successful multinational companies often have strong domestic roots. Nestlé, with 96.5% of its employees outside of its home country, remains firmly in Swiss control by limited foreign shareholding voting rights to 3%. With the exception of Sony, most Japanese companies remain controlled by domestic senior management. As Whittington (1993) notes, the main message of the systemic theorists is that the formulation of strategy must be sociologically sensitive.

These four approaches to strategy offer different advice to management. Their main characteristics are summarised in Table 19.1. An appreciation of these alternative approaches is useful since individual managers and organisations probably tend, more or less, to follow one of these directions. Managers should also appreciate that, for fairly obvious reasons, accountants by their training tend to see strategy through the eyes of the classicists, and hence their accounting systems tend to be somewhat rigid by conforming to fairly rigid norms.

The importance of the nature of the environment cannot be stressed enough when it comes to determining the organisational structure of a particular company. This structure tends to define the 'style' of management practised and, in turn, has profound influences on the way that accounting information is prepared and used. Table 19.2 provides an outline of environmental influence on organisational structure.

In environments that are simple and static organisations tend to be more concerned with operational efficiency and their management styles, and accounting systems tend to be mechanistic and centralised. However, in environments that are simple and dynamic there is a real need to increase the extent to which managers are capable of sensing what is going on around them, identifying change and

Table 19.1 The four perspectives on strategy

	Classic	*Processual*	*Evolutionary*	*Systemic*
Strategy	Formal	Crafted	Efficient	Embedded
Rationale	Profit maximisation	Vague	Survival	Local
Focus	Internal (plans)	Internal (politics/ cognitions)	External (markets)	External (societies)
Processes	Analytical	Bargaining/learning	Darwinian	Social
Key influences	Economics/military	Psychology	Economics/biology	Sociology
Key authors	Chandler	Cyert and March	Hannan and Freeman	Granovetter
	Ansoff	Mintzberg	Williamson	Marris
	Porter	Pettigrew		
Key period	1960s	1970s	1980s	1990s

Source: Whittington (1993).

Table 19.2 Environmental influences on organisational structure

	Stable	*Dynamic*
Complex	Decentralised bureaucractic (e.g. hospitals)	Decentralised organic (e.g. advanced electronics)
Simple	Centralised bureaucratic (e.g. mass production)	Centralised organic (e.g. retailing) *or* decentralised bureaucratic

Source: adapted, with permission, from Mintzberg (1979: 268).

responding to it. A more organic style of management is therefore needed and this applies equally to the type of accounting models that are required. Increased complexity in stable environments is handled by devolving decision responsibility to specialists. At least for operational purposes, they tend to have more decentralised management structures and there is a need for interactive management accounting systems. Finally, where the environment is both complex and dynamic there is a need for speed and flexibility that only organic styles of management can provide; and the level of complexity is such that they must devolve responsibility and authority to specialists who either have a good level of financial management skills or dedicated accounting support.

Strategy evaluation and accounting

From the foregoing debate it is clear that accountants can work positively with managers if both parties are influenced by the underlying philosophy of either the classicist or the systemicist proponents of strategy evaluation. Elsewhere in this text we have examined accounting approaches to both short-term and long-term decisions. We have also recognised, from the outset, that it is cash that keeps organisations 'alive' and viable, and not accounting profit – companies become insolvent when they run out of cash to pay their bills (Chapter 17).

In this section we reconsider the value that certain accounting approaches can have in assisting managers to determine the strategic direction(s) that they wish to follow. The first issue is that of **added value**:

> The creation of added value is governed by two factors – the value of the good or service to the customer and the cost of production to the firm. Added value is the difference between the two. The firm can never appropriate the whole of that added value. As the intensity of the competitive environment increases, prices will bid down the costs of other firms, and added value can only be the result of competitive advantages. In hot wars (i.e. unstable competitive environments), price is driven by the marginal cost of production. In cold wars (i.e. stable economic environments with markets in which firms have adopted compatible repeated game strategies[1]), firms are generally able to earn some of the value of the goods and services they provide.
>
> (Kay 1993: 226)

As Kay goes on to discuss, the costs which are relevant in measuring the value added from a particular productive activity are the **incremental** costs associated with that product or activity. These are the costs that arise from either increasing or decreasing activity as demand either rises or falls. Although every introductory economics text-book stresses the importance of marginal costs, in reality they play little role in business decisions. The cost estimates that form the background to pricing decisions tend to arise as a result of the allocations of accounting costs, in which virtually the whole of the business's expenses are attributed to some product or service. Activities are therefore monitored and driven by reference to their contribution – the amount which they yield over and above the direct (variable) costs associated with them. Most managers and accountants tend to see marginal cost pricing as a recipe for going broke. Recall, in relation to earlier discussions on contributions, that all too often management tends to see too high a proportion of the operational costs as fixed. While this may be true in the short term, it is folly necessarily to presume so into the longer term. In the long term every cost can be varied in line with the scale and operational requirements of the firm.

The more recent promotion of activity-based costing systems (see Chapter 12) can be seen as an approach to bridging the gap between the more mechanical approaches to cost allocation and the measurement of the direct costs associated with particular outputs. Again to quote Kay: 'Building up the structure of costs in this way links the value chain of the firm, the overall added value statement, and the incremental costs associated with individual products' (Kay 1993: 227). This is sound advice; the strategic imperative is to see such a cost structure as setting the basis for a pattern of minimum prices across all markets, with the additional recovery related to the value of products/services to customers/clients, and the state of competition in the variety of markets that exist from time to time.

Managers need also to understand the concept of **market segmentation**. This is particularly so in relation to the provision of services rather than to manufactured goods. Curiously, while from a marketing standpoint segmentation is almost seen as a nuisance – customers insisting that they be treated differently – from an economic perspective this presents an opportunity to enhance profitability and increase sales by distinguishing economic market opportunities and resisting the application of the law of one price. What managers need to appreciate is that market segmentation is a strategic imperative of economic survival. This can be achieved by individual pricing (one-on-one negotiation), group pricing (as often practised in the transport industry) and by product/service proliferation (similar but distinctive products/ services offered in different markets). However, underlying these strategies must be a clear recognition that the price must always cover relevant costs.

Supply-chain management represents another strategic focus that managers and accountants should pay more attention to. Some writers describe this as either vertical relationships management or the life cycle approach to product/service delivery. It is a concept which considers the whole supply chain from the sourcing of inputs through to processing and finally to customer delivery. All too often attention is too focused on internal processes. Many large organisations have to deal with too many suppliers and pay scant attention to the importance and mode of service/product delivery. Lateral thinking can radically improve cost reduction throughout all the links in the supply chain. For example, suppliers can be invited to send their personnel on to the shop floor to examine issues of quality and efficiency. Cost savings can then be shared pro rata. In Australia BHP Steel has various of its major suppliers provide personnel to work directly with its workers at identifying cost savings. It has also reduced its suppliers from thousands to only a few hundred by outsourcing some if its supply requirements to 'group' suppliers. As Baversox and Closs (1996) have noted, supply-chain relationships are among the most complex and least understood areas of logistics operations.

The final aspect that needs re-emphasis in this section is that of risk analysis. Again, we have already briefly introduced the contribution of portfolio analysis to the management of risk (Chapter 13). This is not the only approach to be considered. Simulation techniques such as Monte Carlo simulation analysis may also be useful in mapping out various probability-weighted scenarios. Pragmatic solutions such as insurance and the introduction of price-indexation clauses into contracts help to reduce the operational risks faced by both buyers and sellers. Hedging is also another strategy for adding value through contract design. In fact, management often does not spend enough time on good contract design and, while it may consult lawyers, it seldom discusses contract details with accountants. Contracts should be clear as to which party bears which risk. There are two basic principles (Kay 1993) of risk-sharing in contracts. Identifiable risks should be assigned to the party that has more control over them. If both have equal control (or if neither has control) risk should be assigned to which ever of the parties can manage it cheaply, often the larger of the parties. In the automobile industry the assembler invariably takes most of the risk associated with specific input costs. More general economic uncertainties, which neither party can particularly influence, tend to be shared between the parties in proportions that vary according to their current negotiating strength.

Assessing strategic direction

In this section we consider the information requirements that management needs to consider when carrying out a strategic assessment of the organisation. In many ways it is a review reflective of many of the issues earlier in this text. While it is formed around a strategic analysis of a private-sector organisation, those in the public sector will see obvious parallels with their own organisations.

As Kay (1993) has said, successful strategy requires a company to choose the market(s) in which its distinctive capabilities yield the greatest competitive advantage. How can this be achieved? First, it is important to collect appropriate quantitative and qualitative information on your own company, on the industry or sector it is in, and on a range of broader contextual (environmentally related) factors that have an impact on all companies in general. Ellis and Williams (1993) have set out a nine-cell table that defines this set of information needs (see Table 19.3). It should be recognised that there is considerable overlap between the different areas. A broad range of sources can be sought from which to compile this information, including annual reports, the business press, information-retrieval systems (such as FT Profile, Textline and Datastream) and industry/company-sponsored reports and books. It is important to remember that focusing on the non-financial components of the analysis and virtually ignoring the assessment of financial statements will give rise to a distorted picture. The same is also true in reverse, so it is important to ensure a balance in the information collected.

Careful attention should be paid to both the profitability and the cash-flow position of your own company as well as of your competitors. With respect to profitability, management needs to focus on:

Table 19.3   Key information requirements

	Assessing strategic direction	Financial-statement analysis	Stock-market assessment
Company	1 Identify and assess corporate and business unit strategies, management resources, product market positions, etc.	2 Assess current and future outcomes of the company's strategies – sales, profitability, cash flow, etc.	3 Understand the market assessment and rating of the company
Industry/sector	4 Evaluate competitive forces and the relative strengths and strategies of competitors Review key industry drivers and the likely future pattern of industry development	5 Make comparisons with other companies operating in the same or similar product markets	6 Compare the company's rating with those of other companies in the same sector Review performance of the sector against the overall market
Broad context	7 Assess key PEST change agents, i.e. political, economic, social and technological factors	8 Evaluate opportunities for raising funding (debt and equity), likely tax and interest-rate changes, etc.	9 Identify movements in the overall stock market and likely future pattern of share prices

Source: Ellis and Williams (1993).

- the extent to which turnover and profits/losses have been influenced by the various sectors/units of the company, and whether any of these business sectors/units have been acquired or disposed of during the year;
- significant notes to the accounts that might cover significant provisions and/or contingencies;
- change to or differences between accounting policies – key areas can relate to items such as depreciation, goodwill, pension-fund accounting and brand accounting;
- the identification of activities which are the key profit drivers and those areas/units which are underperforming;
- its strategies to improve areas of underperformance.

With respect to the company's overall cash position, management needs to focus on:

- assessing the cash-flow statement to see whether it is a generator or user of funds;
- establishing whether funds generated are from trading activities or are a result of restructuring – in both cases the use to which such funds have been put should be reviewed;
- considering whether the position in relation to the use of funds (if the company is a user of funds) has deteriorated or improved over the last twelve months and what has been done to improve matters;
- examining whether additional shares have been issued or borrowed funds raised, and for what purpose;
- identifying activities that are either cash-generators or cash-wasters;
- identifying strategies for maintaining or improving the cash-flow position.

Key financial ratio analysis should be undertaken to compare the company's position relative to its competitors. With this background management should endeavour to assess the extent to which the market is suggesting that future returns are likely to come from dividends or changes in share price and the basis on which this assessment is made. With respect to share prices, an analysis should be made of movements over the last twelve months and why these have occurred. Management needs to consider, for example, whether the market has already discounted certain future events in determining the share price. Management needs to consider the broader strategic future of the company. Is it, for example, a potential takeover target? If so, what is the management view on this? Is the takeover to be fought or should there be a concentration on what the company might be valued at? If management, to take another tack, believes the share price undervalues the company, what is it going to do to improve the company's standing? Financial-statement analysis and stock-market assessment are critical to the assessment of strategic direction.

The 'new' accounting?

In the previous section we discussed a new, and emerging, feature of management accounting – that of companies, as part of their strategic management process, starting to use accounting concepts and techniques in the measurement of their external environment, and, in particular, assessing their own position vis-à-vis that of their competitors. This is indicative of a broader change in management accounting. Increasingly, accountants, in collaboration with managers, are starting both to measure new things and to measure existing things in different ways. The emergence of activity-based costing in recent years is one example of this. The drive behind this trend is the need for managers to have more relevant and more focused information in today's increasingly competitive environment. Closely associated with this 'new' accounting has been the emergence of new management techniques, a number of which have emerged either from Japan or as a response to changing technologies.

Thus, for example, increasing emphasis is placed these days on 'total quality management' concepts. There is an extensive and growing literature dealing with quality-management issues (see, e.g. Oakland 1994). Here, we are concerned with the impact of the quality movement on management accounting. Increasingly, the costs of quality (or the lack of it) are becoming significant to organisations; hence, they need to know what these costs are so that they can be managed. The following costs must be measured:

- **Prevention costs**: these are the costs of the systems an organisation installs to prevent quality falling below the required level. They will typically include items such as staff training, preventative maintenance, planning and design costs, re-engineering and technical support costs.
- **Appraisal costs**: these are the costs of ensuring that the required level of quality is being achieved. They will include items such as inspection and testing, supervisory and quality audit costs.
- **Internal failure costs**: these are the costs that the organisation bears when quality standards are not achieved and this failure is recognised prior to delivery to the customer. They include items such as downtime, rework and scrap costs.
- **External failure costs**: these are the costs that the organisation bears when quality standards are not achieved and sub-standard delivery is made to customers. Typically, they will include items such as warranty and product liability costs, as well as the opportunity costs of lost business as customers go elsewhere.

The costs of prevention and appraisal are normally referred to as the 'costs of conformance', and the internal and external failure costs as the 'costs of non-conformance'. The objective of management should be to minimise the total of these costs. To achieve this, it needs to understand the trade-offs between these two types of costs.

A related example of accounting seeking to measure costs that are directly relevant to management's information needs come with the assessment of supplier performance. There will be a trade-off between the price (per unit) charged by a supplier and the quality (broadly defined as 'fitness for purpose') of what is supplied. It is very tempting for a management facing intense competition to go for the lowest-price supplier, and traditional cost accounting systems may well encourage this. However, if the 'quality' is not right additional costs may well be incurred, and it becomes important to know what these costs are. There are a variety of ways this might be calculated but, in essence, they all involve approaches such as the computation of a 'supplier cost index', calculated by:

$$\frac{\text{Cost of purchased materials} + \text{Cost of non-value-adding activities}}{\text{Cost of purchased materials}} \tag{19.1}$$

Here, the cost of non-value-adding activities includes items such as the costs associated with inspection, rejection, reworking and non-scheduled delivery. The objective of the measurement is to help managers identify the lowest-*total*-cost suppliers rather than the lowest-price suppliers. Of course, other issues (see Chapter 17) will be involved in the final selection of suppliers, but the cost will remain an important element.

Another area where accounting is starting to work more closely with management is that of production design and planning. Again, the thrust is that of providing managers with more relevant information. Two examples of this are 'target costing' and 'life-cycle costing'.

The first of these completely reverses old-fashioned notions of 'cost-plus' pricing. In essence, cost-plus pricing involves designing a product (service), costing it (probably on a conventional absorption-costing basis) and then trying to market it at a price which will produce an acceptable level of profit. Target costing involves assessing what the market is likely to be prepared to pay for a product (service) with a specified set of features and then, allowing for an acceptable profit margin, determining a target cost for it. The product design and subsequent manufacture is then focused on the achievement of this target cost. Partridge and Perren (1997) provide a good summary of the benefits of target costing, emphasising its links with notions of 'continuous improvement'. However, they rightly emphasise the fact that the real opportunity of continuous improvement is at the pre-production stage (Partridge and Perren 1997).

This is where life-cycle costing comes into play. Life-cycle costing recognises that the decisions made at the early stages of product design and specification frequently commit management to future patterns of cost, giving only restricted freedom of choice (and cost management) once production starts. Thus great emphasis needs to be placed on managerial understanding of decisions being made during product development. Accountants have a major role to play here as part of a multi disciplinary team which works to produce product designs that will meet target costs over the life-cycle of the product.

At the same time, new production techniques, such as 'advanced manufacturing technologies' and 'just-in-time' management, are reinforcing the need for change in traditional management and cost accounting systems. Fortunately, there is evidence that management accountants are responding to these challenges (see, e.g., Bromwich and Bhimani 1989, 1994; Green and Amenkheinan 1992; Shank and Govindarajan 1992; Drury and Dugdale 1996).

Similar moves are taking place with regard to customers. For too long, management accounting's emphasis has been on the profitability of product (service) lines. Little attention has been paid to the profitability of servicing individual customers. In part, this issue is addressed by activity-based costing, with its questioning of the costing of small bespoke batches of product. It is now also being addressed by 'customer-profitability' analysis. This involves looking not just at the sales (and contribution generated therefrom) that are being made to individual customers, but also at the costs of generating those sales. Thus it looks at issues such as the number of orders (and the cost of processing them), the balance between standard and non-standard product ordered (and the associated costs), and the costs of support and servicing for individual customers. A commonly found result when customer-profitability analysis is first introduced is that servicing some customers (even quite large ones) costs money rather than makes money.

A major stimulus to these developments was the work of Johnson and Kaplan (1987). This has been followed up in the UK by the work of people such as Bromwich and Bhimani (1989, 1994), and further work by Cooper and Kaplan (1991) and Kaplan and Norton (1996). The emphasis of all this work has been on the importance of *relevance* in the work of management accounting, on the need to integrate financial and operating information and, perhaps more importantly, on the need for a 'balanced scorecard', both for strategic planning and for the subsequent implementation and control of plans.

Conclusions

In this chapter we have been able to give only a flavour of the changes that are taking place in accounting. In earlier chapters we discussed the changes that are taking place in financial accounting (reporting). However, the authors believe that the most significant changes are taking place in management accounting. The pace of change in this area over the last decade has been significant, although that much of this change has been limited to large multinational companies. Hopefully these changes will soon be reflected in the practices of smaller enterprises and the public sector. The core elements of this change have been a renewed focus on the need for management accountants to provide management with *relevant* information. This has led them to seek to measure old things differently; to measure new things; to break away from the dominance of financial accounting; and to integrate financial and operating information. Greater emphasis is being placed on the role of performance indicators and involvement in the whole value-chain of business, and on the need to integrate accounting practices with strategic planning (Wilson 1995).

At the beginning of this book we stated that its focus would be primarily on the contribution that accounting and accountability systems can make towards the more efficient and effective management of business enterprises, because of the rapidly changing nature of the financial consequences of the activities of organisations and individuals.

The first part of the book dealt essentially with financial reporting. The principal areas covered were the importance and bases of accounting records, a review of the key financial statements and their interpretation, together with the legal and regulatory requirements associated with their publications. Financial reports are important because they provide outsiders with financial information on the organisation's performance. They are also an important means by which management understands how competitors are doing. However, as indicated, there have been a number of concerns over the reliability of the financial information provided in these reports. Why was it that during the recession of 1990–91 some companies which reported record profits were almost simultaneously going into administration? The most dramatic of these collapses was that of Polly Peck, the consequences of which remain with us today. We have covered in some detail the remit undertaken by the Accounting Standards Board to improve the quality and reliability of financial reporting.

One of the major confusions with financial reporting for many ill-informed users of annual reports is the basic fact that profit does not equal cash. This confusion, regrettably, often also resides with sections of management. Other 'profitable' enterprises that have gone bust in recent years include Coloroll, British & Commonwealth and Maxwell Communications. Shareholders have lost their investment, their interests being failed by the professionals, management and the regulators who were employed to protect them. Even in the stock market it remains the case that far too much attention is given to the 'magic' earnings-per-share number (see Smith 1992). Financial reports should be read only if due attention is given to the accounting policies and footnotes that accompany the main financial statements. Always remember:

PROFIT REPRESENTS AN OPINION(S); CASH IS FACT.

It is cash that pays wages, invoices, dividends and funds reinvestment.

The need to generate cash effectively came to the fore in the second half of the book. The basics of costing, having been considered, attention was paid to both short- and long-term investment strategy. All the time we considered the contribution, in cash terms, that was likely to arise from following a particular course of action. Despite recognising that the basic economic objective of maximising shareholder wealth underpins much of the theory of decision-making, we also had to recognise that the behavioural sciences also have much to offer us in this area. In reality, managers tend not to be maximisers; they tend to be risk-averse satisfiers. By examining aspects of behavioural accounting we were then able to consider aspects of financial control and issues associated with the measurement of management accountability. Time and again we pointed out that often financial control systems fail because the means by which management is evaluated are not necessarily congruent with overall organisational objectives. This was particularly illustrated when we considered the evaluation of managers in a divisionalised organisation. What became clear was that there was no ideal way of measuring management's performance.

Corporate strategy develops as a result of compromise; organisations tend to develop multiple objectives rather than a unitary objective. Multiple objectives tend to mean that managers have to trade on the importance of one priority relative to another. The quality of information, including accounting information, is critical to aiding our understanding of whether, overall, the organisation is achieving its targets. Managers tend to operate in a market or quasi-market environment. As such, all have to be commercially accountable. It is important that they demand and use good-quality accounting information when they make decisions and monitor performance. If they are to use this information they must understand the principles and assumptions that underly its presentation. They must also be prepared to help to make decisions on the underlying assumptions that will have an impact on the quality and relevance of the accounting information provided.

Further reading

In the last few years a number of texts have been published that have sought more closely to combine accounting and strategic management. There are also some excellent tests that deal with strategy in a way that is very accessible for managers. Whittington's *What is Strategy?* (1993) is an excellent, short and challenging read which challenges basic assumptions of management orthodoxy. Johnson and Scholls's *Exploring Corporate Strategy* (1993) is a popular standard text on corporate strategy. Ellis and Williams, in *Corporate Strategy and Financial Analysis* (1993) uniquely seek to interface managerial accounting and stock-market perspectives in terms of strategies that companies follow. Kaplan and Norton's *The Balanced Scorecard* (1996) focuses on the implementation of strategies and the role of performance measurement. Kay's *Foundations of Corporate Success* (1993) integrates organisation and financial perspectives on the performance of successful firms. In addition, journals such as *Journal of Management Accounting Research* and *Management Accounting* are replete with articles reflecting changes in management accounting practice.

Questions and exercises

1 To compete and cooperate in a dynamic business environment we need to be sensitive to the diverse textures of different business systems. Discuss.

2 To what extent is it fair to state that the success of Far East economies, the entry of the Eastern European countries into the capitalist world and the closer interaction of Western European countries are compelling a proper appreciation of the diversity of practice within capitalist economies?

3 Marginal cost pricing is seen by most firms and accountants as a recipe for going broke, yet every elementary economics textbook stresses the importance of marginal costs. Who is right, the accountants or the economists?

4 Why is it that activity-based costing helps build up the structure of costs in ways which link the value-chain of the firm, the overall added-value statement and the incremental costs associated with individual products?

5 For an organisation with which you are familiar, define its value-chain and associated competitive advantages and disadvantages?

6 Using the structure set out in Table 19.2, analyse a company with which you are familiar both in relation to its industry sector and against the broader economic framework of the UK economy.

7 How useful are companies' annual reports in assessing their strategic direction?

8 'Analysts should be focusing their energies on reviewing the cash position of companies rather than focusing on levels of profit and balance sheets.' Do you agree?

9 Assume that your analysis of your company's share price leads you to believe it is undervalued in the market. Why would this be of concern and how would you endeavour to promote its revaluation upwards?

10 To what extent do you believe that all managers also need to be competent financial managers?

Notes

2 The background to traditional accounting statements

1 Conventionally the symbol Δ is used to indicate a change in the amount of a quantity. Thus, in equation (2.5) Δ (equity) represents the change in equity over a period of time.

18 Accounting for social responsibility and the environment

1 This concept is aimed at encouraging organisations to provide both quantitative and qualitative analysis of a chosen project's environmental impact and to be able to justify the hurdle rates used.

19 Strategic business accounting

1 It should be noted that governments may object to certain 'cold war' strategies as these are in fact often cartels or other groupings which are deemed to be acting against the public interest.

Glossary of terms

abridged accounts The Companies Acts exempt small and medium-sized companies from the full financial reporting requirements specified in the Acts. In particular, small companies can file an abbreviated balance sheet with the Registrar of Companies and do not have to file a profit and loss account. Medium-sized companies can file an abbreviated profit and loss account. Full accounts are still required for shareholders, and an audit is still required. The qualifying criteria for these exemptions are specified in section 247 of the Companies Act 1989.

absorption costing A method of determining the unit cost of products, normally on a full-cost basis, inclusive of direct costs and indirect costs or overheads. The overhead charges are proportional to some measure of direct work done on the product, rather than to a measure of actual work done in the support services (as under activity-based costing).

accelerated depreciation An approach to depreciation in which the cost of the asset being depreciated is written off over a period of time shorter than its forecast useful life.

acceptance credit An arrangement via which a bank allows a customer to issue bills of exchange up to an agreed limit. It is normally used by enterprises in place of overdrafts where large amounts are involved.

account As a noun, the generic name of the subdivisions of an entity's accounting records used for the purposes of analysis. As a verb, the generic name for the process whereby an entity (individual) renders a statement about its actions and their outcomes to those having a right to such a statement.

accountability The generic name for the relationship which exists between an entity (individual) which has to account for its actions and the entity (person) to whom the account is rendered.

accountant A person suitably trained to prepare, update and analyse accounts.

accounting The setting up, maintenance and analysis of financial records and the preparation of financial reports from such records. (Also referred to as accountancy.)

accounting bases The accounting measurement methods that are available to entities in the preparation of their financial statements. The range of accounting bases is very wide and there is frequently more than one recognised accounting basis for dealing with a particular item, e.g. depreciation.

accounting period   The period of time spanning the date between two consecutive balance sheets and to which the profit and loss account relates. For companies it is normally twelve calendar months.

accounting policies   These are the specific accounting bases adopted by an enterprise in the preparation of its financial statements. Companies have to disclose their accounting policies as part of the notes to their financial statements.

accounting rate of return   A technique for the evaluation of investment projects which compares the potential average annual increase in profit which would result from a project to the amount of the investment required by the project. This technique is analogous to the return on capital employed and return on investment measures of corporate and divisional performance.

accounting reference period   The period by reference to which accounts have to be prepared and submitted to members of the company. Section 3 of the Companies Act 1989 lays down the regulations for determining the accounting reference period.

accounting standards   The generic name given to the statements issued by professional bodies (and others) in an attempt to standardise (regulate) the preparation of financial statements by companies.

accounts payable   An alternative term, of American origin, to creditors for describing amounts owed by an entity to third parties.

accounts receivable   An alternative term, of American origin, to debtors for describing amounts owed to an entity by third parties.

accrual   An amount included in the creditors of an entity in the preparation of its financial statements to allow for expenditure which has not yet been recorded in the accounting records of the entity.

accruals basis   The normal basis of preparing accounts for trading enterprises. In this basis the income and expense effects of transactions are incorporated in the entity's financial statements, whether or not they have as yet resulted in cash-flow consequences, and matched with one another so far as a relationship can be established.

accumulated depreciation   The cumulative amount of depreciation charged against an asset during the period from its acquisition to the date of the financial statements.

acid test   The ratio of an enterprise's liquid assets to its short-term liabilities. Also referred to as the liquid ratio and the quick ratio, it provides a measure of the enterprise's liquidity.

acquisition   Normally refers to one company obtaining control of another by means of purchasing at least 50% of the voting shares in the company being acquired. Often referred to as a takeover.

acquisition cost   The original historical cost of acquiring an asset.

activity-based costing   An approach to the costing of individual products and services which focuses on the identification of 'cost drivers', i.e. those activities which lead to indirect production costs being incurred, and which charges the individual products or services with these indirect costs on the basis of their demand for these 'cost drivers'.

activity-based management   The use of information derived from activity-based costing in order to improve cost control, work and value-added analysis, pricing and product-mix decisions, etc.

administration A part of the corporate insolvency process whereby it is possible for qualified insolvency practitioners (administrators) to take over the management of a failing company with a view to reviving it and avoiding receivership or liquidation.

advanced corporation tax The income tax paid by a company on behalf of its shareholders in relation to dividend payments. Later, subject to certain restrictions, it can be offset against the company's mainstream corporation tax.

agreed bid A takeover offer which has obtained the support of the directors of the target company, who recommend to their shareholders that the offer should be accepted.

allocation The process by means of which costs or revenues are assigned to a business segment, responsibility centre, product or service. There are numerous different bases on which this process can be conducted. However, wherever possible, an attempt is made to carry it out according to logical measures of production or use.

allotment The process by means of which shares in a new issue are allotted to those who have applied for such shares. Frequently, the terms of the offer will specify the basis of such allotment in the event of the offer being oversubscribed.

amortisation The writing off over a number of accounting periods of the original (historical) cost of an asset or a liability. It is sometimes used as a synonym for depreciation. In the context of assets it is most commonly used to describe the writing off of intangible rather than tangible assets.

annual general meeting A meeting which a company must hold each year and which all shareholders are entitled to attend. The business to be conducted at this meeting normally includes consideration of the directors' report and accounts, election of directors, appointment of auditors and the declaration of dividends. Shareholders must be given twenty-one days' notice of the meeting in writing.

annual report A report produced each year by a company. *Inter alia*, it contains the directors' report and accounts. It normally contains a statement by the chairman and a range of information on the company's activities. Such a report is required by the Companies Acts, which also specify a number of specific items of information that it must contain. Accounting standards and stock-exchange regulations (for listed companies) also specify disclosure requirements.

annual return A requirement of the Companies Acts (s. 363), it is a document detailing various information regarding the company (e.g. details of directors, where the register of shareholders is kept, and where any register of debenture holders is kept), which must be filed annually with the Registrar of Companies within forty-two days of a company's annual general meeting. The Companies Acts specify the information required in an annual return. Copies of the accounts and other statutory reports must be annexed to the return. The return and the other reports are available for public inspection at the Companies Registry.

annuity An annuity is a cash flow of a contractually agreed amount which lasts for a specified number of years. A common form of annuity is where individuals pay an insurance company a lump sum in exchange for annual (monthly) payments from the insurance company for the rest of their life.

APB A professional body formed in 1991 to take over the work of the APC for the issuing of Auditing Standards and Guidelines.

APC   A subcommittee of the CCAB, containing representatives of the three Institutes of Chartered Accountants and the ACCA, which issues authoritative statements on auditing. It issued the first auditing standards in 1980, and subsequently issued a number of other Auditing Standards and Guidelines. Its work has now been taken over by the APB.

Articles of Association   Every company requires a set of Articles of Association, which are in effect part of the constitution of the company. They specify how the company shall conduct its affairs, and the rights and obligations of various parties involved with the company.

ASB   A subcommittee of the Financial Reporting Council which was set up in 1990 and has taken over the work previously carried out by the ASC in relation to the issuing of authoritative statements on accounting standards.

ASC   Originally set up in 1970, when it was called the ASSC, the ASC sought by the issue of SSAPs to narrow the range of accounting bases that could be adopted in accounts and to ensure greater comparability between the accounts of different enterprises. Its work has been taken over by the ASB.

asset   'Assets are rights or other access to future economic benefits controlled by an entity as a result of past transactions or events' (ASB 1995a: para. 3.5).

asset–turnover ratio   The ratio of the sales turnover of the enterprise to the net assets employed. It is commonly regarded as a measure of the efficiency with which the assets are employed in generating sales.

associated companies   An associated company is a company in which another company has a participating interest and over which it has significant influence but not control. The consolidated accounts of a group of companies must account for their share of the associated company's profits.

attributable cost   The cost per unit (or, sometimes, per product line or per organisational unit) which could be avoided or escaped if a particular product or other segment of a business was discontinued while leaving the supporting organisational structure (and costs) intact.

audit   The role of auditors is 'to provide objective assurance on an entity's published financial reports, principally for the benefit of the primary stakeholders to whom the auditors owe a duty of care, but also for the information of other stakeholders' (APB 1994: para. 4.7).

auditing standards   Authoritative statements on auditing from the APB, which issues them as Statements of Auditing Standards.

auditor   The person who carries out an audit. To carry out an audit of the accounts of a company such a person must be a member of one of the professional bodies approved for this purpose by the secretary of state and must hold a current practising certificate. The 1989 Companies Act introduced a number of changes regarding the activities of auditors pursuant to the 8th Directive of the European Union. In practice, most auditors are partnerships of qualified accountants rather than individuals.

authorised share capital   The maximum amount of share capital which the company is authorised by its Memorandum of Association to issue at any point in time. The amount can be altered by means of a resolution of the company in general meeting and is disclosed each year in the accounts.

avoidable cost   The amount of cost which will not continue to be incurred if an existing activity ceases, or that amount of cost that will not be incurred if a potential activity is not undertaken.

bad debts The amount of money owed to an entity by its debtors which will not be collectible from them.

balance sheet One of the primary financial statements, being a statement of an entity's assets, liabilities and equity at a particular date. In the case of companies it is a statutory annual requirement; the Companies Acts specify its form and content in some detail, and require that it presents a 'true and fair' view of the state of the company's affairs at the relevant date.

bankruptcy The state of an individual being unable to pay his/her debts. There are various legal rules dealing with bankruptcy, most notably the Insolvency Act of 1986.

bearer securities A security (e.g. share or bond) where simple possession of the certificate is proof of ownership, as ownership of the security is not registered.

bill of exchange 'An unconditional order in writing addressed by one person to another signed by the person giving it requiring the person to whom it is addressed to pay on demand, or at some fixed or determinable future time, a sum certain in money to or to the order of a specified person or to the bearer' (section 3(1), Bills of Exchange Act 1882).

bill of materials A schedule of the direct materials required for the manufacture of a specified type and quantity of product.

bonds Documentation evidencing medium- or long-term borrowing by an enterprise, a government or other organisation.

bonus shares An issue of fully paid shares to shareholders by way of a dividend out of a company's undistributed profits.

book value The amount at which an asset is stated in an entity's balance sheet, as opposed to its market value. It is sometimes referred to as carrying value.

break-even point That volume of activity at which the revenues an entity generates are just equal to the costs that it incurs, and it accordingly makes neither profit nor loss.

budget A formal quantified statement (normally expressed in financial terms) of a plan of action.

budget appropriation An authorisation made via a budgetary process to spend a specified amount of resources for a specified purpose.

budget variance The difference between the amount contained in a budget and the corresponding actual cost or revenue.

budgetary control The continual comparison of budget forecasts with actual performance.

call A demand by a company for additional capital from its shareholders, most commonly where shares have been issued on a part-paid basis and the company wants the whole, or part, of the unpaid balance to be paid.

called-up share capital The amount of the issued share capital that the shareholders have been 'called upon' to pay. It is equal to the amount of the issued share capital in the absence of calls in advance or in arrears.

capital allowances The amounts which an entity is permitted under taxation legislation to charge against its earnings in lieu of depreciation of its fixed assets. As part of computing an entity's taxable profit, the accounting depreciation is added back to profit and the capital allowances deducted. Capital allowances and accounting depreciation may differ significantly.

capital asset pricing model An economic model for determining the required rate of return on an investment, taking into account the required rate of return on a risk-free investment, the difference between the risk-free rate of return and that for the capital market as a whole, and the relationship between the risk of the investment in question and that of the market as a whole.

capital budgeting The process by means of which an enterprise formally plans its capital investment programme. It incorporates, but is not restricted to, the appraisal of individual capital-investment projects.

capital employed The resources utilised by a business in the conduct of its trading activities to generate profit. Its two main components are working capital and fixed assets.

capital expenditure on fixed assets. The Companies Acts have a number of disclosure requirements relating to such expenditure, whether already made or for which future commitments have been entered into or authorised by the directors.

capital gains tax A tax on surpluses made on the disposal of capital (fixed) assets. It applies to individuals and not to companies, which pay corporation tax on all gains.

capital gearing The relationship between the amount of debt finance and the amount of equity finance on an entity. The relationship can be either in terms of the capital amounts of the finance or in terms of its consequences for income distribution. It is sometimes referred to as leverage.

capital investment appraisal The process of determining whether or not it is worthwhile investing in longer-term capital projects. A range of accounting techniques are available to assist in this process. It is one part of capital budgeting.

capital maintenance A concept stating that an enterprise cannot be regarded as having made a profit in an accounting period unless the value of its capital at the end of the period is at least equal to the value of its capital at the start of the period, after allowing for any equity distributions or contributions. The different approaches to measuring capital for this purpose are the subject of much debate in accounting, especially because of the effects of price-level changes on capital values.

capital redemption reserve A non-distributable reserve created on the redemption of redeemable preference shares other than by the issue of new shares.

capital reserves These are either legally not available for distribution (e.g. unrealised revaluation reserves and share premiums) or not regarded as being available for distribution by the directors for other reasons.

cash basis A method of accounting under which transactions are recognised only at the time they lead to the payment or receipt of monies.

cash budget A plan, covering a specific period of time, summarising the anticipated future receipts and payments of an enterprise, i.e. its forecast cash flow.

cash flow The actual cash receipts and payments of an enterprise for a particular accounting period.

cash-flow accounting A system of accounting based on actual cash flows as opposed to the accruals basis of accounting.

cash-flow forecast   A forecast, covering a specific period of time, of the estimated receipts and payments of an enterprise.

cash-flow statement   One of the primary financial statements, being a statement which summarises the principal components of an entity's receipts and payments during a specified financial period.

chairman's report   A report by the chairman on the activities of the enterprise which is normally included as part of its annual report.

charge   to secure debentures   A form of security, with similarities to a mortgage, offered to lenders whereby the enterprise pledges assets as security for repayment of loans. A charge issued by a company can be a fixed charge, in which case specific assets are the subject of the charge, or a floating charge over all assets of the company. Charges have to be registered with the Registrar of Companies to be effective. The lender has a prior claim for repayment out of the proceeds of selling the charged assets.

collateral   Commonly used to refer to security given to secure a loan. More precisely, it refers to security given by a third party rather than the borrower.

commitment accounting   A system of accounting which records the expenditure which an entity has committed itself to making, as opposed to the expenditure it has actually incurred. It enables management of the entity better to assess the extent of 'free' resources available for fresh initiatives.

committed costs   Costs which have not yet been incurred but which are the subject of a contract such that they will be incurred in the future.

common costs   A cost the benefits of which are enjoyed by a number of different segments of an entity and which cannot be logically allocated to the individual segments.

Companies Acts   Statute law regulating the affairs of companies. The most recent is the 1989 Companies Act, which updates the 1985 Companies Act, which itself was a consolidation of previous Acts.

company   An entity with a legal personality separate from its members, registered under and subject to the requirements of the Companies Acts.

conglomerate   A large company, often with numerous subsidiary companies, which operates in a number of different, and apparently unrelated, commercial and industrial sectors.

conservatism   An accounting concept, rooted in nineteenth-century ideas of creditor and investor protection, which requires accounts to be prepared on a cautious rather than an optimistic basis as regards the valuation of assets and liabilities, and the measurement of revenues and expenses. It is similar to the fundamental accounting concept of prudence.

consistency   This fundamental accounting concept states that there should be 'consistency of accounting treatment of like items within each accounting period and from one period to the next' (ASSC 1971: para. 14c). It is a requirement of both SSAP 2 (Accounting Policies), and the Companies Acts, and is important for the purposes of intertemporal comparison.

consolidated accounts   Consolidated accounts are accounts which incorporate the accounts (balance sheet, profit and loss account, statement of total recognised gains and losses, and cash-flow statement) of the parent company and those of its subsidiary undertakings. These accounts are required by the Companies Acts to give a 'true and fair' view, relating to the undertakings included in the consolidation as a whole, as far as they concern the members of the parent company.

contingencies These are the subject of SSAP 18 (Accounting for Contingencies), which defines them as 'a condition which exists at the balance-sheet date, where the outcome will be confirmed only on the occurrence or non-occurrence of one or more uncertain future events.' (ASSC 1980: para. 14). The SSAP requires that contingencies be taken into account when preparing financial statements based on the best information available at that time.

contingent liability A liability the crystallisation of which is contingent on some future event occurring or not occurring. The Companies Acts require disclosure of such contingent liabilities in the accounts.

continuity convention Another name for the 'going-concern' convention.

continuous budget Also called a rolling budget, this is a budget which constantly covers a specified future period of time by adding another accounting period at the conclusion of each accounting period completed.

contracting out The process of taking a service/function previously provided by a public-sector organisation (such as a local authority) and, via a tendering process, offering it to alternative providers on very carefully specified contractual terms (both operational and financial). It is sometimes referred to as outsourcing.

contribution The difference between the variable revenues and the variable costs attaching to a particular course of action.

contribution approach A method of preparing profit and loss accounts which separates variable from fixed costs and emphasises the difference between variable revenues and variable costs (contribution). The object of the approach is to emphasise the dynamics of cost and revenue behaviour for planning and control purposes.

contribution margin The difference between sales revenue and variable costs.

controllable cost A cost that can be directly controlled at a given level of management.

convertible loan stock Loan stock which carries the option of being converted into shares on specified terms at some future date or on the occurrence of some future event.

corporate report The annual report of an enterprise, intended to give useful information to its recipients.

corporation tax The taxation that companies pay on their taxable profits.

cost The sacrifice that is entailed in acquiring or using goods or services. There are a number of different bases for measuring cost, most notably acquisition cost and opportunity cost.

cost–benefit analysis An approach, derived from economics, for appraising the overall costs and benefits (including ones not normally measured in financial terms, and particularly public ones) of a particular activity or set of activities.

cost centre A responsibility centre within an enterprise, the performance of which is assessed in terms of the service it provides and the costs that it incurs in providing that service.

cost driver A measurable characteristic of work activity (e.g. number of transactions, or time devoted to a particular beneficiary product, service, client, etc.)

which can be recorded and used as the basis for the assignment of costs (especially in activity-based costing).

cost of capital The cost to an enterprise of its sources of finance. It is normally expressed as an annual percentage of the finance, and reflects the relative costs and proportions of debt (provided by lenders) and equity (provided by shareholders) finance.

cost of sales The cost to an enterprise of the goods or services it supplies to its customers. In financial accounts it is normally calculated on an absorption-costing basis.

cost-plus A measure of cost to which is added some mark-up, contribution or profit margin for the purpose of setting external prices or internal (transfer) prices. The measure of cost can be direct/variable cost, full production cost or total cost.

cost–volume–profit analysis An accounting technique based on analysing the cost and revenue structure of an enterprise into component elements based on their variability relative to the volume of activity. This form of analysis, which is sometimes referred to as 'break-even' analysis, is most commonly used as an aid to budgeting and profit planning.

costing The process whereby the cost of a business activity or product is measured and analysed.

credit rating An evaluation of the creditworthiness of an individual or firm.

creditors The amounts owed by an enterprise to those who have supplied it with goods or services for which they have not as yet been paid, or to those who have lent it money.

cumulative preference shares Preference shares on which arrears of dividends have to be paid before any dividend can be paid to ordinary shareholders. The amount of any arrears of such dividends has to be disclosed in the accounts.

currency conversion The process of exchanging an amount in one currency for the equivalent amount in another.

currency translation The calculation of the equivalent of an amount in one currency in terms of another for accounting purposes. Unlike currency conversion, it does not involve the actual exchange of an amount in one currency for the equivalent amount in another.

current assets Assets which are held by an enterprise for the short term and are expected to be converted to cash within that term, normally regarded as being within twelve months of the date of the accounts. They are sometimes referred to as circulating assets.

current cost accounting A basis of preparing accounts under which non-monetary items in the accounts are valued at their current cost equivalent (i.e. market or replacement-cost valuation) rather than their historical cost. This system of accounting, which proved highly contentious, was the subject of SSAP 16 (Current Cost Accounting), which was withdrawn in 1988.

current liabilities Liabilities which are due for settlement within the short term, which is normally regarded as being within twelve months.

current purchasing power accounting A basis of preparing accounts under which items in the accounts are stated in terms of their equivalent purchasing power as at the end of the accounting period. This system of accounting was the subject of Provisional SSAP 7 (Accounting for Changes in the Purchasing Power of Money), which was withdrawn in 1978.

current ratio   The ratio of an entity's current assets to its current liabilities. The ratio is regarded as being a measure, albeit a relatively crude one, of an enterprise's liquidity.

debentures   A document issued by a company to a lender as evidence of a debt due to the lender. Such debts usually arise out of a loan and are normally the subject of a fixed and/or floating charge. There are various kinds of debentures, but commonly they involve more than one lender and involve the creation of a deed of trust charging the property of the company in favour of a trustee for the debenture holders. Debenture holders, or their trustee, have various legal rights to ensure the value of their security.

debtors   Amounts owing to an enterprise, normally arising from the sale of goods or services on a non-cash (or credit) basis.

debtor turnover   The ratio between an entity's debtors and its sales on a credit basis. It is usually expressed in terms of the average number of days credit sales that debtors represent or in terms of the multiple that credit sales are of debtors. It is commonly regarded as an indicator of the efficiency of an entity's debtor-collection practices.

decision package   Documentation used in the implementation of zero-base budgeting (typically involving the use of pro formas). It describes the decision unit involved (typically a cost or profit centre with delegated authority for its actions) and the costs/revenues of its operation.

deferred asset   An asset the worth of which is contingent on some reasonably certain future event. It is most commonly encountered in the case of a deferred taxation asset.

deferred taxation   A provision for taxation which recognises the differences in timing in the recognition of profit for accounting and taxation purposes. It is the subject of SSAP 15 (Accounting for Deferred Tax).

depletion   A means of computing depreciation for an asset the economic life of which is limited by the speed at which it is used up. It is most commonly applied in the extractive industries and involves depreciating the asset in line with the rate of extraction.

depreciation   The process of allocating the net cost (original acquisition cost less estimated scrap value) of a long-lived asset over its estimated life. There are a number of accounting techniques for doing this, including straight-line depreciation, the reducing-balance method and usage-based methods. Depreciation is the subject of SSAP 12 (Accounting for Depreciation).

depreciation charge   This is the amount of depreciation included in an entity's profit and loss account for a particular accounting period and represents that accounting period's share of the total depreciation of the asset(s) in question.

deprival value   A basis of valuing assets based on the loss that an enterprise would suffer if it were to be deprived of those assets. This idea of value was an important element in the development of the current cost accounting methodology.

differential cost   The difference in future costs that an enterprise will incur depending on what courses of action it chooses to pursue, compared to the continuation of present policy.

dilution The decrease in earnings per share and/or control that existing shareholders suffer when new shares are issued wholly or in part to parties other than themselves.

direct cost A cost which is specifically and measurably identified with a particular product or activity within an enterprise. Such costs are sometimes referred to as separable costs.

direct labour organisation (DLO) That part of a local authority responsible for undertaking maintenance and construction work for which separate annual accounts and reports are required. Extension of this into office and other non-manual local-authority work has led to the further and related concept of the direct service organisation (DSO).

directors' emoluments The amounts that directors receive from a company. The Companies Acts require extensive and detailed disclosure of these amounts.

directors' report An annual report from the directors of a company to its shareholders. This report is required by the Companies Acts, which specify its minimum contents. The report accompanies the company's annual accounts.

direct taxation Taxes on individuals and organisations based on their income or profits, e.g. income tax and corporation tax. It is a tax on income rather than spending.

discounted cash flow A method of investment appraisal based on the present value, after allowing for the cost of capital and timing, of the future cash flows associated with an investment project. There are two principal variants of the method (net present value and the internal rate of return).

discretionary costs Costs the incurring of which is a matter of discretion for management. Typically, they relate to items of expenditure which are not an essential part of the entity's short-term activities, e.g. research and development, advertising, staff development, etc. Thus they are clearly matters for management policy decisions.

dividend That part of the profits of a company that is distributed to the shareholders of the company in proportion to the numbers of shares that they hold and the respective rights attaching to those shares. The Companies Acts contain regulations relating to dividend payments and there have been a number of legal cases dealing with them. An important general principle is that dividends can be paid only out of realised profits, whether from the current trading year or from previous years.

dividend cover The multiple that the profits available for paying a dividend are of the actual amount of the dividend paid.

dividend policy Relates to the policy of the company (directors) on how it divides its profits between paying dividends to shareholders and retaining them for reinvestment.

dividend yield The ratio between the dividend per share and the market price of a share. Effectively it is a measure, albeit fairly crude, of the return on investment in shares, ignoring any possible capital gains.

division A major responsibility centre within an enterprise which has devolved responsibility for a particular activity or set of activities, the performance of which is appraised in terms of the profitability of these activities.

drawings The amount of money a sole trader or the partners in a partnership withdraw from their business for their personal use.

earnings   A synonym for profit. However, like profit, earnings can be measured at a variety of different levels, e.g. operating earnings (profit), earnings (profit) before taxation, earnings (profit) after taxation, earnings (profit) per share, depending on the purpose for which it is being measured.

earnings per share   The profit for an accounting period attributable to ordinary shareholders divided by the number of ordinary shares in issue.

earnings yield   The ratio of earnings per share of a company to the market price of an ordinary share. It is the inverse of the price–earnings ratio.

ED   Part of the process of formulating and promulgating SSAPs. An Exposure Draft is a preliminary draft of the text of a proposed SSAP issued for comment by interested parties prior to the statement being finalised.

EU Directives   The mechanism via which the European Commission is attempting to achieve harmonisation within the Community with regard to the regulation of corporate entities. After due process, and with some flexibility, member states are expected to incorporate the contents of these Directives into local legislation.

efficient-market hypothesis   A hypothesis to the effect that the capital market efficiently imputes all available information into the market prices of securities. There are three variants of the hypothesis: the weak version, the semi-strong version and the strong version. The hypothesis is relevant to accounting as annual accounts are a source of information available to the market. However, the hypothesis is the subject of some contention.

entity   That set of activities having an independent existence for which accounts are prepared.

equity   Ownership interest in the entity.

equity share capital   That part of the share capital of a company which has unfettered rights to share in the distribution of dividends or in the capital of a company after all preferential and prior claims have been met. In effect, it is the pure risk capital.

exceptional items   'Material items which derive from events or transactions that fall within the ordinary activities of the reporting entity and which individually, or, if of similar type, in aggregate, need to be disclosed by virtue of their size or incidence if the financial statements are to give a true and fair view' (ASB 1993a: para 5).

expense   'Expenses are decreases in economic benefits during the accounting period in the form of outflows or depletions of assets or the incurring of liabilities that result in decreases in equity, other than those relating to distributions to equity participants' (IASC 1989: para. 705).

external financial limits   The limits imposed by central government on the annual use of external finance by public-sector organisations.

extraordinary items   'Material items possessing a high degree of abnormality which arise from events or transactions that fall outside the ordinary activities of the reporting entity and which are not expected to recur. They do not include exceptional items nor do they include prior period items merely because they relate to a prior period' (ASB 1993a: para. 6).

factoring   A generic term to describe the raising of finance by the 'sale' of debtors to a financial institution. There are a number of different forms of factoring, ranging from ones involving the 'sale' of individual large invoices to ones involving whole sales ledgers and ones with differing entitlements in the case of bad debts.

fair value A feature of the acquisition method of accounting for business combinations which requires that the values of these items should be their fair (arm's-length) values at the date of the combination. It is the subject of FRS 7 (Fair Values in Acquisition Accounting).

FIFO An approach to valuing stocks in which it is assumed that those items remaining in stock at the end of the accounting period are those that were purchased most recently. The acronym stands for 'first in, first out'.

finance lease A finance lease is a lease which effectively transfers the risks and rewards associated with ownership of the leased asset from the lessor to the lessee. Thus the substance of the arrangement is a purchase transaction rather than a rental one, and it is accounted for as such. Finance leases are dealt with in SSAP 21 (Accounting for Leases and Hire Purchase Contracts).

Financial Management Initiative An initiative introduced by central government in the 1980s aimed at developing better management information systems.

financial ratio A generic term for the comparison of related figures in financial statements so as to assess corporate performance.

financial statements Statements showing the financial position of an enterprise at a given date (the balance sheet); the profit for the accounting period ended on the given date (the profit and loss account); the gains and losses recognised in the accounting period (statement of total recognised gains and losses); and the flow of cash through the enterprise in that accounting period (cash-flow statement). The statements are normally supported by explanatory notes.

fixed assets Assets owned by an enterprise for long-term use in its activities rather than for resale.

fixed capital Items such as premises or equipment.

fixed charge The charge of a specific asset(s) as security for a debt.

fixed costs Costs the amount of which are not expected to vary in the period being considered, typically one year, whatever the level of activity engaged in by an enterprise.

fixed overheads Costs, other than direct costs, the amount of which is not expected to vary in the period being considered by an enterprise.

fixtures and fittings A term used to describe things which are attached to premises, and articles of furniture etc. which did not form part of the original building.

floating charge A charge on all the assets of an enterprise, to the extent that individual assets or groups of assets are not the subject of a fixed charge, as security for a debt.

flotation Introduction of a company to the stock exchange by offering its securities for sale to the 'public' and its inclusion in the stock-exchange list.

flow-of-funds statement A financial statement summarising the principal sources of funds and the application of funds of an entity during an accounting period.

formats of accounts The Companies Act of 1985, as amended by the Companies Act 1989, specifies the formats that companies must adopt in preparing their annual accounts. The formats are set out in Schedule 4 to the 1985 Act.

franked investment income Income consisting of dividends previously charged to corporation tax in the hands of the company paying the dividend.

FRC A body set up in 1990 with members drawn from preparers and users of accounts as well as the accounting profession. Its principal function is the oversight of financial reporting in the UK, including setting of accounting standards and monitoring of their implementation.

FRED A draft of a FRS issued for comment by the ASB.

FRS An accounting standard issued by the ASB following a period of consultation after the issue of a draft standard (FRED).

full costing See absorption costing.

functional budget A budget which charges costs (resource inputs) to individual functions or activities. It is sometimes referred to as a programme budget.

fundamental accounting concepts The broad basic assumptions underlying periodic financial accounts. In the absence of a clear statement to the contrary in the accounts it is assumed that these basic assumptions (the going-concern concept, the accruals concept, the consistency concept and the prudence concept) have been applied in the preparation of the accounts. Fundamental accounting concepts are dealt with in SSAP 2 (Disclosure of Accounting Policies) and in the Companies Act 1985.

gains 'Gains are increases in ownership interest, other than those relating to contributions from owners' (ASB 1995a: para. 3.47).

gearing The relationship between the amount of debt finance and the amount of equity finance of an enterprise. The relationship can be expressed either in terms of the capital amounts of the finance or in terms of its consequences for income distribution. It is sometimes referred to as leverage.

general reserve A reserve which has not been appropriated by the directors for any specific purpose.

going concern One of the four fundamental accounting concepts dealt with in SSAP 2 (Disclosure of Accounting Policies). The essence of the concept is an assumption that an enterprise will continue in existence throughout the foreseeable future and that there is no necessity to reflect 'break-up' or liquidation values in the financial statements.

goodwill The value of the commercial advantages that an entity enjoys because of its prior existence. It reflects such things as the entity's particular expertise and trade reputation. In the case of some entities, particularly ones in the service/knowledge sectors, it may represent the major trading 'asset' of the enterprise. However, it is not separable/saleable from the enterprise, is very difficult to place a value on, and is not normally valued in corporate financial statements.

goodwill on consolidation Appearing only in a consolidated balance sheet, this is the excess of the amount paid to acquire an interest in a subsidiary over the corresponding proportion of the fair value of net assets of the subsidiary at the date of acquisition.

gross profit The difference between the selling price of an article and the cost of the materials and labour which are required to produce it.

group A parent company together with its subsidiary undertakings. The parent company of a group is required, under the Companies Acts, to publish consolidated accounts.

group accounts The accounts of a group of companies. Under the provisions of the Companies Act 1989, these must take the form of consolidated accounts.

historical cost The traditional measurement basis employed in accounting, under which assets and liabilities are recorded at their original cost and revenues and costs are recorded at their monetary values. The historical-cost basis does allow for some deviations from the foregoing, particularly with regard to revaluations of fixed assets and the substitution of market value for cost in the case of current assets where market value is lower than historical cost.

holding company Another name for the parent company of a group of companies.

IASC A grouping of professional accountancy bodies from over eighty countries which is trying to standardise/harmonise international financial reporting practices.

IFAC A grouping of professional accountancy bodies from over eighty countries which is trying to harmonise accounting practice.

income 'Income is increases in economic benefits during the accounting period in the form of inflows or enhancements of assets or decreases in liabilities that result in increases in equity, other than those relating to contributions from equity participants' (IASC 1989: para. 70a).

income statement Another name for a profit and loss account.

incremental budgeting An approach to the preparation of budgets which uses the previous budget as the starting point and concentrates on changes (increments/decrements) from that budget. Such an approach does not challenge the relevance of the volume/cost assumptions on which the previous budget was based.

indirect costs Costs which are not directly identifiable or measurable with the individual products or activities of an enterprise.

indirect taxation Where the tax is not collected directly from the taxpayer, e.g. VAT. It is a tax on spending rather than income.

insolvency The state of an entity being unable to meet its liabilities. The legal regulations dealing with insolvency are contained in the Insolvency Act 1986.

intangible assets These are assets which have no underlying physical substance. Examples include goodwill, trade marks, copyrights and, more controversially, brand names.

interim accounts Financial information about an enterprise which relates to a period shorter than a financial year.

interim dividend A dividend distributed prior to approval of dividends by a company's annual general meeting.

interim report A report issued by a company during the course of a financial year. Such reports are a stock-exchange requirement for listed companies.

internal control An internal control system 'includes all the policies and procedures (internal controls) adopted by the directors and management of an entity to assist in their objective of ensuring, as far as practicable, the orderly and efficient conduct of its business, including adherence to internal policies, the safeguarding of assets, the prevention and detection of fraud and error, the accuracy and completeness of accounting records, and the timely preparation of reliable financial information' (APB 1995a: para. 8).

internal rate of return A method of discounted cash-flow analysis which involves calculating that discount rate which just equates the present value of the cash inflows attaching to an investment project to the present value of the cash outflows attaching to it. This discount rate, the internal rate of return, is then used as a basis for deciding whether or not the investment project should be undertaken, on the basis of comparing it with the entity's cost of capital.

inventory   An overall term, of American origin, for describing an enterprise's holding of stocks and work-in-progress.

investment centre   A responsibility centre, the performance of which is assessed in terms of the rate of return on capital invested in its resources. Used especially in association with a divisional management structure and transfer pricing.

issued share capital   The nominal value of the share capital actually issued at any point in time. It is disclosed in the accounts.

job order costing   A costing system under which product costs are charged, allocated and apportioned on the basis of individual jobs or contracts.

joint costs   Broadly the same concept as common costs. To be distinguished from joint product costs, which arise where a single set of resources becomes transformed in a joint process into two or more main products and/or by-products (often with separate additional processing).

leasing   A method under which the use of assets for a specified period of time is secured by an entity, the lessee, entering into a contract for hire with another party, the lessor. Accounting for leases is the subject of SSAP 21 (Accounting for Leases and Hire Purchase Contracts).

leverage   See capital gearing.

liabilities   'Liabilities are obligations of an entity to transfer economic benefits as a result of past transactions or events' (ASB 1995a: para. 3.21).

life-cycle costing/pricing   The process of planning a product's development, production and marketing over its (economic) lifetime, costing all this and pricing it. If prices seem non-viable all cost elements will be reiterated to obtain a profitable outcome or the product will be abandoned.

LIFO   An approach to valuing stocks which assumes that those items remaining in stock at the end of the accounting period are those that were the first to be purchased. The acronym stands for 'last in, first out'.

limited-liability company   A company incorporated with limited liability under the provisions of the Companies Acts. The limited liability relates to the liability of the members of the company in case of insolvency. This limit may be determined by the nominal value of the shares in the company or by the amount of a guarantee given by the members.

limited partnership   A partnership in which the liability of some of the partners for the debts of the partnership is limited. However, limited partners are not permitted to engage in the management of the affairs of the partnership and there must be at least one unlimited partner.

limiting factor   A 'bottleneck', or a point in the production or distribution cycle at which volume becomes capped while other resources are still not fully utilised. It is important to identify this, for feasible removal, and meanwhile to analyse which products maximise profit contribution while fully utilising the capacity of the limiting factor.

line-item budgets   Budgets which detail income/costs in terms of individual categories of revenue/expenditure (e.g. rents, salaries, printing, telephones, etc.).

liquid assets   Assets which are either cash or readily convertible to cash.

liquidation   The process by which the assets of a company are realised into cash, its liabilities paid off and any surplus distributed to the shareholders.

liquidity   A term referring to the net short-term funding position of an enterprise. A 'liquid' enterprise is one which has sufficient short-term funding to meet its financial obligations and, perhaps, a sufficient surplus of funding to engage in new opportunities as they present themselves.

loan capital   Long-term finance which an entity obtains by borrowing.

losses   'Losses are decreases in ownership interest, other than those relating to distributions to owners' (ASB 1995a).

margin of safety   The difference, in units or as a percentage of sales, between actual (forecast) sales volume and the volume at which profit break-even is achieved. Used in evaluating alternative products or production methods, etc., often in association with cost–volume–profit analysis.

marginal cost   A concept derived from economics which measures the increase in total costs associated with an increase in output/activity levels (normally of one unit).

master ratio   See return on capital employed.

matching   Another name for the accruals concept, derived from the principle of 'matching' the costs and the revenues for transactions included in the accounts of a particular accounting period.

materiality   An accounting concept which recognises that accounts cannot report with complete accuracy every minute detail of an enterprise's affairs on the grounds of both practicality and limited potential benefit to the readers of the accounts. However, accounts should contain all material information. 'Information is material if its omission or misstatement could influence the economic decisions of users taken on the basis of the financial statements' (IASC 1989: para. 30).

Memorandum of Association   Part of the constitution of a company registered under the Companies Acts. The Memorandum of Association is a legal requirement and its minimum contents are specified in the Companies Acts.

merger   A combination of two business enterprises conducted in such a way that one enterprise is not in substance acquiring the other. The Companies Acts and FRS 2 (Accounting for Subsidiary Undertakings) specify conditions which must be met if a combination is to be treated as a merger.

minority interest   Arises when one company acquires another but acquires less than 100% of the shares. The remaining shareholders in the company acquired are referred to as the minority shareholders, and their interests in the assets and profits of the acquired company are referred to as minority interests.

mixed costs   Costs which contain both fixed and variable elements (which often cannot easily be separately measured). See semi-fixed costs and semi-variable costs.

monetary assets   Assets which are cash or whose value in cash terms is fixed.

national insurance   The system whereby the government takes money from employers and employees, and makes payments to persons who are sick, unemployed or retired, etc. The amount of the contribution is related to income.

net assets   The value of assets less liabilities, which equals the amount of the ownership interest.

net current assets The difference between an entity's current assets and its current liabilities.

net present value The net current equivalent value of the net of the future cash inflows and cash outflows of an investment project discounted at the enterprise's cost of capital. The net-present-value technique is one of the discounted cash-flow techniques for investment appraisal.

net profit ratio The relationship between the net profit for an accounting period and the sales turnover for that period.

net realisable value The amount which an asset would realise, net of selling expenses, if it were to be sold.

net worth The book value of an enterprise's equity, i.e. the book value of its assets less the book value of its liabilities.

neutrality 'To be reliable, the information contained in financial statements must be neutral, that is, free from bias. Financial statements are not neutral if, by the selection or presentation of information, they influence the making of a decision of judgement in order to achieve a pre-determined result or outcome' (IASC 1989: para. 36).

nominal share capital Another name for a company's authorised share capital, i.e. the maximum amount of share capital that a company is authorised by its Memorandum of Association to issue at a point in time.

non-voting shares Shares which do not carry any entitlement to vote at general meetings of the company.

objectivity See neutrality.

off-balance-sheet finance Arises where entities secure the use (control) of assets in such legal forms as do not provide ownership. It is a topic which is covered by FRS 4 (Reporting the Substance of Transactions).

operating lease Any lease other than a finance lease, i.e. one which does not substantially transfer all the risks and rewards of ownership to the lessee.

operating profit Profit for an accounting period before charging taxation and interest. It is widely regarded as indicating the profit generated by management on the resources under its control independently of how those resources are financed.

opportunity cost An economic concept which regards the cost of utilising a resource as being the benefit forgone by not using it in its best alternative use.

ordinary shares Those shares entitled to participate in the profits and capital of a company after all prior claims against profits and capital have been met.

output measures measures of the quantity of service/product produced. Such measures are often used in the performance appraisal of managers responsible for the provision of particular services/products.

overdraft A arrangement which an individual or company has with a bank to enable him/her to borrow money on a short-term basis up to an agreed overdraft limit. Interest is chargeable only on the amount that is actually borrowed rather than on the total of the facility. Accordingly, overdrafts can offer a flexible means of short-term borrowing. However, the interest rates that are charged are often relatively high and the borrowing may be repayable on demand.

overhead costs Costs which are not directly identified with a particular product or activity. They are also referred to as indirect costs. However, many indirect costs are variable costs, whereas many 'true' overhead costs are relatively fixed.

paid-up share capital The amount of a company's share capital which has actually been subscribed by the shareholders.

parent company A company which has subsidiary companies or undertakings. Also sometimes referred to as a holding company.

par value The nominal value of a share.

participating preference shares Preference shares which in addition to their preferential rights also have some rights to participate in profits and capital after other prior claims have been met.

partnership A form of business entity involving two or more owners (partners) or 'The relation which subsists between persons carrying on a business in common with a view of profit' (Partnership Act 1890, s.1). Except in the case of a limited partnership, all partners carry a joint and several liability for the debts of the partnership.

payback period The amount of time it will take for the cash inflows arising from an investment project to repay the cash investment that was made in the project.

planning, programming, budgeting (PPB) A budgetary approach, initially developed within the USA, which attempts to establish clearly defined goals and objectives for each area of an organisation's operations. These are then linked with quantification of the benefits and costs of operations and used for identifying, and subsequently monitoring, the most desirable programmes.

ploughing back The retention of profits for further investment in the enterprise as opposed to distributing profits to the equity owners.

pre-acquisition profits Profits earned and retained by a subsidiary prior to its acquisition.

preference shares Shares which have prior claims over those of ordinary shares as regards either dividends or repayment of capital, or both. The rights of different types of share capital are normally contained in a company's Articles of Association.

preferential creditors Creditors who have a prior claim over other creditors as regards the settlement of their debt out of the assets of the company. Their prior claim may be established by statute law (Insolvency Act 1986) or by contract.

prepayments Payments for goods or services where the payment has been made prior to the end of the accounting period but the goods or services are not received or completed until after the end of the period. Shown as an asset in an enterprise's accounts, they are the counterpart to accruals.

price–earnings ratio The relationship between the earnings per share and the market price of a share. Effectively, it shows how many years' earnings, at the last reported rate, will be needed to cover the cost of buying a share.

primary ratio See return on capital employed.

prior charges Claims against the assets or profits of a company that have a right to settlement before other claims.

private company A company which is not a public company.

profit The difference between an enterprise's revenues and its expenses.

profit and loss account A primary financial statement giving details of an enterprise's revenues and expenses. In the case of companies a profit and loss account is required to show a 'true and fair' view of the profit, or loss, for the accounting period.

profit centre   A responsibility centre within an enterprise the performance of which is assessed in terms of the profit that it generates from its activities. It may incorporate subsidiary cost and revenue centres.

prospectus   An invitation to subscribe to the share or debenture capital of a company. The contents of prospectuses are closely regulated by the Companies Acts.

provision   An amount put aside in the accounts relating to an anticipated liability or to a reduction in the value of an asset where the amount cannot be identified with a high degree of accuracy.

prudence   A fundamental accounting concept defined as follows: 'the concept of prudence: revenue and profits are not anticipated, but are recognised by inclusion in the profit and loss account only when realised in the form either of cash or of other assets the ultimate cash realisation of which can be known with reasonable certainty; provision is made for all known liabilities (expenses and losses) whether the amount of these is known with certainty or is a best estimate in the light of the information available' (ASSC 1971: para. 14a). However, prudence is not the same as taking a 'doomsday' view: 'a prudent reaction to uncertainty [is] to ensure that uncertainties and risks inherent in business situations are adequately considered . . . not the deliberate, consistent understatement of net assets and profits' (FASC 1980).

public company   A public limited company, which has the designation 'plc' after its name. To be a public company, a company's Memorandum of Association must permit this, and it must have a minimum authorised capital of £50 000 (or such higher amount as the secretary of state may determine) and comply with certain other legal regulations. Only a public company may offer its shares and debentures to the public or have its shares listed on a stock exchange.

purchase method   This is a method of consolidating the accounts of subsidiary companies with the parent company. The basis of this method is that the assets and liabilities of the subsidiaries are aggregated with those of the parent company, and that the cost of the parent company's investment in the subsidiary company is eliminated. Any differences between the book value of the subsidiaries' net assets at the time of acquisition and the cost of the parent company's investment, allowing for minority interests, is treated either as purchased goodwill or as a capital reserve on acquisition. One consequence of this method of consolidation is that the pre-acquisition profits of the subsidiaries are frozen and are not available for distribution. It is also known as the acquisition method.

quick assets   Another name for liquid assets. Essentially these are assets that can be readily and rapidly converted into cash. A common way of defining them is: current assets less stocks and work-in-progress. However, for some purposes this approach may be inadequate and an alternative one is to regard liquid assets as being: debtors, excluding prepayments, plus cash and marketable securities.

quick ratio   The relationship between the liquid assets of an enterprise and its short-term (current) liabilities. Also referred to as the acid test and the liquid ratio.

rate of return   The relationship between profit and the resources (net assets) employed to generate those profits.

ratio analysis   An approach to interpreting the information contained in financial statements based on relating significant figures to each other.

receivables   Another term, of American origin, for debtors.

reducing-balance depreciation   An approach to calculating depreciation in which the depreciation charge for a period is based not on the original cost of the asset but on its net book value at the beginning of the relevant financial period.

replacement cost   The amount it would cost to replace an asset with a similar one.

reserves   See capital reserves.

retained profits   Profits earned by an enterprise but not distributed to owners.

return on capital employed (ROCE)   The relationship between the profit of an enterprise and the capital employed in generating that profit. The most common variants are return on equity capital employed (which relates profit attributable to equity owners to equity capital) and return on total capital employed (which relates operating profit to total long-term capital). It is commonly regarded as a measure of the effectiveness with which management have utilised the capital available to them.

return on investment (ROI)   A measure analogous to return on capital employed but relating to units within a business (e.g. divisions), or to specific projects or capital outlays.

revaluation   The process whereby an asset (normally a fixed asset) is stated in the accounts at its current value rather than its historical cost. The difference between the two is shown as a reserve arising on revaluation and, as it is not realised, it is not distributable.

revenues   See income.

sales   The revenues an entity generates from its trading activities.

segmental reporting   An aspect of financial reporting in which the overall profits and revenues of an entity (or group of entities) are disaggregated into significant business or geographical segments to provide more detailed information about activities.

semi-fixed costs   Costs which are not permanently fixed for all volumes. They arise, and therefore become fixed, at intermediate stages in the volume range, and are sometimes termed 'step costs'.

semi-variable costs   Costs which change with a variation in volume of work or activity, but whose rate of change is not constant, linear or necessarily always predictable for any given volume.

sensitivity analysis   Any method which takes alternative data on costs, sales (demand), the timing of events, etc. to check the possible consequences of failure to achieve the target (or most probable) outcome of a decision. May be combined with profitability analysis.

share capital   The amount of a company's capital, divided into shares of a fixed amount the rights of which are determined by the company's Articles of Association.

shareholder   A member of a company by virtue of ownership of a share(s).

shareholders' funds   The total of share capital and reserves. Also referred to as equity capital.

share premium   This arises when shares are issued at an amount exceeding their nominal value. This excess is a non-distributable reserve.

SORP   These are statements of accounting practice prepared by recognised 'industry groups' dealing with current and best accounting practice specific to their industry.

SSAP These are authoritative statements on accounting practice intended to narrow areas of difference and variety in financial reporting. They were drafted by the ASC, and accepted and issued by the councils of the professional accounting bodies. They were intended to apply to all accounts whose purpose is to give a 'true and fair' view. The work of the ASC has now been taken over by the ASB and SSAPs are being replaced by FRSs. However, until a SSAP is replaced by an FRS it remains in force.

step costs See semi-fixed costs.

stock turnover An accounting ratio which measures the relationship between an entity's inventories and its cost of sales. In general, it is thought that efficient management of inventories (stocks and work-in-progress) will result in inventory holdings which are relatively low in relation to cost of sales. The ratio is expressed either as the number of days cost of sales represented by inventories or as the multiple that cost of sales are of inventories.

straight-line depreciation A method of calculating depreciation based on subtracting a fixed asset's forecast salvage value from its original cost and dividing the result by the estimated life of the asset.

substance over form An accounting doctrine, which is the subject of some debate, stating that accounting statements should reflect the underlying economic substance of an event or transaction rather than its precise legal form. It is the subject of FRS 5 (Reporting the Substance of Transactions).

tangible fixed assets Fixed assets having an underlying physical substance.

target costing/pricing Prices are taken or forecast from the market, in the light of market share/volume sought. Profit margin is deducted to determine allowable total costs. Products and production methods/efficiency are then designed/engineered/ adapted to be completed within allowable cost. May be used with life-cycle costing/ pricing.

timing differences Differences in the accounting periods within which an item is recognised for taxation purposes as opposed to accounting purposes.

transfer pricing The internal mechanisms via which goods or services transferred from one part of an enterprise to another are charged for.

true and fair view The requirement imposed by the Companies Acts on the accounts of companies is that they should present a 'true and fair' view of the state of affairs at balance-sheet date and of the profit, or loss, for the period ending on that date. Counsel's opinion on the meaning of the phrase forms part of the ASB's Foreword to Accounting Standards (1993c).

turnover Sales revenues.

two-part tariff A method of transfer pricing, or other pricing or charging, in which a fixed or time-related charge is used for resources committed, and a variable cost-plus charge is used to cover the direct and variable costs (with some profit contribution usually added) of the actual volume of goods or services supplied/ transferred.

unit cost The total (full) cost of producing one unit of a good or service.

unlimited company An unusual type of company where the liability of the members of the company is not limited, either by shares or by guarantee.

variable costs   Costs the total amount of which vary as the level of an entity's activity changes.

window dressing   A pejorative term referring to the practice of companies trying to put the 'best gloss' on their financial position (as reported in their financial statements) by the incorporation of 'questionable' elements.

working capital   Current assets less current liabilities.

zero-base budgeting (ZBB)   A system of budgeting, originally developed in the USA for non-trading organisations. Its approach is a 'bottom-up' one involving the ranking of the contribution that differing activities make to the achievement of organisational objectives in cost–benefit terms.

References and further reading

AAA (1966) *A Statement of Basic Accounting Theories*, New York: AAA.

—— (1972) *Report of the Committee on Concepts of Accounting Applicable to the public sector*, Sarasota, USA.

ASB (1991) *FRS 1: Cash Flow Statements*, London: ASB.

—— (1992) *FRS 2: Accounting for Subsidiary Undertakings*, London: ASB.

—— (1993a) *FRS 3: Reporting Financial Performance*, London: ASB.

—— (1993b) *Operating and Financial Review*, London: ASB.

—— (1993c) *Foreword to Accounting Standards*, London: ASB.

—— (1994a) *FRS 5: Reporting the Substance of Transactions*, London: ASB.

—— (1994b) *FRS 6: Acquisitions and Mergers*, London: ASB.

—— (1994c) *FRS 7: Fair Values in Acquisition Accounting*, London: ASB

—— (1995a) *Statement of Principles for Financial Reporting*, London: ASB.

—— (1995b) *FRED 10: Cash Flow Statements*, London: ASB.

—— (1996) *FRS 1 (Revised): Cash Flow Statements*, London: ASB.

—— (1997) *Amendment to SSAP8: The Treatment of Taxation under the Imputation System in the Accounts of Companies, Exposure Draft*, London: ASB.

ASC (1986) *SSAP 6: Extraordinary Items and Prior Year Adjustments*, London: ASC.

—— (1988) *SSAP 9: Stocks and Long Term Contracts*, London: ASC.

—— (1992) *SSAP 12: Accounting for Depreciation*, London: ASC.

ASSC (1971) *SSAP 2: Disclosure of Accounting Policies*, London: ASSC.

—— (1975a) *The Corporate Report*, London: ASSC.

—— (1975b) *SSAP 9: The Valuation of Stocks and Work in Progress*, London: ASSC.

—— (1975c) *SSAP 10: Funds Flow Statements*, London: ASSC.

Aldis, J. and Renshall, M. (1990) *The Companies Acts 1985 and 1989: Accounting and Financial Requirements*, London, KPMG Peat Marwick McLintock and ICAEW.

Alexander, D. and Britton, A. (1996) *Financial Reporting*, 4th edn, London: International Thomson Business Press.

Alexander, D. and Nobes, C. (1994) *A European Introduction to Financial Accounting*, Hemel Hempstead: Prentice-Hall International (UK).

Amey, L.R. and Egginton, D.A. (1975) *Management Accounting: A Conceptual Approach*, London: Longman.

Ansoff, H.I. (1965) *Corporate Strategy*, Harmondsworth: Penguin.

—— (1968) *Administrative Behaviour*, Harmondsworth: Penguin.

Argyris, C. (1964) *Integrating the Individual and the Organisation*, Chichester: John Wiley & Sons.

Arnold, D. and Turley, S. (1996) *Accounting for Management Decisions*, 3rd edn, Hemel Hempstead: Prentice-Hall.

Arnold, D., Cooper, M.J.D. and Shaw, J.C. (1990) *Financial Reporting: The Way Forward*, London: ICAEW and ICAS.

AGCAS (1997) *Accountancy, Taxation and Financial Management*, Manchester: CSU Publications.

Audit Commission (1986) *Performance Review in Local Government*, London: Audit Commission.

APB (1991) *Consultative Paper: Proposals for an Expanded Auditors Report*, London: APB.

—— (1993) *Statement of Auditing Standards: 600 – Auditors' Reports on Financial Statements*, London: APB.

—— (1993a) *Revision of Auditing Standards and Guidelines*, London: APB.

—— (1994) *The Audit Agenda*, London: APB.

—— (1995a) *Statement of Auditing Standards: 300 – Accounting and Internal Control Systems and Audit Risk Assessments*, London: APB.

—— (1995b) *Statement of Auditing Standards: 500 – Considering the Work of Internal Audit*, London: APB.

—— (1995c) *Statement of Auditing Standards: 160 – Other Information in Documents Containing Audited Financial Statements*, London: APB.

—— (1996) *The Audit Agenda – Next Steps*, London: APB.

Bailes, J. C. and Kleinsorge, I. K. (1992) 'Cutting waste with JIT', *Management Accounting*, May.

Bartlett, S. A. and Chandler, R. A. (1997) 'The corporate report and the private shareholder: Lee and Tweedie twenty years on', *British Accounting Review* 29(3): 245–62.

Baversox, D. J. and Closs, D. J. (1996) *Logistical Management*, New York, London: McGraw-Hill.

Brearley, R. and Myers, S. (1991) *Principles of Corporate Finance*, New York, London: McGraw Hill.

Bright, J., Davies, R. E., Downes, C. A. and Sweeting, R. C. (1992) 'The deployment of costing techniques and practices: a UK study', *Management Accounting Research* 3(3): 201–11.

Bromwich, M. (1976) *The Economics of Capital Budgeting*, Harmondsworth: Penguin.

Bromwich, M. and Bhimani, A. (1989) *Management Accounting: Evolution not Revolution*, London: CIMA.

—— (1994) *Management Accounting: Pathways to Progress*, London: CIMA.

Brownell, P. (1982) 'The role of accounting data in performance evaluation, budgetary participation and organisational effectiveness', *Journal of Accounting Research*, spring: 12–27.

Butler, R. (1993) *Strategic Investment Decisions: Theory and Practice*, London: Routledge.

Burrit, R. L. and Lehman, G. (1995) 'The Body Shop wind farm: an analysis of accountability and ethics', *British Accounting Review* 27(3): 167–86.

Butterworths (1997) *Butterworth's UK Tax Guide, 1997–98*, London: Butterworth & Co.

Cadbury Committee (1992) *The Financial Aspects of Corporate Governance*, London: Gee.

Carey, A. (1992) ' A questioning approach to the environment', in D. Owen (ed.) *Green Reporting: Accountancy and the Challenge of the Nineties*, London: Chapman & Hall.

Carsberg, B. V. (1969) *Introduction to Mathematical Programming for Accountants*, London: George, Allen & Unwin.

Chandler, I. (1962) *Strategy and Structure*, Cambridge, MA: MIT Press.

CIMA (1990a) *Corporate Reporting: The Management Interface*, London: CIMA.

—— (1990b) *The Costs to Industry of Adopting Environmentally Friendly Practices*, CIMA Research, London: CIMA.

—— Cm 918 (1990) *Financial Reporting to Parliament*, London: HMSO.

Collier, P. A., Cooke, T. E. and Glynn, J. J. (1988) *Financial and Treasury Management*, Oxford: Heinemann Professional Publishing.

CBI (1990) *Waking Up to a Better Environment*, London: CBI/PA Consulting.

Cooke, T. E. and Glynn, J. J. (1981) 'Fixed asset replacement in a recession', *Accountancy*, November: 83–5.

Cooper, R. (1990), 'Cost classification in unit-based and activity-based manufacturing cost systems', *Journal of Cost Management*, winter: 4–13.

Cooper, R. and Kaplan, R. S. (1988) 'Measure costs right: make the right decisions', *Harvard Business Review*, September/October: 96–103.

Cyert, R. M. and March J. G. (1963) *A Behavioural Theory of the Firm*, New York: Prentice-Hall.

DePaula, F. C. and Attwood, F. A. (1982) *Auditing Problems and Practice*, London: Pitman.

Dean, J. (1951) *Managerial Economics*, New York: Prentice-Hall.

Dearing, R. (1988) *The Making of Accounting Standards: Report of the Review Committee*, London: CCAB.

Dominiak, G. F. and Louderback, J. G. (1988) *Managerial Accounting*, 5th edn, Boston, MA: Kent Publishing Company.

Drury, C. (1996) *Management and Cost Accounting*, 4th edn, London: International Thomson Business Press; 3rd edn (1992), London: Chapman & Hall.

—— (1997) *Management Accounting for Business Decisions*, London: International Thomson Business Press.

Drury, C., Braund, S., Osbourne, P. and Tayles, B. (1992) *A Survey of Management Accounting Practices in UK Manufacturing Companies*, London: ACCA.

Drury, C. and Dugdale, D. (1996) 'Surveys of management accounting practices', in C. Drury (ed.) *Management Accounting Handbook*, London: Butterworth–Heinemann.

Ellis, J. and Williams, D. (1993) *Corporate Strategy and Financial Analysis*, London: Pitman Publishing.

Emmanuel, C., Otley, D. and Merchant, K. (1990) *Accounting for Management Control*, 2nd edn, London: Chapman & Hall.

Ernst & Young (1992) *UK/US GAAP Comparison*, London: Ernst & Young.

Estes, R. (1976) *Corporate Social Reporting*, New York: John Wiley & Sons.

Fava, J. A. (1991) 'Product life cycle assessment: improving environmental quality', *Integrated Environmental Management* 3, October.

Fayol, H. (1949) *General and Industrial Management*, London: Pitman.

FASB (1978) *Statement of Financial Accounting Standards (SFAC) 1: Objectives of Financial Reporting by Business Enterprises*, Stanford, CT: FASB.

—— (1980) *Statement of Financial Accounting Concepts (SFAC) 2: Qualitative Characteristics of Accounting Information*, Stanford, CT: FASB.

FRC (1991) *The State of Financial Reporting: A Review*, London: FRC.

Fisher, I. (1907) *The Rate of Interest*, London: Macmillan.

—— (1930) *The Theory of Interest*, London: Macmillan.

Freeman, M. A. (1985) 'The implications of agency theory for behavioural research', *AAANZ Conference paper*.

French, E. A. (1977) 'The revolution of the dividend law of England', in W. T. Baxter and S. Davidson (eds) *Studies in Accounting*, 3rd edn, London: ICAEW.

Glynn, J. J. (1987) *Public Sector Financial Control and Accounting*, Oxford: Blackwell; 2nd edn (1993).

—— (1993) *Public Sector Accounting and Control*, Oxford: Blackwell.

Glynn, J. J., Gray, A. G. and Jenkins, W. I. (1992) 'Auditing the three Es: the challenge of effectiveness', *Public Policy and Administration*, winter.

Goldman, A. and Barlev, B. (1974) 'The auditor–firm conflict of interests: its implications for independence', *Accounting Review*, October: 707–18.

Granovetter, M. (1985) 'Economic action and social structure: the problem of embededdness', *American Journal of Sociology* 93(1): 481–510.

Gray, R., Bebbington, J. and Walters, D. (1993) *Accounting for the Environment*, London: Paul Chapman Publishing.

Green, F. B. and Amenkhienan, F. E. (1992) 'Accounting innovations: a cross sectional survey of manufacturing firms', *Journal of Cost Management for the Manufacturing Industry*, spring.

Griffiths, I. (1995) *New Creative Accounting*, London: Macmillan.

Guthrie, J. and Parker, L. D. (1989) 'Corporate social disclosure practice: a comparative international analysis', in M. Neimark (ed.) *Advances in Public Interest Accounting*, Greenwich, CT: JAI Press.

Hancock, D. (1997) *Taxation Policy and Practice (1997–98 Edition)*, London: International Thomson Press.

Hannan, M. T. and Freeman, J. (1988) *Organisational Ecology*, Cambridge, M.A.: Harvard University Press.

Hathery, D. J. (1980) *The Audit Evidence Process*, London: Anderson Keen Publishing.

Hatry, H. P. (1979) *Efficiency Measurement for Local Government Services*, Washington, DC: Urban Institute.

Henderson, B. D. (1989) 'The origin of strategy', *Harvard Business Review*, November–December: 139–43.

Henley, D., Likeirman, A., Perrin, J. *et al.* (1992) *Public Sector Accounting and Financial Control*, 4th edn, London: Chapman & Hall.

Herzberg, F. B. (1959) *The Motivation to Work*, Chichester: John Wiley & Sons.

Hill, N. C. and Sartoris, W. L. (1995) *Short-term Financial Management*, 3rd edn, Englewood Cliffs, NJ: Prentice-Hall.

Hirschleifer, J. (1958) 'On the theory of optimal investment decisions', *Journal of Political Economy* 66(4): 329–52.

Hofstede, G. H. (1968) *The Game of Budget Control*, London: Tavistock Publications.

HM Treasury (1984) *Investment Appraisal in the Public Sector: A Technical Guide for Government Departments*, London: HMSO.

—— (1988) *Output and Performance Measurement in Central Government: A Technical Guide*, London: HMSO.

Holmes, G. and Sugden, A. (1994) *Interpreting Company Reports and Accounts* 5th edn, Hemel Hempstead: Woodhead-Faulkner.

Hopwood, A. G. (1988) 'Accounting and organisational action', *Accounting from the Outside: The Collected Papers of Anthony G. Hopwood*, New York: Garland.

Horngren, C. T., Foster, G. and Datar, S. M. (1994) *Cost Accounting: A Managerial Emphasis*, 8th edn., London: Prentice-Hall International (UK).

Humphrey, C. G., Moizer, P. and Turley, S. W. (1992) *The Audit Expectations Gap in the United Kingdom*, London: ICAEW.

Inflation Accounting Committee (1975), Cmnd 6225, (The Sandilands Report), London: HMSO.

Innes, J. and Mitchell, F. (1990) *Activity-based Costing: A Review With Case Studies*, London: CIMA.

—— (1995) 'A survey of activity-based costing in the UK's largest companies', *Management Accounting Research* 6(2): 137–53.

ICAS (1988) *Making Corporate Reports Valuable*, Edinburgh: ICAS.

—— (1993) *Auditing into the Twenty-first Century*, Edinburgh: ICAS.

ICAS/ICAEW (1991) *The Future Shape of Financial Reports*, London: ICAS and ICAEW.

IFAC (1987) *Preface to Statements on International Management Accounting*, New York: IFAC.

IIA (1987) 'Standards for the professional practice of internal auditing', reproduced in A. D. Chambers, G. M. Salim and G. Vinten (eds) *Internal Auditing*, London: Pitman.

IASC (1989) *Framework for the Preparation and Presentation of Financial Statements*, New York: IASC.

IAPC (1989) *Exposure Draft 35: Analytical Procedures*, New York: IAPC.

James, S. and Nobes, C. (1997) *The Economics of Taxation (1997–98 Edition)*, Hemel Hempstead: Prentice-Hall.

Johnson, G. and Scholes, K. (1993) *Exploring Corporate Strategy: Text and Cases*, London and New York: Prentice-Hall.

Johnson, H. T. and Kaplan, R. S. (1987) *Relevance Lost: The Rise and Fall of Management Accounting*, Boston, MA: Harvard Business School Press.

Jones, C. (1990) 'Corporate social accounting and the capitalist enterprise', in D. Cooper and T. M. Hopper (eds) *Critical Accounts*, Basingstoke: Macmillan.

Jupe, R. (1994) 'How green are UK company accounts? An exploration of changing corporate environmental disclosures', *Social and Environmental Accounting* 14(2): 2–4.

—— (1997) 'How green are UK company environmental reports? An exploration of corporate voluntary disclosures', *Social and Environmental Accounting* 17(1).

Kaplan, R. S. and Norton, D. P. (1996) *The Balanced Scorecard*, Boston, MA: Harvard Business School Press.

Katz, D. and Kahn, R. L. (1966) *The Social Psychology of Organisations*, Chichester: John Wiley & Sons.

Kay, J. (1993) *Foundations of Corporate Success*, Oxford: Oxford University Press.

Kay, J. A. and King, M. A. (1978) *The British Tax System*, Oxford: Oxford University Press.

Keynes, J. M. (1939) 'National self-sufficiency', *Yale Law Review* 22: 755–63.

Lapsley, I. (1986) 'Investment appraisal in UK non-trading organisations', *Financial Accountability & Management* 2(2), summer: 135–51.

Layfield Committee (1976) *Local Government Finance*, Cmnd 6453, London: HMSO.

Lee, J. Y. (1987) *Managerial Accounting Changes for the 1990s*, Wokingham: Addison Wesley.

Lee, T. A. (1986) *Company Auditing*, 3rd edn, New York: Van Nostrand Reinhold.

Lee, T. A. and Tweedie, D. P. (1975a) 'Accounting information: an investigation of shareholder usage', *Accounting and Business Research*, autumn: 280–91.

—— (1975b) 'Accounting information: an investigation of shareholder understanding', *Accounting and Business Research*, winter: 3–17.

—— (1977) *The Private Shareholder and the Corporate Report*, London: ICAEW.

Lester, K. (1992) 'Protecting the environment: a new managerial responsibility', in D. Owen (ed.) *Green Reporting: Accountancy and the Challenge of the Nineties*, London: Chapman & Hall.

Levy, H. and Sarnatt, M. (1986) *Capital Investment and Financial Decisions* 2nd edn, Hertfordshire: Prentice-Hall.

Likert, R. (1961) *New Patterns of Management*, New York: McGraw-Hill.

London Stock Exchange (1997) *Fact File 1997*, London: London Stock Exchange.

Lowe, T. and Machin, J. L. J. (eds) (1983) *New Perspectives in Management Control*, London: Macmillan.

Lumby, S. (1991) *Investment Appraisal and Financing Decisions*, London: Chapman & Hall.

Macdonald Commission (1988) *Report of the Commission to Study the Public's Expectations of Audits*, Toronto: Canadian Institute of Chartered Accountants.

McGregor, D. (1960) *The Human Side of Enterprise*, New York: McGraw-Hill.

McInnes, W. (1993) *Auditing into the Twenty-first Century*, Edinburgh: ICAS.

McIntyre, A. D. and Coulthurst, N. J. (1986) *Capital Budgeting Practices in Medium-sized Businesses*, London: CIMA.

Maslow, A. H. (1954) *Motivation and Personality*, London: Harper & Row.

Mautz, R. K. and Sharaf, H. A. (1961) *The Philosophy of Auditing*, Sarasota, FL: AAA.

Mintzberg, H. (1979) *The Structuring of Organisations*, Englewood Cliff, N.J.: Prentice-Hall.

—— (1987) 'Crafting strategy', *Harvard Business Review*, July-August: 65–75.

Mishan, E. (1971) *Cost–Benefit Analysis*, London: George Allen & Unwin.

Moore, P. G. (1976) *Basic Operational Research*, London: Pitman.

Murphy, M. P. (1996) 'Management audit', in J. J. Glynn, D. A. Perkins and S. Steward (eds) *Achieving Value for Money in the NHS*, London: Saunders.

Nobes, C. (1997) *Introduction to Financial Accounting*, 4th edn., London: International Thomson Press.

Nobes, C. and Parker, R. H. (1995) *Comparative International Accounting*, 4th edn., Hemel Hempstead: Prentice-Hall International (UK).

Oakland, P. (1994) *Total Quality Management*, Oxford Butterworth-Heinemann.

Otley, D. T. (1977) *Behavioural Aspects of Budgeting: Accountants' Digest No. 49*, London: ICAEW.

—— (1980) 'The contingency theory of management accounting: achievement and prognosis' *Accounting, Organisations and Society* 5(1): 194–208; reprinted in C. Emmanuel, D. Otley and K. Merchant (eds) *Readings in Accounting for Management Control*, London: Chapman & Hall.

Owen D. (ed.) (1992) *Green Reporting: Accountancy and the Challenge of the Nineties,* London: Chapman & Hall.

Page, M. (1992a) 'The ASB's proposed objective of financial statements: marching in step backwards: a review essay', *British Accounting Review* 24(1): 77–85.

—— (1992b) 'Turn again Professor Whittington', *Accountancy*, February: 30.

Parker, R. H. (1984) *Macmillan Dictionary of Accounting*, London: Macmillan.

Partridge, M. and Perren, L. (1997) 'Vice versa', *Accountancy*, November: 54.

Perkins, D. (1996) 'Control and VFM', in J. J. Glynn, D. Perkins and S. Stewart (eds) *Managing Healthcare: Achieving Value for Money*, London: Saunders.

Perrin, J. (1988) *Resource Management in the NHS*, London: Van Nostrand Reinhold and Chapman & Hall.

Perrow, C. (1970) *Organisational Analysis*, Tavistock: Wadsworth.

Pike, R. H. and Wolfe, M. B. (1988) *Capital Budgeting in the 1990s*, London: CIMA.

Pinches, G. E. (1990) *Essentials of Financial Management*, New York: Harper & Row.

Porter, M. E. (1980) *Competitive Strategy: Techniques for Analysing Industries and Firms*, New York: Free Press and Macmillan.

Price Waterhouse (1990) *Value for Money Auditing*, London: Gee & Co.

Roberts, C. (1992) 'Environmental disclosures in corporate annual reports in Western Europe', in D. Owen (ed.) *Green Reporting: Accountancy and the Challenge of the Nineties*, London: Chapman & Hall.

Samuels, J. M., Wilkes, F. M. and Brayshaw, R. E. (1995) *Management of Company Finance*, 6th edn., London: International Thomson Press.

Sealy, L. S. (1996) *Cases and Materials in Company Law* 6th edn., London: Butterworths.

Shank, J. K. and Govindarajan, V. (1992) 'Strategic cost management and the value chain', *Journal of Cost Management* 5(4): 5–21.

Sharpe, W. F. (1964) 'Capital asset prices: a theory of market equilibrium under conditions of risk', *Journal of Finance*, September: 10–18.

Shillinglaw, G. (1963) 'The concept of attributable cost', *Journal of Accounting Research* 1(1): 73–85; reprinted in D. Solomons (ed.) *Studies in Cost Analysis* 2nd edn. London: Sweet & Maxwell, 1968.

Sikha, P., Puxty, T., Wilmott, H. and Cooper, C. (1992) *Eliminating the Expectations Gap?*, Research Report No. 28, London: ACCA.

Simon, H. A. (1957) *Administrative Behaviour*, New York: Free Press.

Simmonds, A. and Azières, O. (1989) *Accounting for Europe: Success by 2000 AD?*, London: Touche Ross & Co.

Singleton-Green, B. (1990) 'Bridging the expectation gap', *Accountancy*, October: 79–84.

Sizer, J. (1989) *An Insight into Management Accounting*, 3rd edn., Harmondsworth: Penguin.

Sloan, A. P. (1963) *My Years with General Motors*, Sidgewick & Jackson.

Smith, T. (1996) *Accounting for Growth: Stripping the Camouflage from Company Accounts*, 2nd edn., London: Century Business.

Solomons, D. (1952) *Studies in Costing*, London: Sweet & Maxwell.

—— (1965) *Divisional Performance: Measurement and Control*, Illinois: Financial Executives' Research Foundation and R. D. Irwin; republished 1983.

—— (1983) *Divisional Performance: Measurement and Control*, New York: Marcus Weiner Publishing, Inc.

Stacey, R. D. (1993) *Strategic Management and Organisational Dynamics*, London: Paul Chapman.

Stedry, R. C. (1960) *Budget Control and Cost Behaviour*, New York: Prentice Hall.

Steen, D. C. M. E. (1989) *Audits and Auditors: What the Public Thinks*, London. KPMG Peat Marwick McLintock.

Taylor, F. W. (1947) *Scientific Management*, London: Harper & Row.

Taylor, P. A. (1996) *Consolidated Financial Reporting*, London: Paul Chapman.

Tobin, J. (1958) 'Liquidity preference as a behaviour toward risks', *Review of Economic Studies*, February: 65–86.

Touche Ross Management Consultants (1990) *Head in the Clouds or Head in the Sands? UK Managers' Attitudes to Environmental Issues: A Survey*, London: Touche Ross & Co.

Whittington, R. (1993) *What is Strategy – And Does It Matter?*, London and New York: Routledge.

Williamson, O. E. (1991) 'Strategising, economising and economic organisation', *Strategic Management Journal* 12: 75–94.

Wilson, R. M. (1995) 'Strategic management accounting', in D. Ashton, T. Hopper, and R. W. Scapens (eds) *Issues in Management Accounting*, Hertfordshire Prentice-Hall.

Wilson, R. M. S. and Chua, W. F. (1993) *Managerial Accounting: Method and Meaning*, 2nd edn, London: International Thomson Business Press.

Index